Best Practices in the Behavioral Management of Chronic Disease

Volume I
NEUROPSYCHIATRIC DISORDERS

Edited by Jodie A. Trafton, Ph.D. and William P. Gordon, Ph.D.
Institute for Disease Management

Published by Institute for Brain Potential

Best Practices in the Behavioral Management of Chronic Disease
Institute for Disease Management, Los Altos, CA

Acknowledgements:

We would like to acknowledge the research assistance of Tatiana Mejia, M.A., Marie Gordon and Brie Linkenhoker, Ph.D., the editorial assistance of Joan Zimmerman and Linda Williams, and the production assistance of Patricia Fullerton and Emmit Hancock.

Jodie A. Trafton, Ph.D. and William P. Gordon, Ph.D., Editors

All guidelines and discussions are presented as examples or generalized information only and should never be used as the basis for a legal document. They are intended as resources that can be selectively used and adapted with the advice of legal and medical resources to meet state, local and individual hospital, and specific departmental needs and requirements.

The editors have made every effort to ensure the accuracy of the information herein, particularly with regard to drug selection, dose and behavioral treatments. However, appropriate information sources should be consulted, especially for new or unfamiliar drugs or procedures. It is the responsibility of every practitioner to evaluate the appropriateness of a particular opinion in the context of actual clinical situations and with due consideration to new developments. Authors, editors and the publisher cannot be held responsible for typographical or content errors found in this publication.

Orders: 866-992-9399
Customer Service: 650-960-3536

Library of Congress Cataloging-in-Publication Data
Best Practices in the Behavioral Management of Chronic Disease
Volume I: Neuropsychiatric Disorders
ISBN 978-1-932745-15-3   Library of Congress Control Number: 2007932255

Best Practices in the Behavioral Management of Chronic Disease
Volume II: Other Medical Disorders
ISBN 978-1-932745-32-0   Library of Congress Control Number: 2007932255

IBP is a non-profit organization dedicated to providing advances in Behavioral Medicine through publications and conferences. IBP is a 501 (c) (3) organization (tax identification number 77-0026830) founded in 1984 as Institute for Cortext Research and Development. The Institute has trained over one million health professionals in the neurobehavioral sciences and has published books in the fields of Neuropsychology and Behavioral Medicine.

Printed in the United States of America

Volume I: NEUROPSYCHIATRIC DISORDERS

Contact Information and Additional Grant Support

Chapter 1: AN UPDATE ON MAXIMUM IMPACT PRACTICES FROM A TRANSTHEORETICAL APPROACH
James Prochaska, Ph.D.[1,2], Janice M. Prochaska, Ph.D.[1]
[1]Pro-Change Behavior Systems, Inc.
[2]Cancer Prevention Research Center
University of Rhode Island
2 Chafee Road
Kingston, RI 02881
[1]Jop@uri.edu
[2]JanicePro@aol.com

Chapter 2: INCREASING SELF-EFFICACY FOR HEALTH BEHAVIOR CHANGE: A REVIEW OF SELF MANAGEMENT INTERVENTIONS
John McKellar, Ph.D.
Center for Health Care Evaluation
795 Willow Road (152-MPD)
Menlo Park, CA 94025
John.McKellar@med.va.gov

Chapter 3: USING MESSAGE FRAMING TO PROMOTE HEALTHFUL BEHAVIORS: A GUIDE TO BEST PRACTICES
Alexander J. Rothman, Ph.D.[1], Emily N. Stark, M.A.[1], Peter Salovey, Ph.D.[2]
[1]Department of Psychology
University of Minnesota
N321 Elliott Hall
75 East River Road
Minneapolis, MN 55455-0344
Rothm001@umn.edu

[2] Department of Psychology
Yale University
PO Box 208205
New Haven, CT 06520-8205
Peter.salovey@yale.edu

Chapter 4: REVIEW OF INTERVENTIONS TO CHANGE PATIENT AND PROFESSIONAL BEHAVIORS IN STROKE MANAGEMENT AND PREVENTION

Judith Redfern, M.S., Christopher McKevitt, Ph.D., Anthony Rudd, Ph.D., Charles Wolfe, Ph.D.
Department of Public Health Medicine
5th Floor, Capital House
Guy's Hospital
42 Weston Street
London SE1 3QD
Judith.m.redfern@kcl.ac.uk
christopher.mckevitt@kcl.ac.uk
charles.wolfe@kcl.ac.uk

Chapter 5: BEHAVIORAL MANAGEMENT OF DEMENTIA

Cornelia Beck, Ph.D., RN, FAAN[1], Valorie Shue[2]
[1]Department of Geriatrics
[2]Department of Psychiatry
University of Arkansas for Medical Sciences
4301 W. Markham, Slot 808
Little Rock, AR 72205
[1]Beckcornelia@uams.edu
[2]ShueValorieM@uams.edu

Chapter 6: ANXIETY DISORDERS

David Barlow, Ph.D.[1], Todd J. Farchione, Ph.D.[2]
Boston University
648 Beacon St. 6th floor
Boston MA 02215
[1]Dhbarlow@bu.edu
[2]tfarchio@bu.edu

Chapter 7: MAJOR DEPRESSION

David J. Knesper, M.D.
Department of Psychiatry
University of Michigan
UH8D8806, Box 0116
1500 East Medical Center Drive
Ann Arbor, Michigan 48109-0116
Dknesper@med.umich.edu

Chapter 8: AN UPDATE ON THE PSYCHOTHERAPEUTIC TREATMENT OF SUICIDAL BEHAVIOR

M. David Rudd, Ph.D.
Baylor University
One Bear Place 97334
Waco, TX 76798-7334
M_Rudd@baylor.edu

Chapter 9: LONG-TERM EFFICACY OF INTERVENTIONS TO REDUCE SUBSTANCE USE

Jodie Trafton, Ph.D.[1], Jared Minkel[2], Elizabeth Oliva[2], Doyanne Horst[2]
[1]Institute for Disease Management
PO Box J, Los Altos, CA 94023
In4brain@mindspring.com

[2]Center for Health Care Evaluation
795 Willow Road (152-MPD)
Menlo Park, CA 94025
Additional funding was provided by a Merit Review Entry Program award from Veteran's Health Care Administration Health Services Research and Development

Chapter 10: PREVENTION OF YOUTH SMOKING

Raymond Niaura, Ph.D[1], Alessandra N. Kazura, M.D.[2]
Department of Psychiatry & Human Behavior
Centers for Behavioral & Preventive Medicine
The Miriam Hospital
Coro Center, Suite 500
One Hoppin Street
Providence, RI 02903
[1]Raymond_Niaura@brown.edu
[2]Akazura@lifespan.org

Chapter 11: EVIDENCE-BASED RECOMMENDATIONS FOR THE TREATMENT OF TOBACCO DEPENDENCE

David W. Wetter, Ph.D., Ludmila Cofta-Gunn, Ph.D., Kelli L. Wright, Ph.D.
UT M.D. Anderson Cancer Center
Department of Behavioral Sciences
1515 Holcombe Blvd., Box 243
Houston, TX 7030
Dwetter@mdanderson.org

Chapter 12: DUAL DIAGNOSIS DISEASE MANAGEMENT
Robert Drake, M.D., Ph.D.
Dartmouth University
2 Whipple Place, Suite 202
Lebanon, NH 03766
Robert.E.Drake@dartmouth.edu

Chapter 13 META-ANALYSIS OF LONG-TERM EFFECT OF PSYCHOSOCIAL INTERVENTIONS ON PAIN IN ADULTS WITH CANCER
Elizabeth C. Devine, Ph.D., RN, FAAN
University of Wisconsin-Milwaukee School of Nursing
PO Box 413
Milwaukee, WI 53201
Ecd@uwm.edu
This research was supported in part by a grant from the National Institutes of Health (R15 NR04750).

Chapter 14 BEHAVIORAL MANAGEMENT OF CHRONIC PAIN
Robert J. Gatchel, Ph.D., ABPP, Yuan Bo Peng, M.D., Ph.D.
Department of Psychology, College of Science
The University of Texas at Arlington
501 South Nedderman Drive
Arlington, TX 76019-0528
gatchel@uta.edu
Supported in part by grants 2R01 DE1No. 0713, 2R01 MH46452 and 1K05 MH071892 from the National Institutes of Health and grant No. DAMD17-03-1-0055 from the Department of Defense

Chapter 15: MANAGEMENT OF MIGRAINE AND TENSION-TYPE HEADACHES
Kenneth A. Holroyd
Psychology Department
Ohio University
Athens, OH 45701-2979
Holroyd@ohio.edu
Support for this review was provided in part by a grant from The National Institute of Neurological Disorders and Stroke (NINDS # NS32374)

Chapter 16: BEHAVIORAL TREATMENT OF PERSISTENT INSOMNIA

Charles M. Morin, Ph.D.
École de Psychologie,
Université Laval,
Sainte-Foy, Québec, Canada G1X 4V4
cmorin@psy.ulaval.ca
Acknowledgements: Preparation of this chapter was supported in part by grants from the National Institute of Mental Health (MH-60413) and from the Canadian Institutes of Health Research (MT-42504).

Chapter 17: PRIMARY PREVENTION OF OBESITY

Nancy Sherwood, Ph.D[1], Robert Jeffery, Ph.D.[2]
[1]HealthPartners Research Foundation
8100 34th Avenue South
Post Office Box 1524
Minneapolis MN 55440-1524
Nancy.E.Sherwood@HealthPartners.com

[2]University of Minnesota Twin Cities
Department of Epidemiology, Room 300 WBOB 7525
1300 South 2nd St
Minneapolis MN 55454
Jeffery@epi.umn.edu

Chapter 18: BEHAVIORAL MANAGEMENT OF OBESITY

G. Ken Goodrick, Ph.D., Suzanne Kneuper, Donna Laws-Gallien
Baylor College of Medicine
Family and Community Medicine
Clinical Effectiveness Program
Research Division
5615 Kirby Dr., Suite 610
Houston, TX 77005
Goodrick@storge.fm.bcm.tmc.edu

Preface to the 2006 Edition

The Centers for Disease Control estimate that chronic and preventable diseases kill over 1.7 million Americans annually, and almost half of the population has at least one chronic disease. The World Health Organization's 2005 report on chronic disease lays out a global objective of reducing chronic disease mortality by 2 percent annually over the next decade. If this goal were realized, 36 million lives would be saved. The report emphasizes that the scientific knowledge to achieve this goal already exists, however, with over 100,000 peer-reviewed articles concerning behavioral medicine, it is difficult to keep pace with advances.

Best Practices in the Behavioral Management of Chronic Disease is designed to be the most comprehensive review of evidence-based research of its kind. Written by national and international experts in the management of chronic diseases, *Best Practices* is divided into two volumes.

Volume I presents advances in preventing and managing Neuropsychiatric Disorders. The work includes three chapters on theoretical approaches, and new chapters for the 2006 edition focusing on Message Framing, Insomnia, and the Prevention of Suicide. Over half of the chapters were updated for 2006 edition including those concerning the management of stroke, as well as the management of chronic pain, cancer pain, and obesity.

Volume II presents advances in preventing and managing other medical disorders. The 2006 Edition contains new chapters on Cancer screening, secondary prevention of heart disease, prevention and management of osteoporosis, and management of hypertension. Revised chapters include those concerning adherence to anti-retroviral medication, managing type 2 diabetes, medication adherence, and physical activity.

The chapters are organized to review the best controlled clinical trials, focusing on long-term, randomized samples. The results are summarized in helpful tables. Authors present key insights, important advances, practice recommendations, and limitations of current knowledge.

The book identifies effective clinical, community and public health interventions for reducing chronic disease, and is a valuable resource for health professionals, decision-makers, researchers, and students. We hope you find this work helpful in your efforts to prevent and manage chronic disease.

AN UPDATE ON MAXIMUM IMPACT PRACTICES FROM A TRANSTHEORETICAL APPROACH

James O. Prochaska, Ph.D. & Janice M. Prochaska, Ph.D.

INTRODUCTION

Historically, best practices were evaluated by their efficacy, the percentage of participants who were successful at long-term follow-up. If one smoking cessation program, for example, generated long-term abstinence rates of 30%, it would be judged to be a 50% better practice than a program generating only 20% abstinence or efficacy. The problem was that the best practices in smoking cessation generated 1% or less participation, even when offered for free (Lichtenstein and Hollis, 1999; Prochaska, 1996). Such practices could have little impact on one of the most important behaviors for disease prevention and management. Low participation was the rule rather than the exception for participation with most health and mental health behaviors (Prochaska and Norcross, 2002).

Impact has been defined as the participation rate times efficacy. If the best practice that produces 30% abstinence, generates 5% participation, its impact is 1.5%. If an alternative practice that produces 20% abstinence generates 75% participation, its impact is 15%. The apparently lesser practice actually has ten times as much impact on high-risk behaviors in terms of maximum population impacts for the purposes of disease prevention and disease management. This chapter will present a systematic review on Transtheoretical research designed to produce increasing impacts and to raise the standard for best practices.

This is not a comprehensive review of research from a Transtheoretical perspective. More comprehensive reviews are available for research on smoking (Spencer et al., 2002), diet (Horwath, 1999) and exercise (Marshall and Biddle, 2001).

This is also not a review of practices based on stages of change or stages of readiness. Stage of change is a variable; it is not a theory. A theory involves systematic relationships amongst a set of variables. The Transtheoretical Model (TTM) is a theory involving systematic relationships between five stages of change, ten processes of change, the pros and cons of changing, self-efficacy and temptations. There is no reason to assume that interventions driven by any single variable, including stages or self-efficacy, can produce consistent outcomes or best practices. There is reason to assume that interventions that are theory-driven are likely to produce greatest efficacy, participation and impacts.

TTM Interventions

Figure 1 presents an overview of the Transtheoretical Model. It shows how different processes of change are emphasized at different stages of change. Consciousness raising techniques, like education, information and feedback, are used to help people progress from Precontemplation (not intending to take action in the foreseeable future) to Contemplation. Self-reevaluation (how I think and feel about myself as a couch potato and how I will think and feel about myself as a physically active person) is applied more to help people progress from Contemplation to Preparation (ready to take action now). Self-liberation is what the public calls willpower and is emphasized more for progressing into Action. Action is the stage in which people have made an overt behavior change like quitting smoking. In this stage, people have to work the hardest to keep from regressing and it takes about six months of concerted effort to progress into the

Maintenance stage. Processes like counter conditioning (substituting healthy alternatives for unhealthy behaviors), reinforcement, helping relationships or social support and stimulus control (removing tempting cues like ashtrays and providing helpful cues like no smoking signs) are all applied during the action stage. Counter conditioning and stimulus control are also emphasized during the Maintenance stage.

Figure 1 also illustrates other principles of change such as the pros of changing having to increase to progress from Precontemplation, the cons of changing having to decrease to progress from Contemplation, self-efficacy having to increase and temptation having to decrease to progress from Preparation to Action and into Maintenance.

Figure 1. Integration of the Stages, Processes and Principles of Change.

Precontemplation	Contemplation	Preparation	Action	Maintenance

Consciousness
  Raising →
Dramatic Relief →
Environmental
  Reevaluation →

            Self-
          Reevaluation→

                Self-Liberation →

                        Reinforcement Management
                        Helping Relationships
                        Counter Conditioning→
                        Stimulus Control→

        Pros of Changing Increasing
            Cons of Changing Decreasing
                        Self-Efficacy Increasing
                        Temptation to Relapse Decreasing

Social Liberation has been found to not have differentiate emphasis across all five stages.

Basic TTM research on how people progress through the stages of change served as a major impetus for the development of tailored communications for disease prevention and management (e.g. Campbell et al., 1994; Prochaska et al., 1993; Velicer et al., 1993). These basic findings provided a clear guide for tailoring processes and principles of change for participants at each stage of change.

Stage tailoring is particularly important when targeting entire at risk populations. Research has consistently shown that across adolescent and adult populations in the U.S. less than 20% of smokers, for example, are prepared to quit smoking (Velicer et al., 1995). In nations like China, Germany, Spain, and Switzerland with smoking prevalence rates over 30%, less than 5% of adult smokers are prepared to quit (Etter, 1997). Providing traditional non-tailored action oriented interventions would match the needs of only those relatively small segments of populations of smokers. The Transtheoretical Model is one of the most commonly applied theories for developing population based tailored communications.

Another finding, the stage effect, has immediate implications for tailoring goals for each stage. The stage effect involves the ability to predict people's performance over time depending on the stage they are in at baseline. The classic stage effect involved the amount of abstinence smokers show following treatment as a function of their stage prior to treatment. In 570 smokers randomly assigned to four different self-help treatments the stage effect was seen over 18 months with 25% abstinence in smokers in Preparation at baseline, 15% for those in Contemplation and only about 8% for those originally in Precontemplation (Prochaska et al., 1992). This stage effect with smokers has been replicated with Mexican Americans in small towns in Texas (Gottlieb et al., 1990); cardiovascular patients entering the hospital for surgery (Ockene et al., 1992); middle-age men in Finland at risk for CVD (Pallonen et al., 1992); and head and neck cancer patients in California (Gritz et al., 1992). In a recent HMO population of smokers the stage effect was replicated in 66 out 70 predictions (Prochaska et al., 2004).

Helping patients in Precontemplation progress to Contemplation with a brief tailored intervention can allow them to reach the increased abstinence rates for those in Contemplation over time. From a stage paradigm such a tailored goal is much more realistic and attainable than trying to persuade or pressure smokers in Precontemplation to set a quit date in the next month. A one size fits all action goal for smokers in Precontemplation is likely to lead to low participation rates, low retention rates or low abstinence rates.

Tailored interventions require an assessment of current status on a battery of behavior change variables. Assessments are typically performed either by a telephone interview, mailed questionnaires that can be optically scanned, or the Internet. The assessments are entered into a computer and an expert system report is generated to help guide people from their current stage to the next stage. The first report is also accompanied by a stage-based self-help manual that participants can use to progress between interventions. Three to six months later the person is assessed again and a second report is generated. A third assessment occurs three to six months later and a final report is generated. The individual reports are assembled from a large number of available paragraphs on the basis of a complex set of decision rules. These rules are derived from prior longitudinal studies of how smokers change.

The first report is based on a comparison of the responses of the smoker to a large comparative sample of successful and unsuccessful quitters. This report relies only on normative comparisons. The norms differ by stages. The initial norms were derived from a naturalistic sample of smokers. Evaluation trials of the expert system provide updated norms at periodic intervals. The second and all subsequent reports compare the smoker to both the normative group and to their own previous responses and provide both ipsative, i.e., self-comparisons, and normative comparisons. The ipsative comparisons involve access to the database for the results of the previous contact. On the basis of these comparisons, a 3-4-page report is generated that makes individualized recommendations for change.

REVIEW OF TTM TRIALS
Study 1

In the first major clinical trial (Study 1), a computer-based tailored intervention was compared to a leading standardized action-oriented program for smoking cessation (Prochaska et al., 1993). The stage-matched manuals were tailored on only one TTM variable, namely stage. Though this stage-matched manual produced 18% abstinence at 18 months compared to 11% for the standardized action manual, the difference was not statistically significant. The fully tailored expert system, however, produced more than twice as much abstinence as the action manuals (24% vs. 11%), which was significant. Surprisingly stage tailored telephone counseling did not enhance the tailored expert system and produced abstinence rates comparable to the stage matched manuals alone (18% and 18%). There were four proactive counseling calls delivered at 0, 1, 3 and 6 months. The calls were based in part on the expert system reports sent to the participant and, in part, on special concerns of the participant (e.g., emotional distress that is a barrier to progress). This was one of the first studies to demonstrate the advantages of tailored communications when compared not to placebo or no-treatment but to one of the leading home based treatment programs for smoking cessation, ALA's non-tailored action-oriented manuals.

Study 1 relied on traditional reactive recruitment that involves a cessation program reacting when smokers call for help. The problem with such procedures is that only a small percentage of smokers respond to such reactive programs. So, in Study 1 only efficacy could be assessed and the tailored expert system was the best practice based on efficacy.

Study 2

In subsequent clinical trials, proactive recruitment, where programs reach out to entire populations at all stages of change to recruit them to behavior change programs, was used. Combining proactive recruitment with stage tailored interventions has consistently produced high recruitment rates. With high recruitment rates, most participants are not prepared to take action. In studies with smokers, for example, over 40% of the smokers were in the Precontemplation stage,

about 40% in the Contemplation stage, and less than 20% were prepared to quit.

With an 80% recruitment rate in Study 2 (Prochaska et al., 2001), outcomes were produced that were remarkably similar to results in the reactive study 1. With a fully tailored expert system providing three inter-active interventions over six months, the abstinence rates at 18 months were 24% for the reactive recruitment study 1 and 23% for the proactive study 2. The tailored communication program was significantly more effective than proactive assessment alone at 6, 12, 18 and 24-month follow-ups. More striking was that the absolute differences between the treatment and assessment groups increased at each follow-up. These results suggest that the tailored interventions continued to produce beneficial effects in the population 18 months after the last intervention at 6 months. This proactive study shifted the focus from efficacy to impact.

The reactive and proactive studies produced comparable efficacy (24% vs. 23%), but the impact in the proactive trial was much greater (80% x 23% = 18%). As far as we know this was the highest impact produced by a cessation intervention.

Study 3

In the next major clinical trial (Study 3), the program proactively recruited 85% of 4653 smokers in an HMO sponsored program. In one study we compared stage-matched manuals and the manuals plus fully tailored expert system communications (Velicer et al., 1999). These two treatments were compared on four different doses: 1, 2, 3 and 6 contacts. With each number of doses, fully tailored communications produced more abstinence at every six-month follow-up than did the manuals matched only at baseline on the stage variable. This was the first study to demonstrate the advantages of maximally tailored interactive communications over non-

Table 1: Trials based upon the TTM model

Study	Participants	Interventions	Outcomes
1. Prochaska et al., 1993	741 Smokers reactively recruited	1. ALA Action and Maintenance Manuals 2. Stage-based manuals 3. Three expert system reports at 0, 3 and 6 months and manuals. 4. Four counselor calls plus condition #3	1. 11% abstinent at 18 months 2. 18% abstinent at 18 months 3. 24% abstinent at 18 months 4. 18% abstinent at 18 months
2. Prochaska et al., 2001	80% proactive random digit dial recruitment of 5,130 smokers	1. Three expert system reports at 0, 3 and 6 months and manuals.	1. 25% in TTM and 19.7% abstinent in control at 24 months.
3. Velicer et al., 1999	85% proactive recruitment of 4,653 smokers in HMO	1. 1 ,2, 3, or 6 expert system tailored communications over 1 to 12 months. 2. 1, 2, 3, or 6 non-tailored, stage-based manuals over 1 to 12 months. 3. Interactive expert system vs. manuals	1. No significant dose-response relationships for interactive communication. 2. No dose response relationship for non-interactive manuals 3. Interactive tailored communications significantly higher abstinence across all doses.
4. Prochaska et al., 2001	Shared sample with Study 3	1. 3 expert system tailored communications at 0, 6 and 12 months. 2. Condition 1 plus 3 telephone counselor calls at 0, 6 and12 months. 3. Condition 1 plus hand held nicotine fading computer.	1. 23.2% abstinence at 18 months compared to 17.5% in control. 2. 23.2% abstinence at 18 months compared to 23.2% in Condition #1. 3. 13% abstinence at 18 months compared to 23.2% in condition #1.

Study	Participants	Interventions	Outcomes
5. Velicer et al.,in press	64% proactive recruitment of 2,054 smokers from V.A. system.	1. Stage-based manuals alone 2. Manuals plus NRT 3 3. NRT plus expert system reports at 0, 6 and 12 months. 4. Condition 3 plus 12-month access to voice activated computer counseling.	1. 20.3% abstinent at 30 months 2. 19.3% abstinent at 30 months 3. 17.6% abstinent at 30 months 4. 19.9% abstinent at 30 months
6. Evers et al., under review	70% proactive recruitment of 1,200 people with stress symptoms	Three expert system tailored communications at 0, 3 and 6 months and stage-based manual.	1. 62% of TTM group in Action or Maintenance for effective stress management at 18 months compared to 40% in control group
7. Johnson et al., 2004	Proactive recruitment of 1227 adult HMO members who had been prescribed anti- hypertensive medication.	Three expert system tailored interventions at 0, 3 and 6 months plus stage-based manual.	80% of the treatment group vs. 65% of control reached Action and Maintenance at 6 months. At 18-month follow-up 75% of the treatment group was in Action or Maintenance vs. 69% of control.
8. Prochaska et al., 2004	83.6% proactive recruitment of parents of teens (N = 2,460)	Three expert systems tailored communications at 0, 6 & 12 months for each at-risk behavior of parent (smoking, diet and sun exposure) and multiple behavior manual.	1. Smoking: 22% of TTM abstinent at 24-months compared to 17% of control. 2. Diet: 33.5% in Action or Maintenance for low-fat diet at 24 months compared to 25.9% of control. 3. Sun exposure: 29.7% in Action or Maintenance at 24 months compared to 18.1% of control.
9. Prochaska et al., in press	65% proactive recruitment of primary care patients (N = 5,545)	Same as Study 7 plus tailored communications for mammography screening.	1. Smoking: 25.4% of TTM abstinent vs. 18% control at 24 months. 2. Diet: 28.8% of TTM in Action or maintenance for low-fat diet vs. 19.5% of controls. 3. Sun exposure: 23.4% of TTM in Action or Maintenance for safe sun vs 14.4% of controls. 4. Mammography: 3% relapse for TTM vs. 6% for controls at 24 months.

Study	Participants	Interventions	Outcomes
10. Jones et al., 2003	Proactively recruited Canadian patients with diabetes (N = 1,040)	12 monthly contacts including 3 quarterly proactive assessments, 3 tailored communications, 3 counselor contacts, and stage-matched newsletters for multiple behaviors (SMBG, diet and smoking).	1. Diet: 40.6% of TTM in Action or Maintenance for diet at 12 months vs. 31.8% of usual care 2. SMBG: 38% of TTM in Action or Maintenance at 12 months vs. 25% of usual care. 3. Smoking: 25% of TTM vs. 15% of usual care abstinent at 12 months (N.S.).
11. Rossi et al., 2002	Proactively recruited 400 patients with diabetes in Hawaii	Same as Study 9 minus the counselor contacts	1. Diet: 24.1% of TTM in Action or Maintenance for diet at 12 months vs. 11.5% of usual care. 2. SMBG 28% of TTM in Action or Maintenance for diet at 12 months vs. 18% of usual care. 3. Smoking: 25.9% of TTM in Action or Maintenance for diet at 12 months vs. 15.9% of usual care.
12. Evers et al., under review	Proactive recruitment of a diverse sample of 1,237 M.S. students from 12 schools and 1,202 H.S. students from 13 schools.	Internet based expert system program used 3 times over a 3-month period designed to increase respect and decrease the three roles (bully, victim & passive bystander) associated with bullying.	32% of M.S. treatment groups progressed to Action or Maintenance compared to 19% of control. 42% of the H.S. treatment groups progressed to Action or Maintenance compared to 22% of control.

interactive stage based manuals while controlling for number of contacts.

Study 3 also examined dose response relationships for stage-matched manuals and full TTM tailored communications (Velicer et al., 1999). For neither the manuals nor the TTM tailored interventions was there any evidence for a dose response relationship. There were no significant differences between doses 1, 2, 3 or 6 communication contacts for either type of intervention. This study demonstrated that doubling the number of tailored communications from 3 to 6 failed to increase

efficacy (23.2%) for three contacts vs. 19.7% for six contacts, (Velicer et al., 1999).

Study 4

Another study based on the HMO sample (Study 4), compared computer generated tailored communications to computers plus counselors (Prochaska et al., 2001). The counselor protocol was enhanced based on counselors' previous experience where they did not outperform the computers alone in Study 1. The original protocols were experienced as pressuring participants to progress too rapidly or with too big of steps. The new protocol provided smaller steps or challenges that participants could take with more confidence. With the improved protocol the counselors plus computers did outperform the computer alone at a 12-month follow-up (25% vs. 20%). But at 18 months the computers alone were tied with the combined condition (23.2%). The two studies with counselors compared to computers suggest that tailored communications from computers may generate greater self-reliance for changing behaviors like smoking than does reliance on professional counselors.

Given that counselors have been shown to be helpful in other behavior change interventions, this suggests that counselors function by some of the same mechanisms as tailored messages. These mechanisms probably include individualized and interactive guidance. Counseling may also produce a reliance on social controls (e.g., monitoring) and social support that may need to be faded out if participants have become dependent on such social sources of change.

Study 4 also combined stage tailored computer communications with an action-oriented hand held computer designed to bring smoking under stimulus control. The stimulus control computer was then designed to produce nicotine fading by having longer and longer duration between each stimulus that cued the smoker to have a cigarette. Combining stage tailored communication with a standardized action-oriented computer resulted in significantly poorer outcomes than the tailored communication alone (13% vs. 23.2%). These results suggest that adding one-size fits all interventions to tailored communications may hurt outcomes when the one-size doesn't actually fit the needs of all smokers, particularly those who are not prepared to quit.

Summary across Studies 1 - 4

Two consistent findings emerge across these first four studies. First, the computer-based tailored intervention produces a point prevalence smoking cessation rate of 22 to 25% at the end of the study. Figure 2 summarizes the results for this intervention from the four studies. These results were achieved with a total population in the last three studies and the intervention was of low intensity and delivered at home. A second important finding from the last three studies (involving only two samples) is the high participation rates achieved. Except for Study 1, the studies relied on self-reports which is the accepted standard for population cessation studies (Velicer et al., 1992).

Study 5

In the next clinical trial in a population of 2054 smokers in a V.A. health care system, adding nicotine replacement (NRT) also showed no evidence of increasing efficacy with only 17.6% abstinent at 30 months with NRT plus tailored print communications (Velicer et al., in press). Adding telecommunications with computers calling smokers on a set schedule and interacting with them on the telephone or smokers calling into the computers, also failed to significantly increase efficacy with this combined condition producing 19.9% abstinence at 30 months (Velicer et al., in press). None of the treatments outperformed a self-help manual alone comparison condition.

Study 6

With a national population suffering from stress symptoms, Study 6 proactively recruited over 70% (N = 1,200) to a single behavior change program for effective stress management (Evers et al., under review). The TTM program involved three expert system tailored communications over six months and a stage-based self-help manual. At the 18-month follow-up, the TTM group had over 60% of the at-risk sample reaching Action or Maintenance compared to 40% for the proactive

Figure 2. Summary of the Point Prevalence Cessation Rates Across 4 Studies

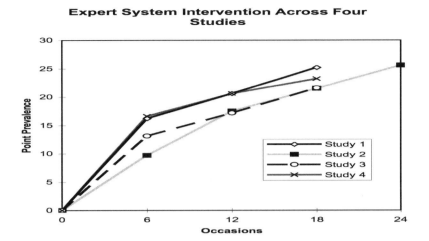

assessment alone control group. Compared to studies on smoking cessation, Study 6 produced much more effective action at 6 months in the TTM group (about 60%) and this outcome was maintained over the next 12 months. To see a demo of this program go to www.prochange.com/stressdemo.

Study 7

As many as 50-75% of hypertensive patients' blood pressure is not controlled, primarily because of inadequate adherence to treatment. This study examined the efficacy of a TTM expert system intervention in a sample of 1227 adult HMO members who had been prescribed anti-hypertension medication. The sample was proactively recruited and randomly assigned to receive usual care or three individualized expert system reports and a stage-matched manual over 6 months. Participants were surveyed at baseline, 6, 12 and 18 months. Significantly more of the intervention group participants reported being in Action and Maintenance at follow-up time points. 80% of the treatment group vs. 65% of control reached Action and Maintenance at 6 months. At 18 month follow-up 75% of the treatment group was in Action and Maintenance vs. 69% of control.

Scores on a behavioral measure of non-adherence differed significantly at follow-up time points. TTM-based expert system interventions have the potential to have a significant impact on entire populations of individuals who fail to adhere, regardless of their readiness to change. This intervention could be easily adapted into clinical practice without increasing provider burden by having physicians give prescriptions for this program in conjunction with anti-hypertension prescriptions.

Multiple Behaviors

More than a decade of efforts failed to increase impacts on smoking cessation by increasing the efficacy of the best practice of tailored communications for smoking cessation. Doubling the number of tailored communication contacts, adding telephone counselors, computers to cue nicotine fading, NRT and telecommunications all failed to increase abstinence.

Faced with a real ceiling on recruitment and a practical ceiling on efficacy, impacts have not improved since the first population based clinical trial more than a decade ago. One potential alternative was to treat multiple behaviors in a population, since populations with multiple behavior risks are at greatest risks with chronic disease and premature death. Those populations also account for a disproportionate percentage of health care costs. The best estimates are that about 60% of health care costs are due to about 15 % of the population, all of who have multiple behavior risks (Eddington, 2001).

The research literature indicates that changing multiple behaviors on a population basis would be a particularly risky test, since it would not be likely to work. A thorough review of the literature funded by the Robert Wood Johnson Foundation failed to find adequate evidence for the consistent efficacy of treating multiple behaviors (Orleans et al., 2002). Ebrahim and Smith (1997) also failed to find support for multiple behavior interventions and they concluded that, " . . . such interventions implemented through standard health channels have limited use in the general population" (p. 1666). The established wisdom in disease management has been that it is not possible to successfully treat multiple behaviors simultaneously, because it places too many demands on a population (Patterson, 2001).

The literature to date, however, was limited by reliance on the action paradigm, the frequent use of quasi-experimental designs and the lack of applying the most promising interventions, such as interactive and individualized stage-based tailored communications (Orleans et al., 2002). Applying the action paradigm to multiple behaviors would indeed risk overwhelming populations, since Action is the most demanding stage and taking action on two or more behaviors at once could be overwhelming. But in individuals with four health behavior risks, like smoking, diet, sun exposure and sedentary lifestyles, less than 10% of the population is ready to take action on two or more behaviors (Prochaska and Velicer, 1997). The same thing is true with populations with diabetes who need to change four behaviors (Ruggiero et al., 1997).

Study 8

Applying the best practices of a stage-based multiple behavior manual and three expert system feedback reports over 12 months, Study 8 proactively intervened on three behaviors in a population of parents of teens who were participating in parallel projects at school (Prochaska et al., 2004). First, the study had to demonstrate that it could proactively recruit a high percentage of parents if impacts were to be high. This study recruited 83.6% (N = 2,460) of the available parents. The treatment group received up to three expert system reports at 0, 6 and 12 months and the control group received proactive assessments only. At 24-month follow-up, the smoking cessation rate was significantly greater in the treatment group (22% abstinent) than the controls (17%). The parents did even better on diet with 33.5 % progressing to the Action or Maintenance stage and going from high-fat to low-fat diets compared to 25.9% of the controls. With sun exposure 29.7 % of the at-risk parents had reached Action or Maintenance stages compared to 18.1% of the controls.

Study 9

With a population of 5,545 patients from primary care practices, Study 9 proactively recruited 65 % for a multiple behavior change project. This represents the lowest recruitment rates in any of these studies and appeared to be due to patient concerns that project leaders had received their names and phone numbers from their managed care company, which many did not trust.

With this population, mammography screening was also targeted, but most of the women over 50 were in the Action or Maintenance stages, so relapse prevention was targeted. Of the four targeted behaviors, significant treatment effects were found for all four. At 24 months, the smoking cessation rate for the treatment group was 25.4% compared to 18% for the controls. With diet,

28.8% of the treatment group had progressed from high-fat to low-fat diets compared to 19.5% of the control group (Prochaska et al., in press). With sun exposure 23.4% of the treatment groups were in Action or Maintenance compared to 14.4% of the controls. And, with mammography screening, twice as many in the control had relapsed (6%) compared to the treatment group (3%).

Study 10

With a population of patients in Canada with Type 1 and Type 2 diabetes, Study 10 proactively recruited 1,040 patients to a multiple behavior change program for diabetes self-management (Jones et al., 2003). With this population, self-monitoring for blood glucose (SMBG), diet and smoking were targeted. Patients were randomly assigned to standard care or TTM. The TTM program involved monthly contacts that included three assessments, three expert system reports, three counseling calls and three newsletter mailings targeted to the participant's stage of change. At 12-month assessments, the TTM group had significantly more patients in Action or Maintenance for diet (40.6% vs. 31.8%) and for SMBG (38% vs. 25%). With smoking, 25% of the TTM group were abstinent compared to 15% of usual care. This was not significant due to statistical power, but the abstinent rate fell within the 22% to 25% rate seen in single and multiple behavior change programs for disease prevention.

Study 11

With a population of patients in Hawaii with type 1 and 2 diabetes, Study 11 proactively recruited 400 patients to a multiple behavior change program for diabetes self management (Rossi et al., 2002). The same three behaviors were targeted as in Study 9. The TTM program, however, did not include counselor contacts but did have monthly contacts. At the 12-month

assessment, the TTM group had significantly more patients in Action or Maintenance for diet (24.1% vs. 11.5%) and for SMBG (28% vs. 18%). There were too few smokers to do statistical comparisons, but the abstinence rates were 25.9% for TTM versus 15.9% for the controls.

While the absolute level of change for TTM in Study 10 was less than those in Study 9 using counselors, the relative difference compared to usual care was actually greater in Study 10. These informal comparisons across Studies 9 and 10 suggest that with diabetes management, telephone counselors may not increase the efficacy of tailored communications alone, which would be similar to what was found in Studies 1 and 4 for disease prevention.

Study 12

Tailored interventions based on TTM and delivered over the Internet for middle school and high school students were designed to reduce participation in each of three roles related to bullying (bully, victim, and passive bystander). Effectiveness trials were completed in 12 middle schools and 13 high schools in the U.S. A diverse sample of 1237 middle school and 1202 high school students were available for analyses. At follow-up in the middle schools, there was about a 32% reduction in each of the three roles for each of two intervention groups compared to about 19% in the control group. In the high school, here was about a 42% reduction in each of two intervention conditions in each of the roles compared to about 22% in the control group. Given the relative ease of dissemination, these programs could be applied as stand-alone practices or as part of more intensive interventions.

TTM INTERVENTION STRATEGIES RANKED FOR IMPACT

1. A series of three proactively delivered and computer-generated tailored communica-

tions plus stage-based manuals for multiple behaviors for participants at each stage of change. This strategy has the most empirical support for producing the greatest impacts for disease prevention.

2. A series of three proactively delivered and computer-generated tailored communications with 12 monthly contacts for multiple behavior changes for patients with diabetes at each stage of change. This strategy has the best support to date for producing the greatest impacts for disease management.

3. A series of three proactively delivered tailored communications plus self-help manuals for single behaviors for participants at each stage of change.

4. A single proactively delivered tailored communication plus self-help manuals for a single behavior for participants at each stage of change. This strategy has support from a single study.

5. A single or series of stage-matched self-help manuals for single behaviors have been found to produce about 70% of the efficacy of tailored communications plus manuals in two studies.

6. A series of three proactively delivered tailored communications plus self-help manuals plus other enhancements (e.g., telephone counselors, hand-held computers and nicotine replacement therapy) for a single behavior for participants at each stage of change. These enhancements and more costly strategies have not been found to increase efficacy across a series of studies.

FUNDAMENTAL RESEARCH QUESTIONS

1. Why has the field been unable over the past 30 years to increase the efficacy of action-oriented or stage-based interventions for behavior medicine?

2. Why has there been no increase in efficacy for some of the most important biological medicines for disease management, such as anti-hypertensives and anti-depressants?

3. Are multi-level interventions, such as individual and family or individual, family, worksite organizations and community the most promising approaches to increased efficacy, as many leaders recommend, even though the evidence for these complex and costly interventions have little evidence from randomized clinical trials?

4. How many behaviors can be treated simultaneously and effectively as a way to increase impacts?

5. Are there integrative ways to treat more multiple behaviors while reducing demands on patients and providers, such as teaching patients the principles and processes of effective change that they could then apply to any risk behavior or organizing behaviors around clinical themes, such as proactive lifestyles for preventing cancer or managing diabetes?

RECOMMENDED READINGS
A. Journal Articles

1. Velicer WF, Prochaska JO. (1999) An expert system intervention for smoking cessation. Patient Education and Counseling 36: 119-129.

2. Prochaska JO, DiClemente CC, Norcross JC. (1992) In search of how people change: Applications to addictive behavior. American Psychologist 47: 1102-1114.

3. Prochaska JO, Velicer WF, Rossi JS, Goldstein MG, Marcus BH, Rakowski W, Fiore C, Harlow LL, Redding CA, Rosenbloom D, Rossi SR. (1994) Stages of change and decisional balance for twelve problem behaviors. Health Psychology 13: 39-46.

4. Prochaska JO, Velicer WF. (1997) The Transtheoretical Model of health behavior change. American Journal of Health Promotion 12: 38-48.

B. Books

1. Prochaska JO, Norcross JC, DiClemente CC. (1994) <u>Changing for Good</u>. New York: Morrow. Released in paperback by Avon, 1995.

2. Velasquez MM, Maurer GG, Crouch C, DiClemente CC. (2001) <u>Group Treatment for Substance Abuse: A Stages of Change Therapy Manual</u>. New York: Guilford Press.

3. Pro-Change Behavior Systems (2003) <u>Stress Management: A Stage-based Manual</u>. www.prochange.com.

C. Chapters

1. Prochaska JO. (1999) Change at differing stages. In CR Snyder and RE Ingram (Eds.), <u>Handbook of Psychological</u> Change. New York: John Wiley and Sons.

2. Prochaska JO, Redding C, Evers K. (2002) The transtheoretical model and stages of change. In K Glanz, FM Lewis and BK Rimer (Eds.), <u>Health Behavior and Health Education: Theory, Research and Practice</u> (3rd Edition). Jossey-Bass Publications, Inc.

3. DiClemente CC, Prochaska JO. (1999) Toward a comprehensive transtheoretical model of change: Stages of change and addictive behaviors. In WR Miller and N Heath (Eds.), <u>Treating Addictive Behaviors</u> (2nd Edition). New York and London: Plenum Press.

REFERENCES

Campbell MK, DeVelllis BM, Strecher VJ, Ammerman AS, DeVellis RF, Sandler RS. (1994) Improving dietary Behavior: the Effectiveness of Tailored Messages in Primary Care Settings. Am J Public Health 84: 783-787.

Ebrahim S, Smith G. (1997) Systematic review of randomized controlled trials of multiple risk factor interventions for preventing coronary heart disease. Br Medical J 314: 1666-1674.

Eddington DW. (2001) Emerging research: A view from one research center. Am J Health Promotion 15: 341-369.

Etter JF, Perneger TV, Ronchi A. (1997) Distributions of smokers by stage: International comparison and association with smoking prevalence. Preventive Medicine 26: 580-585.

Evers KE, Prochaska JO, Mauriello LM, Johnson JL, Padula JA, Prochaska JM. (under review) A randomized clinical trial of a population and transtheoretical-based stress management intervention.

Evers KE, Prochaska JO, VanMarten D, Johnson JL, Prochaska JM. (under review) Transtheoretical-based bullying prevention effectiveness trials in middle schools and high schools.

Gottlieb NH, Galavotti C, McCuan RS, McAlister AL. (1990) Specification of a social cognitive model predicting smoking cessation in a Mexican-American population: A prospective study. Cognit Therapy Research 14: 529-542

Gritz E, Car C, Chang C. (1992) Quality of life and smoking cessation in head and neck patients. Presented at 16th Annual Meeting of the American Society of Preventive Oncology. Bethesda, MD.

Horwath CC. (1999) Applying the trans-theoretial model to eating behavior change: Challenges and opportunities. Nutrition Research Review 12: 281-317.

Johnson SS, Driskell MM, Johnson JL, Prochaska JM, Zwick W, Prochaska JO. (under review) Efficacy of a trans-theoretical model-based expert system for anti-hypertensive adherence.

Jones H, Edwards L, Vallis MT, Ruggiero L, Rossi S, Rossi JS, Greene G, Prochaska JO, Zinman B. (2003) Changes in diabetes self-care behaviors make a difference to glycemic control: The diabetes stages of change (DiSC) study. Diabetes Care 26: 732-737.

Lichtenstein E, Hollis J. (1992) Patient referral to smoking cessation programs: Who follows through? J Family Practice 34:739-744.

Marshall SJ, Biddle SJ. (2001) The transtheoretical model of behavior Change: A meta-analysis of applications to physical activity and exercise. Annals Behavior Medicine 23: 229-246.

Ockene J, Kristeller JL, Goldber R, Ockene I, Merriam P, Barrett S, Pekow P, Hosmer D, Gianely R. (1992) Smoking cessation and severity of disease: The coronary artery smoking intervention study. Health Psychology 11: 119-126.   .

Orleans CT, Prochaska JO, Redding CA, Rossi JS, Rimer B. (2002) Multiple behavior change for cancer prevention and diabetes management. Symposium presented at the Society for Behavior Medicine, Washington, DC, April 2002.

Pallonen UE, Fava JL, Salonen JT, Prochaska JO. (1992) Readiness for smoking change among middle-aged Finnish men. Addictive Behavior 17: 415-424.

Patterson R. (2001) Changing Patient Behavior: Improving outcomes in health and disease management. San Francisco: Jossey-Bass.

Prochaska JO. (1996) A stage paradigm for integrating clinical and public health approaches to smoking cessation. Addictive Behavior 21: 721-732.

Prochaska JO, DiClemente CC, Norcross JC. (1992) In search of how people change: Applications to the addictive behaviors. Am Psychol 47: 1102-1114.

Prochaska JO, DiClemente CC, Velicer WF, Rossi JS. (1993) Standardized, individualized, interactive and personalized self-help programs for smoking cessation. Health Psychol 12: 399-405.

Prochaska JO, Norcross JC. (2002) Systems of psychotherapy: A Transtheoretical Analysis (Fifth Edition) Pacific Grove, CA: Brooks-Cole.

Prochaska JO, Velicer WF. (1997) The transtheoretical model of health behavior change. (Invited paper). Am J Health Promotion 12: 38-48.

Prochaska JO, Velicer WF, Fava JL, Rossi JS, Tsoh J. (2001) Evaluating a population-based recruitment approach and a stage-matched expert system intervention for smoking cessation. Addictive Behavior 26, 583-602.

Prochaska JO, Velicer WF, Fava JL, Ruggiero L, Laforge RG, Rossi JS, Johnson SS, Lee PA. (2001) Counselor and stimulus control enhancements of a stage-matched expert system intervention for smokers in a managed care setting. Preventive Med 32: 23-32.

Prochaska JO, Velicer WF, Prochaska JM, Johnson J. (2004) Size, consistency and stability of stage effects for smoking cessation. Addictive Behavior 29: 207-213.

Prochaska JO, Velicer WF, Redding CA, Rossi JS, Goldstein M, DePue J, Greene GW, Rossi SR, Sun X. (in press) Stage-based expert systems to guide a population of primary care patients to quit smoking, eat healthier, prevent skin cancer and receive regular mammograms. Preventive Medicine.

Rossi JS, Ruggiero L, Rossi S, Greene G, Prochaska JO, Edwards L, Vallis M, Jones H, Zinman B, Chung R, Skikuman N. (2002) Effectiveness of stage-based multiple behavior interventions for diabetes management in two randomized clinical trials. Annals Behavioral Med 24: S192.

Ruggiero L, Glasgow RE, Dryfoos JM, Rossi JS, Prochaska JO, Orleans CT, Prokhorov AV, Rossi SR, Green GW, Reed GR, Kelly K, Chobanian L, Johnson S. (1997)

Diabetes Self-management. Diabetes Care 4: 568-576.

Spencer L, Pagell F, Hallion EH, Adams TB. (2002) Applying the transtheoretical model to tobacco cessation and prevention: A review of literature. Am J Health Promotion 17: 7-71.

Velicer WF, DiClemente CC. (1993) Understanding and intervening with the total population of smokers. Tobacco Control 2: 95-96.

Velicer WF, Fava JL, Prochaska JO, Abrams DB, Emmons KM, Pierce J. (1995) Distribution of smokers by stage in three representative samples. Preventive Med 24: 401-411.

Velicer WF, Keller S, Friedman R, Fava JL, Gulliver S, Ward R, Ramelson H, Prochaska JO, Robins AG, Cottrill SD. (in press) Comparing participants and non-participants recruited for an effect-iveness study of nicotine replacement therapy. Annals Behavioral Medicine

Velicer WF, Prochaska JO, Bellis JM, DiClemente CC, Rossi JS, Fava JL, Steiger JH. (1993) An expert system intervention for smoking cessation. Addictive Behavior 18: 269-290.

Velicer WF, Prochaska JO, Fava JL, Laforge RG, Rossi JS. (1999) Interactive versus non-interactive interventions and dose-response relationships for stage-matched smoking cessation programs in a managed care setting. Health Psychol 18: 21-28.

Velicer WF, Prochaska JO, Rossi JS, Snow M. (1992) Assessing outcome in smoking cessation studies. Psychol Bull 111: 23-41.

INCREASING SELF-EFFICACY FOR HEALTH BEHAVIOR CHANGE: A REVIEW OF SELF MANAGEMENT INTERVENTIONS

John McKellar

INTRODUCTION

The concept of self-efficacy refers to one's perceived ability to carry out a particular behavior or course of action. People's beliefs about their ability have been found to have a large impact on their ability to achieve goals because beliefs can influence such factors such as whether they initiate actions or whether they persist in the face of obstacles (Bandura, 1997). Individuals with strong efficacy beliefs persevere in particular actions or behaviors longer than those with weaker beliefs, as those with weaker beliefs may consume emotional energy in dealing with feelings of inadequacy that might otherwise be focused on the task at hand (Strecher et al., 1986). The concept of self-efficacy was first outlined in a paper by Bandura (Bandura, 1977) entitled "Towards a unifying theory of behavior change." This paper was recently cited as one of the key writings in the area of social psychology in the last century (Baumeister, 1999).

Self-efficacy is not a global personality trait (Bandura, 1997) but, instead, pertains to a person's view of their ability to carry out a particular activity or a specific course of action. For example, although track runners may indicate that they possesses athletic efficacy in a general sense they are less likely to do so when asked specifically if they also possess athletic efficacy in pole vaulting, hurdling, or discus throwing. Accordingly, specific self-efficacy beliefs are more robust predictors of performance than are global efficacy beliefs (Martin and Gill, 1991; Pajares and Graham, 1999).

Self-efficacy has proven to be a potent predictor of an individual's likelihood of engaging in health protective or health maintaining behaviors for a variety of health disorders. For instance, a medline search for the terms "self-efficacy" and "health" yielded over 1700 citations. The theory has been applied to the adoption of health protective behaviors such as smoking cessation (Gwaltney et al., 2002), decreased substance abuse (Ritter et al., 2002) and sun exposure (Rodrigue, 1996). Evidence suggests that self-efficacy also plays an important role in adjustment to chronic conditions such as fibromyalgia (Buckelew et al., 1996), arthritis (Barlow et al., 1996), chronic low back pain (Lackner and Carosella, 1999), diabetes (Grossman et al., 1987), multiple sclerosis (Schwartz et al., 1996), and chronic obstructive pulmonary disease (Wigal et al., 1991). While an individual's level of self-efficacy is predictive of their ability to carry out behaviors and actions as cited above, the concept also appears to be an active ingredient in many self-management interventions (Lorig et al., 2001; Rhee et al., 2000). Studies of self-management interventions find that pre-post changes in self-efficacy are predictive of important changes such as improved medication adherence, decreased medical utilization, and decreased functional impairment (Gowans et al., 2001).

Given the large body of evidence supporting the use of the self-efficacy construct as both a predictor of behavior change and as an active ingredient involved in self-management interventions, this review will focus on theoretical and empirical factors that contribute to increased self-efficacy. The review will begin by briefly discussing some background and basic concepts related to self-efficacy and self-care behaviors. Next, the review turns attention to sources of self-efficacy as outlined in Social Cognitive Theory. Following this theoretical discussion, the review will evaluate studies that focus on increasing self-efficacy for specific self-management behaviors. Finally, by combining theory and empirical evidence, clinical and research recommendations will be offered for how providers can improve a patient's self-efficacy for health-related behaviors.

Self-Care Behaviors and Self-Efficacy

Initiation and maintenance of health behaviors, self-management strategies, and health-protective behaviors have become a growing healthcare focus since the emergence of the self-care movement in the 1970's (Shoor and Lorig, 2002). This movement was born out of the steep rise in health care costs propelled by the shift from treating predominantly acute illness to treating chronic illness. Those at the forefront of the self-care movement in the 1970's quickly discovered that their patients with chronic diseases were accustomed to a more traditional medical system where patients were passive recipients of care (Shoor and Lorig, 2002). Attempts to shift patients into taking a more active role in their health care proved challenging, as health providers became increasingly aware of the difficulty of changing health behaviors. Concordant with the growing emphasis on patient self-care, was the increasing awareness that health maintaining or health protective behaviors might contribute more to morbidity and mortality than clinical health interventions. With this new focus on behavior and behavior change researchers and clinicians sought out theoretical formulations of behavior change that might be applied to health settings. It was at this point that the theory of self-efficacy began to be applied to health behavior change.

Theoretical Sources of Self-Efficacy

Bandura (Bandura, 1997) identifies four sources of efficacy information: enactive attainments, vicarious experience, verbal persuasion, and observations of one's own physiological state. An enactive attainment involves "doing it" or carrying out the specific behavior. The experience of successfully carrying out a particular behavior provides an information store that directly informs an individual's efficacy expectations. The impact of carrying out the behaviors is especially potent when the behavior is either difficult or previously feared. Successive or repeated mastery over subtasks required to engage in the behavior helps the person to develop and refine skills and assists the individual in overcoming obstacles that occur. Some factors that may moderate the impact of the behavior on efficacy expectations are the ease with which the behavior is completed and the degree to which the individual attributes success to their own accomplishments and not external or temporary factors.

The second source of efficacy expectations, vicarious experience, involves learning that occurs though observation of events and/or other people. These events or people are referred to as "models" when they display a set of behaviors or "stimulus array that illustrates a certain principle, rule or response"(Bandura, 1993). Observation of an individual confronting their fear of a snake provides a prototypical example of modeling for people with snake phobias. As the model progressively masters different behavioral sub-tasks such as seeing a picture of a snake, seeing a snake in a cage, and, eventually, handling a snake, the observer experiences an increase in his or her efficacy expectations. The potency of the modeling experience is moderated by factors such as the degree to which the model is viewed as overcoming difficulties with ease or with determined effort (expert modeling vs. mastery modeling), and the degree to which the model is seen as being similar to the observer in characteristics such as age or gender.

The third source of efficacy expectations is verbal persuasion. This source simply

17

involves provision of encouragement and exhortation to an individual. Encouragement is most effective when a positive outcome is expected, as unrealistically positive persuasion will discredit the persuader and undermine the recipient's self-efficacy (Bandura, 1997). Persuasion is only effective when the persuader is seen as credible, such as when the persuader is perceived as skilled and experienced related to the particular behavior.

The fourth source of efficacy expectation is the person's current physiological state or anxiety. High physiological arousal, as evidenced by sweaty palms, racing heartbeat, and trembling knees, not only impairs performance directly (i.e., stuttering, word finding problems, decreased concentration) but also serves as source of negative feedback for self-monitoring of performance. The effect of physiological arousal or anxiety on self-efficacy is bi-directional in that arousal undermines confidence and increased confidence can decrease arousal. One direct manner to try and counteract the effects of physiological arousal is through the use of relaxation techniques such as progressive muscle relaxation, autogenic relaxation, or imagery.

Self-management Interventions that Increase Self-Efficacy

Studies reviewed in this section met the following criteria, (1) the study evaluated a self-management intervention; (2) the study included pre- and post-treatment measures of self-efficacy. Table 1 summarizes the results of this group of studies. The first column identifies the self-management focus of the intervention and indicates the name(s) of the author(s). Study design and sample size information is included in column two and includes studies from randomized trials (8) or effectiveness/cohort studies (4). Column three includes the elements of the intervention to allow for identification of common elements across this diverse group of studies. Finally, column four includes effect sizes estimates for self-efficacy measures that were computed with the "d" statistic. For the randomized studies the "d" statistic refers to the difference in self-efficacy scores at follow-up between the experimental and control group(s), whereas the "d" statistic refers to pre-post differences for the effectiveness studies.

Kaplan and colleagues (Kaplan et al., 1984) investigated whether efficacy expectations mediate exercise compliance in patients with chronic obstructive pulmonary disease (COPD). In this study, 60 older adult patients with COPD were given a prescription to increase their exercise (walking) and randomly assigned to either control or experimental groups. All groups received attention but only the experimental groups received an intervention that focused on increasing walking. The experimental groups included a behavior modification group that focused on goal setting and functional analysis of walking, a cognitive therapy group that focused on decreasing negative thoughts and promoting positive self-talk, and a cognitive behavioral therapy group that included all of both above elements plus relaxation training. Subjects completed measures of self-efficacy (related to different forms of physical exertion) and health locus of control (Wallston et al., 1976) at baseline and then three months later. Health Locus of Control Scale measures the degree to which an individual believes that health behaviors/outcomes are under one's control (internal) or not under one's control (external). Interventions that included behavioral components produced the greatest changes in walking self-efficacy while health locus of control less strongly related to behavior change. Interestingly, the change in efficacy beliefs appeared specific to thetarget behavior (walking) as efficacy beliefs about other behaviors (climbing, exertion, pushing,

Study	Study Design	Elements of Intervention	Magnitude of Self-Efficacy Δ
Randomized Studies			
COPD Kaplan, Atkins and Reinsch, 1984	*Randomized Trial* BM: Behavior Modification (N=15) CT: Cognitive Treatment (N=15) CBT: Cognitive Behavior – Therapy (N=15) AC: Attention Control (N=15)	BM: goal setting, functional analysis of walking CT: Id. Negative thoughts, promote pos. self-talk CBT: All of both above plus relaxation training AC: Attention without focus on walking (all condit. 6 sessions)	Effect Size Walking Efficacy Post-Intervention: BM v. AC = 1.29 CT v. AC = 1.16 CBT v. AC = 1.58
Memory Dellefield and McDougall, 1996	*Randomized Trial* Intervention Control (N=145)	-Performance Accomplishment -Modeling -Feedback (4 sessions 90m)	Effect Size Memory Self-Efficacy: Post Intervention: .21 2 week f/u: .17
Oral Hygiene Stewart, Wolfe, Maeder and Hartz, 1996	*Randomized Trial* EI: Education Intervention (N=40) PI: Psychological Intervention (N=37) Control: (N=40)	EI: Information only PI: Initially used Stage of Change, Self-monitoring, Contingency Management, Goal Setting, Control: Usual Care (4 session 40m for EI and PI groups)	Effect Sizes Flossing Self-Efficacy: PI vs. Control = .75 EI vs. Control = .27
Sun Exposure Rodrigue, 1996	*Randomized Trial* IOC: Information only Intervention NIC: No-Information Control CPP: Comprehensive Prevention Program (N=55)	CPP: Knowledge Behavioral Skills Attitudes and Beliefs (Parents and children) IOC: Increase Knowledge (1 session 90m)	Insufficient information for self-efficacy effect size estimation.

Study	Study Design	Elements of Intervention	Magnitude of Self-Efficacy Δ
Rheumatoid Arthritis Barlow, Pennington, and Bishop, 1997	Randomized Education Trial Intervention: Leaflet Control: No Leaflet (N=108)	Education	No change in S.E. for either condition
Child's Asthma Hanson, 1998	*Randomized Trial* IG: Standard Education, Group Education, Home visits CG: Standard Education during Clinic Visit (N= 303 baseline) (N=158 follow-up)	Social Support Education (6 in-home sessions beyond Usual Care, 5 sessions at Clinic)	Equal change in S.E. in Intervention and Control Groups
Fibromyalgia Buckelew, Conway, Parker, Deuser, Read et al., 1998	*Randomized Trial* RG: Relaxation (N=29) EG: Execise (N=30) CG: Combination (N=30) ACG: Attention Control N=30	RG: Cognitive and Muscular Relaxation, practice, self-monitoring EG: Strengthening and walking exercises CG: Both of above ACG: Educational (Training: Weekly sessions 90-120m, 6 weeks: Maintenance: Monthly sessions 1hr up until 24 months)	Effect size for Fibromyalgia <u>Self-Efficacy Function Score</u> <u>2-yr post training phase</u> CG v. RG = 1.98 CG v. EG = .78 CG v. ACG = 2.57 RG v. ACG = 2.89 EG v. ACG = 1.92
Macular Degeneration Brody, Williams, Thomas, Kaplan, Chu, and Brown, 1999	*Randomized Trial* SM: Self-Management Intervention (N=44) WLC: Wait-List Control (Cross-over) (N=48)	-Modeling Adapt. Behav. -Guided Practice -Persuasion -Cognitive Restructuring -Goal Setting (6 sessions 120m)	Effect Size for Self-Efficacy <u>Post- Intervention:</u> SM v. WLC = .60

Study	Study Design	Elements of Intervention	Magnitude of Self-Efficacy Δ
Fibromyalgia Gowans, deHueck, Voss, Silaj, Abbey and Reynolds, 2001	*Randomized Trial* Exp (N=27) Cont. (N=23) Measure: Arthritis Self-Efficacy Scale (for Fibromyalgia)	-Practice -Modeling -Persuasion -Feedback (3, 30-minute exercise classes/week for 23 weeks)	Effect size for Fibromyalgia Self-Efficacy Post-Intervention: Pain = .68 Function = .55 Symptoms = .47
Effectiveness Studies			
Safe Sex Thomas, Cahill and Santilli, 1997	*Effectiveness Study* (N=211)	Modeling Practice Education (1 computer session)	Statistically significant change reported. Insufficient information for effect size estimation.
Memory MacDougall, 1998	*Effectiveness Study* (N=23)	-Practice -Feedback -Modeling -Persuasion -Relaxation (8 sessions 60m)	Pre-Post effect size for Memory Self-Efficacy: At 3 mos.= .26
Chronic Disease Lorig, Ritter, Stewart, Sobel, Brown, Bandura, Gonzalez, Laurent and Holman, 2001	*Effectiveness Study* (N=683, 1-yr) (N=533, 2-yr)	-Modeling -Social Persuasion -Practice -Feedback -Goal Setting (7 peer-led sessions 2.5 hrs)	Pre-Post effect size for Self-Efficacy At 1-yr = .13 At 2-yr = .10
Binge Eating Wolff and Clark, 2001	*Effectiveness Study* (N=12)	-Education -Practice -Relaxation -Self-Monitoring (15 sessions- weekly)	Pre-Post effect size for Self-Efficacy.: Post-treatment: 1.71

behavior (walking) as efficacy beliefs about other behaviors (climbing, exertion, pushing, lifting, anger, tension) changed only to the degree to which they were similar to walking. With regard to Social Cognitive Theory (SCT), this study provides support for enactive attainments as a crucial factor changing efficacy expectations.

Dellefield and McDougall (Dellefield and McDougall, 1996) investigated the effects of an intervention designed to increase memory self-efficacy and memory performance. The study included 145 older adults who were randomized to either a control condition or the experimental condition which involved 2-weeks of group intervention. The four 1.5 hour intervention sessions involved teaching participants memory aid techniques, providing ample time for in-session practice and feedback, and assigning participants between-session exercises. Memory self-efficacy (Hertzog et al., 1990) and memory performance was assessed in both intervention and control participants at baseline, post-treatment, and 2-week follow-up. The results revealed that the control group's memory self-efficacy declined significantly over the course of the study while the experimental group experienced a significant increase in memory self-efficacy. The experimental group also experienced a significant increase in memory performance (memory performance was not measured in the control group). In terms of SCT, the authors hypothesized that both enactive experiences and vicarious experiences accounted for the improvement in memory and memory self-efficacy.

Stewart and colleagues (Stewart et al., 1996) investigated changes in self-efficacy following an intervention to change oral hygiene behavior. In this study, 123 male veterans were randomized to either four educational sessions about causes and prevention of dental disease, four psychological sessions based upon a stage of change model (see Volume 1, Chapter 1), and a control group. In addition to following the stage of change process, the psychological intervention used cognitive behavioral techniques of self-monitoring, contingency management, and goal setting. All participants completed dental self-efficacy estimates and received a 10-minute demonstration of correct brushing and flossing techniques prior to any interventions. Results indicated that both the intervention groups improved in dental knowledge as compared with the control group. All groups improved in terms of flossing efficacy, but the psychological intervention group demonstrated significantly greater flossing efficacy changes when compared to either the educational or control groups. Thus, while all groups improved in terms of dental self-efficacy the greatest improvement was demonstrated with the intervention that first focused on increasing the participant's readiness for change and then on increasing monitoring of enactive attainments.

Barlow and colleagues (Barlow et al., 1997) conducted an intervention for patients with rheumatoid arthritis (RA) using educational leaflets. One hundred and eight participants were randomized to either the intervention (leaflet) or control group. Participants completed measures of functional impairment, pain, arthritis knowledge, and arthritis self-efficacy (Lorig et al., 1989) at baseline and then three weeks later. Although the pamphlets did result in significant improvements in arthritis knowledge and pain for the intervention group, arthritis self-efficacy was not impacted by the intervention.

Hanson (Hanson, 1998) evaluated the benefits of a self-efficacy program in helping parents manage their child's asthma. The study assigned 303 participants (92% mothers) into either the intervention group or the usual care group. Both the treatment and control groups received standard education (i.e., asthma pathophysiology, symptoms, triggers, environmental control) from nurse educators during normal clinic visits. The intervention group received group education based upon the Open Airways Asthma Self-Management Program that included 2 one-hour classes at the initial visit, 2 additional one-hour sessions, a review at 6 months, and a problem solving session at 1-year. The intervention group also received scheduled home visits from a lay health advisor at 2, 4, 8, 14, and 20 months to provide social support and advice. All participants completed measures of asthma self-efficacy and asthma management at baseline, 6, 12, and 24 months. Both control and intervention groups displayed modest improvements in asthma self-efficacy but no differences emerged between the groups at any of the time points. Significant attrition occurred in both samples as only 65% of the control group and 58% of the intervention group completed the 2-year follow-up.

Buckelew and colleagues (Buckelew et al., 1998) compared the effectiveness of relaxation, exercise, and a combined treatment program for the treatment of fibromyalgia. The study randomly assigned one hundred and nineteen participants to one of four groups (1) relaxation training, (2) exercise training, (3) a combination treatment, or (4) an educational/attention control group. The relaxation group consisted of training in cognitive and muscular relaxation techniques and involved didactics, self-monitoring, and practice. The exercise group received training in increasing range of motion, strength, and aerobic capacity through walking. The combination group consisted of exercise and relaxation training as described above while the attention/educational control group received educational instruction about fibromyalgia. All groups met weekly for the first six weeks of the intervention (training phase) and then met on a monthly basis thereafter (maintenance phase). All participants completed measures of fibromyalgia symptoms, psychological distress, sleep quality, and self-efficacy. Results indicated improvements for all intervention groups in terms of fibromyalgia symptoms and self-efficacy. The combination group alone, however, maintained the self-efficacy gains at 2-year follow-up. Active ingredients of this intervention, as applied to SCT, include decreasing anxiety, modeling, enactive attainments, and persuasion.

Brody and colleagues (Brody et al., 1999) used a randomized clinical trial to assess whether a self-management group could improve mood, self-efficacy, and activity in people with central vision loss due to age-related macular degeneration. The study randomly assigned ninety-two older adults to the self-management intervention or to the wait-list control group (who crossed-over to intervention status in stage 2). The intervention consisted of 6 weekly 2-hour group sessions providing education about disease, group discussion, and skills training aimed at addressing barriers to independence. Participants completed measures of self-efficacy, psychological distress, and use of visual aids. Results indicated significant improvements in self-efficacy for the intervention group when compared to the control group (before cross-over) and improvements in self-efficacy, mood, and use of visual aids. Similar improvements appeared in the control group after they received the intervention. Likely sources of self-efficacy change include enactive attainments, modeling, and persuasion.

Gowans and colleagues (Gowans et al., 2001) evaluated the effect of exercise on mood and physical functioning in patients with fibromyalgia. Their study randomized fifty participants to either an exercise intervention or control group. The exercise intervention involved participation in three 30-minute exercise classes per week for 23 weeks. The graduated exercise program began with exercises in a therapeutic pool before moving on to walking classes in a gymnasium and finally to intermittent jogging. Assessments completed at baseline, 6, 12, and 23 weeks included completion of measures of mood, fibromyalgia self-efficacy (adapted from AES, (Lorig et al., 1989)), and physical functioning (6-minute walk distance). At 23-week follow-up the intervention group displayed significant improvements in mood, physical functioning, and fibromyalgia self-efficacy compared to their own baseline scores and to the control group. As in the previous study, the likely sources of self-efficacy involved in this intervention include enactive attainments, modeling, and persuasion.

Thomas and colleagues (Thomas et al., 1997) designed an interactive computer game to increase skill and self-efficacy regarding safer sex negotiation for adolescents. This study involved 211 out-of-school adolescents at 13 different sites ranging from group homes to private substance abuse residential facilities to federal Job Corps sites. The naturalistic study placed a computer kiosk at these sites where participants could elect to anonymously participate in an interactive video game. The game supplied information on safe sex practices by presenting the participant with negotiating tasks (i.e., turn down sex, ask a partner to use a condom) and then providing behavioral options along with pros and cons of the different options. Later, the participant is presented with negotiating situations and given the opportunity to record their own response to the situation. The game sessions typically lasted 50-60 minutes. Participants completed measures of HIV transmission knowledge and safe sex self-efficacy at the beginning and at the end of their computer session. A significant increase in HIV knowledge and self-efficacy was evidenced in those who completed the computer game. Interestingly, those who reported the highest levels of self-efficacy at

beginning of the game lowered their estimations significantly at the final assessment. The authors interpreted this finding as evidence of their more "cocky" participants receiving a "reality check" when they actually had to produce their responses to negotiating tasks. The sources of self-efficacy included in this intervention include enactive attainments and modeling (provided by computer generated peers).

McDougall (McDougall, 1998) tested the effects of a group intervention to increase memory self-efficacy in a cohort of 23 Hispanic older adults. This effectiveness trial included 9 sessions over a 4-week period and a booster session 3 months later. Components of the intervention included education about memory loss as people age and factors that affect memory such as mood, practicing memory techniques in a group setting, and receiving feedback from the instructor. All measures and classes were provided in Spanish. Participants completed measures of memory self-efficacy and frequency of use of memory techniques at baseline and again after the booster sessions 3 months after the intervention. The intervention produced pre-post improvements in memory self-efficacy and in use of memory techniques. Framed from the perspective of SCT, active ingredients involved in this intervention included enactive attainments, modeling, and persuasion.

Lorig and colleagues (Lorig et al., 2001) assessed the long-term impact of The Chronic Disease Self-Management Program (CDSMP) on health outcomes for a heterogeneous group of patients with chronic illnesses (lung disease, stroke, or arthritis). A total of 831 participants who completed the initial intervention provided data at 1 and 2 years post-intervention. A prior study involving this cohort, (Lorig et al., 1999) found that that patients randomized to the intervention achieved better health outcomes and lower health utilization. The intervention involved

7 weekly 2.5-hour sessions that were led by peer facilitators. Content of the sessions included adoption of exercise programs, use of cognitive symptom management techniques, fatigue and sleep management, mood management, and training in communicating with health providers. Participants completed measures assessing health status, health utilization, and disease management self-efficacy. The 1 and 2 years assessment indicated that, compared to baseline, participants increased their disease management self-efficacy and reduced their health distress and health utilization. Interestingly, improvements in self-efficacy were correlated with decreased health utilization. The authors noted the following elements in the intervention related to SCT: modeling, persuasion, and guided mastery.

Wolff and Clark (Wolff and Clark, 2001) investigated changes in eating self-efficacy and body image following cognitive-behavioral group therapy for binge eating disorder. Participants were 12 obese women diagnosed with binge eating disorder who completed the 15-week program. The cognitive behavioral program included psychoeducational material, self-monitoring of eating behavior, learning about cues and consequences of eating behavior, coping with negative thoughts, body image enhancement, assertiveness training, and relapse prevention strategies. At baseline and post-treatment participants completed measures of mood, self-efficacy, frequency of binge eating, and body image. Results indicated a reduction in binge episode frequency and significant improvements in self-efficacy, mood and body image. Active ingredients from SCT included enactive attainments, modeling, and persuasion.

Summary of Empirical Studies

The above studies suggest that self-efficacy for a particular behavior or set of behaviors can be increased and that the increases appear to follow pathways suggested by Social Cognitive Theory. One particularly strong lesson to be learned from the above studies is the importance of focusing on learning, changing, or practicing actual behaviors in order to change a given individual's perceived self-efficacy. Those programs that focused solely on education, and not on enactive attainments, produced relatively smaller or non-existent effects on self-efficacy. For instance, the intensive intervention study by Hanson (Hanson, 1998) may have failed to produce significant results because it focused primarily on education and support while neglecting the more central issue of ensuring that participants learn and practice behaviors related to managing their child's asthma.

A number of the studies found that changes in self-efficacy were related to important changes in health behaviors or improvements in health outcomes. Increases in self-efficacy for targeted behaviors were concordant with improved physical functioning (Gowans et al., 2001; Kaplan et al., 1984) increased health behaviors (Brody et al., 1999; McDougall, 1998; Wolff and Clark, 2001), improved mood (Brody et al., 1999; McDougall, 1998; Wolff and Clark, 2001), and decreased use of medical services(Lorig et al., 2001).

Most of the above interventions incorporated several sources of self-efficacy from SCT into their interventions: enactive attainment, vicarious experiences, and persuasion. Only two studies (Kaplan et al., 1984), however, included a component of the intervention that directly addresses physiological arousal or anxiety. This is surprising given the extensive literature reporting beneficial effects of stress management techniques such as applied relaxation (Kiecolt-Glaser et al., 2002; Mandle et al., 1996) for a wide range of disorders such as hypertension, insomnia, anxiety, and pain.

RECOMMENDATIONS FOR INCREASING PATIENT'S SELF EFFICACY

A voluminous body of literature exists relating high levels of self-efficacy to a number of health protective or health restorative behaviors for a variety of disorders. The purpose of this review is to focus on factors that are specifically associated with increasing self-efficacy. Having reviewed both the theoretical and empirical contributions to the question of how to increase a patient's self-efficacy, this discussion will now turn to recommendations for how to use SCT to help patients change their health behaviors. Although the following three recommendations apply equally well to either group or individual encounters with patients it should be recalled that one source of self-efficacy, vicarious experiences, is greatly enhanced by the use of a group interventions.

Traditional approaches to changing a patient's health behaviors typically involve only one source of self-efficacy enhancement: persuasion/exhortation. Although this activity is one of the four sources of self-efficacy described in SCT, it is not seen as a good "stand alone" method for increasing self-efficacy (Bandura, 1997). A more direct route to building self-efficacy for a behavior is actual performance of the behavior (enactive attainments). Thus, one recommendation is that performance of the target behavior and repetition of a target behavior should be considered as a routine component of medical care. Having a patient perform the health behavior in front of the health provider would be particularly effective for complex health regimens such as when a patient is learning glucose monitoring or when a patient is learning self-injection for management of diabetes. Educational information is beneficial in that the patient can refer back to such information at home, but it's clear from the above reviewed studies

that information alone is not sufficient for increasing a patient's self-efficacy to carry out a behavior such as glucose monitoring. Being able to carry out the behavior, whether in a clinic appointment or in a diabetes management class, will increase the individual's self-efficacy related to the behavior and increase the likelihood that they will carry out the behavior at home (Piette et al., 2000). In addition to having a patient perform the target behavior in the initial clinic appointment or education class, patients should be given opportunities to again perform the behavior at subsequent appointments or classes (practice). Not only does this ensure that the health behavior is being carried out properly at home but it gives the patient additional practice, which increases self-efficacy, which increases the likelihood that the patient will continue to engage in the behavior.

An additional recommendation for increasing a patient's self-efficacy for a behavior involves targeting the efficacy intervention at very specific aspects of the behavior. Self-efficacy for one behavior (i.e., glucose monitoring) may or may not be related to a patient's self-efficacy for other behaviors (i.e., self-injection or remembering oral medications). For complex regimens such as the management of diabetes it can be helpful to explore a patient's efficacy expectations for separate parts of the regimen and then spend time trying to help the patient improve upon their perceived areas of weakness. However, when targeting different aspects of adherence the behavioral foci will change, as will the efficacy targets. For example, targeting injection behavior could involve the patient practicing the actual injection of insulin while targeting diet could involve having the patient record frequency of eating contraindicated foods. Breaking down the regimen will not only help target the patient's efficacy for specific behaviors but it will also help the patient to view the regimen as manageable.

Increasing a patient's self-efficacy for a behavior can decrease their anxiety related to performance of the behavior. However, the converse is also true. Decreasing anxiety can increase a patient's self-efficacy for performing a behavior. A recommendation for providers, often overlooked, is that teaching patients stress management techniques can lead to increased self-efficacy and improved performance of the target health behavior and thus improved health outcomes. Stress management typically involves teaching relaxation techniques such as progressive muscle relaxation (Wadden and de la Torre, 1980), autogenic relaxation, or imagery. Despite a multitude of relaxation techniques, they all serve the function of decreasing physiological arousal. Relaxation techniques can be readily found either in the form of scripts that can be read for group instruction or in the form of audio cassettes/compact discs which patients can use at home or at work.

FUTURE DIRECTIONS FOR RESEARCH

Several important questions for future research on increasing self-efficacy for health behaviors remain unanswered. One important question relates to the relative importance of different sources of self-efficacy and the degree to which they work to increase self-efficacy. Although many of the studies included in this review cite different factors that are believed to contribute to self-efficacy there is no indication about the relative strength of these factors as they impact a patient's subsequent levels of self-efficacy. The apparent benefits of increasing self-efficacy, combined with the time-constrained nature of health care, point to the importance of identifying what theoretical sources of self-efficacy are most central. Related to the question of expediency are questions of what

conditions are necessary or sufficient for promoting self-efficacy in patients. While focusing on practicing of a specific behavior may be necessary to changing behavior, what benefits are accrued by seeing others successfully practice this behavior? Are benefits of learning in a group additive beyond the benefits of actually practicing the health behavior and gaining confidence in one's abilities?

Another direction for future research that has been alluded to previously is the introduction of stress management techniques to interventions and further investigation of the relationship between decreased stress and increased self-efficacy. Most of the research pertaining to self-efficacy and stress has focused on how increases in self-efficacy lead to decreases in physiological arousal or anxiety; much less has been focused on the reverse. Even though many researchers include both measures of self-efficacy and stress management interventions they overlook the potential direct relationship that stress management exerts on self-efficacy. For example, increases in self-efficacy might be related to frequency of practicing forms of relaxation or to the self-reported degree that a person feels less tense from practicing relaxation. It is also the case that learning stress management techniques might facilitate enactive attainments by relieving the patient of performance anxiety or by decreasing negative thoughts. Such hypotheses might account for Buckelew and colleagues' (1998) finding that relaxation combined with exercise produced greater change in self-efficacy over a longer period of time than exercise (enactive attainments) alone.

CONCLUSIONS

Numerous reports in recent years (see Trafton and Gordon this volume) point to the large impact that health behaviors exert on morbidity and mortality rates in the population. Since the 1970's self-care movement, clinicians have become increasingly aware of the inherent challenge of changing health behaviors in their patients. The targeting of self-efficacy for specific health behaviors has empirical support (Purdie and McCrindle, 2002; Shoor and Lorig, 2002) as an effective method for changing patient health behaviors since patients appear more likely to engage in behaviors when they feel competent or efficacious. Health care providers can help enhance the self-efficacy of their patients by incorporating SCT into their health behavior change interventions. By focusing on their patient's self-efficacy for health behaviors clinician's can increase the patient's perceived control over their illness and decrease future morbidity.

RECOMMENDATIONS FOR HEALTH PRACTITIONERS

The following recommendations are ranked by their respective level of empirical support.

1. Have patients practice the target behavior
2. Focus on specific behaviors
3. If necessary, break behavior down into components for practice
4. Take advantage of vicarious experiences inherent in group interventions
5. Incorporate stress management techniques

ADDITIONAL SOURCES OF INFORMATION ON SELF-EFFICACY AND SOCIAL COGNITIVE THEORY

1. Bandura, A. (1999). Self-efficacy: Toward a unifying theory of behavioral change, Baumeister, Roy F. (Ed). (1999). The self in social psychology. Key readings in social psychology. (pp. 285-298). ix, 492pp.

2. Bandura, A. (1998). Health promotion from the perspective of social cognitive theory. Psychology and Health, 13(4), 623-649.

REFERENCES

Bandura A. (1977) Self-efficacy: toward a unifying theory of behavioral change. Psychol Rev, 84(2): 191-215.

Bandura A. (1993) Perceived self-efficacy in cognitive development and functioning. Educational Psychologist, 28(2): 117-148.

Bandura A. (1997) Self-Efficacy: The Exercise of Control. New York: W. H. Freeman and Company

Barlow JH, Pennington DC,Bishop PE. (1997) Patient education leaflets for people with rheumatoid arthritis: A controlled study. Psychology Health and Medicine, 2(3): 221-235.

Barlow JH, Williams B, Wright C. (1996) The Generalized Self-Efficacy Scale in people with arthritis. Arthritis Care Res, 9(3): 189-196.

Baumeister RF. (Ed.). (1999) The self in social psychology: (1999). ix, 492 pp.

Brody BL, Williams RA, Thomas RG, Kaplan RM, Chu RM, Brown SI. (1999) Age-related macular degeneration: A randomized clinical trial of a self-management intervention. Annals of Behavioral Medicine, 21(4): 322-329.

Buckelew SP, Conway R, Parker J, Deuser WE, Read J, Witty TE, Hewett JE, Minor M, Johnson JC, Van Male L, McIntosh MJ, Nigh M, Kay DR. (1998) Biofeedback/relaxation training and exercise interventions for fibromyalgia: a prospective trial. Arthritis Care Res, 11(3): 196-209.

Buckelew SP, Huyser B, Hewett JE, Parker JC, Johnson JC, Conway R, KayDR. (1996) Self-efficacy predicting outcome among fibromyalgia subjects. Arthritis Care Res, 9(2): 97-104.

Dellefield KS, McDougall GJ. (1996) Increasing metamemory in older adults. Nursing Research, 45(5) : 284-290.

Gowans SE, deHueck A, Voss S, Silaj A, Abbey SE, Reynolds WJ. (2001) Effect of a randomized, controlled trial of exercise on mood and physical function in individuals with fibromyalgia. Arthritis Rheum, 45(6): 519-529.

Grossman HY, Brink S, Hauser ST. (1987) Self-efficacy in adolescent girls and boys with insulin-dependent diabetes mellitus. Diabetes Care, 10(3), 324-329.

Gwaltney CJ, Shiffman S, Paty JA, Liu KS, Kassel JD, Gnys M, Hickcox M. (2002) Using self-efficacy judgments to predict characteristics of lapses to smoking. J Consult Clin Psychol, 70(5): 1140-1149.

Hanson J. (1998) Parental self-efficacy and asthma self-management skills. Journal of the Society of Pediatric Nurses, 3(4) :146-154.

Hertzog C, Dixon RA, Hultsch DF. (1990) Relationships between metamemory, memory predictions, and memory task performance in adults. Psychol Aging, 5(2): 215-227.

Kaplan RM, Atkins CJ, Reinsch S. (1984) Specific efficacy expectations mediate exercise compliance in patients with COPD. Health Psychol, 3(3): 223-242.

Kiecolt-Glaser JK, McGuire L, Robles TF, Glaser R. (2002) Psychoneuroimmunology: psychological influences on immune function and health. J Consult Clin Psychol, 70(3): 537-547.

Lackner JM, Carosella AM. (1999) The relative influence of perceived pain control, anxiety, and functional self efficacy on spinal function among patients with chronic low back pain. Spine, 24(21:, 2254-2260; discussion 2260-2251.

Lorig K, Chastain RL, Ung E, Shoor S, Holman HR. (1989) Development and evaluation of a scale to measure perceived self-efficacy in people with arthritis. Arthritis Rheum, 32(1): 37-44.

Lorig KR, Ritter P, Stewart AL, Sobel DS, Brown BW Jr, Bandura A, Gonzalez VM, Laurent DD, Holman, HR. (2001) Chronic disease self-management program: 2-year health status and health care utilization outcomes. Med Care, 39(11): 1217-1223.

Lorig KR, Sobel DS, Ritter PL, Laurent D, Hobbs M. (2001) Effect of a self-management program on patients with chronic disease. Eff Clin Pract, 4(6): 256-262.

Lorig KR, Sobel DS, Stewart AL, Brown BW Jr, Bandura A, Ritter P, Gonzalez VM, Laurent DD,Holman HR. (1999) Evidence suggesting that a chronic disease self-management program can improve health status while reducing hospitalization: a randomized trial. Med Care, 37(1): 5-14.

Mandle CL, Jacobs SC, Arcari PM, Domar AD. (1996) The efficacy of relaxation response interventions with adult patients: a review of the literature. J Cardiovasc Nurs, 10(3): 4-26.

McDougall GJ. (1998) Increasing memory self-efficacy and strategy use in Hispanic elders. Clinical Gerontologist, 19(2): 57-76.

Pajares F, Graham L. (1999) Self-efficacy, motivation constructs, and mathematics performance of entering middle school students. Contemporary Educational Psychology, 24(2) : 124-139.

Piette JD, Weinberger M, McPhee SJ. (2000) The effect of automated calls with telephone nurse follow-up on patient-centered outcomes of diabetes care: a randomized, controlled trial. Med Care, 38(2): 218-230.

Purdie N, McCrindle A. (2002) Self-regulation, self-efficacy and health behavior change in older adults. Educational Gerontology, 28(5): 379-400.

Rhee SH, Parker JC, Smarr KL, Petroski GF, Johnson JC, Hewett JE, Wright GE,

Multon, KD, Walker SE. (2000) Stress management in rheumatoid arthritis: What is the underlying mechanism? Arthritis Care and Research, 13(6): 435-442.

Ritter A, Bowden S, Murray T, Ross P, Greeley J, Pead J. (2002) The influence of the therapeutic relationship in treatment for alcohol dependency. Drug Alcohol Rev, 21(3): 261-268.

Rodrigue JR. (1996) Promoting healthier behaviors, attitudes, and beliefs toward sun exposure in parents of young children. Journal of Consulting and Clinical Psychology, 64(6): 1431-1436.

Schwartz CE, Coulthard-Morris L, Zeng Q, Retzlaff P. (1996) Measuring self-efficacy in people with multiple sclerosis: a validation study. Arch Phys Med Rehabil, 77(4): 394-398.

Shoor S, Lorig KR. (2002) Self-care and the doctor-patient relationship. Med Care, 40(4 Suppl): II40-44.

Stewart JE, Wolfe GR, Maeder L, Hartz GW. (1996) Changes in dental knowledge and self-efficacy scores following interventions to change oral hygiene behavior. Patient Education and Counseling, 27(3):269-277.

Strecher VJ, DeVellis BM, Becker MH, Rosenstock IM. (1986) The role of self-efficacy in achieving health behavior change. Health Education Quarterly, 13(1): 73-92.

Thomas R, Cahill J, Santilli L. (1997) Using an interactive computer game to increase skill and self-efficacy regarding safer sex negotiation: Field test results. Health Education and Behavior, 24(1): 71-86.

Wadden TA, de la Torre CS. (1980) Relaxation therapy as an adjunct treatment for essential hypertension. J Fam Pract, 11(6): 901-908.

Wallston BS, Wallston KA, Kaplan GD, Maides SA. (1976) Development and validation of the health locus of control (HLC) scale. J Consult Clin Psychol, 44(4): 580-585

Wigal JK, Creer TL, Kotses H. (1991) The COPD Self-Efficacy Scale. Chest, 99(5): 1193-1196.

Wolff GE, Clark MM. (2001) Changes in eating self-efficacy and body image following cognitive-behavioral group therapy for binge eating disorder: A clinical study. Eating Behaviors, 2(2).

USING MESSAGE FRAMING TO PROMOTE HEALTHFUL BEHAVIORS: A GUIDE TO BEST PRACTICES

Alexander J. Rothman, Emily N. Stark, and Peter Salovey

INTRODUCTION

"Be safe this summer: Use Sunscreen." "Failing to immunize your children will put their health at risk." "Don't forget: There are costs to not screening for breast cancer." People constantly see and hear messages about health and their health practices and, in many cases, these messages provide critical information about behaviors they need to adopt. Thus, the primary goal of these messages is to persuade people to either initiate a new pattern of behavior (e.g., get a mammogram) or sustain a current pattern of behavior (e.g., obtain regular mammograms).

What makes a health message persuasive? The effective communication of health information is a complicated process that depends on a myriad of factors (for reviews, see Salovey et al., 1998; Salovey and Wegener, 2003). However, one aspect of health messages that has been shown to be particularly important is how the information is framed (Rothman and Salovey, 1997; Rothman et al., 2003).

Information about a health behavior can emphasize the benefits of taking action (i.e., a gain-framed appeal) or the costs of failing to take action (i.e., a loss-framed appeal). For example, a brochure to promote breast cancer screening could emphasize the health benefits afforded by being screened or the health costs that arise if you fail to get screened (See Table 1 for examples of gain- and loss-framed appeals). The frame that is used has been shown to have a systematic effect on people's behavioral decision.

Table 1. Examples of Gain and Loss-Framed Statements

Gain Frame		Loss Frame	
Prevention Behavior	Detection Behavior	Prevention Behavior	Detection Behavior
'You can significantly decrease your chances of ultimately getting skin cancer by not exposing your skin to the sun without protection'	'We will show that detecting breast cancer early can save your life.'	'You can significantly increase your chances of ultimately getting skin cancer by exposing your skin to the sun without protection'	'We will show that failing to detect breast cancer early can cost you your life.'

Note: The framed statements for a prevention behavior are from material developed by Rothman et al (1993) and those for a detection behavior are from material developed by Banks et al. (1995).

In this chapter, we review how the decision to disseminate either a gain- or a loss-framed message affects people's decision-making and subsequent behavior. First, we provide a brief overview of the conceptual framework that has guided research on message framing and health behavior. Second, we summarize the empirical evidence available regarding the differential impact of gain- and loss-framed messages on health practices. Third, we address several technical issues regarding the development of framed messages. Finally, we consider the critical questions in this area that still need to be addressed. Taken together, this review should provide investigators with an understanding of the differential impact of gain- and loss-framed messages that will inform and guide professional decisions regarding the optimal way to communicate health information.

THE APPLICATION OF MESSAGE FRAMING TO HEALTH MESSAGES

Research on the differential influence of gain- and loss-framed health messages was motivated by the observation in the decision-making literature that people's preferences are sensitive to how a decision-making dilemma is framed. According to the framing postulate of Prospect Theory (Tversky and Kahneman, 1981), people act to avoid risks (they are risk-averse in their preferences) when considering the potential gains afforded by a decision, but are willing to take risks (they are risk-seeking in their preferences) when considering the potential losses afforded by their decision. The empirical basis for this postulate rests primarily on people's responses to hypothetical scenarios framed in terms of gains or losses (for a meta-analytic review, see Kuhberger et al., 1999). For example, in one scenario people were informed about an illness expected to affect 600 individuals and asked to choose between two interventions to combat the disease (Tversky and Kahneman, 1981). Although the two interventions afforded the same expected utility, one offered a certain outcome, whereas the other offered an uncertain or risky outcome. In the gain-framed condition, the two interventions were described in terms of the number of lives that would be <u>saved</u> (e.g., If Program A is adopted, 200 people will be saved; if Program B is adopted, there is a 1/3 probability that all 600 people will be saved, and a 2/3 probability

that nobody will be saved), whereas in the loss-framed condition, the interventions were described in terms of the number of lives that would be <u>lost</u> (e.g., If Program C is adopted, 400 people will die; if Program D is adopted, there is a 1/3 probability that nobody will die, and a 2/3 probability that all 600 people will die). Consistent with the theory, when informed about the number of lives that could be saved, people preferred the intervention program that provided a certain gain, but when informed about the number of lives that could be lost, people's preferences shifted and they consistently preferred the intervention program that offered a risky outcome.

Why do preferences depend on how the programs are framed? Although the specific cognitive processes that underlie the impact of framed information on choice are not well-specified, the differential response to gain- and loss-framed information is thought to reflect the shape of the value function that relates objective outcomes (e.g., losing 200 lives) to subjective values (e.g., the distress elicited by losing 200 lives). In the domain of losses, the value function is steep as people find even modest losses distressing (Taylor, 1991). Furthermore, the shape of the function is convex, such that increases in potential losses have a rapidly diminishing impact on the perceived value of the outcome. If the subjective cost of losing 600 lives is not appreciably greater than losing 400 lives, people accept the risk of a larger loss in order to try to avoid any losses. In the domain of gains, the shape of the value function is concave, and thus the satisfaction derived from any increase in potential gains is associated with relatively smaller increases in perceived value. However, in the domain of gains, the modest improvement in value leads people to be risk-averse rather than risk-seeking in their preferences (i.e., the increase in value associated with saving 600 rather than 400 lives is not worth the risk of saving no lives).

Although research on Prospect Theory had focused primarily on explaining the choices people make when faced with a hypothetical decision problem, several investigators have relied on this perspective to understand how altering the framing of a health message might affect people's willingness to perform a particular behavior (e.g., Meyerowitz and Chaiken, 1987; Rothman et al., 1993). In fact, Rothman and Salovey (1997) have argued that predictions regarding the relative influence of gain- and loss-framed messages on health behavior can be derived from the conceptual framework outlined in Prospect Theory. Given the premise that people are more willing to take risks when faced with loss-framed information but are more risk-averse when faced with gain-framed information, the influence of a given frame on behavior should be contingent on whether the behavior under consideration is perceived to reflect a risk-averse or risk-seeking course of action.

Consistent with this perspective, Rothman and Salovey (1997) provided a taxonomy of situations – classifying them as risk-averse or risk-seeking -- that affords predictions as to when gain- or loss-framed health appeals are maximally persuasive. When people are considering a behavior that they perceive involves some risk or uncertainty (e.g., it may detect a health problem), loss-framed appeals are more persuasive, but when people are considering a behavior that they perceive involves a relatively certain outcome (e.g., it prevents the onset of a health problem), gain-framed appeals are more persuasive. Moreover, the function served by a health behavior can operate as a reliable heuristic to predict the behaviors people tend to perceive as risky or as relatively certain or safe. Detection behaviors such as breast self-examination (BSE) or mammography serve to detect the presence of a health problem, and because they can inform people that they may be symptomatic or ill, initiating the behavior

may be considered a risky decision. Although detection behaviors such as mammography provide critical long-term benefits, characterizing them as risky accurately captures people's subjective assessment of these behaviors (e.g., Lerman and Rimer, 1995; Mayer and Solomon, 1992; Meyerowitz and Chaiken, 1987). In fact, one reason why women delay scheduling their regular screening mammogram is concern that it might reveal that they have a problem. In contrast, prevention behaviors such as the regular use of sunscreen or condoms forestall the onset of an illness and maintain a person's current health status. In fact, these behaviors are risky only to the extent that one chooses not to take action. Taken together, this framework suggests that loss-framed appeals would be more effective in promoting the use of detection behaviors but gain-framed appeals would be more effective in promoting the use of prevention behaviors (Rothman and Salovey, 1997).

We believe research findings on message framing are best understood when examined within the two broad domains of prevention and detection behaviors. However, even within a single health domain, prevention and detection behaviors can differ on a range of dimensions such as cost, familiarity, difficulty, and frequency. Is there evidence to support the premise that the function of the behavior (i.e., prevention vs. detection) moderates the influence of frame?

A series of laboratory studies have confirmed that the function of the behavior regulates the influence of gain- and loss-framed appeals. For example, in one study, college students read either a gain- or a loss-framed pamphlet about gum disease and a mouth rinse (Rothman et al., 1999, Experiment 2). Some students read either gain or loss-framed messages suggesting that a mouth rinse was an effective way to prevent the build-up of plaque (i.e., a prevention behavior), whereas other students read either gain- or loss-framed messages suggesting that a mouth rinse was an effective way to <u>detect</u> the build-up of plaque (i.e., a detection behavior). Consistent with predictions, the persuasiveness of gain- vs. loss-framed pamphlets was contingent on the function of the mouth rinse. When the mouth rinse prevented the build-up of plaque, students were more likely to request a free sample of the product after having read the gain-framed pamphlet, but when the mouth rinse detected the build-up of plaque, students were more likely to request a free sample after having read the loss-framed pamphlet. Given these findings, we rely on this framework to organize our summary of the empirical findings that have been generated by experimental tests of the influence of message framing on health behavior.

REVIEW OF TRIALS OF THE IMPACT OF MESSAGE FRAME ON BEHAVIOR

In this section, we summarize the findings that have been obtained in experiments that have assessed the differential effect of gain- and loss-framed messages on health behavior. Tables 2A and 2B provide a detailed summary of these experiments. Consistent with the theoretical framework outlined above, we have divided the review into two sections. The first section summarizes the findings from studies that have tested the impact of frame on detection behaviors (e.g., mammography, HIV testing; see Table 2A), and the second section summarizes the findings from studies that have tested the impact of frame on prevention behaviors (e.g., sunscreen, exercise; see Table 2B).

Detection behaviors

Are loss-framed messages more effective at promoting interest in and the performance of detection behaviors? The first experiment to test this premise was conducted with ninety female undergraduates who read either a gain-framed or a loss-framed pamphlet about breast cancer and BSE. Meyerowitz and Chaiken (1987) chose to focus on BSE because women had reported that concern about the risk of finding a health problem (i.e., a lump) was an important barrier to performing an exam. Four months after reading the pamphlet, participants were contacted by phone to assess performance of BSE. Consistent with predictions, a loss frame advantage was obtained. Women who had read the loss-framed pamphlet performed more breast self-exams than did those who had read the gain-framed pamphlet. Although a subsequent study (Lalor and Hailey, 1989) failed to replicate this finding, several other studies have found a significant advantage for loss-framed appeals and have been able to extend these results to other populations and behaviors.

For example, Banks and colleagues (1995) attempted to replicate the findings of Meyerowitz and Chaiken in a sample of women over age 40 who were not compliant with mammography screening guidelines. The hypothesis was that a loss-framed appeal would be the most effective way to promote mammography, and this prediction was supported. Twelve months after having viewed a video about breast cancer and mammography, 66.2% of women who had viewed the loss-framed video had a mammogram, whereas only 51.5% of women who had viewed the gain-framed video had a mammogram.

This finding was subsequently replicated in an intervention that targeted an ethnically diverse sample of women recruited from community health clinics and public housing developments (Schneider et al., 2001). It should be noted, however, that the framing effect was obtained only when the video presented the information in a multicultural context. Videotapes that presented information only about women of the same ethnicity as the participant did not produce a framing effect. Although the reason for this

Table 2a. Trials that have tested the Impact of Gain- and Loss-Framed Health Messages: Screening Behaviors.

Study	Participants	Health Domain/ Targeted Outcome	Frames Used / Method	Relevant Moderators	Results
Meyerowitz & Chaiken (1987)	Female undergraduates N=90	Breast self-exams (BSE) **BSE 4 months after intervention**	Gain frame Loss frame No frame control **Pamphlets**	None	**Loss frame advantage** Loss: 1.42 exams Gain: 0.74 exams Control: 0.75 exams
Lalor & Hailey (1989)	Female undergraduates N=55	Breast self-exams **BSE 4 months after intervention**	Gain frame Loss frame **Pamphlets**	None	**No effect of frame** Loss: 2.62 exams Gain: 2.23 exams [a]
Lauver & Rubin (1990)	Women with abnormal pap test N=116	Cervical cancer screening **Attendance at follow-up within 6 weeks of intervention**	Gain frame Loss frame **Phone call script**	None	**No effect of frame** Loss: 77% Gain: 71%
Lerman et al. (1992)	Female members of an HMO with previous abnormal mammograms N=446	Mammography screening **Screening 3 months after intervention**	Gain frame Loss frame No frame control **Educational booklets**	None	**No effect of frame** [b] Loss: 67% Gain: 66% Control: 53%
Banks et al., (1995)	Women over age 40, not compliant with mammography screening guidelines N=133	Mammography screening **Mammogram 12 months after intervention**	Gain frame Loss frame **Video**	None	**Loss frame advantage** Loss: 66% Gain: 52%
Kalichman & Coley (1995)	African-American women from a women's clinic N=100	HIV testing **HIV testing 2 weeks after intervention**	Loss frame No frame control **Videotapes**	None	**Loss frame advantage for HIV testing** Loss: 63% Control: 23%

Table 2a. cont. Trials that have tested the Impact of Gain- and Loss-Framed Health Messages: Screening Behaviors.

Study	Participants	Health Domain/ Targeted Outcome	Frames Used / Method	Relevant Moderators	Results
Schneider et al., (2001)	Women over age 40, not compliant with mammography screening guidelines N=752	Mammography screening **Screening 6 months after intervention**	Gain frame Loss frame **Video**	Multicultural vs. targeted to ethnicity	**Loss frame advantage** *only for multicultural intervention Loss: 50% Gain: 36% **Ethnically targeted intervention:** Loss: 36% Gain: 41%
Finney & Iannoti (2002)	Female hospital patients over age 40 N=929	Mammography screening **Screening 1 & 2 months after intervention**	Gain frame Loss frame No frame control **Hospital mammography reminder screening letter**	Family history of breast cancer	**Loss frame advantage at 1 month only** * only for positive family history Loss: 33.0% Gain: 23.5% Control: 29.4% **Negative family history:** Loss: 23.2% Gain: 22.4% Control: 23.1%
Apanovitch et al., (2003)	Low income, ethnic minority women N=480	HIV testing **HIV testing 6 months after intervention**	Gain frame Loss frame **Videos**	Perceived certainty that HIV testing will produce a favorable outcome	**Gain frame advantage** *only for people who were certain testing would be favorable Loss: 26% Gain: 38% **Uncertain outcome:** Loss: 48% Gain: 47%

Table 2b. Trials that have tested the Impact of Gain- and Loss-Framed Health Messages: Prevention Behaviors.

Study	Participants	Health Domain/ Targeted Outcome	Frames Used / Method	Relevant Moderators	Results
Rothman et al., (1993) Exp. 2	Undergraduates N=146	Skin cancer / sunscreen use **Mailed postcard requesting sunscreen sample with SPF of 15**	Gain frame Loss frame **Pamphlets**	Gender	**Gain frame advantage** *only for women Loss 45% Gain: 79% **Men** Loss: 47% Gain: 50%
Detweiler et al., (1999)	Beach-goers N=217	Skin cancer / sunscreen use **Redeem coupon for free sunscreen**	Gain frame Loss frame **Brochure**	None	**Gain frame advantage** Loss: 53% Gain: 71%
McCaul et al., (2002)	Medicare recipients who had not received a flu shot in the past year N=23,733	Flu immunizations **Vaccination 6 months after intervention**	Gain frame Loss frame No frame control letter No letter received **Reminder letter**	None	**No effect of frame** [b] Loss: 24.5% Gain: 23.4% No Frame Control: 24.5% No letter: 19.6%
Jones et al., (2003)	Undergraduates N=192	Physical exercise **Amount of strenuous exercise 2 weeks after intervention**	Gain frame Loss frame **Pamphlets**	Credible vs. non-credible author of message	**Gain frame advantage** *only for credible source Loss: 1.86 exercise sessions Gain: 2.22 exercise sessions **Non-credible source:** Loss: 2.11 exercise sessions Gain: 1.90 exercise sessions

[a] Condition mean was estimated because mean levels were not separately given in text.
[b] All letter/booklet conditions produced a significantly greater response than the no letter/control condition

discrepancy is not well-understood, it may be that these latter videos were viewed as patronizing or offensive in some way by viewers and thus may not have been as carefully watched. As we will discuss later, framing effects may depend on participants paying sufficient attention to the framed material.

Kalichman and Coley (1995) conducted one of the few studies that tested the impact of frame on a detection behavior unrelated to breast cancer. They tested messages designed to promote HIV testing among African-American women recruited from a women's health clinic. In this study, women who viewed a loss-framed videotape about HIV testing were more likely to get tested for HIV two weeks after the intervention than were women who viewed a control tape that did not include any framed information (63% to 23%, respectively).

Several studies have examined participants' attitudes toward a behavior or their intentions to perform the behavior, in lieu of assessing actual behaviors. The results of these studies generally support the findings already described: Loss-framed information is more effective than gain-framed information in increasing attitudes toward and intentions to perform a detection behavior. For example, Cox and Cox (2001) found that a loss-framed appeal increased intentions to get a mammogram and elicited more positive attitudes toward mammography. Shiloh, Eini, Ben-Neria, and Sagi (2001) examined recommendations for amniocentesis to detect possible birth defects, and again, a loss frame advantage was found. Women who received a loss-framed summary sheet about amniocentesis were more likely to recommend the procedure than were women who received a gain-framed summary sheet. Lastly, Arora (2000) found that a dental ad that contained loss-framed information elicited greater intentions to go to the dentist for a check-up than did a gain-framed version of the ad.

Two studies of framing effects on detection behaviors have reported no effect of frame. Lerman et al. (1992) tested messages designed to encourage women who previously had abnormal mammograms to get a follow-up mammogram. Women who received a gain or a loss-framed booklet were equally likely to get a follow-up mammogram during the three month follow-up (66% and 67%, respectively). The second study (Lauver and Rubin, 1990) targeted women who had received an abnormal PAP test. Each woman received either a gain- or a loss-framed phone call encouraging her to return for a follow-up screening. Again, there was no differential effect of frame. Seventy-seven percent of women who received a loss-framed call and 71% of women who received a gain-framed call returned within 6 weeks for further screening.

One unique feature of these two studies is that they involved participants who needed to take action after having received an abnormal test result. In both cases, there was a relatively high rate of compliance, which may suggest that in situations where people know they have a medical problem, they are sufficiently motivated to return for more testing and, thus, do not benefit from the added motivation afforded by a loss-framed appeal. Alternatively, in response to the fact that the initial test had already detected a potential health problem, women may have changed how they think about the screening test. Some women might see the follow-up test as even riskier and hence be responsive to a loss-framed appeal. Yet other women might no longer see being screened as risky and, in fact, might even see the follow-up test as an opportunity to reaffirm that they are healthy. In this case, they might be more responsive to a gain-framed appeal. As we discuss briefly later in this chapter, to the extent there is variability in how people think about a test procedure, evidence of a systematic effect of framing will be harder to discern.

Several investigators have begun to identify factors that may constrain or moderate the impact of message framing on behavior. One variable of interest is people's level of involvement with a health issue. It is possible that people need to be highly invested in the health issue for a framing effect to occur (for a more complete discussion of this issue, see Rothman and Salovey, 1997; Rothman et al., 2003). One study has tested this thesis by using the presence or absence of a family history of breast cancer as a proxy for involvement with breast cancer (Finney and Iannoti, 2002). Consistent with prior research, this study found an advantage for loss-framed information at a 1 month follow-up: 33% of women who received a loss-framed letter from the hospital returned for a mammogram, compared to only 23.5% of those who received a gain-framed letter and 29.4% of those who received the standard (unframed) letter. However, this effect held only for people with a family history of breast cancer; people with no family history of breast cancer were not affected by frame. Although a woman's family history of breast cancer moderated the effect of frame on behavior, any strong conclusions about the role of involvement is limited by the absence of any direct evidence that women without a family history of breast cancer are not involved with this issue. It could be that having a family history of breast cancer affected how women construed the act of getting a mammogram. These women might be particularly likely to see getting a mammogram as "risky" as it would be more likely to detect a sign of cancer.

Some investigators have begun to examine how variation in how people view a detection behavior can affect the influence of message framing. Several studies have provided suggestive evidence that the persuasive impact of a loss-framed message is obtained only among people who construe the behavior as risky (see Rothman et al., 2003). However, to date, only one study has assessed a behavioral outcome. Apanovitch, McCarthy, and Salovey (2003) tested the impact of gain- and loss-framed videos about HIV testing on the behavior of a sample of low-income women. Prior to viewing the video, women indicated their beliefs about the outcome of a potential HIV test. The investigators differentiated between people who were certain the test result would be negative (making the test a low-risk behavior) and those who were uncertain about the test result (making the test a high-risk behavior). Six months after the video, women who construed the test as a low-risk behavior were more likely to get tested if they had seen the gain-framed video, whereas those women who construed the test as a high-risk behavior were somewhat more likely to get tested if they had seen the loss-framed video.

Taken together, research has shown that loss-framed messages are more effective than gain-framed message in promoting detection behaviors. This pattern of results would appear to reflect the fact that by choosing to be screened people believe they run the risk of finding a health problem. Although people typically construe detection behaviors in terms of their ability to find a health problem, variability in how people think about a given behavior will have a systematic effect on the observed impact of gain- and loss-framed messages. In particular, to the extent that people believe being screened will afford an opportunity to affirm their health, a gain-frame appeal will be more effective.

Although the studies reviewed have included a range of populations and health behaviors, the majority of the work that has been done has involved breast cancer screening behaviors. We expect these findings will generalize to other detection behaviors, but investigators should be mindful of this issue as they develop framed messages to target detection behaviors for other health concerns.

Prevention behaviors

A smaller number of studies have tested the hypothesis that gain-framed messages are more effective than loss-framed messages in promoting prevention behaviors. Of the four studies that have assessed a behavioral outcome, three have reported an advantage for gain-framed messages.

Two studies tested the effect of receiving framed information about skin cancer on a person's willingness to use sunscreen. Both Rothman et al. (1993) and Detweiler et al. (1999) found that people were more likely to request a sample of sunscreen with a sun protection factor of 15 after having read a gain-framed brochure about skin cancer and sunscreen. Although in the initial study (Rothman et al., 1993) the framing effect was obtained only among women, the follow-up study (Detweiler et al., 1999) revealed a gain-framed advantage for both men and women. In this latter study, 71% of beach-goers who read a gain-framed brochure redeemed a coupon for free sunscreen compared to only 53% of those who read a loss-framed brochure.

Two other studies have looked at the effect of framed information on physical exercise (Jones et al., 2003) and flu immunizations (McCaul et al., 2002). Jones et al. (2003) found that people who read the gain-framed message subsequently engaged in more sessions of strenuous exercise than did those who read the loss-framed message (2.22 exercise sessions over a two week period to 1.86, respectively). McCaul et al. (2002) tested whether gain-framed appeals would be an effective way to encourage Medicare recipients to get a flu shot. The study involved over 23,000 Medicare recipients who had not received a flu shot in the previous year. Although the investigators found that receiving a letter about the flu vaccine increased vaccination rates, there was no differential effect of message frame.

Several studies have examined the impact of message framing on people's intentions to perform prevention behaviors and they have generally supported the thesis that gain-framed messages will be more effective. For example, Donovan and Jalleh (2000) found that adult women who read gain-framed information about a hypothetical immunization available for children up to 1 year of age were more likely to report that they would get this immunization or seek more information about it compared to women who read loss-framed information. However, this effect was more pronounced in women who did not have a child less than one year of age and were not considering having a child within the next year. Women who had a child younger than one year of age showed very high intentions to immunize regardless of frame (Mean gain = 4.36, Mean loss = 4.12, on a scale of 1 to 5), indicating that women in this situation may not need any additional motivation to seek out immunization.

A second study examined the impact of framed information on intentions to engage in safe driving behaviors (Millar and Millar, 2000). As predicted, participants reported stronger intentions to use safe driving behaviors after having read the gain-framed message. However, this effect was found only for those individuals who, prior to the study, indicated that they were very interested in the issue of safe driving; no framing advantage was found for those individuals who did not consider themselves involved. This finding converges with others (e.g., Finney and Iannoti, 2002) to suggest that people need to be sufficiently involved or interested in a health issue for framing effects to be obtained. Defining what level of interest is needed is an issue for future research.

Although only a handful of studies have tested the impact of framed appeals on the performance of prevention behaviors, they have provided relatively strong support for the thesis that gain-framed messages are more effective than loss-framed messages. To date, no studies of prevention behavior have shown loss-framed messages to be more persuasive. This is striking given the consistent finding that loss-framed messages were more effective when promoting the performance of detection behaviors. Although a compelling body of evidence has developed to support the thesis that gain-framed messages are more effective when promoting a prevention behavior and loss-framed messages are more effective when promoting a detection behavior, it is important to recognize that the distinction between these two classes of behaviors rests on the premise that people perceive engaging in detection behaviors as posing some risk and engaging in prevention behaviors as posing little to no risk. The function of the behavior serves as a heuristic that investigators can use to anticipate how people construe a given behavior. Thus, prior to designing a framed appeal to promote a new prevention or detection behavior, investigators need to consider how people tend to construe the behavior. For example, if a prevention behavior is perceived to involve some risk (e.g., a vaccination that only works for some people), a loss-framed message may prove to be more effective than a gain-framed message (Bartels et al., 2004). To the extent that there is variability in how people construe a given detection or prevention behavior, the relative influence of gain- and loss-framed appeals is more complex.

Unfortunately, not every behavior of interest to health professionals can be categorized as a prevention behavior or a detection behavior. For example, it is not readily apparent how to think about efforts to lose weight. Weight loss can afford a variety of health benefits including the prevention of further health problems, but people may not think about weight loss behaviors in these terms. In fact, given that people who lose weight are typically unable to maintain the change in their weight, choosing to participate in a weight loss program might be construed as a risky endeavor. To date, the empirical literature is unable to provide much guidance as to recommendations for framing messages that target behaviors that are not clearly prevention or detection behaviors. This is clearly an important issue for future research.

DEVELOPING FRAMED MESSAGES

Prior to developing gain- and loss-framed messages there are several issues about which investigators should be mindful. First, there are several ways information about a disease or health behavior can focus on positive outcomes or aspects (gain framing) or negative outcomes or aspects (loss framing). For example, numerical information could be presented as either '19 out of 20 people are cured' or '1 out of 20 people die'. In this case, the gain frame describes the positive consequences of a behavior or situation, whereas the loss frame describes the negative consequences of the same behavior or situation. This type of frame represents what Rothman and Salovey (1997) referred to as *different consequences* framing, due to the presentation of distinct positive or negative consequences. This type of framing typically involves the presentation of numerical information.

However, most health messages are not comprised of arguments that afford different, but complementary consequences. When investigators want to frame information about the same consequences, gain- or loss-framed wording is used to emphasize either the presence or absence of this outcome. For example, a gain-framed appeal about mammography would be, 'If you have a mammogram, you have the best chance of detecting breast cancer before it is life-threatening', whereas the loss-framed appeal would be, 'If you do not have a mammogram, you will miss the best chance of detecting breast cancer before it is life-threatening.' Although the two messages differ in their emphasis, they both describe the same consequence. Rothman and Salovey (1997) referred to this type of framing as *same consequences* framing. Within this approach, a gain-framed message can take two forms. It can describe the presence of a good outcome ('you will get better') or the absence of a negative outcome ('you won't get sick'). The loss frame can also take two forms, describing either the absence of a good outcome ('you won't get better') or the presence of a negative outcome ('you will get sick'). To date, the only study to test whether there are differences in the persuasiveness of different types of gain and loss-framed messages found them to be equally effective (Detweiler et al., 1999). Further research is needed before any strong conclusions can be drawn.

Second, because framing manipulations generally involve altering only a small part of the message, there are many different contexts in which framed health information can be presented. Typically, pamphlets or brochures are created to describe procedures such as mammography (e.g., Lerman et al., 1992), or sunscreen use (e.g., Detweiler et al., 1999; Rothman et al., 1993). For example, Meyerowitz and Chaiken (1987) developed a 5-page pamphlet about BSE that was designed to match one produced by the American Cancer Society. The framing manipulation was imbedded only on the second page of the pamphlet. The gain-framed version included six bulleted arguments about the positive consequences of performing breast self-exams (e.g., 'By doing BSE now, you can learn what your normal, healthy breasts feel like so that you will be better prepared to notice any small, abnormal changes that might occur as you get older'), whereas the loss-framed version included six bulleted arguments about the negative consequences of not doing BSE (e.g., 'By not doing BSE now, you will not learn what your normal, healthy breasts feel like so that you will be ill prepared to notice any small, abnormal changes that might occur as you get older'). In a similar manner, framed argu-

ments can be inserted into educational booklets as well as reminder letters that are used to alert patients of upcoming visits or tests (e.g., Finney and Iannoti, 2002; McCaul et al., 2002).

Framed educational videotapes have also been used (Apanovitch et al., 2003; Banks et al., 1995). Apanovitch et al. (2003) created 15-minute educational videos designed to encourage HIV testing. Gain- and loss-framed arguments comprised 30% of the information provided in the video and addressed four topics: medical consequences, psychological consequences, responsibility to family members, and responsibility to the community. In videos, the gain-and loss-framed text is accompanied by visual images that reinforce the message. The only study to date to compare the differential impact of framed audio and framed video content found no difference between the two modalities; in this study, gain-framed audio and video content was more persuasive than loss-framed content in affecting young adult smokers' interest in reducing their tobacco use (Schneider et al, 2001). Although the issue has received limited empirical scrutiny, it would appear that framed messages are equally effective across a broad range of media. In addition, based on comparisons across studies, the impact of a framed message does not seem to depend on the presentation of a critical amount of framed information.

FUTURE DIRECTIONS

There are a number of important issues that need to be addressed in order to maximize the ability of investigators to use message framing effectively. Over the past decade, we have developed a more sophisticated understanding of the conditions under which gain- and loss-framed messages are most effective. However, the process by which framed appeals affect behavior remains poorly understood. Advances in the understanding of these underlying processes would provide an invaluable framework to guide predictions regarding the relative impact of gain- and loss-framed appeals on behaviors beyond the categories of prevention and detection behaviors. As we previously noted, distressingly little is known about the impact of message framing on complex behaviors that are not easily categorized as well as on adherence to treatment regimens. Research on message framing would benefit from advances in our understanding of how people think about different classes of health behaviors and, in particular, the development of tools to assess these construals. For example, we have emphasized differentiating between behaviors based on the risks they afford. Although investigators have been able to capture differences in how risky a given behavior is thought to be (e.g., Apanovitch et al., 2003; Bartels et al., 2004), a systematic, well-validated method for assessing the risk posed by a behavior is needed.

Research on message framing has also focused exclusively on changing single behavioral decisions. Messages are tested based on their ability to get people to seek a mammogram or receive a vaccination. Yet, most recommended health practices involve an on-going series of behaviors. Given that the benefits afforded by most health practices require people to follow a sustained pattern of behavior, the practical value of understanding how people make decisions regarding ongoing behavioral practices is clear (Rothman, 2000; Rothman et al., 2004). At present, little attention has been paid to how message frames could be used to motivate ongoing behavioral practices. For example, what is the most effective way to promote regular screening mammography? Should women consistently be sent a loss-framed appeal? To the extent that people's perceptions of a behavior determine their response to a framed appeal, the continued influence of a loss- or gain-framed message should depend on how performing the behavior affects people's representation of it (Rothman et al., 2003).

For example, how might the experience of having had a series of mammograms that were all negative affect how a woman perceives having a mammogram? If a woman responds to these favorable results by feeling reassured by the news that she is in good health, over time she may begin to construe having a mammogram as an opportunity to affirm her health and no longer perceive the behavior as an illness-detecting – or risky – behavior. If this were to happen, a gain-framed appeal would likely be a more effective way to promote continued screening. On the other hand, if a woman responded to the favorable results with a sense of anxiety that she's been lucky and that the next screen will find a problem, a loss-framed appeal would likely be the most effective way to promote continued screening. Although intriguing, these ideas remain untested. Further research is needed that can detect the impact of framed appeals on on-going patterns of behavior and thus inform how investigators can use message frames to promote an even broader array of health practices.

RECOMMENDED READINGS

1. Meyerowitz B, Chaiken S. (1987) The effect of message framing on breast self-examination attitudes, intentions, and behavior. J Personality Social Psychol, 52: 500-510.

2. Rothman AJ, Kelly KM, Hertel A, Salovey P. (2002) Message frames and illness representations: Implications for interventions to promote and sustain healthy behavior. In L.D. Cameron and H. Leventhal (Eds.), The self-regulation of health and illness behavior (pp. 278-296). Routledge.

3. Rothman AJ, Martino SC, Bedell BT, Detweiler JB, Salovey P. (1999) The

systematic influence of gain- and loss-framed messages on people's interest in and use of different types of health behaviors. Personality Social Psychol Bull *11*: 1355-1369.

4. Rothman AJ, Salovey P. (1997) Shaping perceptions to motivate healthy behavior: The role of message framing. Psychol Bull *121*: 3-19.

REFERENCES

Apanovitch AM, McCarthy D, Salovey P. (2003) Using message framing to motivate HIV testing among low-income, ethnic minority women. Health Psychol *22:* 60-67.

Arora R. (2000) Message framing and credibility: Application in dental services. Health Marketing Quarterly *18:* 29-44.

Banks S, Salovey P, Greener S, Rothman A, Moyer A, Beauvais J, Epel E. (1995) The effects of message framing on mammography utilization. Health Psychol 14: 178-184.

Bartels RD, Elo L, Rothman AJ. (2004) An analysis of how construal of inoculation interacts with message-based framing appeals. Presented at the annual meeting of the American Psychological Society, Chicago, IL.

Cox D, Cox A. (2001) Communicating the consequences of early detection: The role of evidence and framing. J Marketing, 65: 91-103.

Detweiler J, Bedell B, Salovey P, Pronin E, Rothman A. (1999) Message framing and sunscreen use: Gain-framed messages motivate beach-goers. Health Psychol 18: 189-196.

Donovan R, Jalleh G. (2000) Positive versus negative framing of a hypothetical infant immunization: The influence of involvement. Health Education Behav 27: 82-95.

Finney L, Iannoti R. (2002) Message framing and mammography screening: A theory-driven intervention. Behav Med 28: 5-14.

Jones L, Sinclair R, Courneya K. (2003) The effects of source credibility and message framing on exercise intentions, behaviors, and attitudes: An integration of the elaboration likelihood model and prospect theory. J Appl Social Psychol 33: 179-196.

Kalichman S, Coley B. (1995) Context framing to enhance HIV-antibody-testing messages targeted to African-American women. Health Psychol *14:* 247-254.

Kuhberger A, Schulte-Mecklenbeck M, Perner J. (1999) The effects of framing, reflection, probability, and payoff on risk preference in choice tasks. Organizational Behavior and Human Decision Processes 78: 204-231.

Lalor K, Hailey BJ. (1989) The effects of message framing and feelings of susceptibility to breast cancer on reported frequency of breast self-examination. Int Quarterly Commun Health Education 10: 183-192.

Lauver D, Rubin M. (1990) Message framing, dispositional optimism, and follow-up for abnormal papanicolau tests. Research Nursing Health 13: 199-207.

Lerman C, Rimer BK. (1995) Psychosocial impact of cancer screening. In R.T. Croyle (Ed.), *Psychosocial effects of screening for disease prevention and detection* (pp. 65-81). Oxford: Oxford University Press.

Lerman C, Ross E, Boyce A, Gorchov P, McLaughlin R, Rimer B, Engstrom P. (1992) The impact of mailing psycho-educational materials to women with abnormal mammograms. Am J Pub Health *82:* 729-730.

Mayer JA, Solomon L. (1992) Breast self-examination skill and frequency: A review. Ann Behavioral Med 14: 189-196.

McCaul K, Johnson R, Rothman A. (2002) The effects of framing and action instructions on whether older adults obtain flu shots. Health Psychol *21:* 624-628.

Meyerowitz B, Chaiken S. (1987) The effect of message framing on breast self-examination attitudes, intentions, and behavior. J Personality Social Psychol *52:* 500-510.

Millar M, Millar K. (2000) Promoting safe driving behaviors: The influence of message framing and issue involvement. J Applied Social Psychol 3*0:* 853-856.

Rothman AJ. (2000) Toward a theory-based analysis of behavioral maintenance. Health Psychol *19*: 64-69.

Rothman AJ, Baldwin A, Hertel A. (2004) Self-regulation and behavior change: Disentangling behavioral initiation and behavioral maintenance. To appear in K. Vohs and R. Baumeister (Eds.), *The handbook of self-regulation* (pp. 130-148). Guilford Press: New York, NY.

Rothman AJ, Kelly KM, Hertel A, Salovey P. (2003?). Message frames and illness representations: Implications for interventions to promote and sustain healthy behavior. In L.D. Cameron and H. Leventhal (Eds.), *The self-regulation of health and illness behavior* (pp. 278-296). Routledge.

Rothman AJ, Martino SC, Bedell BT, Detweiler JB, Salovey P. (1999) The systematic influence of gain- and loss-framed messages on people's interest in and use of different types of health behaviors. Personality Social Psychol Bull 11: 1355-1369.

Rothman AJ, Salovey P. (1997) Shaping perceptions to motivate healthy behavior: The role of message framing. Psychol Bull 121: 3-19.

Rothman A, Salovey P, Antone C, Keough K, Martin CD. (1993) The influence of message framing on intentions to perform health behaviors. J Experimental Social Psychol *29:* 408-433.

Salovey P, Rothman AJ, Rodin J. (1998) Health behavior. In D. Gilbert, S. Fiske, and G. Lindzey (Eds.), *Handbook of social psychology (4th edition)* (Vol. 2, pp. 633-683). New York: McGraw-Hill.

Salovey P, Wegener DT. (2003) Communicating about health: Message framing, persuasion, and health behavior. In J. Suls & K.A. Wallston (Eds.), *Social psychological foundations of health and illness.* Malden, MA: Blackwell Publishing.

Schneider T, Salovey P, Apanovitch A, Pizarro J, McCarthy D, Zullo J, Rothman A. (2001) The effects of message framing and ethnic targeting on mammography use among low-income women. Health Psychol 20: 256-266.

Schneider T, Salovey P, Pallonen U, Mundorf N, Smith N, Steward W. (2001) Visual and auditory message framing effects on tobacco smoking. J Applied Social Psychol 31: 667-682.

Shiloh S, Eini NJ, Ben-Neria Z, Sagi M. (2001) Framing of prenatal test results and women's health-illness orientations as determinants of perceptions of fetal health and approval of amniocentesis. Psychol Health 16: 313-325.

Taylor SE. (1991) Asymmetrical effects of positive and negative events: The mobilization-minimization hypothesis. Psychol Bull 110: 67-85.

Tversky A, Kahneman D. (1981) The framing of decisions and the rationality of choice. Science 221: 453-458.

REVIEW OF INTERVENTIONS TO CHANGE PATIENT AND PROFESSIONAL BEHAVIORS IN STROKE MANAGEMENT AND PREVENTION

Judith Redfern, Christopher McKevitt, Anthony Rudd and Charles Wolfe

INTRODUCTION

Stroke is the 3rd leading cause of death in the Western world, accounting for around 5.5 million deaths per year (10%-12% of all deaths) (Giroud et al., 2002). It is also the leading cause of adult disability both in the US and in Europe, with around a third of stroke survivors estimated to suffer some form of disability (Wade, 1994). Stroke can lead to physical limitations such as incontinence, difficulty walking or carrying out day to day personal tasks. It can also lead to communication problems affecting speech, language and memory, and one of the most common psychological consequences of stroke is depression (see Wolfe et al., 1996 for a discussion of the consequences of stroke). Families and those who care for stroke patients may also be affected by the consequences of stroke (Wade et al., 1986).

Stroke affects mainly older people, with 88% of stroke deaths occurring in the over 65 age group. Stroke incidence has also been associated with gender, family history, socio-economic status and ethnic group, with men, those who are socially deprived, and Black African and Black Caribbean ethnic groups being at higher risk (Wolfe et al., 2002). In addition stroke incidence has also been associated with numerous risk factors including physiological, socio-economic, genetic and behavioral risk factors (Wolfe et al., 1996).

In the past, stroke was considered a 'Cinderella' disease, the poor relative to other chronic diseases in terms of health care services and research. Unlike other chronic diseases (such as heart disease) for which interventions have been developed (including sophisticated surgical procedures), there were few interventions that could either prevent strokes or improve outcomes after stroke. Now, with the introduction of new drug therapies and the focus more generally on chronic disease prevention through modifying risk factors, stroke prevention is becoming an increasing public health priority (Warlow et al., 2001) and in certain countries there are targets for the reduction of stroke risk.

In terms of prevention, the most common modifiable risk factors are similar to those associated with coronary heart disease including high blood pressure, diabetes, atrial fibrillation, high cholesterol, smoking, heavy alcohol and illicit drug use and obesity (for a detailed discussion of stroke risk factors see Wolfe et al., 1996). Epidemiologists have developed mathematical equations to predict future risk of stroke using population estimates generated from large scale cohort studies (Anderson et al., 1991; Coppola et al., 1995). Such studies emphasise the importance of controlling multiple rather than just single risk factors. Treatments include surgical procedures (carotid endarterectomy), pharmaceutical therapies (antithrombotics, antihypertensives, statins for cholesterol, diabetes medications) and lifestyle modification (smoking cessation, dietary modification including reduction in salt and cholesterol intake, and increased exercise).

Different areas for intervention

Health promotion interventions to improve risk factor control can be implemented at a number of different levels, at national or local policy level, at an organisational or health service level, or at an individual level (Nutbeam and Harris, 2001). The UK NHS Centre for Reviews and Dissemination outlines relevant literature on interventions in stroke prevention (Rees et al., 2000). National and local policy level interventions include smoking taxation, policies to tackle poverty, and smoking restrictions e.g. on public transport. Interventions targeted at individuals include health promotion literature to target smoking and other behavioral risk factors, and organisational or service interventions include the introduction of specialist clinics for delivering health promotion or individuals such as nurses to coordinate stroke care.

Warlow et al. (2001) argue that for primary stroke prevention, policy level interventions or those targeting socio-economic, environmental, or individual behavioral factors are likely to have more impact than health service based interventions (such as pharmaceutical therapies or surgical interventions). Interventions delivered via health services might not be appropriate for reaching the general population since many people who might benefit from these interventions do not access health services at the relevant time. Ebrahim and Davey-Smith (2000) also argue that interventions to improve management of multiple risk factors are more cost effective when used in secondary prevention rather than primary prevention.

Aim of this review

This review reports on interventions that aim to change professional or patient behaviors to reduce the risk of stroke or lessen the severity of a stroke. Different types of interventions will be described along with their reported impact on stroke specific outcomes. Pharmaceutical, surgical and therapeutic interventions not aimed at targeting behavior change (physiotherapy, speech therapy or occupational therapy) have not been included. The review is also not concerned with evaluations of methods of service delivery such as the impact of stroke units versus care on general medical or elderly care wards (Stroke Unit Trialists Collaboration, 2002) or interventions to investigate whether home based or hospital based rehabilitation settings lead to improved health outcomes (Early Supported Discharge Trialists, 2002).

Since stroke has similar risk factors to cardiovascular disease, risk factor management interventions reported in other chapters may also be relevant for stroke prevention and secondary prevention. For instance simple advice from a primary health care practitioner has been shown to be effective in encouraging smoking cessation (Lancaster et al., 2000). Since smoking is an important risk factor for both stroke and cardiovascular disease, adopting this strategy would bring benefits for prevention of both diseases. However, since smoking cessation interventions have been covered elsewhere, this review only includes interventions specifically aimed at improving stroke outcomes.

METHODS

A literature search was conducted using Web of Science (Science and Social Science databases) and PubMed using key words: stroke, prevention, recurrence, risk factor, intervention, compliance, adherence, concordance, information, education, knowledge, communication, screening, guidelines, access, support, rehabilitation, qualitative, long term, psychology, health promotion, and decision making.

In addition the following individual journals were also searched electronically: Stroke; BMJ; Cerebrovascular Diseases; JAMA; Social Science and Medicine; Sociology of Health and Illness; Health Psychology; British Journal of Health Psychology; Clinical Rehabilitation; Health Education; Health Education Research; Journal of Advanced Nursing; Health Promotion International; Patient Education and Counselling. Existing reviews of stroke health promotion interventions were searched for using the Cochrane Database of Systematic Reviews, as well as UK health education and health policy documents.

A total of 46 different interventions aimed specifically at improving stroke outcomes were identified (21 of which were evaluations using randomised controlled trial methods). In addition 5 reviews of interventions to improve stroke outcomes and 5 other reviews (interventions to prevent heart disease, smoking cessation, or improve exercise or compliance with medication prescriptions) were identified. Seven studies were excluded because they referred to a type of therapeutic intervention (occupational therapy, physical therapy, leisure therapy, music therapy and counseling) rather than a behavioral intervention.

RESULTS

While there is a large literature on stroke risk factors, the majority of studies evaluating interventions to improve risk factor management have been designed for treating heart disease, using heart disease outcomes rather than stroke specific outcomes. In many ways the findings of these studies are relevant for stroke prevention, particularly in the case of primary prevention since the risk factors for heart disease and stroke are similar, although the relative risks and risk reductions will be different. These studies have been reviewed in detail (Ebrahim and Davey-Smith, 1996; Lancaster et al., 2000; McAlister et al., 2001; Haynes et al., 1996; Ebrahim and Davey-Smith, 1997). However since this review focuses on interventions to improve stroke specific outcomes, findings from heart disease interventions have not been included.

Stroke interventions fell into three main categories, interventions to change professional behaviors in preventing and managing stroke, interventions targeted at patients and people from the general population to improve stroke prevention and secondary prevention, and interventions targeted at stroke patients and care-givers to improve recovery and adjustment after stroke. Interventions were targeted both at an individual level (general public, stroke patients, care-givers and health professionals) and at a health service level. The majority of interventions were targeted at an individual behavioral level rather than at a social or environmental level. This may reflect the search criteria used to identify studies since environmental and social interventions are more likely to be targeted at the general population and aimed at preventing a range of diseases. Such studies might not have been found unless they included stroke specific outcomes.

Interventions targeting health professionals
Stroke prevention

The majority of stroke prevention interventions were targeted at the patient rather than the professional. However four interventions were targeted at professionals (Table 1).

Two studies investigated the process of dissemination of locally adapted guidelines on stroke risk factor management. Silagy et al. (2002) found that guideline distribution enhanced health professionals' knowledge of aspirin use and investigations for stroke prevention. Jackson et al. (2004) demonstrated an increase in warfarin prescribing and use following production of guidelines and academic detailing visits for patients defined as being at high risk of stroke. However neither study investigated the impact of guideline dissemination on improving health outcomes.

The other two studies aimed to improve medical decision making in the management of risk factors. Coppola et al. (1995) described a risk factor scoring system to help professionals identify those patients at high risk of having a stroke. By identifying risk factors for individual patients (including smoking status, diagnosis of hypertension and age), scores were produced associated with the patient's future risk of stroke. The scoring system was tested against existing patient data and found to adequately predict 80% of all strokes happening in the next 5 years.

In another study by Thomson et al. (2000), decision analysis guidelines were made even more explicit. They produced algorithms using an economic decision analysis tool to define appropriate antithrombotic treatments (e.g. Aspirin or

Warfarin) for patients with atrial fibrillation (an important clinical risk factor for stroke). The tool attempts to take into account the patient's preference for treatment as well as the estimated risks of stroke and haemorrhage for patients of different ages and with different risk factors. However neither intervention has been tested for use in stroke prevention.

Table 1. Interventions targeting professionals in stroke prevention

Author + date	Subjects	Intervention	Duration of intervention	Method (e.g. RCT)	Outcome
Silagy et al. 2002	243 GPs	Locally adapted clinical practice guidelines on stroke prevention and lower urinary tract symptoms in men.	1 time dissemination of guidelines.	RCT	GPs in the intervention arm reported knowledge and practices more consistent with the guidelines on appropriate aspirin use in stroke prevention and initial investigations for carotid stenosis.
Coppola et al. 1995	7735 patients on the British Regional Heart Study	A computer scoring system to predict 5 year risk of stroke using individual data on age, systolic blood pressure, cigarette consumption, and anginal chest pain.	not applicable	Descriptive – data from a cohort study	The scoring system was able to detect 80% of all stroke occurring within five years in the top fifth of the score distribution.
Thomson et al. 2000	not applicable	Decision analysis guidelines for anticoagulant therapy in patients with atrial fibrillation.	not applicable	descriptive	not applicable
Jackson et al. 2004	162/272 general practitioners in Southern Tasmania	Locally produced guidelines on risk factors for stroke, risk stratification, stroke risk reduction and antithrombotic drug use for atrial fibrillation, plus academic detailing visits from a research pharmacist	one-time dissemination of guidelines and detailing visit lasting approximately 15 minutes	Before and after study	Prescribing data before and after the intervention showed a significant increase in warfarin prescribing post intevention for patients prior to hospital admission (33% to 46%). Hospital admission data also showed an increase in warfarin use on discharge amongst those at high risk of stroke (39% to 53%).

Stroke management

Interventions to change professional behaviors to improve management after stroke are presented in Table 2. Three types of intervention were identified: using evidence based guidelines, professional skills training, and decision support.

Evidence based guidelines and integrated care pathways

Interventions aimed at improving health professionals' practices include development of stroke guidelines to inform best practice (Gorlick et al., 1999; European Stroke Initiative, 2000; Royal College of Physicians, 2001). These guidelines summarise the main evidence on appropriate stroke management including recommendations for service organisation, diagnosis, treatments and preventive measures, rehabilitation and specific aspects of stroke care such as disability management. Guideline development is essential so that clinicians can have a reliable source of best evidence. However getting guideline recommendations into routine practice is a complex process.

One structured method for disseminating best evidence to health professionals is through integrated stroke care pathways. Integrated care pathways for stroke can be defined as plans, protocols or algorithms identifying different activities to be carried out over a certain time period in order to achieve best practice in stroke management. Such activities include referral requests, tests and investigations, medication and therapy, and patient education. Integrated care pathways have been reviewed elsewhere (Kwan and Sandercock, 2002; Sulch and Kalra, 2000). In their Cochrane Review, Kwan and Sandercock identified 10 studies investigating integrated care pathways, only three of which were randomised controlled trials (RCT). While evidence from RCTs suggests that use of care pathways has no significant impact on death, dependence or discharge arrangements, evidence from non randomised trials suggests that care pathways may influence some of the processes of care (increase in brain scanning and carotid duplex study), decrease in readmission to hospital, as well as clinical outcomes (decrease in urinary tract infection) (Kwan and Sandercock, 2002). Non-randomised studies also suggest an association with reduced length of stay in hospital and a reduction in costs of care (Sulch and Kalra, 2000).

Table 2. Interventions targeted at professionals in stroke management

Author + date	Subjects	Intervention	Duration of intervention	Method (e.g. RCT)	Outcome
Royal College of Physicians 2001		Guidelines on stroke management		Descriptive	
European Stroke Initiative 2000; Hacke 2003		Guidelines on stroke management		Descriptive	
Gorelick et al. 1999		Guidelines on stroke management		Descriptive	
Forster et al.. 1999	32/40 nurses	Lectures and practical demonstrations about physiological aspects of stroke recovery, delivered by physiotherapists.	9 hours	Before and after design + qualitative study	Total attitude score improved after the training programme. Qualitative analysis revealed that the training helped nurses get over some of the conflicts between a traditional caring nursing role and that of a therapist. The training also helped them with communication, and provided them with new insights into practice.
Crotty et al. 2004	715 patients, 121 physicians, 452 residential care staff at 10 hostels (low level care) and 10 nursing homes (high level care)	Pharmacy outreach detailing visits by a pharmacist in the physician's surgery. Key messages combined evidence based guidelines on falls prevention with information from a case-note audit and survey. Physicians were also provided with audit data on fall rates, prescribing patterns and risk reduction practices.	Two 30-minute visits	RCT	Fall rates increased in both intervention and control arms over the 3-month study period. There were no statistically significant differences between intervention and control groups in fall rates, risk factor management outcomes or pschotropic drug use, except for greater use of 'as required' psychotropic drug use in the intervention arm.

Heinemann et al. 2003	131/352 doctors; 134/244 non doctors (nurses, physical therapists, occupational therapists, case managers, social workers, speech therapists, students, psychologists and educators)	A one-time lecture on covering the clinical practice guidelines. Plus a packet of information on post stroke rehabilitation. Evaluation of impact on knowledge score 6 months post intervention	One hour	Pre test-post test	21% of respondents reported changes in referral practice after the presentation, with 42% of these attributing the changes to information received during the presentation. These included changes in referral to rehabilitation, and education for staff family and friends. A further 37% reported that they had plans to change referral practices.
Williams et al. 2003	Professionals admitting patients at Morriston Hospital, Swansea	Paper and electronic guidelines on hospital guidelines and protocols, pharmacy information and databases such as Cochrane. Evaluation of compliance with guidelines after paper and electronic introduction measured in case notes.	3 months	Before and after study - multiple-interrupted time series design + interviews with doctors	Compliance with stroke guidelines decreased slightly after distribution of paper guidelines but increased significantly after the guideline was made available electronically. Average compliance with stroke guideline was 28%. Guidelines were widely supported and actively promoted by doctors.
Eo et al. 2002	164 Paramedics in Seoul.	Training in stroke knowledge from 3 emergency specialists. Training covered stroke definition, signs and symptoms of stroke and how to recognize a stroke.	6 months	Before and after comparative study	Post intervention, paramedics showed an increase in knowledge about stroke.
PRISM study group. 2003	1952 patients attending 16 hospital centres for initial assessment (inpatient or outpatient) with a clinical diagnosis of acute ischaemic stroke or TIA. No. of clinicians not known	Computer based decision support system (CDSS) for prescribing 6 potential antithrombotic therapies. The CDSS calculates event rate estimates for each therapy based on aspects of medical history and patient and clinical findings. *Intervention hospitals* clinicians are presented with CDSS output in the form of a graph. Data are calculated as soon as possible after patients presented at hospital/clinic and CDSS output faxed to staff. Output is placed in medical record for use in future prescribing decision. *Control hospitals*: usual care	One-off intervention calculated when patient is admitted to hospital/ attends outpatient clinic. However all prescribing decisions in 6 month study period could be influenced by CDSS	Cluster RCT, hospitals randomised, before – after design	Primary outcome: The CCDS did not significantly affect the estimated relative risk reduction (RRR) achieved by prescribing antiplatelet or anticoagulant therapy, or the proportion of patients receiving optimal therapy. Secondary outcomes: significant reduction in RRR was achieved for patients with certain clinical features: AF, previous MI, active peptic ulcer, CAD. CDSS did not influence long-term anticoagulation prescribing in 271 patients with AF. 9 clinicians reported that CCDS output was available for assisting prescribing decision.

Training interventions

The majority of interventions to promote better psychosocial outcomes have focused on the patient. However four studies were identified focusing on the impact of training or academic detailing on professionals (Forster et al., 1999; Crotty et al., 2004; Heinemann et al., 2003; Williams et al., 2003; Eo et al., 2002). Forster et al (1999) focused on the impact of a physical therapist led training program on nurses' attitudes in caring for stroke patients. The authors hypothesised that training in rehabilitation skills could improve nurses' negative attitudes toward stroke rehabilitation and consequently the rehabilitation they provide to patients. The training sessions provided by a team of professionals (physical thera-pists, doctors and occupational therapists) consisted of 10 hours in total of teaching, videos, demonstrations and participation. The intervention was shown to have some effect in changing nurses' attitudes toward rehabilitation but the impact on the subsequent rehabilitation provided was not measured. A parallel qualitative evaluation also revealed that the training helped the nurses resolve some of the problems resulting from their change in role from a traditional caregiver to a therapist, helped them with communication and provided them with new insights into practice.

Three studies aimed to improve pro-fessionals' compliance with recommend-ations for stroke management in best practice guidelines. In the study by Crotty et al (2004) detailing was provided by an outreach pharmacist, Heinemann et al., delivered lectures to health professionals presented by a psychiatrist practicing in stroke rehabilitation, and Williams et al, (2003) delivered guidelines on paper and electronically to health care professionals. Dissemination of guidelines appeared to influence professionals' perceptions of their practice and there is some evidence that compliance with guidelines increased after the intervention. However, only Crotty et al's (2004) study evaluated their inter-vention using RCT methods and they showed no statistically significant diffe-rences in patients' fall rates as a result of disseminating guidelines on falls pre-vention.

Eo et al (2002) conducted a simple before-and-after study investigating the impact of training on paramedics' knowledge of stroke. They showed that 6-months post intervention, levels of knowledge on how to recognise the symptoms of a stroke had increased.

Decision support

The PRISM study group conducted a cluster RCT of an intervention to enhance clinical decision making for prescribing of 6 antithrombotic therapies for patients with a diagnosis of acute ischaemic stroke. Clinicians in the intervention arm were provided with a graphical representation of their patients' future event rates for each of the 6 therapies based on details from the individual's clinical history. The invest-igators hypothesised that the intervention would improve 'optimal' prescribing lead-ing to a relative risk reduction (RRR). Overall the intervention had no significant effect on these outcomes, however it was associated with a RRR for patients with specific clinical risk factors – those with atrial fibrillation, previous myocardial infarction (MI) and coronary artery disease (CAD).

Interventions targeting patients and the general population

Interventions aimed at improving stroke prevention and secondary prevention are presented in Tables 3 and 4. Twelve studies were identified, only three of which used a randomised controlled trial design to evaluate outcomes (Banet and Felchia, 1997; Kreuter and Strecher, 1995; Man-Son-Hing, 1999).

Primary prevention of stroke

Nine of the twelve interventions identified focused on primary prevention with the general population as the target audience (Table 3). All of the interventions included an educational component, but this ranged from providing patients with information and feedback about aspects of their stroke (medical history, test results, feedback on risk estimates), to formal teaching and more complex interventions in which education was only a supplementary component. Other components included decision support, nurse counseling, screening, and mass media campaigns.

Information and feedback interventions

One study conducted a mass media campaign to educate the general public about stroke and encourage them to call emergency services if they had stroke symptoms (Becker et al., 2001). The educational information was delivered through television, newspapers and through public screenings. The intervention package was evaluated using a pre-test post-test telephone survey. The intervention was associated with an increase in the level of knowledge of stroke symptoms and risk factors six months later. Of the three different types of media, television was identified as the most memorable with few respondents remembering messages about stroke from newspaper advertisements.

Two studies provided patients with information and feedback about stroke and stroke risk factors (Kreuter and Strecher, 1995; Banet and Felchia, 1997). Kreuter and Strecher (1995) provided information and feedback to patients recruited from general practices. This consisted of risk information (based on 'Healthier People' risk appraisal algorithms, Healthier People Network Inc., 1992) about a range of diseases (stroke, heart disease, cancer) and feedback about behavior change. Feedback had four main components: lists of 'risky' behaviors together with illustrations of which risky behaviors are most important to change, presentations of individual 10 year mortality risk, explanations of what to do to reduce

the risks, and a table of the patient's present and ideal levels of weight, blood pressure and cholesterol. Members of the enhanced intervention also received individually tailored messages about behavior change concerning their perceived barriers to and benefits of changing behavior. Feedback was successful in increasing perceived risk of stroke amongst patients who under estimated their own risk but had no impact on patients' subsequent use of GP services two months later. The impact on subsequent behavior change was not investigated.

Formal training

Stern et al. (1999) investigated the impact of an educational intervention using a slide/audio program to provide education on warning signs for stroke. Participants either received the program alone or the program plus a discussion afterwards. The program was associated with increased knowledge of stroke risk factors, warning signs and recommended action to take if they had symptoms of stroke. The post program discussion did not however achieve any additional improvements in knowledge.

One study investigated the impact of formal training on risk factor change (Eriksson et al., 1997). Heart attack survivors and people with a diagnosis of diabetes or hypertension were provided with education about changing risk factors including physical exercise, food preparation, relaxation and physiology and various forms of addiction (specific types of addiction not stated). The education was

Table 3. Interventions targeted at patients and people in the general population in primary stroke prevention

Author + date	Subjects	Intervention	Duration of intervention	Method (e.g. RCT)	Outcome
Becker et al. 2001	547/6087 English speaking respondents to a telephone survey	A social marketing campaign educating people about stroke and the need to call 911. Interventions were delivered through public service announcements, television, and advertising in newspapers and public stroke screenings. 'Brain attack' fliers were distributed. advertising the screenings	Assessment 6 months post intervention	Pre-test, post-test design.	Respondents were 50% more likely to know a risk factor for stroke and 35% more likely to know a symptom of stroke (although less than 50% could name a symptom). TV spots were the most often remembered media for campaign delivery , only 9% remembered newspaper education.

Stern et al. 1998	657 adults living in the community or senior independent-living settings	Intervention 1. A 12 minute professionally produced slide/audio educational program defining stroke and describing different types of stroke, the warning signs for stroke. Intervention 2: the slide/audio programme plus review of content with a facilitator.	Assessment immediately after the program	Pre-test post test evaluation	The slide show was associated with a 10% increase in knowledge score. There was no added increase in knowledge associated with facilitation (intervention 2).
Kreuter and Strecher 1995	1317 patients in primary care	Computer generated risk feedback, risk feedback + behavior change feedback or no feedback. Risk estimates generated from 'Healthier People' algorithms. Feedback consisted of a list of the patient's 'risky' behaviors, graphic and numeric illustrations of which risky behaviors are most important to change, graphic and numeric presentations of the patient's 10 year mortality risk, explanations of what they can do to reduce their risk, and a table of the patient's present and ideal levels of weight, blood pressure and cholesterol. Members of the enhanced intervention also received individually tailored messages about behavior change concerning patients' perceived barriers to, and benefits of changing behavior.	1 time intervention. Outcomes assessed 2 months post intervention.	RCT	Individualised risk feedback was effective in increasing perceived stroke risk amongst patients who underestimated their risk of stroke, and in reducing perceived risk of cancer among patients who overestimated their risk. No impact on heart attack perceptions or motor vehicle crash perceptions. Patients who were pessimistic about cancer risk were more likely to seek follow up from their doctor two or more times in the 2 months post intervention.
Eriksson et al. 1997	295 patients with hypertension diabetes or post MI attending county health institutions	Patient education on physical exercise, relaxation and knowledge of physiology, selecting and preparing food for cooking, addiction, plus discussion on healthy living and personal experiences. Formal lectures on hypertension, diabetes and MI, and nutrition. Individual guidance from a dietician, physiotherapist, fitness assistant, nurse and a physician.	38 hours initial training per patient plus a 4-day refresher course 1 year later.	Before and after design	Overall stroke risk reduced: Systolic BP reduced by 9mmHg, diastolic by 5mmHg. On average patients lost 4kg of weight and BMI decreased by 1.4kg/m^2. Proportion of smokers decreased from 20% to 10%. Medication doses for hypertension decreased from 0.6 to 0.5 daily doses.
Man-Son-Hing et al. 1999	287 patients with atrial fibrillation from an aspirin cohort study	29 page booklet and personal worksheet about consequences of stroke, Warfarin monitoring, plus risk estimates of stroke depending on therapy (Warfarin versus aspirin). Estimates were presented as smiley or sad faces. The worksheet asked patients to place values on specific outcomes and list questions about their medication and to indicate a preference for being involved in the decision making process. Physicians also received a manual on the decision aid.	1-time intervention	RCT	Patients in the intervention arm were more likely to perceive they had input into decisions about medication choices; no difference in patient satisfaction; no difference in adherence to medication choice. Possible differences in proportion of patients switching from Warfarin to aspirin 6 months after stroke but numbers were too small to investigate.

Willoughby et al. 2001	107 volunteers from general population attending the screening program.	Tests for cholesterol, BP, weight, body fat %, blood glucose, carotid artery auscultation, pulse palpitation; nurse counselling on ways to reduce stroke risk; dietician and pharmacist advice; National Stroke Association stroke reduction plan.	1 time screening + telephone survey at 1, 3, 6 months after screening.	Before and after design	Subjects take less time to answer questions testing stroke knowledge. 86% of questions where answered correctly, 54% changed to a low fat/cholesterol diet,, 34% improved awareness/monitoring of cholesterol, 23% began weight loss measures, 11% improved monitoring/control of blood pressure. 4/7 smokers tried to give up. Subjects found the screening helpful, 98% reported that it increased stroke awareness and knowledge.
Iso et al. 1998	General population: 3219 (full) , 1468 (minimal)	Minimal intervention (control): blood pressure screening + follow up every 2 years. Full intervention (cases): Blood pressure screening; referral to clinics for high risk individuals; health education at screening sites, adult classes and nurse home visits; training about healthy diet; community-wide media disseminated education to encourage participation in screening	Follow up every 2 years between 1963 and 1987.	Population survey	Stroke incidence declined in both full and minimal intervention groups. Stroke incidence declined more in the full intervention group for men but there was no difference in decline in incidence between full and minimal intervention for women.
Fang et al. 1999	General population: 18786 intervention, 18876 control	Biweekly visits to a clinic for patients with hypertension or diabetes. BP and therapy recorded at each visit. Treatment was individualised by special intervention doctors. Health education program to all the residents.		Community intervention study in 2 villages in rural China	The intervention group had a lower incidence of stroke. Increase in hypertension over 3.5 years was less in the intervention group than the control group.
Lin et al. 2004	4977/5965 people in the general population aged 40+ years in rural Taiwan.	Hypertension screening, follow-up, health education, village based hypertension campaigns (yearly weight control and smoking cessation classes and yearly television broadcasts). Screening and follow-up delivered by 143 volunteer villagers trained in blood pressure measuring. Health education was delivered by outside experts.	March 1994 – August 1997. Participants screened at 1 year and 3.5 years.	Before and after study	Compared to baseline scores, higher knowledge and behaviour scores were recorded at 3.5 years. Mean systolic and diastolic blood pressure readings were significantly reduced at the 1-year and 3.5-year time points. Mean waist-hip ratio was also significantly less than at baseline. Stroke mortality in the intervention declined by 40% between 1994 and 1997.

Table 4. Interventions targeted at patients in secondary prevention of stroke

Author + date	Subjects	Intervention	Duration of intervention	Method (e.g. RCT)	Outcome
Banet andFelchia 1997	52 patients discharged after first stroke	Shared medical record (medical history, and test results), inpatient teaching and brochures from the American Stroke Association.	1 time intervention in hospital	RCT	No differences in Glasgow Outcome Scale or Global outcome at 6 months post stroke. No difference in diet, smoking or medication taking practices. Subjects in the intervention group reported higher satisfaction and reported learning more about strokes than controls.

Rimmer et al. 2000	35 stroke survivors at least 6 months post stroke	Education classes on exercise (fitness class), nutrition (hands on meal preparation) and health behavior (psychosocial intervention incorporating Stages of Change model).	3 sessions a week for 12 weeks.	Pre-test/post-test lag control design	Total cholesterol decreased amongst treatment group compared with controls where it increased. Treatment group lost an average of 2.8lbs but there was no change in the control group. Treatment group improved exercise measures (bench press, leg press and flexibility). Both treatments and controls improved nutrition. Treatment group improved in some aspects of psychosocial measures, while controls did not.
Jiang et al. 2004	1558 people with first in a lifetime stroke, 736 in the intervention arm, 820 in the control arm	Comprehensive risk factor management (high blood pressure screening, monitoring and counselling) and community-based health education. Difference in 3-year survival and recurrence rates between groups	3 years	Controlled trial	42% of patients in the intervention arm and 40% of those in the control arm died within 3 years of stroke. Differences were not significant. However the survival probability for haemorrhagic stroke was slightly higher for the intervention arm and marginally significant. Patients in the control arm were significantly more likely to have a recurrence within 3 years (21% compared to 12% respectively)

provided as part of a course (based on training of medical students) and had a practical emphasis. It included formal lectures covering hypertension, diabetes, myocardial infarction and nutrition and individual guidance from a range of health professionals. One year later, the patients had lower blood pressure readings, had lost weight, and the prevalence of smoking had decreased from 20% to 10%. The average amount of antihypertensives taken had also decreased from 0.6 to 0.5 defined daily doses. Reduction in medication use presumably represents a positive outcome since less medication was needed whilst at the same time improvements in average blood pressure were achieved (although this is not clear, nor is it clear how these data were measured). Differences between patients with different diagnoses were not presented.

Decision making

Apart from simply improving the quality of information and education, interventions also aimed to improve the process of using information in decision-making. One study aimed to improve patient concordance with

treatment and advice by incorporating the patient's preferences for treatment into the decision making process (Man-Son Hing et al., 1999). This study has a similar theoretical basis to the study by Thomson et al. (2000), as it accounts for patient preferences for treatment. However this intervention is targeted at the patient rather than the professional. Patients were randomised to receive a booklet and personal worksheet about the consequences of stroke, together with anti-coagulation monitoring, and estimates of their future stroke risk based on whether they took Warfarin or Aspirin. Patient estimates were designed for a lay audience and presented in picture form using smiley faces. Patients were also asked a list of questions to illicit their preference for treatment. Those receiving the intervention were more likely to perceive that they had input into the treatment decision but there was no subsequent difference in satisfaction with care or medication concordance.

Screening

Four more complex interventions were based around screening for stroke risk factors but included multiple components. Willoughby et al. (2001) conducted a non-randomised study of a screening and health education intervention about stroke amongst healthy volunteers. Participants were screened for serum cholesterol, blood pressure, weight, body fat percentage, blood glucose, carotid artery auscultation and pulse palpitation. All participants were then provided with individualised counselling from a registered nurse about risk factors and ways to reduce their personal risk. A dietician and a pharmacist were also available to provide additional advice. Participants took less time to answer questions testing their stroke knowledge and showed significant improvements in a number of behavioral outcomes 6 months later (54% changed to a low cholesterol diet, 34% improved monitoring of cholesterol and 23% were attempting to lose weight) although actual changes in cholesterol, and weight were not measured.

Lin et al, 2004 conducted an intensive multi-factorial intervention in a rural area of Taiwan. The intervention combined population hypertension screening with village based media campaigns, risk factor management classes and health education. After receiving the intervention, participants had higher knowledge scores, reduced mean blood pressure measurements, and reduced waist-hip ratio measures. Mortality rates in the area (although not specifically those who received the intervention) declined by 40% over a three-year period during which the intervention was delivered. However since this was not an RCT there is no way of knowing whether this reduction was due to the intervention itself.

Two studies (Iso et al., 1998; Fang, 1998) actually showed reductions in stroke incidence. Iso et al. (1998) compared a minimal intervention which involved blood pressure screening every two years with a full intervention involving screening plus a referral system to specialist services for individuals at high risk of stroke, health education and a community wide media campaign. Health education involved adult classes on blood pressure together with nurse home visits, and training of 150 'healthy diet' volunteers. The media campaign was aimed at encouraging participation in blood pressure screening and reduced salt intake. Stroke incidence declined over time in both the full intervention group and the minimal intervention group but men in the full intervention group showed a greater decline in incidence (42% decrease 1970-1975, 53% decrease 1976-1981 and 75% decrease 1982-1987) compared to minimum intervention group (5% increase, 20% decrease, 29% decrease in incidence).

Fang et al. (1999) conducted a study in urban China in which communities were assigned to receive either the intervention or control. A selected cohort of patients at high risk of stroke (those with hypertension or diabetes) living in those communities received biweekly blood pressure and medication checks at a clinic and then individualised treatment from doctors. All residents in the intervention communities received health education (leaflets, posters and stickers explaining the role of hypertension, diabetes and CHD in stroke risk) delivered door to door. Patients in the intervention group had a lower incidence of stroke three and a half years post intervention. The prevalence of hypertension increased in both groups but less so in the intervention group (4.3% compared to 7.8% in the control group). Awareness of hypertension, and the proportion of hypertensives regularly taking their medication also increased more in the intervention group than in the control group.

Secondary prevention of stroke

Only three studies focused on secondary prevention of stroke (Table 4). Banet and Felchia (1997) conducted a randomised controlled trial in which community stroke patients in the intervention group received a shared medical record together with standard leaflets from the American Stroke Association. Controls received only the standard leaflets. The shared medical record contained details about the individual patient's medical history, clinical diagnoses and test and investigation results, as well as information about community resources. The authors state that 'teaching' was reinforced at outpatient visits although no details are provided. Six months post- intervention there was no difference in prevention practices (diet, smoking, medication concordance) between patients who received the intervention and those who did not.

In Rimmer et al.'s study (Rimmer et al., 2000) the patients took part in 'hands on' education including physical exercise classes involving gym sessions to encourage strength and flexibility, and practical food preparation classes. Patients also received health behavior classes based around the Transtheoretical Model of Change (Prochaska and DiClemente, 1984). Patients in the intervention group significantly decreased their average cholesterol by 12.49 mg/dl while those in the control arm increased their cholesterol by 8.58 mg/dl. Those in the intervention group also lost an average of 2.8lbs compared to controls who showed no difference in weight. Treatment group patients also improved on measures of cardiovascular fitness and increased strength and flexibility, compared to controls who showed no significant differences 3 months later.

Jiang et al. (2004) conducted a non-randomised controlled trial of a comprehensive risk factor management intervention in people with first in lifetime stroke. The intervention included blood pressure screening and monitoring, counselling, and community based health education. Participants in the intervention arm were less likely to have a recurrence within 3 years of the first stroke but there was no difference in mortality between the two trial arms.

Interventions targeted at stroke patients and caregivers to improve recovery and adjustment after stroke

Table 5 lists behavioral interventions to improve recovery and adjustment after

stroke. Interventions to improve psychosocial outcomes after stroke have been reviewed elsewhere (Knapp et al., 2000) and this review presents the main findings from published studies.

Interventions have been targeted mainly at the patient but also at caregivers (van den Heuval et al., 2002; van den Heuval et al., 2000; Clark, 2003; Lincoln, 2003; Hartke, 2003; Pierce et al, 2004; Steiner & Pierce, 2002), and include information booklets or leaflets, education and counseling from a nurse or psychologist, social support, worker interventions, and video conferencing, telephone and web-based education and support.

Information booklets

Five studies used information booklets to improve psychosocial outcomes (Mant et al., 1998; Lorenc et al., 1992; Pain and McLellen, 1990; Frank et al., 2000; Nir et al., 2004). Mant et al. (1998) provided patients with an information pack containing leaflets produced by The Stroke Association (national stroke charity for England and Wales). The intervention was delivered using a single mailing and had no success in improving knowledge or other psychosocial outcomes 1 month later. Lorenc et al. also used an information pack but had two intervention arms, one in which the pack came with instructions to enhance understanding and recall. Both interventions had a positive effect on stroke knowledge with the intervention plus instructions achieving the best results. However the interventions made no difference to patient satisfaction or health status outcomes. Pain and McLellen (1990) delivered an individualised booklet to patients including more detailed information about their own condition and instructions about the exercises they had been prescribed. Nevertheless, again the intervention had no significant impact on psychosocial outcomes.

Frank et al. (2000) and Nir et al. (2004) took a different approach aiming to improve

Table 5. Interventions targeted at stroke patients and caregivers to improve adjustment and recovery after stroke.

Author + date	Subjects	Intervention	Duration of intervention	Method (e.g. RCT)	Outcome
Mant et al. 1998	71 acute stroke patients	Information pack containing Stroke Association publications.	1 time mailing 1 month after stroke.	RCT	After adjusting for age there were no significant differences in knowledge or satisfaction between intervention and control arms. No differences in contact with health care services. Caregivers in the intervention arm scored better on one domain of the SF36.
Lorenc et a.l 1992	30 patients hospitalised as a result of stroke	Control: no information. Intervention one: information pack. Intervention two: information plus instruction on how to read and understand the information.	1 time intervention. Assessment period not known.	RCT	Significant differences in knowledge scores post intervention, with those in the information and comprehension intervention group scoring higher than the other two groups. Both intervention groups were less likely than controls to ask questions after the test. No difference in satisfaction between groups.
Pain and McLellen 1990	36 patients admitted to hospital with a CVA for at least 10 days and discharged home with a relative or caregiver	A booklet containing information about the patient's condition: persisting symptoms, aims of rehabilitation, instructions on daily living activities, description of exercises prescribed, local and national addresses and contacts for people with stroke.	1 time mailing. Outcome assessment at 3 months post intervention.	RCT	Patients in the intervention arm more often cited the activities mentioned in the booklets. No clinically significant differences in physical improvement or social activity. Patients and therapists thought the intervention booklets were useful.
Frank et al. 2000	39 community patients less than 2 years post stroke	Workbook intervention designed to increase perceptions of control. The workbook was delivered in 2 parts, part 1: information about stroke (causes, management, recovery) and quizzes testing knowledge; part 2: methods of coping, relaxation tape, recovery plan with daily tasks. Weekly telephone follow up to give patients the opportunity to ask questions.	Intervention delivered over 2 weeks with weekly follow-up. Assessment at one month post intervention.	RCT	Patients receiving the intervention found it useful and easy to understand. There were no differences between patients receiving the workbook and controls in terms of functional limitations (FLP), or anxiety and depression (HADS).
Evans and Held 1984	43 stroke patients and caregivers/family members	Stroke classes including a folder with resource materials. Classes included formal teaching and group discussion on: stroke physiology and the effects of cognitive and perceptual changes. This was followed by OT led teaching on home visits, home modifications and architectural barriers.	1 time stroke class. Outcomes assessed using test immediately after the class.	pre test-post test	A significantly higher proportion of respondents answered questions correctly on 5 of the 10 concepts covered in the educational session: right brain damage, emotional lability, prognosis, depression and result of stroke.

van Den Huevel et al. 2000 2002	100 stroke caregivers	Educational sessions including information on causes of stroke, disabilities, recovery and prognosis. Discussion of the social consequences of stroke. Education about OT e.g. using lifts, stress, organising support from friends, and holidays as well as problem solving strategies.	8 week program starting 4 weeks after recruitment. 16 hours of education.	RCT	Both interventions achieved small increase in confidence in knowledge of patient care and use of active coping strategies (decreased between 1 and 6 months). The group program achieved a small increase in social support seeking. No differences between home and group support.
Johnson and Pearson 2000	41/430 community stroke survivors responding to a mailing	Structured education classes. Topics included stroke facts, disability, emotional aspects of stroke, self esteem, ways of encouraging a positive active lifestyle.	Eight 2-hour classes over a 4 week period.	RCT	Patients in the intervention arm had higher average scores on the 'Hearth Hope Scale' (73.68 compared to 66.33) and lower average scores on the 'Beck Depression Inventory' (8.5 compared to 12.61). No difference in scores on the 'Ways of coping' scale.
Rogers et al. 1999	204/398 patients, and 176 caregivers	1 hour small group education sessions for patients and caregivers. Intervention was delivered by a range of healthcare professionals and covered: nature of stroke; role of physiotherapist and occupational therapist in stroke care; psychological effect of stroke; caring for a stroke patient; communication and swallowing problems; reducing risk of stroke. In addition patients were given leaflets and access to a hotline to telephone for more information.	Six 1-hour sessions.	RCT	Patients and carers had higher knowledge scores but there were no differences in SF36 health status or emotional outcomes. Patients but not caregivers were more satisfied with care they had received.
Glass et al. 2000	Not applicable	Education, social support network cohesion and training in problem solving.	Not applicable	Descriptive	Intervention aims to improve functional recovery through increasing knowledge, efficacy, and control.
Dennis et al. 1997	417 stroke patients	Stroke family care worker. Aimed to coordinate between health care services, social services and voluntary agencies. Also provided some counselling.	6 months	RCT	No significant differences in physical measures between intervention patients and controls. Patients in the treatment group were less well adjusted socially and more depressed than controls. Caregivers of patients in the intervention arm were less anxious. Both patients and caregivers in the intervention arm were more satisfied with care.

Mant et al. 2000	323 patients with stroke and 267 caregivers	Visit from a Family support worker (number of visits up to their discretion), information leaflets.	Not known	RCT	No significant differences in use of health services except physiotherapy where intervention patients used less. Intervention patients used Stroke Association Stroke clubs more, and SLT less (non significant), Non significant differences in activities of daily living score in favour of the intervention. Caregivers were more satisfied with their understanding of stroke.
Towle et al. 1988	44 patients with depression at least 1 year post stroke	Control: received an information booklet including addresses of stroke clubs, social services and OT departments, descriptions of financial benefits. Intervention: the information booklet plus visits from a social worker (action depended on the individual).	Twice weekly visits from the social worker for 16 weeks.	RCT	No difference between intervention and control groups in financial benefits received, social independence, or number of services or aids received.
Friedland and McColl 1992	88 community stroke survivors recently discharged from an OT agency	Social support intervention involving specially trained OTs, stroke patients and members of their social support system (personal, friends, professionals, groups and community support members). Social support members were mapped and deficiencies identified. Goal setting used develop support in problem areas. Support system continually re-evaluated over the course of the intervention.	8-12 weekly sessions. Assessment 3 months post intervention.	RCT	No significant differences in on social support measures or psychosocial outcomes.
Evans et al. 1988	188 stroke caregivers	Intervention 1 Education: OT led education classes during 3rd week of hospitalisation, lecture + video on consequences of stroke. In addition a social worker led class within 3 days of first class on treatments. Intervention 2 Counselling: education as above plus seven 1 hour sessions with a social workers trained in cognitive behavioral therapy between 3rd week of hospitalisation and 12 weeks post discharge. Aim was to develop coping strategies.	Intervention 1: 2 weekly sessions Intervention 2: 12 or more weeks	RCT	Significant differences between interventions and control scores on knowledge, family function, communication and behavioral control, affective involvement, global family function, and patient adjustment. Both education and counselling were better at 1 year than controls (on some of above measures). Family function benefits deteriorated over time but less so in the intervention groups.
Forster and Young 1996 Dowswell et al. 1997	240 patients with stroke	Visits from a nurse support worker trained in counselling and listening based on patient's reported requests for information identified after the first year of stroke. The nurses used goal setting, problem solving techniques and gave advice on specific issues. They also had information packs containing detailed information on benefits.	On average patients received 8 visits in 6 months. Outcomes evaluated at 1 year.	RCT + qualitative evaluation	No significant difference in social improvement between intervention and controls. No difference in perceived well being, Barthel Index, stress in caregivers. Qualitative analysis revealed that less tangible aspects of the nursing role (concern, attention, empathy and interest) were valued by the patients and caregivers.

Nir et al. 2004	155 stroke survivors aged 57-93. 82 intervention arm, 73 control arm	Controls received standard rehabilitation (half an hour of physical and occupational therapy 5 days/wk). Intervention arm received standard rehabilitation plus + structured written nursing program. Intervention consisted of a guidebook with topics that addressed common stroke problems. Each topic contained goals, a guide to achieving the goals and a feedback form. The intervention was tailored to the individual patient and care giver and focused on affective, cognitive and instrumental domains.	Intervention lasted 19 days. Evaluation took place at 3 and 6 month intervals after stroke	RCT with stratified random sampling	All participants improved their Functional Independence Measure (FIM) scores and dietary change over time. However, intervention scores were significantly more improved than control scores. Three months post intervention, the intervention group was more likely to perceive their health status as good, and had higher self esteem scores compared to controls. They were also less likely to be depressed. There were no differences between groups in activities of daily living (IADL) scores or locus of control scores.
Clark et al., 2003	62 stroke patients living in the community with a spouse, and their spouses: 32 intervention; 30 control.	Stroke information package plus 3 visits from a social worker trained in family counselling. Information covered stroke and its consequences, measure to reduce the risk of further stroke, practical coping suggestions and details of community services and support structures.	Three 1-hour sessions at three time points: 3-weeks, 2-months and 5-months post discharge.	RCT	Family functioning of patients and spouses remained stable in the intervention arm but declined in the control arm. Disability outcomes (Barthel Index) were slightly better in the intervention group than control group. Social recovery (measured by the Adelaide Activities Index) was better in the intervention group than control group for domestic chores, household maintenance and social activities. The intervention had no impact on health status (SF-36) or depression.
Lincoln et al., 2003	250 patients admitted to hospital and their informal caregivers: 126 intervention arm, 124 control arm	Patients were randomised to receive a family support worker (FSO) service, or usual care. Intervention patients were contacted by the FSO 2 weeks after recruitment. The FSO participated in case conferences and liased with the rehabilitation team whilst in hospital. The FSO visited patients at home after discharge to discuss problems, offer information and support and direct them to appropriate services.	Intervention delivered for up to 9 months. Outcomes assessed at 4 weeks and 9 months post stroke	RCT	There were no significant differences in patients or carers in the intervention and control arms in terms of mood (GHQ-12) independence in extended activities of daily living (EADL), or caregiver strain (Caregiver Strain Index). Patients and carers in the intervention arm were significantly more knowledgeable about: stroke, information and community resources, and measures to reduce the risk of recurrence. They were also significantly more satisfied with the information and emotional support they had received.
Lai et al., 2004	21 stroke patients living at home in Hong Kong	Video conferencing for community-based stroke rehabilitation including educational talks, exercise and social support provided by a physiotherapist. Education covered stroke physiology, symptoms, medical management, rehabilitation pathways, risk factor modification, psychosocial impact and community support, and home safety. Exercise sessions lasted 30 min and focused on strength and balance.	The intervention was delivered in weekly 1.5h sessions for 8 weeks.	Before and after study plus qualitative study	Post intervention patients reported significant improvements in balance (Berg Balance Scale - BBS), and self esteem (State Self Esteem Scale – SSES), knowledge (stroke knowledge test), and health status (all subscales of the SF36). Qualitative findings suggested that patients found video conferencing acceptable

Hartke & King, 2003	88/500 spouses of stroke survivors acting as primary caregivers for at least one month.	Telephone support group sessions for stroke caregivers. Groups varied from 3-6 members and were facilitated by a psychologist, social worker or nurse. Sessions included: introduction, facts about stroke, communication, dealing with spouse's problems and behaviour, caregiver stress, taking care of yourself, conclusion and goal setting.	8 one-hour sessions. Outcomes assessed 6 months post intervention.	RCT	Participants in the intervention group showed decreased levels of stress but differences between intervention and control groups were non-significant. Control participants experienced an increase in measures of 'burden'. Intervention participants showed a significant increase in competence.
Pierce et al, 2004; Steiner & Pierce 2002.	5 caregivers stroke survivor sin a rural setting (Ohio)	Internet-based social support. "Caring-Web". Caregivers are able to ask questions of a nurse specialist and rehabilitation team via specially designed web pages. They are able to discuss rehabilitation issues with other caregivers and nurses via email and obtain educational information about stroke.	3-months	Pilot survey	Some technical problems were identified in using Caring-Web but users were generally satisfied with the intervention and liked the design of the web pages.

psychological aspects of recovery (perceived control) with workbooks rather than just improving knowledge. In Frank's study although patients receiving the workbook gave it an average rating of 7.8 on a scale from 1 to 10 of its 'usefulness', it had no impact on functional limitations, anxiety or depression. However, in the RCT conducted by Nir et al, patients receiving the workbook intervention (which included individually tailored goal setting and problem solving tasks) had improved functional independence and dietary change outcomes. They were also more likely than controls to perceive their health as 'good', had higher self esteem scores and were less likely to be depressed at 6 months post stroke.

Education and counselling

Five studies investigated the impact of formal education classes with patients and caregivers of stroke survivors (Evans and Held, 1984; van den Heuval et al., 2000; van den Heuval et al., 2002; Johnson and Pearson, 2000; Rogers et al., 1999; Glass et al., 2000). Interventions were evaluated for their impact on patient knowledge and patient satisfaction, as well as other psychological, physical, and social outcomes (including measures of coping, depression, hope, emotional outcomes, self efficacy and control, social support seeking behavior, and SF36 health status measures). Evans and Held (1984) improved patients' knowledge measured by a test administered before and after education classes delivered by an occupational therapist. Van den Heuval et al. (2000, 2002) and Johnson and Pearson (2000) both aimed to improve coping strategies. Van den Heuval et al. achieved a small increase in patients' knowledge of stroke care and in coping strategies which they defined as 'confronting' and 'seeking social support' one month post intervention (van den Heuval et al., 2000). However this increase was not sustained in the longer term (six months post intervention, van de Heuval et al., 2002). Johnson and Pearson (2000) found no improvement in the coping measure they had devised (The Ways of Coping-Cardio-vascular Accident scale, WOC-CVA), as a result of structured educational classes but did achieve improvements in their hope and depression measures.

Rogers et al. (1999) aimed to improve emotional outcomes, disability and handicap. Patients and caregivers were given six one-hour small group education sessions on stroke and stroke services including information about psychological and physical effects of stroke and how to care for people with stroke. Patients and caregivers were also given information leaflets and a telephone hotline number they could phone for more information. Rogers et al. found a positive association between taught education sessions and increased knowledge about stroke and satisfaction with information received. However there were no differences in emotional or functional outcomes.

Glass et al. (2000) described an intervention based on psychological theory to increase self efficacy as well as enhancing network cohesion and problem solving abilities. This study has not yet been evaluated.

Social support

A number of studies have looked at the effect of a family support (social support) intervention on stroke outcomes (Dennis et al., 1997; Mant et al., 2000; Towle et al., 1988; Friedland and McColl, 1992, Evans et al., 1988; Forster and Young, 1996; Clarke et al., 2003; Lincoln et al., 2003). Family support workers came from a range of different backgrounds. In two studies the social support was provided by a social worker (Dennis et al., 1997; Towle et al., 1988), in Friedland and McColl's study the social support was provided by an occupational therapist (Friedland and McColl, 1992) and in Forster and Young's study by a nurse (Forster and Young, 1996). However in each case the social support intervention aimed to enhance social support by improving social support networks, or coordinating between different health and social services, and in some cases provided counselling. In most cases the number of visits for each patient was defined by the social support worker and varied from 6-12 visits (Friedland and McColl, 1992), 1 hospital visit, 1 home visit and 3 phone calls (Mant et al., 2000) to educational classes in hospital plus 7 one-hour counselling sessions from a social worker at home.

Although these studies all evaluated the impact of an intervention delivered by a person responsible for providing social support after stroke, the role of the social support worker is not a standardised one. This is reflected in the variation in skill mix and content of the social support between studies. For a discussion of the role of one type of social support worker (a Stroke Association funded non-clinical social support worker), see Pound and Wolfe (1998).

Evaluations of family support interventions suggest that they had a positive impact on patient and caregiver satisfaction and most showed a positive impact on patient or caregiver mood (Dennis et al., 1997; Mant et al., 2002; Evans et al., 1988) but little impact on other psychological outcomes, social outcomes (use of health care services, Oxford handicap scale) or physical outcomes (Barthel Index).

In one RCT in which the social support worker also delivered a stroke information package for patients and caregivers (Clark, 2003), the intervention group had better disability outcomes, and more improvement in certain aspects of social recovery but the intervention had no impact on health status.

Although Forster and Young's trial is described as a nursing intervention, the aim of the specialist outreach nurse was similar to that of a family support worker, to improve perceived health, social integration and emotional adjustment rather than provide a traditional nursing role. They found no differences between the intervention group and controls in terms of perceived health, social activities or caregiver stress, but disabled patients in the intervention arm did report a small increase in social activities (measured by the Frenchay Activities Index). A parallel qualitative study was also conducted to evaluate the impact of the trial from patients' perspectives (Dowswell et al., 1997). Although the quantitative study found no impact on professionally derived clinical outcomes, the qualitative study showed that patients valued the service and that they perceived it to have had a positive impact on their recovery.

In three studies social support was delivered not by a 'person' but using a range of technologies (Lai et al., 2004; Hartke & King, 2003; Pierce et al., 2004). In the first study a video conferencing intervention was evaluated using before-and-after methods (Lai at al., 2004). The intervention included an educational component, exercises and social support provided by a physiotherapist. Post- intervention, participants reported improvements in balance, stroke knowledge and health status. In the second study (Hartke and King, 2003), psychological and educational support was provided via telephone follow-up in a RCT, but no significant differences were found. In the third study (Pierce et al., 2004), a social support intervention was delivered via the internet. The intervention provides the opportunity for stroke caregivers to ask questions of the rehabilitation team, and the opportunity to email other caregivers and rehabilitation professionals. This inter-vention has not yet been evaluated.

DISCUSSION

This review aimed to describe and evaluate two types of behavioral inter-ventions in stroke, those aimed at preventing stroke and stroke recurrence, and those aimed at lessening in the impact of stroke. A total of 46 interventions were identified in the published literature. Interventions aimed to achieve a range of health outcomes, targeting health profess-ionals, stroke patients, caregivers and healthy individuals. A range of different methods was used, from raising awareness and increasing knowledge to intervening in complex psychological and social processes. Outcomes of evaluations differed depending on whether the interventions were aimed at preventing strokes or improving adjustment and recovery after stroke.

Not all the interventions outlined here had been evaluated sufficiently, with many studies using non-randomised participants or not incorporating a control group to compare outcomes. Some of the inter-

ventions documented have not yet been evaluated (National guidelines on best practice, decision making interventions and booklets to increase self efficacy and personal control, web-based interventions to provide social support for patients and caregivers).

Which interventions are most effective?

Since interventions have been so diverse in content, and evaluations so diverse in terms of methodology, it is difficult to prioritise interventions in terms of those which work and those which do not.

Although some of the interventions aimed at improving professional practice were not evaluated in relation to patient outcomes, we do know that guidelines are perceived as helpful by physicians and that computerised decision support has been used to help get evidence based recom-mendations into routine practice in other areas of chronic disease (Lobach and Hammond, 1996; Hunt, 1998). We know from research in patients with atrial fibrillation that patients and professionals prioritise treatment risks differently (Devereaux et al., 2001) therefore interventions such as those designed by Thomson et al. (1999) and Man-Son Hing et al. (1999) which take into account patient preferences could be useful in making treatment prescriptions more appropriate for individual patients. The impact of such interventions on stroke prevention and secondary prevention at a population level may be small (since only a approximately 2% of the population have atrial fibrillation, the main indication for anticoagulant therapy). However inclusion of preferences may make a huge difference to those patients who do have atrial fibrillation and would have failed to adhere with treatment had their preferences not been included. This approach may also benefit a wider population if it is possible to generalise these decision-making approaches to other types of treatment such as antihypertensives or cholesterol lowering medication.

Positive associations were found between skills training and improvements in professional attitude toward stroke patients and stroke care. More research is needed to establish whether such interventions also translate into improvements in professional practice and subsequently patient care.

Interventions to improve stroke prevention had surprisingly successful outcomes. This is in contrast to heart disease prevention interventions which have had limited success (Ebrahim and Davey-Smith, 1997). Two studies found associations between screening and education interventions and a decrease in stroke incidence (Iso et al., 1989; Fang et al., 1989). Whilst relatively dramatic reductions in stroke incidence were documented in both studies, results should be interpreted with caution since it is not known to what extent incidence would have declined naturally over this period. WHO MONICA data from 10 countries (including a Chinese population relevant to Fang et al.'s study) have shown a decline in stroke incidence worldwide since 1982. Similar results have been found from studies of incidence in rural Japan, relevant to the population studied by Iso et al. (Morikawa et al., 2000). However, even assuming a general decline in incidence, both studies included control groups and comparisons showed decreases in incidence amongst people in the intervention arms over and above those in controls arms. Both these interventions were relatively intensive and complex involving multiple components (regular screening checks, referral to specialist care, media campaigns and education). It is difficult to assess which components were most effective but other more simple interventions achieved more modest results. Thus it may be the package as a whole which is important, reflecting the complexity of changing behavior.

Patient decision making aids were associated with increased patient choice. Although this did not subsequently enhance adherence to treatment, it may actually have achieved an equally important goal, that of allowing the patient to make an educated decision not to take their treatment.

While these results are encouraging, it should be noted that only 3 of the 10 studies were randomised controlled trials. That is not to say that the other methodologies were inappropriate, rather that without this experimental design it is difficult to establish whether the positive results found are truly due to the interventions described.

Forster et al. (2001) has already reviewed the impact of educational interventions to improve recovery and adjustment after stroke. Information-only approaches were judged to be less effective than more intensive educational packages. In general, educational interventions were found to influence patient knowledge but whether this has a subsequent impact on behaviour or recovery and adjustment is not known. Knapp et al. (2000) outline some of the methodological difficulties, which may explain the poor association between psychosocial interventions and patient outcomes. One of the key messages is that although it is not clear whether such interventions do improve health outcomes, it cannot be assumed that they do not have an impact. In the study by Forster and Young (1996), a parallel qualitative evaluation was conducted which found opposing results (Dowswell et al., 1997). Social support interventions may have little impact on current health outcome measures after stroke but may still have an important impact on aspects of recovery and adjustment not currently measured or aspects which may not be measurable.

Areas where interventions are lacking

One area in which few interventions were identified was in stroke secondary prevention. There have been numerous studies conducted into heart disease secondary prevention involving education, patient recall and reminders, and nursing interventions (Ebrahim and Davey-Smith, 1997; McAlister et al., 2001) but only two studies were identified focusing on secondary prevention in stroke patients.

While the findings from heart disease interventions may be generalisable to stroke populations, stroke patients may also present different challenges.

One example where there may be differences is in the underlying knowledge base and current levels of education post-stroke. There has been considerable research investigating patient knowledge, and information provision in this area. Some studies have argued that individual knowledge and awareness about stroke is lacking both in stroke populations and high risk groups (Yoon and Byles, 2002; Gupta and Thomas, 2002; Samsa et al., 1997). Studies have shown that patients have unmet needs in terms of information and advice about stroke. Rogers et al. (2001) conducted a review of patient information and concluded that many patients have both a lack of understanding and a desire for further knowledge about stroke. Hanger et al. (1998) and Wiles et al. (1998) both investigated patients' information needs at different time points after stroke. Patients wanted information about many aspects of stroke (stroke causes, stress, recovery, treatment, prognosis, practical tasks, social activities and community resources, memory and concentration, and balance problems). Hanger et al. (1998) argue that patients' needs for information change over time. Two years after stroke 14% still had unmet needs for information. Given that there is evidence of such unmet needs, it seems strange that so few interventions have been conducted aiming to address this gap.

Apart from education about prevention, other needs of caregivers and patients have been reported. In a qualitative study of community support after stroke, patients reported difficulties accessing aids and adaptations for the home after stroke, and felt that they had been denied clinical care such as physiotherapy, which might potentially improve recovery. Caregivers have described emotional and psychological difficulties such as fear and frustration as a consequence of the stroke but do not necessarily want or need a health profes-sional such as a support worker to solve their problems (McKevitt and Wolfe, 2000). It will be interesting to see whether new technologies such as email and the internet can be used as a tool for improving social support.

Summary of key findings

1. Intensive multifaceted interventions were shown to improve blood pressure awareness and control and reduce stroke incidence. However more research is needed to confirm the generalisability of these findings, and ensure they are not simply an artefact of a more general downward trend in stroke incidence.

2. It is not known which aspects of multi-faceted interventions lead to behavior change. It was unclear whether single component interventions such as screening, education, decision-making tools, or feed-back influence patient behavior and risk factor control.

3. Educational interventions lead to improv-ed patient knowledge about risk factor control and aspects of stroke recovery and adjustment. However this does not necess-arily translate into more robust outcomes such as improved risk factor control, patient satisfaction, psychological or physical stroke outcomes.

REFERENCES

Anderson KM, Odell PM, Wilson PWF, Kannel WB. (1991) Cardiovascular disease risk profiles. Am Heart J 121: 293-298.

Banet GA, Felchia MA. (1997) The potential utility of a shared medical record in a "first-time" stroke popu-lation. J Vasc Nurs 1: 29-33.

Becker KJ, Fruin MS, Gooding TD, Tirshwell DL, Love PJ, Mankowski TM. (2001) Community based education improves stroke knowledge. Cerebro-vasc Dis 11: 34-43.

Clark MS, Rubenach S, Winsor A (2003). A randomised controlled trial of an education and counselling intervention for families after stroke. Clinical Rehabil 17: 703-712.

Coppola WGT, Whincup PH, Papacosta O, Walker M, Ebrahim S. (1995) Scoring system to identify men at high risk of stroke: a strategy for general practice. Brit J Gen Pract 45: 185-189.

Crotty M, Whitehead C, Rowett D, Halbert J, Weller D, Finucane P, Esterman A (2004). An outreach intervention to implement evidence based practice in residential care: a randomised controlled trial. BMC Health Serv Res 4:6.

Dennis M, O'Rouke S, Slattery J, Staniforth T, Warlow C. (1997) Evaluation of a stroke family care worker: results of a randomised controlled trial. BMJ 314: 1071-1076.

Devereaux PJ Anderson RDR, Gardner MJ, Putnam W, Flowerdew GJ, Brownell BF, Nagpal S, Cox JL. (2001) Differences between perspectives of physicians and patients on anticoagulation in patients with atrial fibrillation: an observational study. BMJ 323: 1-7.

Dowswell G, Lawler J, Young J, Forster A, Hern J. (1997) A qualitative study of specialist nurse support for stroke patients and care-givers at home. Clin Rehabil 11: 293-301.

Ebrahim S, Davey-Smith G. Bennet R. (2000) Health promotion activity should be retargeted at secondary prevention. BMJ 320: 185-186.

Ebrahim S, Davey-Smith G. (1997) Systematic review of randomised controlled trials of multiple risk factor interventions for preventing coronary heart disease. BMJ 314: 1666-1674.

Ebrahim S, Davey-Smith G. (1996) Health Promotion in older people for the prevention of heart disease and stroke. Health Education Authority London: Health Education Authority.

Eo EK, Ryu JY, Cheon YJ, Jung KY, Kim YJ, Choi GK, Song HS, Yoo JH, Kim JS (2002). Effects of training paramedics on prehospital stroke management. Neurol Psychiatr Brain Res 10: 165-172.

Eriksson S, Kaati Gunnar, Bygren O. (1998) Personal resources and patient education leading to changes in cardiovascular risk factors. Patient Education Counseling 34: 159-168.

European Stroke Initiative, 2000. (2000) European Stroke Initiative Recommendations for Stroke Management. Cerebrovasc Dis 10:335-351.

Evans RL, Held S. (1984) Evaluation of family stroke education. Int J Rehabil Res 7: 47-51.

Evans RL, Matlock AL, Bishop DS, Stranahan S, Pederson C. (1998) Family intervention after stroke: does counselling or education help? Stroke 19: 1243-1249.

Fang X, Kronmal RA, Li A, Longstreth WT, Cheng X, Wang W, Wu S, Du X, Siscovick D. (1999) Prevention of stroke in Urban China: a community based intervention trial. Stroke 30:495-501.

Forster A, Dowswell G, Young J, Sheard J, Write P, Bagley P. (1999) Effects of a physiotherapist-led stroke training programme for nurses. Age Ageing 28: 567-574.

Forster A, Dowswell G, Young J. (1999) Effect of physiotherapist-led training programme on attitudes of nurses caring for patients after stroke. Clin Rehabil 13: 113-122.

Forster A, Smith J, Young J, Knapp P, House A, Wright J. (2002) Information Provision for stroke patients and their caregivers (Cochrane Review) In: The Cochrane Library, Issue 3, 2002. Oxford: Update Software.

Forster A, Young J. (1996) Specialist nurse support for patients with stroke in the community: a randomised controlled trial. BMJ 1642-1646.

Frank G, Johnston M, Morrison V, Pollard B, MacWalter R. (2000) Perceived control and recovery from functional limitations: preliminary evaluation of a workbook-based intervention for discharged stroke patients. Br J Health Psychol 5: 413-420.

Friedland JF, and McColl M. (1992) Social support intervention after stroke – results of a randomised trial. Arch Phys Med Rehabil 73: 573-581.

Giroud M, Czlonkowska A, Ryglewicz D, Wolfe C. (2002) The problem of interpreting variations in health status (morbidity and mortality) in Europe. In Stroke Services: policy and practice across Europe, (Wolfe C, McKevitt C, Rudd A, eds.) pp 1-16. Oxford: Radcliff Medical Press.

Glass TA, Greenburg S, Rintell D, Roesch C, Berkman LF. (2000) Psychosocial intervention in stroke: Families in recovery from stroke trial (FIRST). Am J Othropsychiatry 70: 169-181.

Gorelick PB, Sacco RL, Smith DB, Alberts M, Mustone-Alexander L, Rader D, Ross JL, Raps E, Ozer MN, Brass LM, Malone ME, Goldberg S, Booss J, Hanley DF, Toole JF, Greengold NL, Rhew DC. (1999) Prevention of a First Stroke. A review of guidelines and multidisciplinary consensus statement from the National Stroke Association. JAMA 281: 1113-1121.

Gupta A, Thomas P. (2002) General perception of stroke. BMJ 325-329.

Hacke W (2003). European Stroke Initiative recommendations for stroke management – Update 2003. Cerebrovascular diseases; 16: 311-337.

Hanger HC, Walker LA, Paterson LA, McBride S, Sainsbury R. (1998) What do patients and carers want to know about stroke? A two-year follow up study. Clin Rehabil 12: 45-52.

Hartke RJ, King RB (2003). Telephone group intervention for older stroke caregivers. Topics Stroke Rehabil 9: 65-81.

Haynes RB, McKibbon KA, Kanani R. (1996) Systematic review of randomised controlled trials of interventions to assist patients to follow prescriptions for medications. Lancet 348: 383-386.

Healthier People Network Inc. (1992) Healthy living: a health risk appraisal for older adults (brochure). Center for Disease Control.

Heinemann AW, Roth EJ, Rychlik K, Pe K, King C, Clumpner J (2003). The impact of stroke practice guidelines on knowledge and practice patterns of acute care health professionals. J Eval Clin Practice 9:203-212.

Hunt DL, Hayne RB, Hanna SE, Smith K. (1998) Effects of computer-based clinical decision support on physician performance and patient outcomes - a systematic review. JAMA 280:1339-1346.

Intercollegiate working party for stroke. (2000) National clinical guidelines for stroke. London: Royal College of Physicians.

Iso H, Shimamoto T, Naito Y, Sato S, Kitamura A, Iida M, Konishi M, Jacobs DR, Komachi Y. (1998) Effects of long term hypertension control program on stroke incidence and prevalence in a rural community in north-eastern Japan. Stroke 29: 1510-1518.

Jackson SL, Peterson GM, Vial JH (2004). A community-based educational intervention to improve antithrombotic drug use in atrial fibrillation. Ann Pharmacother 38: 1794-1799.

Jiang B, Wang W, Wu S, Du X, Bao Q (2004). Effects of urban community intervention on 3-year survival and recurrence after first-ever stroke. Stroke 35: 1242-1247.

Johnson J, Pearson V. (2000) The effects of a structured education course on stroke survivors living in the community. Rehabil Nurs 25: 59-65.

Knapp P, Young J, House A, Forster A. (2000) Non-drug strategies to resolve psychosocial difficulties after stroke. Age Ageing 29:23-30.

Kreuter MW, Strecher VJ. (1995) Changing inaccurate perceptions of health risk – results from a randomised trial. Health Psychol 14: 56-63.

Kwan J, Sandercock P. (2002) In-hospital care pathways for stroke (Cochrane Review). In The Cochrane Library. Oxford: Update Software.

Lai JCK, Woo HE, Chan WM (2004). Telerehabilitation – a new model for community-based rehabilitation. J Telemed Telecare 10: 199-205.

Lancaster T, Stead L, Silagy C, Sowden A. (2000) Effectiveness of interventions to help people stop smoking: findings from the Cochrane Library. BMJ 321: 355-358.

Lin T, Chen C-H, Chou P (2004). Impact of the high risk and mass strategies on hypertension control and stroke mortality in primary health care. J Human Hypertens 18: 97-105.

Lincoln NB, Francis VM, Lilley SA, Sharma JC, Summerfield M (2003). Evaluation of a stroke family support organiser. A randomised controlled trial. Stroke 34: 116-121.

Lobach DF, Hammond E. (1997) Computerized decision support based on a clinical practice guideline improves compliance with care standards. Am J Med 102:89-98.

Lorenc L, Sturmey P, Brittain H. (1992) Evaluation of a meta cognitive strategy to improve the information gained from a stroke education pack. Stress Med 8:111-112.

Man-Son Hing M, Laupacis A, O'Conner AM, Biggs J, Drake E, Yetisir E, Hart RG. (1999) A patient Decision Aid regarding anti-thrombotic therapy for stroke prevention in atrial fibrillation: a randomised controlled trial. JAMA 282:737-743.

Mant J, Carter J, Wade DT, Winner S. (2000) Family Support for stroke: a randomised controlled trial. Lancet 256: 808-813.

Mant J, Carter J, Wade DT, Winner S. (1998) The impact of an information pack on patients with stroke and their carers: a randomised controlled trial. Clin Rehabil 12:465-476.

McAlister F, Lawson FME, Teo KK, Armstrong PW. (2001) Randomised controlled trials of secondary prevention programmes in coronary heart disease: systematic review. BMJ 323: 957-962.

McKevitt C, Wolfe C. (2000) Community support after stroke: patients and carers views. Br J Therapy Rehabil 7: 6-10.

Morikawa Y, Nakagawa H, Naruse Y, Nichijo M, Miura K, Tabata M, Hirokawa W, Kagamimori S, Honda M, Yoshida K, Hayashi K. (2000) Trends in stroke incidence and acute case fatality ina Japanese rural area – The Obabe study. Stroke 31: 1583-1587.

Nir Z, Zolotogorsky Z, Sugarman H (2004). Structured nursing intervention versus routine rehabilitation after stroke. Am J Phys Med Rehabil 83:522-529.

Nutbeam D, Harris E. (2002) Theory in a nutshell: a guide to health promotion theory. Australia: McGraw Hill.

Pain HSB, McLellen DL. (1990) The use of individualised booklets after stroke. Clin Rehabil 4:265-272.

Pierce LL, Steiner V, Govini AL, Hicks B, Cervantez Thompson TL, Friedmann ML. (2004). Internet-based support for rural caregivers of persons with stroke shows promise. Rehabil Nurs 29: 95-99.

Pound P, Wolfe C. (1998) Stroke in the community: the role of the family support organizer. Br J Therapy Rehabil 5: 482-488.

Prescription in Ischaemic Stroke Management (PRISM) Study Group (2003). Cluster-randomised, controlled trial of computer-based decision support for selecting long-term anti-thrombotic therapy after acute ischaemic stroke. Quarterly J Med 96:143-153.

Rees K, Lawlor DA, Ebrahim S, Mant J. (2000) A national contract on coronary heart disease and stroke. In Evidence from systematic reviews of research relevant to implementing the wider public health agenda. Report for the NHS Centre for reviews and Dissemination.

Rimmer JH, Braunschweig C, Silverman K, Riley B, Creviston T, Nicola T. (2000) Effects of a short term health promotion intervention for predominantly African American group of stroke survivors. Am J Prev Med 18: 332-338.

Rogers H, Atkinson C, Bond S, Suddes M, Dobson R, Curless R. (1999) Randomised controlled trial of a comprehensive education program for patients and caregivers. Stroke 20: 2585-2591.

Rogers H, Bond S, Curless R. (2001) Inadequacies in the provision of information to stroke patients and their families. Age Ageing 30: 129-133.

Samsa GP, Cohen SJ, Goldstein LB, Bonito AJ, Duncan PW, Enarson C, DeFriese GH, Horner RD, Matcher DB. (1997) Knowledge of risk among patients at increased risk of stroke. Stroke 28: 916-921.

Silagy CA, Weller DP, Lapsley H, Middleton P, Shelby-James T, Fazekas B. (2000) The effectiveness of local adaption of nationally produced clinical practice guidelines. Fam Pract 19:223-230.

Steiner V, Pierce LL. (2002). Building a web of support for caregivers of persons with stroke. Topics Stroke Rehabil 9: 102-111.

Stern EB, Berman M, Thomas JJ, Klassen AC. (1999) Community education for stroke awareness.. An efficacy study. Stroke 30: 720-723.

Stroke Unit Trialists Collaboration. (2001) Organised inpatient (stroke unit) care for stroke. (Cochrane Review). In the Cochrane Library. Oxford Update Software.

Sulch D, Kalra L. (2000) Integrated care pathways in stroke management. Age Ageing 29: 349-352.

Thomson R, Parkin D, Eccles M, Sudlow M, Robinson A. (2000) Decision analysis and guidelines for anticoagulant therapy to prevent stroke in patients with atrial fibrillation. Lancet 355: 956-962.

Towle D, Lincoln NB, Matfield LM. (1989) Service provision and functional independence in depressed stroke patients and the effects of social work intervention on these. J Neurol Neurosurg Psychiatry 52: 519-522.

van den Heuval ETP, deWitte LP Nooyen-Haazen I, Sanderman R, Meyboom-de Jong B. (2000) Short-term effects of a group support program and an individual support program for informal caregivers of stroke patients. Patient Education Counselling 40: 109-120.

Wade D, Legh-Smith J, Langton Hewer R. (1986) Effects of living with and looking after survivors of a stroke. BMJ 293: 418-420.

Wade D. (1994) Stroke (acute cerebrovascular disease) in Health Care Needs Assessment volume 1. (Stevens A, Raftery J, ed), Oxford: Radcliffe Medical Press.

Warlow CP, Dennis MS, van Gijn J, Hankey GJ, Sandercock PAG, Bamford JM, Wardlow JM. (2001) Stroke: a practical guide to management (Second Edition). Oxford: Blackwell Science.

WHO MONICA Project (prepared by P Thorvaldsen, K Kuulasmaa, AM Rajakangas, D Rastenyte, C Sarti and L Wilhelmsen). Stroke Trends in the WHO MONICA Project. Stroke. 28:500-506.

Wiles R, Pain H, Buckland S, McLellen L. (1998) Providing appropriate information to patients and carers following stroke. J Adv Nurs 28: 794-801.

Williams JG, Cheung WY, Price DE, Tansey R, Russell IT, Duane PD, Al-Ismail A, Wani MA. (2004). Clinical guidelines online: do they improve compliance? Postgrad Med J 80: 415-419.

Willoughby DF, Sanders L, Privette A. (2001) The impact of a stroke screening program. Public Health Nurs 18: 418-423.

Wolfe C, Rudd T, Beech R. (1996) Stroke Service and Research. London: Stroke Association.

Wolfe CDA, Taub NA, Woodrow E, Richardson E, Warburton FG, Burney PGJ. (1993) Patterns of acute stroke care in three districts of southern England. J Epidemiol Community Health 47: 144-148.

Yoon SS, Byles J. (2002) Perceptions of stroke in the general public and patients with stroke: a qualitative study. BMJ 324: 1065-1070.

BEHAVIORAL MANAGEMENT OF DEMENTIA

Cornelia Beck and Valorie Shue

INTRODUCTION

People with dementia often display functional dependency and behavioral symptoms. Behavioral symptoms have the potential for or are perceived by caregivers as: 1) endangering the person with dementia or others; 2) stressing, frightening or frustrating to the person with dementia or others; or 3) being socially unacceptable or isolating (Beck et al., 1997). These characteristics can overwhelm home caregivers and force them to place persons with dementia in nursing homes (Gibbons et al., 2002; Hebert et al., 2001; Smith et al., 2000). Such facilities have relied on the medical model since the 1950s and cast residents in passive roles (Post and Whitehouse, 1995). The environment is often both over responsive and over protective and does not consider the person's preserved strengths and abilities (Baltes and Horgas, 1997).

Cohen-Mansfield (2000) has identified four main theoretical frameworks as explanations of how behavioral symptoms evolve. They are the *direct impact of dementia-biological model* (Cohen-Mansfield, 2000), the *behavioral model* (Cohen-Mansfield, 2000), the *environmental vulnerability model* (Hall and Buckwalter, 1987) and the *unmet needs model* (Cohen-Mansfield and Taylor, 2000; Algase et al., 1996). These models are not mutually exclusive and can be used interactively. The direct impact of dementia-biological model has two premises: behavioral symptoms result directly from neurological changes in the brain, and severe organic brain deterioration results in behavioral disinhibition. According to the behavioral model, the behavior's antecedents and consequences control the behavioral symptom. For example, residents learn many behaviors through reinforcement by staff members who provide

attention when residents display the behavior. The environmental vulnerability model posits that the dementia process results in greater sensitivity to the environment and a lower threshold at which stimuli affect behavior.

The unmet needs model describes how the dementia process results in a decreased ability to meet one's needs because of a decreased ability to communicate the needs and to provide for oneself (Cohen-Mansfield, 2000). Algase and colleagues (Algase et al., 1996) have developed the *need-driven dementia-compromised behavior model*. Rather than viewing the behaviors globally as "disruptive" or "agitated" without regard to their origin, they maintain that they arise partly as expressions of needs and reflect the interaction of salient background and proximal variables. Background variables represent the more stable characteristics that influence behavior. Proximal variables represent the need states of a person and the changing environmental characteristics that influence fulfillment of certain needs. Although disruptive, dysfunctional or ineffective, need-driven behaviors may constitute the patients' most integrated and meaningful attempt to communicate needs, given the limitations imposed by their condition, the preserved strengths of their basic abilities and personality (background variables), and the constraints, challenges or supports in their environment (proximal variables).

REVIEW OF RECENT STUDIES

Only in the past decade have researchers started conducting randomized clinical trials investigating the behavioral management of institutionalized persons with moderate to severe dementia. Therefore, we will review studies from 1994 to 2004. We conducted searches in Medline and CINAHL with the terms Alzheimer's Disease (AD) or dementia and randomized controlled trial, PsychLit with the terms Alzheimer's Disease or dementia and clinical trial, reviews (Cohen-Mansfield, 2001; Burgio and Fisher, 2000; Doody et al., 2001) and personal holdings. Of the studies reviewed here only five had follow-up periods to measure the sustained effect of an intervention. The longest follow-up period was two months (Beck et al., 2002), We will describe investigations that address: 1) improving functioning in activities of daily living using strategies to mitigate the incongruence between actual cognitive abilities and levels of assistance; and 2) reducing or extinguishing behavioral symptoms of dementia through sensory stimulation and multiple strategies.

RESULTS

Incongruence between cognitive abilities and levels of assistance

Three randomized studies sought to bridge the gap between actual cognitive abilities and levels of assistance (Table I). Tappen (1994) compared a targeted program of skills training in basic Activities of Daily Living (ADLs) to a more general stimulation program and to regular nursing home care. The skills training program concentrated on grooming, eating, bathing, dressing, toileting, standing and walking. The general stimulation program incorporated traditional recreational activities such as dominoes, music, relaxation and discussion groups. The 63 demented subjects were randomly assigned to the three groups. A gerontological clinical nurse specialist, assisted by a rehabilitation aide, taught the skills training and general stimulation groups five days a week, 2.5 hours per day, for 20 weeks in a group setting. Each subject practiced all skills during daily group sessions guided by verbal prompting, physical demonstration and positive reinforcement. A gerontological nurse practitioner blinded to treatment groups made assessments. Post-testing occurred at the end of the 20 weeks of intervention. Compared to the other two groups, the skills training group improved the most on ability to perform basic ADLs (p=0.01) and meeting individual ADL-related goals (p=0.0023). However, subjects did not maintain the improvements after training ended nor did they generalize the training to actual ADL performance, suggesting that it is necessary to train behaviors during normal daily performance of them. The skills training intervention would be expensive to establish in today's nursing homes. The author suggested that shorter, less intensive programs might be equally successful. Coyne and Hoskins (1997) tested the effect of directed verbal prompts and positive reinforcement on eating independence in 24 female nursing home residents. Both experimental (n=12) and control (n=12) groups consisted of three groups of four women. The interventionist used directed verbal prompts focused on improving eating behaviors and positive reinforcement to increase appropriate eating behaviors. The study occurred across a 13-day time period during three daily meals: Days 1 and 2 (pre-test), Days 3-5 (treatment for experimental group), Days 6 and 7 (post-test I) and Days 12 and 13 (post-test II). The experimental group achieved higher task performance when consuming solid food (p=0.011) and liquid food (p=0.007) than the control group did. Treatment effects were retained at post-test I and decreased slightly at post-test II. These findings indicate that persons with dementia often retain the capacity to increase eating independence when caregivers use specific behavioral strategies. This suggests that the strategies helped stimulate dormant functional capacity. Nursing home personnel can learn directed verbal prompting and positive reinforcement (Beck et al., 1997), which would defer the human and financial costs of enteral nutrition.

Tappen, Roach, Applegate and Stowell (2000) compared assisted walking and walking combined with conversation to a conversation-only intervention. Sixty-five subjects randomly assigned to treatment group were tested at baseline and at the end of treatment. Treatment occurred three times a week for 30 minutes for 16 weeks. Functional mobility declined significantly in the walking group (20.9% decline, p=0.01) and tended to decline in the talking group (18.8% decline, p=0.09). Functional mobility did not significantly change in the combined group (2.5% decline, p>0.10). The addition of conversation with walking in the combined treatment appears to have improved compliance with the intervention and thus treatment outcome. Results indicate that assisted walking with conversation can contribute to maintenance of functional mobility in nursing home residents with dementia.

Table 1: Controlled trials of interventions to reduce congruence between cognitive abilities and levels of assistance

Study	Subjects/ Group	Intervention	Outcomes
Skill training, a traditional stimulation approach and usual care on ability to perform basic ADL Tappen,1994	1: 21 2: 21 3: 21	1: Skill training: repeated practice and use of verbal prompts, physical demonstration and positive reinforcement; 2: Traditional stimulation: games, group discussions, music and simple relaxation 3: Regular nursing home care	Significant difference on skill performance between the skill training and control group (p=0.01). No difference between the traditional stimulation and other groups
Directed verbal prompts and positive reinforcement on eating behaviors Coyne and Hoskins, 1997	Treated = 12 Control = 12	Directed verbal prompts and positive reinforcement when a subject completed eating tasks Control: usual nursing home care	Differences between treatment and control groups for both solid (p=0.011) and liquid (p=0.007) food consumption
Combined walking and conversation Tappen et al., 2000	1: 23 2: 22 3: 20	1: Walking with intervener who did not initiate conversation but responded to subject; 2: Conversation about objects, events and personal interests; 3: Combined 1 and 2 interventions	Significant ↑ in functional mobility for 1 (p=0.0119), ↑ approaching significance for 2 (p=0.0874), and no significant ↑ in 3

Sensory stimulation

Nursing homes frequently over- or understimulate residents' senses, which can induce behavioral symptoms. Four studies used sensory stimulation to ameliorate behavioral symptoms (Table 2).

Visual stimulation. Mishima et al. (1994) reported that residents with dementia in the treatment group (n=14) received daily light therapy of 3000-5000 lumens bright light for four weeks every morning between the hours of 9 a.m. and 11 a.m. One nursing staff member stayed with each resident and instructed the resident to glance frequently at the desktop light therapy device equipped with full-spectrum fluorescent lamps. The control group (n=10) received usual care. Nursing staff observed the residents hourly and indicated when a resident displayed a behavioral symptom. They made these observations two weeks before, one month during and two weeks after the light therapy. Before light therapy, patients averaged 23.9 on a measure of behavioral symptoms. During light therapy, patients significantly decreased behavioral symptomatology to 11.6 (p<0.05). The article did not report follow-up findings.

In a sample of 71 residents with severe dementia, Ancoli-Israel *et al.* (2003) randomly assigned 23 residents to morning bright light, 23 to morning dim red light, and 25 to evening bright light. Treatment lasted 10 days followed by five days of post-treatment. For bright light therapy, Apollo "Brite-Lite" boxes were placed one meter from the resident for an exposure of 2,500 lux. A red light box, which emitted dim red light and resulted in <300 lux exposure, was no brighter than room light levels in nursing homes. Nursing and research staff could not be kept blind to light condition, but investigators told them that they expected both bright and dim light to have an effect. Trained research staff observed the residents for 20 seconds every 15 minutes for 24 hours every other day for 9 days and from 0730 to 2000 hours on the other 9 days. Nursing staff rated agitation once at baseline and once after treatment.

Bright light had little effect on observational ratings of agitation. The peak of physical agitation for the morning bright light group was delayed by 1.63 hours (p=.03) from 12:51 to 14:47 hours. Overall caregiver ratings of agitation decreased. This could indicate that agitation occurred when caregivers could more easily cope with it, for example when the staff-to-resident ratio was higher or when caregivers were more alert.

Since residents typically had lunch at around 11:30 a.m., it is likely that the agitation peak levels at baseline coincided with nursing staff breaks after the noontime meal.

Caregiver ratings showed decreased agitation from both bright and dim red light, which may indicate a caregiver expectation effect stemming from the extra attention residents received from research staff. The lack of objective behavioral effects of bright light in this study may be a result of greater brain deterioration in this severely demented sample. Degeneration of the suprachiasmatic nucleus (SCN) may prevent regulation of circadian patterns of activity and agitation. Persons with more intact SCNs (i.e., those with mild or moderate dementia) might benefit more from light therapy than those with severe dementia.

Auditory stimulation. Camberg *et al.* (1999) introduced a highly individualized intervention, Simulated Presence Therapy (SPT), in which nursing assistants played an audiotape that contained one side of a conversation with a family member or surrogate on selected memories and positive emotions whenever a resident became agitated. They tested SPT against a placebo, which was an audiotape of a person reading emotionally neutral articles from the newspaper. Residents (n=54) received SPT (n=18), placebo (n=18) or usual care (n=18) in randomly selected sequences, with each continuing for 17 days over a four-week course followed by a 10-day washout. Trained non-participant observers used a structured time-sampling technique to observe each resident in 20-minute segments for at least 3 hours and 20 minutes a week between 9 a.m. and 7 p.m. Staff indicated on a log, Monday through Friday, when they used an intervention for agitated or withdrawn behaviors. Staff did not always play the tapes as needed. Instead they used them when they had time; therefore, they played them much less than the researchers had expected. From direct observations, staff used SPT 11.7% of the time compared with placebo, which staff used 10.5% of the time. Staff logs showed that SPT reduced agitation 69% of the time and was significantly better (p<0.001) at reducing agitation than usual care and placebo. No follow-up data collection occurred.

Olfactory stimulation. In the United Kingdom, 71 persons residing in National

Table 2: Controlled trials of Sensory Stimulation Interventions

Study	Subjects/ Group	Intervention	Outcomes
Visual Stimulation			
Light therapy Mishima et al., 1994	Treated =14 Control =10	Illumination of 3000-5000 lx of full-spectrum fluorescent light 2 hours daily for 4 weeks	Morning light therapy ↑ total (p<0.05) and nocturnal sleep (p<0.01) and ↑ daytime sleep (p<0.05) and behavior disorders (p<0.05)
Bright light therapy Ancoli-Israel et al., 2003	1:23 2:23 3:25	1: 0930 to 1130 hours bright light of 2,500 lux exposure 2: 0930 to 1130 hours red light of < 300 lux exposure to control for placebo and staff-patient interaction effects 3: 1730 to 1930 hours bright light of 2,500 lux. Treatment lasted 10 days.	Nurse-rated ↑ physical agitation (p=.008) across all light treatment conditions while observational ratings showed little change. Peak of physical agitation in group #1 only was delayed (p=.034)
Auditory Stimulation			
Simulated presence therapy (SPT) vs. placebo and usual care Camberg et al.,1999	Treated =18 Placebo = 18 Control = 18	SPT: a telephone conversation of memories using a continuous play audio tape system; Placebo: audio tape of a person reading the newspaper Control: usual care	Staff nursing logs revealed that SPT reduced agitation more than placebo (p<0.001) and usual care (p<0.001)
Olfactory Stimulation			
Aromatherapy Ballard et al., 2002	Treated =35 Placebo =36	Essential oil of Melissa Officinalis (lemon balm) or placebo (sunflower oil) in a base lotion applied to persons' faces and arms 2x/day by care-giving staff for 4-weeks	60% of treated and 14% of placebo experienced a 30% ↑ in agitation, with an overall improvement in agitation of 35% in treated and 11% in placebo (p<0.0001). Treated subjects showed a ↑ in time spent socially withdrawn (p=0.005) and ↑ in % of time engaged in constructive activities (p=0.001)

Health Service care facilities with clinically significant agitation and severe dementia were randomly assigned to aromatherapy with *Melissa Officinalis* (lemon balm) oil (n=35) or placebo (sunflower oil) (n=36) (Ballard et al., 2002). Researchers combined the active treatment or placebo oil with a base lotion. Care-giving staff applied the lotion to the residents' faces and arms twice a day for a total of 6 doses per day, providing a total of 200 mg of oil, for 4 weeks. The full application process, which involved gently applying the cream onto the skin, took 1 to 2 minutes to complete. The participants receiving the active treatment (p<0.0001) and those receiving the placebo (p=0.005) experienced significant improvement in agitation with a 35% reduction in the treatment group and an 11% reduction in the placebo group. Twenty-one subjects (60%) in the treatment group, but only five (14%) in the placebo group attained a 30% improvement (p<0.0001), which is the threshold generally defined as clinically significant. Further, there was a significant reduction in the percentage of time spent socially withdrawn (p=0.005) and a significant increase in the percentage of time engaged in constructive activities (p=0.001) among those receiving active treatment, suggesting that, unlike neuroleptic treatments to reduce agitation the treatment did not have a sedating effect (McShane et al., 1997). No follow-up data collection occurred.

Multiple Intervention Strategies

Multiple component interventions included the AGE dementia care program (Rovner et al., 1996), validation group therapy (Toseland et al., 1997), physical activity and improved sleep environment (Alessi et al., 1999), aromatherapy massage (Smallwood et al., 2001), activities of daily living/psychosocial activities (Beck et al., 2002), individualized interventions (Opie et al., 2002), calming music/hand massage (Remington, 2002) and person-centered showering and towel bath (Sloane et al., 2004).

Rovner *et al.* (1996) developed a three-part treatment. In an activity program held weekdays from 10 a.m. to 3 p.m., a creative arts therapist and two nursing aides developed and implemented the program activities, which included music, exercise, crafts, relaxation, reminiscence, word games and food preparation. Psychotrophic prescriptions were managed by a psychiatrist instead of the primary care physician. Guidelines were developed to reduce or eliminate psychotropic medications, when efficacious. Education rounds involved the study psychiatrist meeting with the activities staff weekly for one hour to discuss each patient's behavioral, functional, and medical status. Discussion focused on conditions like delusions and their causes (notable environmental changes). Then, a research psychiatrist blind to treatment assignment directly observed participants between 3 and 5 p.m., when no activity occurred. The treatment group was less likely to have behavioral symptoms than was the control group (p=0.037). Interventions lasted six months. Twelve of 42 intervention patients (28.6%) had behavior symptoms compared to 20 of 39 control patients (51.3%). Intervention participants were much more likely to engage in activities (p=0.001). The authors acknowledged that the AGE program cost more than usual nursing home care. The cost per patient per day for the intervention activity was $8.94 while the cost per patient per day for nursing home-provided activity was $1.13. In addition, the intervention psychiatrist's cost was $3,900.

Toseland *et al.* (1997) compared validation group therapy with a social contact group and usual care. Nursing home residents who completed the study (n=66) were randomly assigned to validation (n=23), social contact (n=21) or usual care (n=22). Validation and social contact groups met in groups of six or nine for four 30-minute sessions each week for a total of 52 weeks. Validation therapy involved four 5- to 10-minute segments: introduction and fostering warm greetings, discussing a topic of interest, a program activity such as a sing-along, and a closing with refreshments and goodbyes. The social contact group participated in one of 54 activities in each session. The activities fell into eight categories: music, art, literature and writing, dance/exercise, games/trivia, holiday and event planning, discussion and other activities. The usual care group received regular nursing home care. Non-participant observers and nursing home staff collected data two weeks before intervention (baseline) and at three and 12 months post-intervention. No follow-up data were collected. Compared to the social contact and usual care groups, the validation group showed a significant reduction in physically aggressive behaviors both at three months (p<0.001) and at one year (p<0.001), according to nursing staff data. A significant reduction occurred in verbally aggressive behaviors for both the validation and social contact groups (p<0.01) when compared with the usual care group; however, no significant differences emerged between validation and social contact groups, according to nursing staff data. In contrast, data from non-participant observers revealed that compared to the validation and usual care groups, the social contact group displayed significantly lower scores on verbally aggressive behaviors both at three months (p<0.05) and at one year (p<0.01). Physically non-aggressive behaviors declined for the social contact and usual care groups (p<0.01) at one year but not for the validation group, according to nursing staff data. The data seem to suggest that validation therapy is effective for reducing physically aggressive behaviors while social contact (as well as usual care) is effective for reducing physically non-aggressive behaviors. Results were equivocal for verbally aggressive behaviors.

Alessi et al. (1999) randomized subjects to receive either an intervention combining increased daytime physical activity (14 weeks) plus a nighttime program (5 nights) to decrease noise and sleep-disruptive nursing care practices (intervention group) or the nighttime program alone (control group). The physical activity intervention was performed during, or incidental to, daily nursing care routines such as toileting. Trained research personnel performed the sessions every two hours from 8 a.m. to 4 p.m. for a maximum of four sessions a day Monday through Friday. Sessions involved a structured series of arm and leg exercises, sit-to-stands, and walking or wheelchair propulsion based on the subject's ability. After 14 weeks of the physical activity alone to reach a maintenance level of physical function, the nighttime program was added. It involved reducing noise, light and sleep-disruptive nursing care practices. The control subjects also received the nighttime intervention. Research personnel made observations of agitation for one minute every 15 minutes from 8 a.m. to 4 p.m. The intervention group had a 22% decrease in the mean percent of observations of agitation, whereas, controls had a 150% increase in mean percent of observations of agitation (p=0.009). No follow-up data were reported.

Smallwood, Brown, Coulter, Irvine and Copland (2001) tested the relaxing effects of an aromatherapy massage on behavioral symptoms of dementia. They randomized 21 persons to aromatherapy massage, conversation and aromatherapy or massage only. Behavior was recorded using a video camera for 15 minutes between 10-11 a.m., 11-noon, 2-3 p.m. and 3-4 p.m. A baseline measure of behavior was recorded over a two-week period. The treatment phase directly followed the last week of baseline measurement. During the treatment phase each individual received treatment twice weekly, after which the patient's behavior was recorded. Treatment was rotated across each period so that each individual received treatment twice in each period of the day. Aromatherapy massage decreased agitated behavior across all time periods and showed the greatest reduction in excessive motor behaviors. This reached statistical significance between 3 and 4 p.m. ($p<0.05$) when aromatherapy massage consistently reduced motor behavior compared with conversation and aromatherapy ($p=0.05$). It appears that of the three treatments examined, massage and oil components are needed for maximum therapeutic change. In comparison to neuroleptic medication, aromatherapy massage has low costs and negligible side effects.

Beck *et al.* (2002) conducted a clinical trial of two behavioral interventions--an activities of daily living (ADL), a Psychosocial Activity (PSA) and a combined ADL and PSA (CB) intervention-- using a five-group experimental design with a placebo group for the PSA intervention and a no-intervention control group. The ADL intervention employed environmental and behavioral strategies to promote functional independence during morning care and the noon meal. The PSA intervention consisted of 25 standardized modules designed to engage the resident in a meaningful activity and meet psychosocial needs. The combined intervention included both the PSA and ADL interventions conducted daily with the participant. The PSA placebo intervention involved one-to-one interaction 30 minutes each day to control for the effect of one-to-one attention in the PSA intervention. Certified Nursing Assistants employed specifically for this study received training to perform the interventions. A master's level clinical nursing specialist supervised them. The no-intervention control participants received routine morning care and noon meal care by a nursing home nursing assistant. The sample consisted of 127 subjects. The females were randomized to groups, but the males were assigned to groups

to ensure the even distribution of their small number. Multivariate tests revealed no significant treatment effects by group or time. One month and two months after the research team left the nursing home, follow-up data collection occurred. A videotape analysis of 84 subjects supported increased positive affect and decreased negative affect. Compared to the control groups, the treatment groups had significantly more positive facial expressions ($p<0.001$), positive body movements ($p<0.001$), contentment ($p=0.037$) and interest ($p=0.028$). They also had a shorter duration of sadness ($p=.007$) and anger ($p=.054$). These results suggest that future intervention research should consider the individual characteristics of the person with dementia (Maslow, 1996) and the triggers of the behavior (Algase et al., 1996). Studies that have individualized interventions, as well as the one described next, have demonstrated decreased behavioral symptoms of dementia (Gerdner, 2000; Hoeffer et al., 1997).

A team consisting of a psychiatrist, a psychologist and two nurses conducted detailed assessments of 99 nursing home residents with dementia (Opie et al., 2002). Residents were then randomly assigned to an early (n=48) or late (n=51) intervention group and observed for four weeks. Interventions included medical (e.g., change in pain management), nursing (e.g., timing/approach to activities of daily living) and psychosocial (e.g., radio, audiotapes) components. Of the 99 residents, 73 received at least one medical intervention, 75 received at least one nursing intervention and 90 received at least one psychosocial intervention. Strategies were intended to be simple, inexpensive, practical and respectful of staff resources. Staff did not implement 8.1% of medical interventions, 2.8% of nursing interventions or 3.8% of psychosocial interventions. At post-intervention, both groups had significant reductions in restlessness ($p<0.0005$), physical aggression ($p<0.01$), verbal disruption (p<0.0005), inappropriate behaviors (p<0.01) and overall behavioral symptoms (p<0.0005). There were no significant 'group' (early group versus late group) effects. Within the four-week period, 30% of the variance could be attributed to the intervention, indicating that this intervention produced clinically meaningful improvement in outcomes (p<0.005). At one-month follow-up, senior staff rated changes in behavior on a four-point scale. Staff reported that targeted behaviors had decreased in at least one behavioral category for 75% of residents and that severity had decreased in at least one category for 60%. They reported reductions in restlessness (44.8%), physical aggression (40%), verbal disruption (39.4%) and inappropriate behaviors (27.6%). Staff noted reductions in severity for restlessness (34.5%), physical aggression (35.6%), verbal disruption (37.9%) and inappropriate behaviors (28.9%). They rated 73.5% of interventions as very acceptable or accept-able, 14.3% as neutral and 12.2% as unacceptable. Individually-tailored medical, nursing and psychosocial interventions led to reductions in challenging behaviors over and above changes originating from the presence of interested and knowledgeable consultants.

Remington (2002) conducted a four-group, repeated measures experiment to test the effect of 10-minute exposure to either calming music, hand massage, calming music and hand massage simultaneously or no intervention on the frequency and type of agitated behaviors in 68 nursing home residents with dementia. Each of the experimental interventions reduced agitation more than no intervention. The benefit lasted and increased up to one hour following the intervention (p<0.01). The increase in benefit over time was similar for each intervention group. When types of agitated behaviors were examined separately, none of the inter-ventions significantly reduced physically aggressive behaviors, while physically non-

aggressive behaviors decreased during each intervention (p<0.01). No additive benefit resulted from simultaneous exposure to calming music and hand massage. Calming music has an advantage over hand massage because caregivers can perform other tasks while the treatment is occurring.

Sloane et al. (2004) evaluated the efficacy of person-centered showering and the towel bath (a person-centered, in-bed bag-bath with no rinse soap) in reducing agitation and aggression. A randomized controlled trial, with a usual-care control group and two experimental groups with crossover between the experimental groups occurred in 15 nursing homes. Facilities were randomized into three groups (five facilities each): a control group, which received showering without person-centered bathing techniques, and two treatment groups based on the order of treatment administration. One treatment group received the towel bath during the first 6-week intervention period and person-centered showering the second 6-week intervention period. The other treatment group received the same interventions in reverse order. Three certified nursing assistants in each nursing home performed the intervention.

Person-centered bathing focused on resident comfort and preferences, viewed behavioral symptoms as expressions of unmet need, employed communication techniques appropriate for the resident's level of disease severity, applied problem-solving approaches to identify causes and potential solutions, and regulated the physical environment to maximize resident comfort.

Person-centered showering used a wide variety of techniques such as providing choices, covering with towels to maintain resident warmth, distraction, and using preferred bathing products to individualize interventions.

The towel bath, an in-bed method, involved the caregiver using two bath blankets, two bath towels, a no-rinse soap, and 2 quarts of warm water; keeping the resident covered at all times; and cleansing the body using gentle message.

A clinical nurse specialist or psychologist who worked alongside the nursing assistant two days a week for 4 weeks introduced the interventions. Videotaping occurred during the 2 weeks after intervention training; study research assistants conducted the videotaping and had no other responsibilities in the project. Intensively-trained undergraduate and graduate students rated the videotaped baths.

Across all measures of agitation studied, ratings of baths after both interventions produced significantly fewer agitated behaviors than at baseline or under the control condition. No significant differences emerged between the towel-bath and person-centered showering on any agitation measure, but discomfort was less (p=.003) with the towel bath when compared with person-centered showering. Further, bath time did not increase significantly with the towel bath while it did increase significantly (p<.001); mean of 3.3 minutes) with person-centered showering.

Table 3: Controlled trials of Multi-component Interventions

Study	Subjects/Group	Intervention	Outcomes
Multi-Strategies			
AGE dementia care program Rovner *et al.*, 1996	Treated = 42 Control = 39	Activities, guidelines for psychotropic medications and educational rounds	28.6% intervention patients exhibited behavior disorders compared with 51.3% controls (p=0.037). Intervention patients were much more likely to participate in activities (p=0.001)
Validation and social contact therapy Toseland *et al.*, 1997	1: 23 2: 21 3: 22	Four 30 minute group sessions/week for 52 weeks of 1: validation therapy 2: social contact therapy or 3: Usual Care	Nursing staff observations revealed ↑ in physically aggressive behavior (p<0.001) at 3 mo and 1 yr for 1; ↑ in verbally aggressive behavior (p<0.01) at 1 yr for 1 and 2; and ↑ in physically non-aggressive behaviors (p<0.01) at 1 yr for 2 and 3. Non-participant observers found ↑ in verbally aggressive behaviors for 2 (3 mo: p<0.05; 1 yr: p<0.01)
Physical activity and improved sleep environment Alessi *et al.*, 1999	Treated = 15 Control = 14	Combined intervention of increased daytime physical activity (14 wks) plus a nighttime program (5 nights) to decrease noise and sleep-disruptive care practices vs. nighttime program alone	Intervention group had a 22% ↑ in observations of agitation while controls had a 150% ↑ (p=0.009)

Study	Subjects/ Group	Intervention	Outcomes
Aromatherapy, massage, conversation Smallwood *et al.*, 2001	1: 7 2: 7 3: 7	1: Lavender essential oil massage 2: Conversation and lavender essential oil disseminated by diffuser 3: Plain oil massage	Between 3 and 4 p.m., motor behavior ↑ in 1 compared with 2 (p=0.05)
Activities of Daily Living (ADL) and Psychosocial activities (PSA) Beck *et al.*, 2002	1: 28 2: 29 3: 22 4: 29 5: 19	1: ADL intervention 2: PSA intervention 3: combined intervention 4: placebo 5: no intervention	No significant effect on behavior between groups; compared to control groups 1-3 had ↑ positive facial expression (p<0.001), positive body/posture/movements (p<0.001), contentment (p=0.037) and interest (p=0.028) and ↑ sadness (p=.007) and anger (p=.054)
Individually tailored strategies Opie *et al.*, 2002	Early group =48 Late group =51	Medical, nursing and psychosocial interventions based on residents' characteristics	At post intervention, ↑ in restlessness (p<0.0005), physical aggression (p<0.01), verbal disruption (p<0.0005), inappropriate behaviors (p<0.01) and all behaviors combined (p<0.0005) in both groups
Calming music and hand massage Remington, 2002	1: 17 2: 17 3: 17 4: 17	1: Calming music 2: Hand massage 3: Calming music and hand massage 4: Usual care	Interventions reduced agitation more than no intervention. Benefit up to 1 hour after treatment (p<0.01)
Person-centered showering & the towel bath Sloane *et al.*, 2004	1: 24 2: 25 3: 24	1: Person-centered shower 2: Person-centered towel bath 3: Usual care control	All measures of agitation & aggression ↑ in treatment groups but not control group. Aggression ↑ 53% in #1 (p<.001) and 60% in towel bath (p<.001)

DISCUSSION

Although the studies have not examined long-term effects, it is generally accepted that graded assistance, practice and positive reinforcement increase functional independence and that music, particularly during meals and bathing, and light exercise reduce behavioral symptoms (Doody et al., 2001). However, many unanswered questions surround the use of non-pharmacological interventions to treat the behavioral symptoms of dementia. This section lists 10 areas that require further study.

First, most noticeably, none of the studies in this review included a yearlong follow-up, which is greatly needed to determine the long-term effects of interventions.

Second, many of the interventions presented were not individualized to the person's needs and capabilities. Issues of cognitive level, sensory deficits, mobility, social abilities and environmental resources all have an effect on the tailoring of a specific treatment for a given behavior and need consideration in study designs (Cohen-Mansfield, 2001). Before introducing an intervention, it is important to identify the relevant individual characteristics to assess and design algorithms for prescribing the interventions.

Third, since behaviors may respond selectively to interventions, targeting interventions requires much greater specificity. For example, aggressive behaviors may respond to validation therapy, whereas pacing may respond to social contact but not validation therapy (Burgio and Fisher, 2000).

Fourth, it is important to understand what characteristics (i.e., timing, duration, location, intensity) of the interventions optimize their impact (Cohen-Mansfield, 2001). Similarly, the effect of attention alone requires evaluation by including placebo groups, as does the amount of maintenance necessary to sustain treatment effects.

Fifth, not many studies have systematically explored the effects of caregiver variables as moderators or mediators of treatment effect (Davis et al., 1997). Simultaneously treating the patient and altering the social and physical environment of the caregiver-patient dyad may produce important synergies (Burgio and Fisher, 2000).

Sixth, few studies have examined the resource use, cost or organizational facilitators and barriers of enacting interventions. If clinicians are to adopt efficacious interventions, more health services studies are needed (Beck, 2001).

Seventh, including outcome measures more consistent with those used in pharmacologic trials, such as the Alzheimer's Disease Assessment Scale-Cognition, would allow for easier comparisons of effect sizes between studies. It also is important that the outcomes measured in behavioral intervention trials include multiple measures rather than just focusing on only cognition, ADL functioning or behavior. Quality of life and caregiver measures are also important outcomes to consider.

Eighth, the effect of genotype on the type of behavioral symptoms that persons display needs further exploration. Studies of persons in the early stages of AD suggest that there is no association between behavioral symptoms and the Apolipoprotein E ε4 alleles. However, Craig et al. (2004a) found that in 400 persons with moderate to severe AD, a significantly higher frequency of the ε4 allele was found in persons with aggression/agitation (p=.03). Comparisons between ε4 genotypes and non-ε4 genotypes revealed an additional risk for aggression/agitation with ε4 genotypes (p=.02). Craig et al. (2004b) also found that males with a history of agitation/aggression were more likely to possess a polymorphic variation at the tryptophan hydroxylase gene (p=.044). In an earlier study, Cacabelos (1996) noted that agitation and motor disorders were slightly more frequent in persons with APOE-4/4 than in those with APOE 3/4.

Ninth, researchers need to start conducting trials that involve both behavioral and pharmacologic treatments to answer such questions as, "Does an enhanced environment potentiate the effect of acetylcholinesterase inhibitors (AChEIs)? Are the effects of an ADL program improved with AChEIs? How do caregiver interventions interact with drug therapies?"

Tenth, incorporating computer technology and robotics into care may have beneficial effects. Technology-based interventions could include remote presence, digital family portrait, family intercom, gesture pendant and gesture panel, and assisted cognition systems.

SUGGESTED READINGS

Beck C. (2001) Identification and assessment of effective services and interventions:

The nursing home perspective. Aging Ment Health 5(Suppl 1): S99-S111.

Burgio LD, Fisher SE. (2000) Application of psychosocial interventions for treating behavioral and psychological symptoms of dementia. Int Psychogeriatr 12(Suppl 1): 351-358.

Cohen-Mansfield J. (2001) Nonpharmacologic interventions for inappropriate behaviors in dementia. Am J Geriatr Psychiatry 9: 361-381.

Doody RS, Stevens JC, Beck C, Dubinsky RM, Kaye JA, Gwyther L, Mohs RC, Thal LJ, Whitehouse PJ, DeKosky ST, Cummings JL. (2001) Practice parameter: Management of dementia (an evidence-based review). Neurology 56: 1154-1166.

REFERENCES

Alessi CA, Yoon EJ, Schnelle JF, Al-Samarrai NR, Cruise PA. (1999) A randomized trial of a combined physical activity and environmental intervention in nursing home residents: Do sleep and agitation improve? J Am Geriatr Soc 47: 784-791.

Algase DL, Beck C, Kolanowski A, Whall A, Berent S, Richards K, Beattie E. (1996) Need-driven dementia-compromised behavior: An alternative view of disruptive behavior. Am J Alzheimers Dis Other Demen 11: 10, 12-19.

Ancoli-Israel S, Martin JL, Gehrman P, Shochat T, Corey-Bloom J, Marler M, Nolan S, Levi L. (2003). Effect of light on agitation in institutionalized patients with severe Alzheimer Disease. Am J Geriatr Psychiatry 11: 194-203.

Ballard CG, O'Brien JT, Reichelt K, Perry EK. (2002) Aromatherapy as a safe and effective treatment for the management of agitation in severe dementia: the results of a double-blind placebo-controlled trial with *Melissa*. J Clin Psychiatry 63: 553-558.

Baltes MM, Horgas AL. (1997) Long-term care institutions and the maintenance of competence: A dialectic between compensation and overcompensation. In Societal Mechanisms for Maintaining Competence in Old Age (S. L. Willis, K. W. Schaie, and M. Hayward, eds.), pp. 142-164. New York: Springer Publishing Company.

Beck C. (2001) Identification and assessment of effective services and interventions: The nursing home perspective. Aging Ment Health 5(Suppl 1): S99-S111.

Beck CK, Heacock P, Mercer SO, Walls RC, Rapp CG, Vogelpohl TS. (1997). Improving dressing behavior in cognitively impaired nursing home residents. Nurs Res 46(3): 126-132.

Beck C, Heithoff K, Baldwin B, Cuffel B, O'Sullivan P, Chumbler NR. (1997). Assessing disruptive behavior in older adults: The Disruptive Behavior Scale. Aging and Mental Health, 1: 71-79.

Beck CK, Vogelpohl TS, Rasin JH, Uriri JT, O'Sullivan P, Walls R, Phillips R, Baldwin B. (2002) Effects of behavioral interventions on disruptive behavior and affect in demented nursing home residents. Nurs Res 51(4): 219-228.

Burgio LD, Fisher SE. (2000) Application of psychosocial interventions for treating behavioral and psychological symptoms of dementia. Int Psychogeriatr 12(Suppl 1): 351-358.

Cacabelos R, Rodriguez B, Carrera C, Caamano J, Beyer K, Lao JI, Sellers MA. (1996). APOE-related frequency of cognitive and noncognitive symptoms in dementia. Methods Find Exp Clin Pharmacol 18(10): 693-706.

Camberg L, Woods P, Ooi WL, Hurley A, Volicer L, Ashley J, Odenheimer G, McIntyre K. (1999) Evaluation of simulated presence: A personalized approach to enhance well-being in persons with Alzheimer's Disease. J Am Geriatr Soc 47: 446-452.

Cohen-Mansfield J. (2000) Theoretical frameworks for behavioral problems in dementia Alzheimers Care Q 1(4): 8-21.

Cohen-Mansfield J. (2001) Nonpharmacologic interventions for inappropriate behaviors in dementia. Am J Geriatr Psychiatry 9: 361-381.

Cohen-Mansfield J, Taylor L. (2000) Assessing and understanding agitated behaviors in older adults. In Behaviors in Dementia: Best Practices for Successful Management (M. Kaplan and SB.Hoffman, eds.), Baltimore, Maryland: Health Professions Press.

Coyne ML, Hoskins L. (1997) Improving eating behaviors in dementia using behavioral strategies. Clin Nurs Res 6(3): 275-290.

Craig D, Hart DJ, McCool K, McIlory SP, Passmore AP. (2004a). Apolipoprotein E e4 allele influences aggressive behaviour in Alzheimer's disease. J Neurol Neurosurg Psychiatry 75: 1327-1330.

Craig D, Hart DJ, Carson R, McIlroy SP, Passmore AP. (2004b). Allelic variation at the A218C tryptophan hydroxylase polymorphism influences agitation and aggression in Alzheimer's disease. Neuroscience Letters 363: 199-202.

Davis LL, Buckwalter K, Burgio LD. (1997) Measuring problem behaviors in dementia: Developing a methodological agenda. ANS Adv Nurs Sci 20(1): 40-55.

Doody RS, Stevens JC, Beck C, Dubinsky RM, Kaye, JA, Gwyther L, Mohs RC, Thal LJ, Whitehouse PJ, DeKosky ST, Cummings JL. (2001) Practice parameter: Management of dementia (an evidence-based review). Neurology 56: 1154-1166.

Gerdner LA. (2000). Effects of individualized versus classical "relaxation" music on the frequency of agitation in elderly persons with Alzheimer's disease and related disorders. Int J Psychogeriatr 12(1): 49-65.

Gibbons LE, Teri L, Logsdon R, McCurry SM, Kukull W, Bowen J, McCormick W, Larson E. (2002) Anxiety symptoms as predictors of nursing home placement in patients with Alzheimer's Disease. J Clin Geropsychol 8(4): 335-342.

Hall GR, Buckwalter KC. (1987) Progressively lowered stress threshold: A conceptual model for care of adults with Alzheimer's disease. Arch Psychiatr Nurs 1(6): 399-405.

Hebert R, Dubois MF, Wolfson C, Chambers L, Cohen C. (2001) Factors associated with long-term institutionalization of older people with dementia: Data from the Canadian Study of Health and Aging. J Gerontol A Biol Sci Med Sci 56(11): M693-M696.

Hoeffer B, Rader J, McKenzie D, Lavelle M, Stewart B. (1997) Reducing aggressive behavior during bathing cognitively impaired nursing home residents. J Gerontological Nurs 23(5): 16-23.

Maslow K. (1996) Relationship between patient characteristics and the effectiveness of nonpharmacologic approaches to prevent or treat behavioral symptoms. Int J Psychogeriatr 8(Suppl. 1): 73-76.

Mishima K, Okawa M, Hishikawa Y, Hozumi S, Hori H, Takahashi K. (1994) Morning bright light therapy for sleep and behavior disorders in elderly patients with dementia. Acta Psychiatr Scand 89: 1-7.

Opie J, Doyle C, O'Connor DW. (2002) Challenging behaviours in nursing home residents with dementia: A randomized controlled trial of multidisciplinary interventions. Int J Geriatr Psychiatry 17(1): 6-13.

Post SG, Whitehouse PJ. (1995) Fairhill guidelines on ethics of the care of people with Alzheimer's disease: A clinical summary. J Am Geriatr Soc 43: 1423-1429.

Remington R. (2002) Calming music and hand massage with agitated elderly. Nurs Res 51(5): 317-323.

Rovner BW, Steele CD, Shmuely Y, Folstein, MF. (1996) A randomized trial of dementia care in nursing homes. J Am Geriatr Soc 44: 7-13.

Sloane PD, Hoeffer B, Mitchell CM, McKenzie DA, Barrick AL, Rader J, Stewart BJ, Talerico KA, Rasin JH, Zink RC, Koch GG. (2004). Effect of person-centered showering and the towel bath on bathing-associated aggression, agitation, and discomfort in nursing home residents with dementia: A randomized controlled trial. J Am Geriatr Soc 52: 1795-1804.

Smallwood J, Brown R, Coulter F, Irvine E, Copland C. (2001) Aromatherapy and behaviour disturbances in dementia: a randomized controlled trial. Int J Geriatr Psychiatry 16: 1010-1013.

Smith GE, Kokmen E, O'Brien PC. (2000) Risk factors for nursing home placement in a population-based dementia cohort. J Am Geriatr Soc 48(5): 519-525.

Tappen RM. (1994) The effect of skill training on functional abilities of nursing home residents with dementia. Res Nurs and Health 17: 159-165.

Tappen RM, Roach KE, Applegate EB, Stowell P. (2000) Effect of a combined walking and conversation intervention on functional mobility of nursing home residents with Alzheimer Disease. Alzheimer Dis Assoc Disord 14(4): 196-201.

Toseland RW, Diehl M, Freeman K, Manzanares T, Naleppa M., McCallion P. (1997) The impact of validation group therapy on nursing home residents with dementia. J Applied Gerontology 16(1): 31-50.

ANXIETY DISORDERS

David H. Barlow and Todd J. Farchione

INTRODUCTION

Anxiety disorders are chronic, often lasting a lifetime if untreated, costly to our health care system, and associated with sustained impairment (Barlow, 2002). Since the 1960's, treatment techniques have been refined greatly, although early systematic invest-igations provided the basis for many of the treatment techniques used today (Agras et al., 1968). Exposure-based treatments in which patients face the triggers and cues for their anxiety under clinical supervision have consistently been shown to produce significant improvement in symptomatology for most phobic disorders, while additional techniques including psychoeducation about the nature of anxiety and reappraisal of maladaptive cognitions have also proved beneficial for all anxiety disorders. Psychopharmacological interventions have offered additional relief for many individuals suffering from some specific anxiety disorders as well. However, a number of problems still exist with our current treatments, including limited efficacy (Barlow, 2002). In addition, the high cost of treatment and lack of effective dissemination have left far too many people suffering with chronic fear and anxiety.

One potential remedy to these problems exists in a new theoretical understanding of emotional disorders. Integrative approaches suggest that all emotional disorders stem from similar underlying difficulties. In particular, general avoidance of emotional arousal (which may take the form of avoiding emotion based thoughts, feelings, and/or behaviors) characterizes all emotional disorders, such that only by facilitating processing of emotions and their cues will the cycle of anxiety be broken (Barlow et al., 2004). Furthermore, single integrative

protocols applicable to all disorders will assist dissemination of treatment techniques and have significant implications for reducing cost of treatment. While still in its infancy, preliminary data suggest that integrated treatment techniques increasing emotional exposure are the next frontier for treating chronic anxiety difficulties (Barlow and Allen, 2004).

Currently, clinicians tend to use a wide variety of strategies in managing their patients' symptoms. While there is an abundance of research on current cognitive-behavioral and psychopharmacological treatments for anxiety disorders, some debate exists as to which practices are more helpful for which disorder and for whom. To better understand these complex findings, the existing data for each of the anxiety disorders with the exception of post-traumatic stress disorder (PTSD) will be reviewed in the following sections, and suggestions for future research directions presented. Research reviewed will focus on data from randomized clinical trials (RCTs). Due to space limitations and because RCTs covering PTSD are just beginning to appear, PTSD will not be covered in this review.

PANIC DISORDER WITH AND WITHOUT AGORAPHOBIA (PDA)
Description

To receive a diagnosis of PDA, an individual must experience recurrent unexpected, panic attacks consisting of a number of physical symptoms, some of which include a racing heart, sweating, trembling or shaking, and shortness of breath that rapidly become very intense. In addition, these attacks must be followed by at least one month of persistent concern about having another attack, worry about the implications of these attacks, and/or significant behavioral changes in response to the attacks. Although panic attacks do occur in the context of other anxiety disorders, the anxiety and worry characteristic of panic disorder results from catastrophic misinterpretations about and subsequent fear of the attack itself. Agoraphobia often accompanies panic disorder, as situations or places often become conditioned to elicit cues for panic. Literally meaning "fear of the marketplace," this fear of situations or places perceived as likely to produce panic attacks can be extremely disabling. Over time, the number of situations deemed "safe" are reduced, and some people with PDA can eventually become housebound.

Cognitive-behavioral treatments of PDA

Cognitive-behavioral treatments (CBT) for PDA have proven highly effective (results from selected studies are summarized in Table 1). On average, approximately 90% of patients complete CBT and of these, approximately 80% will be panic-free at the end of treatment. The majority of these individuals will maintain their treatment gains for follow-up periods as long as two-years (Craske and Barlow, 2001). Results from a meta-analytic review of controlled studies by Gould, Otto, and Pollack (1995) suggest that cognitive-behavioral treatments yield higher effect sizes than pharmacological interventions (such as imipramine, alprazolam, and propanolol) and combination treatments (E=0.68, 0.47, and 0.56, respectively). Furthermore, CBT was found to be more durable than pharmacotherapy, with regard to long-term maintenance of treatment gains, highly tolerable (attrition was estimated at 5.6%) and cost-effective. These treatments have also been shown to improve quality of life (Telch et al., 1995).

Current cognitive-behavioral treatments typically involve a combination of strategies for modifying misappraisals of bodily sensations, managing anxiety, and reducing agoraphobic avoidance. While the emphasis on specific treatment components varies across studies, the prototypical CBT package includes situational (*in vivo*) exposure, exposure to the physical sensations of anxiety (interoceptive exposure), and cognitive restructuring. These treatment approaches are described in further detail below.

***In Vivo* Exposure**

"*In vivo* exposure" refers to repeated, systematic, exposure to real-life agoraphobic situations. In the treatment of panic disorder, exposure involves having the patient confront situations that are likely to elicit anxiety and panic-sensations. Exposure treatment typically begins with the development of a rank order listing of situations that the patient is avoiding or enduring with great anxiety (i.e., fear and avoidance hierarchy). Examples of avoided situations include shopping in crowded malls alone, going to a movie theatre, or driving on the freeway. Once a hierarchy is developed, patients are encouraged to systematically face their feared situations and by doing so, elicit increasingly higher levels of anxiety. Exposures may be conducted with the assistance of the therapist, particularly for patients with more severe agoraphobia. But eventually, patients are encouraged to engage in exposures by themselves, preventing any potential reliance on another person to provide a feeling of safety to an otherwise frightening situation.

Studies on situational exposure over the past few decades have found this approach to be an effective treatment for the agoraphobic component of PDA. A number of meta-analyses and reviews from the 1980's found that 88% of patients completed situational exposure treatment, and of these 60 to 75% of patients showed clinical improvement in panic symptoms and related avoidance behaviors (Barlow, 1988; Jacobson et al., 1988; Jansson and Öst, 1982; Munby and Johnston, 1980;

Table 1. Clinical Trials of Cognitive-Behavioral Treatments for Panic Disorder: Intent-to-Treat Analysis[*]

Clinical Trial	Length of Follow-Up (Months)	Treatment type/ Number of Patients/ % Panic free	Treatment Comparisons (Percentage Panic Free)[a]
Shear et al. (2001)	6	CBT (n = 22), 91%	Yes: EFT = 61%
			Yes: IMI = 100%
			Yes: PL = 50%
Barlow, Gorman et al. (2000)	12	PCT (n = 77), 41%	Yes: PCT+PL= 31.9%
			Yes: PL = 13%
			Yes: IMI = 19.7%
			Yes: PCT+IMI = 26.3%
Black et al. (1993)	PT	CT (n = 25), 32%	Yes: FL = 68%
			Yes: PL = 20%
Beck et al. (1992)	PT	CT (n = 17), 94%	Yes: ST = 25%[d]
Craske et al. (1991)[b]	24	PCT (n = 15), 81%	Yes: AR = 36%
			Yes: PCT and AR = 43%
Craske et al. (1995)	PT	CBT (n = 16), 53%	Yes: NPT = 8%
Clark et al. (1994)	12	CT (n = 17), 76%	Yes: AR = 43[c]
			Yes: IMI = 48[c]
Cote et al. (1994)	12	CBTM, (n = 13), 92%	---
		CBTNM (n = 8), 100%	
Klosko et al. (1990)	PT	PCT (n = 15), 87%	No: AL = 50%
			Yes: PL = 36%
			Yes: WL = 33%
Margraf and Schneider (1991)	1	CT (n = 22), 91%	Yes: WL = 5%
Newman et al. (1990)	12	CTM (n = 24), 87%	---
		CTNM (n = 19), 87%	
Öst et al. (1993)	12	CT (n = 19), 89%[c]	No: AR = 74%[c]
Shear et al. (1994)	6	CBT (n = 23), 45%	No: NPT = 45%
Telch et al. (1993)	PT	PCT (n = 34), 85%	Yes: 30%

[*] Abbreviations. AL = alprazolam; AR = applied relaxation; CBT = cognitive-behavioral therapy; CBTM = cognitive-behavioral therapy and medication; CBTNM = cognitive-behavioral therapy without medication; CT = cognitive therapy; CTM = cognitive therapy and medication; CTNM=cognitive therapy without medication; EFT = Emotion Focused Therapy; FL = fluvoxamine; IMI = imipramine; NPT = nonprescriptive treatment; PL = pill placebo; PCT= exposure and cognitive restructuring; PT = posttreatment; ST = supportive therapy, WL = wait list.
[a] Yes = comparison was significant, No = comparison was not significant, --- = comparison was not made.
[b] Follow-up study of Barlow et al. (1989). [c] Percentage of patients who were panic free at follow-up and who had received no additional treatment during the follow-up period. [d] At 8 weeks (the end of supportive therapy), 71% of CT patients were panic free.
Source: Modified with permission from Barlow and Lehman (1996), © 1996 American Medical Association.

Trull et al., 1988). Although few patients were completely symptom free following treatment, follow-up studies revealed long-term maintenance of treatment gains, even after several years (Burns et al., 1986; Cohen et al., 1984; Jansson et al., 1986). In a more recent study by Fava et al. (1995), 87% of patients who had received 12 sessions of graduated self-directed exposure-based treatment for PDA were panic-free at the end of treatment. Using a survival analysis to estimate the long-term maintenance of treatment gains, the authors reported that 96% of treatment responders remained in remission for the first two years following treatment, 77% remained panic-free throughout the first five years, and 67% maintained treatment gains even after seven years.

Conducting situational exposures is rather straightforward and most patients are able to conduct these exercises without continuing assistance from a therapist. However, there are a number of modifications that can be made to the administration of exposure exercises that may maximize therapeutic gains. For instance, many researchers have examined variations in the pacing of treatment. Results from a number of studies comparing massed and intensive exposure sessions to spaced and graduated expose sessions have demonstrated some superiority of more intensive, massed exposure sessions, especially at long-term follow-up (Chambless, 1990; Feigenbaum, 1988; Foa et al., 1980). On the other hand, Barlow (1988) discussed several advantages of spaced and graduated *in vivo* exposure, including lower attrition and relapse rates (Hafner and Marks, 1976; Jansson and Öst, 1982).

Interoceptive Exposure

Consistent with the idea that physical sensations can become conditioned stimuli for the occurrence of a fear or panic response (Bouton et al., 2001), newer cognitive-behavioral treatments typically target anxiety

focused on somatic sensations through repeated and systematic exposure to those sensations. This is often accomplished in treatment by having patients induce panic-like physical sensations through repeated symptom-induction "exercises" such as hyperventilation, running in place, and breathing through a thin straw.

Induction of panic related sensations through a variety of methods (e.g., sodium lactate infusions, carbon dioxide inhalation, and exercise) has been shown to reduce the frequency of panic attacks and elicit a decrease in fearful responding (Griez and van den Hout, 1986) but does not appear to significantly impact agoraphobic avoidance (Beck et al., 1997). On the other hand, interoceptive exposure may confer a *significant advantage on situational exposure procedures*. In the aforementioned meta-analysis by Gould et al. (1995), cognitive-behavioral treatments that included interoceptive exposure yielded larger mean effective sizes (E=0.88) than interventions combining CBT techniques and situational exposure (E=0.68).

Cognitive Restructuring

Cognitive therapy (CT) for PDA involves modification of an individual's anxious thoughts about panic attacks. Patients with PDA typically overestimate the probability of disastrous outcomes as a result of panic and assume that the worst possible outcome will ensue. So this component of treatment involves identifying anxious thoughts about the panic sensations and replacing them with more accurate interpretations. Restructuring may facilitate interoceptive and *in vivo* exposures by helping patients reduce their anxiety in the situation and consequently make them more likely to confront their fear.

A number of studies have examined the efficacy of using CT alone for the treatment of PDA. Results generally indicate that CT is as effective, if not more helpful than other, non-cognitive, active treatments (i.e., applied relaxation) (Beck et al., 1994; Öst and Westling, 1995). In a controlled randomized study by Clark et al. (1994), patients receiving a variation of CT that emphasized misappraisals of bodily sensations showed greater long-term maintenance of treatment gains when compared to patients receiving either imipramine or applied relaxation.

Efficacy of Panic Control Treatment

Barlow and Craske (2000) developed one of the first manualized treatments for PDA in the mid 1980's. This CBT protocol, termed panic control treatment (PCT), consists of the three core components described above. The original PCT program also included a breathing retraining component (in addition to the standard CBT techniques) designed to provide patients with a "tool" to decrease the acute symptoms of hyperventilation often present during panic. However, the efficacy of this component has been questioned, as it can be conceptualized as a safety behavior for reducing panic sensations, thereby reinforcing the belief that they are dangerous. In fact, some researchers have found that eliminating breathing retraining from CBT protocols may actually significantly improve treatment outcome (Schmidt et al., 2000). Current treatments at our research center emphasize "facing the fear" to its fullest, without any compensatory strategies or "safety signals" (e.g., carrying a cell phone, water bottle, or prescription medications) that might lessen the fear response.

Several studies have shown that PCT is more effective than wait-list or other active treatments such as relaxation training (Barlow et al., 1989; Craske et al., 1991). For instance, in a study by Barlow and colleagues (1989) comparing PCT, relaxation training, and a combination of these techniques to a wait-list control, all three treatments were superior to the control condition, though significantly fewer patients receiving relaxation training were panic-free at the end of treatment relative to the PCT and combined conditions (60% vs. 85% vs. 87%). In addition, a controlled study by Klosko et al. (1990) found superiority of PCT over a high potency benzodiazepine, alprazolam. More recently, Barlow, Gorman, Shear, and Woods (2000) conducted a large multi-site randomized clinical trial comparing PCT alone, imipramine alone, PCT plus imipramine, placebo alone, and PCT plus drug placebo. Following three months of acute treatment and six months of maintenance treatment, all treatment conditions were superior to placebo, and the combined condition was slightly better than comparison groups after maintenance only. However, at 6-months post-maintenance follow-up assessment (after all treatments had been discontinued), patients in the imipramine and the combined PCT plus imipramine conditions were more likely to relapse than those in PCT alone and PCT plus placebo conditions who were not administered drugs; PCT alone or with placebo was now significantly better than the drug conditions.

Summary and Future Directions

PDA has been the most widely researched anxiety disorder of the past twenty years. This extensive work has led to the development of effective cognitive-behavioral treatments for this disorder. Overall, these approaches appear to be superior to other alternative treatments such as applied relaxation and are equally effective to pharmacotherapy, with superior long-term results. Despite these promising results, however, cognitive-behavioral treatments for panic disorder are far from perfect. For instance, in a study by Brown and Barlow (1995) more than one-third of the patients showed some degree of relapse during a 2-year follow-up period and many received additional treatment for their panic. Further, the majority of effectiveness studies include patients with only mild to moderate levels of agoraphobia. Consequently, these studies may be overestimating the efficacy of CBT. Indeed, these treatments do not appear to be as effective for patients with more severe agoraphobia, as less than 60% of these patient's show significant improvement at long-term follow-up (Craske and Barlow, 2001), partly because of higher attrition rates. Continuing efforts are needed to improve these treatments, particularly in patients with more severe agoraphobic avoidance.

SOCIAL ANXIETY DISORDER
Description

According to DSM-IV criteria (DSM-IV, American Psychiatric Association, 1994), social anxiety disorder refers to persistent fear of a number of social and performance situations in which there is the potential for scrutiny by others. Individuals with this disorder are excessively concerned that they may act in a way that will be embarrassing or humiliating or that they will manifest anxiety symptoms (e.g., blushing, sweating, or shaking) that will be visible to others. Feared social situations are often avoided but may also be endured with extreme discomfort or dread. In order to receive a diagnosis of social anxiety disorder, the fear and avoidance must cause significant impairment in social or occupational functioning and/or significant distress.

Cognitive Behavioral Treatment for Social Anxiety Disorder

CBT approaches have consistently been shown to be effective for the treatment of social phobia (for review see Hofmann and Barlow, 2002). Treatment typically consists of a combination of strategies aimed at modifying faulty appraisals (cognitive therapy) and increasing exposure to feared social situations (*in vivo* exposure). There is some evidence to suggest that integrating these components with other CBT approaches, such as social skills training and applied relaxation, might also lead to positive outcome (Turner et al., 1994).

Results from studies on the efficacy of combined treatments have been encouraging (Table 2). Butler and colleagues (1984) compared a combination treatment consisting of *in vivo* exposure plus distraction and rational self-talk to exposure with a nonspecific filler and a wait list control. While both therapy groups were superior to the waitlist control at post-treatment, the combined condition demonstrated some superiority at six-month follow-up. Similarly, in a study by Mattick and Peters (1988), a combination of guided exposure plus cognitive restructuring was compared to guided exposure alone. Patients in both groups showed improvements following treatment but those in the combined treatment fared better at the 3-month follow-up. A second study by Mattick and colleagues (Mattick et al., 1989) yielded similar results. In this study, patients were randomly assigned to one of the following four conditions: guided exposure alone, cognitive restructuring alone, a combined treatment of cognitive restructuring and guided exposure, or a wait list control. At the end of treatment, all active treatments were superior to the wait list condition across measures of behavioral and cognitive change, with the combined treatment showing the greatest improvement, overall. On a composite measure of improvement, 72% of patients in the combined condition achieved high to very high improvement, compared to 45% patients in the exposure condition and only 27% of patients receiving cognitive treatment alone.

Despite the effectiveness of these integrated treatments, however, there is still considerable debate as to which components are necessary for treatment effectiveness and a number of studies have failed to demonstrate superiority of combined treatments over *in vivo* exposure alone (Hope et al., 1995; Scholing and Emmelkamp, 1983a). In four meta-analytic studies examining controlled investigations of cognitive behavioral treatments, both CT and exposure were more effective than a wait-list control (Federoff and Taylor, 2001; Feske and Chambless, 1995; Gould et al., 1997; Taylor, 1996) but the combination of these strategies did not appear to improve treatment outcome.

Table 2. Controlled Trials of Cognitive Behavioral Treatments for Social Phobia*

Study	Length of Follow-up (months)	Treatment	Percentage Clinical Improvement of Completers (If Available)	Treatment Comparisons (Percentage Clinical Improvement)[a]	
				Other Treatment	Wait-list
Davidson et al. (2004)	PT	CCBT (n=60)		No: FLU No: CCBT/FLU No: CCBT/PL Yes: PL	
Clark et al. (2003)	12	CT (n=20)		Yes: FLU/SE Yes: PL/SE	
Butler et al. (1984)	6	AMT and E (n=15)		Yes: E	Yes
Mattick and Peters (1988)	3	E and CT (n=11)	86%	Yes: E = 52%	Yes
Mattick et al. (1989)	3	E and CT (n=25)		Yes: E	Yes
Heimberg et al. (1990)	6	CBGT (n=20)	81%	Yes: ES = 47%	
Heimberg et al. (1993)[b]	54-75	CBGT (n=10)		Yes: ES (most)	
Heimberg et al. (1998)	PT	CBGT (n=28)	75%	No: PH = 77% Yes: PL = 41% Yes: ES = 35%	
Lucas and Telch (1993)	PT	CBGT (n=18) CBTI	61% 50%	Yes: ES = 24%	
Liebowitz et al. (1999)[c]	6-12	CBGT (n=14)		Yes: ES = 27% No: PH	
Gelernter et al. (1991)	2	CBGT (n=20)		No: PH, AL, PL	

*AL = alprazolam; AMT = anxiety management training; CBGT = cognitive behavioral group therapy; CBTI = cognitive behavioral treatment – individual; CCBT = Comprehensive Cognitive Behavioral Group Therapy; CT = cognitive therapy; E = exposure; ES = educational supportive group psychotherapy (placebo treatment); FLU = Fluoxetine; PL = pill placebo; PH = phenelzine; PT = posttreatment; SE = self-exposure
[a]Yes indicates the comparison was significant; no, comparison not significant
[b]Follow-up study of Heimberg et al. (1990).
[c]Follow-up study of Heimberg et al. (1998).
Source: Modified with permission from Barlow and Lehman (1996), © 1996 American Medical Association.

Cognitive Behavioral Group Treatment

A number of manualized cognitive-behavioral programs have been developed for the treatment of social phobia. In the early 1990's, Heimberg and colleagues developed a 12-week treatment package called cognitive behavioral group treatment (CBGT), consisting of education and cognitive restructuring, simulated in-session exposures to feared social situations, and *in vivo* situational exposures conducted between group sessions. The efficacy of CBGT has been demonstrated in a number of controlled studies (Gelernter et al., 1991; Heimberg et al., 1985; Heimberg et al., 1990; Heimberg et al., 1998; Heimberg et al., 1993) and it is currently listed as an "empirically supported treatment" by the Society of Clinical Psychology's (Division 12 of the American Psychology Association) Task Force on Promotion and Dissemination of Psychological Procedures. In a study by Heimberg and colleagues (1990) comparing CBGT to a credible placebo condition consisting of psycho-education and group support, both groups showed significant improvement on most measures at post-treatment and a 6-month follow-up, but CBGT patients were more improved on an individualized behavioral avoidance task and were rated as being less impaired overall by independent clinical assessors. Following treatment, seventy-five percent of the CBGT group showed clinically significant improvement compared to only 40% of the placebo control condition. Both groups maintained gains through the 6-month follow-up period, with similar differences between the groups. In addition, at a five-year follow-up of a subset of participants from the original sample, individuals in the CBGT group demonstrated slightly better maintenance of their already superior treatment gains when compared with participants in the placebo condition (Heimberg et al., 1993).

CBT versus Pharmacotherapy for Social Phobia

To date, there have been only a few controlled studies directly comparing cognitive-behavioral and pharmacological interventions. In one such study by Turner, Beidel, and Jacob (1994), behavioral treatment (intensive exposure) produced greater improvements on a number of outcome measures relative to atenolol (a beta-blocker) and pill placebo. Similar results were obtained in a more recent study comparing cognitive therapy to fluoxetine plus self-directed exposure or pill placebo plus self-exposure (Clark et al., 2003). Cognitive therapy produced the greatest improvement on a composite measure of social phobia severity at mid-treatment, post-treatment, and a 12-month follow-up. In a recent randomized clinical trial by Davidson and colleagues (2004), a comprehensive cognitive group therapy, fluoxetine, and the combination of these interventions were all found to be superior to placebo on a number of self-report and clinician-rated measures. However, there was no significant advantage of the combined treatment over CBT and fluoxetine alone..

Studies examining differential efficacy between the CBGT protocol and pharmacotherapy have produced mixed results. In a randomized study comparing CBGT to alprazolam plus self-directed exposure and phenelzine plus self-directed exposure, both CBGT and medication treatments were found to be equally effective relative to a wait-list control (Gelernter et al., 1991). On the other hand, Otto and colleagues (2000) found that patient's reported greater benefits from clonazepam plus self-directed exposure than CBGT following a 12-week treatment, although the medication condition resulted in greater attrition. However, the implications of this study are not entirely clear, as there was no long-term follow-up assessment.

The largest controlled investigation of this kind was a multi-site collaborative project comparing CBGT, phenelzine (a monoamine oxidase inhibitor), a psychosocial placebo, and a pill placebo (Heimberg et al., 1998). After 12-weeks of treatment, CBGT and phenelzine were equally effective, with approximately 60% of patients completing treatment in each group showing significant improvement, and phenelzine showing somewhat more effectiveness than CBGT on some self-report measures. Both active treatments were clearly superior to psychosocial and pill placebo. Following acute treatment, a subset of treatment responders in the active treatment groups participated in a 6-month maintenance phase and then a 6-month treatment-free phase. At the end of the maintenance phase, no differences were detected between the CBGT and phenelzine patients with regards to drop-out or relapse (Liebowitz et al., 1999). At a 6-month follow-up, however, relapse was somewhat higher in the phenelzine group (3/14) compared to no relapse in the CBGT condition, though this difference only approached significance, most likely due to a very small N.

Summary and Future Directions

Cognitive-behavioral approaches for the treatment of social phobia have consistently been shown to be superior to placebo and wait-list conditions. These treatments typically include a combination of components including social skills training, applied relaxation, *in vivo* exposure, and cognitive restructuring. Results on the effectiveness of multifaceted treatments have been encouraging. However, some studies have not found clear benefit from combining cognitive and behavioral components. Likewise, results from dismantling studies comparing various components of cognitive-behavioral treatments have been inconsistent and no specific component has definitively been shown to be superior to *in vivo* exposure alone. Additional research is needed to resolve this issue.

SPECIFIC PHOBIAS
Description
Specific phobias are defined as a marked or persistent fear of circumscribed objects or situations, which are avoided or endured with great dread. The fears must be deemed excessive or unreasonable and must be severe enough to cause interference in life functioning or produce high levels of subjective distress. In the DSM-IV, specific phobias are classified according to one of the following five categories: animal, natural environment, blood-injection-injury, situational, or other (a catchall category used to classify fears that do not fit into one of the other four categories). Individuals rarely seek treatment for a specific phobia, as the feared object or situation can often be avoided without producing significant impairment in daily functioning. However, in the clinical setting, specific fears often accompany other anxiety disorders as well as depression.

Cognitive Behavioral Treatment for Specific Phobias
In vivo exposure is the most widely used and effective treatment for specific phobias and has emerged as the treatment of choice among experts in the field (Antony and Barlow, 2002). Detailed procedures for each of the specific phobias are available in manualized format (Antony et al., 1995). These guides typically include sections on general treatment procedures (e.g., psychoeducation, cognitive restructuring, *in vivo* exposure, skills training, and relaxation techniques) as well as more phobia-specific techniques (for example, applied tension in the treatment of blood-injury-injection phobia). The following is a brief description of treatment procedures common to all of the specific phobias.

Treatment usually begins with education about the etiology of specific phobias and the basis of exposure treatment. Based on a functional analysis of the patient's fear, the therapist works with the patient on developing a fear and avoidance hierarchy. Patients may also be provided with additional information about the phobic object or situation to correct misappraisals about the dangerousness of the feared stimulus. Relaxation and breathing retraining are sometimes used to help patients manage physiological arousal during the exposure. However, as previously stated, these techniques may be counterproductive to treatment if they impede natural habituation of the fear response. Once a treatment plan has been developed, repeated exposures to the feared stimulus are conducted in a systematic and controlled manner. Confrontation of the feared stimulus can be conducted imaginally or through virtual reality, but more direct in vivo exposures are recommended whenever possible.

Efficacy of Cognitive Behavioral Treatment for Specific Phobias

The effectiveness of in vivo exposure has been demonstrated across a wide range of specific phobias, including animals (e.g., Muris et al., 1998; Öst, 1989a; Öst et al., 1997; Öst et al., 1991), heights (Baker et al., 1973; Bourque and Ladouceur, 1980), enclosed places (Craske et al., 1995; Öst et al., 1982), thunder and lightning (Öst, 1978), water (Menzies and Clark, 1993b), blood-injection-injury (Öst, 1989a; Öst and Sterner, 1987), flying (Beckham et al., 1990; Howard et al., 1983; Öst et al., 1997; Solyom et al., 1973), choking (McNally, 1986; McNally, 1994), and dental procedures (Jerremalm et al., 1986; Liddell et al., 1994). In a review of controlled studies by Öst (1996), 76% of patients receiving cognitive-behavioral intervention (including exposure, relaxation, modeling, and applied tension) showed improvement after only 4.8 hours of therapy. Treatment gains were maintained and actually improved slightly to 78% at 11-month follow-up. Attrition was very low, with less than 2% of patients discontinuing treatment.

A few studies have also investigated the benefit of adding pharmacologic interventions to exposure-based procedures. In a study by Zoellner and colleagues (1996), the addition of the benzodiazepine medication alprazolam did not lead to better treatment outcome over exposure alone. In fact, benzodiazepine medications may actually impede long-term outcome (Wilhelm and Roth, 1996). Results from two studies investigating the effectiveness of selective serotonin reuptake inhibitors (SSRIs) have been promising (Abene and Hamilton, 1998; Benjamin et al., 2000). But additional controlled studies are needed to investigate the efficacy of these medications relative to other proven treatment methods.

Methods of In Vivo Exposure Delivery

Concentrated, one-session exposure treatments have been shown to be effective across a number of specific phobias, including spiders (Arntz and Lavy, 1993; Hellström and Öst, 1995; Öst et al., 1997), blood (Hellström et al., 1996), injection (Öst et al., 1992), and flying (Öst et al., 1997). And, in general, massed exposure schedules appear to be superior to spaced schedules for the desensitization of specific fears (Foa et al., 1980; Marks, 1987). An expanding-spaced schedule, one in which inter-trial intervals become progressively longer over time, has also shown promise for the treatment of specific fears (Lang and Craske, 2000). In a study by Rowe and Craske (1998), this method of exposure delivery was shown to be even more effective than massed exposure in preventing return of fear. In this study, participants who received massed exposure reported greater habituation of their fear during treatment and superior outcome at post-treatment relative to participants who were treated according to an expanding-spaced schedule. However, participants in the massed exposure condition experienced a clear return of fear after one-month, whereas participants in expanding-spaced exposure condition continued to improve.

In accordance with animal studies demonstrating the contextual basis of learning (e.g., Bouton et al., 2001; Gunther et al., 1998), a number of studies were recently conducted investigating the contextual dependency of extinguished fears. Although results from an early investigation of context specificity in treatment were mixed (Tsao and Craske, 1996), more recent studies by this group have provided some evidence to support context effects during exposure (Mystkowski et al., 2002; Rodriguez et al., 1999). More specifically, individuals with spider fear showed greater return of fear when tested in a different context than the one in which treatment was originally conducted.

Craske and colleagues have also studied the effects of random and variable exposure practices on treatment outcome. In a study by Lang and Craske (1998), patients who attempted items on their fear hierarchy in a random order reported less return of fear one month following treatment, despite higher levels of fear during treatment. Likewise, exposures conducted in a variety of formats (e.g., spiders of different colors and sizes) appear to produce less fear reduction during treatment but better maintenance of treatment gains over time. Taken together, these data suggest that conducting variable-stimulus and random exposures across a number of contexts may lead to superior treatment generalization.

Summary and Future Directions

Current treatments for specific phobias are highly effective, with up to 90% of patients achieving long-term improvement or complete recovery (Antony and Barlow, 2002; Gitin et al., 1996; Öst et al., 1997). However, researchers have only recently begun to examine differences between the five subtypes (animal type, natural environment type, blood-injection-injury [BII] type, situational type, and a residual "other" category) and further understanding of more specific characteristics will inform future treatment approaches and may even

enhance outcome. Studies examining variations in the administration of exposure-based procedures suggest that intensive, massed exposures may be most effective. But a number of other factors, such as the spacing of exposure sessions and the level of therapist involvement, may have an impact on the effectiveness of treatment as well. Cognitive interventions show some promise, but further research on this approach, both alone and in combination with in vivo exposure, is needed. Finally, studies on the effects of pharmacologic interventions are lacking. However, given the effectiveness of behavioral treatment, it may be difficult to show incremental benefits of additional interventions.

OBSESSIVE-COMPULSIVE DISORDER
Description

According to the DSM-IV, individuals with obsessive-compulsive disorder (OCD) experience recurrent obsessions and/or compulsions that interfere substantially with their daily functioning. Obsessions are anxiety-provoking thoughts, images or impulses. Common obsessive thoughts are fear of contamination, doubting whether something was accurately completed, and fear of accidental harm to others. Compulsions, on the other hand are repetitive behaviors or mental acts that prevent or reduce anxiety or distress. Although the majority of patients (over 90%) primarily manifest behavioral rituals (e.g., washing, checking, etc.), helping individuals with OCD identify and refrain from mental compulsions such as counting, praying, and reassurance seeking is also important to treatment outcome. This is particularly true for a subset of patients characterized by more covert mental rituals (i.e., "pure obsessionals"). Functionally, though, both behavioral and mental rituals serve a similar purpose. That is, both are aimed at reducing distress brought on by obsessions (Foa et al., 1995).

Treatment of Obsessive Compulsive Disorder

Both behavioral strategies and pharmacological treatments have been shown to reduce the symptoms associated with OCD. Cognitive approaches have also gained interest as a potential treatment as well, though the research in this area is less established. These approaches are described in greater detail below. Results of recent treatment outcome studies are summarized in Table 3.

Table 3. Controlled Trials of Cognitive Behavioral Treatments for Obsessive Compulsive Disorder*

Study	Length of Follow-up (months)	Treatment	Percentage Responders (If Available)	Treatment Comparisons (Percentage Responders) [a]	
				Other Treatment	Wait-List
Cottraux et al. (2001)	12	CT (n=33)		No: ERP	
Freeston et al. (1997)	12	CBT (n=15)			Yes
van Oppen et al. (1995)	PT	CT (n=28)		Yes: ERP (some measures)	
Lindsay et al. (1997)	PT	ERP (n=9)		Yes: AM	
Fals-Stewart et al. (1993)	6	ERP (n=31)		No: Group ERP / Yes: PMR	
van Balkom et al. (1998)	PT	CT (n=19)		No: ERP / No: CT + FL / No: ERP + FL	
Kozak et al. (2000)	3	ERP (n=18)	85%	Yes: CMI = 50% / No: ERP + CMI = 71%	Yes

*AM = anxiety management treatment; CBT = cognitive behavioral therapy; CMI = clomipramine; CT = cognitive therapy; ERP = exposure with response prevention; FL = fluvoxamine; PL = pill placebo; PMR = progressive muscle relaxation; PT = posttreatment; WL = wait list.
[a]Yes indicates the comparison was significant; no, comparison not significant

Behavioral Treatment for OCD

In 1966, Victor Meyer reported on two patients who responded favorably to a treatment that included prolonged exposure to obsessional cues and strict prevention of ritualized behaviors. Since then, this procedure, termed exposure and response prevention (ERP), has been found to be extremely successful for the treatment of OCD.

There are many variants of ERP treatment and several factors, such as exposure duration and frequency, have been shown to influence treatment outcome. Foa and colleagues developed an intensive variation of ERP treatment that has achieved excellent results (Foa et al., 1992; Franklin et al., 2000). Their treatment, outlined in Foa and Franklin (2001), involves 2-information gathering sessions and 15 daily 2-hour exposure sessions. Similar to treatment for other anxiety disorders, a fear hierarchy of increasingly more difficult exposures related to obsessional material is developed at the beginning of treatment. Patients are then asked to engage in systematic exposure exercises designed to elicit obsessional material while refraining from all rituals, both mental and behavioral, that serve to neutralize the obsession. In this protocol, exposures are conducted both imaginally and *in vivo*, for a period between 90 minutes and two hours, and are typically practiced with the assistance of a therapist. Additionally, patients are asked to continue exposures for homework, sometimes up to another two hours a day.

Although intensive ERP treatments, such as the one described above, are effective in reducing OCD symptomatology, there are a number of practical problems associated with a more concentrated protocol. For instance, the cost may be prohibitive for some patients and the time commitment for treatment can be impractical for patients whose daily functioning is less constrained by the disorder. Patients with mild OCD symptoms may require less frequent exposure sessions, such as one or two visits per week. And positive results have been obtained using more widely spaced exposure sessions (see for example, DeAraujo et al., 1995). But for more severe patients, an intensive treatment, such as the one developed by Foa and colleagues, may be necessary to produce significant treatment gains.

Efficacy of Behavioral Treatment for OCD

In a review of ERP treatment, Stanley and Turner (1995) concluded that 63% of patients across studies showed some improvement following treatment. Foa and Kozac (1996) found even more promising results in their review of outcome studies reporting treatment responder rates, with 83% of patients responding favorably to ERP treatment. Additionally, these researchers reported that 76% of patients who entered an ERP program were classified as treatment responders at long-term follow-up (the mean follow-up period for the reviewed studies was 29-months). More recently, Franklin et al. (2000) found that 86% of OCD patients who completed intensive outpatient treatment achieved significant clinical improvement.

Despite these encouraging results, however, many patients continue to be symptomatic following treatment and up to 50% require further therapy (Öst, 1989b). Furthermore, when accounting for drop-out and treatment refusal, which can be upwards of 12% in some cases, the final rate of improvement may not be nearly as high (Keijsers et al., 1994). Nevertheless, ERP is superior to a variety of other treatments, including relaxation training (Fals-Stewart et al., 1993), anxiety management training (Lindsay et al., 1997), and exposure alone (Abramowitz, 1996; Foa et al., 1984).

A number of studies have examined the benefit of adding imaginal exposures to *in vivo* exposure treatment. In general, treatments involving the combination of *in vivo* and imaginal exposure appear to be superior to *in vivo* exposure alone (Abramowitz, 1996; Foa et al., 1980; Ito et al., 1995), although there have been some data to the contrary (DeAraujo et al., 1995). In addition, factors that appear to improve treatment outcome in other anxiety disorders, such as therapist-assisted exposures and longer treatment sessions, may enhance ERP treatment for OCD as well (Abramowitz, 1996). Results from a study by Hiss, Foa, and Kozac (1994) suggest that the addition of a relapse prevention program may also help to improve long-term treatment outcome. In this study, 75% of patients receiving a relapse prevention program were classified as responders at 6-month follow-up ("response" was defined as 50% or greater reduction in OCD symptoms), compared to only 33% of patients receiving a credible but ineffective control treatment. And finally, there is some evidence to suggest that behavioral therapy may be enhanced by family involvement (Mehta, 1990). Although there have not been any controlled studies on the role of family members in treatment, this support is often enlisted in clinical settings. Family members are typically provided with information about

OCD and instructed on ways to constructively assist the patient in treatment, for instance by providing encouragement and by refraining from participation in rituals.

ERP versus Cognitive Treatment

Early cognitive approaches targeting suppression (i.e., "thought stopping") or restructuring of obsessional content met with limited success. In fact, there is reason to believe that challenging the irrational content of obsessions via more traditional cognitive techniques (e.g., examining the probability that a loving mother would actually poison her child) functions as a form of neutralization which can actually increase the frequency and intensity of obsessions in the long-term (Salkovskis, 1989). Since then, a more comprehensive cognitive model of OCD has developed and newer cognitive therapies use restructuring techniques to specifically address misappraisals about obsessions rather than the obsessional content itself (see Freeston et al., 1996 and van Oppen and Arntz, 1994, for a detailed description of these procedures). In addition, newer cognitive therapies include specific techniques aimed at modifying problematic beliefs typical of individuals suffering with OCD such as overimportance of thoughts, intolerance of uncertainty and perfectionistic expectations (Foa and Franklin, 2001).

CT has been shown to be an effective treatment for OCD, both alone and in combination with ERP procedures. Findings from a number of studies suggest that outcome from CT is comparable to that obtained from ERP treatment (Emmelkamp and H., 1991; Emmelkamp et al., 1988; Jones and Menzies, 1997; van Oppen et al., 1995). Combining CT and ERP procedures has also been shown to be effective for the treatment of OCD, particularly in patients with primarily mental rituals (Freeston et al., 1997). However, the extent to which more formal cognitive restructuring may enhance the effectiveness of behavioral treatment for OCD is not entirely clear, as research in this area is very limited.

ERP versus Pharmacotherapy

A number of controlled studies have demonstrated the effectiveness of serotonergically targeted medications for the treatment of OCD. In a meta-analysis of the major clinical trials comparing individual drugs to placebo, clomipramine was found to be more effective than fluvoxamine, fluoxetine, and sertraline (Effect sizes were 1.48, 0.69, 0.50, and 0.35, respectively) (Griest et al., 1995). Approximately 60% of patients show some response to serotonergic medications. However, while all of these treatments are clearly superior to placebo control, overall treatment gains are moderate at best (Griest, 1990). In addition, discontinuation of these medications is associated with high rates of relapse and worse long-term treatment outcome (Hembree et al., 2003). In a controlled double-blind substitution trial, 90% of OCD patients relapsed within 7 weeks of clomipramine discontinuation (Pato et al., 1988).

Information on the relative and combined efficacy of medication treatment and ERP is relatively scarce and many of these studies have been limited by design complications. In a study by van Balkom and colleagues (1998), the sequential addition of fluvoxamine to cognitive and behavioral therapies was not superior to either treatment alone. One recently completed study has shown clear superiority of combined medication treatment and ERP over medication alone, with no advantage (or disadvantage) of combined treatment over ERP alone, with the exception of added cost (71% of responders in combined treatment vs. 85% in ERP alone and 50% in clomipramine alone) (Kozak et al., 2000). Likewise, in a study by Simpson and colleagues (2004) examining the long-term effects of ERP, clomipramine, and a combination of these interventions in patients who responded favorably to treatment, ERP, both alone and in combination with clomipramine, resulted in less relapse relative to medication alone over the course of 12-week follow-up period. Here again, the combination treatment was not superior to ERP alone.

Summary and Future Directions

In summary, ERP is the treatment of choice for obsessive-compulsive disorder. Despite the effectiveness of this treatment approach, ERP is far from perfect and many patients remain symptomatic following treatment. Renewed interest in the cognitive basis of OCD has led to the development of newer cognitive therapies targeting misappraisals about obsessions and cognitive errors characteristic of this disorder (e.g., intolerance of uncertainty, perfectionistic expectations, etc.). The results from several studies examining these newer cognitive strategies have been encouraging, but cognitive therapy does not appear to be any more effective than ERP treatment alone nor does the addition of cognitive strategies to ERP appear to maximize treatment outcome. Nevertheless, further research on cognitive treatment for OCD is warranted. Pharmacologic treatments for OCD have been shown to be superior to placebo control. However, studies on these treatments relative to and in combination with ERP show less effectiveness. As medications are often combined with ERP in the clinical setting, additional research in this area is needed, although combined treatment does not provide incremental support based on studies available thus far.

GENERALIZED ANXIETY DISORDER
Description

Generalized anxiety disorder (GAD) is characterized by excessive and uncontrollable anxiety and worry about a number of topics, lasting at least six months. The anxiety and worry are associated with a number of physical symptoms including restlessness, fatigue, irritability, difficulty sleeping, muscle tension, and impaired concentration. Individuals with GAD typically find it so difficult to control their worry that it pervades most aspects of their daily lives and significantly impairs social and occupational functioning. Furthermore, GAD is a chronic and insidious disorder, with little chance of remission if left untreated (Brown et al., 1994).

As with the other anxiety disorders, generalized anxiety disorder is also conceptualized in terms of increased arousal in response to uncomfortable thoughts and feelings. Unlike panic disorder or specific phobias, however, individuals with GAD are not fearful of *a specific* stimulus. As the name suggests, their concerns are more generalized and are characterized by pervasive negative affect and avoidance of emotional arousal. Efforts to control emotional responding and ubiquitous perceived threat results in a desire for "preparedness" (usually seen as excessive worry or "planning"), safety behaviors (i.e., carrying cell phones and prayer books), and withdrawal from significant activities. Unfortunately, while these individuals feel their worry is an "active" attempt to prevent a negative outcome, it is typically seen as lacking in any problem-solving capabilities.

Cognitive Behavioral Treatments for GAD

Early treatments based on relaxation and biofeedback produced only marginal improvement in GAD symptoms (e.g., LeBoeuf and Lodge, 1980). Since that time, a number of CBT packages for GAD have been developed. These "active" treatments typically include cognitive restructuring, relaxation training, anxiety-management training, or a combination of these components. Numerous studies have shown that CBT produces greater improvement in GAD symptoms than no treatment (see for example, Barlow et al., 1984; Barlow et al., 1992; Blowers et al., 1987; Butler et al., 1987). Even more encouraging, studies that include long-term follow-up assessments report substantial maintenance of treatment gains (see for example, Barlow et al., 1992; Butler et al., 1991; White and Keenan, 1992). A summary of these results are presented in Table 4.

Table 4. Controlled Trials of Cognitive Behavioral Treatments for Generalized Anxiety Disorder*

Study	Length of Follow-up (months)	Treatment	Percentage Clinical Improvement of Completers (If Available)	Treatment Comparisons, (Percentage Clinical Improvement)[a]	
				Other Treatment	Wait-list
Barlow et al. (1984)	6	CBT (n=5)			Yes
Blowers et al. (1987)	6	CBT (n=20)		Yes: ND (some measures)	Yes
Borkovec et al. (1987)	6-12	CT + PR (n=16)		Yes: ND + PR (some measures)	
Butler et al. (1987)	6	CBT (n=22)	58.5%		Yes
Borkovec and Mathews (1988)	12	CT + PR (n=6)		No: SCD + PR No: ND + PR	
Power et al. (1989)	PT	CBT (n=10)		Yes: PL (one central measure) No: DZ (one central measure)	
Power et al. (1990)	PT	CBT (n=21)	61.9%	No: CBT + DZ = 69.8% No: CBT + PL = 55.6% Yes: DZ = 30.3% Yes: PL = 17.5%	
Butler et al. (1991)	6	CBT (n=18)	42%	Yes: BT = 5%	Yes
Barlow et al. (1992)	6	CBT (n=29)	55%	Yes: ES (most)	Yes
White and Keenan (1992)	6	CBT (n=26)		No: BT, CT	Yes
Borkovec and Costello (1993)	12	CBT (n=18)	57.9%	Yes: ND = 26.7% Yes: AR = 37.5%	
Durham et al. (1994)[b]	6	CT (n=40)	>60%	Yes: AP<31% Yes: AMT<37%	

*AMT = anxiety management training; AP = analytic psychotherapy; APL = attention placebo; AR = applied relaxation; BT = behavior therapy; CBT = cognitive behavioral therapy; DZ = diazepam; ND = nondirective therapy; PL = pill placebo; PR = progressive relaxation; PT = posttreatment; SCD = self-control desensitization; ES = educational supportive psychotherapy (placebo treatment). [a]Yes indicates the comparison was significant; no, comparison not significant [b] Intent-to-treat
Source: Modified with permission from Barlow and Lehman (1996), © 1996 American Medical Association.

A recent randomized controlled study by Borkovec, Newman, Pincus, and Lytle (2002) compared cognitive therapy alone, self-control desensitization alone, and a combination of these components. All three treatments produced comparable improvement on measures of anxiety and depression, but patients in the combined condition appeared to make greater gains over the 6-month follow-up period. Differences between the groups were no longer present at either the 1-year or 2-year follow-up assessments, though both groups were still significantly improved over baseline.

In a recent review of randomized controlled studies (Borkovec and Ruscio, 2001), CBT approaches were found to yield significant improvements that were maintained for up to 12-months. Average effect sizes for anxiety measures were 2.48 at post-treatment and 2.44 at follow-up, suggesting substantial improvement in anxiety symptoms. Furthermore, a number of recent studies have found that psychosocial treatments may result in a substantial reduction in the use of anxiolytic medications, providing even further evidence of clinically significant improvement. For instance, in a study by Barlow and colleagues (1992), virtually all patients who were using benzodiazepine medications at the beginning of treatment (33%-55% of patients) had discontinued them by 2-year follow-up. Cognitive-behavioral approaches have also shown some promise for the treatment of GAD in both children (Barrett et al., 1996; Kendall et al., 1997) as well as older adults although relative efficacy is yet to be determined (Stanley et al., 1996; Wetherell et al., 2003).

But despite general improvements and reductions in medication use, many patients remain symptomatic, with only 40%-60% of patients meeting criteria for high end-state functioning (defined as scoring within the "normal" range on a set number of measures examining overall clinical severity, anxiety and depression, and interference with functioning). Relative to the efficacy of CBT procedures for other anxiety disorders, overall treatment gains reported by these studies can only be considered modest, at best. And although these treatments are more effective than the passage of time, most studies have failed to find differences between active treatment components and a credible nonspecific "placebo" (Blowers et al., 1987; Borkovec and Mathews, 1988; White and Keenan, 1992), with one notable exception (Borkovec and Costello, 1993). In addition, whereas most studies have found the treatments to be effective to some degree, most have failed to demonstrate differential efficacy between active treatment components (Barlow et al., 1992; Blowers et al., 1987; Borkovec and Mathews, 1988; Borkovec et al., 2002; Durham and Turvey, 1987; White et al., 1990), although some find cognitive treatments to be superior to behavioral approaches (Butler et al., 1991; Durham et al., 1994).

Thus, although cognitive behavioral interventions for GAD are associated with reliable and significant change, more work is needed in this area. Fortunately, in accordance with recent theoretical developments on the nature of GAD and chronic worry, several research groups are in the process of developing and investigating new treatment methods for this disorder. For instance, Craske and colleagues (Craske, 1999; Craske et al., 1992; Zinbarg et al., 1993) developed a comprehensive treatment package that includes a procedure that targets worry more directly (i.e., worry exposure). Ladoucer and colleagues (e.g., Ladouceur et al., 2000) have been targeting intolerance of uncertainty in their cognitive behavioral treatment and Wells (Wells, 1997; Wells, 1999) recently developed a metacognitive therapy for GAD. Borkovec and colleagues recently examined the role of interpersonal/experiential factors in treatment and Roemer and Orsillo (Roemer and Orsillo, 2002) are currently investigating a treatment that integrates a mindfulness/acceptance-based treatment with existing cognitive-behavioral methods.

Summary and Future Directions

Cognitive behavioral approaches have been shown to produce some improvement in GAD symptoms relative to no treatment. However, current treatments for this disorder are less effective than those for other anxiety disorders and overall treatment gains are modest at best. This may be due to the fact that until recently, treatments for GAD were relatively nonspecific. Recent efforts by researchers to refine their conceptualization of this disorder have led to the development of newer cognitive-behavioral treatments that will hopefully produce more successful outcomes. Preliminary data from these studies have been encouraging but further clinical investigation is needed.

CONCLUSIONS

Decades of research on the nature of fear and anxiety have led to the development of efficacious treatments for a variety of emotional disorders (see Table 5 for recommended procedures for each disorder). However, there are a number of limitations that have yet to be addressed and further refinement of these procedures is necessary. While we now have treatments that are clearly effective in a research setting, the clinical utility and cost effectiveness of these procedures is not entirely clear. For instance, many practicing clinicians don't have access to empirically supported treatments. This is especially true in primary-care settings, where pharmacological treatments are most often used (Barlow, 1996; Barlow et al., 1999). As we move into the era of managed care, identifying and training clinicians in empirically supported treatments will be essential. Currently, manualized treatments are somewhat complex and training in the various protocols can be both costly and time consuming. So developing more concise treatment strategies is necessary to make CBT approaches more readily available to clinicians in the real world setting.

As noted at the outset, recent research has suggested that emotional disorders may have a common underlying basis and forthcoming

Table 5: Recommended Psychosocial Treatments by Disorder*

Disorder	PDA	Social Phobia	Specific Phobia	OCD	GAD
Treatment	PCT	CBGT	Exposure	ERP	CBT

*CBGT = cognitive behavioral group treatment; CBT = cognitive behavioral therapy; ERP = exposure and response prevention; GAD = generalized anxiety disorder; PCT = panic control treatment; PDA = panic disorder with agoraphobia; OCD = obsessive compulsive disorder

treatments may develop from a unified theoretical understanding (Brown and Barlow, 2002; Barlow et al., 2004). In accordance with this integrated model, it would no longer be necessary for clinicians to learn numerous distinct protocols. Rather, a number of essential treatment guidelines could be applied to a variety of disorders. While facilitating emotion recognition and acceptance, these new treatments will also target avoidance of the emotional experience, a common thread throughout many disorders. As we move towards a more comprehensive understanding of both psychosocial and pharmacological interventions, unification of treatment strategies and dissemination of knowledge will pave the road for even more effective approaches to treating emotional disorders.

REFERENCES

Abene M V, Hamilton JD. (1998) Resolution of fear of flying with fluoxetine treatment. J Anxiety Dis 12: 599-603.

Abramowitz JS. (1996) Variants of exposure and response prevention in the treatment of obsessive compulsive disorder: A meta-analysis. Behav Ther 27: 583-600.

Agras WS, Leitenberg H, Barlow DH. (1968) Social reinforcement in the modification of agoraphobia. Arch Gen Psychiatry 19: 423-427.

American Psychiatric Association. (1994) Diagnostic and statistical manual of mental disorders (4th ed.). Washington, DC: Author.

Antony MM, Barlow DH. (2002) Specific phobias. In D. H. Barlow, Anxiety and its disorders: The nature and treatment of anxiety and panic (2nd ed.). New York: Guilford Press.

Antony MM, Craske MG, Barlow DH. (1995) Mastery of your specific phobia: Client workbook. Boulder CO: Graywind Publications Incorporated.

Arntz A, Lavy E. (1993) Does stimulus elaboration potentiate exposure in-vivo treatment? Two forms of one-session treatment of spider phobia. Behav Psychotherapy 21: 1-12.

Baker BL, Cohen DC, Saunders JT. (1973) Self-directed desensitization for acrophobia. Behav Res Ther 11: 79-89.

Barlow DH. (1988) Anxiety and its disorders: The nature and treatment of anxiety and panic. New York: The Guilford Press.

Barlow DH. (1996) The effectiveness of psychotherapy: Science and policy. Clinical Psychological: Science Practice 3: 236-240.

Barlow DH. (2002) Anxiety and its disorders: The nature and treatment of anxiety and panic (2nd Ed.). New York: The Guilford Press.

Barlow DH, Allen LB. (2004) The scientific basis of psychological treatments for anxiety disorders: Past, present, and future. In J. M. Gorman (Ed.), Fear and anxiety: Benefits of translational research. Washington, DC: American Psychiatric Press.

Barlow, DH, Allen, LB, Choate, ML. (2004) Toward a unified treatment for emotional disorders. Behav Ther, 35, 205-230.

Barlow DH, Cohen AS, Waddell MT, Vermilyea JA, Klosko JS, Blanchard E B, Di Nardo PA. (1984) Panic and generalized anxiety disorders: Nature and treatment. Behav Ther 15: 431-449.

Barlow DH, Craske MG. (2000) Mastery of your anxiety and panic: Client workbook for anixety and panic. San Antonio, TX: Graywind Psychological Corporation.

Barlow DH, Craske MG, Cerny JA, Klosko JS. (1989) Behavioral treatment of panic disorder. Behav Ther 20: 1-26.

Barlow DH, Gorman JM, Shear MK, Woods SW. (2000) Cognitive-behavioral therapy, imipramine, or their combination for panic disorder: A randomized controlled trial. JAMA 283: 2529-2536.

Barlow DH, Lehman C. (1996) Advances in the psychosocial treatment of anxiety disorders: Implications for national health care. Arch Gen Psychiatry 53: 727-735.

Barlow DH, Levitt JT, Bufka LF. (1999)The dissemination of empirically supported treatments: A view to the future. Behav Res Ther 37: S147-S162.

Barlow DH, Rapee RM, Brown TA. (1992) Behavioral treatment of generalized anxiety disorder. Behav Ther 23: 551-570.

Barrett PM, Dadds MR, Rapee RM. (1996) Family treatment of childhood anxiety: A controlled trial. J Consult Clin Psychol 64f: 333-342.

Beck AT, Shipherd JC, Zebb BJ. (1997) How does interoceptive exposure for panic disorder work? An uncontrolled case study. J Anxiety Dis 11: 541-556.

Beck AT, Sokol L, Clark DA, Berchick R, Wright F. (1992) A crossover study of focused cognitive therapy for panic disorder. Am J Psychiatry 149: 778-783.

Beck AT, Stanley MA, Baldwin LE, Deagle EA, Averill PM. (1994) Comparison of cognitive therapy and relaxation training for panic disorder. J Consult Clin Psychol 62: 818-826.

Beckham JC, Vrana SR, May JG, Gustafson DJ, Smith GR. (1990) Emotional processing and fear measurement synchrony as indicators of treatment outcome in fear of flying. J Behav Ther Exp Psychiatry 21: 153-162.

Benjamin J, Ben-Zion IZ, Karbofsky E, Dannon P. (2000) Double-blind placebo-controlled study of paroxetine for specific phobia. Psychopharmacology 149: 194-196.

Black DW, Wesner R, Bowers W, Gabel J. (1993) A comparison of fluvoxamine, cognitive therapy, and placebo in the treatment of panic disorder. Arch Gen Psychiatry 50: 44-50.

Blowers C, Cobb J, Mathews A. (1987) Generalized anxiety: A controlled treatment study. Behav Res Ther 25: 493-502.

Borkovec TD, Costello E. (1993) Efficacy of applied relaxation and cognitive-behavioral therapy in the treatment of generalized anxiety disorder. J Consult Clin Psychology 61: 611-619.

Borkovec TD, Mathews AM. (1988) Treatment of nonphobic anxiety disorders: A comparison of nondirective, cognitive, and coping desensitization therapy. J Consult Clin Psychol 56: 877-884.

Borkovec TD, Mathews AM, Chambers A, Ebrahimi S, Lytle R, Nelson R. (1987) The effects of relaxation training and cognitive therapy or nondirective therapy and the role of relaxation -induced anxiety in the treatment of generalized anxiety. J Consult Clin Psychol 55: 883-888.

Borkovec TD, Newman MG, Pincus A, Lytle R. (2002) A component analysis of cognitive behavioral therapy for generalized anxiety disorder and the role of interpersonal problems. J Consult Clin Psychol 70: 288-298.

Borkovec TD, Ruscio AM. (2001) Psychotherapy for generalized anxiety disorder. J Clin Psychiatry 62: 37-45.

Bourque P, Ladouceur R. (1980) An investigation of various performance-based teratments with acrophobics. Behav Res Ther 18: 161-170.

Bouton ME, Mineka S, Barlow DH. (2001) A modern learning theory perspective on the etiology of panic disorder. Psychol Rev 108(1): 4-32.

Brown TA, Barlow DH. (1995) Long-term outcome in cognitive-behavioral treatment of panic disorder: Clinical predictors and alternative strategies for assessment. J Consult Clin Psychol 63: 754-765.

Brown TA, Barlow DH. (2002) Classification of anxiety and mood disorders. In D.H. Barlow, Anxiety and its disorders: The nature and treatment of anxiety and panic (2nd ed., pp. 292-327). New York: The Guilford Press.

Brown TA, Barlow DH, Liebowitz MR. (1994) The empirical basis of generalized anxiety disorder. Am J Psychiatry 151: 1272-1280.

Burns LE, Thorpe CL, Cavallaro LA. (1986) Agoraphobia 8 years after behavioral treatment: A follow-up study with interview, self-report, and behavioral data. Behav Ther 17: 580-591.

Butler G, Cullington A, Hibbert G, Klimes I, Gelder M. (1987. Anxiety management for persistent generalized anxiety. Br J Psychiatry 151: 535-542.

Butler G, Cullington A, Munby M, Amies P, Gelder M. (1984) Exposure and anxiety management in the treatment of social phobia. J Consult Clin Psychol 52: 642-650.

Butler G, Fennell M, Robson P, Gelder M. (1991) Comparison of behavior therapy and cognitive behavior therapy in the treatment of generalized anxiety disorder. J Consult Clin Psychol 59:167-175.

Chambless DL. (1990) Spacing of exposure sessions in treatment of agoraphobia and simple phobia. Behav Ther 21: 217-229.

Clark DM, Ehlers A, McManus F, Hackman A, Fennell M, Campbell H, Flower T, Davenport C, Louis B. (2003) Cognitive therapy vs. fluoxetine plus self-exposure in the treatment of generalized social phobia (social anxiety disorder): A randomized placebo controlled study. J Consult Clin Psychol.

Clark DM, Salkovskis PM, Hackmann A, Middleton H, Anastasiades P, Gelder M. (1994) A comparison of cognitive therapy, applied relaxation and imipramine in the treatment of panic disorder. Br JPsychiatry 164,: 759-769.

Cohen SD, Montiero W, Marks IM. (1984) Two-year follow-up of agoraphobics after exposure and imipramine. Br J Psychiatry 144: 276-281.

Cote C, Gauthier J G, Laberge B, Cormier H J,Plamondon J. (1994) Reduced therapist contact in the cognitive behavioral treatment of panic disorder. Behav Ther 25: 123-145.

Cottraux J, Note I, Yao SN, Lafont S, Note B, Mollard E, Bouvard M, Sauteraud A, Bourgeois M, Dartigues JF. (2001) A controlled trial of cognitive therapy versus intensive behavior therapy in obsessive compulsive disorder. Psychother Psychosom 70: 288-297.

Craske MG. (1999) Anxiety disorders: Psychological approaches to theory and treatment. Boulder, CO: Westview Press.

Craske MG,Barlow DH. (2001) Panic disorder and agoraphobia. In D. H. Barlow (Ed.), Clinical handbook of psychological disorders (3rd ed., pp. 1-59). New York: Guilford Press.

Craske MG,Barlow,DH, O'Leary T. (1992) Mastery of your anxiety and worry. Boulder CO: Graywind Publications Incorporated.

Craske MG, Brown TA, Barlow DH. (1991)Behavioral treatment of panic disorder: A two-year follow-up. Behav Ther 22: 289-304.

Craske MG, Mohlman J, Yi J, Glover D, Valeri S. (1995) Treatment of claustrophobia and snake/spider phobias: Fear of arousal and fear context. Behav Res Ther 33: 197-203.

Davidson J, Foa EB, Huppert JD, Keefe FJ, Franklin ME, Comptom JS, Zhao N, Connor KM, Lynch TR, and Gaddle KM. (2004) Fluoxetine, comprehensive cognitive behavioral therapy, and placebo in generalized social phobia. Arch Gen Psychiatry 61: 1005-1013.

DeAraujo LA, Ito LM, Marks IM, Deale A. (1995) Does imaginal exposure ot the consequences of not ritualizing enhance live exposure for OCD? A controlled study: I. Main outcome. Br J Psychiatry 167: 65-70.

Durham RC, Murphy T, Allen T, Richard K, Treliving LR, Fenton GW. (1994) Cognitive therapy, analytic psychotherapy and anxiety management training for generalzied anxiety disorder. Br J Psychiatry 165: 315-323.

Durham RC, Turvey AA. (1987) Cognitive therapy vs behaviour therapy in the treatment of chronic general anxiety. Behav ResTher 25: 229-234.

Emmelkamp PMG, HB. (1991) Cognitive therapy with obsessive-compulsive disorder: A comparative evaluation. Behav ResTherapy 29: 293-300.

Emmelkamp PMG, Visser S, Hockstra RJ. (1988) Cognitive therapy vs. exposure in vivo in the treatment of obsessive-compulsives. Cogn Ther Res 12: 103-114.

Fals-Stewart W, Marks AP, Schafer J. (1993) A comparison of behavioral group therapy and individual behavior therapy in treating obsessive compulsive disorder. J Nerv Ment Dis 181: 189-193.

Fava GA, Zielezny M, Savron G, Grandi S. (1995) Long-term effects of behavioural treatment for panic disorder and agoraphobia. Br J Psychiatry 166: 87-92.

Federoff IC, Taylor S. (2001) Psychological and pharmacological treatments of social phobia: A meta-analysis. J Clin Psychopharmacology 21: 311-324.

Feigenbauw W. (1988) Long-term efficacy of ungraded versus graded massed exposure in agoraphobics. In I. Hand and H. Wittchen (Eds.), Panic and phobias: Treatments and variables affecting course and outcome (pp. 83-88). Berlin: Springer-Verlag.

Feske U, Chambless DL. (1995) Cognitive behavioral versus exposure only treatment for social phobia: A meta-analysis. Behav Ther 26: 695-720.

Foa E, Jameson JS, Turner RM, Payne LL. (1980) Massed vs. spaced exposure sessions in the treatment of agoraphobia. Behav ResTher 18: 333-338.

Foa E, Steketee G, Grayson JB, Turner RM, Latimer P. (1984) Deliberate exposure and blocking of obsessive-compulsive rituals: Immediate and long-term effects. Behav Ther 15: 450-472.

Foa EB, Franklin ME. (2001) Obsessive-compulsive disorder. In D. H. Barlow (Ed.), Clinical handbook of psychological disorders: A step-by-step treatment manual (3rd ed.). New York, NY: Guilford Press.

Foa EB, Kozak MJ. (1996) Psychological treatments for obsessive compulsive disorder. In M. R. Mavissakalian and R. P. Prien (Eds.), Long-term treatments of anxiety disorders (pp. 285-309). Washington, DC: American Psychiatric Press.

Foa EB, Kozak MJ, Goodman WK, Hollander E, Jenike MA, Rasmussen S. (1995) DSM-IV field trial: Obsessive compulsive disorder. Am J Psychiatry 152: 90-96.

Foa EB, Kozak MJ, Steketee G, McCarthy PR. (1992) Treatment of depressive and obsessive-compulsive symptoms in OCD by imipramine and behavior therapy. Br J Clin Psychol 31: 279-292.

Franklin ME, Ambramowitz JS, Kozak MJ, Levitt JT, Foa EB. (2000) Effectiveness of exposure and ritual prevention for obsessive compulsive disorder: Randomized versus non-randomized samples. J Consult Clin Psychol 68: 594-602.

Freeston MH, Ladouceur R, Gagnon F, Thibodeau N, Rhéaume J, Letarte H, Bujold A. (1997) Cognitive-behavioral treatment of obsessive thoughts: A controlled study. J Consult Clin Psychol 65: 405-413.

Gelernter CS, Uhde TW, Cimbolic P, Arnkoff DB, Vittone BJ, Tancer ME, Bartko JJ. (1991) Cognitive-behavioral and pharmacological treatment of social phobia. Arch Gen Psychiatry 48: 938-945.

Gitin NM, Herbert JD, Schmidt C. (1996) One-session in vivo exposure for odontophobia. Paper presented at the 30th Annual Convention of the Association for Advancement of Behavior Therapy, New York.

Gould RA, Buckminster S, Pollack MH, Otto MW, Yap L. (1997) Cognitive-behavioral and pharmacological treatment for social phobia: A meta-analysis. Clin Psychol Sci Pract 4: 291-306.

Gould RA, Otto MW, Pollack MH. (1995) A meta-analysis of treatment outcome for panic disorder. Clin Psychol Rev 15: 819-844.

Griest JH. (1990) Treatment of obsessive-compulsive disorder: Psychotherapies, drugs, and other somatic treatments. J Clin Psychiatry 51: 44-50.

Griest JH, Jefferson JW, Kobak KA, Katzelnick DJ, Serlin RC. (1995) Efficacy and tolerability of serotonin reuptake inhibitors in obsessive compulsive disorder: A meta-analysis. Arch Gen Psychiatry 46: 53-60.

Griez E, van den Hout MA. (1986) CO_2 inhalation in the treatment of panic attacks. Behav ResTher 20: 323-328.

Gunther LM, Denniston JC, Miller RR. (1998) Conducting exposure treatment in multiple contexts can prevent relapse. Behav Res Ther 36: 75-91.

Hafner J, Marks IM. (1976) Exposure in vivo of agoraphobics: Contributions of diazepam, group exposure, and anxiety evocation. Psychol Med 6: 71-88.

Heimberg RG, Becker RE, Goldfinger K, Vermilyea JA. (1985) Treatment of social phobia by exposure, cognitive restructuring, and homework assignments. J Nerv Ment Dis 173: 236-245.

Heimberg RG, Dodge CS, Hope DA, Kennedy CR, Zollo LJ, Becker RE. (1990) Cognitive-behavioral group treatment for social phobia: Comparison with a credible placebo control. Cognit Ther Res 14: 1-23.

Heimberg RG, Liebowitz MR, Hope DA, Schneier FR, Holt CS, Welkowitz LA, Juster HR, Campeas R, Bruch MA, Cloitre M, Fallon B, Klein DF. (1998) Cognitive behavioral group therapy vs. phenelzine therapy for social phobia: 12-week outcome. Arch Genl Psychiatry 55(12): 1133-1141.

Heimberg RG, Salzman DG, Holt CS, Blendell KA. (1993) Cognitive-behavioral group treatment for social phobia: Effectiveness at five-year followup. Cognit Ther Res 17: 325-339.

Hellström K, Fellenius J, Öst L-G. (1996) One versus five sessions of applied tension in the treatment of blood phobia. Behav Res Ther 34: 101-112.

Hellström K, Öst L-G. (1995) One-session therapist directed exposure vs. two forms of manual directed self-exposure in the treatment of spider phobia. Behav Res Ther 33: 959-965.

Hembree EA, Riggs DS, Kozak MJ, Franklin ME, Foa EB. (2003) Long-term efficacy of exposure and ritual prevention therapy and serotonergic medications for obsessive-compulsive disorder. CNS Spectrums 8: 363-366, 369-371.

Hiss H, Foa EB, Kozak MJ. (1994) A relapse prevention program for treatment of obsessive compulsive disorder. J Consult Clin Psychol 62: 801-808.

Hofmann SG, Barlow DH. (2002) Social Phobia (Social Anxiety Disorder). In D. H. Barlow, Anxiety and Its Disorders (2nd ed., pp. 454-476). New York: Guilford Press.

Holt CS, Heimberg RG, Hope DA, Liebowitz MR. (1992) Situational domains of social phobia. JAnxiety Dis 6: 63-77.

Hope DA, Heimberg RG, Bruch MA. (1995) Dismantling cognitive-behavioral group therapy for social phobia. Behav Res Ther 33: 637-650.

Howard WA, Murphy SM, Clark JC. (1983) The nature and treatment of fear of flying: A controlled investigation. Behav Ther 14: 557-567.

Ito LM, De Araujo LA, Hemsley DR, Marks IM. (1995) Beliefs and resistance in obsessive-compulsive disorder: Observations from a controlled study. J Anxiety Dis 9(4): 269-281.

Jacobson NS, Wilson L, Tupper C. (1988) The clinical significance of treatment gains resulting from exposure-based interventions for agoraphobia: A reanalysis of outcome data. Behav Ther 19: 539-554.

Jansson L, Jerremalm A, Öst L-G. (1986) Follow-up of agoraphobic patients treated with exposure in vivo or applied relaxation. Br J Psychiatry 149: 486-490.

Jansson L, Öst L-G. (1982) Behavioral treatments for agoraphobia: An evaluative review. Clin Psychol Rev 2: 311-336.

Jerremalm A, Jansson L, Öst L-G. (1986) Individual response patterns and the effects of different behavioral methods in the treatment of dental phobia. Behav Res Ther 24: 587-596.

Jones MK, Menzies RG. (1997) The cognitive mediation of obsessive-compulsive handwashing. Behav Res Ther 35: 843-850.

Keijsers GPJ, Hoogduin CAL, Schaap CPDR. (1994) Predictors of treatment outcome in the behavioural treatment of obsessive-compulsive disorder. Br J Psychiatry 165: 781-786.

Kendall PC, Flannery-Schroeder E, Panichelli-Mindel SM, Southam-Gerow M, Henin A, Warman M. (1997) Therapy for youths with anxiety disorders: A second randomized clinical trial. J Consult Clin Psychol 65: 366-380.

Klosko JS, Barlow DH, Tassinari R, Cerny JA. (1990) A comparison of alprazolam and behavior therapy in treatment of panic disorder. J Consult Clin Psychol 58: 77-84.

Kozak MJ, Liebowitz MR, Foa EB. (2000) Cognitive-behavior therapy and pharmacotherapy for OCD: The NIMH-sponsored collaborative study. In W. Goodman and M. Rudorfer and J. Maser (Eds.), Obsessive-compulsive disorder: Contemporary issues in treatment (pp. 501-530). Mahwah, NJ: Erlbaum.

Ladouceur R, Freeston MH, Léger E, Gagnon F, Thibodeau N. (2000) Efficacy of a new cognitive-behavioral treatment for generalized anxiety disorder: Evaluation in a controlled clinical trial. J Consult Clin Psychol 68: 957-964.

Lang AJ, Craske MG. (1998) Long-term benefits of maximizing memory for exposure-based treatment of fear. Paper presented at the World Congress of Behavioural and Cognitive Therapies, Acapulco, Mexico.Lang AJ, Craske MG. (2000) Manipulations of exposure-based therapy to reduce return of fear: A replication. Behav ResTher 38: 1-12.

LeBoeuf A, Lodge J. (1980) A comparison of frontalis EMG feedback training and progressive muscle relaxation in the treatment of chronic anxiety. Br J Psychiatry 137: 279-284.

Liddell A, Di Fazio L, Blackwood J, Ackerman C. (1994) Long-term follow-up of treated dental phobics. Behav Res Ther 32: 605-610.

Liebowitz MR, Heimberg RG, Schneier FR, Hope DA, Davies S, Holt CS, Goetz D, Juster HR, Lin S-H, Bruch MA, Marshall RD, Klein DF. (1999) Cognitive-behavioral group therapy versus phenelzine in social phobia: Long-term outcome. Depress Anxiety 10: 89-98.

Lindsay M, Crino R, Andrews G. (1997) Controlled trial of exposure and response prevention in obsessive-compulsive disorder. Br J Psychiatry 171: 135-139.

Lucas JA, Telch MJ. (1993) Group versus individual treatment of social phobia. Paper presented at the annual meeting of the Association for Advancement of Behavior Therapy, Atlanta, GA.

Margraf J, Schneider S. (1991). Outcome and active ingredients of cognitive-behavioral treatment for panic disorder. Paper presented at the annual meeting of the Association for Advancement of Behavior Therapy, New York City.

Marks IM. (1987) Fears, phobias, and rituals: Panic, anxiety, and their disorders. New York: Oxford University Press.

Mattick RP, Peters L. (1988) Treatment of severe social phobia: Effects of guided exposure with and without cognitive restructuring. J Consult Clin Psychol 56: 251-260.

Mattick RP, Peters L, Clarke JC. (1989) Exposure and cognitive restructuring for social phobia: A controlled study. Behav Ther 20: 3-23.

McNally RJ. (1986) Behavioral treatment of a choking phobia. J Behav Ther Exp Psychiatry 17: 185-188.

McNally RJ. (1994) Panic disorder: A critical analysis. New York: Guilford Press.

Mehta M. (1990) A comparative study of family-based and patients-based behavioural management in obsessive-compulsive disorder. Br J Psychiatry 157: 133-135.

Menzies RG, Clark JC. (1993b) A comparison of in vivo and vicarious exposure in the treatmen of childhood water phobia. Behav Res Ther 31: 9-15.

Munby J, Johnston DW. (1980) Agoraphobia: The long-term follow-up of behavioral treatment. Br J Psychiatry 137: 418-427.

Muris P, Mayer B, Merckelbach H. (1998) Trait anxiety as a predictor of behavior therapy outcome in spider phobia. Behav Cognit Psychotherapy 26: 87-91.

Mystkowski JL, Craske MG, Echeveri AM. (2002) Treatment context and return of fear in spider phobia. Behav Ther 33: 399-416.

Newman CF, Beck JS, Beck AT. (1990) Efficacy of cognitive therapy in reducing panic attacks and medication. Paper presented at the annual meeting of the Association for Advancement of Behavior Therapy, San Francisco.

Öst LG. (1989b) A maintenance program for behavioral treatment of anxiety disorders. Behav ResTher 37: 123-130.

Öst L-G. (1978) Behavioral treatment of thunder and lightning phobias. Behav Res Ther 16: 197-207.

Öst L-G. (1989a). One-session treatment for specific phobias. Behav Res Ther 27: 1-7.

Öst L-G. (1996). Long term effects of behavior therapy for specific phobia. In M. R. Mavissakalian and R. F. Prien (Eds.), Long-term treatments of the anxiety disorders. Washington, DC: American Psychiatric Press.

Öst L-G, Brandberg M, Alm T. (1997) One versus five sessions of exposure in the treatment of flying phobia. Behav Res Ther 35: 987-996.

Öst L-G, Ferebee I, Furmark T. (1997) One-session group therapy of spider phobia: Direct versus indirect treatments. Behav ResTher 35: 721-732.

Öst L-G, Hellström K, Kaver A. (1992) One versus five sessions of exposure in the treatment of injection phobia. Behav Ther 23: 263-282.

Öst L-G, Johansson J, Jerremalm A. (1982) Individual response patterns and the effects of different behavioral methods in the treatment of claustrophobia. Behav Res Ther 20: 445-460.

Öst L-G, Salkovskis PM, Hellström K. (1991) One-session therapist directed exposure vs. self-exposure in the treatment of spider phobia. Behav Ther 22: 407-422.

Öst L-G, Sterner U. (1987) Applied tension: A specific behavioural method for treatment of blood phobia. Behav Res Ther 25: 25-30.

Öst L-G, Westling BE. (1995) Applied relaxation versus cognitive behavior therapy in the treatment of panic disorder. Behav Res Ther 33: 145-158.

Öst L-G, Westling BE, Hellstrom K. (1993) Applied relaxation, exposure in vivo and cognitive methods in the treatment of panic disorder with agoraphobia. Behav Res Ther 31: 383-395.

Otto MW, Pollack MH, Gould RA, Worthington JJ, McArdle ET, Rosenbaum JF, Heimberg RG. (2000) A comparison of the efficacy of clonazepam and cognitive-behavioral group therapy for the treatment of social phobia. J Anxiety Dis 14: 345-358.

Pato MT, Zohar-Kadouch R, Zohar J, Murphy DL. (1988) Return of symptoms after discontinuation of clomipramine in patients with obsessive-compulsive disorder. Am J Psychiatry 145: 1521-1525.

Piccinelli M, Pini S, Bellantuono C, Wilkinson G. (1995) Efficacy of drug treatment of obsessive-compulsive disorder. A meta-analytic review. Br J Psychiatry 166: 424-443.

Power JG, Jerrom DW, Simpson RJ, Mitchell MJ, Swanson V. (1989) A controlled comparison of cognitive-behavioral therapy, diazepam, and placebo in the management of generalized anxiety. Behav Psychotherapy 17: 1-14.

Power JG, Simpson RJ, Swanson V, Wallace L, Feistner ATC, Sharp D. (1990) A controlled comparison of cognitive-behaviour therapy, diazepam, and placebo, alone and in combination, for the treatment of generalized anxiety disorder. J Anxiety Dis 4: 267-292.

Rodriguez BI, Craske MG, Mineka S, Hladek D. (1999) Context-specificity of relapse: Effects of therapist and environmental context on return of fear. Behav Res Ther 37: 845-862.

Roemer L, Orsillo SM. (2002) Expanding our conceptualization of and treatment for generalized anxiety disorder: Integrating mindfulness/acceptance-based approaches with existing cognitive-behavioral models. Clinical Psychology: Science and Practice 9: 54-68.

Rowe MK, Craske MG. (1998) Effects of an expanding-spaced vs. massed exposure schedule on fear reduction and return of fear. Behav ResTher 36: 701-717.

Schmidt NB, Woolaway-Bickel K, Trakowski J, Santiago H, Storey J, Koselka M, Cook J. (2000) Dismantling cognitive-behavioral treatment for panic disorder: Questioning the utility of breathing retraining. J Consult Clin Psychol 68: 417-424.

Scholing A, Emmelkamp PMG. (1983a) Cognitive and behavioural treatments of fear of blushing, sweating, or trembling. Behav Res Ther 31: 155-170.

Shear MK, Houck P, Greeno C, et al. (2001) Emotion-focused psychotherapy for patients with panic disorder. Am J Psychiatry 158: 1993-1999.

Shear MK, Pilkonis PA, Cloitre M, Leon AC. (1994) Cognitive behavioral treatment compared with nonprescriptive treatment of panic disorder. Arch Gen Psychiatry 51: 395-401.

Simpson BH, Liebowitz MR, Foa EB, Kozak MJ, Schmidt AB, Rowan V, Petkova E, Kjernisted K, Huppert JD, Franklin ME, Davies SO, Campeas R. (2004) Post-treatment effects of exposure therapy and clomipramine in obsessive-compulsive disorder.

Solyom L, Shugar R, Bryntwick S, Solyom C. (1973) Treatment of fear of flying. Am J Psychiatry 130: 423-427.

Stanley MA, Beck JG, Glassco JD. (1996) Treatment of generalized anxiety in older adults: A preliminary comparison of cognitive-behavioral and supportive approaches. Behav Ther 27: 565-581.

Stanley MA, Turner SM. (1995) Current status of pharmacological and behavioral treatment of obsessive-compulsive disorder. Behav Ther 26: 163-186.

Taylor S. (1996) Meta-analysis of cognitive-behavioral treatments for social phobia. J Behav Ther Exp Psychiatry 27: 1-9.

Telch MJ, Lucas JA, Schmidt NB, Hanna HH, Jaimez TS, Lucas RA. (1993) Group cognitive-behavioral treatment of panic disorder. Behav Res Ther 31: 279-287.

Telch MJ, Schmidt NB, Jaimez TS, Jacquin KM, Harrington PJ. (1995) Impact of cognitive-behavioral treatment on quality of life in panic disorder patients. J Consult Clin Psychol 63: 823-830.

Trull TJ, Nietzel MT, Main A. (1988) The use of meta-analysis to assess the clinical significance of behavior therapy for agoraphobia. Behav Ther 19: 527-538.

Tsao JCI, Craske MG. (1996) Contextual control of the return of fear in spider-fearful individuals. Unpublished master's thesis, University of California, Los Angeles.

Turner SM, Beidel DC, Cooley MR, Woody SR, Messer SC. (1994) A multicomponent behavioural treatment for social phobia: Social effectiveness therapy. Behav Res Ther 32: 381-390.

van Balkom AJLM, de Haan E, van Oppen P, Spinhoven P, Hoogduin KAL, Vermeulen AWA, van Dyck R. (1998) Cognitive and behavioral therapies alone and in combination with fluvoxamine in the treatment of obsessive compulsive disorder. J Nerv Ment Dis 186: 492-499.

van Oppen P, de Haan E, van Balkom AJLM, Spinhoven P, Hoogduin K, and van Dyck R. (1995) Cognitive therapy and exposure in vivo in the treatment of obsessive compulsive disorder. Behav Res Ther 33: 379-390.

Wells A. (1997) Cognitive therapy of anxiety disorders: A practice manual and conceptual guide. New York: Wiley.

Wells A. (1999) A metacognitive model and therapy for generalized anxiety disorder. Clin Psychol Psychotherapy 6: 86-95.

Wetherell JL, Gatz M, Craske MG. (2003) Treatment of generalized anxiety disorder in older adults. J Consult Clin Psychol 71; 31-40.

White J, Keenan M. (1992) Stress control: A controlled comparative investigation of large group therapy for generalized anxiety disorder. Behav Psychotherapy 20 97-114.

White J, Keenan M, Brooks N. (1990) Stress control: A pilot study of large group

therapy for Generalized Anxiety Disorder. Behav Psychotherapy 18: 143-146.

Wilhelm FH, Roth WT. (1996). Acute and delayed effects of alprazolam on flight phobics during exposure. Paper presented at the 30th Annual Convention of the Association for Advancement of Behavior Therapy, New York.

Zinbarg RE, Craske MG, Barlow DH. (1993) Therapist's guide for the mastery of your anxiety and worry. Boulder CO: Graywind Publications Incorporated.

Zoellner LA, Craske MG, Hussain A, Lewis M, Echeveri A. (1996) Contextual effects of alprazolam during exposure therapy. Paper presented at the 30th Annual Convention of the Association for Advancement of Behavior Therapy, New York.

MAJOR DEPRESSION

David Knesper

MAJOR DEPRESSION: FUNDAMENTAL PERSPECTIVES

Epidemiological and World Health Organization perspective

Depression is a recurrent and potentially chronic and often lethal disease. Among all diseases, major depressive disorder (unipolar affective disorder) ranks fourth in terms of disease burden, and major depression is the leading cause of disability in market economies according to the World Health Organization's Global Burden of Disease Study (Murray and Lopez, 1997). This study projects that by 2020, major depression will rank second in terms of disease burden. At this present time, the disease burden from major depression outranks diabetes, cerebrovascular diseases, dementia, lung cancer and other diseases of great disease burden (Murry and Lopez, 1996; Greden, 2001). Worldwide, major depressive disorder is the *leading cause of disability* for ages 15 – 44 years (World Health Organization, 1996).

Rates of current major depressive episode range from 4.6% to 7.4%, depending on country (Smith and Weissman, 1992); 4.5% to 5.8% is the rate in the United States (Blazer et al., 1994; Narrow, 2002); 7.4% of adolescents report symptoms consistent with the diagnosis of major depression (Riolo et al., 2002). Large-scale community surveys find that the lifetime prevalence rates for major depression are approximately 21.3% for females and 12.7% for males. Accordingly, a large minority of people in the general population is at risk for the majority of episodes of affective disorders.

Major depressive disorder is all too often lethal. Compared to individuals without a mood disorder, individuals with major depression are at 11 times greater risk for making a suicide attempt. The tragedy of suicide is somehow intensified by our limited knowledge about preventative means. The compelling belief that treating depression can prevent suicide has minimal factual support. In fact, a recent review (Hollen et al., 2002) was unable to identify a single randomized controlled trial testing this hypothesis.

Diagnostic perspective

The collection of signs and symptoms that define disorders of mood has been developed largely by a consensus of experts. The resulting diagnostic criteria have been revised several times and mood disorders may be viewed as a fluid concept. None of the criteria sets have been validated by a clear and compelling concept of disease. That two distinct major mood disorders are recognized does not eliminate the very real possibility that unipolar and bipolar disorders are part of a larger etiologically heterogeneous group of mood disorders. Moreover, it is reasonable to assert that a differential combination of genetic vulnerability and environmental experiences and exposures produces the affective profile that distinguishes each subtype. This categorical approach to psychopathology is less reasonable at the boundaries of these disorders. At the boundary of severity, the differences between non-disorder and disorder are often objectively obscure. Under these circumstances, diagnostic decisions are made often on the bases of self-reported excessive disability, significant distress, deviations from age-appropriate expectations, and so forth.

Risk and vulnerability factor perspective

Ideally, a risk factor for major depressive disorder is identified by persuasive, empirical evidence that the factor substantially increases the probability of occurrence, regardless of causal mechanisms. The necessary evidence is established with longitudinal prospective studies and comparison groups. Prevention studies demonstrating that treatment meaningfully reduces risk provide additional evidence. Unfortunately, the vast bulk of risk factors mentioned subsequently are based on cross-sectional studies and many of the conclusions presented must be considered tentative.

Representing a subset of risk, vulnerability implies some knowledge of the causal mechanisms that predispose an individual to a major depressive disorder; such processes are active even in the absence of mood symptoms (Ingram and Price, 2001). Many of the major categories of vulnerability will be mentioned (e.g., genetic vulnerability), but more specific biological markers and possible neural substrates will go unmentioned because of the preliminary nature of the research in this area.

A GUIDE TO THE TEXT

This chapter identifies a range of primary and secondary prevention strategies that can be used to reduce the severity of symptoms of major depressive disorder. The primary goal of this chapter is to compare preventative interventions across classes. So, for example, the efficacy and effectiveness of antidepressant medications will be compared to the efficacy and effectiveness of various forms of psychotherapy. This comparison suggests these two classes of intervention be separated by a boundary as if they each produced distinct effects. Advances in brain imaging technologies demonstrate that both psychotherapy and antidepressants affect the same portions of the brain; therefore, separation simply identifies alternative procedures. Less attention will be given to comparisons within classes of interventions (e.g., Drug A compared to Drug B). This chapter is based on the categorical construct

of major depressive disorder as defined by the DSM-IV (American Psychiatric Association, 1994).

At the very least, the topic of suicide prevention demands its very own thoughtful review. Rather than minimize the urgency of suicide prevention with an abbreviated section, this present review will avoid a consideration of the topic for the most part.

The emphasis is on providing a useful overview as opposed to an academic investigation and synthesis. To achieve utility, some precision has had to be sacrificed in the following ways:

• The examined longitudinal studies have been selected on the basis of historical relevance, recent completion, and important conclusions. Unless otherwise specified, all studies reviewed used randomization and, where applicable, blinded procedures.

• Comparisons across studies are promoted by converting all depression severity measurements to scores based on the 17-item Hamilton Rating Scale for Depression; scores range from 0 – 50. There is considerable correspondence and agreement among scales used to rate the severity of depressive symptoms and to monitor symptom changes (Senra, 1996).

• The outcomes of interventions and control conditions are given as percentages so that the reader can judge how these compare to a true placebo control condition. In clinical trials of medications, the mean (SD) proportion of patients in the placebo group who respond with a ≥ 50% reduction in symptom severity is approximately 30% (8%) (range 12.5% - 51.8%). The placebo response rate tends to move opposite to the severity score—the higher the severity score, the lower the placebo response rate (Peselow et al., 1992).

• Many individual studies reviewed will end with *Comments* pertaining to that single study; collections of studies will end with *Summary Comments*.

MAJOR DEPRESSIVE DISORDER: DEFINITION, CHRONICITY AND SEVERITY

Major depressive episode defined

An uncomplicated major depressive episode (unipolar depression) is different from simple unhappiness or normal grief following a loss. The diagnosis of major depression is made only when significantly depressed mood and loss of interest and/or pleasure in most activities are constant for two weeks. The other core features of a depressive episode may include altered sleep and eating patterns, excessive guilt, diminished concentration and memory as well as limited energy and motor behaviors and increased risk of suicide (American Psychiatric Association, 1994). Concurrently, persons suffering from this disorder feel like less valuable and confident human beings and have poor motivation and excessively pessimistic thoughts and attitudes. Many depressed people are generally slowed down and disengaged and have a reduced frequency of gestures and smiling and laughing in comparison to the person's non-depressed state. Little things overwhelm a more seriously depressed person; the simplest decisions may reduce them to tears. In agitated forms of major depression, individuals have difficulty sitting still; instead, they pace and wring their hands. A large minority of patients will complain of somatic symptoms primarily; motor weakness, heart palpitations, headaches, chest pain, nausea and abdominal pain are examples of many such possible complaints (Kronke, 1994). The expressions of these symptoms vary depending on age, developmental level, culture, and life experiences (Cove, 2002; Garber and Flynn, 2001). This variability in expression has led to the identification of subgroups such as "postpartum depression," "seasonal affective disorder," "melancholic/endogenous depression," and others. Unlike traditional disease models, most theoretical models of major depression do not assume discontinuity between dysfunctional behavior and normal behavior.

What is the evidence that major depressive disorder is a chronic disease?

See Figure 1. The course of major depression for most patients is one of variable severity that alternates between the specific episodes of depression and phases of improvement or even complete recovery (Figure 1). The chance of a second episode of depression is 80%; this figure is 100% if subsyndromal depression is the criteria. Without treatment, most patients experience multiple episodes; four is the median number (Judd, 1997; Judd et al. 1998). Often major depression begins at a young age; thereafter, depression tends to be recurrent and chronic (Kovacs, 1996; Pine, 1999). "Relapse" references the reemergence of symptoms within the first 6 to 9 months after a remission (Frank et al., 1991); thereafter, any recurrence of symptoms is considered to be a new episode. This lifelong episodic pattern is so characteristic of major depression that the illness is positioned rightfully as a chronic disorder (Lavori et al., 1984; Consensus Development Panel, 1985; Hammen, 1991; Judd, 1997).

The Severity of Major Depressive Disorder

Once completed, rating scales for the assessment and management of major depression give a numerical score, and a range of severity scores corresponds to a specific category of severity (Yonkers and Samson, 2000). The Hamilton Rating Scale for Depression (HRSD) is a widely used scale (Hamilton, 1960) that is clinician-administered. Of the 21 item on the checklist, the first 16 items are scored; 9 items are scored 0-4 and 7 items 0-2 for maximum 50 points. The score-ranges corresponding to

Figure 1: **Prototypical Course of Major Depression with Suboptimal Treatment**

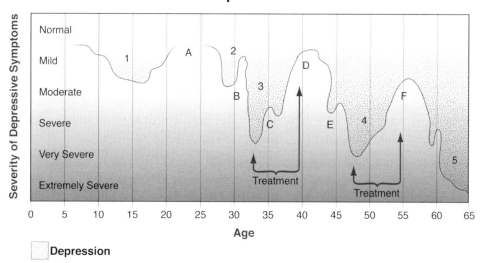

Depression

depression severity are: very severe, > 23; severe, 22-19; moderate, 18-14; mild, 13-8; and normal ≤ 7.

There is no category for "extremely severe"; however, patients with scores of greater than 30 are common and a score of 40 or above characterize many patients. Many of the studies reviewed hereafter claim to pertain to patients with "severe depression," but persons in this category may be able to go to work daily and exhibit little visible distress. *No study reviewed hereafter pertains to "extremely severe" major depression.*

"Involutional melancholia" may best describe this unbelievably catastrophic state of depression (Rosenthal, 1968; Thase, 2000). Features may include any or all of the following: loss of appetite with significant weight loss; several to many somatic symptoms (e.g., nausea, pain, unsteady gait, etc.); weeping for hours on end; incapacitating fatigue and tiredness yet unable to get more than a couple hours of sleep; inability to even consider decisions; inattention and memory impairment of dementia-like proportions; pacing and general agitation or catatonic forms of psychomotor retardation; self-condemnation; numerous

worries about improbable catastrophes; preoccupation with death and/or suicide; and other disabling symptoms. This depressive syndrome and its variations are not at all rare. Because most people and many doctors have never seen this state of extremely severe or melancholic depression, there is a gross underestimation of the true nature of severe depression and the associated challenges of treatment.

RISK AND VULNERABILITY ASSESSMENT: PREDICTING THE LIKELIHOOD OF THE FIRST EPISODE OF MAJOR DEPRESSION

See Table 1. Risk assessment is an established and effective means of preventing and managing the vast bulk of medical disorders—except for psychiatric disorders. Most physicians and mental health professionals are unaccustomed to integrating the assessment of major depression risk factors into their clinical practices. Knowing "weight" of risk factors for major depression associated with particular individual permits the clinician to estimate the likelihood that the individual will either have a first episode or a subsequent episode of major depression.

Moreover, in the face of diagnostic uncertainty the "weight" of risk factors provides strong or weak support for a tentative diagnosis. For example, when the clinical examination finds subsyndromal depression, the provision of treatment is made more urgent when the patient is at increased risk based on a comprehensive assessment of risk factors. Providing the means and evidence for this more comprehensive approach to the diagnosis and management of major depressive disorder is the goal of this section.

For this section, the umbrella term "risk factors" include both intra-personal and extra-personal attributes associated with an increased probability of the occurrence of a disorder. "Vulnerability factors" refer to a subset of risk factors that are personal characteristics that predispose to a particular disorder. Table 1 provides a summary.

Genetics

Undeniably, depression is, in part, inherited. In both males and females inheritance accounts for about 37% - 39% of the risk for a major depressive episode; the remaining 63% - 61% of the risk results from personal attributes (e.g., cognitive style) and environmental factors (e.g., serious adversity). These percentages are derived from a recent analysis of twin pairs (Kendler and Prescott, 1999; Sullivan et al., 2000). Compared to children of non-depressed parents, children of depressed parents have a three-fold greater risk of having major depression (Beardslee et al., 1998) and a 40% chance the episode will occur before the age of 18 (Weissman et al., 1987). Also, inheritance predicts more severe forms of depression (e.g., recurrences, longer episode duration, higher levels of impairment) (Rutter et al., 1990; Lyons et al., 1998; Kendler et al., 1999). In a study of identical female cotwins, the combination of genetic risk for major

depression and significant personal adversity during the 12 months prior to onset, predicts higher rates of major depression (Kendler et al., 1995). Compared to the general population, relatives of depressed probands have higher rates of depression, as expected; but, in addition they may have higher rates of severe psychosocial adversity, suggesting a genetic-environmental interaction (McGuffin, 1988). There are some people who seem prone to contribute to their own misfortune (Daley and Hammen, 1997). Perhaps, the capacity to generate adversity and be interpersonally difficult is, in part, inherited!

Gender and age

Sex is the intra-personal risk factor that best predicts major depression. Until the early teenage years, major depression is about equally distributed among males and females. In adult populations, females with major depression outnumber men by a ratio of 2:1 (Weissman and Olfson, 1995). Genetic factors may play a larger role for females then for males for whom environmental factors may play a larger role (Bierut et al., 1999). For females the lifetime prevalence of major depression is 21.3%; for males 12.7% (Kessler et al., 1993). One-month prevalence rates are highest between the ages of 15 to 24 years old (Blazer et al., 1994). A birth cohort effect is likely; individuals born more recently are more likely to have depression (Klerman and Weisman, 1989; Burke et al., 1991).

Middle to late adolescence may be the origin of depression found in adults (Hankin et al., 1998). On average, serious symptoms of depression for females begin in the teenage years; males begin in their 20's (Pajer, 1995). Compared to males, females may have longer depressive episodes (Kornstein, 1997) and are more likely to report atypical symptoms (e.g., appetite and weight increase) and have a chronic and recurring illness (Frank et al., 1988; Winokur, 1993). The data describing

Table 1. Risk Factors Predicting Adult-Onset Major Depressive Disorder

Risk Factors Predicting the Initial Episode
1. Inheritance; a parent, parents and/or a close biological relative with a mood disorder
2. Female gender
3. Pre-pubescent significant sub-clinical depressed feelings and/or anxiety, hostility, poor peer acceptance, poor physical health (boys), death of a parent and/or poor academic performance (girls).
4. History of physical, sexual, emotional abuse
5. Depressotypic cognitive styles (e.g., profound sense of diminished control; pessimistic and/or self-defeating misattributions; excessive-to-the-situation helplessness and/or hopelessness; others)
6. Minor or sub-syndromal depressive symptoms (e.g., chronic dysthymia)
7. Major psychosocial adversity (e.g. learning disorder, death of child, divorce, traumatic experience, etc.)
8. Convictions about low self-esteem, low personal effectiveness, etc.
9. Chronic illness, especially hypothyroidism and chronic neurological illness
10. Medications to treat a medical condition that may cause or worsen depressive symptoms (e.g., glucocorticosteroids, some antihypertensives, interferons, others)
11. Living in poverty without means to improve

Risk Factors Predicting a Subsequent Episode
1. Continuation of or newly acquired risk factors associated with an initial episode
2. Subsequent episode; each episode confers added risk and progressively shorter intervals between episodes
3. Incomplete recovery from previous episode; failure to achieve remission
4. Insufficient dose and duration of antidepressant and/or psychotherapeutic treatment
5. Significantly reduced fidelity of intervention provided (e.g., provider inadequately trained to provide cognitive-behavioral therapy)
6. Non-adherence to treatment due to negligible therapeutic alliance, drug side effects, misinformation, many others
7. Psychotic and/or catatonic and/or atypical features
8. Comorbid conditions (e.g., alcohol or substance abuse or dependence, panic disorder, sub-clinical or clinical bipolar disorder, personality

the increased vulnerability of women is very persuasive; data about differential variability in clinical course has not been firmly established (Lewis-Hall et al., 2002).

Childhood psychosocial adversity

Childhood abuse is a tragedy and a poorly quantified epidemic. There is substantial evidence that children who are traumatized by various forms of abuse, neglect and parental deprivation are at substantially increased risk for the development of mood and anxiety disorders in adolescence and adulthood (Berent and Stein, 1999; Glaser, 2000; Heim and Nemeroff, 2001). Moreover, childhood abuse alters the brain and neurophysiological response systems so as to predispose to mood and anxiety disorders (Dettling et al., 2002).

There is considerable certainty about the linkage between abuse and risk. Both prenatal, postnatal and childhood mal-treatment, neglect and abuse and similar horrific experiences are associated with depression (Kaufman, 1991; Kaufman et al.,

2000). Most studies find that other psychiatric disorders (e.g., conduct and oppositional disorders, attention-deficit/hyperactivity disorder) antecede or accompany depression in youngsters (Rhode et al., 1991; Costello et al., 1999). High quality and responsive parenting offers protection from depression (Werner and Smith, 2001). On the other hand, growing up with a depressed parent or parents (or caretaker) or dysfunctional role models likely results in increased risk for the involved children; the magnitude of this risk is unknown (Costello et al., 2002).

Reinherz and colleagues (Reinherz, 2000) have identified specific age-related, psychosocial risk factors. Greater risk for major depression a decade or more later is associated at age 5 with hostility; and at age 9 with poor peer acceptance, anxiety, and sub-clinical depressed feelings. There are gender differences; subsequent major depression is predicted for boys at ages 3-5 by poor physical health; for girls at age 9 by the history of death of a parent and by poor academic performance.

Behavioral, interpersonal conflict and personality traits

The concept of vulnerability due to extra-personal factors is central to psychosocial and maturational theoretical models that assert a relationship between childhood and adult psychopathology and is part of the foundation for primary prevention in mental health (Price and Lento, 2001). This approach identifies persons at risk based on their behavioral and personality traits. The following formulation illustrates this approach.

Child and adolescent development consists of phases, each of which contains difficulties and obstacles encountered in affective, cognitive, social-behavioral, and biological systems. Unsuccessful negotiation of these encounters results in diminished competencies and, thereby, makes the "scared" youngster more vulnerable to

affective disorders and other forms of mental illness later in life (Strofe, 1997). Toxic interpersonal dynamics serve to shape patterns of thinking and beliefs (Garber and Flynn, 2001). For example, an adult may be more vulnerable to depression if s/he has come to believe that certain events are beyond his or her control and/or that assertiveness and self-defense are to be avoided at all costs. A belief system based on absence of control tends to result from the complex interaction between a shy or fearful temperament, overprotective or abusive parents, and early life experiences during which the child has diminished control (Chorpita and Barlow, 1998).

The profile of personal and/or cognitive attributes that pertain to depression and that are developed in childhood have been given various names: "learned helplessness" (Abramson and Alloy, 1978; Nolen-Hoeksema et al., 1986)," "maladaptive self-control" (Rehm, 1977), "depressive self-schema" (Beck, 1979), "low self-esteem" (Brown and Harris, 1989) and others. The depressotypic cognitive styles or coping systems that produce hopelessness have drawn considerable attention. The Hopelessness Theory of Depression (Abramson and Alloy, 1999) asserts that highly desired but unattainable outcomes and undesired aversive outcomes are proximal factors that mediate depression in vulnerable individuals.

Childhood and adolescent major depression

There is a growing consensus that various forms of childhood and early adolescent depression predate the mood disorders found in adults. There is a growing amount of population-based and prospective evidence for this assertion (Garber and Flynn, 2001; Costello et al., 2002). Indeed, an episode of adolescent depression confers a very high risk for recurrences in adulthood which tend to be more severe and recurrent, especially for those with a family history of depression (Weissman et al., 1988; Rao et al., 1999; Weissman et al., 1999a; Fergusson and Woodward, 2002). Prepubertal depression may lead to later problems with drugs and conduct (Weissman et al., 1999b), or lead to later depression, often with a recurrent and chronic course (Kovacs, 1996; Pine et al., 1999).

Adult psychosocial adversity; stressful life events

It has long been recognized that the first episode of depression is preceded by psychosocial adversity (Pakel, 1982; Hammen, 2001). Abuse, loss/abandonment/ death, separation, rejection, public humiliation, and interpersonal conflict are some of the more common themes. The mixture of serious life adversity and a vulnerable personality profile appears to activate a psychoneurophysiological cascade of events that, together, result in symptoms (e.g., depressed affect) of depression (Monroe and Simon, 1991). Major depression is predicted by the occurrence of significant personal adversity in the 12 months prior to onset (Kendler et al., 1995). Such an event is experienced by approximately 70 to 90% of seriously depressed persons; 25 to 40% is the figure for non-depressed comparison groups (Brown and Harris, 1989). Moreover, after several episodes, each new episode may occur autonomously without a preceding significant stressor (Post, 1992). However compelling this theory may be, it is unknown why an affective response to psychosocial stress leads to clinically significant depression for one at risk individual and not for another. A seemingly similar individual, when faced with a similar or even more severe stressor, has an affective response without becoming clinically depressed. Surely, what constitutes a severe psychosocial stress varies across quite similar individuals. Presumably, the

individualized, unique meaning of the stress and a combination of other risk factors and protective factors (e.g., genetics, number of prior episodes, female sex, age, social supports, etc.) come into play (O'Hara, 1995; Kendler et al., 2001).

Lower education and income, separation and divorce, and Hispanic ethnicity are all predict higher rates of major depressive episode (Blazer et al., 1994). In some situations, psychosocial adversity appears to be one of the behavioral consequences of depression and appears not to contribute to its immediate cause. Strong, supportive intimate relationships predict lower risk (Brown and Harris, 1978; Roberts and Gotlib, 1997).

There is abundant evidence that aversive life events, subjectively defined as meaningful and extremely stressful, are prominent factors associated with the onset of most mood disorders. This linkage is established for children, adolescents and adults. Less is known about what factors perpetuate and maintain the depressed state.

Depressotypic cognitive interpretations of one's circumstances

Aaron Beck (1967) was among the first investigators to argue that cognitive mechanisms developed in childhood and adolescence place an individual at increased risk for major depression later in life. Beck proposed that traumatic situations that end poorly are prototypical of subsequent experiences that activate a recurrent cognitive-behavioral response that fosters depression. Numerous variations of Beck's model exist. The core of each variation is quite similar: Information is processed in a fashion that distorts aspects of reality and yields conclusions that magnify misattribution and that are excessively pessimistic and ultimately self-defeating (Hammen, 2001). Anyone who has worked with depressed individuals readily accepts the accuracy of this description, but do such cognitions qualify as a risk factor? Alternatively, are such cognitions merely symptoms of the disease?

The most recent research suggests that dysfunctional attitudes are present in both the depressed and non-depressed state, with decreases in the non-depressed state (Zuroff et al., 1999). Hopelessness, however, may be the core cognitive inference most associated with depression and suicide (Abramson and Alloy, 1999; Abramson et al., 2002). Another possibility is that there is a depressogenic cognitive trait that is latent and becomes activated by on or a series of unacceptable, adverse life events (Hedlund and Rude, 1995; Segal et al., 1999). Despite its intuitive appeal, "inconclusive" seems to best fit the hypothesis that forms of cognitive processing *predict* risk for major depression. Further research is needed to more precisely identify and specify the relationships that this cognitive construct has to the antecedents of serious depression.

Prodromal depressive symptoms; minor or subsyndromal depression

In general, antecedent subsyndromal depressed states have a high probability of being transformed into major depressions (Horwath et al., 1992). Alternatively, early symptoms may rightfully be viewed as early manifestations that arise consequent to unidentified causal factors.

Precursors and prodromal symptoms that occur before the onset of depression are non-specific; they do not invariably lead to depression, even in the absence of an intervention. Such attributes as dysthymia and depressive personality and subthreshold depressive symptomatology may place some individuals at high risk for a first episode of major depression. Moreover, often the interval is very short between the onset of mild depressive affective symptomatology and the onset of major depression (Klein and Anderson, 1995). Course modifiers remain to

be definitely identified and understood in mechanistic terms. However compelling is this continuum model of depression, there have been an insufficient number of prospective studies to persuasively confirm the proposed linkages and the extent of the risk is unclear. For some individuals with minor forms of depression, it is quite possible that their lifelong subsyndromal depressive profile remains relatively stable over time. Such individuals may simply adapt to a life of low-grade depression.

Older adults; serious medical and neurological illness; medications

For older adults and most certainly the elderly, various medical and neurological conditions appear to be major risk factors for depression (Ranga and Krishnan, 2002). Although it is uncommon for medications to cause or worsen depression, the list of possible offenders is lengthy (Margolis and Swartz, 2002). While not insignificant, genetic factors are likely less significant for this age group (Maier, 1991). Since serious medical illness has to be a major life adversity, any resulting increased risk may be more due to general stress and adversity than due to the specific illness. Major depression is quite common following many neurological conditions (e.g., stroke, Parkinson's disease, Alzheimer's disease, various cerebrovascular changes, and others) (Starkstein and Robinson, 1993). A head injury in early adulthood increases risk for major depression for subsequent decades by about 5% compared to matched controls (Holsinger and Steffens, 2002). Accordingly, almost any neurological condition affecting the central nervous system should be considered a risk factor for subsequent major depression. Procedures and criteria vary for diagnosing depression in the context of or concurrent with medical diseases (Alexopoulos et al., 2002). Therefore, the numerical values for rates of depression in the medically and neurologically ill are always suspect and are without reference to the location of the diagnosis along the continuum of depressive symptomatology and without further knowledge about the heterogeneous nature of depression in late life.

There is a collection of well-known and often expected unfortunate life events that come with age. Besides medical illness, there is death of a loved one, less desirable living circumstances, disability, reduced cognitive capacity, increasing social isolation, financial problems and so forth. All such changes have been identified as risk factors for major depression (Bruce, 2002). In aged populations, medical conditions are found in close association with major depression; however, cause and effect relationships are most uncertain (Ranga and Krishnan, 2002). Furthermore, cognitive impairment and/or cerebrovascular disease may result in excessive disability and poor antidepressant and psychotherapeutic treatment responses (Alexopoulos et al., 1996; Alexopoulos et al., 2000). Whether risk is best explained by the general term "adverse life events," or one or more specific adverse events or the sequence of events is the subject of ongoing research. The familiar negative effects of adversity do not necessarily all have to be expected. Counterbalancing psychosocial factors may alter expectations, sometime dramatically. Successful aging may have less to do with genetics and more to do with the many lifestyle choices made over the course of a lifetime. Examples include exercise and dietary habits, meaningful involvement with people, seeking mental challenges and so forth (Rowe and Kahn, 1998).

PREVENTING THE INITIAL EPISODE OF MAJOR DEPRESSION AND REDUCING INCIDENCE

See Table 2. Depression has been identified by the Institute of Medicine Committee on the Prevention of Mental Disorders as the most preventable of all the mental disorders (Institute of Medicine, 1994; Munoz et al., 1996). Unfortunately, for primary prevention of depression this assertion is without much empirical evidentiary support. Research concerning the primary prevention of depression is undernourished; the research that has been done shows great promise. *The distinction between primary prevention and early detection and intervention is blurred since there is not a distinct boundary separating depressive symptoms and major depression.*

Prevention programs that target youth below the age of 12

The origins of depression stem from an early age. Recent advances in the diagnosis of youth depression permit empirical prevention studies to be based on valid and reliable diagnoses (Ryan, 2001), and high-risk youth can be identified in both population- and in home-based samples (Beardslee and Gradstone, 2001). Such studies are methodologically difficult and require large samples and appropriate sub-samples that permit longitudinal surveillance. These substantial constraints account for the small number of target programs aimed at the prevention of depression in youth. Two such studies have been completed (Table 2); strict randomization or placebo controls were impossible because the interventions took place in the public school system.

Kellam et al. 1994.

In theory, poor academic achievement is a risk factor of depression and improving competence reduces depressive symptoms. This ambitious study targeted 685 first-grade children in 44 classrooms in 19 different schools in Baltimore, Maryland. On average, the children had baseline depression severity scores consistent with major depression. From fall to spring, the experimental group was exposed to an enriched curriculum

Table 2. Preventing the Initial Episode of Major Depression in Children, Adolescents and Adults

Authors	Questions Asked	Age	Severity (average or lowest score)	n	Participants' Clinical Features	Treatments	Months of Follow-up	Clinical Outcomes
Kellam SG, et al., 1994	Does improved reading skills reduce depressive symptoms?	6.3	13.5	685	First-graders in one of 44 classrooms in 19 schools.	Classroom-based enriched reading curriculum vs. behavior management strategy.	9	Regression models link improvements in the course of depressive symptoms and progress in learning to read for boys only.
Jaycox LH, et al., 1994	Does group teaching of cognitive techniques prevent depressive symptoms in youth at risk for depression?	11.4	≥ 9.5	143	Adolescents with sub-clinical symptoms: conduct problems, low social competence, etc.	Manual-based, cognitive-behavioral training and/or social problem solving skills vs. control.	6	Incidence of moderate depressive symptoms: 14%=intervention, 25%=control.
Clark GN, et al., 2001	Does teaching cognitive behavioral skills and strategies prevent depression?	14.5	< 4	94	Adolescents; 67% history of major depression. Parent(s) depressed within past 12 months. HMO-based.	15, one-hour manual-based group sessions teaching cognitive behavioral skills and strategies, and usual care vs. Usual care done.	15 24	Incidence of major depression: 9.3% = intervention, 28.8% = control. 21% = intervention, 32% = control.
Clarke N, et al., 1995	Does group teaching of cognitive techniques prevent unipolar depression in "demoralized" youth?	15.3	≥ 18.2	150	Adolescents with sub-clinical symptoms and at elevated risk for future major depression; 72% had hx. major depression.	15-session, manual-based, cognitive group prevention vs. usual care control.	13	Unipolar depression incidence rates: 14.5% = intervention, 25.7% = control; but minimal change in pre/post severity scores.

Study	Research question			N	Population	Intervention		Results
Seligman EP, et al., 1999	Does group plus individual CBT[a] education prevent major depression in at risk college freshman?	19	≤ 15	231	College freshman with a pessimistic attributional style.	16 hours over 8 weeks of group plus 6 hours of individual sessions; CBT[a] strategies vs. control	36	Incidence of major depression: 13.2% = intervention, 10.9% = control. Not significant.
Peden AR, et al., 2001	Does a course aimed at reducing negative symptoms decrease depressive symptoms?	19.3	12.7	92	Single college women without hx. of depression or previous psychiatric care.	Six 1-hour small group sessions vs. controls.	18	Women with severity score ≥ 7: 15% = intervention, 29% = control.
Vinokur AD, et al., 1995	Does skill enhancement prevent increased depressive symptoms and promote reemployment?	34.7	≤ 7	1,801	Unemployed adults at low- or high-risk for increases in depressive symptoms.	Five 4-hour manual-based, skill building seminars vs. controls.	6	High-risk intervention group had greatest reduction in depressive symptoms; 56% reemployed vs. 46% controls.
Munoz RF, et al., 1995	Does a course on cognitive behavioral methods prevent major depression in a sample of primarily minority participants?	52.5	13	150	Low-income, mostly jobless, minority from primary care clinics.	8-session, manual-based course on cognitive-behavioral methods vs. controls.	12	5% overall incidence of depressive disorders. No differences between groups.

[a] "CBT" is cognitive-behavioral psychotherapy

designed to improve reading achievement; the control group received behavioral management aimed at reducing aggressive behavior. Regardless of countermeasures, there was considerable intervention variability across classrooms. Hypotheses are tested with regression models. In general, lower achievement predicted more depressive symptoms. Improvements in reading achievement for boys were linked to reductions in depressive symptoms. For boys, high depression severity appeared to be an impediment to achievement gains. For girls, achievement and reduction in depressive symptoms occurred in both the experimental and the control groups. Several hypotheses are suggested to account for the differential outcomes by gender. *Comment. The high prevalence of significant depressive symptoms among first-graders is a significant finding.*

Jaycox et al. 1994.

On the basis of current level of depressive symptoms and perception of parental conflict, 5th and 6th grade children self-selected for participation; 10-12 students formed a group—one group in each of six schools. There were three active and three control groups. Prior to receiving the intervention 24% of the children were above a severity score indicating moderate depressive symptoms. The intervention taught skills (e.g., assertiveness and negotiation, social problem solving, etc.) and gave weekly homework assignments. The treatment group was expected to have fewer depressive symptoms and behavior problems at six-month follow-up. No information is given about the frequency, timing, or number of sessions. Attendance is unstated. From the information provided, it is reasonable to conclude that there was considerable variability in compliance and participation. After six months the incidence of moderate depressive symptoms for the intervention

group was 14% versus 25% for controls—not statistically significant. Overall, the level of behavior problems was unchanged.

Prevention programs that target ages 13 – 20 (college freshman)
Clark et al. 1995.

This study demonstrated that depressive disorders may be prevented among adolescent offspring (aged 13-18) of adults treated for depression in a health maintenance organization. The adolescents received 15, one-hour sessions of a manual-based course titled Coping With Stress. Attendance averaged 9.5 sessions; homework completion was 46% of the sessions attended. The control group received "usual care," meaning any mental and/or physical health services offered by their HMO. The 94 adolescent participants were judged to be at risk for future depression based on their performance on the Center for Epidemiological Studies Depression Scale (CES-D) plus other measures and based on a history depression in one or both parents. At baseline, the adolescents were judged to have "medium-severity depression." The incidence of depression was assessed at 6 and 12 months using the change in scale scores. The results derived from a survival analysis are impressive. At 15 months (median), 9.3% was the cumulative major depression incidence in the intervention group versus 28.8% for controls. At 24 months, these figures were 21% versus 32%, indicating that gains fade over time. No "booster" sessions were provided after the conclusion of the 15-session course.

Comments. The short-term impressive results are qualified. This study does not qualify for primary prevention because 67% of participants had a history of major depression. There was no placebo group. Placebo response could easily account for the percentage differences between intervention and control. The average baseline CES-D scores were about 24 on average; a score of 16 or higher is used to identify persons with depressive illness. From the CES-D the authors "extracted" scores for the Hamilton Rating Scale for Depression (Ham-D) which averaged about 3—clearly not depressed. These differences in severity measures are unexplained. The intervention group CES-D at 12 months averaged 15.1; 19.5 at baseline. While these are significant differences, many adolescents remained in the depressed range subsequent to the intervention. Given the variability of adolescent depression over time and the high placebo response rate in general, the linkage between intervention and outcome is weakened. Clearly, this sort of study requires replication.

Clarke et al. 2001.

This investigation sought to prevent unipolar depressive disorder in a sample of 9th and 10th grade high school students who were at risk due to having depressive symptom scores on the CES-D and on the Schedule for Affective Disorders and Schizophrenia for School-Age Children. The "demoralized" 150 participants were randomly assigned to either a "usual care" control condition or 15, forty-five minute, after-school sessions of a manual-based course titled Coping With Stress. The median follow-up was 13 months and the follow-up measure was *DSM III-R* diagnostic criteria for unipolar depression. A survival analysis found incidence rates of 14.5% for the intervention; 25.7 for the control.

Comments. The investigators' conclusion that "depressive disorder can be successfully prevented…" cannot go unchallenged. There was a 26.7% total dropout rate which sensors many participants from the survival analysis. Moreover, differences in the continuous measures (e.g., CES-D) were not significant. The explanation of "statistical artifact" is questionable.

Peden et al. 2001.

This investigation if of particular interest because the 92, unmarried, college women participants had no prior exposure to psychiatric care of any sort and had never been diagnosed with clinical depression. Nevertheless, these women had minimal to mild depressive symptom scores on the Beck Depression Inventory (BDI), which provides self-report data. The participants were randomized to either six, one-hour small group sessions that emphasized reducing negative thinking and related cognitive-behavioral strategies or a no-treatment control. At the 18-month follow-up, 15% of the intervention group and 29% of the control group had severity scores above the non-depressed cut-off. BDI severity scores were obtained at 1, 6 and 18 months. Differences between the control and intervention were generally significant; a last-observation-carried-forward analysis strategy was used. The intervention group demonstrated a greater decline in the prevalence of high BDI scores across time; the control group had a less striking decline.

Comments. Only 46% of participants completed the study. The investigators' statement that "no special training is required to implement the intervention" suggests a relatively weak intervention. No information is provided about session attendance and adherence. Moreover, numerous factors are unaccounted for. The emotional life and experiences of freshman are enormously variable; self-reports done at self-selected times has the potential for major distortions.

Seligman et al. 1999.

Male (48%) and female (52%) college freshman entered this study between 1991 to 1993 and were followed for three years. Qualifications included scoring in the most pessimistic quartile on attributional explanatory style, scoring less than 19 on the Beck Depression Inventory (BDI), without any other major mental illness, and without current treatment for mental health problems. The average BDI scores qualified the participants for mild-moderate severity of depressive symptoms—clearly at risk for or meeting criteria for major depression. The experimental group received 16 hours of group sessions and homework over eight weeks (i.e., a workshop) and 6 hours of individual sessions spread over two years (i.e., booster sessions). Attendance at the workshop averaged 85%; there was a $400 incentive for completing all phases of the research. The 231, Ivy League participants were randomized to intervention or an assessment-only control group; the attrition rate was a mere 3.5%. At 36 months the incidence of major depression was 13.2% for the experimental group; 10.9% for the controls. This outcome is not significant, although the workshop tended to improve measures of explanatory style.

Prevention programs that target adults
Vinokur et al. 1995.

Job loss is surely a major stress and a risk factor for major depression. For this study, participants were recruited from the Michigan agency that provides unemployment payments. Excluded were participants with more severe depressive symptoms. The investigators developed an index that partitioned the sample into low or high risk for depression. The 1,801 identified participants were randomized to five, four-hour seminars (n = 671) designed to foster job-search and problem-solving skills. The control group (n = 487) received a mailed booklet. Depression was measured by self-reporting symptoms on the Hopkins Symptom Checklist. At six months, the intervention primarily benefited the high-risk participants; 56% were re-employed versus 46% of controls. In terms of reduction in depressive symptoms, 16% separated the two high risk groups. Across all

groups, no one qualified for the diagnosis of depression at six months.

Comments. Comparisons with the other prevention studies reviewed here are made difficult because the Vinokur study used non-clinical measures. The major conclusion from this study is that skill enhancement enhances mental health and re-employment, but determining prevention requires a longer follow-up period and more rigorous measures. This is more of a feasibility study than a prevention study.

Munoz et al. 1995.

An older, largely unemployed minority sample of 150 participants was randomized to either an eight-session course on cognitive behavioral methods or one of two control groups—an information-only or a no-intervention group. The course was based on a manual of procedures adapted for the minority population; 20% never arrived at class. The Beck Depression Inventory (BDI) was used to screen depressive symptoms. At baseline the average participant qualified for mild severity depression; participants with more severe depressive symptoms were screened out. Over the 12-month follow-up the National Institute of Mental Health Diagnostic Interview schedule was used to identify major depression. The overall incidence of depression was 5% and group differences were non-significant. *Comment.* This sample was too small to test the hypothesis, making this a feasibility study.

Summary Comments

Primary prevention strategies show considerable promise, but they are insufficiently developed and are not really available for implementation in community settings (Costello et al., 2002). Selecting heterogeneous samples and providing short-term teaching to improve cognitive skills seems like a weak intervention compared to the long-term strength of likely risk factors.

Among the eight prevention studies to be reviewed, there is not one that begins with a population of participants that at baseline are both unambiguously devoid of depressive symptoms and unambiguously devoid of a history of major depressive disorder. These "prevention" studies begin with participants with risk factors for developing major depressive disorder and with either sub-syndromal symptoms and/or major depressive disorder of low or higher severity. In this context, "prevention" is aimed at reversing severity scores and stopping an early form of depression from being transformed into a more serious depressive condition that might, for example, lead to taking an antidepressant drug for the first time ever.

For an expanded analysis and an alternative viewpoint, the reader is referred to the recent article by William Beardslee and Tracy Gladstone in which they examine most of the above mentioned studies (Beardslee and Gladstone, 2001).

Should antidepressants be used to prevent the first episode of depression?

There is one study that provided antidepressant medication to *asymptomatic* individuals who have never had an episode of major depression but who are at considerable risk (Musselman et al., 2001b). This is a new and highly controversial approach to the prevention of major depression but one that is based on sound scientific underpinnings (Stahl, 2002). For example, it is likely that pathways in the central nervous system altered by major depressive disorder progressively habituate such that over time they become activated by lower and lower severity provocation (Heim and Nemeroff 2001). Moreover, actual brain damage (e.g., hippocampal atrophy) occurs if depression is severe and prolonged (Elzinga and Bremner 2002). If prophylactic antidepressants and/or depression-specific psychotherapy will delay or prevent the first episode of major depression, prevent relapse and prevent treatment resistant depression, these treatments may be preferable to the alternatives. This is the rationale for investigations underway that administer atypical antipsychotics to youths who are at high risk for developing schizophrenia (Yung and McGorry 1997; Tsuang et al., 1999; Tsuang et al., 2002).

SCREENING FOR MAJOR DEPRESSION

The majority of persons with major depressive disorder come to the attention of primary care physicians (Regier et al., 1993), but major depression is unrecognized for about half of these patients (Von Korff et al., 1987). Major depression can be diagnosed effectively with help from any one of a number of screening tools that have considerable clinical utility in primary care settings (Shade, 1998). For these reasons, routinely screening adults for depression is recommended by the United States Preventive Services Task Force (U.S. Preventive Task Force, 2002). The Task Force based its recommendation on an analysis of 14 randomized, controlled trials examining the effectiveness of depression screening in primary care practices (Pignone et al., 2002).

The Task Force was persuaded by the work of Whooley and others (1997) that just *two questions may be as effective as more complicated questionnaires*. "Over the past 2 weeks, have you felt down, depressed or hopeless?" and "Over the last 2 weeks have you felt little interest or pleasure in doing things?" are recommended. Affirmative responses require a more comprehensive assessment. When non-physician clinical personnel feedback the screening information to the primary care physician, the recognition of depression increases two- to three-fold, and the relative risk for major depression is reduced by 13% (Pignone, 2002). There is no data to recommend how often to screen, but screening is indicated in the presence of risk factors. Both the American Academy of Pediatrics and the American Medical Association recommend screening adolescents for depresssion, but their analysis of the relevant data did not persuade the U.S. Preventive Services Task Force to do the same (Pignone et al., 2002).

Does screening improve outcomes? None of the seven outcome studies completed prior to 1998 found screening to have any measurable benefit (Shade, 1998). More recent studies yield somewhat mixed results, but many of these studies lacked sufficient statistical power to detect clinical meaningful differences (Pignone et al., 2002). However, the meta-analysis done by the U.S. Preventative Services Task Force suggests that "overall, screening and feedback reduced the risk of persistent depression."

THE EFFICACY AND EFFECTIVENESS OF ANTIDEPRESSANT MEDICATION

Antidepressants for major depression are both efficacious and effective for major depression. This can be stated unequivocally and is based, in part, on the Agency for Health Care Policy and Research Depression Guideline Panel's comprehensive review of the evidence (1993) provided by over 200 randomized clinical trials. Additional and more recent support comes from a meta-analyis of 81 placebo-controlled, randomized trials of newest antidepressants (Mulrow et al., 1998).

Placebo-response in clinical trials of antidepressants

Nevertheless, questions about the efficacy and the effectiveness of antidepressants stem from the variable but substantial response (10% to 50%) to inert placebos in randomized, industry-funded, controlled trials of antidepressant medications (Walsh, 2002). Based on these sorts of findings it would be *wrong* to conclude that antidepressants are

devoid of clinically meaningful effects. The primary aim of the industry sponsors of these trials is to obtain U.S. Food and Drug Administration (FDA) approval; these trials are *not* designed to prove or disprove whether antidepressants are beneficial to patients who persuasively meet criteria for major depression (Thase, 2002a). As the market for antidepressant has expanded, industry-sponsored trials have more and more included participants with less severe subtypes of depression that respond less favorably to antidepressants (Robinson and Rickles, 2000). Severe forms of major depression tend to be more antidepressant medication responsive, and the less severe subtypes of depression tend to be more placebo-responsive (Kahn et al., 2002; Simon et al., 2002).

Comparative efficacy versus "real world" effectiveness

No single antidepressant or group of antidepressants has been shown consistently to have superior efficacy over any other (Anderson, 2000; Donogue and Hylan, 2001). To demonstrate even modest differences between two effective medications requires procedures that are uncommonly employed (Thase, 2002b).

The "real world" of clinical practice has numerous specific decisions, constraints and complexities that are avoided during clinical trials. Each major element that is essential to the success of a clinical trial is violated commonly in community-based primary care practices. Commonly, primary care physicians and non-psychiatric physicians administer subtherapeutic doses for an insufficient number of months (Katon et al., 1992; Donoghue and Hylan, 2001; Young and Klapp, 2001).

Antidepressant medication selection and dosage adjustments

See Tables 3 and 4. Since there are no clearly superior antidepressants, selection is based on the profile of side effects that are desirable or undesirable. Generally, antidepressants classified as monoamine oxidase inhibitors and tricyclic antidepressants are associated with more and more dangerous side effects and drug interactions. Thus these classes are prescribed almost exclusively by psychiatrists. The newer agents are prescribed by all types of physicians. Tables 3 and 4 provide guidelines for selecting one of the newer agents.

Generally, patients begin taking an antidepressant at the smallest tolerated dose and at 2-7 day intervals increase the dose until the drug manufacture's recommended minimum dose is reached. In the absence of a meaningful therapeutic response in two to eight weeks, the dose is increased; if there is still no response, the dose is increased again and so forth (Schmidt et al., 2000). *An antidepressant is considered ineffective only after there has been no response at maximum dosage for six to eight weeks.* If, rather than full remission, there is a partial response, it is reasonable to recommend that the patient remain on the antidepressant at the maximum dosage for at least a year or more. Most patients with major depressive disorder who adhere faithfully to taking an antidepressant at the maximum therapeutic dose will have a full remission given sufficient time. Generally, the longer the period of major depression, the longer it will take to achieve full remission. The few long-term follow-up studies that have been done find that the vast bulk of patients recover from major depression during the first year on maximum dose antidepressant medication; however, about 20% of patients will take two years to recover, and 10% will take five years. *Most often, antidepressant medication dosages are too small, and the duration of treatment is too short.*

If the first selective serotonin reuptake inhibitor (SSRI) is ineffective, another SSRI product will have a response rate of 50-70%

(Thase et al., 1997; Zarate et al., 1996; Brown and Harrison, 1995). After failing two SSRIs *and assuming the diagnosis of major depression is correct*, the patients should be switched to an antidepressant in another class (e.g., bupriopion, duloxetine, mirtazapine, venlafaxine). The question of what to do when patients fail to respond to a standard trial of treatment with an antidepressant medication is the subject of a national, multisite clinical trial called "Sequenced Treatment Alternatives to Relieve Depression (STAR-D)". Combinations of antidepressants and other psychotropic medications are essential to achieve recovery for some depressed patients. There are guidelines for this sort of polypharmacy (Nassir and Appleton, 2002; Stahl, 2000), but none are based on careful randomized clinical trials.

Better antidepressants are needed

Not only do antidepressants take four to eight weeks have a meaningful clinical response but also some side effects may remain for the entire duration of therapy. For example, one common cause of non-adherence is the sexual dysfunction associated with all but a few antidepressants (Zajecka, 2001). The antidepressants associated with minimal or no sexual dysfunction are: bupropion (Wellbutrin≥), nefazodone (Serzone≥), and mirtazapine (Remeron≥).

THE DIFFERNTIAL EFFICACY AND EFFECTIVENESS OF DEPRESSION-SPECIFIC PSYCHOTHERAPY ALONE COMPARED TO ANTIDEPRESSANT MEDICATION ALONE OR THE COMBINATION

See Table 3. Although numbers of perceptive skeptics remain, there is now a consensus that antidepressants and/or depression-specific psychotherapy are efficacious treatments for mild to moderate major depressive disorder. Depression-specific psychotherapy is any well-defined, empirically-tested, manual- and discussion-based intervention; cognitive behavioral therapy (CBT) and interpersonal psychotherapy (IPT) are used most clinically. These psychotherapies are matched to specific procedures, making it possible to check the fidelity of intervention provision. What remains controversial is the: (1) appropriateness of depression-specific psychotherapy for the more high severity patients (e.g., melancholic depression), (2) capacity of each mode of treatment to achieve remission and prevent relapse, (3) speed of onset of the therapeutic effect, (4) duration of prophylactic efficacy, (5) effectiveness of depression-specific psychotherapy in real world clinical practice, and (6) long-term cost effectiveness. Note: Psychoanalysis is not considered in this class; however, supportive-expressive psychodynamic therapy (SEDT) for depression uses analytic strategies but waits controlled clinical trials (Crits-Christoph et al., 2002) as do other psychodynamic-, psychoanalytic-based strategies adapted for use in major depression.

The most recent published review of this field (Casacalenda et al., 2002) available to this author identified only six randomized, double-blind efficacy studies with the endpoint of full remission from depression that directly compared antidepressants, depression-specific psychotherapy, and controls. Their meta-analysis recorded remission for 46.4% receiving antidepressants, 46.3% receiving depression-specific psychotherapy, and 24.4% receiving a control condition. The patients in these six studies all had mild to moderate severity scores and treatment duration ranged from 10 to 34 weeks. Both treatments were equally effective. This meta-analysis is noteworthy for its focus on full remission. Casacalenda and her colleagues concluded: "Both antidepressant medication and psychotherapy may be considered first-line treatments for mildly to moderately depressed outpatients."

A somewhat modified conclusion is reached by Robert DeRubis (DeRubeis et al., 1999) after doing a meta -analysis of four major randomized comparisons pertaining to the acute outcomes of antidepressant medication and CBT in severely depressed outpatients. DeRubis writes: "Cognitive behavioral therapy has fared as well as antidepressant medication with severely depressed outpatients in four major comparisons. Until findings emerge from current or future comparative trials, antidepressant medication should not be considered, on the basis of empirical evidence, to be superior to cognitive behavior therapy for the acute treatment of severely depressed outpatients."

Hereafter will be reviewed those recent studies that, together, shed additional light on some of the controversial issues (Table 3). No claim is made that these are the most important studies or that bias is totally absent.

Elkin I et al, 1989.

This major study from the National Institute of Mental Health Treatment of Depression Collaborative Program has generated much of the controversy. All outpatients met standard criteria for major depressive disorder ranging from mild to moderate severity; post-intervention follow-up came after four months. Antidepressant (ADM) and case management, interpersonal psychotherapy (IPT), and cognitive behavioral therapy (CBT) were effective. However, antidepressants combined with therapy were not studied. One analysis of a 61-participant sub-sample with more severe depression (HDRS ≥ 20) found ADM + case management versus IPT alone to be equally effective. A related analysis found ADM superior to IPT. The researchers concluded: "Significant differences among treatments were present only for the subgroup of patients who were more severely depressed…there was some evidence of the effectiveness of

Table 3. Depression-Specific Psychotherapy Compared to Antidepressant Medication or the Combination

Authors	Questions Asked	Age	Severity (average or lowest score)	n	Participants' Clinical Features	Treatments	Months Follow-up	Clinical Outcomes
Elkin I, et al., 1989	What is the differential effectiveness of CBT[a], IPT[b], imipramine and clinical management, placebo and clinical management for treating major depressive disorders of various severities?	35	19.5	239	Psychiatric outpatients meeting criteria for major depressive disorders for ≥ 2 weeks.	16-20, fifty-minute sessions of CBT or IPT; ≥ 150 mg imipramine and "clinical management"; placebo and "clinical management".	40	For the 162 participants completing treatment and scored ≤ 6 on the HRSD[c]: 57%=imipramine&case management 55%=IPT, 51%=CBT, 29%=placebo & case management
Schulberg HC, et al., 1996	Comparing antidepressant therapy to ITP to usual care, which is most effective for treating major depression?	38.1	23.1	276	Primary care patients with major depression; 33% of antidepressant and 42% of ITP arm completed treatment.	16 weekly ITP sessions and 4 continuation phase sessions. Nortriptyline at therapeutic blood levels for 3 consecutive visits. Usual care.	8	Percentage Patients ≥ 50% decrease severity: 70% = each intervention, 20% = usual care.
Keller MB, et al.,2000	Is the combination of cognitive-behavioral therapy and antidepressant more efficacious than either treatment alone for treatment of chronic major depression?	43	27	662	Patients with ≥ 2 years of major depressive disorder.	≥ 12 sessions manual-based CBT and/or ≤ 600 mg nefazodone.	4	Rate of response among 519 participants who completed the study: 52% = CBT 55% = nefazodone 85% = combined.
Mynors-Wallace LM, et al., 2000	Is the combination of problem-solving therapy and antidepressants more effective than either treatment alone for management of major depression?	35	19.8	151	Primary care patients; 95% with major depression.	1, one-hour and five, 30-minute therapy sessions ≤ 12 weeks and SSRI vs. each alone.	12	No significant differences. Regardless of intervention: 20-24% recovered; 5-9% partially recovered, 7-9% not recovered.

Table 3. Depression-Specific Psychotherapy Compared to Antidepressant Medication or the Combination

Authors	Questions Asked	Age	Severity (average or lowest score)	n	Participants' Clinical Features	Treatments	Months of Follow-up	Clinical Outcomes
Clark GN, et al., 2002	Does teaching cognitive behavioral skills and strategies add incremental benefit to usual care?	15.3	11.7	88	Adolescents with major depression or dysthymia and with parent(s) depressed within past 12 months. HMO-based.	Manual-based 16, two hour group sessions teaching about cognitive behavioral skills & strategies and usual care vs. usual care alone.	24	Both groups recovered and CBT had no added benefit.
DeRubeis RJ, et al., 2002.	What is the comparative efficacy of CBT vs. antidepressants for acute response and relapse prevention in severe depression?	40.4	23.9	240	Outpatients with moderate to severe depression with average duration = 46.2 months; average number prior episodes = 2.4.	2, one-hour CBT sessions per week vs. ≥35 mg paroxetine vs. placebo.	2	% responders (≤ 12 severity): 49% = paroxetine, 40% = CBT, 25% = placebo.
DeRubeis RJ, et al. 4 months ACUTE PHASE		?	?			CBT continues; paroxetine may be augmented; placebo group stops.	4	57% = paroxetine, 58% = CBT.
DeRubeis RJ, et al. 12 months CONTINUATION PHASE		?	≤ 12	104	Patients responding to acute phase treatment.	3 CBT booster sessions; paroxetine arm divided to drug vs. placebo.	12	% sustained improvement: 30% = paroxetine, 39% = CBT + boosters, 16% = placebo drug.

a   "CBT" is cognitive-behavioral psychotherapy.

b   "IPT" is interpersonal psychotherapy.

c   "HRSD" is Hamilton Rating Scale for Depression.

IPT…and strong evidence of the effectiveness of imipramine plus clinical management." It is noted that "clinical management" is therapy in the form of focused sympathetic attention and encouragement; this is not "usual care."

Schulberg HC et al, 1996.

This investigation attempted to prove that IPT and ADM therapy for major depression are effective in a primary care setting. Intensive IPT (16 weekly sessions and 4 booster sessions) was contrasted with the antidepressant, nortriptyline or usual care. ADM adherence was monitored with blood levels. Both active interventions produced a 70% recovery rate (i.e., at least a 50% decrease in severity score) versus 20% for usual care.

Comments. This widely cited study is compromised because of a high attrition rate (only 33% completed ADM and only 42% completed IPT). Additionally, participants who failed to respond in six – ten weeks were dropped from the study. The major tentative finding, therefore, was that ADM broke away from usual care at one month; by six months, IPT and ADM were equally effective. The combination of therapy and ADM was not tested.

Keller MB et al, 2000.

Keller and his colleagues work is remarkable because the combination of ADM and CBT was rigorously examined; the large sample of 681 adults met standard criteria for major depression with seven to eight years duration, on average. Depression scores were in the very severe range. Acute response is studied. Both interventions were intensive— 20 IPT sessions and, on average, over 450 mg of nefazodone. At four months, 85% of the ADM + CBT group responded compared to about 53% for either alone. The placebo response for depression of this severity is about 12% (Kocsis et al., 1988). Moreover,

at the last follow-up ADM + IPT averaged the lowest severity score (11 vs 16 on the HDRS).

Comments. This study is significant. Short-term, the combination of ADM + CBT is significantly more effective than either intervention alone. Psychotherapy tends to be less effective in the short-term; this study reveals nothing about long-term efficacy.

Mynors-Wallis LM et al, 2000.

This is another widely referenced study; unfortunately, the study is flawed and the results are misstated. For a sample with moderate to severe depression, the interventions dose is too low. The therapy is 3.5 hours over no more than 12 weeks, and patients receiving medication did so for a 10.7 weeks, on average; only one patient received 40 mg of paroxetine (maximum dose is 60 mg). It comes as no surprise that all interventions were equally ineffective at the 12-month follow-up.

Comments. The authors conclusion that "the combination of (problem solving) treatment with antidepressant medication is no more effective than either alone" is simply incorrect! The major conclusion from this study is that even with considerable effort it is difficult to provide adequate doses of antidepressant medication and psychotherapy in a primary care setting.

Clarke GN et al, 2002.

Adolescents at risk for or experiencing major depression received 32 hours of group teaching about cognitive behavioral skills and strategies and usual care; the control group received usual care. All participants were from one health maintenance organization and care was provided in this community setting. "Usual care" could be any mental health services. All the usual mental health services were provided to some members of both groups; on average, over 100 days of antidepressant medications were provided; a very few patients were hospitalized. At 2-

year follow-up there were no significant differences, and the conclusion offered is "group CBT does not appear to be incrementally beneficial…"

Comments. Rather than showing CBT to be a failure, this study is an example of the problems demonstrating CBT's effectiveness in community settings.

DeRubeis RJ et al, 2002.

Because this research is being reviewed for certain publication and not available in print, this study will be reviewed at length. Robert DeRubeis most generously provided the data to be summarized; this reviewer is most appreciative. After hearing the presentation and then going over the data page by page, there is one inescapable conclusion: This investigation is a monumental achievement.

Robert DeRubeis and his many colleagues have the longest-running study that compares antidepressants to cognitive behavioral therapy for patients with more severe depressions—a major feature that distinguishes DeRubeis' research. The mean Hamilton Depression Rating Scale for Depression scores are 23.9 $\pm$ 3.5 (one standard deviation), clearly in the moderate to severe range—but not very severe (i.e. all participants score 23 or more) or extremely severe. However, further attribution of severity is evidenced by an average of 2.4 $\pm$ 2.6 prior episodes. Two sites are used: the University of Pennsylvania (Penn) and Vanderbilt University (Vandy); 240 patients with moderate to severe depression are randomly assigned to cognitive behavioral psychotherapy or paroxetine or placebo. The dose of cognitive behavioral therapy is significant: two, hour-long sessions each week for 16 weeks provided by well-trained therapists. The study has three phases: acute treatment for 16 weeks; continuation treatment for 12 months, and a follow-up phase lasting 12 months. At 8 weeks patients who did not respond to paroxetine could be

augmented with either lithium or desipramine—making the antidepressant arm analogous to good clinical practice. Single-blinded procedures were used; however, the comparison of antidepressant to placebo is triple-blind for the first eight weeks of acute treatment.

At *eight weeks* the Hamilton-scored severity was 13.4 for the antidepressant arm (50% of patients improved) and 16.1 for the placebo arm; no other significant differences. Approximately 45% of cognitive therapy patients improved but this score is not statistically significant. Antidepressants appear to work faster than cognitive therapy. Hereafter, the no treatment arm of the study ceases.

At *sixteen weeks* antidepressants and cognitive behavioral therapy yielded nearly identical mean levels of symptom reduction (53% vs 52%) and response rates (57% vs 58%). Also, antidepressants were more likely than cognitive-behavioral therapy to produce a full remission (45% vs 37%). At 16 weeks the mean dose of paroxetine was 35-40 mg per day—a reasonable but not a maximum dose (i.e., 60 mg).

There were differences across the two sites: at Vandy antidepressants did signify-cantly better than cognitive therapy; whereas at Penn the reverse was true.

The *twelve-month continuation phase* (i.e, 16 months of treatment—4 months of initial plus 12 months continuation treatment) included responders only. Continuing patients receiving antidepressants for the first 16 weeks are randomized in a triple-blind fashion to either antidepressant or placebo—a means of testing for relapse due to stopping an antidepressant. Recall that patients on the antidepressant paroxetine may receive augmentation (41% were augmented) with lithium or desipramine. For this continuation phase, patients who responded to cognitive therapy received no more than three booster sessions—insurance against relapse.

The following rates are from a survival analysis of the 100% who began the 12-month continuation phase. Relapse was avoided by: 75% of those who received cognitive therapy and 60% on antidepressants. Placebo-pills achieved almost no benefit; a mere 19% avoided relapse. While the differences across sites were less pronounced, Penn patients tended to do better with cognitive therapy and Vandy patients with antidepressants, perhaps reflecting the relative strengths of each site.

A preliminary analysis suggests that patients with comorbid generalized anxiety disorder are less likely to respond to cognitive therapy—a surprise since CBT deals with unrealistic worry. Post-traumatic stress disorder (PTSD) was the only comorbidity that predicted relapse. This study is on-going; additional information will become available at the conclusion of the 36 month maintenance/follow-up phase.

Comments. It is reasonable to conclude that for moderately to severely ill patients with major depression: (1) Intensive prior (and booster) cognitive therapy from highly trained therapists is at least as effective as antidepressants in preventing relapse in the near-term; (2) Relapse may be prevented by either continuous use of antidepressants or discontinuous treatment with cognitive behavioral therapy. Moreover, CBT may instill some measure of resilience and enduring usefulness that may be unavailable from antidepressants—surely an important but very tentative conclusion. Unfortunately, there is no test of the efficacy of combination antidepressant medication and depression-specific psychotherapy.

The University of Pennsylvania and Vanderbilt University are major research centers, yet the University of Pennsylvania patients appeared to receive more effective CBT because of their known strength in providing this intervention. This finding leads to one inescapable conclusion: Since there are no measurable differences among patients, high-quality cognitive behavioral therapy appears to be difficult to consistently provide—even in major academic research health care systems.

Cumulative direct costs were calculated. At 16 months, (indefinite) medications cost about $2,590 and (intensive) cognitive therapy cost about $2,250 per patient. Since cognitive therapy is discontinuous, it may be more cost-effective in the long term. Of course, insurance reimbursements favor drugs; few, if any, insurance plans would allow the intensity of psychotherapy provided the study patients.

Summary Comments. None of the samples consisted entirely of very severely depressed patients, and extremely severe depression was not considered. For moderate to very severe patients, antidepressants (ADM) work faster. After about four months, either antidepressants or cognitive-behavioral psychotherapy (CBT) appear to be equally effective when each is administered intensively. The combination of ADM and CBT appears to produce the best results in the short-term. There has been no long-term, rigorous study of ADM versus CBT versus the combination.

PREVENTING THE REOCCURENCE OF MAJOR DEPRESSIVE DISORDER: REDUCING EPISODE SEVERITY AND MAINTAINING RECOVERY

See Table 4. If, after the initial episode of major depression, enough time elapses without therapeutic interventions, almost all patients will have a recurrent episode. Following recovery from the index episode, 20 months is the median length of time to recurrence. In general, the recurrence rate after five years is 60%; after 10 years 75%; and after 15 years 87% (Keller and Boland, 1998). More prior episodes predict a higher frequency of relapse. Indeed, almost 100% of

Table 4. Preventing Reoccurrence and Maintaining Remission

Authors	Questions Asked	Age	Severity (average or lowest score)	n	Participants' Clinical Features	Treatments	Months of Follow-up	Clinical Outcomes
Evans MD, et al., 1992	What is the differential effectiveness in relapse prevention: CBT[a], antidepressant medication (ADM), or the combination?	32.6	≤ 11	38	Responded to 12 weeks of acute treatment with CBT, ADM, or combination.	Imipramine at ≥ 50% of acute treatment dose vs. discontinued CBT and/or drug.	12	Percentages with ≥ 12 on HRSD[b]: 15% = combined CBT + ADM; 21% = CBT discontinued at 3 months; 32% = ADM continued for 1 year; 50% = ADM discontinued at 3 months.
Kupfer DJ, et al., 1992	How long should maintenance treatment last to prevent relapse or recurrence of major depression?	39.2	3.3	20	Prior treatment of major depressive disorder for 3 years without relapse or recurrence.	Imipramine 236 mg average dose/d vs. placebo vs. discretionary monthly IPT[c] or clinic visits (78% received).	24	≤15 on HRSD: 89% = antidepressant ±IPT, 33% = placebo ±IPT, 11% = placebo & no IPT.
Keller MB, et al., 1998	Does maintenance antidepressant treatment prevent recurrence of depression in high-risk patients?	40.7	5.9	161	Outpatients; responded to sertraline after 1-month acute and 4-months continuation treatment.	Variable doses (mean = 146 mg/d) of sertraline vs. placebo.	18	Relapse rate: 6% = antidepressant, 23% = placebo.
Harkness KL, et al., 2002	Does maintenance interpersonal psychotherapy prevent recurrence of unipolar depression due to potentially triggering life events?	40.2	≤ 8	83	Women with prior episode(s) of unipolar depression, now in full remission. Subjects receiving fluoxetine (n = 23) discontinued drug.	Biweekly maintenance interpersonal psychotherapy.	24	The 32% relapse rate predicted by fluoxetine discontinuation but not by life events.
Lenz EJ, et al., 2002	What is the differential effectiveness of alternative maintenance treatments for late-life depression for preventing recurrence and improving social functioning?	≥ 60	≤ 10	49	Outpatients with major depressive disorder that responded to 16 weeks of continuation therapy.	Monthly IPT & nortriptyline vs. IPT & clinic visits vs. IPT & placebo drug vs. clinic visits and placebo drug.	12	Regardless of active intervention 100% avoided relapse; most of the placebo group relapsed; only IPT & nortriptyline improved scores on social functioning.

[a] "CBT" is cognitive-behavioral psychotherapy.   [b] "HRSD" is Hamilton Rating Scale for Depression.
[c] "IPT" is interpersonal psychotherapy.

138

patients with three or more previous episodes will have a recurrent episode of major depression (Keller and Berndt, 2002). Unfortunately, less than 10% of individuals with unipolar depression receive adequate treatment for a sufficient length of time (Hirschfeld et al., 1997). Prophylactic treatment using maintenance therapy is indicated. The research summarized below provides guidelines about the constituents of such therapy.

Preventing a subsequent episode after one or more episodes of major depression
Evans MD et al, 1992.

All patients met standard criteria for unipolar major depression and responded to three-months of antidepressant medication, CBT, or the combination. For 12 months, antidepressant medication continued for one half of the sample. CBT and the combination stopped at three months. The majority of responders had been depressed for less than six months; 52% had three or more previous episodes; 22% were first-episode patients. At the beginning of the two-year follow up period, patients had either recovered or had mild depressive symptoms. At follow-up 15% of the CBT + ADM relapsed; 21% for CBT discontinued at 3 months; 32% for ADM continued for a year; and 50% relapse for ADM discontinued at 3 months. Patients treated to recovery with CBT had a 64% reduction in risk compared to patients treated with ADM for only 3 months.

Comments. Importantly*, ADM was allowed to fall to one-half of the maximum dosage that resulted in the response at 3 months.* While this study concludes that CBT prevents relapse as well as CBT + ADM, the quailfication is that ADM is ineffective if continued at a lower dosage than the dose that produced a response.

Kupfer DJ et al, 1992.

Prior to entry, the patients in this study had been successfully treated for three years. In contrast to the previous investigation, this two-year follow-up study (5 years total) continued ADM at or near the maximum dose (236 mg imipramine, on average). Also, the majority of patients continued to receive once monthly psychotherapy. By far the best outcome was that 89% of the ADM group remained well; 33% for the psychotherapy and placebo drug intervention; and a mere 11% for the no treatment group. The investigators recommend prophylaxic treatment for at least 5 years. *Comments.* This has been a very influential study of only 20 patients.

Keller MB et al, 1998.

The 161 patients in this study responded to sertraline by 5 months. Thereafter, the patients were randomly assigned to up to 200 mg of sertraline (the maximum dose) or placebo and followed for 18 months. Recurrence occurred in only 6% of the ADM patients versus 23% of the placebo group. Depressive symptoms reemerged in 23% of the ADM patients as opposed to 50% of placebo patients.

Harkness KL et al, 2002.

Due to a history of previous episodes of major depression, the 83 female participants were at high risk for recurrence. The sample was randomly bifurcated: 28% achieved remission on fluoxetine (ADM), and the remaining 72% achieved remission with interpersonal psychotherapy (IPT) alone. ADM is discontinued, and all participants receive biweekly maintenance IPT. After two years, 32% have relapsed, and those who discontinued fluoxetine had a three-fold higher risk of recurrence compared to those who remitted on IPT alone.

Comments. Because life events failed to predict recurrence, the investigators concluded that IPT reduces the capacity of life events to trigger recurrences. Since the statistical models fail to include severity scores from prior depressive episodes, this interpretation is weak. An alternative interpretation may be more persuasive: Maintenance IPT alone is unlikely to prevent recurrent depression of high-risk patients who discontinue ADM therapy at the beginning of the maintenance period. The quality of the IPT is an unmeasured variable.

Lenze EJ et al, 2002.

The subjects in this study were aged 60 and over. All 49 outpatients remitted after 16 weeks of ADM (nortriptyline) and IPT provided without blinded procedures. Thereafter, patients were randomly assigned to one of four experimental conditions: ADM + IPT, ADM + medication visits, placebo + IPT, or placebo + medication visits. Follow-up after 12 months excluded the placebo + medication visit group—almost all had recurrent major depression. A prior study (Reynolds et al., 1999) found that these individual were more likely to remain in recovery if they were maintained on ADM + IPT. This present study considered effects on social adjustment and found that combination therapy is more likely to maintain social adjustment than treatment with ADM or IPT alone.

Comments. This study suggests strongly that antidepressant medications or depression-specific psychotherapy is mandatory if relapse is to be avoided; however, the combination appears benefit social functioning.

Summary Comments

Relapse is predicted by either discontin-uing or lowering the therapeutic dose of antidepressant medications.While depression-specific psychotherapy appears to prevent relapse, these studies do not reveal the patient attributes that best predict a favorable outcome for depression-specific psycho-therapy. If, for example, there is a history of three severe episodes of major depression that included suicidal ideation, is relapse avoided

if the patient receives depression specific psychotherapy? If so, what is the dose of the psychotherapy?

MAJOR DEPRESSION HAS CONSEQUENCES FOR CARDIOVASCULAR AND OTHER CHRONIC DISEASES

Depression's consequences for chronic diseases

Major depression is bad for your health. Although depression is brain disease, it has consequences for the entire body (Thakore , 2001). Depression has been persuasively linked to morbidity and/or mortality associated with heart disease, stroke, diabetes, dementia, osteoporosis, and immune system-related disorders (Wulsin et al., 1999; Appels et al., 2000; Jonas and Mussolino, 2000; Kronfol and Remick, 2000). Depression is associated with premature death from cancer (Newport and Nemeroff 1998; Musselman et al., 2001a). Certain medical drugs can trigger a major depression that can be successfully prevented and/or treated with antidepressants (Musselman et al., 2001b). Because of depression's capacity to profoundly reduce overall sense of wellbeing, depression can result in excessive disability for nearly every disease and treatment for depression leads to significant improvement (Coulehan et al., 1997; Thakore, 2001). Additionally, de-pression is a risk factor for noncompliance with medical treatment (DiMattteo et al., 2000).

Depression's consequences for heart disease

There is burgeoning scientific evidence that depression is related to increased morbidity and mortality in patients with acute and chronic cardiac syndromes (Connerney et al., 2001; Jiang et al., 2001; Musselman et al., 1998; Frasure-Smith et al., 1993). Depression predicts mortality from cardiac events regardless of one's baseline history of cardiac disease; the excess mortality risk is more than twice as high for major as compared to minor depression (3.0-3.9 versus 1.5-1.6) (Penninx et al., 2001).

If depression symptoms improve, do cardiac outcomes improve?

The initial results from two major longitudinal studies consider the relationship between the treatment of depression and changes in cardiac outcomes. Enhancing Recovery in Coronary Heart Disease Patients (ENRICHD) is a multicenter, randomized, controlled trial that targets 2481 individuals with low social support, a known psychosocial risk factor for poor cardiac outcomes. Cognitive behavioral therapy for depression is the intervention, and survival and reinfarction for both men and women are the outcome variables (ENRICHD investigators, 2001). Preliminary information from this trial is not encouraging. In a sample of post-myocardial infarction patients, the mortality rate for patients undergoing cognitive behavioral therapy is nearly identical to the rate for the control condition, usual care (Berkman et al., 2001).

The relationship between improvements in depression severity and mortality was the subject of another large multicenter clinical investigation (Lesperance et al., 2002). The sample consisted of 896 acute myocardial patients. Severity scores were obtained when each of these patients was hospitalized and again one year later. Mortality was assessed over a five-year period; only 2.9% of patients were lost to follow-up. All patients received usual care. Depression severity scores at one year predicted mortality in dose-response relationship. As depression severity scores increased so did mortality rates. Regarding improvements in depression severity, the difference between baseline severity and severity at one year was just enough to permit a regression analysis. For patients with moderate to severe depressive symptoms at

baseline, symptom improvement had no effect on outcome. However, for patients with mild depressive symptoms, change in depression severity scores was linked to perceived social support and predicted a better prognosis.

Summary Comments

Death from cardiovascular disease is the result of the long-term accumulation of multiple risk factors and physiological events. Short-term changes in behavior or mood are unlikely to have much impact on this relentless, long-term course. Mood and behavior change is surely best integrated into a standard cardiovascular risk reduction program that targets dietary, exercise, biologic, and mood and behavior change targets. There is every reason to treat depression in the cardiovascular patient, but intervention early in the course of both diseases will likely result in the best outcomes.

THE INTEGRATION AND FINANCING OF MENTAL AND BEHAVIORAL HEALTH AND PRIMARY CARE SERVICES IN ORGANIZED MEDICAL SETTINGS

See Table 5. Historically, the provision of primary care medicine has been done by organizations designed to provide "walk-in" services. After all, the concept of health maintenance organizations and health promotion gained momentum with the Health Maintenance Organization Act of 1973 (Luft and Harold, 1981; Druss, 2002). While considerable organizational heterogeneity exists across health provision systems, it is expected that primary care providers treat common illnesses rather than refer them to specialists. Since the vast bulk of depressed patients come to the attention of a primary care provider (Pincus et al., 1998), primary care medical settings need to be organized to both diagnose and treat depressed patients. Unfortunately, depression is under-diagnosed

Table 5. Integrating Mental Health and Primary Care Service in Organized Medical settings

Authors	Questions Asked	Severity (average or lowest score)	n	Participants' Clinical Features	Treatments	Months of Follow-up	Clinical Outcomes
Katon W, et al., 1995	Does improvements in antidepressant adherence improve outcomes for *major depression?*	43	91	≥ 16	*Major depression;* 72% history of ≥ 2 prior depressive episodes.	Collaborative management vs. usual care.	12	Adherence: 76% = intervention, 50% = usual care. $\geq 50\%$ severity score improvement: 75% = intervention, 44% = usual care.
Katon W, et al., 1995	Does improvements in antidepressant adherence improve outcomes for *minor depression?*	51	126	≥ 9	*Minor depression;* 73% history of ≥ 2 prior depressive episodes.	Collaborative management vs. usual care.	12	Adherence: 88% = intervention, 48% = usual care. $\geq 50\%$ severity score improvement: 60% = intervention, 68% = usual care.
Katon W, et al., 1999	After failing usual care, does collaborative care for major depression improve antidepressant adherence and outcomes?	47	228	≥ 11	Dysthymia (55%) and major depression (80%); ≥ 3 prior depressive episodes.	After failing 6-8 weeks usual care, provided collaborative care or continued usual care.	6	Adherence: 69% = intervention, 44% = usual care. Symptom remission: 44% = intervention, 31% = usual care.
Katzelnick DJ, et al., 2000	If depressed high utilizers of medical services receive extensive depression management from their primary care clinic, is services utilization reduced?	46	407	19	Major depression; 34% visited a mental health professional in last 2 years.	Extensive case management by non-psychiatrists vs. usual care.	12	Antidepressant adherence at 6 months: 69% = intervention, 19% = usual care. Symptom remission at 12 months: 45% = intervention, 28% = usual care. Outpatient visit frequency: no difference.
Unützer J, et al., 2002	Is depression treatment outcomes improved when mental health services are a component of primary care?	71	1,801	≥ 11	Major depression (17%), dysthymia (30%), both (53%); ≥ 2 prior depressive episodes.	Mental health services from a depression clinic specialist vs. usual care.	12	$\geq 50\%$ severity score improvement: 60% = intervention, 30% = usual care. Symptoms remission: 25% = intervention, 7.5% = usual care.

12/18/2002

142

and under-treated in primary care and most other medical settings (Hirschfeld et al., 1997). If this unsatisfactory situation is to change, the coordination and integration of mental health and primary care services is essential. There has been considerable research in this area that will be reviewed selectively. Most of the work pertains to the management of uncomplicated mild to moderate depression, which can be successfully treated in primary care.

Models of collaboration between mental health professionals and primary care physicians
Katon WL et al, 1995.

This investigation asserts that despite the proven efficacy of antidepressant medication, most depressed primary care patients are not benefited because of under dosing and overly short periods of administration. To rectify this, a collaborative management intervention was designed to achieve the dosage recommendations of the Agency for Health Care Policy and Research. Over a 12-month period, 217 patients with major (42%) and minor (58%) depression were randomized either to usual care or intensive care. Intensive care included patient education, additional and more frequent visits with the primary care doctor and with a consulting psychiatrist, and surveillance of medication adherence. Usual care could include referral for mental health services. The analysis compared 12-month results for major and minor depression.

Compared to usual care, both diagnostic groups had significantly better medication adherence (e.g., 76% vs 50%), and considered antidepressants helpful (e.g., 88% vs 63%). At least a 50% improvement in depression severity occurred for 75% of patients with major depression versus 44% for usual care, a highly significant difference. This measure of improvement was achieved by nearly

identical percentages (60% vs 67%) with minor depression; for this diagnosis more intensive services had the same outcome as less intensive usual care.

Katon WL et al, 1999.

If patients with major depression and a new antidepressant prescription remained depressed after six to eight weeks of usual primary care, they were "stepped up" to collaborative care. This second step consisted of educational materials (book and videotape about depression), one 50-minute and two 25-minute sessions with a psychiatrist, and psychotherapy and additional psychiatry visits as clinically indicated. The mental health team gave verbal and written consultation reports to the primary care physician and monitored antidepressant adherence with pharmacy records. Usual care provided antidepressant medication, two to three visits with the primary care doctor over three months, and provider or patient-initiated referrals for mental health services.

Dysthymia (55%) and mild to severe major depression (80%) characterized the 228 adult participants from four large clinics; 73% completed the six-month study. Antidepressant adherence was 73% for the intervention versus 50% for usual care; 69% of intervention and 44% of usual care received doses recommended by the Agency for Health Care Policy and Research. Symptom remission was achieved by 44% of the intervention group versus 31% usual care. Intervention patients were more satisfied with the care received. All results are statistically significant.

Katzelnick DJ et al, 2000.

A disproportionately high percentage of patients with unrecognized or under treated depression consume general medical services. Accordingly, this research targeted this consumer group. Sampling was done in 163 primary care practices in one of three health maintenance organizations (Northwest, Midwest, New England). The 407 patients enrolled met criteria for moderate to severe major depression and had numbers of regular outpatient visits in the 85th percentile for the two prior years. At least one chronic medical problem characterized 47% of participants. The patients were randomly assigned to either a depression management program (DMP) (physician and patient education, anti-depressant medication, treatment coordin-ation, follow-up phone monitoring) or usual care. Under the DMP, the primary care doctors were provided two hours of training about the assessment and antidepressant treatment of major depression and explicit antidepressant medication algorithms. Patients were prescheduled to have supplementary visits with the doctor. At each site, one or two psychiatrists provided consultation to the DMP. No information is provided about the exact nature of the psychiatric consultation, but face-to-face patient contact with the consulting psychiatrist was likely infrequent. Blinded assessments yielded outcome measures.

Over 93% of the sample completed the 12-month assessment. At six months, anti-depressant adherence was 69% in the DMP versus 18% receiving usual care. A 50% reduction in depression severity was achieved by 53% of the DMP patients versus 33% usual care patients. Full remission from major depression was obtained by 45% in DMP versus 28% in usual care. While the intervention group improved more on scales measuring mental health, social functioning, and general health perceptions, *the change in outpatient visit frequency was not significantly different between groups.* Of those in usual care, 42% became involved in mental health services; this percentage is unreported for the intervention group.

Comments. The absence of help from psychiatry and depression-specific psycho-therapy is noteworthy. This study seems to demonstrate that with considerable support primary care physicians are able to improve the overall quality and outcomes of care for patients with major depression. Since the frequency of ambulatory visits is determined by a lifetime of experience and habit, even a year of outstanding treatment for major depression is unlikely to be of much impact.

Unützer J et al, 2002.

Project IMPACT (Improving Mood: Promoting Access to Collaborative Treatment for Late Life Depression) has enrolled 1,801 depressed older patients across 18 participating primary care clinics in five states. The collaborative treatment model for the management of depression interfaces a Depression Clinical Specialist (DCS) with the patient's regular primary care physician. A designated psychiatrist provides the DCS with supervision, consultation and back-up. Patients may self-select treatment with antidepressants or six to eight sessions of problem-solving psychotherapy. By allowing patients to switch or combine therapy, the project IMPACT attempts to duplicate standard practices.

Patients are randomized to the usual care offered at each site or the enhanced care available from the DCS. In addition to brief psychotherapy, the DCS provided close follow-up to assess symptom improvement and medication side-effects for patients taking antidepressants. Over a two-year period all participants will be followed with independent telephone surveys. Here is reported the *preliminary results* from year one. The self-report Hopkins Symptom Check List subscale for depression (SCL-20) was the primary measurement tool.

At entry, 17% of participants had major depressive disorder; 30% dysthymia; 53% had both; and 71% had a history of at least two prior episodes of depression. In the 3 months prior to the study, 42% received a prescription for antidepressant medication. At the end of one year, a 50% or more improvement in depressive symptoms was obtained by 60% of the enhanced care group versus 30% for usual care. Compete remission of depressive symptoms occurred for 25% of the enhanced care participants versus a mere 7.5% for usual care. The patients had on average 3.2 chronic physical illnesses. At 12 months there was an overall improvement in functional disability.

Summary Comments

These are feasibility trials. The intervention is a medical model with an emphasis on consultation from mental health professionals and adherence to antidepressant medication. Psychological services and/or depression specific psychotherapy is largely ignored as a component of these interventions; psychological services are the subject of related investigation (Katon et al., 1996). The severity of depression is mild to moderate. Is it possible to manage more serious and persistent forms of mental illness in the primary care setting?

Why is mental health different? If primary care physicians had access to an endocrinologist and/or a nurse specialist and monitored medication adherence routinely, the care of diabetes and thyroid disease would surely improve. For these case management models to be implemented, they may be best incorporated into care pathways for "best practices" in general. Some changes could be made at relatively low cost. For example, medication surveillance could be automated! At modest cost, a program of systematic follow-up and care management by telephone significantly improved adherence to antidepressant medication (Simon et al., 2000).

Strategies for referral to a psychiatrist

Primary care physicians can provide effective treatment for depression for more than 75% of depressed patients (Depression Guideline Panel, 1993). Non-response to

maximum doses of two antidepressants, matching to a specific psychotherapy, diagnostic uncertainty, multiple psychiatric diagnoses, symptoms of bipolar disorder, psychosis or suicide risk recommend referral to a psychiatrist for consultation or treatment. Seven specific referral strategies (e.g., "just like another test") are described by Kerber and Knesper (1997).

Expenses associated with the integration of mental health and primary care services

Not all health systems favor the integration of mental health and primary care services. Many health maintenance organizations (HMOs) "carve out" mental and behavioral health services; patients seeking these services must call a designated center for diagnosis and referral, staffed by mental health professionals who authorize services provided by a mental health specialist on the HMO's panel of approved providers. About 70% of HMOs favor this arrangement and maintain separate financial databases—one for reimbursed medical-surgical service and another for the reimbursed and "carved out" behavioral health services. Roger Kathol (2002) asked what are the *overall* health care expenses attributed to patients receiving behavioral health services and medical-surgical services compared to patients receiving medical-surgical services alone? The answer required combining the claims/reimbursement records of a large health insurance organization in the Midwest United States. The preliminary results are astonishing. In general and in comparison to consumers using medical-surgical services only, consumers with added behavioral health services of any sort have double the reimbursements paid providers. Patients with added behavioral health and chemical dependency services have five times the reimbursements; and rates of 10 times exist for some combinations (Kathol, personal communication). These findings recommend strongly designing health care systems that treat mental and behavioral health services and medical-surgical services within one organizational framework.

The expenses associated with such integration have been considered. The differential expenses associated with alternative collaborative care models for the treatment of major depression have been investigated in two major studies (Lave et al., 1998; Von Korff, 2002). Both reach similar conclusions: compared to usual care, collaborative care is more expensive and produces better outcomes, with outcomes measured by reductions in severity of depression and disability or depression free days. Moreover, both studies found a modest increase in cost-effectiveness (e.g., average annual cost of treating major depression divided by the proportion of patients successfully treated). The Von Korff analysis found a modest cost offset; collaborative care reduced the expenses due to specialty behavioral health services. Of course, the available data pertain to relatively short-term care and fail to consider the overall societal gains of increases in work productivity and the like.

Treatment-resistant depression and other poor outcomes: Expenses associated with the absence of prevention and resulting chronic major depression

Doing nothing to prevent major depression and/or providing suboptimum treatment has financial consequences of major proportions. Perhaps the most emotionally painful and tormenting result is treatment-resistant depression. Interventions that are effective in first- and second-episode major depression are of limited benefit for third- or fourth-episodes. During this unfavorable course of major depression, long-term, chronic and treatment-resistant forms of major depression are established (Greden, 2001; Sackeim, 2001). Unfortunately, treatment-resistance is all too common, and it characterizes

approximately one-third of depressed patients (Fava and Davidson, 1996).

The impact of treatment-resistant depression on health care utilization and costs has been quantified. William Crown and his associates (2002) analyzed a fee-for-service medical and prescription claims database retrospectively. Using criteria based on antidepressant dosing, duration of administration, the use of antidepressant augmentation strategies (Lam et al., 2002) and psychiatric hospitalization, a reasonable definition of treatment-resistant depression was developed. These 3370 patients were contrasted with 7335 patients who were provided reasonable standard of care treatment for depression but who did not meet criteria for treatment resistance. After sorting into these two groups, all patients were followed for a minimum of nine months.

Treatment-resistant depression patients made more extensive and costly use of medical services. Among the many findings from this remarkable study were the following. Treatment-resistance patients had double or more the combined general medical and depression-related hospitalization rates. The subset of patients (n = 483) who were hospitalized for treatment-resistance had over six times the average total medical expenses of non-treatment resistant patients ($42,344 versus $6,512). Moreover, the total depression-related expenses were 19 times greater for the treatment resistant group ($28,001 versus $1,455).

STRATEGIES TO DECREASE THE PREVALENCE OF MAJOR DEPRESSION IN POPULATIONS
Eradicating the stigma of mental illness

"When my depression was first diagnosed, I felt both relief and shame—relief that my condition had a name, and possibly a cure; shame that I was afflicted with a mental disorder. I still felt that I should have been able to rise above it, to use my will to overcome it on my own, and that my inability to do so was proof of my weak nature. I kept the diagnosis and my condition a secret from all but my husband and family at first." These words from Kathy Cronkite typify societal stigmatization of mental illness in general and major depression in particular. Kathy Cronkite is Walter's daughter; in her book, *On the Edge of Darkness: Conversations about Conquering Depression,* celebrities tell about their experiences of depression and stigma.

Stigma is the major impediment to strategies aimed at the prevention of major depression. Of course stigma is not unique to mental illness; issues of stereotyping prejudice and labeling are features of all chronic illnesses (Saylor et al., 2002; Goffman, 1963). So what's so different about mental health? Depression is considered a character flaw—your body is fine, it's your personality that is weak. Your identity is spoiled. Those who have achieved and been successful have much to loose by disclosing their stigmatized mental disorder. In *Telling is Risky Business*, Otto Wahl summarizes what patients have to say about their personal experiences of stigmatization. This book is the result of a year-long, nationwide study of over 1,300 survivors of mental illness. *Telling is Risky Business* eloquently describes the double burden of mental illness—disability and stigmatization.

Stigmatization plays itself out in primary care. Primary care physicians point to patient attitudes and beliefs about depression as the major barrier to diagnosis and initiating treatment (Nutting et al., 2002). Of course, physicians could set a better example. Art Buchwald, Kathy Cronkite, Patty Duke, Kay Jamison, Mike Wallace are among the dozens of celebrities that have made their struggles with depression public. Surely, physicians should do no less.

Founded in 1979, NAMI, the National Alliance for the Mentally Ill, was among the

first advocacy group to be formed. The National Stigma Clearinghouse; the Carter Center Mental Health Program; DBSA, Depression and Bipolar Support Alliance; NMHA, the National Mental Heath Association Program; the National Empowerment Center; the National Mental Health Consumers Self-Help Clearinghouse; and GAMIAN, Global Alliance of Mental Illness Advocacy Networks are national resources that fight sigma and advocate strongly for the mentally ill. Agencies of national and state government are involved as well. Providing donations of time and/or money to any one or all of these organizations is one way each of us can become active and contribute to the fight against stigmatization, the provision of equitable and fair services, and to the prevention of depression and mental illness.

Improving health care provision systems

Wayne Katon and his colleagues have done many randomized, longitudinal clinical trials with large health maintenance organizations. Katon's research has consistently and persuasively demonstrated that collaborations between primary care physicians and clinics and mental health professions improve the outcomes of care for depressed patients (Katon and Korff, 1997). Katon's collaborative care models for health care provision systems take into account the fact that about 80% of patients with depression initially present with such physical symptoms as weakness and fatigue, insomnia, headaches and so forth (Kirmayer et al., 1993). Collaboration has several attributes: diagnostic screening tools, making the patient a partner in care by means of education and encouraging self-management, adoption and adherence to standards of care for pharmacotherapy and psychotherapy, ongoing surveillance of patient progress and adherence to treatment, placement of a mental health care professional in the primary care clinic, access to psychiatric consultation using a consultation-liaison model, and implementing effective strategies for preventing relapse and/or recurrence and chronic treatment-resistant depression. Not only do these strategies work but they appear to be quite cost-effective.

INTERVENTION STRATEGIES AVAILABLE TO THE PRACTICING CLINICIAN

The following recommendations are based on the studies reviewed and the scientific literature mentioned, the American Psychiatric Association's Practice Guidelines for the Treatment of Patients with Major Depressive Disorder (Karasu, 2002), the clinical practices of the University of Michigan's Depression Center, and the relevant sections in *Primary Care Psychiatry* (Knesper et al., 1997). Clinical decisions that may be made by primary care physicians are emphasized. To increase the utility of this section, reference materials that have been previously mentioned are excluded from this section.

Depression risk and vulnerability assessment

See Table 1. Most physicians and mental health professionals are unaccustomed to integrating the assessment of major depression risk factors into their clinical practices. Knowing the "weight" of risk factors for major depression associated with particular individual permits the clinician to estimate the likelihood that the individual will either have a first episode or a subsequent episode of major depression. Moreover, in the face of diagnostic uncertainty the "weight" of risk factors provides strong or weak support for a tentative diagnosis. For example, when the clinical examination finds subsyndromal depression, the provision of treatment is made more urgent when the patient is at increased risk based on a comprehensive assessment of risk factors.

The use of risk assessment information in routine clinical practice is without much research support. Nevertheless, it is recommended that a depression risk assessment be part of a comprehensive evaluation for any mood disorder. The evaluated patient should be informed about each risk factor that pertains to his or her risk and should be educated about the symptoms of major depression and mood disorders in general.

Screening for major depression

Routinely screening adults for depression is recommended by the United States Preventive Services Task Force. *The following two questions may be as effective as more complicated questionnaires*: "Over the past 2 weeks, have you felt down, depressed or hopeless?" and "Over the last 2 weeks have you felt little interest or pleasure in doing things?" Affirmative responses require a more comprehensive assessment.

Clinical personnel are to feedback the screening information to the primary care physician. This procedure increases the recognition of depression two- to three-fold and reduces the relative risk for major depression by 13% (Kronke et al., 1994).

Establishing the diagnosis of major depression and quantifying its severity

Multiple depression case finding tools have been validated for primary care practice (Williams et al., 2002). Each takes no more that 5 minutes to complete. The Center for Epidemiologic Studies Depression Scale (CES-D) and the Zung Self-Rating Depression Scale were developed specifically to identify depression. Each has been thoroughly evaluated for use in primary care settings. They can be used to rate the severity of depression and monitor response to treatment. Each may be downloaded from various web sites; for example, go to http://www.google.com/, enter the rating scale name and do a search.

Rating scales are tools that help to make the diagnosis of major depression; confirmation of the diagnosis requires a clinical interview. At the end of his article, John Williams Jr. (2002) considers how primary care physicians may improve their depression diagnostic skills.

Severity may be assessed using a simple visual analog scale (Ahearn, 1997). Draw a ten-centimeter line and write zero at one end and 10 at the other. Tell the patient that zero represents not depressed at all and 10 is "the worst depression imaginable." Have the patient draw a line between these two extremes, and the centimeter distance from zero is the severity score.

Preventing the reoccurrence of major depression and maintaining recovery

Treating the first and any subsequent episodes of major depression to full remission of symptoms and maintaining a normal mood is the best practice for preventing recurrence or relapse. The following sections provide guidelines for implementing this recommendation. For all the examples and recommendations, therapeutic decision-making requires a periodic re-consideration of the diagnosis; the material below applies to major depressive disorder and does not necessarily apply to subsyndromal depressive conditions. In the absence of risk factors, antidepressant medication is of limited value for treating symptoms of acute or chronic dysphoria (Ackerman and Williams, 2002).

The phases of treatment: definitions

Initial or acute phase is defined as the first 6 to 8 weeks of treatment; if in this period there is no or minimal response, the acute phase continues for another 6 to weeks or until there is a response. Since longer duration depressions are less likely to quickly benefit from treatment, for chronic depressions the initial treatment phase may last for a year or longer.

Response means at least a 50% reduction in the severity score.

Remission means a full recovery and a return to the patient's baseline state of normal mood for a minimum of six months.

Relapse means the return of depressive symptoms in the six months following a remission, aresponse to treatment or a spontaneous recovery.

Recurrence means a new episode of depression occurring after at least a six-month period of remission.

Continuation phase is defined as the treatment period beginning at the end of the initial phase of treatment and ending with treatment discontinuation or treatment maintenance. With the recognition that major depression is a chronic illness, the continuation phase has lengthened—a one year continuation phase is frequently recommended.

Maintenance phase is defined as the continuation of treatment subsequent to the continuation phase; this phase could last a lifetime.

Frequency of appointments or visits is determined by the phase of treatment and the severity of illness. For primary care practices, visits are weekly to monthly during the initial phase of treatment; thereafter, every two to four months may be appropriate.

The decision to treat with antidepressant medication and/or depression-specific psychotherapy

See Tables 6 and 7. Maximum episode severity (severity includes the results from a suicide assessment), number of prior episodes, symptom severity between episodes and persistence of risk factors, adverse experiences with prior treatment, patient preferences and requirements for more immediate symptom relief, and the availability of high-quality, depression-specific psychotherapy determine the treatment. The following clinical examples illustrate how these variables may be combined to decide among treatment options.

Example clinical situation one: *Low overall severity, first episode, and few risk factors.*

Depression specific-psychotherapy and/or medications are the options. If the patient favors psychotherapy and depression-specific psychotherapy (i.e., cognitive-behavioral or interpersonal) is available, psychotherapy alone is a very reasonable choice. Otherwise, antidepressant medication is best. See Table 6 and 7.

Example clinical situation two: *Low overall severity, first episode, and multiple risk factors (e.g. female, father and brother died from suicide, history of mild depressive symptoms as an adolescent, ongoing, overwhelming adversity and absence from work).*

See clinical situation one. While depression-specific psychotherapy is quite reasonable, in addition most psychiatrists would prescribe antidepressant medications and some would recommend life-long because of the risk factor profile. Since antidepressant medication works faster than does psychotherapy, the patient's desire for more immediate symptom relief, for example to get back to work soon, is a strong argument for initiating treatment with an antidepressant medication.

Example clinical situation three: *Moderate to severe major depression with near-lethal suicide attempt, second episode, and several risk factors.*

As the severity of depression increases, administering antidepressant medication becomes more and more compelling. For this generic situation, both medication and depression-specific psychotherapy is best practice. If depression-specific psychotherapy is unavailable, medication alone should be prescribed and psychotherapy should be started as soon as this treatment option becomes available.

Example clinical situation four: *Very severe to extremely severe depression (e.g., confined to bed mostly but unable to sleep, 30 pound weight loss, near constant crying, etc.), second episode, several risk factors.*

Antidepressant medication (or electoconvulsive therapy) is best practice for the initial treatment phase. Once a biological foundation supports a lower-severity depression, thereby making the patient more accessible to depression-specific psychotherapy, psychotherapy is indicated in combination with medication.

The dosage of antidepressant medication and/or depression-specific psychotherapy

Failure to respond to an antidepressant is recognized when the patient has been on the manufacturer's recommended maximum dose for six to eight weeks. If major depression has been present for a year or more, many psychiatrists continue the maximum dose for two to six or more months before declaring a failed trial. If the patient fails to respond to a below-maximum dose, increasing the dose is indicated. See Tables 6 and 7 for guidelines.

Continuation or maintenance antidepressant medication therapy is always at the same dose that was used to gain remission of symptoms. Lowering the dose places the patient at substantial risk for relapse.

Depression-specific psychotherapy requires about ten therapy hours over as many weeks. Additional hours are indicated for unresolved issues and to better fasten new skills to cognitive-behavioral responses. Similar to antidepressant medications, if depressive symptoms remain unchanged or are worse, the intensity of psychotherapy should be increased. If symptoms re-emerge at any time in the continuation or maintenance phase of treatment, "booster" psychotherapy sessions are recommended. The optimal

Table 6: SEROTONIN SELECTIVE REUPTAKE INHIBITORS: PRACTICAL GUIDELINES FOR MATCHING ANTIDEPRESSANTS TO PATIENTS

SELECTION CRITERIA[a] / Antidepressants (Brand Name)	citalopram (Celexa)	escitalopram (Lexapro)	fluoxetine (Prozac & Sarafem)	fluoxetine weekly (Prozac Weekly)	paroxetine (Paxil)	paroxetine controlled-release (Paxil CR)	sertraline (Zoloft)
Side Effects and Other Attributes Used in Patient Selection	May be initially sedating or initially increase alertness. Mild initial sedation is dose-dependent. May be least stimulating SSRI. Negligible drug-drug interaction.	10 mg/d comparable to 20 mg/d citalopram. Negligible drug-drug interactions.	Tends to produce more initial nervousness, and arousal than other SSRI's. Very long half-life of 7-15 days.	Tends to produce more initial nervousness, and arousal than other SSRI's. Very long half-life of 7-15 days.	Anticholinergic properties tend to reduce arousal and insomnia effects common with SSRI's.	Initial nausea rate is 14% vs 23% for immediate release; otherwise side-effect profiles nearly identical.	Tends to initially increase alertness; patients with psychomotor retardation may benefit. Minimal drug-drug interactions.
All SSRI's: During the initial phase of treatment all SSRI's may produce one or all of the following: Increased arousal (agitation), insomnia, nausea, diarrhea (due to increased GI motility), initial weight gain after about 6 months, sexual dysfunction. Uncommon adverse events include: akathisia (restlessness), psychomotor slowing, mild parkinsonism, apathy. Note: Dosage should be decreased 50% in patients with hepatic impairment; 3-fold increase in plasma levels possible.							
Sexual dysfunction	Common	Common	Common	Common	Common	Common	Common
DO NOT COMBINE WITH MONOAMINE OXIDASE INHIBITORS (MAOIs)							
Selected Important Drug-Drug Interactions[b,c]	Minimal inhibitor of CYP 2D6 isoenzymes. Good choice for medical/surgical patients *without* renal impairments.	Comparable to citalopram.	Potent inhibitor of CYP 2D6 isoenzymes.	Potent inhibitor of CYP 2D6 isoenzymes. Potent inhibitor of CYP 2D6. Inhibitor recommends avoiding phenytoin (Dilantin).	Potent inhibitor of CYP 2D6 isoenzymes.	Potent inhibitor of CYP 2D6 isoenzymes.	Weak inhibitor of CYP 2D6 isoenzymes. Good choice for medical/surgical patients. Contraindicated with pimozide (Orap).
Patient Profile Most Likely to Benefit Because …	Elderly patient with an agitated depression and GI sensitivity.	Elderly patient with agitated depression and GI distress or GI sensitivity. Claims of more rapid efficacy may be exaggerated.	Noncompliant or "forgetful" patient (i.e., used as a "depot" oral antidepressant); excessive fatigue.	Identical to fluoxetine; also once weekly may reduce personnel costs in institutional settings.	Less likely to produce initial anxiety and/or insomnia.	Less likely to produce initial nausea. Nausea rate at 25 mg/d comparable to escitalopram at 20 mg/d.	The medical/surgical patient on one or more medical drugs. Initial activation and increased alertness desired.
Patient Profile Least Likely to Benefit Because …	Do not use if creatinine clearance ≤ 20 mL/min; drug 20% excreted by kidney. Elderly patient with excessive sleep and apathy.	Do not use if creatinine clearance ≤ 20 mL/min; drug 20% excreted by kidney. Elderly patient with excessive sleep and apathy.	Patient on several medications and/or frequent medication changes anticipated.	Identical to fluoxetine.	Elderly or similar patient who might require high dose and, therefore, be more prone to anticholinergic effects (e.g., delirium). Half-life increased by 170% in elderly.	Elderly or similar patient who might require high dose and, therefore, be more prone to anticholinergic effects (e.g., delirium). Half-life increased by 170% in elderly.	Patient sensitive to any of the typical SSRI side-effects (e.g., increased arousal).
Available Preparations And Doses	20, 40 mg scored, coated tablets.	5 (unscored), 10, 20 mg scored tablets.	10,20,40 mg capsules; 10 mg scored tablets; 20 mg/5 ml concentrate.	90 mg capsule containing enteric-coated pellets.	10,20,30,40 mg tablets; 10 mg/5 ml concentrate.	12.5 and 25 mg enteric-coated tablets.	25,50,100 mg scored, coated tablet; 20 mg/ml concentrate.
Usual Therapeutic Doses; Maximum Dose	20-40 mg/d; 60 mg/d.	15-20 mg/d; 60 mg/d.	20-40 mg/d; 80 mg/d.	90 mg/week; 90 mg twice weekly.	20-40 mg/d; 60 mg/d.	25-50 mg/d; 62.5 mg/d.	75-150 mg/d; 200 mg/d.
Suggested Dosing Strategies — Youthful Reasonable Health	20 mg P.O. Qam (or QHS if sedating.) Uptaper if no response after 6 weeks.	10-20 mg/d P.O. Qam (or QHS if sedating); 15-20 mg/d thereafter. Uptaper if no response in 6 weeks.	20 mg P.O. Qam; increased doses may be given a.m. and noon, if excessive arousal. Uptaper if no response in 6 weeks.	20 mg/d fluoxetine X 7 d; thereafter, 90 mg/wk. Uptaper if no response in 6 weeks.	20 mg P.O. Qam; increased doses may be given a.m. and noon; if excessive arousal. Give QHS if sedating.	25 mg/d P.O. Qam X 7 d; 50 mg/d thereafter; increase to 62.5 mg/d if no response in 6 weeks.	50 mg P.O. Qam X 1 week; 75 mg P.O. Qam thereafter; increased doses may be given a.m. and noon, if excessive arousal.
Suggested Dosing Strategies — Frail, Elderly, Medically Ill	5-10 mg P.O. Qam X 3 d, 10-20 mg P.O. Qam X 3 d, etc. until desired initial dose.	5 mg/d P.O. Qam (or Qpm if sedating); uptaper weekly to 15 mg/d initial dose.	5-10 mg P.O. Q every other a.m. for 3-4 days (i.e., two doses) then similarly uptapered to 20 mg P.O. Qam initial dose.	Identical to fluoxetine; slowly uptaper to 40-60 mg/d before switching to 90 mg/weekly.	5-10 mg/d P.O. Qam X 3-4 d, 10-20 mg P.O. Qam X 3-4 d, etc. until desired initial dose.	12.5 mg/d P.O. Qam X 7 d; 25 mg/d P.O. Qam, etc. until desired initial dose.	12.5-25 mg P.O. Qam X 3 d; 25-50 mg P.O. Qam X 3 d, etc. until desired initial dose.

Notes: [a] If a patient fails one SSRI class of antidepressants, another SSRI class may be tried (i.e., don't try a third SSRI).
[b] Do not combine any of the listed antidepressants with monoamine oxidase inhibitors (MAIOs),
[c] Drug interaction data bases: <http://drug-interaction.com> and <http://www.hanstenandhom.com> and <http://medicine.iupui.edu/flockhart/> are recommended.
IT IS THE RESPONSIBILITY OF THE TREATING PHYSICIAN TO STAY CURRENT WITH THE PSYCHOPHARMACOLOGY OF ANTIDEPRESSANTS AND TO DETERMINE DOSAGES AND DRUG INTERACTIONS, AND THE BEST TREATMENT FOR THE PATIENT.
Developed by David J. Knesper, M.D., University of Michigan, Department of Psychiatry. Last revised December 10, 2002.

Table 7. NOREPINEPHRINE, SEROTONIN AND/OR DOPAMINE MECHANISMS: PRACTICAL GUIDELINES FOR MATCHING ANTIDEPRESSANTS TO PATIENTS

SELECTION CRITERIA	norepinephrine/dopamine reuptake inhibitor	serotonin/norepinephrine reuptake inhibitor	Serotonin & alpha-2 receptor blocker; (increases release of serotonin and norepinephrine)	serotonin-2 antagonist/reuptake inhibitor	serotonin/norepinephrine reuptake inhibitor
Mechanisms of Action					
Antidepressants (Brand Name)	bupropion sustained-release (Wellbutrin SR)	duloxetine[c] (Cymbalta)	mirtazapine (Remeron)	nefazodone (Serzone)	venlafaxine extended release (Effexor XR)
Side Effects and Other Attributes Used in Patient Selection	Least likely to switch patient to mania. Most activating antidepressant available. DO NOT USE if history of seizure, head trauma, substance abuse/bulimia/anorexia or electrolyte disturbance.	Similar to SSRIs but more exaggerated. Mild, blood pressure elevations $\leq 4\%$ of patients. Nausea, dry mouth, somnolence and constipation may lead to discontinuation.	Produces sleep; *lower* doses produce more sleep than do higher doses. Weight gain may be ≥ 10 lbs. Some represent product's antiemetic properties by "the poor man's ondansetron" (Zofran).	BLACK-BOX WARNING: Liver damage and/or liver failure in 1/250,000 patients. Corrects sleep disturbances and reduces anxiety in about a week. Side effects somewhat opposite to SSRIs. Fatigue and dizziness common complaints.	Identical to those common to all SSRIs with > nausea. Sustained hypertension risk is 3% at ≥ 300 mg. BP increases are dose-dependent. Low protein binding and linear dose-response. Constipation is unusual but may cause discontinuation.
DO NOT COMBINE WITH MONOAMINE OXIDASE INHIBITORS (MAOIs)					
Sexual Dysfunction	Rare	Less common	Unlikely	Unlikely	Less Common
Selected Important Drug-Drug Interactions[a]	Complex biotransformation is relatively unstudied. However drug-drug interactions are uncommon. Recent report finds clinically significant inhibition of CYP2D6.	Insufficient information.	Usually clinically insignificant due to extensive metabolism via CYP1A2, 2D6, 3A4. Does not appear to interfere with the metabolism of other drugs.	Potent inhibitor of CYP 3A/34. 15% decreased oral clearance of digoxin. Contraindicated with: cisapride (Propulsid), cyclosporine, simvastatin (Zocor). Potential inhibitor of CYP 3A/34; moderate of PGP. 15% decreased oral clearance of digoxin. Contraindicated with: cisapride (Propulsid), cyclosporine, simvastatin (Zocor). Avoid with: pimozide (Orap), sildenafil (Viagra).	Usually clinically insignificant due to low protein binding and weak inhibition of P450 enzymes.
Patient Profile **Most Likely to Benefit Because ....**	The now depressed, actually or potentially, bipolar patient. The apathetic, low energy patient. Patients motivated to stop smoking. Helpful for ADHD[b].	Patient with depression and chronic pain (effects on pain are dose-dependent). Patient failing an SSRI trial.	The medically ill patient with weight loss, insomnia and nausea.	The depressed, over-anxious patient with marked difficulty sleeping.	Dual reuptake inhibitor an added benefit at 225 mg or more. Patients failing an SSRI trial. When used at higher doses, patients with chronic pain.

Antidepressants (Brand Name)		bupropion sustained-release (Wellbutrin SR)	duloxetine [c] (Cymbalta)	mirtazapine (Remeron)	nefazodone (Serzone)	venlafaxine extended release (Effexor XR)
Patient Profile Least Likely to Benefit Because ...		Patients who are agitated, very anxious and/or panicky. Patients at risk for seizures and/or with history of head trauma, substance abuse, eating disorder, or electrolyte disturbance.	Patient with significant anorexia and/or constipation and/or other GI symptoms.	The obese patient with fatigue and hypersomnia. Patients with neutropenia: risk of neutropenia = 1.5%; risk agranulocytosis = 0.1%.	Patients who sleep excessively with life-long underachievement and excessive contentment. Patients with severe depression tend to require maximum dose.	Patients with unstable BP, and perhaps, those who are GI sensitive. A clinically significant withdrawal syndrome requires slow downtaper.
Available Preparations and Doses		100, 150, 200 mg coated tablet (immediate release tablets available).	Insufficient information.	15, 30 mg scored tablets; 45 mg unscored tablet; 15, 30, 45 mg unscored orally disintegrating (not orally dissolving) tablet (Remeron SolTab).	100, 150 mg scored; 50, 200, 250 mg unscored tablets.	37.5, 75, 150 mg capsules (immediate release tablets available)
Usual Therapeutic Doses; Maximum Doses		300-400 mg/d; 450 mg/d.	60 mg at night; 60 mg bid.	30-45 mg/d; 60 mg/d.	300-400 mg/d; 600 mg/d.	150-225 mg/d; 375-450 mg/d.
Suggested Dosing Strategies	Youthful, Reasonable Health	100-150 mg SR with breakfast and before 7 pm.; increase to minimum dose: 150 mg bid. DO NOT DOUBLE-UP MISSED DOSES.	Slow uptaper from smallest dose.	7.5 (more sleep) to 15 mg (less sleep) night one; 30 mg night two; increase to 45 mg if no improvement after two weeks. See below: liver and kidney.	Use 150 mg tablets: ½ tab at HS x 4 nights; 1 tab x 4 nights; ½ tab in am and 1 tab at HS x 4 nights; ½ tab in am and 1½ tabs HS x 4 nights; ½ tab in am and 2 tabs HS x 4 nights; 1 tab am and 2 tabs HS thereafter.	Every 3-7 day uptaper, starting at 37.5 mg reduces risk of nausea; initial trial at 225 mg/d. Reduce dose 50% for hepatic impairment; 25% for renal.
	Frail, Elderly, Medically Ill	Every 3-4 day uptaper, starting at 100 mg; initial trial at 150 mg bid; last dose before 7 pm. DO NOT DOUBLE-UP MISSED DOSES.	Insufficient information to make a recommendation.	15 mg at night X 3; 30 mg thereafter; increased to 45 mg if no improvement in two weeks. Reduce dose by 50% for hepatic impairment; 25% for renal.	Ever 3-4 days uptaper, starting at 25-50 mg bid; 150 mg bid initial trial.	Every 7 day uptaper, starting at 37.5 mg; initial trial at 150 mg/d. Reduce dose 50% for hepatic impairment; 25% for renal.

Notes: [a] Drug interaction databases: <http://Drug-interactions.com> and <http://www.handstenandhorn.com> and <http://medicine.iupui.edu/flockhart/> are recommended.

[b] "ADHD" means attention deficit hyperactivity disorder.

[c] Duloxetine should be available in 2003; all information is preliminary.

IT IS THE RESPONSIBILITY OF THE TREATING PHYSICIAN TO STAY CURRENT WITH THE PSYCHOPHARMACOLOGY OF ANTIDEPRESSANTS AND TO DETERMINE DOSAGES AND DRUG INTERACTIONS, AND THE BEST TREATMENT FOR THE PATIENT.
Developed by David J. Knesper, M.D., University of Michigan, Department of Psychiatry. Last revised December 10, 2002.

number, length and frequency of sessions of depression-specific psychotherapy have been understudied.

Antidepressant administered by a primary care physician and psychotherapy from psychologist or social worker

This arrangement is understudied however frequent it may be. It is essential that the primary care doctor and the therapist have contact frequently. The primary care doctor must encourage this sort of contact. Impediments to communication may provide patients a path to deterioration and even suicidal behaviors. Emergency situations are avoidable with just a little effort.

Switching to a different antidepressant medication or adding a second antidepressant

It is recommended that a failed trail of one serotonin reuptake inhibitor (SSRI) may be followed by a different SSRI. Failing two SSRIs recommends switching to an antidepressant with an entirely different mechanism of action. See Table 6 and 7.

If a patient has not responded to a first antidepressant, it is common practice among psychiatrists to use an augmentation strategy. This combines two (or more) antidepressants each with a different but complementary mechanism of action. There is no systematic research to guide augmentation strategies nor is there research to guide conversion to monotherapy.

Alternative therapy: herbal medicine and exercise

St. John's wort (*Hypericum perforatum*) is promoted for both depression and anxiety. Regarding use in primary anxiety disorders, data from randomized trials does not exist. St. John's wort was investigated for use in outpatients with major depression in three recent randomized, placebo controlled trials. A recent review of these studies by Peter De

Smet and published in the *New England Journal of Medicine* (December 19, 2002) concludes: "On the basis of available evidence, St. John's wort should not be substituted for a conventional antidepressant in patients with moderately severe or severe major depression." De Smet reviews the numerous side effects associate with St. John's wort and describes the high potential for drug-drug interactions.

Exercise for the prevention and treatment of depression is an undeveloped area of research. The few studies that have been done have been reviewed by Egil Martinsen and Thomas Stephens (1994), who conclude that both aerobic and nonaerobic exercise is of benefit in both the short- and the long-term for depression and other psychiatric disorders. The available evidence does not allow for a good estimate of the size of the benefit. More to the point, exercise is a simple strategy that can be a useful supplement to traditional treatment, and if injury is avoided, exercise has only beneficial side effects.

Discontinuation of treatment

Because the exact timing and method of discontinuing treatment has not been systematically studied, it is important to consider the percentage risk of recurrence and relapse before recommending discontinuation of treatment. Approximately 50% of patients will make a full recovery from an episode of depression within 6 months. Even after two years, 20% of patients will remain in an episode despite adequate treatment. On average, 50% to 85% of patients with a single episode will have a second. The risk of recurrence is 95% in two years for patients with three or more episodes. Consequently, the consensus among psychiatrists is to continue aggressive treatment (i.e., full dose treatment) until there has been a remission and to consider discontinuation only for those patients who are at low risk for relapse or reoccurrence. The longer the patient has been depressed, the longer therapy should continue. Patients in a third episode of major depression of moderate or higher severity should be considered for life-long treatment. Many psychiatrists would recommend life-long treatment to anyone over 50 years old who has recovered from a severe to extremely severe episode of major depression.

If antidepressant medications and/or depression-specific psychotherapy are to be discontinued, a slow downtaper is recommended, although there is little research support for this recommendation. What is a slow downtaper? If a patient begins discontinuation at 100% of the maximum dose, a 10% to 20% dose reduction per month is suggested. This approach, coupled with an educated patient, permits any reemergence of symptoms to be met with a rapid uptaper in dose. This recommendation pertains both to medications and depression-specific psychotherapy.

Changes in the provision of mental health services in primary care settings

The average 10 to 15 minutes for a return primary care visit is of insufficient length to foster any therapeutic alliance, promote treatment adherence, or reassess the clinical problem. In the absence of a major reorganization of health care provision, it is possible to make some low cost changes that appear to impact outcomes. A program of systematic follow-up and care management by telephone significantly improved adherence to antidepressant medication.

Eradicating the stigma of mental illness

Educational materials should be provided to patients and families who are recipients of mental health services. Also, patients and families should be informed about the following advocacy groups. NAMI, the National Alliance for the Mentally Ill, was among the first advocacy group to be formed. The National Stigma Clearinghouse; the

Carter Center Mental Health Program; DBSA, Depression and Bipolar Support Alliance; NMHA, the National Mental Heath Association Program; the National Empowerment Center; the National Mental Health Consumers Self-Help Clearinghouse; and GAMIAN, Global Alliance of Mental Illness Advocacy Networks are national resources that fight sigma and advocate strongly for the mentally ill. All have web sites. Agencies of national and state government are involved as well. Providing donations of time and/or money to any one or all of these organizations is one way each of us can become active and contribute to the fight against stigmatization, the provision of equitable and fair services, and to the for prevention of depression and mental illness.

UNANSWERED RESEARCH QUESTIONS

The section below titled "For Further Reading" references several recent issues of *Biological Psychiatry: A Journal of Psychiatric Neuroscience*. The journal volumes referenced contain superb reviews and each review considers unanswered research questions and suggests research strategies. The problems with psychiatric diagnoses are the subject of *A Research Agenda for DSM-V* (Kupfer et al., 2002), and this excellent book contains recommendations for research.

These scholarly resources provide a research agenda for the next decade. To this agenda will be added only four categories of research relevant to prevention.

Risk factors. Risk factor assessment and the incorporation of risk factors with clinical decision-making is common in all of medicine—except for psychiatry. Since knowledge about risk factors pertains to prevention, investigations are needed that link the clinical assessment of risk factors for major depression to prevention.

Behavioral change. The prevention of many diseases such as cardiovascular disease, dementia, hypertension, cancer and so forth involves making behavioral changes at an early age. So, for example, exercise, diet and weight loss are components of an overall prevention strategy for cardiovascular disease. The most preliminary research on the primary prevention of major depression would be strengthened greatly by just following in the methodological footsteps that have been applied to other diseases.

Abuse and neglect prevention. It is difficult to find word to describe the tragedies of childhood abuse and neglect that predisposes individuals to a multitude of mental and physical problems. This is an epidemic that seems to go unrecognized. Abuse prevention research must be made a national priority. Let's get to the root of the problems.

Health care provision systems that place mental and physical health under one roof. Wayne Katon and others have given us collaborative care models that combine mental health and physical health services and bring mental health professionals and primary care physicians together and working on common goals. Additional health services research is mandatory if these models are to be refined and are to serve as a basis for providing health care in general. A less fragmented and better overall health care provision system is surely one means of decreasing the prevalence of major depression and all other diseases for populations of patients.

PUBLISHED RESOURCES
For further reading

Several outstanding resources became available during the writing of this chapter. These remarkable works are the products of the many of the most accomplished and talented clinicians and researchers working today in the field of psychiatry, psychology and mental heath services research. This chapter benefited in immeasurable ways.

Charney DS & Babich KS eds (2002). Workgroup reports: NIMH strategic plan for mood disorders research. In Biological Psychiatry: A Journal of Psychiatric Neuroscience, Volume 52, Number 6, September 15, 2002. NY: Elsevier Science.

Coyle JT & Lewis L eds (2001). The unmet needs in diagnosis and treatment of mood disorders in children and adolescents. In Biological Psychiatry: A Journal of Psychiatric Neuroscience, Volume 49, Number 12, June 15, 2001. NY: Elsevier Science.

Gotlib IH & Hammen CL eds (2002). Handbook of Depression. NY: Guilford Press.

Karasu TB, Chair, Work Group on Major Depressive Disorder, et al (2002). Practice guidelines for the treatment of patients with major depressive disorder. In American Psychiatric Association Practice Guidelines for the Treatment of Psychiatric Disorders: Compendium 2002 (American Psychiatric Association Steering Committee on Practice Guidelines) pp 463-545. Washington DC: American Psychiatric Association.

Medina J (1998). Depression: How it happens. How it's healed. Irvine, CA: CME, Inc.

Nemeroff CB (ed) (2002). Remission: Today's target in the Treatment of Mood and Anxiety Disorders. In Psychopharmacology Bulletin, Volume 36, Supplement 2, Summer 2002. NY: MedWorks Media.

Reynolds CF, Charney DS eds (2002). Unmet needs in diagnosis and treatment of mood disorders in late life. In Biological Psychiatry: A Journal of

Psychiatric Neuroscience, Volume 52, Number 3, August 1, 2002. NY: Elsevier Science.

Solomon A (2001). The Noonday Demon: An Atlas of Depression. NY: Scribner.

REFERENCES

Abramson LY, Alloy LB (1978) Learned helplessness in humans: critique and reformulation. J Abnorm Psychol 87:49-74.

Abramson LY, Alloy LB (1999) Cognitive vulnerability to depression: Theory and evidence. J Cognit Psychother 13:5-20.

Abramson LY, Alloy LB, et al (2002) Cognitive vulnerability to depression: Theory and evidence. In Clinical Advances in Cognitive Psychotherapy: Theory and Application (Leahy RL, Dowd ET, eds) pp 75-92. New York: Springer Publishing.

Ackerman RT, Williams JW Jr. (2002) Rational treatment choices of non-major depression in primary care: an evidenced-based review. J Genl Intern Med 17:293-301.

Ahern EP (1997) The use of visual analog scales in mood disorders: a critical review. J Psychiatr Res 31:569-579.

Alexopoulos GS, Borson S et al (2002) Assessment of late life depression. Biol Psychiatr 52:164-174.

Alexopoulos GS, Meyers BS et al (2000) Executive dysfunction and risk for relapse and recurrence of geriatric depression. Archives of General Psychiatry 57:285-290.

Alexopoulos GS, Vrontou C et al (1996) Disability in geriatric depression. Am J Psychiatr 153:877-885.

Alloy LB, Abramson LY (2000) Cyclothymic personality. In The Corsini Encyclopedia of Psychology and Behavioral Sciences, 3rd ed. (Craighead WE, Nemeroff C, eds), Volume 1, pp 417-418. John Wiley & Sons.

American Psychiatric Association (1994) Diagnostic and Statistical Manual of Mental Disorders, 4th ed. Washington, DC: American Psychiatric Press.

Anderson IM (2000) Selective serotonin reuptake inhibitors versus tricyclic antidepressants: a meta-analysis of efficacy and tolerability. J Affective Disord 58:19-36.

Appels AD, Frits W et al (2000) Inflammation, depressive symptomatology, the coronary artery disease. Psychosom Med 62:601-605.

Beardslee WR, Gladstone TRG (2001) Prevention of childhood depression: recent findings and future prospects. Biol Psychiatr 49:1101-1110.

Beardslee WR, Salt P, et al (1997a) Sustained change in parents receiving preventative interventions for families with depression. Am J Psychiatr 154:510-515.

Beardslee WR, Versage EM et al (1998) Children of affectively ill parents: A review of the past 10 years. J Am Acad Child Adolesc Psychiatr 37:1134-1141.

Beardslee WR, Wright C et al (1997b) Examination of children's responses to two preventive intervention strategies over time. J Am Acad Child Adolesc Psychiatr 36:196-204.

Beck AT (1967) Depression: Clinical, Experimental, and Theoretical Aspects. New York: Harper & Row.

Beck AT, Rush AJ (1979) Cognitive Therapy of Depression. New York: The Guilford Press.

Berkman L, ENRICHD investigators (2001) Initial results. Presented at the American Heart Association Annual Meeting, November 14, 2001.

Bernet CZ, Stein MB (1999) Relationship of childhood maltreatment to the onset and course of major depression in adulthood. Depression & Anxiety 9:169-74.

Bierut LJ, Heath AC et al (1999) Major depressive disorder in a community-based twin sample: Are there different genetic and environmental contributions for men and women? Arch Gen Psychiatr 56:557-563.

Blazer DG, Kessler RC et al (1994) The prevalence and distribution of major depression in a national community sample: the National Comorbidity Survey. Am J Psychiatr 151:979-986.

Brown GW, Harris TO (1978) Social Origins of Depression: A Study of Psychiatric Disorder in Women. New York: Free Press.

Brown GW, Harris TO (1989) Depression. In Life Events and Illness Psychopathology (Brown GW, Harris TO, eds), pp49-93. New York: The Guilford Press.

Brown W, Harrison W (1995) Are patients who are intolerant to one serotonin selective reuptake inhibitor intolerant to another. J Clin Psychiatr 56:30-34.

Browne G, Steiner M et al (2002) Sertraline and/or interpersonal psychotherapy for patients with dysthymic disorder in primary care: 6-month comparison with longitudinal 2-year follow-up of effectiveness and costs. J Affective Disord 68(2-3):317-30.

Burke KC, Burke JD et al (1991) Comparing age at onset of major depression and other psychiatric disorders by birth cohorts in five community populations. Arch Gen Psychiatr 48:789-795.

Casacalenda N, Perry JC et al (2002) Remission in major depressive disorder: a comparison of pharmacotherapy, psychotherapy and controlled conditions. Am J Psychiatr 159:1354-1360.

Chorpita BF, Barlow DH (1998) The development of anxiety: The role of control in the early environment. Psychol Bull 124:3-21.

Clark GN, Hornbrook M et al (2001) A randomized trial of a group cognitive intervention for preventing depression in adolescent offspring of depressed parents. Arch Gen Psychiatr 58:1127-1134.

Clark GN, Hornbrook M et al (2002) Group cognitive-behavioral treatment for depressed adolescent offspring of depressed parents in a health maintenance organization. J Am Acad Child Adolesc Psychiatr 41:305-313.

Clarke GN, Hawkins W et al (1995) Targeted prevention of unipolar depressive disorder in an at-risk sample of high-school adolescents: a randomized trial of a group cognitive intervention. J Am Acad Child Adolesc Psychiatr 34:312-321.

Cohen LS, Sichel DA et al (1995) Postpartum prophylaxis for women with bipolar disorder. Am J Psychiatr 152:1641-1645.

Connerney I, Shapiro PA et al (2001) Relation between depression after coronary artery bypass surgery and 12-month outcome: a prospective study. Lancet 358(9295):1766-1771.

Consensus Development Panel (1985) NIMH/NIH consensus development conference on mood disorders: Pharmacological prevention of recurrences. Am J Psychiatr 142:469-476.

Costello EJ, Erkanli A et al (1999) Development of psychiatric comorbidity and substance abuse in adolescents: Effects of timing and sex. J Clin Child Psychol 28:298-311.

Costello EJ, Pine DS et al (2002) Development and natural history of mood disorders. Biol Psychiatr 52:529-542.

Coulehan JL, Schulberg HC et al (1997) Treating depressed primary are patients improves their physical, mental, and social functioning. Arch Intern Med 157(10):1113-20.

Cove S (2002) Classification and Diagnosis of Psychological Abnormality. New York: Routledge.

Crits-Christoph P, Mark D et al (2002) Supportive-expressive psychodynamic therapy for depression. In Comparative

Treatments of Depression (Reinecke MA and Davison MR, eds), pp 166-194. New York: Springer Publishing.

Crown WH, Finkelstein S et al (2002) The impact of treatment-resistant depression on health care utilization and costs. J Clin Psychiatr 63:963-971.

Daley S, Hammen C (1997) Predictors of the generation of episodic stress: A longitudinal study of late adolescent women. J Abnorm Psychol 106:252-259.

Davidson RJ, Lewis DA et al (2002) Neural and behavioral substrates of mood and mood regulation. Biol Psychiatr 52:478-502.

De Smet PAGM (2002) Drug therapy: herbal remedies. N Engl J Med 347:2046-2056.

Demyttenaere K (1997) Compliance during treatment with antidepressants. J Affect Disord 43:27-39.

Depression Guideline Panel (1993) Clinical Practice Guideline Number 5: Depression in Primary Care. Volume 1: Detection and Diagnosis. (AHCPR publication number 1993:93-0550) Rockville, MD: U.S. Department of Health and Human Services, Agency on Health Policy Research.

DeRubeis RJ, Hollon SD et al (2002) Cognitive therapy vs medications for severe depression: acute response and relapse prevention. American Psychiatric Association Annual Meeting, Philadelphia, Pennsylvania, May 23, 2002.

Dettling AC, Feldon J et al (2002) Repeated parental deprivation in the infant common marmoset (Callithrix Jacchus, Primates) and analysis of its effects on early development. Biol Psychiatr 52:1037-1046.

DiMatteo MR et al (2000) Depression is a risk factor for noncompliance with medical treatment. Arch Intern Med 160:2101-2107.

Donoghue J, Hylan TR (2001) Antidepressant use in clinical practice: efficacy v. effectiveness. Br J Psychiatr 179 (suppl.42) S9-S17.

Druss BG, (2002) The mental health/primary care interface in the United States: history, structure, and context. Gene Hospital Psychiatr 24:197-202.

Elkin I, Shea MT (1989) National Institute of Mental Health treatment of depression collaborative research program. Arch Gen Psychiatr 46:971-982.

Elzinga BM, Bremner JD (2002) Are the neural substrates of memory the final common pathway in posttraumatic stress disorder (PTSD)? J Affect Disord 70:1-17.

ENRICHD Investigators (2001) Enhancing recovery in coronary heart disease (ENRICHD) study intervention: rationale and design. Psychosomatic Med 63(5):747-755.

Evans MD, Hollon SD (1992) Differential relapse following cognitive therapy and pharmacotherapy for depression. Arch Gen Psychiatr 49:802-808.

Fava M, Davidson KG (1996) Definition and epidemiology of treatment-resistant depression. Psychiatr Clin North America 19(2):179-200.

Fergusson DM, Woodward LJ (2002) Mental health, educational, and social role outcomes of adolescents with depression. Arch Gen Psychiatr 59:225-231.

Frank E, Prien RF et al (1991) Conceptualization and rationale for consensus definitions of terms in major depressive disorder: Remission, recovery, relapse, and recurrence. Arch Gen Psychiatr 48:851-855.

Frasure-Smith N, Lesperance F et al (1993) Depression following myocardial infarction. Impact on 6-month survival. JAMA 270(15):1819-1825.

Garber J, Flynn C (2001) Vulnerability to depression in childhood and adolescence.

In Vulnerability to Psychopathology (Ingram RE, Price JM, eds), pp175-225. New York: The Guilford Press.

Ghaemi S and Appleton A (2002) Polypharmacy of depression. In Polypharmacy in Psychiatry (Ghaemi S, ed), pp 79-99. NY: Marcel Decker.

Glaser D (2000) Child abuse and neglect and the brain – a review. J Child Psychol Psychiatr Allied Disciplines 41:97-116.

Goffman E (1963) Stigma: Notes on Management of Spoiled Identity. Englewood Cliffs, NJ: Prentice-Hall.

Gold PW, Chrousos GP (1999) The endocrinology of melancholic and atypical depression: relation to neurocircuitry and somatic consequences. Proc Assoc Am Physicians 111(1):22-34.

Goldberg D, Blackwell B (1970) Psychiatric illness in general practice: a detailed study using a new method of case identification. BMJ 2:439-43.

Greden JF (2001) The burden of disease for treatment-resistant depression. J Clin Psychiatr 61 (suppl 16):26-31.

Hamilton M (1960) A rating scale for depression. J Neurol Neurosurg Psychiatr 23:56-62.

Hammen C (1991) Depression Runs in Families: The Social Context of Risk and Resilience in Children of Depressed Mothers. New York, NY: Springer-Verlag.

Hammen C (2001) Vulnerability to depression in adulthood. In Vulnerability to Psychopathology (Ingram RE, Price JM, eds), pp226-257. New York: The Guilford Press.

Hankin BL, Abramsom LY et al (1998) Development of depression form preadolescence to young adulthood: emerging gender differences in a 10-year longitudinal study. J Abnorm Psychol 107:128-140.

Harkness KL, Frank E et al (2002) Does interpersonal psychotherapy protect women from depression in the face of stressful life events? J Consult Clin Psychiatr 70.4:908-915.

Hayes SC, Barlow DH et al (1999) The Scientist-Practitioner: Research and Accountability in Clinical and Educational Settings, 2nd ed. New York: Pergamon Press.

Hedlund S, Rude SS (1995) Evidence of latent depressive schemas in formerly depressed individuals. J Abnorm Psychol 104:517-525.

Heim C, Nemeroff CB (2001) The role of childhood trauma in the neurobiology of mood and anxiety disorders: preclinical and clinical studies. Biol Psychiatr 49(12):1023-1039.

Hendrick V, Altshuler LL et al (1996) Course of psychiatric disorders across the menstrual cycle. Harvard Review of Psychiatry 4:200-207.

Hirschfeld RM, Keller MB et al (1997) The National Depressive and Manic-Depressive-Association consensus statement on the undertreatment of depression. JAMA 22;277(4):333-340.

Hollon SD, Munoz RF et al (2002) Psychosocial intervention development for the prevention and treatment of depression: Promoting innovation and increasing access. Biol Psychiatr 2002:610-630.

Holsinger T, Steffens DC (2002) Head injury in early adulthood and the lifetime risk of depression. Arch Gen Psychiatr 59:17-22.

Horwath E, Johnson, J et al (1992) Depressive symptoms as relative and attributable risk factors for first-episode major depression. Arch Gen Psychiatr 49:817-823.

Ingram RE, Price JM (2001) The role of vulnerability in understanding psychopathology. In Vulnerability to Psychopathology (Ingram RE, Price JM, eds), pp3-18. New York: The Guilford Press.

Institute of Medicine (1994) <u>Reducing Risks of Mental Disorders: Frontiers for Preventive Intervention Research.</u> Washington, DC: National Academy Press.

Jaycox LH, Reivich KJ et al (1994) Prevention of depressive symptoms in school children. Behav Res Therapy 32:801-816.

Jiang W, Alexander J et al (2001) Relationship of depression to increased risk of mortality and rehospitalization in patients with congestive heart failure. Arch Intern Med 161(15):1849-1856.

Johnson SL, Sandrow D et al (2000) Increases in manic symptoms after life events involving goal attainment. J Abnorm Psychol 109:721-727.

Johnson SL, Winett CA et al (1999) Social support and the course of bipolar disorder. J Abnorm Psychol 108:558-556.

Jonas BS, Mussolina ME (2000) Symptoms of depression as a prospective risk factor for stroke. Psychosomatic Med 62:463-471.

Judd LL (1997) The clinical course of unipolar major depressive disorders. Arch Gen Psychiatr 54:989-991.

Judd LL, Akiskal HS et al (1998) A prospective 12-year study of subsyndromal and syndromal depressive symptoms in unipolar major depressive disorders. Arch Gen Psychiatr 55:694-700.

Kathol RG. Financing integrated medical and psychiatric care: Role of psychiatrists inn the medically ill. The Academy of Psychosomatic Medicine Annual Meeting, Tucson, Arizona, November 21, 2002.

Katon W, Robinson P et al (1996) A multifaceted intervention to improve treatment of depression in primary care. Arch Gen Psychiatr 53:924-932.

Katon W, Von Korff M et al (1992) Adequacy and duration of antidepressant treatment in primary care. Med Care 30:67-76.

Katon W, Von Korff M et al (1995) Collaborative management to achieve treatment guidelines. JAMA 273:1026-1031.

Katon W, Von Korff M et al (1997) Population-based care of depression: Effective disease management strategies to decrease prevalence. Gen Hospital Psychiatr 19:169-178.

Katon W, Von Korff M et al (1999) Stepped collaborative care for primary care patients with persistent symptoms of depression. Arch Gen Psychiatr 56:1109-1115.

Katzelnick DJ, Simon GE et al (2000) Randomized trial of a depression management program in high utilizers of medical care. Arch Fam Med 9:345-351.

Kaufman J (1991) Depressive disorders in maltreated children. J Am Acad Child Adolesc Psychiatr 30:257-265.

Kaufman J, Plotsky PM et al (2000) Effects of early adverse experiences on brain structure and function: Clinical implications. Biol Psychiatr 48:778-790.

Kellam SG, Ling X et al (1998) The effect the level of aggression in the first grade classroom on the course and malleability of aggressive behavior into middle school. Development Psychopathol 10:165-185.

Kellam SG, Rebok GW et al (1994) Depressive symptoms over first grade and their response to a developmental epidemiologically based preventive trial aimed at improving achievement. Development Psychopathol 6:463-481.

Keller MB, Berndt ER (2002) Depression treatment: A lifelong commitment? Psychopharmacol Bull 36 (Suppl 2):133-141.

Keller MB, Boland RJ (1998) Implications of failing to achieve successful long-term maintenance treatment of recurrent unipolar major depression. Biol Psychiatr 44:348-360.

Keller MB, Kocsis JH et al (1998) Maintenance phase efficacy of sertraline for chronic depression. JAMA 280:1665-1672.

Keller MB, Lavori PW, et al (1992)Time to recovery, chronicity, and levels of psychopathology in major depression. A 5-year prospective follow-up. Arch Gen Psychiatr 49:809-816.

Keller MB, McCullough JP et al (2000) A comparison of nefazodone, the cognitive behavioral analysis system of psychotherapy, and their combination for the treatment of chronic depression. N Engl J Med 342:1462-1470.

Kendler KS, Gardner CO et al (1999) Clinical characteristics of major depression that predict risk of depression in relatives. Arch Gen Psychiatr 56:322-327.

Kendler KS, Neale MC et al (1995) Stressful life events, genetic liability, and onset of an episode of major depression in women. Am J Psychiatr 152:833-842.

Kendler KS, Prescott CA (1999) A population-based twin study of lifetime major depression in men and women. Arch Gen Psychiatr 56:39-44.

Kendler KS, Thornton LM et al (2001) Genetic risk, number of previous episodes, and stressful life events in predicting onset of major depression. Am J Psychiatr 158:582-586.

Kerber KB, Knesper DJ (1997) Making referrals for psychiatric care: clinical advice and managed care implications. In Primary Care Psychiatry (Knesper DJ, Rib MB, Schwenk TL eds), pp85-94. New York: W.B. Saunders.

Kessler RC, McGonagle KA et al (1993) Sex and depression in the National Comorbidity Survey, I: Lifetime prevalence, chronicity, and recurrence. J Affect Disord 29:85-96.

Kessler RC, McGonagle KA et al (1994) Lifetime and 12-month prevalence of DSM-III-R psychiatric disorders in the United States. Arch Gen Psychiatr 51:8-19.

Khan A, Leventhal RM et al (2002) Severity of depression and response to antidepressants and placebo: an analysis of the Food and Drug Administration database. J Clin Psychopharmacol 22:40-45.

Kirmayer L, Robbins J et al (1993) Somatization and the recognition of depression and anxiety in primary care. Am J Psychiatr 150:734-741.

Klein DN, Anderson RL (1995) The behavioral high-risk paradigm in the mood disorders. In The Behavioral High-Risk Paradigm in Psychopathology (Miller GA ed), pp199-221. New York: Springer-Verlag.

Klerman GL, Weisman MM (1989) Increasing rates of Depression. JAMA 261:2229-2235.

Knesper DJ, Riba MB et al (1997) Primary Care Psychiatry. NY: WB Saunders.

Kocsis JH, Frances AJ et al (1988) Imipramine treatment for chronic depression. Arch Gen Psychiatr 45:253-257

Kornstein SG (1997) Gender differences in depression: Implications for treatment. J Clin Psychiatr 58(suppl 15):12-18.

Kovacs M (1966) Presentation and course of major depressive disorder during childhood and later years of the life span. J Am Acad Child Adolesc Psychiatr 35:705-715.

Kronfol Z, Remick DG (2000) Cytokines and the brain: Implications for clinical psychiatry. Am J Psychiatr 157:683-694.

Kronke K et al (1994) Physical symptoms (of depression) in primary care. Arch Fam Med 3:774-779.

Kronkite K (1994) On the Edge of Darkness: Conversations about Conquering

Depression. NY: Bantam Doubleday, p10.

Kupfer DJ, First MB et al (2002) A Reasearch Agenda for DSM-V. Washington, DC: American Psychiatric Association.

Kupfer DJ, Frank E et al (1992) Five-year outcome for maintenance therapies in recurrent depression. Arch Gen Psychiatr 49:769-773.

Lam RW, Wan DD et al (2002) Combining antidepressants for treatment-resistant depression. J ClinPsychiatr 68(8):685-93.

Lave J, Frank R et al (1998) Cost-effectiveness of treatments for major depression in primary care practice. Arch Gen Psychiatr 55:645-651.

Lavori PE, Kessler MB et al (1984) Relapse in affective disorder: a reanalysis of the literature using life table methods. J Psychiatr Res 18:13-25.

Lecrubier Y, Clerc G et al (2002) Efficacy of St. John's Wort Extract vs 5570 in major depression: A double-blind, placebo-controlled trail. Am J Psychiatr 159:1361-1366.

Lenze EJ, Drew MA et al (2002) Combines pharmacotherapy and psychotherapy as maintenance treatment for late-life depression: Effects on social adjustment. Am J Psychiatr 159:466-468.

Lesperance, F, Frasure-Smith N et al (2002) Five-year risk of cardiac mortality in relation to initial severity and one-year changes in depression symptoms after myocardial infarction. Am Heart Assoc J 105:1049-1053.

Lewis-Hall F, Williams TS et al (2002) Psychiatric Illness in Women. Washington, DC: American Psychiatric Press.

Luft, Harold S, (1981) Health Maintenance Organizations, dimensions of performance. New York: John Wiley & Sons.

Lyons MJ, Eisen SA et al (1998) A registry-based twin study of depression in men. Arch Gen Psychiatr 55:468-472.

Maier W, Lichtermann D et al (1991) Unipolar depression in the aged: Determinants of familial aggregation. J Affect Disord 23:53-61.

Margolis S, Swartz KL (2002) Depression and Anxiety (The Johns Hopkins White Papers), p 5. New York: Medletter Associates.

Martinsen EW and Stephens T (1994) Exercise and mental health in clinical and free-living populations. In Advances in Exercise Adherence (Dishman RK, ed), pp55-72. Champaign, IL: Human Kinetics.

Merikangas KR, Chakravarti A et al (2002) Future of genetics of mood disorders research. Biol Psychiatr 52:457-477.

Merikangas KR, Swendsen J (1997) Genetic epidemiology of psychiatric disorders. Epidemiol Rev 19:144-155.

Monroe SM, Simons AD (1991) Diathesis-stress theories in the context of life stress research: Implications for the depressive disorders. Psychol Bull 110:406-425.

Mulrow C, Williams JJ et al (1998) Treatment of depression—newer pharmocotherapies. Psychopharmacol Bull 34:409-479.

Munoz RF, Le HN et al (2002) Preventing the onset of major depression. In Handbook of Depression (Gotlib IH, Hammen CL eds.) pp383-403. New York: The Guilford Press.

Munoz RF, Mrazek PJ et al (1996) Institute of Medicine Report on Prevention of Mental Disorders—summary and commentary. Am Psychol 51:1116-1122.

Munoz RF, Ying YW et al (1995) Prevention of depression with primary care patients: a randomized controlled trial. Am J Community Psychol 23:199-222.

Murray CJL, Lopez AD (1996) The Global Burden of Disease and Injury Series, Volume 1: A Comprehensive Assessment of Mortality and Disability from Diseases, Injuries and Risk Factors in 1990 and Projected to 2020. Cambridge, MA:

Harvard University Press. (Published on behalf of the World Health Organization and the World Bank.)

Murray CJL, Lopez AD (1997) Global mortality, disability, and the contribution of risk factors: Global Burden of Disease Study. Lancet 349:1436-1442.

Musselman DL, Evans DL et al (1998) The relationship of depression to cardiovascular disease: epidemiology, biology and treatment. Arch Gen Psychiatr 55:580-592.

Musselman DL, Lawson DH et al (2001b) Paroxetine for the prevention of depression induced by high-dose interferon alfa. N Engl J Med 344(13):961-966.

Musselman DL, Miller AH et al (2001a) Higher than normal plasma interleukin-6 concentrations in cancer patients with depression: preliminary findings. Am J Psychiatr 158(8):1252-1257.

Mynors-Wallace LM, Gath DH et al (2000) Randomised controlled trial of problem solving treatment, antidepressant medication, and combined treatment for major depression in primary care. BMJ 320(7226):26-30.

Nolen-Hoeksema S, Girgu J et al (1986) Learned helplessness in children: A longitudinal study of depression, achievement, and explanatory style. J Personal Social Psychol 51:435-442.

Nutting PA, Rost K et al (2002) Barriers to initiating depression treatment in primary care practice. J Gen Intern Med 17:103-111.

O'Hara MW (1995) The cognitive diathesis for depression. In The Behavioral High-Risk Paradigm in Psychopathology (Miller GA ed), pp250-270. New York: Springer-Verlag.

Pajer K (1995) New strategies in the treatment of depression in women. J Clin Psychiatr 56(suppl 2):30-37.

Pakel ES (1982) Life events and early environment. In Handbook of Affective Disorders (Pakel ES, ed), pp 146-161. New York: The Guilford Press.

Peden AR, Rayens MK et al (2001) Preventing depression in high-risk college women: A report of an 18-month follow-up. J Am College Health 49(6):299-306.

Penninx BW, Beekman AT et al (2001) Depression and cardiac mortality: results from a community-based longitudinal study. Arch Gen Psychiatr 58:221-227.

Peselow ED, Sanfilipo MP et al (1992) Melancholic/endogenous depression and response to somatic treatment and placebo. Am J Psychiatr 149(10): 1324-34.

Pignone MP, Gaynes BN et al (2002) Screening for depression in adults: a summary of the evidence for the U.S. Preventive Services Task Force. Ann Intern Med 136:765-776.

Pincus HA, et al (1998) Prescribing trends in psychotropic medications: primary care, psychiatry, and other medical specialties. JAMA 279(7):526-531.

Pine DS, Cohen P et al (1999) The risk for early-adulthood anxiety and depressive disorders in adolescents with anxiety and depressive disorders. Arch Gen Psychiatr 55:56-59.

Post RM (1992) Transduction of psychosocial stress into the neurobiology of recurrent depression. Am J Psychiatr 149:999-1010.

Price JM, Lento J (2001) The nature of child and adolescent vulnerability: history and definitions. In Vulnerability to Psycho-pathology: Risk Across the Lifespan (Ingram RE, Price JM, eds), pp 20-38. New York: The Guilford Press.

Price RH, van Ryn M et al (1992) Impact of a preventive job search intervention on the likelihood of depression among the unemployed. J Health Social Behav 33:158-167.

Ranga K, Krishnan R (2002) Biological risk factors in late life depression. Biol Psychiatr 52:185-192.

Ranga K, Krishnan R et al (2002) Comorbidity of depression with other medical diseases in the elderly. Biol Psychiatr 52:539-588.

Rao U, Hammen C et al (1999) Continuity of depression during the transition to adulthood: A 5-year longitudinal study of young women. J Am Acad Child Adolesc Psychiatr 38:908-915.

Regier D, Narrow WE et al (1993) The de facto US mental and addictive disorders service system: epidemiologic catchment area prospective 1-year prevalence rates of disorders and services. Arch Gen Psychiatr 50:85-94.

Rehm LP (1977) A self-control model of depression. Behavior Therapy 8:787-804.

Reichenberg-Ullman J, Ullman R (1999) Homeopathic Alternatives to Conventional Drug Therapies. Berkley, CA: North Atlantic Books.

Reubgerz HZ, Giaconia RM et al (2000) General and specific childhood risk factors for depression and drug disorders by early childhood. J Am Acad Child Adolesc Psychiatr 39:223-231.

Reus VI, Freimer NB (1977) Understanding the genetic basis of mood disorders: Where do we stand? Am J Human Genetics 60:1283-1288.

Reynolds CF,Frank E et al (1999) Nortriptyline and interpersonal psychotherapy as maintenance therapies for recurrent major depression: a randomized controlled trial in patients older than 59 years. JAMA 281:39-45.

Riolo SA et al (2002) National data on depression prevalence and treatment among adolescents. Presented at the American Academy of Chile & Adolescent Psychiatry Annual Meeting, October 24, 2002.

Roberts JE, Gotlib IH (1997) Social support and personality in depression: Implications for quantitative genetics. In Sourcebook of Social Support and Personality (Pierce GR, Lakey B, eds), pp 187-214. New York: Plenum Press.

Robinson DS, Rickels K (2000) Concerns about clinical drug trails. J Clin Psychopharmacol 20:593-596.

Rohde P, Lewinsohn PM et al (1991) Comorbidity of unipolar depression: II. Comorbidity with other mental disorders in adolescents and adults. J Abnorm Psychol 100:214-222.

Rowe JW, Kahn RL (1998) Successful Aging. New York: Pantheon Books.

Roy-Byrne P, Post RM et al (1985) The longitudinal course of recurrent affective illness: Life chart data from research patients at the NIMH. Acta Psychiatr Scandinavia (suppl) 317:2-34.

Rutter M, Macdonald H et al (1990) Genetic factors in child psychiatric disorders—II. Empirical findings. J Child Psychol Psychiatr 31:39-83.

Ryan ND (2001) Diagnosing pediatric depression. Biol Psychiatr 49:1050-1054.

Sackeim HA (2001) The definition and meaning of treatment-resistant depression. J Clin Psychiatr 62 (suppl 16):10-17.

Satcher D (2001) From the Surgeon General. Global mental health: it's time has come. JAMA 285:1697.

Saylor, C, Yoder M et at (2002) Stigma. In Chronic Illness: Impact & Interventions. p 53. Sudbury, MA: Jones & Bartlett Publishers.

Schade CP, Jones ER et al (1998) A ten-year review of the validity and clinical utility of depression screening. Psychiatr Serv 49:55-61.

Schmidt ME, Fava M et al (2000) The efficacy and safety of a new enteric-coated formulation of fluoxetine given once weekly during the continuation treatment of major depressive disorder. J Clin Psychiatr 61(11):851-857.

Schulberg HC, Block MR et al (1996) Treating major depression in primary care practice: Eight-month clinical outcomes. Arch Gen Psychiatr 53(10):913-919.

Segal ZV, Gemar M et al (1999) Differential cognitive response to a mood challenge following successful cognitive therapy or pharmacotherapy for unipolar depression. J Abnorm Psychol 108:3-10.

Seligman ME, Schulman P et al (1999) Prevention of depression and anxiety. Prevention & Treatment 2, Article 8 (ejournal).

Senra C (1996) Evaluation and monitoring of symptom severity and change in depressed outpatients. J Clin Psychiatr 52(3):317-324.

Simon GE, VonKorff M et al (2000) Randomised trial of monitoring, feedback, and management of care by telephone to improve treatment of depression in primary care. BMJ 320:550-554.

Smith AL, Weissman MM (1992) Epidemiology. In Handbook of Affective Disorders (Paykel ES, ed), pp 111-129. New York: Guilford Press.

Stahl SM (2000) Essential Psychopharma-cology. Neuroscientific Basis and Practical Applications. 2nd ed. Cambridge, UK: Cambridge University Press.

Stahl SM (2002) Can psychopharmacologic treatments that relieve symptoms also prevent disease progression? J Clin Psychiatr 63:961-962.

Starkstein SE, Robinson RG eds (1993) Depression in Neurologic Disease Baltimore: The Johns Hopkins University Press.

Strofe LA (1997) Psychopathology as an outcome of development. Development and Psychopathol 9:252-268.

Sullivan PF, Neale MC et al (2000) Genetic epidemiology of major depression: Review and meta-analysis. Am J Psychiatr 157:1552-1562.

Thakore J (2001) Physical Consequences of Depression. Hampshire, England: Wrightson Biomedical Publishing Ltd.

Thase M, Blomgren S et al (1997) Fluoxetine treatment of patients with major depressive disorder who failed initial treatment with sertraline. J Clin Psychiatr 58:16-21.

Thase ME (2000) Treatment of severe depression. J Clin Psychiatr 61(1):17-25.

Thase ME (2002a) Studying new antidepressants: if there was a light at the end of the tunnel could we see it? J Clin Psychiatr 63(suppl2):24-28.

Thase ME (2002b) Comparing the methods used to compare antidepressants. Psychopharmacol Bull 36(suppl 1):4-17.

Thase ME, Friedman ES, (1999) Is psychotherapy an effective treatment for melancholia and other severe depressive states? J Affect Disord 54(1-2)1-19

Tsuang MT, Faraone SV (1990). The Genetics of Mood Disorders. Baltimore, MD: The Johns Hopkins University Press.

Tsuang MT, Stone WS et al (1999) Treatment of nonpsychotic relatives of patients with schizophrenia: four case studies. Biol Psychiatr 45(11):1412-1418.

Tsuang MT, Stone WS et al (2002) Understanding predisposition to schizo-phrenia: Toward intervention and prevention. Canadian J Psychiatr 47:518-526.

U. S. Preventive Services Task Force (2002) Screening for depression: recommend-ations and rationale. Ann Intern Med 136:760-764.

Unützer J, Katon W et al (2002) Improving care for late life depression: Results from a randomized controlled trial with 1801 depressed older adults. The Academy of Psychosomatic Medicine Annual Meeting, Tucson, Arizona, November 23.

Vinokur AD, Price RH et al (1995) Impact of the JOBS intervention on unemployed workers varying in risk for depression. Am J Community Psychol 23:39-74.

Von Korff M, Katon W (1998) Treatment costs, cost offset, and cost-effectiveness of collaborative management of depression. Psychosomatic Med 60:143-149.

Von korff M, Shapiro S et al (1987) Anxiety and depression in a primary care clinic: comparison of Diagnostic Interview Schedule, General Health Questionnaire, and practitioner assessments. Arch Gen Psychiatr 44:152-156.

Wahl OF (1999) Telling is Risky Business. New Brunswick, NJ: Rutgers University Press.

Weissman MM, Bland RC et al (1996) Cross-national epidemiology of major depression and bipolar disorder. JAMA 276:2983-2991.

Weissman MM, Gammon GD et al (1987) Children of depressed parents: Increased psychopathology and early onset of major depression. Arch Gen Psychiatr 44:847-853.

Weissman MM, Olfson M (1995) Depression in women: implications for health care research. Science 269:799-801.

Weissman MM, Warner V et al (1988) Early-onset major depression in parents and their children. J Affect Disord 15:269-277.

Weissman MM, Wolk S et al (1999a) Depressed adolescents grow up. JAMA 281:1707-1713.

Weissman MM, Wolk S et al (1999b) Children with prepubertal-onset major depressive disorder and anxiety grow up. Arch Gen Psychiatr 56:794-801.

Werner EE, Smith RS (2001) Journeys from Childhood to Midlife: Risk, Resilience and Recovery. Ithaca, NY: Cornell University Press.

Whooley MA, Avins AL et al (1997) Case-finding instruments for depression. Two questions are as good as many. J Gen Intern Med 12:439-445.

Williams JW Jr, Noel PH et al (2002) Is this patient clinically depressed? JAMA 287:1160-1170.

World Health Organization (1996) The Global Burden of Disease. Geneva, Switzerland: World Health Organization Press.

Wulsin LR, Vaillant GE et al (1999) A systematic review of the mortality of depression. Psychosomatic Med 61:6-17.

Yonkers KA, Samson J (2000) Mood disorders measures. In Handbook of Psychiatric Measures. pp 515-529. Washington, DC: American Psychiatric Press.

Young AS, Klap R et al (2001) The quality of care for depression and anxiety disorders in the United States. Arch Gen Psychiatr 58:55-61.

Yung AR, McGorry PD (1997) Is pre-psychotic intervention realistic in Schizophrenia and related disorders? Australian & New Zealand J Psychiatr 31(6):799-805.

Zajecka J (2001) Strategies for the treatment of antidepressant-related sexual dysfunction. J Clin Psychiatr 62 Suppl 3:35-43.

Zarate C, Kando J et al (1996) Does intolerance or lack of response with fluoxetine predict the same will happen with sertraline? J Clin Psychiatr 57:67-71.

Zuroff DC, Blatt SJ et al (1999) Vulnerability to depression: Reexamining state dependence and relative stability. J Abnorm Psychol 108:76-89.

AN UPDATE ON THE PSYCHOTHERAPEUTIC TREATMENT OF SUICIDAL BEHAVIOR

M. David Rudd

REALIZING THE IMPACT AND COSTS OF SUICIDE: A CALL FOR ACTION

Suicide is consistently among the leading causes of death internationally (Delao et al., 2002). Approximately 30,000 people in the United States take their own lives each year and suicides outpaced homicides by 3:2 over the last 100 years (Institute of Medicine, 2002). It has been conservatively estimated that up to 5% of those in the United States have made one or more suicide attempt during their life, with each and every attempt taking an unknown toll on countless family members and friends (Kessler et al., 1999). Suicide is the third leading cause of death among young people age 15-24, with an estimated 12 suicides per 100,000 people (Anderson, 2002). Rates of suicidal ideation vary greatly in the literature; Linehan (1982) estimates that 31% of the clinical population and 24% of the general population have thought about killing themselves at some point. Moreover, there is clearly a link between suicidal thinking and eventual suicide (Beck et al., 1997). In the last decade, there has been a growing consensus that coordinated and targeted action is needed, including improved federal funding for more effective treatment and prevention efforts (DHHS, 2001).

Although the analyses are highly controversial, some have attempted to calculate the economic costs of suicidal behavior. These estimates included medical costs (e.g., emergency transport, hospitalization, rehabilitation), victims' lost wages, and an effort to quantify pain, suffering and quality of life lost by victims' and their family members (e.g., Miller et al., 1995). Miller and colleagues

estimated the cost of suicide was over 15 billion dollars in 1998. These estimates, however, certainly contain erroneous assumptions, and omissions. The emotional scars that survivors carry are difficult to quantify and the true impact is far greater than numbers and dollars can communicate. Nevertheless, such estimates give us a glimpse of the staggering impact of suicide and suicidal behavior in the United States and throughout the world.

The Question of Treatment

The question of what we know about treating suicidal ideation and behavior is a complicated one. Few would disagree that we need to rely on empirical evidence from methodologically sound research; This requires ongoing assessment of research evidence. Here, we evaluate current research on interventions to reduce suicide. We focus on studies specifically targeting suicidal ideation and behavior, not non-fatal self-injury with no associated intent to die and related self-mutilatory behaviors (e.g. O'Carroll et al., 1996). To insure the validity of conclusions drawn from this research, this review particularly addresses issues of terminology, methodology and design, related inclusion and exclusion criteria, and eventual markers of treatment outcome across studies. The number of studies that qualifies for inclusion in this review is limited, but the hope is that such rigor will result in a more accurate understanding of treatment efforts targeting suicidal behavior.

There are many relevant questions about treatment of suicide for researchers and clinicians. Given the limited empirical evidence to date (e.g. Rudd et al., 2004), we are in a position to address only a few fundamental questions:

◆ What treatments have been demonstrated effective specifically for suicidality?

For a treatment to be effective the impact must endure well beyond the last session, particularly when suicide is the issue. To address the question of effectiveness, we will emphasize the specific outcome markers and duration of follow-up assessed in each study.

◆ Among identified treatments, are there common core interventions associated with positive outcome?

The notion of core interventions addresses the potential overlap across successful treatments. By investigating how effective treatments that vary in program description and theory are similar, we hope to find general elements that reduce suicidality and better understand the process of effective treatment of suicidality. Given the limited literature available in this area, this is an issue of particular significance.

◆ Are some treatments better at retaining patients than others?

A fairly robust finding in the suicide risk assessment literature is that active treatment serves a protective function (e.g. Maris et al., 2000). Given the complexities in conducting treatment outcome studies with suicidal patients, simply retaining them in treatment may be an important benefit.

◆ Does treatment setting influence outcome (i.e., inpatient, outpatient, partial hospital-ization, residential, day treatment)?

Very little information is available on the effectiveness of varying treatment settings. For example, little is known about the utility of hospitalization for suicidal behavior, despite the fact that it is almost uniformly accepted as the standard of care during periods of acute risk. Because the cost of providing treatment varies greatly depending on the treatment setting, this is a question of great interest to health care organizations and administrators.

◆ Is treatment duration associated with outcome? Does lengthening treatment duration improve the effectiveness of treatment?

The question of whether or not treatment serves only to delay a suicide is yet to be answered. The question is perhaps most salient for short-term interventions, given the reality that active treatment offers some protective value for patients. Do time-limited interventions result in lasting changes that ultimately reduce lifetime risk for suicide? The only way to know for certain is to track patients for long periods, ultimately for several decades or more.

A Literature Characterized by Limitations

Although a large number of studies about suicidality are available in the literature, including case examples, theoretical articles, and studies without comparison or control groups, this review includes only those studies that are randomized or controlled. Including studies without adequate rigor only serves to further complicate an area of scientific inquiry that already faces significant challenges. Although there are undeniable limitations with this approach, it provides a clear and firm scientific foundation to the treatment of suicidal ideation and behaviors. As is noted below, it is surprising how few studies are available specifically targeting suicidality. However, if we consider the ethical, legal and practical constraints faced by researchers, it is actually surprising that so many rigorous studies have been successfully completed. There are literally hundreds to thousands of studies that explore correlates of suicidal ideation and behavior, but the inherent problem is that these findings are correlational in nature and cannot determine causation. More often than not, such studies raise as many questions as they answer.

A thorough review of the literature (PsycINFO and MEDLINE) yielded a total of 26 randomized or controlled studies targeting suicidality (see Table 1.1 for a detailed summary of all studies discussed). This total incorporates both intervention and treatment studies. I am aware of two additional studies, one by Marsha Linehan and another by Greg Brown and Aaron Beck, that are in press but not available for inclusion at this time. The results of both studies are exciting, with clear implications for the nature of care in this area. These will be added when available. Four studies specifically targeted pharmacological treatment and were excluded from our review due to our focus on psychotherapeutic treatment (Hirsch et al., 1983; March et al., 2004; Montgomery et al., 1981; Montgomery & Montgomery, 1982). With exclusion of the two unpublished and four medication studies, we were left with a total of 22 controlled or randomized studies specifically targeting the psychotherapeutic treatment of suicidality. In the included studies, the goal of the treatment was to reduce suicidality; suicidality was not addressed as a correlate to another disorder or a clinical phenomenon or a peripheral marker of outcome. This review targets adults. None of the studies included are specific to adolescents, although a few include older adolescents (i.e., ages 17-19), most accurately described as young adults. As with adults, there are a limited number of randomized controlled trials targeting suicidal children and adolescents (e.g., Berman et al., 2005 for a review), with many of the same legal concerns inhibiting work in this area.

The indentified studies were catagorized as intervention (n=6) or treatment (n=16) studies. Descriptions provided by the authors were used to make this distinction. Differentiating intervention and treatment studies is important for a number of reasons. Most importantly, these studies have differing implications for the standard of care for suicidal patients.

Intervention studies included studies that specifically stated they were NOT providing any identifiable form of psychotherapy as the study condition. The stated focus was on improved access to care. Intervention studies made procedural changes in the nature of care including improving the ease of access to traditional psychotherapeutic services and exploring subsequent reductions in suicide attempts or related behaviors. It is arguable that a procedural change impacts the nature of treatment provided, but since "treatment" was not specifically controlled it is not possible to arrive at meaningful conclusions outside of a focus on the procedural elements noted in the studies. As is summarized in Table 1.1, several intervention studies faced considerable theoretical and clinical confounds, minimizing the utility and practical application of the findings.

The remaining 16 studies tested psychotherapeutic treatments for suicidality. Given the importance of the topic, it is surprising that the scientific foundation is so limited. However, as noted before, the legal, ethical and practical issues faced by researchers conducting clinical trials with suicidal patients are many and complex.

Among the most serious concerns that limit suicide treatment research is the need to randomly assign participants to treatment conditions and provide comparisons to "treatment as usual". Finding clinicians to agree to serve as the "treatment as usual" comparison group has proven challenging. Similarly, accumulating large clinical samples is difficult since the management of high risk patients is extremely time consuming, expensive and resource intensive.

Most of the treatment studies reviewed incorporated some form of problem solving or skill building activity as the central psychotherapeutic activity (cf. Rudd et al., 2004). More often than not, the conceptual model was consistent with a cognitive-behavioral approach, an approach that is perhaps more amenable to scientific study than other less well defined orientations (e.g., psychoanalytical).

Table 1. Description of Psychotherapeutic Treatment and Intervention Studies Targeting Suicidal Behavior[1]

Author(s)	Inclusion/Exclusion Criteria	Total N (E/C)	Outcome Measures	Follow-up Period	Attrition[2]	Potential Confounds	Conclusions:
Chowdhury, Hicks, & Kreitman, 1973	Included suicide attempters, but excluded those at *high risk* (not clearly defined) for future attempts. However, the potentially low risk nature of the sample is confirmed by the fact that approximately 40% of both the treatment and control groups did not receive a formal psychiatric diagnosis (Axis I or II).	155 (71/84)	Frequency of subsequent attempts, subjective ratings on a *suicidal behavior risk rating scale*, and subjective ratings of *psychiatric* and *social status*. The instruments were not described in any detail nor were psychometric properties provided. However, it appeared that the ratings were simply subjective in nature.	6-months	Not provided	Results are **questionable** due to the following problems: a) confound created by excluding *high risk* cases, b) lack of a *defined* treatment (i.e., content, frequency) or intervention provided in either group. c) failure to assess intent in a standardized manner to select subjects (i.e. subjectively excluding *high risk* cases), and **d)** the lack of psychometrically sound outcome measures.	**Conclusions:** No definitive conclusions can be offered.
Termansen & Bywater, 1975	Included suicide attempters presenting to emergency room, no exclusion criteria were stated.	202 (57/57/50/ 38)	Frequency of subsequent attempts and ratings of anxiety, depression, alcohol abuse, among other variables with an instrument that was not described in any detail. Psychometric properties were not provided. The ratings appeared to be simply subjective in nature, made by the *mental health worker*.	3-months	37% (74/202) Rates for each group were: **E1**=21% **E2**=42% **C1**=36% **C2**=53%	Results are seriously confounded and **questionable** due to the following: a) the lack of equivalence between the groups at intake, b) poorly defined intervention in type (i.e., content) and frequency, c) failure to assess intent in standardized manner for subject selection, **d)** lack of psychometrically sound outcome measures.	**Conclusions:** No definitive conclusions can be offered.

[1] Studies are listed in chronological order; a variation of this summary chart has been used elsewhere.

[2] Attrition for the entire sample at the last identifiable follow-up point, expressed as the overall attrition %, along with the actual N /total sample size. Attrition for each group is also provided, if available.

				Attrited= 160	**No Significant Confounds**	**Conclusions:**
Motto, 1976[3]	Self-selected groups, those accepting treatment following psychiatric admission for depression or a *suicidal state* and those refusing treatment. Of those refusing treatment, only those accepting *contact* were followed.	3,006 **E**=401 **C1**=452 **C2**=1,993	Completed suicide	5-years		**Conclusions:** Simple follow-up contact *can potentially* have preventive value.
Litman & Wold, 1975[4]	*High risk* callers to a suicide prevention center were assigned to 2 groups. The inclusion criteria were not specifically stated, nor were any exclusion criteria summarized.	400 (200/200)	Frequency of suicide attempts, completed suicides, frequency of suicide ideation. Various subjective quality of life measures were also used. Psychometric properties of the instruments were not provided.	2 years	32% (129/400) Not provided for E and C groups separately	Interpretation of the results are seriously limited due to: a) poorly defined intervention both in type and frequency, b) apparent equivalency of intervention provided the 2 groups, failure to define high risk in a standardized way, c) lack of psychometrically sound outcome measures, and d) there were no stated exclusion criteria.	**Conclusions:** Although the study suffers from serious methodological problems, it does offer very limited support for the potential utility of follow-up contact. More specifically, intensive follow-up contact can potentially improve overall quality of life.
Welu, 1977	Suicide attempters were assigned to 2 groups (i.e., intent was addressed, with the author noting a *full gamut of seriousness).* Exclusion criteria were: a) under age 16, b) students in college or university housing, c) individuals living in a care-giving institution (e.g., state hospital), and d) those institutionalized at the time of the attempt.	120 (63/57)	Frequency of subsequent suicide attempts, excessive use of alcohol, drug use, or *purposive accidents.*	4-months	Not provided.	**No Significant Confounds**	**Conclusions:** Results provide evidence that an intensive treatment program (with an *outreach* component) for suicide attempters reduces subsequent attempts and alcohol abuse during a *brief* follow-up period.

---

[3] Not considered *therapy or treatment*, described as intervention.
[4] Not considered *therapy or treatment*, described as intervention, although clearly it is described in a fashion consistent with psychotherapy, as well as incorporating individual and group sessions.

Study	n	Measures	Follow-up	Attrition	Critique	Conclusions
Gibbons, Butler, Urwin, & Gibbons, 1978	400 (200/200)	Frequency of subsequent suicide attempts. Also assessed changes in *depressive mood* (Beck Depression Inventory), *social problems*, and *satisfaction*.	4 and 12-months.	Half (200) were randomly selected for f-u. Of this 159 (79%) were assessed. **E**=81% **C**=78%	Although the results can be interpreted, they are seriously comprised by the exclusion of psychiatric and *high-risk* patients. The resultant sample represents relatively *low risk* patients with limited *personal and social pathology* (p. 116). The implications for treatment of suicidality are therefore limited.	**Conclusions:** Intensive, time-limited follow-up was not effective at reducing attempts among *lower-risk* patients (at 12 months), although it can lead to fewer social problems.

Suicide attempters (i.e., included only attempts by overdose) were assigned to 2 groups. Exclusion criteria were:
a) under age 17,
b) formal *psychiatric illness*,
c) at *high risk* for suicide (i.e., not defined),
d) currently in *another treatment*.

Study	n	Measures	Follow-up	Attrition	Critique	Conclusions
Liberman & Eckman, 1981	24 (12/12)	Frequency of subsequent suicide attempts, Zung Self-Rating Depression Scale, Beck Depression Inventory (BDI), Fear Survey Schedule (FSS), Reinforcement Survey Schedule (RSS), Assertiveness Questionnaire (AQ), and MMPI.	Full assessment at 9-months, at 24-months assessed suicidal ideation & attempts only.	No attrition during follow-up.	Results are potentially compromised by questions raised about *treatment overlap* and *contamination* (p. 1129). Also, the small sample size limits the impact of the findings.	**Conclusions:** Time-limited, intensive behavior therapy was effective at reducing suicidal ideation and related symptomatology over a 9-month follow-up period.

Suicide attempters (i.e., multiple attempters) referred to a 10-day inpatient program. Exclusion criteria included:
a) psychosis,
b) organic brain syndrome, and
c) alcohol or drug dependence.

Study	n	Measures	Follow-up	Attrition	Critique	Conclusions
Hawton, Bancroft, Catalan, Kingston, Stedeford, & Welch, 1981	96 (28/28/20/20)	Frequency of subsequent attempts, mood (i.e., Lorr & McNair Mood Scale), suicidal ideation, social adjustment scale (i.e., Social Adjustment Scale), and *target problems*. The psychometric properties of the instruments were not provided.	12-months	85% (82/96) Not provided for each group separately	Results are highly questionable and have limited value for treatment in light of the following: a) exclusion of psychiatric patients, b) exclusion of *high-risk* suicidal patients, c) poorly defined treatment (i.e., in content), d) considerable variability in application of treatment (e.g., frequency of sessions, inclusion of family members in treatment), e) variable treatment completion rates, f) inclusion of only those making overdose attempt, and g) use of questionable outcome instruments.	**Conclusions;** Home visits were of limited value in reducing subsequent attempts and ideation for *lower risk* suicidal patients in comparison to traditional outpatient care.

Suicide attempters by overdose only. Exclusion criteria included:
a) under 16 years old,
b) in active psychiatric treatment,
c) living outside of the study area,
d) requiring alcohol or drug treatment,
e) requiring inpatient or day treatment,
f) serious suicide risk,
g) *not suitable for random assignment* (e.g., not having a fixed address), or
h) refusal of treatment.

173

Study	Sample (N)	Inclusion/Exclusion Criteria	Measures	Follow-up	Attrition	Findings/Limitations	Conclusions
Patsiokas & Clum, 1985	15 (5/5/5)	Hospitalized suicide attempters. Exclusion criteria included: a) those with psychosis, b) alcohol dependence, and c) drug abuse.	Suicidal ideation (frequency and severity as measured by the Beck Scale for Suicidal Ideation), hopelessness (Beck Hopelessness Scale), and problem solving (Means-Ends Problem-Solving and Alternate Uses Test).	End of treatment and at 3 weeks following treatment.	No attrition.	Findings are limited due to brief follow-up monitoring and small sample size.	**Conclusions:** Brief problem-solving therapy can reduce *acute* suicidality and improve problem solving over an acute time frame.
Hawton, McKeown, Day, Martin, O'Connor, & Yule, 1987	80 (41/39)	Included suicide attempters by overdose only. Additional inclusion criteria were: a) older than 16 years of age, b) living within a reasonable distance of the hospital, considered *suitable* for outpatient *counselling*, c) not in need of formal psychiatric care (i.e., inpatient or day treatment), e) not currently in treatment, f) willing to accept treatment. Exclusion criteria were: a) would not accept help, b) no indicated need for additional care (e.g., resolution of crisis during hospital stay), c) currently in other psychiatric treatment, d) requiring drug or alcohol treatment, and e) relocation out of the study area.	Subsequent suicide attempts, intent (Beck Suicidal Intent Scale, depression (Beck Depression Inventory), social adjustment (Social Adjustment Scale), general health (General Health Questionnaire), and *target problems* (subjective). Psychometric properties of the instruments were not provided.	9-months.	19% (65/80) For each group rates were: **B**=27% **C**=10%	Results are seriously compromised by the fact that only 49% of the **E** group actually completed treatment and analyses included those that were termed *dropouts* and *non-attenders*. Additional problems included the following: a) poorly defined treatment, b) question of comparable treatment and considerable overlap across E and C groups, c) considerable variability in application of treatment (e.g., frequency of sessions, inclusion of family members in treatment), d) highly variable treatment completion rates, e) inclusion of only those making overdose attempts, and f) and exclusion of those with psychiatric diagnoses and potentially higher suicide risk.	**Conclusions:** None noted given the problems referenced above with the E group, primarily with respect to treatment completion rates.

						No Significant Confounds	Conclusions:
Moller, 1989	Included suicide attempt by overdose only. Exclusion criteria were not stated.	141 (68/73)	Frequency of subsequent attempts, treatment compliance.	12-months	4% (5/141) E=3% C=4%		Improved continuity of care did not reduce subsequent attempts during a 12-month follow-up period, but did improve treatment compliance with brief treatment protocol.
Salkovkis, Atha, & Storer, 1990	Suicide attempters (i.e., multiple attempters) were included. Additional inclusion/exclusion criteria were: a) between ages 16-65, b) living in geographic region and in a fixed abode, c) not judged to require immediate psychiatric treatment or would not benefit from the range of treatment options normally available (p. 871), d) no psychosis, and e) no serious organic illness.	20 (12/8)	Frequency of subsequent attempts, suicidal ideation (Beck Scale for Suicidal Ideation), depression (Beck Depression Inventory), mood (Profile of Mood States), hopelessness (Beck Hopelessness Scale), and problem-solving (Personal Questionnaire Rapid Scaling Technique).	12-months	No attrition.	Results are limited by: a) a potential confound of a selection bias, essentially consistent with a *chronic group not in acute crisis,* depending on the initial screening and that those requiring immediate treatment were excluded, b) the small sample is a problem for generalizing findings, c) some concern was also raised about *pretreatment* differences between groups.	Time-limited cognitive behavioral therapy was effective at reducing suicidal ideation and related symptoms among multiple attempters over a 12-month follow-up period relative to treatment as usual. Also, subsequent attempts were reduced for a limited time, that is, six months.
Lerner & Clum, 1990	Inclusion criteria were: a) those experiencing *clinically significant* suicidal ideation, b) ages 18-24. Exclusion criteria were: a) evidence of psychosis, b) substance abuse.	18 (9/9)	Suicidal ideation (Modified Scale for Suicidal Ideation), depression (Beck Depression Inventory), hopelessness (Beck Hopelessness Scale), loneliness (UCLA Loneliness Scale), and problem-solving (Modified Means-Ends Problem-Solving).	3-months	Not provided, but appeared to be 17% (15/18) from df in analyses. Not provided for E and C groups.	Small sample size and clinical composition limits interpretation.	Brief problem-solving group therapy more effectively reduced depression and hopelessness at 3-months follow-up than supportive group therapy among a small sample of ideators.

Citation	Sample	N	Measures	Follow-up	Attrition	Comments	Conclusions
Waterhouse & Platt, 1990	Included suicide attempters by overdose (included those that *were assessed as having no immediate medical or psychiatric treatment needs* (p. 237). Exclusion criteria were: a) suicide attempts by method other than overdose, b) under age 16, c) no *fixed abode*, d) living outside of geographic area, e) current psychiatric inpatients or other treatment needs, f) *self-discharges* from hospital, and g) direct referrals to medical wards.	77 (38/39)	Frequency of subsequent attempts, psychological symptoms (Psychiatric Status Schedule), hopelessness (Beck Hopelessness Scale), and social functioning (Social Behavior Assessment Schedule).	4 months	52% (40/77) **E**=47% **C**=59%	Results are impossible to interpret given the following: a) identified goal of the study, i.e., no treatment provided during hospital stay or discharge home, is unusual, b) excluded high risk patients, c) the average hospital stay was less than one day so the two conditions were essentially identical, and d) unusually high attrition rates at 4 months.	**Conclusions:** None noted given the above problems.
Linehan, Armstrong, Suarez, Allmon, & Heard, 1991	Inclusion criteria were: a) met diagnostic criteria for borderline personality disorder, b) 2 suicide attempts in last 5 years (i.e., multiple attempters), with one during last 2 months, c) between ages of 18 and 45, d) agreed to *study conditions*. Exclusion criteria were: a) diagnosis of schizophrenia, bipolar disorder, substance dependence, or mental retardation.	44 (22/22)	Frequency of subsequent attempts, maintenance of therapy, inpatient treatment, depression (Beck Depression Inventory), hopelessness (Beck Hopelessness Scale), suicidal ideation (Scale for Suicide Ideators), reasons for living (Reasons for Living Inventory).	12-months	No attrition.	Results are compromised by small sample and restriction to borderline personality disordered patients.	**Conclusions:** Severe multiple attempters were safely and effectively treated on a long-term outpatient basis, with reductions in attempts, better treatment compliance and fewer inpatient days.

Study	Sample	Measures	Follow-up	Attrition	Limitations / Confounds	Conclusions
Allard, Marshall, & Plante, 1992	Inclusion criteria were: a) having been seen in the ER following a suicide attempt, b) residing within the catchment area of the hospital, and c) speaking French or English. Exclusion criteria were: a) not having a fixed address, b) already in separate treatment, c) presence of a physical handicap preventing attendance, d) incapacity to give informed consent, e) sociopathy, with physical threat to hospital personnel, and f) the attempt dating back more than one week.	150 (76/74)	Frequency of subsequent attempts.	24-months.	16% (24/150) E=17% C=15%	The primary limitation of the study is the acknowledged variability of the treatment plan implemented. Essentially, all E participants did not receive comparable treatment.	**Conclusions:** More intensive psychosocial treatment (i.e., utilizing a non-specific theoretical approach) following an attempt did not reduce subsequent attempts over a 24-month follow-up period.
Morgan, Jones, & Owen, 1993	Included first time suicide attempters. Exclusion criteria were not stated, aside from multiple attempters.	212 (101/111)	Frequency of subsequent attempts.	12-months.	No attrition.	**No Significant Confounds**	**Conclusions:** Improved ease of access to emergency services reduced subsequent attempts for first-time attempters over a period of one year.
Mcleavey, Daly, Ludgate, & Murray, 1994	Inclusion criteria were: a) age 15-45, b) suicide attempt by overdose, Exclusion criteria were: a) history of psychosis, mental retardation, organic or cognitive impairment (i.e., estimated IQ below 80), b) indicated need for inpatient stay or day treatment.	39 (19/20)	Frequency of subsequent attempts, interpersonal problem solving skills (Means-Ends Problem Solving Procedure, The Optional Thinking Test, The Awareness of Consequences Test, Self Rating Problem Solving Scale), self concept (Self-Perception Scale), problem ratings (Problems Questionnaire).	12-months.	15% E=10% C=20%	Findings are compromised by: a) potential overlap in treatment conditions, b) extremely small sample size, c) stated exclusion of high risk patients, d) failure to include a broad range of attempters, e) failure to assess other psychiatric symptomatology and variables relevant to suicidality.	**Conclusions:** Brief problem solving treatment was effective at improving problem solving skills and reducing attempts for low risk attempters over a 12-month period.

					No Significant Confounds	Conclusions:
Van Heeringen, Jannes, Buylaert, Henderick, DeBacquer, and Van Remoortel, 1995	Inclusion criteria were: c) suicide attempters referred from an Emergency Department, d) age 15 or older, e) living in the catchment area of the hospital. Exclusion criteria were: a) need for inpatient treatment.	516 (218/218)	Frequency of subsequent attempts, treatment compliance.	12-months.	24% (125/516)	**Conclusions:** Treatment compliance was improved over a 12-month period for suicide attempters by use of home visits within two weeks of the original presentation to the Emergency Room.
Rudd, Rajab, Stulman, Orman, Joiner, & Dixon, 1996	Inclusion criteria were: a) suicide attempt precipitating referral, b) mood disorder with concurrent suicidal ideation, c) episodic alcohol abuse with concurrent ideation. Exclusion criteria were: a) substance dependence or chronic abuse requiring separate treatment, b) psychosis or diagnosed thought disorder, c) severe personality disorder in which group treatment was unmanageable.	302 (181/121)	Frequency of subsequent attempts, suicidal ideation (Modified Scale for Suicidal Ideation, Suicide Probability Scale), depression (Beck Depression Inventory), hopelessness (Beck Hopelessness Scale), life stress (Life Experiences Survey), problem-solving (Problem-Solving Inventory), and personality traits (Millon Clinical Multiaxial Inventory).	12-months	73% (193/264)	Findings are compromised by the nature of the sample (military and young age) and the extremely high attrition rate.	**Conclusions:** High-risk suicidal patients were as safely and effectively treated on an intensive, outpatient basis as treatment as usual. Problem-solving therapy may be more effective at retaining those at highest-risk.

							Conclusions:
Van Der Sande, Van Rooijen, Buskens, Allart, Hawton, Van Der Graaf, Van Engeland, 1997	Inclusion criteria were: a) 15 years and older, b) a suicide attempt. Exclusion criteria were: a) self-mutilatory or self-destructive rather than suicidal behavior, b) alcohol and substance abuse, c) inability to understand and write Dutch, d) residing outside of the catchment area, e) psychiatric hospitalization, f) imprisonment, g) acute psychosis, h) or having received *recurrent consultations with a liaison psychiatrist during a prolonged hospital stay.*	274 (140/134)	Frequency of subsequent attempts, suicide intent (Suicidal Intent Scale), depression (Montgomery-Asberg Depression Rating Scale), overall well being (Symptom Checklist-90), and hopelessness (Beck Hopelessness Scale).	12-months.	53% (145/274) Rates for each group were: **E**=37% **C**=67%	Findings are compromised by: f) poorly defined problem solving treatment, g) extremely high attrition rate, h) failure to define *treatment completion* in the experimental group, i.e., the *intent to treat* analysis included individuals that may actually have received no treatment whatsoever.	**Conclusions:** An intensive follow-up program utilizing brief hospitalization, problem solving outpatient treatment, improved access to emergency services, and home visits did not reduce subsequent suicide attempts in comparison to treatment as usual. However, the findings are compromised by a failure to define treatment completion and the *intent to treat analysis* conducted, as well as high attrition rates.
Joiner, Rudd, & Rajab, 1998	Same as above.	Same as above.	Same as above.	Same as above.	Same as above.	**Same as above.**	**Conclusions:** The highest-risk suicidal patients, i.e., those with comorbidity, were more effectively treated with problem-solving therapy than treatment as usual.

Intervention Studies: Do Simple Procedural Changes Make a Difference?

Among the studies reviewed, interventions included the following: a) supportive case management by volunteer workers (Termansen & Bywater, 1975), b) simple follow-up letters and phone calls to those refusing treatment (Motto, 1976), c) incorporation of home visits and more intensive tracking (Litman & Wold, 1975; Van Heeringen et al., 1995), d) brief medical hospitalization with no psychiatric care whatsoever (Waterhouse & Platt, 1990), and e) improved ease of access to 24-hour emergency services (Morgan et al., 1993). In summary, the procedural elements examined included case management, follow-up letters and phone calls, home visits, brief medical (non-psychiatric) hospitalization, and access to emergency services. These procedural changes clearly alter the provision of traditional treatment services, but inadequate controls were in place to address overall treatment effectiveness. As discussed in more detail below, the majority of these intervention studies were plagued by additional theoretical and methodological issues that greatly limit their utility.

Of the six intervention studies reviewed, three had positive findings, but all three are plagued by serious methodological limitations. Termansen & Bywater (1975) found that *intensive case management* by volunteer workers reduced subsequent suicide attempts during the 3-month follow-up period, relative to those receiving no follow-up care. As the authors noted, *"the role* of the volunteers *was not therapeutic in the conventional psychiatric sense; rather it was the role of the helper expressing concern for the person in his total environmental situation"*. The study included four conditions, with each varying as to the nature of initial assessment and follow-up monitoring: the first group received three months of follow-up after presenting in the emergency room; the second group got no

follow-up after and emergency room assessment and the third and fourth groups received no follow-up care of any type and served as controls, with the third receiving initial intervention in the emergency room and the fourth no initial intervention. Groups two and three are essentially similar in the study design. As is clearly detailed in Table 1.1, the findings are highly compromised. Although described as non-psychotherapeutic, the intervention, an evaluation and related crisis intervention, certainly met criteria for a psychotherapeutic intervention, among a host of other problems listed in the table.

VanHeerigan and colleagues (1995) compared the addition of home visits targeting treatment compliance by a community nurse to *usual outpatient care* for enhancing treatment compliance and reducing subsequent attempts. The intervention was fairly simple in nature: *"during the home visits reasons for non-compliance were assessed, needs for treatment evaluated and identified needs matched with the supply of outpatient treatment"*. Findings revealed better treatment compliance among those in the experimental group and, although not significant, a favorable trend (p=.056) was noted in the reduction of subsequent attempts at one year. Overall, the study was well designed for its stated purpose, posing no severe methodological problems. However, it is debatable as to whether or not the intervention constitutes psychotherapeutic services. The intervention certainly included interpersonal contact and the expression of care and concern, both consistent with psychotherapy. The exploration of "reasons for non-compliance" sounds very similar to a problem solving approach. In short, it can be argued that the intervention studied included intensive psychotherapeutic service in addition to the *home visit*. Another significant concern with the study was the exclusion criteria employed. As is common in this area of research, the study excluded the highest risk cases. This limits the utility of the findings. Also of concern, the home visits were not driven by a standard protocol, raising questions about the effective component of the intervention. Without a standard protocol, it is unlikely that clinicians provided comparable interventions across cases.

Morgan, Jones, & Owen (1993) found that improved ease of access to 24-hour emergency services over the period of a year following a first suicide attempt significantly reduced subsequent attempts among those in the experimental group relative to those receiving management as usual (i.e., ranging from inpatient psychiatric admission to referral back to the primary care physician). Improved ease of access was accomplished simply by giving the patient a green card with emergency numbers and encouragment to seek services early in a crisis by going to either the emergency room, calling by telephone, or seeking emergency admission. The authors found that this simple procedural change significantly reduced service demand in the experimental group. Similar to other *intervention* studies, this procedural change arguably resulted in increases or alterations in the quantity or nature of psychotherapeutic services provided to patients (e.g., while at the emergency room or via the telephone during crisis calls). Certainly, an extended phone call during an acute state is a crisis intervention and qualifies as a therapeutic intervention. Another limitation of the study was the fact that it targeted first-time attempters, again excluding the highest risk group, those making multiple attempts and experiencing chronic suicidality. The exclusion of those at highest risk is a noticeable and troubling trend in the treatment outcome literature for suicidality, More often than not, it is secondary to ethical and legal concerns.

Motto (1976) found that simple follow-up letters and phone calls to those refusing treatment after presenting in crisis tended to reduce suicide rates over a 4 year follow-up period, although this difference was not statistically significant. The trend noted by Motto is important, though, indicating that simple follow-up letters reminding patients that care is available may actually have an impact on their emotional health and risk for suicide. Why such a limited intervention may have impact is not fully understood, but we speculate that the simple act of caring can be enormously powerful, even when expressed without direct interpersonal contact.

Litman & Wold (1976) found that telephone calls, home visits, and "befriending contacts" (i.e., what was termed "continuing relationship maintenance") by crisis volunteers did not reduce the frequency of suicide attempts in the experimental group over a period of 24-months, despite an improvement in quality of life.

Waterhouse and Platt (1990) evaluated the utility of simple and brief medical hospitalization (i.e., with no psychiatric care of any type provided) by non-psychiatric staff at reducing subsequent attempts over the next four months. The study has serious methodological flaws. The control group was discharged to home. The average duration of the hospitalization for those in the experimental group was less than a day (i.e., 17 hours) rendering the groups almost completely identical. It is not surprising that no subsequent differences were observed in attempts between groups. Waterhouse and Platt also excluded high risk cases.

What can we learn from the available intervention studies? Despite the limitations mentioned, the best science available suggests that sometimes simple steps have an important impact on complicated clinical phenomena like suicide. Specifically, three interventions were found important: long-term follow-up, home visits and improving the ease of access to emergency services. Why are such simple steps meaningful? I speculate that the common feature of the interventions at the core of their effectiveness is the simple desire to help. Specifically, the three interventions all provide an expression of care and concern for a patient experiencing enormous emotional suffering and pain.

What do Treatment Studies Tell Us? The Potential and Promise of CBT

The treatment studies (n=16) can be divided into two categories, those providing short-term treatment (i.e., less than 6-months, n=14) and those providing longer-term therapy (i.e., 6-months or greater, N=2). As was mentioned at the beginning of this chapter, it is important to differentiate short and long-term care. In particular, such a distinction will help us address the issue of treatment efficiency; What is the minimal care necessary to reduce lifetime risk of suicide? Although a seemingly simple question, the eventual answer is extraordinarily important for setting the standard of care for suicidal patients.

Short term therapies

To date, results of studies of treatment effectiveness have been mixed. Eight studies found positive results about the efficacy of short-term treatments and six negative. Among those with positive findings, the results are consistent and provide some useful information for clinical practice. Among the short-term studies, the majority (N=10) offered some form of cognitive-behavioral therapy including a problem-solving component. More specifically, each intervention integrated a structured and multistepped approach to problem solving. Most problem solving therapies include steps such as: problem orientation, problem identification, generation of alternatives, evaluation of alternatives, and implementation. Additionally, problem solving therapies routinely emphasize the development of interpersonal skills such as assertiveness. Future studies should explore the potential for differential impact of various approaches to problem solving.

The length of treatment varied across the CBT studies but ranged from a low of only ten days (Liberman & Eckman, 1981) to a high of three months (Gibbons et al., 1978). Regardless, these are short-term treatments. The question of long-term impact is one that will require much longer follow-up periods. At present, we simply are unable to determine whether or not such approaches *delay* or *prevent* suicidal behavior. Of the remaining four studies in the brief treatment category, three explored an *additive component* to treatment as usual, that is, additional intensive follow-up care of some type, rather than a comparison of specific treatment modalities (Chowdhury et al., 1973; Hawton et al., 1981; Welu, 1977). The other explored the impact of improved *continuity of care* on subsequent suicide attempts (Moeller, 1989).

Results were generally negative for those studies testing an additive component to short-term treatment (i.e. more intensive follow-up). In some ways, this additive component was similar to the procedural changes described in the *intervention* studies. However, in the studies categorized as *treatment*, the authors specifically noted that the follow-up provided psychotherapeutic services, apparently in recognition of the fact that procedural changes impact the very nature of psychotherapeutic service. Both studies targeting intensive short term follow-up utilized a combination of home visits, telephone contact, and more frequent and flexible routine treatment appointments. They found no impact on subsequent suicide attempts over periods ranging from six to 12-months (Gibbons et al., 1978; Hawton et al., 1981). Hawton et al. (1981) found that home visits did improve treatment compliance, reducing missed appointments. However, improved compliance did not translate into a significant reduction in subsequent attempts over the 12-month follow-up period. Chowdhury et al. (1973) also found that home visits, more frequent outpatient appointments, and improved access to emergency services did not reduce subsequent attempts among multiple attempters compared to *treatment as usual*. Moeller (1989) found that efforts to improve the *continuity of care* by ensuring treatment by the same clinician before and after hospitalization had no noticeable impact on suicide attempts during the year long follow-up period. In all of these studies, *treatment as usual* was simply the routine provision of care to these patients, not dissimilar to the nature of care provided today. More specifically, it amounts to routine appointments, ordinarily one to two times a week.

In contrast, in a well designed study, Welu (1977) found that more intensive follow-up using home visits, telephone contact, and more frequent routine treatment appointments reduced subsequent attempts in the experimental group over the 4-month follow-up period. The results are compromised, though, by the very brief nature of follow-up monitoring. As mentioned before, it is difficult to address the question of treatment effect if it does not endure. In contrast to the above studies that excluded high risk patients, Welu (1977) targeted high risk patients and had positive findings. The pattern of results suggests that more intensive outpatient treatment, irrespective of approach, is effective for those identified as high-risk. High-risk patients are defined as having a psychiatric diagnosis (Axis I or II), a history of multiple attempts, or other comorbidity. However, more intensive outpatient treatment may not improve outcomes for lower risk patients (e.g., Gibbons et al., 1978). This is a important finding for clinicians since the typical suicidal outpatient is a high risk patient whose suicidality may become chronic and difficult to treat (Rudd et al., 2004).

Brief cognitive-behavioral approaches integrating a *core* problem-solving component were found to be effective in seven of ten studies. This is a noticeably consistent finding, particularly in light of some of the methodological challenges faced by researchers in this area. It is argued that cognitive-behavioral approaches are simply more amenable to experimental design and study. Nevertheless, the consistency of these findings cannot be ignored, particularly with this high risk patient population. Differences were not found with respect to suicide attempts, but results indicated reductions in suicidal ideation (Liberman & Eckman, 1981; Salkovkis et al., 1990; Joiner et al., 1998) and related symptomatology such as depression (Lerner & Clum, 1990; Liberman & Eckman, 1981; Salkovkis et al., 1990), hopelessness (Lerner & Clum, 1990; Patsiokas & Clum, 1985), and loneliness (Lerner & Clum, 1990). Follow-up periods ranged from 3-months to one year. This is by no means sufficient. In order to offer some certainty about treatment impact, follow-up periods stretching across 20-30 years are essential. A single study found a reduction in suicide attempts at 12-months post-treatment (McLeavey et al., 1994). The findings by McLeavey et al. (1994) are compromised by serious methodological problems including: a small sample size, failure to include a broad range of attempters, and most importantly, the purposeful exclusion of high-risk patients. Accordingly, the finding is preliminary at best. The three studies with negative findings found no reductions in suicide attempts during nine to 12-month follow-up periods (Gibbons et al., 1978; Hawton et al., 1987; Van Der Sande et al., 1997). As is all too often the case, all excluded those at highest risk for subsequent attempts, among a host of additional methodological problems summarized in Table 1.1.

Long term-therapies

With long-term treatment, the results were mixed. As is frequently cited in the literature, Linehan et al. (1991) demonstrated the efficacy of dialectical behavior therapy (DBT) in reducing subsequent attempts and hospital days, and improving treatment compliance over a year follow-up period. DBT is an intensive long-term treatment that integrates commonly accepted cognitive-behavioral therapy principles. One of the unique features of the treatment, though, is its intensive nature, both in terms of access to emergency services as well as the combination of individual and group treatment. No differences were found between DBT and *treatment as usual*, however, with respect to depression, hopelessness, suicidal ideation, or reasons for living. Linehan's results, along with those of Rudd et al. (1996), comparing outpatient and inpatient care, suggest that outpatient treatment of high-risk suicidal patients is both safe and effective when acute hospitalization is available. In contrast to Linehan et al., Allard, Marshall, & Plante (1992) did not find a reduction in subsequent attempts at 24-months with an eclectic and poorly defined psychotherapy. Although the follow-up period is among the most extensive in the literature, there are a number of problems with the study. The most significant being that they utilized a mixture of poorly defined therapeutic approaches. Its questionable as to whether or not all subjects received a uniform intervention and treatment, and accordingly, it is difficult, if not impossible, to offer meaningful conclusions.

Where Do We Go From Here?

Table 1.2 summarizes available findings across the three categories referenced earlier: intervention studies, short-term treatment, and long-term treatment. As mentioned before, two of the studies were impossible to interpret due to serious methodological flaws. Another four studies rendered questionable findings secondary to methodological problems. The fact that almost 30% of the available studies were, for the most part, impossible to interpret speaks to the methodological challenges of conducting research with suicidal patients.

Among the most serious methodological challenges are: accumulating large enough samples with specific inclusion criteria, ensuring diagnostic comparability across both Axis I and II psychiatric disorders, attaining funding to meet the significant expense in treating and managing high risk patients, and ensuring adequate availability of emergency services and hospitalization if needed. Out of the twenty-two original studies, sixteen provided interpretable results, using sound designs. As indicated, those findings have limited implications for day to day treatment and ongoing clinical management of suicidality.

As stated earlier in this chapter, we can answer only a few of the most fundamental questions raised about the treatment of suicidality. There appears to be emerging evidence for the efficacy of cognitive-behavioral therapy, both over the short and long-term. It appears that cognitive-behavioral therapy, integrating problem-solving as a *core intervention,* is effective at reducing suicidal ideation and related symptoms over the short-term. Reducing attempts appears to require longer-term and more intensive treatment, with a specific focus on skill deficits and related personality dysfunction, similar to the longer-term approach offered by Linehan and her colleagues. There is some indication that simple interventions (e.g., follow-up contact, home visits) can have an impact but only in limited ways. We are not in a position to address the questions about treatment setting, duration, or differential impact of treatment components. Clearly, the most difficult scientific work is ahead of us. Of the questions posed earlier, all are yet to be answered in any definitive manner. Nonetheless, cognitive-behavioral therapy does appear to offer considerable promise in the psychotherapeutic treatment of suicidality. More specifically, we know that approaches that address targeted skill deficits (e.g. problem solving, assertiveness) reduce

Table 1.2. Summary of Current Findings in the Treatment of Suicidality

Study Type	General Implications for Treatment/Intervention
Intervention Studies:	
Termansen & Bywater, 1975	No conclusions, serious methodological problems.
Motto, 1976	Long-term follow-up has some value.
Litman & Wold, 1975	No conclusions serious methodological problems.
Waterhouse & Platt, 1990	Impossible to interpret.
Morgan, Jones, & Owen, 1993	Improved ease of access to emergency services can reduce subsequent attempts for first-time attempters over 12-month period.
Van Heeringen, et al., 1995	Home visits can improve treatment compliance.
Treatment Studies: Short-Term	
Chowdhury & Hicks, 1973	Serious methodological problems.
Welu, 1977	Intensive, time-limited treatment can reduce attempts over a period of weeks.
Gibbons, Butler, Urwin, & Gibbons, 1978	Intensive, time-limited follow-up can lead to fewer social problems and improved social functioning.
Liberman & Eckman, 1981	Time-limited behavior therapy can reduce suicidal ideation and related symptoms over enduring periods, but is effective at reducing attempts for only brief periods of time.
Hawton, Bancroft, Catalan, Kingston, Stedeford, & Welch, 1981	Serious methodological problems.
Patsiokas & Clum, 1985	Brief problem-solving therapy can reduce acute suicidality and improve problem-solving skills.
Hawton, McKeown, Day, Martin, O'Connor, & Yule, 1987	Serous methodological problems.
Moller, 1989	Improved continuity of care from inpatient to outpatient treatment does not reduce suicidality.
Salkovkis, Atha, & Storer, 1990	Time-limited cognitive-behavioral therapy is effective at reducing suicidal ideation and related symptoms over relatively long periods of time, but attempts for only brief periods.
Lerner & Clum, 1990	Brief problem-solving group therapy can reduce suicidal ideation, depression, and hopelessness for brief periods.
Mcleavey, Daly, Ludgate, & Murray, 1994	Brief problem solving treatment was effective at improving problem solving skills and reducing attempts for low risk attempters over a 12-month period.
Van Der Sande, Van Rooijen, Buskens, Allart, Hawton, Van Der Graaf, Van Engeland, 1997	Intensive outpatient treatment did not reduce subsequent suicide attempts in comparison to treatment as usual.
Rudd, Rajab, Stulman, Orman, Joiner, & Dixon, 1996	High-risk suicidal patients can be treated safely and effectively with intensive, brief outpatient problem-solving therapy.
Joiner, Rudd, & Rajab, 2005	The highest-risk patients, i.e. comorbid suicidal patients, are more effectively treated with brief problem-solving therapy than treatment as usual.
Treatment Studies: Long-Term	
Allard, Marshall, & Plante, 1992	Non-specific, intensive follow-up is not effective at reducing attempts over the long-term.
Linehan, Armstrong, Suarez, Allmon, & Heard, 1991	Severe multiple attempters can be effectively treated in long-term outpatient care with DBT, with reductions in suicide attempts, improved treatment compliance and reduced hospitalization.

suicidality, at least temporarily. However, we don't know how long this effect endures and whether or not it has any impact on lifetime risk for suicide. Ultimately, what is needed in this area of research are treatment studies that specifically target those at highest risk for suicide and do so with well-articulated treatment models with very long follow-up periods. Anything short of that will leave the difficult question about lifetime suicide risk unanswered. Are we truly preventing suicide or simply delaying it?

REFERENCES

Allard R, Marshall M, Plante M. (1992) Intensive follow-up does not decrease the risk of repeat suicide attempts. Suicide Life-Threatening Behav 22: 303-314.

Anderson RN. (2002) Deaths: Leading causes for 2000. National Vital Statistics Reports, 50 (16), Hyattsville, MD: National Center for Health Statistics, Centers for Disease Control.

Beck AT, Brown GK, Steer RA. (1997) Psychometric characteristics of the Scale for Suicide Ideation with psychiatric outpatients. Behav Res Ther 35(11): 1039-1046.

Chowdhury N, Hicks R, Kreitman N. (1973) Evaluation of an after-care service for parasuicide (attempted suicide patients). Soc Psychiatr 8: 67-81.

DeLeo D, Bertolote J, Lester D. (2002) Self-directed violence. In E.G. Krug, L.L. Dahlberg, J.A. Mercy, A.B. Zwi & R. Lozano (Eds.), World report on violence and health (pp. 183-240). Geneva, Switzerland: World Health Organization.

Department of Health and Humans Services. (2001) The National Strategy for Suicide Prevention. Washington, DC.

Gibbons J, Butler J, Urwin P, Gibbons J. (1978) Evaluation of a social work service for self-poisoning patients. Brit J Psychiatr 133: 111-118.

Hawton K, Bancroft J, Catalan J, Kingston B, Stedeford A, Welch N. (1981) Domiciliary and outpatient treatment of self-poisoning patients by medical and non-medical staff. Psycholog Med 11: 169-177.

Hawton K, McKeown S, Day A, Martin P, O'Connor M, Yule J. (1987) Evaluation of outpatient counseling compared with general practitioner care following overdoses. Psycholog Med 17: 751-761.

Hirsch S, Walsh C, Draper R. (1983) The concept and efficacy of the treatment of parasuicide. Brit J Clin Psychopharmacol 15: 189S-194S.

Institute of Medicine (2002) Reducing suicide: A national imperative. Washington, DC: National Academies Press.

Joiner T, Rudd M, Rajab M. (2005) An intriguing interaction between comorbid diagnostic status and treatment type in predicting treatment response among suicidal young adults. Under Review.

Kessler RC, Borges G, Walters EE. (1999) Prevalence of and risk factors for lifetime suicide attempts in the National Comorbidity Study. Arch Gen Psychiatr 56(7): 617-626.

Lerner M, Clum G. (1990) Treatment of suicide ideators: a problem-solving approach. Assoc Adv Behav Ther 21: 403-411.

Liberman R, Eckmen T. (1981) Behavior therapy vs insight-oriented therapy for repeated suicide attempters. Arch Gen Psychiatr 38: 1126-1130.

Linehan M. (1982) Suicidal behaviors in among clients in an outpatient clinic versus the general population. Suicide Life-Threatening Behav 12: 234-239.

Linehan M, Armstrong H, Suarez A, Allmon D, Heard H. (1991) Cognitive-behavioral treatment of chronically parasuicidal borderline patients. Arch Gen Psychiatr, 48: 1060-1064.

Litman R, Wold C. (1976) Beyond crisis intervention. In Suicidology: Contemporary Developments. E Shneidman (Ed.), pp. 528-546. New York: Grune & Stratton.

March J, Silva S, Petrycki S, Curry J, Wells K, Fairbank J, Burns B, Domino M, McNulty S, Vitiello B, Severe J; Treatment for Adolescents With Depression Study (TADS) Team. (2004) Fluoxetine, cognitive-behavioral therapy, and their combination for adolescents with depression. JAMA 292: 807-820.

Maris RW, Berman AL, Silverman MM. (2000) Comprehensive Textbook of Suicidology. New York; Guilford.

Miller TR, Covington KL, Jensen AF. (1998) Costs of injury by major cause, United States, 1995: Cobbling together estimates in measuring the burden of injuries. Proceedings of a Conference in Noordwijkerhout, Netherlands, May 13-15, 1998.

Moeller H. (1989) Efficacy of different strategies of aftercare for patients who have attempted suicide. J Royal Soc Med 82: 643-647.

Montgomery S, Montgomery D. (1982) Pharmacological prevention of suicidal behavior. J Affective Dis 4: 291-298.

Montgomery D, Roy D, Montgomery S. (1981) Mianserin in the prophylaxis of suicidal behavior: A double blind placebo controlled trial. In Depression and suicide (Proceedings of the 11th Congress of Suicide Prevention), pp. 786-790. Pergamon Press.

Morgan H, Jones E, Owen J. (1993) Secondary prevention of non-fatal deliberate self-harm: the green card study. Brit J Psychiatr 163: 111-112.

Motto J. (1976) Suicide prevention for high-risk persons who refuse treatment. Suicide Life-Threatening Behav 6 (4): 223-230.

O'Carroll P, Berman A, Maris R, Moscicki E, Tanney B, Silverman M. (1996) Beyond the tower of babel: A nomenclature for suicidology. Suicide Life- Threatening Behav 26: 237-252.

Patsiokas A, Clum G, Luscomb R. (1979) Cognitive characteristics of suicide attempters. J Consult Clin Psychol 47: 478-484.

Rudd MD, Joiner TE, Rajab H. (2004) Treating Suicidal Behavior, New York; Guilford.

Rudd M, Rajab H, Orman D, Stulman D, Joiner T, Dixon W. (1996) Effectiveness of an outpatient problem-solving intervention targeting suicidal young adults: Preliminary results. J Consult Clin Psychol 64: 179-190.

Salkovskis P, Atha C, Storer D. (1990) Cognitive-behavioural problem solving in the treatment of patients who repeatedly attempt suicide: a controlled trial. Brit J Psychiatr 157: 871-876.

Termansen P, Bywater C. (1975) S.A.F.E.R.: A follow-up service for attempted suicide in Vancouver. Canadian Psychiatr Assoc J 20: 29-34.

van der Sande R, Buskens E, Allart E, van der Graaf Y, Van Engeland H. (1997) Psychosocial intervention following suicide attempt: a systematic review of treatment interventions. ACTA Psychiatrica Scandinavica 96: 43-50.

Van Heeringen C, Jannes S, Buylert W, Hendrick H, De Bacquer D, Van Remoortel J. (1995) The management of non-compliance with referral to outpatient after-care among attempted suicide patients: A controlled intervention study. Psycholog Med 25: 963-970.

Waterhouse J, Platt S. (1990) General hospital admission in the management of parasuicide: a randomised controlled trial. Brit J Psychiatr 156: 236-242.

Welu T. (1977) A follow-up program for suicide attempters: Evaluation of effectiveness. Suicide Life-Threatening Behav 7(1): 17-30.

LONG-TERM EFFICACY OF INTERVENTIONS TO REDUCE SUBSTANCE USE

Jodie A.Trafton, Jared Minkel, Elizabeth Oliva, Doyanne Horst

INTRODUCTION

Scope of the problem

Substance use disorders (SUDs) are a pervasive, devastating and costly problem and affect persons and communities of diverse socioeconomic and geographic background. In 2001, an estimated 7.1% of the US population aged 12 and over were current illicit drug users. Rates of current alcohol use were approximately 60% for adults over 21, although the rate of heavy alcohol use (more than 5 days in the last month with more than 5 drinks at one sitting) was much lower, peaking in the 18-25 year old age group (13.6%) and declining with age (1.4% of >65 years age group) (SAMHSA, 2001).

The social costs of substance use disorders are extremely high, as this disease has large impacts on economic, public health and criminal justice systems. In 1998, the overall cost of drug abuse in the US was estimated at $143.4 billion (Office of National Drug Control Policy, 2001), including $12.9 billion in health care costs. Unfortunately, monetary costs are only the beginning of the problem. Drug use contributes to the spread of infectious disease, with 34.3% of AIDS cases in the US attributable to drug use-associated behaviors, and over 90% of intravenous drug users in metropolitan areas infected with hepatitis C. Additionally, roughly 30% of all burglary, larceny and robbery as well as 15.8% of homicide was attributable to drug use, and in 1997 62.6% of inmates in federal prison and 20.7% of inmates in state prisons were incarcerated for drug law offenses. Even without considering the effects of substance use disorders on the personal health and happiness of those afflicted, the necessity for effective SUD treatments is clear.

Nevertheless, the impact of substance use disorders on affected individuals can be enormous, increasing risk of infectious disease, injury, medical and psychiatric conditions, employment, financial and legal problems, family conflict, social isolation and suicide. The multi-faceted damage that may be caused by SUDs is not to be underestimated.

Thankfully, a variety of effective treatments for SUDs have been developed, although they are generally underutilized. Roughly 75% of people diagnosed with substance use disorders never seek treatment for them, and, even for those who do, lack of availability of SUD treatment programs has been identified as a problem. Better understanding and utilization of treatments for SUD would be of great benefit to both afflicted individuals and their families, and society as a whole.

Abuse, dependence and addiction

All problematic substance use is not the same. The least complicated and easiest to treat of substance use disorders is substance abuse. This refers simply to substance use that is dangerous or harmful because it is done in excess or under unsafe conditions. These problems would include, for example, binge drinking, public intoxication, intoxication-related violence, or driving under the influence. As patients who abuse substances are often neither dependent nor addicted, it is relatively easy for these patients to make behavioral modifications and low intensity treatments may be effective.

Substance dependence occurs following repeated use of a substance. In this condition, the patient's body, nervous system included, has made adaptations such that it functions "normally" in the presence of the substance. Because of these adaptations, a dependent patient who is deprived of his substance of choice will develop an abstinence syndrome and will experience withdrawal symptoms. This abstinence syndrome consists of a set of physiological and psychological effects that are opposite to the symptoms of acute intoxication with the substance the patient is dependent on. For example, heroin use produces constipation; withdrawal from heroin includes diarrhea. As all addictive substances produce symptoms that are considered pleasurable by the regular user, symptoms of withdrawal are inevitably unpleasant and generally completely miserable. It is thus believed that dependent patients develop a drive to maintain typical levels of substance use to function "normally" and prevent withdrawal.

Substance addiction is often confused with dependence, although it is a distinct behavioral syndrome. Addiction involves the development of a set of compulsive drug-seeking behaviors, whereby an addicted person learns to repeatedly drug-seek, often times in spite of extremely negative conesquences of continued drug-seeking or use. Addiction is a learned behavior. Addictive behaviors may be context or cue dependent, i.e. they may only occur in specific contexts or in response to particular cues. For example, a cocaine addict may compulsively cocaine binge only in the presence of a set of using friends (his using cue); he may have no urge to use cocaine while at work or visiting relatives. Addictive behaviors must be un-learned or competed out by other behaviors, or substance use related cues or contexts must be avoided to prevent substance use.

As not all substance use disorders are the same, no one treatment is optimal for all patients. Different treatments preferentially target abuse, dependence or addiction, and social circumstances and co-morbid disorders will affect the practical use and success of given interventions. It is important to identify what type of substance use disorder a patient is experiencing and the patient's medical and psychosocial situation when choosing an appropriate treatment method. Proper identi-fication and assessment of SUDs are essential for proper treatment, and techniques and instruments have been developed to facilitate this process. Although discussion of these methods is beyond the scope of this chapter, we emphasize their importance (for a general review of the topic, see Department of Health and Human Services Publication (SMA) 94-2075, 1994).

In this chapter, we will review the long-term outcomes of SUD treatments currently used in the U.S. These therapies include pharmacotherapies such as opioid substitution therapy, naloxone for alcoholism and opioid addiction, and disulfiram for alcohol use disorders, and counseling-based interventions such as brief interventions, cognitive behavioral therapy, couples counseling, contingency management, 12-step facilitation and inpatient treatments. For each type of therapy, randomized controlled trials with at least one-year follow-up are summarized in tables. A brief description of each treatment method and a discussion of its use and efficacy are included. We conclude with a summary of findings, treatment recommen-dations, and questions for future research.

METHODS

We searched PUBMED and PSYCHINFO for English language papers describing randomized controlled trials with at least 1 year of follow-up assessment that tested interventions to alter substance use behaviors. The bibliographies of relevant articles were also searched for additional studies. Studies that evaluated outcomes other than substance use behaviors, tested interventions that have not been approved for use in the US, evaluated treatments for medical management of substance use-related health conditions (e.g. substance withdrawal symptoms or intravenous drug use-related infectious disease), tested interventions for the prevention of substance use or problematic substance use behaviors, or tested interventions for patients with co-morbid substance use disorders and severe mental illness (See Volume I, Chapter 10), were excluded from this review. Nicotine use was also not considered as it is covered in two chapters on smoking prevention and cessation (See Volume I, Chapters 8 and 9). Thus, this chapter focuses on interventions to reduce the problematic use of alcohol and illegal substances. Of note, although we did search for interventions to treat all substance use disorders, we found that long-term studies of substance use disorders treatments generally focused on alcohol, cocaine and opioid use disorders. Studies of other substance use disorders treatments are included when available, however, because of the literature available, the chapter focuses on alcohol, cocaine and heroin use disorders.

RESULTS

Detoxification

Detoxification, a monitored tapering and subsequent discontinuation of substance intake, is not considered a treatment for substance abuse or addiction, but is a treatment for the withdrawal that accompanies the cessation of substance use by a substance-dependent person (Mattick and Hall, 1996). The withdrawal period, lasting a few days to several months, is an uncomfortable, painful and often physically taxing period that may or may not warrant the need for medical attention (Kleber, 1999; Gallant, 1999). Often a patient undergoes detoxification as an inpatient in a medical setting to provide immediate attention to physical compli-cations, access to medications helpful in the treatment of withdrawal, and proper supervision by medical staff. However,

depending on the level of symptom severity, the patient may not require hospitalization and detoxification may be successfully completed in an outpatient setting (Miller and Hester, 1986). Detoxifying a patient will not treat substance addiction or abuse and does not produce long term reductions in substance use when used alone. It is generally used as a preparatory step taken before a patient enters treatment or begins rehabilitation (Alterman et al., 1991). As it is not a treatment for substance use disorders, we will not consider its effectiveness as such; it has been shown to have no benefit for reducing SUD behaviors.

MEDICATION-BASED THERAPIES
Opioid Substitution Therapies
Theory and Practice

Opioid substitution therapy is a treatment for opioid (heroin or opioid medication) dependence that was developed in the 1960's by Dole and Nyswander (although there are reports of this method being used by 19th century physicians). This therapy is based upon the idea that withdrawal symptoms and craving associated with fluctuations in opioid levels in an opioid-dependent individual drive continued drug-seeking and the negative sequela associated with it. Opioid substitu-tion treatment attempts to reduce the with-drawal symptoms and craving and thus drug-seeking by regular administration of an orally administered long-acting opioid to dependent individuals. This essentially normalizes the individual, as the onset of action of these medications is too slow to produce a "high" and individuals become rapidly tolerant to sedative effects of the medication. Patients stop their drug-seeking and can focus on improving their life-situation; although still opioid-dependent, their addiction is treated. Additionally, at high doses of long-acting opioid, the medication blocks the subjective effects of heroin by acting as a competitive antagonist or partial agonist. This further reduces the drive to use heroin.

Three medications have been approved for use in opioid substitution treatment, namely methadone, levomethadyl acetate (LAAM), and buprenorphine. All three are mu opioid receptor agonists and all have been proven effective for the treatment of opioid addiction. Each has its own special properties, and individual subjects often report personal preferences. Methadone has been in use for over 30 years. It is administered orally, generally once per day. It is also an NMDA receptor antagonist, and because of this pharmacological action it has been suggested that tolerance to methadone occurs more slowly than to other opioids. LAAM is a longer acting opioid medication, whose breakdown products are also active MOR agonists. LAAM is also administered orally, but because of its long half-life it is generally only taken once every 2 to 3 days. Buprenorphine is the newest of the medications. It is a partial MOR agonist and thus there is a ceiling on its effects. This is thought to reduce the risk of overdose on the medication, thus increasing its safety. Additionally, buprenorphine is also a kappa opioid receptor (KOR) antagonist. As KOR activation is thought to produce some of the dysphoria associated with withdrawal, it was predicted and patients report that detoxification from opioids with buprenorphine is less noxious.

In the US, opioid substitution treatment with methadone or LAAM is only allowed in specially licensed outpatient opioid substitution treatment clinics. At these clinics patients receive their medication doses as well as counseling and other psychosocial interventions. Generally after successfully maintaining abstinence, patients may be allowed to take increasing amounts of their medication doses home, allowing for reduced clinic contact with treatment success.

In 2002, buprenorphine was approved in the U.S. for use as an opioid substitution treatment administered by individual licensed clinicians. It is thought that this will increase availability of opioid substitution treatment, especially in rural areas, and attract patients uncomfortable with attending an opioid substitution treatment clinic for treatment.

Efficacy and Components of Successful Treatment

Opioid substitution treatment has been shown to be a highly efficacious and effective treatment for heroin and opioid addiction (Table 1). Studies comparing opioid substitution treatment to detoxification have shown substantial benefits to maintenance treatment, with opioid maintained patients having better retention in treatment, reduced heroin use, and lower death rates. An early study by Newman and Whitehill (1979) found that at 3 years, 56% of patients provided opioid substitution therapy compared to 2% of patients receiving placebo treatment were successfully treated (defined as remaining in treatment and being generally heroin abstinent). A similar study by Gunne et al. (1981) comparing patients randomized to methadone maintenance versus drug-free treatment (a treatment program that does not allow pharmacotherapies such as methadone) found that at two years, 76% of methadone maintained patients were clean compared to only 6% of the drug-free patients. A more recent study by Sees et al. (2000) compared a 6-month methadone detoxification program with enhanced psychosocial counseling to methadone maintenance. Even with this extremely slow detoxification and the addition of extra services, methadone maintenance patients had improved outcomes from the fifth month on. Patients on the detoxification program increased their heroin use as their methadone doses were reduced and ended, while those in the methadone maintenance program maintained their early reductions in heroin use. As with many medications, methadone appears to be effective only for the time period over which it is administered. Discontinuation of methadone treatment is associated with a reoccurrence of SUD symptoms, and thus long-term use of opioid substitution treatment is recommended.

A series of randomized controlled trials have identified treatment components that optimize treatment outcomes in patients.

Dose

Higher doses of methadone have been repeatedly shown to reduce heroin use more effectively than lower doses. Strain et al. (1993) demonstrated that after 20 weeks of treatment patients receiving 50 mg of methadone were more apt to still be in treatment and had fewer opioid positive urines than patients receiving 20 mg of methadone or patients who were detoxed off methadone over 35 days. These differences were large, with patients on 50 mg methadone having less than half the number of opioid positive urines as those patients who had been detoxed. Ling et al. (1996) compared treatment with 80 mg methadone to treatment with 30 mg of methadone or 8 mg of buprenorphine per day. At one year, treatment retention was similar for all groups, but patients receiving 80 mg of methadone had more clean urines and less craving than patients in the other 2 groups. Maxwell and Sinderma (1999) investigated whether methadone doses of greater than 100 mg per day would benefit patients who were still not opioid abstinent despite opioid substitution treatment with lower doses of methadone. They found that increasing methadone doses above 100 mg successfully improved drug use outcomes in these treatment resistant patients; after increasing methadone doses in these patients, 97% of their urines were opioid-free, up from 13% on doses less than 100 mg. Based on data from these and shorter studies, clinical guidelines currently recommend using doses equivalent to at least 60 mg of methadone for opioid substitution.

Intensity of psychosocial counseling

The need for intense psychosocial counseling in conjunction with opioid substitution medication has been controversial. While patients provided methadone alone were shown to improve compared to their baseline use, McLellan et al. (1993) demonstrated a intensity-related effect of counseling on treatment outcomes in opioid substitution treatment after 6 months of treatment, with increases in available services improving SUD outcomes. A second study (Calsyn et al., 1994; Saxon et al., 1996), however, found no difference in substance use outcomes between patients randomized to minimal, standard or enhanced counseling services, and an additive effect of a contingency management program only in patients receiving minimal counseling. This study suggested that contingency management techniques could be substituted for additional counseling in these patients.

Based on the results of these studies and concerns surrounding treatment drop-out, practice guidelines recommend providing a variety of psychosocial services or therapies to patients entering opioid substitution treatment.

Naltrexone treatment of opioid addiction
Theory and Practice

Naltrexone is an opioid receptor antagonist that has been used to treat opioid addiction. When taken daily, naltrexone blocks the effects of heroin or other opioids, thereby making use of an opioid pointless. The major caveat of this treatment is that, of course, naltrexone only works when the client takes it; use of this treatment has been plagued by treatment non-compliance and drop-out problems. A patient with major urges to use opioids may not be particularly driven to take a medication that prevents opioid effects.

Efficacy

Generally, naltrexone has not been shown to be more effective than placebo for the treatment of opioid addiction in long-term trials (Table 1). This conclusion is limited however, by the fact that these studies have small sample sizes. Nevertheless, evidence for its effectiveness even as a short-term treatment is lacking (Kirchmayer et al., 2002).

Lack of effectiveness of naltrexone is generally attributed to lack of treatment adherence. Thus, it has been suggested that naltrexone be considered for highly motivated, highly monitored patient populations, such as employed health care professionals with work-site monitoring or parolees who risk reincarceration (Kirchmayer et al., 2002). Nevertheless, further studies are needed to demonstrate the effectiveness of this medication even in special populations.

Naltrexone treatment for alcohol addiction
Theory and Practice

Basic research suggested that the rewarding properties of alcohol were produced through a neuronal circuit that employed endogenous opioids (Gonzales and Weiss, 1998). Thus, it was hypothesized that treatment with an opioid receptor antagonist, such as naltrexone, would block the rewarding effects of alcohol. Without their associated rewarding effects, alcohol-seeking behaviors would extinguish. This was demonstrated in animal models, where rodents given naltrexone gradually decreased their intake of alcohol over time. Thus, naltrexone is theorized to encourage the unlearning of alcohol-seeking behaviors, as subsequent alcohol consumption would not be paired with reward.

In practice, however, naltrexone has not always been used in concordance with its theoretical mechanism of action. In several studies, naltrexone has been administered to abstinent alcoholics as a relapse prevention measure (i.e. in hopes that it would prevent them from trying alcohol again). As behavioral extinction requires experiencing the behavior without the reward, these trials

would not test the above hypothesized medication effect. Possibly because of the variation in the tested use of naltrexone, controlled trials of naltrexone for alcohol addiction have found varied results (Sinclair, 2001).

Efficacy

As has been reviewed in several meta-analyses (Streeton and Whelan, 2001; Srisraponont and Jarusuraisin, 2002), a number of short-term (12 week) randomized trials have demonstrated the efficacy of naltrexone for reducing alcohol consumption, increasing abstinence rates and reducing the number of days of drinking as compared to placebo. The longer-term efficacy of naltrexone has not been as thoroughly addressed. Nevertheless, several studies are informative (Table 1).

A large multisite trial of veterans recently detoxified from chronic severe alcohol dependence compared patients receiving daily naltrexone for 1 year to those receiving 3 months of naltrexone and 9 months of placebo to those receiving only placebo (Krystal et al., 2001). This study found no difference between the groups after 1 year, with all groups showing similar drinking patterns and similar time to relapse to drinking.

Other studies have found more promising effects, however. A study by Rubio et al. (2001) compared treatment with naltrexone to treatment with acamprosate, a drug approved in Europe for treatment of alcoholism, in recently detoxified alcohol dependent patients. They found that patients randomized to naltrexone had significantly superior alcohol use outcomes, with a greater percentage of patients maintaining abstinence, patients remaining abstinent for longer, and patients drinking fewer drinks per sitting. As acamprosate is generally considered an effective treatment for alcohol dependence, this result particularly supports the effectiveness of naltrexone for long-term treatment of alcohol dependence.

Several other long-term studies have demonstrated benefits of naltrexone in conjunction with specific counseling programs or in populations which have previously failed other treatment plans. Heinala et al. (2001) found that naltrexone improved alcohol use outcomes when added to cognitive coping skill therapy sessions. Naltrexone did not improve alcohol use outcome when combined with supportive therapy sessions; the naltrexone with cognitive coping skill therapy produced superior outcomes to supportive therapy with or without naltrexone. This study only followed patients for 32 weeks; it is unclear whether these effects would be maintained for longer periods of time. Interestingly, after a 12-week intensive therapy phase, patients in this study were instructed to only take naltrexone when they were craving alcohol. This dosing technique may have benefits if effective and warrants further investigation. Landabaso et al. (1999) examined the effectiveness of naltrexone given in conjunction with disulfiram in patients who had at least 3 previous treatment attempts with disulfiram. Patients given naltrexone in addition to disulfiram were more likely to remain in treatment and had significantly improved abstinence rates compared to patients treated a fourth time with disulfiram alone. Although abstinence rates decayed over time in both groups, the naltrexone group still had significantly higher abstinence rates at 2 years, a full 18 months after naltrexone treatment was discontinued.

Although evidence for naltrexone's long-term effectiveness is mixed, naltrexone has generally been accepted as an effective treatment for alcohol dependence. Further studies will be necessary to determine naltrexone's long-term effectiveness, the most effective length and dosage schedule of treatment, whether certain sub-populations of alcohol dependent patients have better outcomes on naltrexone, and whether specific counseling modalities improve naltrexone's effectiveness.

Disulfiram for alcohol addiction
Theory and Practice

Disulfiram inhibits the enzyme aldehyde dehydrogenase and blocks the breakdown of acetaldehyde (an ethanol breakdown product) thus encouraging the build-up of acetaldehyde following alcohol drinking. Elevated acetaldehyde levels produce a severely unpleasant and potentially dangerous syndrome, including flushing, throbbing head and neck pain, nausea and vomiting, sweating, thirst, chest pain, palpitation, hyperventilation, tachycardia, confusion, weakness, vertigo, and blurred vision. With more severe reactions, patients may experience respiratory depression, cardio-vascular collapse, myocardial infarction or acute congestive heart failure, convulsions, unconsciousness or even death.

Certain populations have a low-activity isoform of aldehyde dehydrogenase and are thus genetically predisposed to acetaldehyde reactions when consuming alcohol. It has been demonstrated that those with these low-activity isoforms have extremely low rates of alcoholism (Peng et al., 1999, Li, 2000). This "genetic experiment" supports the idea that having unpleasant reactions following alcohol consumption prevents if not reduces alcohol-seeking behaviors.

Nevertheless, this treatment suffers from serious non-compliance problems. Patients are often, understandably, reluctant to take a medication that will make them violently ill if they drink alcohol. Because of this, the effectiveness of this treatment has been questioned. Additionally, concerns about administering this medication to persons unable to control their alcohol consumption have limited its use.

Table 1: Randomized trials of Pharmacotherapies

Study	Subjects/group	Intervention	Outcomes
Opioid Substitution Therapies			
Bale et al., 1980	585 male veterans addicted to heroin 1: 150 2: 59	1: Three separate therapeutic communities 1: One of three separate therapeutic communities A)The Family – abstinence based with intensive group confrontation and support B) Quadrants – less abstinence oriented, uses some medications and limited group confrontation C) Satori – university psychiatric ward staff, medications used, no confrontation, emphasis on historical material and reconstruction in therapy 2: Methadone maintenance program – up to 80 mg/methadone daily plus individual, group and family counseling After 30 days in tx, subjects were allowed to transfer to the program of their choice.	**% of patients that remained in assigned tx program** 1A: 17.7, 1B: 23.8, 1C: 21.9, 2: 30.9 **% of patients assigned to program that decided not to attend any tx program:** 1A: 44.3, 1B: 40.1, 1C: 35.8, 2: 27.7 Patients that remained in 1 for 50 days or 2 for 30 days showed lower heroin use. There was no difference in heroin use between patients that chose to attend 1 versus 2.
Gunne et al., 1981	34 heroin addicts between ages of 20-24 with at least 4 years of IDU 1: 17 2: 17	1: methadone maintenance tx 2: untreated group – offered drug free tx, all refused	**At 24 months,** 1: 12 had no drug use, 5 had ongoing daily abuse (2 expelled from program) 2: 1 had no drug use, 14 had ongoing daily abuse, 2 died **% clean:** 1: 76%, 2: 6%
Kakko et al., 2003	40 adults w/ opioid-dependent for > 1yr who did not meet Sweden's legal criteria for methadone maintenance – multi-substance abusers were excluded	1: buprenorphine maintenance-16 mg/day for 1 year 2: 6 day taper with buprenorphine followed by placebo Both received group CBT and individual counseling weekly, and thrice weekly urinalysis	**Retention in tx after 1 year:** 1: 75%; 2: 0% (p=0.0001) All of 2 failed in tx by 3 mo. 74.8% of urines in 1 were clean **Death rate after 1 year:** 1: 0%; 2: 20% (p=0.015)

Kosten et al., 1993	140 opioid-dependent patients who met criteria for opioid maintenance treatment – 15 dropped out of tx and were left out of analysis	All received opioid substitution treatment with twice weekly relapse prevention groups (reduced to 1 after 6 weeks if clean) 1: 2 mg buprenorphine 2: 6 mg buprenorphine 3: 35 mg methadone 4: 65 mg methadone	**At 24 weeks:** **Retention in weeks:** 1: 17, 2: 15, 3: 21, 4: 19 $p < .005$ methadone better than buprenorphine **% urines clean** 1: 27%, 2: 24%, 3: 52%, 4: 51% $p < .0003$ methadone > buprenorphine **Days used/month:** 1: 6.9 2: 5.4, 3: 2.6, 4: 3.2 $p < .0001$ methadone > buprenorphine
Ling et al., 1996	225 treatment seeking opioid addicts - 75/group	1: 30 mg/d methadone 2: 80 mg/d methadone 3: 8 mg/d buprenorphine	**Retention (% in tx after 1 year)** 1: 19%; 2: 31%; 3: 20% ($p = .16$) ns **Number of clean urines (out of 152)** 1: 40.1; 2: 64.9; 3: 41.9 ($p = .002$) group 2 better than 1 and 3 **Craving** 2 less craving than 1 or 3 ($p = .006$)
Maxwell and Shinderman, 1999	Patients in a methadone clinic who were clinically unstable despite a methadone dose of 100 mg/day 1: 164 versus randomly selected controls from the clinic 2: 101	Methadone maintenance 1: Dosed over 100 mg based on signs and symptoms (average dose 211 mg/day) 2: Given standard doses with 100 mg maximum (average dose 69 mg/day)	**% clean urines:** **Baseline** 1: 13%, 2: 45% **After dose change:** 1: 97%, 2: 64%
Newman and White-hill, 1979	100 male heroin addicts stabilized for 2 weeks on 60 mg/day methadone 1:50 2: 50	1: Received a maintenance dose of methadone (30-130 mg/day) 2: Detoxed off methadone by 1 mg/day and then maintained on placebo Both groups were provided with a broad range of supportive services	**Retention** **at 32 weeks:** 1: 76%, 2: 10% **at 3 years:** 1: 56%, 2: 2% Patients were removed from the study for persistent heroin use. When patients from group 2 were offered tx 1, those who accepted had similar retention as seen in 1.
Saunders et al., 1995	122 opioid-dependent patients entering methadone maintenance 1: 51 2: 65	Methadone maintenance+ 1: Motivational Interviewing – 1 hour session 2: Education control – 1 hour presentation of material in a drug information book	**At 6 months** **Opioid related problems:** Fewer problems in 1 ($p = 0.04$) **Severity of opiate dependence:** Significant decrease from baseline in both groups, no difference between groups **Time until relapse:** No difference between groups `

Saxon et al., 1996 Calsyn et al., 1994	353 admissions to a methadone maintenance clinic	Methadone maintenance with 1: Medication only (referrals only) 2: Standard counseling (Once weekly individual counseling) 3: Enhanced services alone (Standard plus 8-week relapse prevention class, weekly group therapy and additional group and couples counseling) 4: 1+ plus contingency contract (positive urines put patients on a warning that with continued positives led to detoxification) 5:2+contingency contract 6:3+contingency contract	**Over 1 year:** 4 had fewer opioid positive urines than 1 (p<.01) but no difference between 2and5 or 3 and6 There was no difference between 1, 2and3 or 4, 5 and 6 in opioid positive urines. There was no effect of counseling level or contingency contracting on cocaine use.
Sees et al., 2000	179 adults with opioid dependence 1: 91 2: 88	1: methadone maintenance including 2 hours psychosocial therapy/week 2: 180 day methadone detoxification including 3 hours of psychosocial therapy/week + 14 education sessions + 1 hour of cocaine group therapy for 6 months, plus 6 months of non-methadone aftercare	**Tx retention:** 1: 438 days; 2: 174 days (p<.001) **% using heroin at 1 year:** 1: 58, 2: 80, p<.001 **ASI drug score at Intake, 6 and 12 mo., for pts still in tx:** 1: 0.37, 0.25, 0.18 2: 0.37, 0.27, 0.17 p=ns
Strain et al., 1993	247 iv opioid-dependent patients of which 95 remained in treatment for a 15 week stabilization period	Methadone maintenance with: 1: 50 mg methadone 2: 20 mg methadone 3: 0 mg methadone (35 day detox) All patients were detoxed following week 20	**Retention (% drop out by 20 weeks):** 1: 48%, 2: 59%, 3: 79% (p<.05) **Among the 95 who completed tx: % opioid positive urines during period of stable dosing:** 1: 36%, 2: 60%, 3: 73% (p<.05)
White et al., 2002	62 patients in methadone maintenance for at least 6 weeks.	Opioid substitution with: 1: 3 months of methadone then 3 months of LAAM then choice of drug 2: 3 months of LAAM then 3 months of methadone then choice of drug	Patients reported less heroin use while on LAAM (0.7 days/month) than methadone (2.6 days/month), p=.047 More patients chose LAAM when given the choice (27 vs 12, p<.001)
Naltrexone for Opioid Users			
Judson et al., 1981	119 opioid-dependent patients following detox	Thrice weekly dosages of 1: 60 mg naltrexone 2: 120 mg naltrexone for up to 365 days	Of those who stayed in tx for at least 3 months, group 2 remained in tx longer than 1.

Landa-baso et al., 1998	112 heroin addicts in a naltrexone treatment program 1: 56 2: 56	1: Naltrexone treatment alone 2: Naltrexone treatment plus 20 mg/day fluoxetine for the first 6 months	**Retention: (%dropped out)** 1: 52%, 2: 29%at 6 months 1: 68%, 2: 46% at 1 year
Rawson and Tennant, 1984	58 male opioid addicts	1: Naltrexone 2: Naltrexone + behavior therapy 3: Behavior therapy	**At 5 year follow-up:** 90% of naltrexone treated subject became readdicted at some point **At 1 year:** Almost 50% of 1 were opioid free.
Lerner et al., 1992	31 recently detoxed opioid addicts 1: 15 2: 16	1: Naltrexone for 2 months 2: Placebo for 2 months	**% completed 2 months tx:** 1: 60% , 2: 50% **% opioid free for 1 year:** 1: 53% 2: 37%
San et al., 1991	50 heroin-dependent IDUs 1: 28 2: 22	All received a 14-day detox w/ clonidine followed by 1 month of naltrexone treatment (50mg/day week 1; 100 mg every other day week 2-4). Patients were then randomized to: 1: 5 months naltrexone 2: 5 months of placebo	**Retention in Tx:** 1: 17.4%, 2: 40% p=ns **Tx Duration:** 1: 7.5, 2: 8.9 weeks p= ns **Tx visits:** 1: 4.4, 2: 3.1 p=ns **Drug free after 1 year:** 1: 32%, 2: 36% p=ns
Naltrexone for Alcohol Users			
Heinala et al., 2001	121 non-abstinent outpatients with alcohol dependence 1: 67; 2: 54; 3: 63; 4: 58	1: Cognitive coping skill sessions + naltrexone 50 mg/d 2: Supportive therapy + naltrexone 50 mg/d 3: Cognitive coping skill sessions + placebo 4: Supportive therapy +placebo Medication given for 12 weeks and then only when craving alcohol for the next 20 weeks. Supportive therapy emphasized abstinence, cognitive coping group did not.	**% of pts never relapsing to heavy drinking at 32 weeks:** 1: 27%; 2: 7%; 3: 3%; 4: 12% (p=.008 1 v. 3; p=.041 1 v. 2) **Number of pills taken/week in last 20 weeks:** 1: 2.1; 2: 3.4 3: 2.7; 4: 2.4 (p=0.05 1 v. 2)
Landa-baso et al., 1999	30 detoxified alcohol dependent patients who had undergone 3 previous treatments with disulfiram 1: 15 2: 15	1: Naltrexone 25 mg/day for 6 months plus disulfiram for 1 year 2: Disulfiram alone for 1 year	**% abstinent** **at 1 year** 1: 73.3%, 2: 20% **18 months** 1: 66.6%, 6% **2 years** 1: 40%, 2: 0% p>.05 **Tx Retention at 6 months:** 1: 85%, 2: 34% p<.05

Krystal et al., 2001	627 veterans with chronic severe alcohol dependence – 209 pts/group All sober at least 5 days before entering study	1: 12 mo. 50 mg/day naltrexone 2: 3 mo. Naltrexone + 9 mo. Placebo 3: 12 mo placebo	**Number of days til relapse**: 1and2: 72.3, 3: 62.4 (ns) **% of days drinking at 1yr**: 1: 15.1; 2: 19.4; 3: 18.0 (ns) **# of drinks/drinking day**: 1: 9.6; 2: 10.5; 3: 9.3 (ns)
Monti et al., 2001	165 alcoholic	All attended a 2 week partial hospital program for alcoholism plus 12 weeks of aftercare 1: Cue exposure combined with urge specific coping skills training and communication skills training during 2 week program + Naltrexone 50 mg/day during aftercare 2: Same 2 week program as 1 with placebo during aftercare 3: Education and relaxation training during 2 week program + Naltrexone during aftercare. 4: Same 2 week program as 3 + placebo during aftercare	**% Relapsed at 6 and 12 months**: 1+2: 24.2%, 36.7% 3+4: 40.8%, 60.7% (p<.05) There was no difference between naloxone and placebo. **Number of drinks per drinking day during the medication trial**: 1+3: 4.9 drinks 2+4: 8.8 drinks; (p<.05) There was no difference between naloxone and placebo 3 and 6 months after medication was ended.
Rubio et al., 2001	157 recently detoxified alcohol dependent men 1: 77 2: 80	1: naltrexone (50 mg/d) 2: acamprosate (1665-1998 mg/day) Both had weekly psychiatry visits and weekly supportive group therapy	**% subjects abstinent from 6 mo-1 yr of tx**: 1: 54%; 2: 27 % p=.0002 **Days to first relapse (>=5 drinks/day)**: 1: 63; 2: 42 p=0.02 **# drinks consumed at one time**: 1: 4; 2: 9 p=.01 **# of days abstinent**: 1: 243; 2: 180 p=.03

Disulfiram			
Carrol et al., 2000	122 Cocaine and alcohol dependent adults 1: 25 2: 19 3: 27 4: 25 5: 26	1: 12-step facilitation alone 2: Cognitive behavioral therapy alone 3: Clinical management/disulfiram 4: 12-step facilitation/disulfiram 5: Cognitive behavioral therapy/disulfiram Both study treatments were manual-guided 1/week individual sessions for 12 weeks. Disulfiram dose started at 250 mg/day and could be increased up to 500 mg/day. Medication compliance was 66.8%.	Patients receiving disulfiram used less cocaine and alcohol than those that did not (p>.01), however this effect declined over time. There were no differences in cocaine or alcohol use between the 12-step and CBT groups.
Fuller and Roth, 1979	128 alcoholic men	1: Active dose of disulfiram (250 mg/day 2; Inactive dose of disulfiram (1 mg/day) 3: No treatment	**% abstinent at 1 yr:** 1: 21%, 2: 25%, 3: 12%, p=ns No difference in percentage of drinking days between groups.
Fuller et al., 1986	605 men presenting for alcoholism tx at a VA clinic. All were under 60 and did not live alone. 1: 202 2: 204 3: 199	All received 1 year of outpatient treatment with weekly counseling (ind or group) for 6 months and biweekly counseling for the following 6 months. Patients were randomly assigned to receive 1: 250 mg disulfiram 2: 1mg disulfiram 3: no disulfiram	**At 1 year:** **% abstinent for year:** 1: 18.8%, 2: 22.5%, 3: 16.1% p=ns No dif in time to first drink p=.26 **Of pts who reported drinking, # days drinking/year:** 1: 49, 2: 75, 3: 86.5 p=.05
Wilson et al., 1978	20 alcoholics who had just completed detox 1: 10 2: 10	1: Disulfiram implants (100 mg tablet) 2: Placebo implants (saline)	**Total days of abstinence in 2 years post-implant:** 1>2, p<.02

Efficacy

In the few studies that have examined the long-term effectiveness of disulfiram treatment, some improvement in drinking behaviors were observed in patients receiving disulfiram versus controls (Table 1). In the largest long-term study, Fuller et al. (1986) showed that disulfiram did not increase the percentage of patients abstinent from alcohol at 1 year, nor did it increase the time to relapse to drinking. Nevertheless, those on disulfiram who chose to drink consumed alcohol on fewer days in the subsequent year than did controls. This appeared to be the result of patients experiencing the acetaldehyde reaction, as those taking a lower and likely inactive dose of disulfiram drank more often than those on an active dose.

Similarly, Wilson et al. (1978) showed that alcoholics implanted with disulfiram tablets had fewer drinking days over the following two years than those that received placebo implants.

An earlier study by Fuller and Roth (1979) showed no difference in alcohol abstinence rates or drinking days following a year of active disulfiram, inactive disulfiram or no treatment. Nevertheless, there was a trend for patients receiving either active or inactive disulfiram to have higher abstinence rates than untreated controls, suggesting that fear of the acetaldehyde reaction may have some influence towards encouraging abstinence. It is unclear why patients in this study were more hesitant to try drinking while on disulfiram than those in Fuller et al.'s later study (1986).

The general conclusion that has been made from these studies (Garbutt et al., 1999) is that there is some, though not conclusive evidence that disulfiram reduces the number of drinking days in adherent patients, however, there is not evidence that it improves abstinence rates in alcoholic patients.

COUNSELING-BASED INTERVENTIONS
Brief Interventions
Theory and Practice

Brief interventions are interventions, most typically intended for use in primary care, that attempt to correct substance abuse within restricted time constraints. These have most often been directed at correcting problem drinking behaviors, focusing on heavy drinkers (generally defined as >35 drinks/week for men or >21 drinks/week for women) rather than dependent drinkers or illegal substance users. These interventions have been as short as five minutes to as long as approximately 3 hours of sessions.

Most commonly, these sessions include assessment of problematic substance use,

comparison of the patient's substance use to population norms, monitoring of substance use, information on the health and social dangers associated with substance use and recommendations to reduce or abstain from substance use. In some formulations (e.g. motivational interviewing interventions), these brief interventions may include a motivational component focused on increasing the subject's perceived need or drive to reduce substance use. These interventions have most commonly been led by primary care physicians, although nurse-delivered interventions or nurse-delivered follow-ups have been tried. Often these interventions include providing the patient with a self-help book or materials for use on their own.

Efficacy

Brief physician-led interventions for problem drinking have been repeatedly demonstrated to be effective for reducing problem drinking behaviors (Table 2). Most trials comparing brief interventions to no intervention demonstrated significantly greater reductions in alcohol consumption and/or biological correlates of high alcohol consumption than no intervention controls a year or more after the intervention. For example, Anderson and Scott (1992) showed that having a general practitioner provide 10 minutes of feedback and a self-help book to patients screened for excessive alcohol consumption significantly reduced alcohol consumption one year later as compared to patients who were only screened. Similarly, Project TREAT (Fleming et al., 1997; Manwell et al., 2000; Fleming et al., 2002) showed that two 10-15 minute counseling visits with a physician over a month, plus follow-up calls two-weeks later from a nurse significantly reduced alcohol consumption, binge drinking episodes and hospitalizations in patients who screened positive for problem drinking in primary care for four years following the intervention. Other studies using slightly more intensive variations on these interventions obtained similar results with alcohol abusers.

One interesting point demonstrated by Miller et al. (1993) was that therapist style appeared to be important in determining patient's likelihood of reducing alcohol use.

Patients whose therapist employed a confrontational approach had worse outcomes in their study. Based upon observations such as these Miller and Rollnick (1991) recommend a non-confrontational technique termed "motivational interviewing" in which the patients own motivations, life goals and values are discussed, in hopes of increasing

Table 2: Randomized Trials of Brief Interventions

Study	Subjects	Intervention	Outcomes
Brief intervention versus no intervention			
Anderson and Scott, 1992	154 men with excessive alcohol consumption (>350g/week) screened by a general practitioner. 1: 80, 2: 74	1: 10 min of feedback about assessment and information on risks of excessive drinking, benefits of drinking less, and advice to reduce drinking to <210g/week plus patients given a self-help book. 2: No advice from general practitioner.	**Change in g/week drunk over 1 year:** 1: 231 g/week, 2: 151 g/week p<.05
Baer et al., 2001, Marlatt et al., 1998	348 19 year olds entering college who were deemed to be "high risk" based upon history of binge drinking at least once in the last month or having drinking related problems (1and2: 174) plus 113 entering students who were not deemed "high risk" as a natural history control (3: 113)	1: Asked subjects to self-monitor for 2 weeks prior to a session of manual based feedback comparing their drinking behavior and beliefs to actual norms. A summary of this information was mailed to each participant and extremely high-risk subjects were contacted by phone to express concern and offer more sessions. 2: No intervention 3: No intervention	1 showed significantly lower frequency, quantity, and negative consequences of drinking than did 2 over their 4 years in college. The low-risk control consistently had lower drinking frequency, quantity and negative consequences than both groups for the 4 years of college.

Chick et al., 1985	156 male problem drinkers admitted to medical wards	Both groups were assessed by a nurse 1: One session, up to 60 minutes long, of counseling about their drinking habits from a nurse 2: standard care, no advice from nurse	**Drinks (57g) in last week:** 1: Intake: 69, 1 year: 32 2: Intake: 69, 1 year: 35 Both groups decreased consumption (p<.001) but there was no difference between the groups **GGT activity (IU/l):** 1: Intake: 151, 1 year: 89 2: Intake 126, 1 year: 99 Significant decrease in 1 (p<.05) but not 2. 1 showed a greater decrease than 2(p=.03)
Elvy et al., 1988	263 general hospital patients screened as problem drinkers 1: 84 2: 114	1: Approached by a psychologist and who confronted them about their alcohol problems and referred them to an alcohol counselor 2: No treatment	**Time since last drink** **<24 hours:** 12 mo 1: 25%, 2: 48% p<.05 18 mo 1: 33%, 2: 39% p=ns **1-4 days:** 12 mo: 1: 38%, 2: 28% p<.05 18 mo: 1: 29%, 2: 33% p=ns **>5 days:** 12 mo: 1: 38%, 2: 24% p<.05 18 mo: 1: 37%, 2: 27% p=ns **$ spent on alcohol in last week:** 12 mo: 1: $13.7, 2: $19.7 p=ns 18 mo: 1: $9.70, 2: $14.2 p<.05
Fleming et al., 1999	158 older adult problem drinkers in primary care practice 1: 87 2: 71	All received a 30-minute research assessment. 1: Given a general health booklet and scheduled for two 10-15 minute physician-delivered counseling sessions including advice, education and contracting using a scripted workbook. Nurses made follow-up phone calls 2 weeks after each session. 2: Given a general health booklet	**Number of drinks in last week at baseline, 6 mo and 1 year:** 1: 15.5, 10.0, 9.9 2: 16.6, 16.0, 16.3 p<.001 at 6 mo and 1 year **% binge drinking in last month at baseline, 6 mo and 1 year:** 1: 48% 32%, 30% 2: 40%. 42%, 49% p<.025 at 1 year.

Fleming et al., 1997; Manwell et al., 2000; Fleming et al., 2002 Project TrEAT	723 primary care patients who screened positive for problem drinking 1: 392 2: 382	1: Two 10-15 minute counseling visits 1 month apart delivered by physicians using a scripted workbook. Included advice, education and contracting plus a follow-up telephone call from a nurse 2 weeks after each visit. 2: standard care	**% reduction in the number of drinks in last week** 12 mo. FU: 1: 40%, 2: 18%; p<.001, drinking levels and difference was maintained at 48 months. **Number of binge drinking episodes in the last 30 days at 12 months:** 1: 3.07, 2: 4.21; p<.005, difference was maintained at 48 mo although some drift back to original values was seen starting at 24 months. **Days of hospitalizations in the 4 years following intervention:** 1: 420, 2: 664; p<.05 **Cost benefit analysis**: save $43,000 in future health costs with every $10,000 invested.
Persson and Magnusson, 1989	78 patients who had excessive alcohol consumption or raised GGT levels 1: 36 2: 42	1: Assessment by physician then followed by nurse once per month and by a physician every 3rd month for 1 year. Monitored alcohol consumption and laboratory values. Advice to reduce alcohol consumption was given. 2: No intervention control	**GGT levels at baseline and 1 yr:** 1: 0.94 and 0.62 2: 0.63 and 0.51 p=ns (.09) **Weekly alcohol consumption (g)** 1: Baseline: 164, 1-yr: 117 2: Baseline: 160, 1-yr: NA
Scott and Anderson 1990	72 women screening positive for heavy drinking in general practice 1: 33 2: 39	1: 10 minutes of advice from a general practitioner including feedback on drinking, information about the risks of drinking, and a comparison to population drinking norms and a self-help booklet 2: No intervention	**Drinks in last week:** 1: Baseline: 35.3, 1 yr: 23.7 2: Baseline: 36.6, 1 yr: 26.6 Both groups improved significantly, but there was no effect of treatment. Notably, however, many of the patients in 2 were found to have independently had alcohol-related consultations over the last year. Those who had a consultation reduced their drinking significantly more than those who didn't p<.03.

Wallace et al., 1988	909 heavy drinkers screened in general practice	1: Physician-led interview about pattern and amount of alcohol consumption, evidence of drinking problems and societal norms and harmful effects of alcohol. Advice to limit alcohol use was given. Patients received an information pamphlet, a drinking diary, and were offered a follow-up appointment in a month. At follow-up diary was reviewed.
		2: No intervention
			Drinks per week at baseline, 6 mo and 1 year:
			Men: 1: 62.2, 46.7, 44.0
			      2: 63.7, 55.5, 55.6
			Women 1: 35.1, 24.8, 23.6
			      2: 36.8, 28.8, 30.4
			Men: $p<.001$ at 6 mo and 1 year
			Women: $p=ns$ at 6 mo and $p<.05$ at 1 year
			GGT levels at baseline, 6 mo and 1 year:
			Men: 1: 27.8, 26.8, 25.4
			      2: 26.7, 26.7, 27.8
			Women: 1: 13.7, 14.0, 14.0
			        2: 12.0, 12.7, 12.5
			At 12 months, $p<.01$ for men $p=ns$ for women

Comparison of types or intensities of Brief Interventions			
Israel et al., 1996	105 problem drinkers identified by screening patients reporting trauma in the last 5 years for alcohol use in primary care	1: Received 30 minutes of cognitive behavioral counseling from a nurse to encourage controlled drinking and were booked for 20 minute follow-up sessions every 2 months for 1 year. Given pamphlet. 2: Nurse gave advice to reduce alcohol consumption plus a pamphlet with guidelines for achieving abstinence or acceptable drinking. Told GGT levels and their significance.	**Change in drinks/month from baseline to 12 months:** 1: -106, 2: -63 , $p<.05$ **Change in GGT levels (units/L)** 1: -19.8, 2: -5.2, $p<.05$
Miller et al., 1993	42 problem drinkers 1: 14 2: 14 3: 14	Assessment and screening 1: DCU (a 2 hour alcohol assessment and neuropsychological test battery) + check-up at 1 week with assessment feedback plus directive-confrontational counseling 2: DCU + check-up at 1 week with assessment feedback plus client-centered counseling 3: delayed check-up (wait-listed for 6 weeks before DCU)	**Drinking days per week:** 1: Intake: 6.36, 6 weeks: 4.07, 12 months: 5.33 2: Intake: 4.36, 6 weeks: 3.36, 12 months: 4.10 3: Intake: 5.79, 6 weeks: 4.71; 12 months: 6.18 1+2 v. 3 at 6 weeks $p<.01$ Therapist confrontation was associated with increased drinking and worse outcomes.

Nilssen, 1991	338 subjects with elevated GGT 1: 113 2: 113 3: 112	1: Informed of most common reasons for elevated GGT and asked to consider possible reasons for their own elevated GGT. Given information folder on GGT and alcohol consumption. Sent results of second GGT test by mail. 2: Suggested directly that elevated GGT may be from alcohol consumption, asked about drinking habits and alcohol consumption. Given advice about how to reduce alcohol consumption, information folder on GGT and alcohol and monthly GGT consultations until GGT normalized. 3: No assessment or intervention	**GGT levels at baseline and 1 yr:** 1: 78.4, 61.1 2: 70.1, 58.8 3: 79.2, 86.5 p<.001 Both 1 and 2 were different than 3, but not different from each other **Daily alcohol consumption (g/day) at 1 year:** 1: 15.6 2: 13.5 3: 39.2 Both 1 and 2 were different than 3, but not different from each other p<.001
Rich-mond et al., 1995	378 problem drinkers screened in general practice 1: 96 2: 96 3: 93 4: 93	1: A structured behavioral program consisting of 5 short consultations designed to reduce drinking, included a self-help manual, patient diary, motivational interviewing, and goal-setting. 2: 5 minutes of brief advice to reduce drinking, information on health risks of drinking and a self-help manual 3: Assessment only 4: No assessment or intervention	**% drinking above recommended levels at baseline, 6 mo and 1 yr:** 1: 83.3%, 74.0%, 76.0% 2: 79.2%, 74.0%, 77.1% 3: 73.1%, 71.0%, 78.5% p=ns **Proportion of pts with abnormal GGT:** p=ns
Sanchez-Craig et al., 1996	155 media-recruited heavy drinker considering quitting or cutting down on their own	1: Self-help manual, "Saying When", mailed to patient 2: Self-help manual by mail + 30 minute motivational interviewing based assessment by telephone	**Number of drinks in last week** **Admission** Males: 1: 23.5, 2: 25.4 Female: 1: 17.5, 2:16.0 **At 3 months;** Males: 1: 14.1, 2: 11.7 Females: 1: 6.6, 2: 7.5 **At 12 months** Males: 1: 11.2, 2: 10.9 Females: 1: 5.3, 2: 7.7 Both groups reduced their drinking P<.001, but there was no difference between the groups.

Sanchez-Craig et al., 1989	90 problem drinkers recruited through advertisements 1: 28 2: 33 3: 29	1: 3 sessions of advice using a pamphlet outlining basic steps to abstinence or moderate drinking 2: 3 sessions of instruction in the use of a self-help manual 3: 6 or more sessions of instruction in the methods outlined in the self-help manual	**Decrease in # heavy drinking g days in last 90 days from intake to average of 3, 6 and 12 month follow-up:** Males: 1: 9; 2: 15; 3: 22 Females: 1: 36; 2: 30; 3: 30 No significant difference between groups. Women showed greater decreases than men (p<.05) Overall groups heavy drinking days were reduced 53%
Wutzke et al., 2002	554 non-dependent but hazardous drinkers	1: Assessment only 2: 5 min of advice comparing alcohol use with general population, highlighting physical and social problems related to drinking and recommending drinking limits. Given a leaflet. 3: 2 plus 15 min of counseling in problem solving techniques, including identifying problem situations, methods of coping and a support person for assistance. Asked to complete an alcohol use diary. 4: 3 plus 2 additional 20 min counseling sessions over 6 months. Reviewed diary and problem solving techniques and gave results of biochemical tests	At 9 months, there was a lower median weekly alcohol consumption with any intervention (2-4) v. 1, with no dif between 2-4. This effect was gone by 10 yrs. **Median Weekly alcohol consumption:** At 9 months: 1: 262.9 g, (2-4): 208.3; p=.025 At 10 years: 1: 158.0 g, (2-4): 173.7 g; p=ns
Brief interventions versus Intensive interventions			
Burge et al., 1997	175 mexican-american primary care patients who screened positive for alcohol use or dependence.	1: 10-15 minute physician-lead confrontation and discussion with patient recommending abstinence, based on WEEP-F recommendations (Barnes, 1987) 2: 6-week psychoeducational group 3: 1and2 4: no intervention All groups received SUD assessment.	All groups showed significant decreases in drinks per week and Addiction Severity Index Alcohol score at 12 and 18 months. There were no differences in alcohol use outcomes between the groups.

Chapman and Huygens, 1988	113 detoxified alcoholics 1: 36 2: 35 3: 34	1: Inpatient program including individual counseling, medical care, psychotherapy groups, social skills groups, AA, education and recreation 2: 6-week outpatient program including twice weekly evening meetings 3: A single 1-2 hour confrontational interview encouraging abstinence and personal responsibility	**At 18 months:** **% abstinent** 1: 23.1, 2: 36.4%, 3: 30.8% p=ns **Average daily alcohol (g):** 1: 37.7, 2: 33.7, 3: 34.3, p=ns
Chick et al., 1988	152 patients attending an alcohol problems clinic 1: 41 2:55 3:58	1: 5 minutes of simple advice emphasizing that the patient had a drinking problem, needed to stop and must take responsibility for this. 2: 30-60 minutes of advice focusing on enhancing patient motivation to stop drinking. 3: Advice plus further treatment options including detoxification, inpatient or day programs, group therapy, and encouragement to attend Alcoholics Anonymous.	**At 2 years:** **Past 7 days drinking (g)** **% drinking <500 g** 1: 56%, 2: 61%, 3: 71% **% drinking 500-1000g** 1: 29%, 2: 25%, 3: 13% **% drinking > 1000 g** 1: 15%, 2: 14%, 3: 16% p=ns **GGT levels declined** 1and2: 55%, 3: 59%, p=ns Patients in 3 showed a significantly greater reduction in problems but no difference in alcohol consumption compared to 1and2
Edwards et al., 1977	100 married men referred to an outpatient alcoholism clinic 1: 50 2: 50	Patient and wife attended an initial 3 hour assessment, plus one additional session with a social worker, psychologist and psychiatrist to diagnose alcoholism and suggest abstinence, work and focus on marriage then 1: were told that it was their responsibility to attain goals and made one phone call/month to wife to assess progress 2: offered an introduction to Alcoholic Anonymous, a prescription of calcium cyanamide and drugs for withdrawal. Patient continued outpatient tx with psychiatrist; wife with social worker. Patient was offered inpatient tx if progress was lacking	At 12 months, there was no difference in weeks of heavy drinking by either patients or wife's report 1: 24.9; 2: 22.8 p=ns No difference between groups in longest continuous abstinence in last 12 months **Abstinence of > 2 months:** 1: 8%, 2: 8% p=ns

Kristen-son et al., 1983	585 individuals with two consecutive GGT values in the upper decile of the GGT distribution 1: 317 2: 268	1: Subjects were screened for drinking problems and offered continuing follow-up with the physician every third month, GGT tests every month as feedback, and reinforcing contacts with the nurse. Subjects were offered support and encouragement but were given full responsibility for their outcome. 2: Received a letter informing them to be restrictive with their alcohol consumption and that they should get their liver enzymes measured every 2 years.	**Decreases in GGT levels:** 1: 2 years: .466; 4 years: .735 2: 2 years: .450; 4 years: .584 Both groups showed significant decreases from baseline (p<.01) but there was no difference between the groups. **Sick days per year:** 1: Base: 24.0, 2 yr: 28.2, 4 yr: 29.3 2: Base: 24.7, 2 yr: 37.9; 4 yr: 51.9 Difference between groups at 2 and 4 years (p<.05)
Robert-son et al., 1986	37 problem drinkers 1: 21 2: 16	1: 3 or 4 sessions of assessment and advice – identified problem drinking situations and developed individual drinking guidelines 2: Individually tailored cognitive behavioral therapy sessions (ave 9.1 sessions) including problem solving skills training, marital contracting, relaxation training, cognitive restructuring, self-management training, and sexual counseling	**Drinks per month at baseline and 15 months:** 1: 355.4, 268.9 2: 385.9, 129.4 p<.05 1 v. 2
Romelsjo et al., 1989	83 adult participants in a health screening w/ indications of high alcohol consumption (e.g. reported >40g/day ethanol, had elevated GGT) 1: 42, 2: 41	1: Further visits (average of 3) to general practitioner who provided general support and monitoring and feedback based on GGT levels 2: Advice from general practitioner to cut alcohol consumption	Non-significant trend towards greater reduction in GGT and self-reported alcohol consumption in 1 than 2. **GGT levels at 1 year:** 1: 1.5, 2: 1.9; p=ns **Alcohol consumption at 1 year:** 1: 23 g, 2: 28.4 g; p=ns
Sanni-bale, 1988	96 male problem drinkers presenting to a community agency for treatment 1: 9 2: 42 3: 45	1: A single motivational interviewing session. Patients were told they seemed to have an alcohol problem and that it was their responsibility to change. An optional follow-up session was offered. 2: Six sessions of didactic confrontational therapy in individual or group format with an abstinence goal. 3: Seven sessions of Cognitive-behavioral therapy with abstinence or controlled drinking as the goal.	**At 1 year follow-up** **% without drinking problems** 1: 50%, 2: 50%, 3: 45%, p=ns Significant improvements were seen in all groups.

Stephens et al., 2000	291 treatment seeking adult marijuana users	1: 2 90 minute motivational interviewing sessions over 1 month. 2: 14 two hour cognitive behavioral groups sessions over 4 months 3: 4 month delayed treatment control	**Days used per month** **Baseline** 1: 24.24, 2: 25.38, 3: 24.85 **4 months** 1: 7.78, 2: 6.68, 3: 17.1 **13 months:** 1: 11.61, 2: 11.89 **16 months** 1: 12.99, 2: 12.29 Both 1 and 2 significantly improved at all times. There was not difference between 1 and 2.
Zweben et al., 1988	116 couples 1: 70 2: 46	1: 8 outpatient conjoint (alcoholic and spouse) sessions following a communication-interactional approach where alcohol use was considered in terms of its adaptive value for the couple 2: One 1.5 hour conjoint advice counseling session using	**% heavy drinking days:** 12 mo: 1: 17, 2: 18 p=ns 18 mo: 1: 17, 2: 18 p=ns **% days abstinent** 12 mo: 1: 50, 2: 59 p=ns 18 mo: 1: 51, 2: 56 p=ns Both significantly improved with no difference between treatments.

the patient's awareness of behaviors (e.g. substance use) that are inconsistent with his own goals, and thus increasing the patient's desire to reduce substance use.

Studies that investigated different forms or different intensities of brief interventions, however, generally found little to no difference between the treatments. Single brief (5-15 minutes) counseling sessions or simple provision of a self-help book were as successful at reducing alcohol consumption as were longer, more involved counseling sessions. One exception to this was a study by Israel et al. (1996) who showed that 3 hours of cognitive behavioral counseling spread over one year produced superior outcomes to simple advice to reduce drinking when provided by a nurse to patients screening positive for both trauma and excessive alcohol use in primary care. Thus, there may be some benefit in providing more than the minimum of brief interventions, namely advice alone.

Nevertheless, standard brief interventions were generally just as successful in reducing alcohol consumption in alcohol abusers as were extended treatments. All of the studies found in this review found similar reductions in alcohol use in patients receiving brief interventions as compared to more comprehensive ones. Furthermore, a meta-analysis by Moyer et al. (2002) concluded that studies that examined the effectiveness of brief interventions versus more extensive interventions found little added benefit of the more extensive treatment.

The Moyer et al. (2002) meta-analysis also suggested that brief interventions may be more successful with less severe, non-dependent drinkers. This suggests that brief interventions may be useful mainly for the treatment of substance abuse, rather than substance dependence or addiction. Generally, brief interventions have not been tried for treatment of illicit substance use disorders or with severely dependent drinkers. Further investigation into whether brief interventions are successful treatments for alcohol dependence and other substance use disorders is needed.

Inpatient Treatment
Theory and Practice

Inpatient treatment consists of a wide array of treatment methods all containing one similar quality: the patient stays overnight (24 hours) at the treatment site and spends some period of time engaging in treatment in that setting (Finney et al., 1996). The settings vary and include places like hospitals, psychiatric hospitals, specified treatment centers, therapeutic communities and prisons. The type and amount of staff varies widely as well and can include medical doctors, psychiatrists, counselors, social workers, nurses, peer counselors and more. Treatment services available to the patients vary from program to program and include such services as detoxification, AA/12-step-facilitation, psychotherapy, patient education, medication, medical treatment, group therapy and social services (Weiss, 1999). Although treatment setting, staffing and available services all vary by program, essential features of inpatient treatment are the removal of the patient from their general environment into a substance abuse treatment program with 24 hour care. In general a distinction between inpatient treatment and residential treatment is made with inpatient referring to treatment provided in a more medical setting with medical care and medically-trained staff available, and residential referring to treatment that provides less medical care and fewer medically-trained staff. Reasons for prescribing inpatient or residential treatment include; treating and monitoring physically dependent patients for their withdrawal, providing a safe place for patients to recover that separates them from environments that may contribute to their substance use, helping to maintain patients in treatment so that they are able to get adequate treatment, providing an intense amount of treatment, and communicating to patients that the problem is severe and needs to be treated (Finney et al., 1996).

Efficacy

While inpatient treatment generally reduces substance use for over a year (Table 3), the high costs associated with maintaining patients in an inpatient unit spurred a great deal of research examining whether inpatient treatment was superior to outpatient treatment. The resounding answer to this question is no; despite some evidence for improved retention in inpatient treatment (McKay et al., 1995; Guydish et al., 1999; Greewood et al., 2001), one year after the beginning of treatment, patients randomized to outpatient programs showed similar drug use outcomes to patients randomized to inpatient programs (Edwards et al., 1967; McLachlan et al., 1982; Fink et al., 1985; McCrady et al., 1986; McKay et al., 1995; Lam et al., 1995; Guydish et al., 1999; Greenwood et al., 2001). These studies demonstrated that formal inpatient treatment is no more effective than formal outpatient treatment.

The one study that did show improved outcomes with inpatient treatment compared an inpatient program with 3 weeks of compulsory hospitalization followed by Alcoholics Anonymous (AA) meetings 3 times/week for a year to thrice weekly AA meetings for a year alone (Walsh et al., 1991). In this case, patients randomized to the compulsory inpatient treatment program condition had lower rates of relapse to problem drinking, lower intoxication rates and less cocaine use than those sent to AA alone. This study demonstrated that a period of formal inpatient treatment produces better outcomes than self-help alone, speaking to the benefits of a period of formal treatment in patients recovering from alcohol-related disorders.

Table 3: Randomized Trials of Inpatient Treatment

Study	Subjects/group	Intervention	Outcomes
Bale et al., 1984	347 heroin addicted veterans 1: 25 2: 77 3: 79 4: 166	1: "Family' therapeutic community; a residential peer confrontation program, no outside contact, sobriety demanded, therapy once/week 2: "Quadrants" therapeutic community; a residential program with patients working on the weekends, some outside contact, some tolerance of substance use 3: "Satori" therapeutic community; a residential professionally-staffed program with emphasis on individual therapy, some outside contact and alcohol use permitted 4: withdrawal only treatment; 5 day inpatient withdrawal	**Time in treatment:** all programs relatively ineffective at retention. 2 retained less patients than 1 or 3. $p<.05$ 1 and 2 were more likely to lose patients within the first 6 weeks. **Rate of heroin use after 2 years:** 33% of 4 were not using 48% of group 2 were not using: significantly better than all groups at $p<.05$ **Rates of other illegal drug use after 2 years**: 53% of group 3 were not using, significantly more than group 4 (39%), $p<.05$
Edwards et al., 1967	40 alcohol dependent males 1: 20 2: 20	1: inpatient tx; in a general hospital psychiatric ward. tx was abstinence only, 'eclectic'. 2: outpatient tx; same treatment regimen as inpatient Both were 8 weeks with monthly follow-up	Scores given based on amount of drinking over 12 months: $p = NS$
Fink et al., 1985 Mc-Crady et al., 1986	174 Patients originally, 115 made follow-up, from a private university-affiliated psychiatric hospital with a diagnosis of alcohol abuse or dependence	1: extended inpatient treatment; included 1 week of detox, medical and psychiatric assessment, stayed inpatient while attending the 5 week program 2: partial hospital treatment; included 1 week of detox, medical and psychiatric assessment and did not stay inpatient while attending the 5 week program	**12 month outcomes:** **Quantity-Frequency Index (QFI) for drinking**: 1: baseline 6.44, 1 yr 1.24 $p<.001$ 2: baseline 8.74, 1 yr .48, $p<.001$ Between groups $p = NS$ **% days abstinent for the year:** 1: baseline 26%, 1 yr 82%, $p<.005$ 2: baseline 24%, 1 yr 85,% $p<.05$ Between groups $p = NS$ **% days abstinent in the past 30:** 2 was significantly better at $p<.05$. **24 month outcomes**: **Drinking behavior:** both improved significantly on alcohol outcomes throughout the 2 years at $p<.05$ **Overall average of days abstinent over 24 months:** 2 was significantly better at $p<.05$

| Guydish et al., 1999

Green-wood et al., 2001 | 261 mixed race and gender adults from the Walden House in San Francisco, CA with various addictions

1: 114
2: 147 | 1: day treatment: a therapeutic community setting where patients do not stay at the Walden House but attend the program each day.
2: residential-treatment: a therapeutic community setting where patients do stay at the Walden House each night as well as attend the program each day. | **Treatment retention:** lower dropout rate for patients in the first 2 weeks for group 2 **ASI alcohol composite score:** between groups p = NS **Odds of relapse across settings at 6 months:** 1: 47% abstinent 2: 62.6% abstinent 1 has 3x greater odds of relapse than 2, p<.05 **Odds of relapse across settings at 1 year:** 1: 49% abstinent 2: 47.9% abstinent between groups p = NS **Odds of relapse across settings at 18 months:** 1: 55.2% abstinent 2: 50.4% abstinent between groups p= NS |
|---|---|---|---|
| Keso et al., 1990 | 144 employed alcoholics sent by their occupational health agency to the outpatient clinic

1: 74
2: 67 | 1: Hazelden-type inpatient treatment; a structured setting based on the Minnesota model with professional staff, a heavy emphasis on AA principles and abstinence, and therapy lasting 28 days
2: traditional-type inpatient treatment; semi-structured setting where patients are expected to spend some weekends at home. Social work, psychiatric ad medical services are available and AA is not emphasized but recommended for after treatment. Treatment lasts 6 weeks. | **Treatment retention:** 1: 7.9% dropped out 2: 25.9% dropped out p<.02 **Abstinence from alcohol 8-12 month:** 1: 26.3% 2: 9.8% p<.05 **Percent attending no AA meetings:** 1: 40.5%, 2: 80.6% **Percent attending >20 AA meetings:** 1: 18.8%, 2: 4.5% P<.001 |
| Lam et al., 1995 | 294 cocaine abusing men of mixed races living in an urban area 1: 182 2: 112 Follow-up was low at 15 months (150) and 21 months (69) | 1: Grant street partnership (GSP); a 90 day residential shelter and a day treatment program for homeless men 2: community care as usual; a range of services from homeless shelters with case workers to AA groups in the community. | **Percent using cocaine in past 30 days at 15 month f/u:** 1: 28.8% using cocaine 2: 23.9% using cocaine p = NS **Percent using cocaine in past 30 days at 21 month f/u:** 1: 21.2% using cocaine 2: 47.1% using cocaine p = NS **ASI composite scores:** p = NS |

McKay et al., 1995	171 male veterans with a current cocaine use disorder diagnosis 1: 24 2: 24 3: 65 4: 31	1: day hospital; 12-step oriented program attended 5 days a week, provided medical treatment and psychiatric and social counseling 2: inpatient; 12-step oriented program attended 5 days a week, plus patients stayed at the unit, provided medical treatment and psychiatric and social counseling	**Treatment completion** 1: 53%, 2: 88% p=.02 **Mean number of days of alcohol use (past 30) at 12 months f/u:** 1: 3.17, SD 5.35 2: 3.88, SD 6.06 p=NS **Mean alcohol composite score:** 1: .11, 2: .09 p= NS **Days of cocaine use:** 1: 1.52 2: 2.02 p= NS **Drug composite score:** 1: .06 2: .09 p= NS
McLach lan et al., 1982	108 patients from the Dogwood Day Clinic, consisting of male and female alcoholics with a primary addiction to alcohol and not requiring inpatient treatment 1: 50 2: 50	1: day-treatment; at a public hospital, professional staff, medical, psychiatric and social help available, attended for four weeks and attended daily all day 2: inpatient treatment; at a public hospital, professional staff, medical, psychiatric and social help available, attended for four weeks	**Reduced drinking only at 1 year f/u:** 1: 30% 2: 26% p = NS **Abstinence from alcohol at 1 year f/u:** 1: 58% 2: 58% p = NS Relapse at 1 year follow-up: 1: 10% 2: 12% p = NS
Walsh et al., 1991	227 employed adults with an alcohol problem that was interfering with work 1: 73 2: 83 3: 71	1: compulsory hospitalization; 3 weeks of hospitalization and then AA meetings 3 times a week for a year 2: compulsory AA only; AA 3 times a week at least for a year 3: Choice; could choose their own treatment which could include combinations of no treatment, AA or hospitalization	**Drinking outcomes:** All three groups had substantial and fairly stable improvement on all 11 of the self-reported measure of drinking. **Rates of abstinence throughout the 2 yr f/u:** 1 had lower rate of relapse than 2 (p<.01) and 3 (p<.01) Difference between 2 and 3 p=NS **Intoxication rates throughout the 2 yr f/u:** 1 had significantly less intoxication than 2 (p=.0005) and 3 (p=.0148) Difference between 2 and 3 p=NS **Cocaine use at 18 months:** cocaine addicts in group 2 were more likely to report continued use of cocaine (p<.01). Cocaine abusers in group 2 also had worse alcohol outcomes (p<.05)

Randomized trials of inpatient treatment have also identified some components of treatment programs that are associated with improved treatment retention and substance use disorders outcomes. Keso et al. (1990) showed that an inpatient program based on the Minnesota model (12-step) and emphasizing AA principles had better treatment retention and its patients were more likely to be abstinent from alcohol at 12 months than a more traditional inpatient program that did not emphasize AA. Patients rated the Minnesota model program higher in terms of involvement, support and spontaneity and attended significantly more AA meetings in the year following treatment. It is possible that the ongoing treatment contact provided by the availability and familiarity of self-help AA meetings was responsible for the improved outcomes in patients treated with 12-step principles. Alternatively, the more supportive, involving atmosphere of the Minnesota model clinic may have improved engagement and thus outcomes. A study by Bale et al. (1984) that compared the effectiveness of 3 different residential treatment programs demonstrated that those programs employing confrontation as a therapeutic tool had lower retention and worse treatment outcomes than those that did not.

What must be emphasized, however, is that in virtually all cases inpatient treatment was associated with improvements in substance use outcomes at one year. Inpatient treatment is an effective treatment for substance use disorders; it is simply not a more effective treatment than similar programs that are conducted on an outpatient basis. While this knowledge has resulted in a shift away from inpatient treatment in favor of outpatient programs, it is important to consider that in cases where patients are not able to reliably attend outpatient treatment (e.g. in cases where lack of proximity or transportation to an outpatient program is a problem, or with subjects with severe mental illness who lack the organizational skills necessary to maintain regular outpatient attendance), inpatient treatment may be a necessary and effective treatment option.

Cognitive Behavioral Therapy
Theory and Practice

Cognitive behavioral therapy is an approach that conceptualizes addiction as a learned behavior and subject to modification by general behavioral techniques. It encourages individuals to alter maladaptive cognitions and behaviors by teaching skills such as identification of conditioned stimuli associated with addictive behaviors, avoidance of conditioned stimuli, and response-desensitization. By unlearning or relearning behaviors, the individual can free himself from the damaging learned patterns.

The content and length of CBT treatments varies significantly. A number of formal CBT treatments have been developed, including behavioral self-control training, community-reinforcement training, cue identification, relapse prevention, relaxation training and skills training. These treatments generally teach skills to allow an individual greater control over their thoughts, emotions and behaviors but have somewhat different focuses. For example, relapse prevention aims to help individuals maintain desired behaviors and reduce the chance of relapse to substance use disorders by preparing individuals for situations in which they are vulnerable to relapse. Behavioral skills training along with cognitive interventions are employed to help the individual identify what cues or situations lead to relapse, what to do in situations that put him at risk for relapse, how to change maladaptive cognitions that might lead to a lapse to substance use or excessive use following drug sampling, and how to better his coping skills. The length of a treatment program often depends on the severity of the problem being addressed, but

Table 4: Randomized Trials of Cognitive Behavioral Therapies

Study	Subjects/group	Intervention	Outcomes
Cognitive Behavioral Therapies			
Allsop et al., 1997	60 severely dependent male problem drinkers treated in Scotland 1: 20 2: 20 3: 20	All received treatment as usual AND: 1: CBT-based Relapse Prevention program 2: Discussion about relapse 3: No additional treatment 1 and 2 involved eight 1-hr sessions over 2 weeks	**Over 12-mth f/u:** **Days until post-tx drinking lapse:** 1: 107, 2: 31, 3: 25 (p<.04) **Days until post-tx drinking relapse:** 1: 189, 2: 51.5 , 3: 26.5 (p<.03) **% Abstinent at 6 month f/u** 1: 40, 2: 5, 3: 5 (p<.01). **Weeks functioning well:** 1: 17.4, 2: 14.9, 3: 8.1 (p<.01, 1and2>3) Significant difference in non-contact rates b/w gps at 12-mth f/u may have reduced statistical power and affected results. At 12-mth f/u there were no significant differences between groups in weeks functioning well and total abstinence.
Crits-Christoph et al., 1999	487 cocaine dependent patients, multicenter (5 sites)	All tx's were manual-guided with 6-mths tx and a 3-mth booster phase 1: Cognitive therapy (CT) + 12-step based group drug counseling (GDC) 2: Supportive-expressive (SE) psychodynamic therapy + GDC 3: Individual 12-step based drug counseling (IDC) + GDC 4: GDC	**ASI Drug Use Composite average for 12 months:** 1: .12, 2: .11, 3: .10, 4: .12 3 had lower drug use, p=.03. All tx reduced drug use. 1 and 2 were not superior to 4. **Cocaine use in the past 30 days improved across all treatment groups (p<.001), baseline use:** 10.4 days, 12-mths: 3.4 days. **# individual sessions attended:** 1: 15.5, 2: 15.7, 3: 11.9 (p=.004 3<1and2)
Foy et al., 1984	62 male chronic alcoholic veterans	All received 4 wks inpatient tx plus 11 visits of aftercare during the year following discharge All Ss received broad-spectrum behavioral tx AND WERE: 1: Untrained in controlled drinking skills 2: Trained in controlled drinking skills	**Alcohol education (% correct)** **Baseline, Post-triaining:** 1: 50%, 57% p=.03 2: 44%, 60% p=.001 **Blood-alcohol-level accuracy (%)** 2 ONLY **Baseline, Post-training:** .02, .004 p=.0001 All Ss in 2 reached blood-alcohol-level accuracy estimation error less than .01%

Foy et al., 1984 cont.			No overall group differences BUT 1 was superior to 2 for individual dependent measures at 1-6 mths. 2 had more abusive days (p=.03) and less abstinent days than 1 (p=.04) at 6 mths. **Abusive days at pretx and 12-mth:** 1: 165, 46 p<.001 2: 202, 85 p<.001 1>2 p=.08
Graham et al., 1996	Site A: 91 Ss treated in a 26-day residential program for moderate to severe alcohol problems Site B: 101 Ss treated in an evening group counseling program for mild to moderate substance abusers	12 weekly Relapse Prevention sessions (part of aftercare) 1: Individual delivery (Site A: n=42, Site B: n=51) 2: Group delivery (Site A: n=46, Site B: n=50)	No difference between 1 and 2 at either Site A or B for any substance use outcomes at 12 mths
Longa-baugh et al., 1995	229 alcohol abusers	All tx's included maximum of 20 OP sessions 1: Brief broad-spectrum (BBS)—4 modules (CBT, occupational therapy, partners' therapy, didactic sessions) 2: Extended relationship enhancement (ERE)—3 modules (partners' therapy, CBT, didactic sessions) 3: Extended cognitive behavioral (ECB)—All sessions CBT	Abstinence rates increased in all groups (p<.01) **% of days abstinent at baseline and 18 months:** 1: 26%, 83% 2: 38%, 90% 3: 35%, 87% No difference between groups.

Marques et al., 2001	155 Brazilian alcohol and/or drug dependent pts 68% f/u rate at 12-mth f/u	1: Individual cognitive-behavioral psychotherapy 2: Group cognitive-behavioral psychotherapy	Reductions in alcohol consumption in both gps from baseline to 12-mth f/u with no difference between gps. Baseline and 12-mth f/u data: **Number of drinking days:** 1: 47, 30 $p \leq .05$ 2: 51, 29 $p \leq .05$ **Number of heavy drinking days:** 1: 29, 11 $p \leq .05$ 2: 40, 20 $p \leq .05$ **Mean weekly consumption (drinks/wk):** 1: 30, 12 $p \leq .05$ 2: 43, 19 $p \leq .05$ **% w/ partial or total remission** 1: 50%, 2: 45%, p=ns 2 has better cost-benefit ratio
McKay et al., 1999	132 cocaine dependent male veterans referred to continuing care	Tx was a 5-6 months long continuing care program. Patients completing this tx were eligible for longer term aftercare (one session/wk for up to 18 more mths). 1: Standard tx—Two group-therapy sessions/wk using traditional addiction counseling and 12-step practices 2: Relapse prevention—One individual CB relapse prevention session and one gp session/wk	Frequency of cocaine use and heavy drinking decreased in both groups ($p<.01$) with no difference between groups: **Frequency of days of cocaine use:** Baseline—1: 19.54%, 2: 19.15% 19-24 mth f/u—1: 8.29%, 2: 6.97% **Frequency of days of heavy drinking:** Baseline—1: 19.52%, 2: 14.33% 19-24 mth f/u—1:5.98%, 2: 2.54% **ASI drug composite scores also decreased in both groups ($p<.01$) with no difference between groups.** Baseline—1: .096, 2: .074 19-24 mth f/u—1: .057, 2: .061
Miller, 1978	46 problem drinkers who completed tx	All therapies consisted of 10 weekly sessions 1: Aversive counterconditioning using self-administered electrical stimulation 2: Behavioral self-control training 3: Controlled drinking composite (blood alcohol awareness training, discriminated aversive counterconditioning, etc.)	Decrease in drinking for all gps ($p<.001$). No difference b/w gps. **Weekly alcohol consumption (units) at intake and 12-mth f/u:** 1: 39, 14 2: 33, 11 3: 38, 10 3 was the least cost-effective, requiring 4 times as much therapist time as 1 or 2.

Miller et al., 1980a	41 problem drinkers	1: Self-help materials 2: 1 + 6 weekly sessions w/ therapist (Behavioral Self-Control Training—BSCT) 3: 2 + 12 wks standard additional training (muscle relaxation, communication skills, assertiveness) 4: 2 + 12 wks individually tailored additional training (client selected 3 modules out of 10)	All groups decreased drinking (p<.01) **Self-report of weekly alcohol consumption at Intake, Termination and F/U:** 1: 35, 28, 20 2: 34, 26, 23 3: 31, 16, 22 4: 33, 17, 18 No differences in group effectiveness.
Miller et al., 1980b	41 problem drinkers	All groups focused on Behavioral Self-Control Training (BSCT): 1: Bibliotherapy—BSCT self-help manual, self-monitoring cards 2: 1 + Ten individual weekly BSCT sessions 3: 2 + relaxation training 4: 3 in group format (vs. individual)	Decrease in consumption over 12-mth f/u (p<.001) with no difference b/w gps. **Standard Ethanol Content at intake and 12-mth f/u:** 1: 75, 29 2: 32, 25 3: 54, 28 4: 53, 28 1 was cost-effective. Overall improvement was 69% at 12-mth f/u.
Oei et al., 1980	32 chronic alcoholics	1: Group Social Skills Training (SST) 2: Individual SST 3: Group Traditional Supportive Therapy (TST) 4: Individual TST Each gp met for 12 two-hr sessions SST (1and2) and TST (3and4) were compared. Cognitive restructuring was used in SST.	SST superior to TST in reduction of mean alcohol consumption (p<.05) with **mean alcohol consumption pre-intervention and 12-mths (approx):** 1: 33, 15 2: 33, 23 3: 34, 33 4: 32, 32 No difference b/w gp or individual therapy.

Project MATCH Research Group, 1997	2 parallel but independent tx matching studies: 1) 5 OP sites, N=952 2) 5 sites treating aftercare pts, N=774	Ss in each study were randomly assigned to: 1: Cognitive Behavioral Coping Skills Therapy (CBT) 2: Motivational Enhancement Therapy (MET) 3: Twelve-Step Facilitation Therapy (TSF) Tx was manual-guided and individually delivered and lasted 12-wks	Significant improvements at f/u maintained over 12-15 mths. In all cases, at 1-year there were no differences in outcomes b/w gps. **% days abstinent:** **OP** Increased from ~28% at baseline to ~82% at 1-yr f/u for all tx gps. **Aftercare** Increased from ~20% at baseline to ~90% at 1-yr f/u for all tx gps. **Drinks per Drinking Day:** **OP** Decreased from ~12 drinks at baseline to ~3 at 1-yr f/u for all tx gps. **Aftercare** Decreased from ~17 drinks at baseline to ~2 at 1-yr f/u for all tx gps.
Sobell et al., 1973 Sobell et al., 1976 Caddy et al., 1978	70 voluntarily hospitalized male alcoholics 53 inpatient male alcoholics	For all 3 articles: Originally Ss assigned to gps with different tx goals of either: CD=Controlled Drinking ND=Non-drinking (abstinence) Then Ss were randomly assigned to either: 1: Experimental—17 tx sessions in Individualized Behavior Therapy 2: Control— Conventional state hospital tx (abstinence orientation)	1 was superior to 2 in both CD and ND gps (p<.05). **% functioning well at 1-yr f/u** CD-1: 85%, ND-1: 87% CD-2: 32%, ND-2: 27% 1 was superior to 2 in days functioning well at 2nd yr f/u in CD but NOT in ND. **% days functioned well at 2 yr f/u:** CD-1: 85%, CD-2: 42% p<.001 ND-1: 64%, ND-2: 43% ns At 3rd post-treatment year: No difference b/w 1 and 2 for percentage of days abstinent (trend though), percentage of days controlled drinking, and number of days in an abstinent oriented environment. CD-1 had less days drunk than CD-2 (p=.03) but no difference b/w ND-1 and ND-2.

Stephens et al., 1994	212 media-recruited marijuana users 79% f/u rate.	1: Relapse Prevention 2: Social Support Tx consisted of 10 2-hr sessions and additional booster tx sessions conducted at 3 and 6 months.	Fewer days of marijuana use and marijuana problems at each posttreatment assessment compared to pretreatment levels (all ps<.001) for both treatments: **Days of marijuana use:** Pretreatment—1: 27, 2: 26 12-mth f/u—1: 15, 2: 14 **Number of marijuana problems:** Pretreatment—1:7, 2: 7 12-mth f/u—1: 3, 2: 3 No difference between groups regarding marijuana use, marijuana related problems, or abstinence rates.
Vogler et al., 1975	42 inpatient chronic alcoholics	1: Videotaped self-confrontation, alcoholic education, discrimination training, aversion training, discriminated avoidance practice, behavior counseling, alternatives training 2: Alcohol education, alternatives training, behavior counseling	Difference in pre-post alcohol intake (p=.001) with intake prior to tx and at 12-mth f/u being: 1: 184, 39 2: 126, 69 A posteriori comparison b/w post-tx residual intake scores was significant (p<.01). 1 drank less than 2 during 12 mths following tx. Over 12-mth f/u 62% were either abstinent or controlled drinkers.
Vogler et al., 1977	80 problem drinkers with a tx goal of moderation	1: Videotaped self-confrontation, discrimination training, aversion training, alcohol education, behavior counseling, alternatives training 2: Discrimination training, alcohol education, behavior counseling, alternatives training 3: Alcohol education 4: Alcohol education, behavior counseling, alternatives training 1, 2 and 4 had 30-40 contact hrs 3 had 17-20 contact hrs	Pre-post difference (p=.001) in alcohol intake with pre-tx and 12-mth f/u alcohol intake: 1: 94, 34 2: 81, 39 3: 62, 26 4: 79, 42 No differences b/w gps. At intake none of the Ss were moderate drinkers, but during 12-mths after tx, 62.5% were moderate and 4% were abstinent.

typical treatment lengths vary from a single, brief session to upwards of 10 or more sessions. CBT can be administered either individually or in a group setting. It is generally administered by a trained health professional (therapist, psychologist, social worker, etc.).

Efficacy

Studies of cognitive behavioral therapies for SUD have repeatedly and consistently found that CBT programs reduce substance use behaviors by substantial amounts (Table 4). Studies of CBT have been less successful, however, in demonstrating differences in patient outcomes between CBT programs and competing therapeutic techniques or in identifying the important "active ingredients" of the therapy program. The large and influential Project MATCH study (1997) compared patient outcomes following randomization of patients to CBT, 12-step facilitation, or motivational enhancement-based treatment programs for outpatient or aftercare treatment. Project MATCH was designed to address the question of whether identifiable populations of alcohol dependent patients showed better treatment response to a specific treatment technique. This study found that all three treatments were successful in significantly and substantially reducing substance use in patients for more than one year. There was no difference in outcomes depending on the treatment to which patients were randomized, and few predictors of successful outcome in a given type of program were observed. McKay et al. (1999) found similar results in a population of cocaine dependent men; patients randomized to either a traditional, 12-step based program or a CBT- based relapse prevention program significantly reduced their cocaine use and heavy drinking. No main differences between treatment types were found, although it was observed that patients endorsing commitment to abstinence on treatment entry did better in the relapse prevention program, while those with less commitment to abstinence had improved outcomes with the 12-step based program. Crits-Christoph et al. (1999) examined the additional benefit of adding various forms of individual counseling, specifically cognitive therapy, supportive-expressive psychodynamic therapy or

individual 12-step based counseling, to a 12-step based group therapy program. They found that, although all programs were successful in reducing cocaine use over one year, only the addition of individual 12-step based counseling improved outcomes above that seen with 12-step based group counseling alone. The authors suggested that the superiority of the treatment utilizing individual 12-step counseling might be due to the consistency of the message across individual and group therapies or to the fact that the 12-step counseling was performed by substance abuse counselors who were trained and experienced with this population rather than by the general psychotherapists who delivered cognitive or psychodynamic based-therapies. These studies demonstrate that cognitive behavioral therapies are highly successful treatments for SUDs, although they are not superior to the major competing treatment technique, 12-step facilitation, in their current formulation.

Smaller studies comparing cognitive behavioral therapies to supportive discussion sessions have found CBT superior to these non-directive therapy methods. Oei et al., (1980) found that social skills training (a CBT program) produced greater reductions in alcohol consumption than did traditional supportive therapy, where therapists provided support and encouragement during general discussions. Allsop et al. (1997) demonstrated that a CBT-based relapse prevention program was vastly superior to non-specific discussions about relapse for reducing problem drinking in men. Thus, the methods and structure utilized during cognitive behavioral therapies are important to produce their treatment effects; simple support and encouragement from an interested counselor did not produce improvements in SUD outcomes while CBT did.

Studies generally found that the manner in which cognitive behavioral therapies were administered did not affect long-term treatment outcome. For example, Miller et al. (1980b) found that a Behavioral Self-Control Training program for problem drinking produced similar improvements in substance abuse measures regardless of whether it was provided simply as bibliotherapy, or with 10 additional group or individual sessions. Similarly, Graham et al. (1996) found that a Relapse Prevention program consisting of 12 aftercare sessions produced similar results when provided as individual versus group sessions for both a group of alcohol dependent patients in a residential program and for a group of substance abuse patients in outpatient treatment. Marques et al. (2001) replicated this finding in a cohort of Brazilian SUD patients, showing that both individual and group administered cognitive behavioral therapies produced significant reductions in SUD problems over a 12 month period, with no difference between those receiving individual versus group treatments. Thus, the format by which CBTs are delivered appears to be not important so long as the content is maintained.

Contingency Management
Theory and Practice

Contingency management is a psychosocial drug treatment rooted in operant conditioning principles (i.e. using rewarding and punishing consequences to change voluntary behavior). Self-administering drugs is clearly rewarding so contingency management seeks to find competing rewards in order to replace substance use behaviors. It is most often utilized in outpatient settings such as methadone clinics to improve both patient retention and drug use. Patients are offered a behavioral contract at the beginning of treatment that spells out specific rewards and/or punishments for specific behaviors. Patients are rewarded for desired behaviors and not rewarded (or punished) for undesirable behaviors (see Higgins and Petry, 1999 for review).

What behaviors get reinforced, and how, is very flexible (see Petry et al., 2001). Commonly, drug free urines are rewarded with money, vouchers or extra privileges. More frequent and less difficult behaviors can also be reinforced including showing up to the clinic, producing urines with increasingly lower amounts of illicit drugs, and engaging in activities relevant to treatment such as applying for jobs and improving one's parenting. Contingency management has been a promising treatment for substance use disorders for over 20 years, so much is known about its best practices.

Efficacy

Contingency management (CM) has consistently been shown to have strong effects during the first months of treatment on reducing dropout rates and drug use (Petry, 2000; Griffith et al., 2000). Rather than being used as a stand-alone treatment, CM is usually added on to existing treatments like opiate substitution programs, 12-step programs, or group therapy where it has been shown to produce significant additional benefits (Carroll et al., 2002; Preston et al., 2000; Silverman, et al., 1998). The long-term efficacy of contingency management therapies has been less well established however, and there is some evidence that the benefits of contingency management interventions fade after contingency contracts are ended. Generally, outcomes in patients given contingency management interventions in addition to other standard forms of treatment are initially better than those in patients given the standard treatment alone, but these outcomes normalize to levels equivalent to or sometimes slightly better than outcomes in those given standard treatment alone (Epstein et al., 2003; Rawson et al., 2002).

The most successful long-term outcomes were found by Higgins et al. (1995; 2000) in cocaine dependent outpatients. Both studies examined the addition of contingency management interventions to an outpatient program of counseling based on the community reinforcement approach. The contingency management program consisted of rewarding cocaine-free urines with vouchers that could be redeemed for retail items purchased in the community. The value of individual vouchers escalated with consecutive cocaine-free urines and the value of individual vouchers was reset to the initial voucher value when cocaine-positive urines were submitted. The control group received vouchers of equivalent value to those received by the treatment group in a manner not linked to their behavior. This voucher program was employed for the first 12 weeks of treatment. The patients receiving vouchers contingent on their behavior were abstinent from cocaine more often than those in the non-contingent group during treatment and this difference was maintained for at least 18 months after treatment entry, more than 1 year after the contingency management intervention was ended. Higgins et al.'s early study (1995) found similar results comparing this same intervention to a control group that received no vouchers.

Other studies however, did not find lasting effects of contingency management interventions beyond the contracting period. For example, although Epstein et al. (2003) found beneficial effects of contingency management interventions as compared to cognitive-behavior therapy alone during the treatment period, their contingency management intervention was not superior to CBT by 12 months. Schumacher et al. (2002) found similar results. Despite improved outcomes at 6 months when contingency management was added to the standard treatment, there was no added benefit of contingency management by 12-month follow-up. Rawson et al. (2002) found that in methadone maintenance patients with co-occurring cocaine dependence, contingency management or contingency management plus cognitive behavioral therapy improved cocaine abstinence more than cognitive behavioral therapy alone during treatment. However, at one year follow-up, 8 months after both treatments had ended, patients receiving cognitive behavioral therapy alone were at least as likely to be cocaine abstinent as those that had received contingency management interventions. When compared to the control group, only the patients receiving cognitive behavioral therapy without CM had significantly improved rates of cocaine abstinence at 1 year follow up. Clearly, further investigation into how to maintain contingency management induced improvements in SUD outcomes for longer periods of time is needed to improve the consistency with which these interventions produce long-lasting effects.

Shorter-term studies of contingency management interventions have elucidated a number of general principles of successful contingency management. The most proven of these principles are discussed below:

1. For a reinforcer to work it must be experienced. When the criteria for attainment of a reward (or avoidance of a punishment) are too stringent, many patients will fail to receive even a single reinforcer. Under conditions in which rewards are never obtained, contingency management does not modify behaviors. Thus, to insure that contingency management has a chance to work, progressive behavioral shaping can be used (see Preston et al., 2001 for example). Specifically, one begins by rewarding behaviors intermediate to the ultimate behavioral goal and slowly increases the reward criteria toward the behavioral goal as intermediate behaviors are mastered. In this way, difficult or complicated behaviors, such as those required for full recovery from substance use disorders, can

be encouraged and developed using contingency management techniques.

2. Punitive measures increase drop out rates (Stitzer et al., 1986). Although contingency management interventions that contract punishments for inappropriate behaviors can improve behaviors in those patients that choose to remain in the contract, the most typical outcome of these interventions is drop-out from treatment.

3. Consistency of applied rewards and punishments is important (Petry, 2000).

One commonly expressed barrier to the use of contingency management techniques is the potentially high cost of reinforcers. In well-funded experimental studies patients can earn over $1,000 in a 12-week treatment session (e.g. Silverman et al., 1996). Although this amount is not costly in comparison to other medical treatments, most

Table 5: Randomized Trials of Contingency Management Interventions

Study	Subjects/group	Intervention	Outcomes
Epstein et al., 2003	193 cocaine-using methadone-maintained outpatients 1:49, 2:48 3:47, 4:49	1: group CBT + CM 2: group CBT + non-contingent vouchers 3: CM + non-CBT group therapy 4. Control (non-CBT group therapy + non-contingent vouchers) All received daily methadone and weekly indiv. counseling for 29 weeks.	**During Treatment:** **Cocaine use per day** was less frequent in 3 than 2 (self report: p=.016; urinalysis: p<.001) **Number of successive cocaine-free urines** 1: 8.3, 2: 3.7, 3: 11.3, 4: 2.3 (3> 1, 2, or 4, p<.001) 3 showed improvement in % with drug free urine tests (p<.01) while CBT did not **Follow-Up:** At 1 yr there were no significant differences between treatment groups. **Self-reported days of recent drug problems** were higher in 1 and 2 than in 3 and 4 (p=.026) CBT groups (1and2 combined) showed decreased cocaine use from 3-12 month follow up (p=.007) while the non-CBT groups (3and4 combined) did not.
Farabee et al., 2002	97 cocaine dependent subjects 1:24, 2:24 3:25, 4:24	1: 48 ninety minute group sessions of cognitive behavioral therapy 2: Vouchers contingent on providing stimulant-negative urines. Voucher value was escalating with continued abstinence. 3:1+2 4:Methadone Maintenance treatment	No significant differences in self reported cocaine use or cocaine positive urine tests were found between treatment groups at 1 year.

| Higgins et al. 1995 (trials 1 and 2 at 12 months)

Higgins et. al. 1993 (trial 1)

Higgins et al. 1994 (trial 2) | 78 cocaine dependent outpatients

Trial 1
1:19, 2:19

Trial 2
1:20, 2:20 | *Trial 1*
1: 24 weeks counseling under the community reinforcement approach (CRA) with vouchers
2: 24 weeks drug abuse counseling

Trial 2
1:24 weeks CRA with vouchers
2: 24 weeks CRA without vouchers | **Trial 1 during treatment**
Completed treatment:
1: 58%, 2: 11%, (p<.01)
There was no drop in cocaine abstinence in 1 when reinforcer was changed from relatively expensive vouchers to relatively inexpensive lottery tickets.
% achieving 4, 8, and 16 weeks of consecutive abstinence:
1: 74%, 68%, 42%;
2: 16%, 11%, 5%. (p=.005)
Trial 1 follow-up
% cocaine-free urines at 6, 9, and 12 months:
1: 72, 88, 96; 2: 67, 69, 69 (1>2, p=.007).
Provided cocaine-free urines at all 3 follow up points: 1: 58%, 2: 26%, (p=.05).
Reported no cocaine use for past 30 days: 1: 42%, 2: 26% (p=ns)
Entered aftercare: 1: 21%, 2: 0%, (p=.03) Mean days of treatment for 1 = 50 +/- 11.
Received outpatient services such as AA: 1: 37%, 2: 11%, (p=ns) [included to show that CM doesn't interfere with AA]
Trial 2 during treatment
mean weeks of abstinence during tx:
1=11.7; 2=6.0; (P=.03)
% achieving 20 weeks of cocaine free urines: 1: 30%, 2: 5%
Completed Treatment:
1: 75%, 2: 40%, p=.03

Trial 2 at 12 months
ASI drug composite score:
1:.07 vs 2:.12 (p<.01)
ASI psychiatric composite score:
1:.09 vs .2: .29 (p<.05)
Enrolled in Aftercare;
1: 70%, 2: 30%; (p=.01)
ns: number of participants assessed, cocaine free urines during follow up, ASI composite scores on alcohol and family functioning. |

Higgins et al., 2000	70 treatment-seeking cocaine dependent adult men and women. 1:36; 2:34	1: community reinforcement counseling + contingent incentives. 2: community reinforcement counseling + non-contingent incentives.	**Achieved 12 weeks of abstinence during tx:** 1: 38%, 2: 16% (p=.02) **Higher levels of continuous abstinence** in 1 versus 2 (p=.02) at every follow up period (i.e. 6, 9, 12, 15, 18 months) **Abstinent from cocaine for entire follow up period:** 1: 19%, 2: 6%, (p=.09) **ASI composite scores over the 18 month follow up period:** p=ns
Preston et al., 2002	110 methadone patients 1: 55; 2: 55	For 12 weeks: 1: Vouchers and take-home doses contingent on opioid-free urines, followed by step-down maintenance contingency 2: vouchers and take-home doses contingent on providing urines.	At 12 months there were no significant differences in outcome based on intervention. Enrollment in MMT after the intervention was the strongest predictor of outcome.
Rawson et al., 2002 Farabee et al., 2002	120 methadone patients w/ cocaine dependence 1: 30; 2: 30; 3: 30; 4: 30	1: Vouchers contingent on providing stimulant-negative urines. Voucher value was escalating with continued abstinence 2: 48 ninety-minute group sessions of cognitive behavioral therapy. 3:1+2 4:Methadone Maintenance treatment control (all interventions lasted 16 weeks)	1 and 3 did better than 2 during treatment, but by week 26, 2 improved substantially resulting in equal performance to CM groups. There was no additive effect of combined CBT and CM. **Outcomes at 1 year follow up CBT session attendance:** 2: 17.9, 3: 24.7; (p=.04) **% of cocaine-free urines:** 1: 53%; 2: 60%; 3: 40%; 4: :27% (P<.04) **Self-reported days of cocaine use in past 30 days:** 1: 4.5; 2: 3.0 (p<.05 compared to 4); 3: 4.5; 4: 8.5 **% sample with 3wks of cocaine-free urines:** 1:63%; 2: 40%; 3: 57%; 4: 27% (p=.02)
Schuma cher et al., 2002	206 homeless persons with cocaine disorders	1: standard treatment + CM 2: standard treatment	1 did better 6 months after treatment, but at 12 months, both groups were the same. CM enhancement cost was within the range of normal social services, but more than standard treatment alone.

drug treatment clinics do not have extra funds for such programs. Fortunately, more expensive reinforcers have not been found to be more effective than less expensive incentives (see Griffith et al., 2000 for a meta-analysis of CM treatment factors).

Researchers have found two promising inexpensive alternative reinforcers. Clinic privileges, such as take-home methadone doses, are one of patients' favorite reinforcers and also one of the most powerful (Griffith et al., 2000). It is extremely cost-effective for clinics to use these incentives because such privileges are often tacitly and informally given as patients progress through treatment anyway. Simply employing an actual contract with specific contingencies tied to specific clinic privileges can improve patient outcomes. Stitzer et al. (1992) found better outcomes in patients who were given take-home methadone doses explicitly contingent on drug-free urines than in a control group who were given take-homes without regard to urinalysis results. The second promising alternative to reinforcing behaviors with expensive vouchers is to use raffle tickets instead. This method has been used with great success in both alcohol dependent patients (Petry et al., 2000) and polysubstance abusing methadone patients (Petry and Martin, 2002) where the average cost per patient was far less than in other studies ($200 and $137 respectively).

Although many programs have used methadone dose at the primary reinforcer in contingency management, there are several problems with this approach. It is ethically questionable to alter a patient's medication as a reward or a punishment for a behavior. Such an idea would not likely be considered with any other patient population (e.g. diabetics or cardiac patients). Additionally, it is difficult to interpret results because they depend on both operant conditioning principles and pharmacology. Given that many patients at methadone clinics receive less than the recommended 60mg/day minimum dose (D'Annuo and Pollack, 2002), improved outcomes may be due to increasing methadone to therapeutic levels rather than to contingency management. We strongly recommend using an empirically validated reinforcer other than methadone dose and following the clinical guidelines for dispensing methadone as they have an extensive evidence-base.

Self-help and 12-step facilitation
Background (Theory and Practice)

Self-help refers to treatments that are administered by oneself or in a group of peers without without a professional's involvement. Individual self-help programs are generally bibliotherapies, typically consisting of books, pamphlets or more recently webpages that one can use at their own pace and discretion. Self-help groups most typically occur face-to-face in the community, although Internet chat rooms are now fairly commonplace. Alcoholics Anonymous (AA) is the largest and most commonly known self-help group organization and is credited with spurring the growth of the self-help movement. AA developed and utilizes a 12-step program in which participants are encouraged to work their way through 12 steps leading to stable abstinence from substance use. While not all self-help groups utilize the 12-step method all of them have one thing in common: mutual help for people experiencing a similar problem. Examples of other self-help groups are Moderation Management, a self-help organization that promotes moderation of substance use rather than abstinence and Women for Sobriety which focuses on women's needs in achieving sobriety. Most self-help groups are of low- to no-cost to members, making them a cost-effective alternative.

While self-help groups were originally meant to be member-run, the medical community has co-opted some of their techniques and integrated them into their own treatment regimen. Thus, the 12-step program developed by Alcoholics Anonymous is frequently used in medical treatment settings, where the 12-step program is taught and treatment groups are run by a professional addictions counselor. These 12-step facilitation programs often encourage additional participation in self-help groups in the community. As the 12-step philosophy focuses on achieving and maintaining abstinence from all substance use and addictive behaviors, these 12-step facilitation program are typically abstinence-oriented, and promote cessation rather than control of substance use. Because of reference to "a higher power" in the 12-step program, this form of therapy is considered to be more spiritually or religiously oriented than other treatment programs. Nevertheless, 12-step facilitation is not affiliated with any particular religious orientation or organization, and outcomes in these programs have not been found to vary based on patients' religious orientation.

Efficacy

Several studies have demonstrated that mailing self-help materials to persons with

Table 6: Randomized Trials of Self-Help Interventions

Study	Subjects/group	Intervention	Outcomes
Self-help bibliotherapy			
Heather et al., 1987	247 media-recruited problem drinkers 45% 1-yr f/u rate (n=110) Difference in f/u rate b/w gps (p<.05) with 50% in 1 contacted vs. 39% in 2.	Sent either: 1: Self-help manual 2: Educational booklet (general advice and information)—CONTROL	**Drinks/week at Intake and 1-year**: 1: 63 to 40 2: 63 to 46 p=ns 1 had higher scores on control of drinking problems (p<.05) Note: After excluding Ss who received any other form of tx for drinking, 1 had lower f/u consumption than 2 (p<.05) with: 1: 70 to 36 2: 48 to 45 It is possible that Ss in 2 who had high consumption sought help after receiving the booklet.
Sobell et al., 2002	825 media-recruited alcohol abusers who never had help or treatment for an alcohol problem	Mailed one of two materials: 1: Motivational enhancement/personalized feedback 2: Bibliotherapy/drinking guidelines	Reduction in drinking over 1-year for both interventions (p<.001). No difference between interventions for any variable, suggesting that whether or not materials were personalized, they helped reduce drinking. Cost analysis estimated the intervention to cost b/w US $46 to $97 per participant
Spivak et al., 1994	140 problem drinkers desiring to quit or cut down without professional help	1: Manual (30-page workbook) 2: Guidelines (2-page brochure) 3: General Information 1 and 2: given self-monitoring forms for their drinking and coping strategies 3: encouraged to keep track but given no forms	1 and 2 collapsed into "specific advice" group. **Heavy Drinking Days at 1-yr f/u** 1and2: 14 days, 3: 30 days, (p=.018) At 12-mth f/u more Ss in 3 expressed a need for professional help versus 1 and 2 (p=.048)

alcohol problems can reduce problem drinking in these populations (Heather et al., 1987; Sobell et al., 2002, Spivak et al., 1994) (Table 6). Spivak et al. (1994) found that materials that provided specific advice or methods for controlling their drinking were more successful than those that only provided general information. Heather et al.'s (1987) work suggested that some of the effect of the mailed information may be due to persons' deciding to obtain treatment for their alcohol problems after receiving the mailing. When controlling for additional treatment seeking, a specifically designed self-help manual was more helpful than a booklet with general information for reducing substance use in this study as well. These studies support the idea that mailed self-help bibliotherapies can reduce substance use disorders, with more specific and guided information improving outcomes from this intervention. The use of mailed advice as a method for encouraging treatment entry is worth investigating.

Randomized controlled-trials of community self-help groups have not been attempted, due to the technical impossibility of preventing patients from attending a free community meeting. Non-randomized studies, however, support their efficacy in producing and maintaining improvement in SUDs. A trial by Walsh et al. (1991) did demonstrate that addition of a 3-week inpatient treatment program to a year of thrice-weekly compulsory Alcoholics Anonymous (AA) meetings improved outcomes over AA meetings alone, however, patients entering AA alone did show significant and stable improvement in SUD outcomes.

As has been discussed in the section on Cognitive Behavioral Therapies, 12-step facilitation programs have been demonstrated to effectively reduce substance use for over one year. In comparisons of 12-step facilitation treatments to CBT-based programs, 12-step facilitation programs have been shown to be equally effective for treating SUDs (McKay et al., 1999; Project MATCH research group, 1997). 12-step facilitation programs clearly and consistently produce positive outcomes, regardless of whether they are offered in inpatient or outpatient programs (McKay et al., 1995).

Couples and Family Counseling
Theory and Practice

Several approaches to treating addiction have enlisted the help and support of people close to the primary patient. Rather than focusing exclusively on the individual, these approaches to treatment focus on patients' relationships with other people. The best-researched method to date for delivering treatment under this framework is Behavioral Couples Therapy (BCT). As in cognitive behavioral therapy this approach seeks to change maladaptive cognitions and behaviors but focuses on an important relationship as a primary source of rewards and punishments for substance-related behavior. During therapy, the BCT provider seeks to have a close friend, family member, or significant other explicitly reward abstinence while avoiding accidentally or implicitly rewarding problematic behaviors. Additionally, the provider helps the couple develop a better relationship that is less likely to facilitate a relapse to drug use (O'Farrell and Fals-Stewart, 2000).

A typical course of BCT treatment involves 15-20 outpatient sessions with patient and partner over five to six months (O'Farrell and Fals Stewart, 2000). The therapist arranges a daily sobriety contract in which the patient states his or her intention not to drink or use drugs that day. The spouse explicitly supports the patient's efforts for that day and also records his or her performance on a calendar provided by the therapist. The couple is also instructed to carry out activities designed to enhance their relationship such as noting positive things the other has done and sharing enjoyable activities. Communication skills are commonly taught in order to help the couple deal with stressors while avoiding relapse. The couple is then followed up with quarterly visits for the next 2 years. More complete descriptions can be found elsewhere (O'Farrell, 1993; O'Farrell and Fals-Stewart, 2000).

Efficacy

Substance use outcomes for BCT have generally been shown to be better than those for individual treatment. At one year follow up, percent days of abstinence were typically high in patients receiving either individual or couples therapy, with those receiving BCT roughly 10% higher. The superiority of BCT over individual therapies tends to become increasingly apparent at later times, as formal treatment tapers off and patients become more autonomous in their recovery. For example, Fals-Stewart et al. (1996; 1997) compared two 24 week CBT based treatments, one that included 3.5 hours of BCT per week and another that offered the equivalent of this time in additional individual sessions. No differences between the groups were seen until after the 24 week treatment session ended. However, following discharge patients receiving BCT had improved outcomes, with higher abstinence rates and less reported drug use at 9 and 12 month follow-ups (3-6 months after treatment ended) and lower relapse rates in the 90 days following treatment discharge. Similar results were found in a second study by Kelley and Fals-Stewart (2002) that compared a BCT-based program with an individual therapy program, and a couples-based psycho-educational program as a control for general couples-focused attention. There was no difference in abstinence rates between groups at the end of treatment, however, at 6 and 12 months following treatment end, patients that received BCT had abstinence rates 10% higher than either of the other two groups.

These studies and others suggest that behavioral couples therapy may be particularly beneficial for encouraging the maintenance of treatment gains after professional treatment is completed.

In addition to substance use outcomes, BCT has demonstrated impressive improvements in problems indirectly related to drug use. O'Farrell and Murphy (1995) found that while about 30% of husbands engaged in severe violence against their wives in the year before treatment only 9% did so in the year after treatment (p<.001). Severe wife to husband violence showed similar decline (36% to 10%, p<.001). Kelly and Fals-Stewart (2002) found that BCT had a positive impact on children's psychosocial functioning. Rates of clinically significant behavioral and emotional problems of drug abusing couples' children dropped from 50% before treatment to 15% after treatment (p<.01). This improvement was maintained throughout the 12-month follow up. Children of drug abusing couples in the individual therapy condition did not show significant improvement in this domain (50% pretreatment, 38% post-treatment, 44% 12-month follow-up, p=ns).

Although fairly obvious, it is important to note that the biggest differences in treatment were found when BCT was added to an existing intervention and compared to the group that did not receive any additional services. Catalano et al. (1999) demonstrates such an effect in methadone maintenance patients where those who received additional family training and home case management showed markedly improved heroin and cocaine use outcomes. Strong and consistent scientific evidence suggests that adding BCT to existing programs dramatically improves outcomes, especially under conditions in which extensive individual therapies are not already employed. Additionally, as couples therapy is no more expensive to provide than individual therapy and produces improved

Table 7: Randomized Trials of Couples and Family Therapy

Study	Subjects/group	Intervention	Outcomes
Catalano et al., 1999	methadone treated parents with children N=130 1:75 2:55	1: methadone + 33 sessions of family training + 9 months home based case management 2: control group (methadone only)	**Mean days per month of drug use at 6mo and 12mo (adjusted for baseline differences) Marijuana** 1: 4.11, 1.79 (p=ns) 2: 1.54, 3.90 **Heroin** 1: 9.08, 6.89 (p<.01) 2: 6.78, 19.68 **Cocaine** 1: 9.29, 1.78 (p<.10) 2:10.00, 12.16
Fals-Stewart et al., 1996 Fals-Stewart et. al, 1997	80 substance abusing men 1: 40 2: 40	Treatment lasted 24 weeks total for both conditions **1: Behavioral Couples Therapy.** 1 60min individual session + 1 90min group session + 1 60min BCT session per week (BCT lasted 12 weeks). **2: Individual Based Treatment.** 2 60min individual CBT sessions + 1 90min group session per week (primary treatment phase lasted 12 weeks).	**% days abstinent at pre-treatment, post-treatment, 3, 6, 9, and 12 month follow up. (* = p<.05 for 1 vs. 2 comparison) Drug use:** 1:37.9, 97.1, 93.2*, 84.4*, 80.1*, 76.2* 2:38.3, 94.1, 80.4, 73.2, 72.6, 69.4 **Alcohol use:** 1:78.3, 97.4, 92.3*, 84.3, 80.4, 77.4 2:79.4,96.3, 84.2, 78.6, 76.2, 71.6 **Combined Drug and Alcohol:** 1:31.3,95.4, 91.6*, 81.5*, 77.6*, 73.2* 2:28.2, 91.1, 77.5, 70.4, 68.3, 65.1 **Relapse:** Fewer patients in group 1 than group 2 relapsed within 90 days of discharge (p<.01) *Cost Analysis* Total cost of 1 = $1,372.72 per patient while total cost of 2 = $1,359.94. **Total cost of substance-related healthcare at baseline and f/u:** 1:$2,617, $815 2:$2,362, $2,013 (p<.05). **Total cost of Criminal Justice System at baseline and f/u:** 1:$2,832, $925 2:$3,493, $2,383 (p<.01).

Kelley and Fals-Stewart, 2002	alcohol abusing men (n=71) 1:25, 2:22, 3:24 drug abusing men (n=64) 1:22, 2:21, 3:21	1: Behavioral couples therapy 2: Individual behavioral therapy 3: couples based psychoeducational attention control treatment (PACT) All received 32 sessions over 20 weeks.	**% of days abstinent at pre-treatment, post-treatment, 6 month follow up, and 12 month follow-up for alcohol abusing couples.** *=p<.05 compared to the other groups 1: 40, 90.2, 80.6*, 70.9* 2: 36.9, 86.6, 71.4, 60.4 3: 37.4, 87.4, 70.4, 57.9 **% of days abstinent at pre-treatment, post-treatment, 6 month follow up, and 12 month followup for drug abusing couples.** 1:30.4, 85.9, 77.6*, 66.9* 2:32.7, 81.8, 63.6, 53.4 3:34.9, 83.4, 61.5, 51.2
McCrady et al., 1991	45 alcoholics and their spouses 1:14 2:12 3:19	1: control group - minimal spouse involvement (MSI) 2: alcohol-focused spouse involvement (AFSI) 3: AFSI + behavioral marital therapy (ABMT) All received fifteen 90-minute sessions.	**Drinking outcomes across 18mo follow-up** no tx differences were found for continuous days of abstinence, continuous days abstinence plus light drinking, continuous days of heavy drinking, or in drinking-related impairments. group 3 showed improvements in % days abstinent over 18mo (r=+0.78) while groups 1 and 2 deteriorated (r=-0.77; r=-0.32). p<.03 All 3 groups improved over time p<.001
Winters et al., 2002	75 married or cohabiting female drug abusers 1: 37 2: 38	1: behavioral couples therapy 2: equally intense individual treatment All received fifty-six 60-90 minute treatment sessions over 24 weeks	**% days abstinent at pretreatment, post-treatment, 3, 6, 9, and 12 month follow up.** *** =p<.05 for group comparison** 1: 42.3, 94.2, 87.3*, 81.9*, 81.3*, 74.2 2: 45.2, 90.2, 75.3, 71.9, 72.3, 65.4
Yandoli et al. 2002	119 outpatient opiate users 1:41 2:38 3:40	1: family therapy + strict methadone reduction 2: standard methadone treatment + flexible methadone reduction (primary control) 3: low contact intervention, discouraged dependence on therapist + strict methadone reduction (2ndary control)	**At 1 year follow up:** **% heroin free** 1:22%; 2:5.3%; 3:15% (p=.01 1vs2, p=.04 3vs2, 1vs3 not given **% used heroin regularly** 1:48%, 2:78.9%, 3:57.5% (p=.01 1vs.2, p=ns 1vs3) **% drug free** 1:14.6%; 2:0% (p=.02); 3:7.5% (p=ns)

results, it is considered a cost-effective alternative to standard therapies (Fals-Stewart et al., 1997).

In addition to its efficacy, couples therapy has been shown to be versatile; It has been successfully integrated with 12-step facilitation programs (Epstein and McCrady, 1998), opioid substitution treatment, and disulfiram therapy (O'Farrell, 1999).The major limitation of this treatment is that it requires patients to be in fairly stable relationships, a situation which is unfortunately rare in some substance abusing populations. However, for those who are in long-lasting relationships, BCT may be the treatment of choice, largely because of its strong effects on peripheral problems such as relationship adjustment (Fals-Stewart et al., 1996), parenting (Catalano et al., 1999), and domestic violence (Fals-Stewart et al., 2003; O'Farrell and Murphy, 1995). The BCT-associated improvements in these social outcomes may be of greater importance than the substance use effects themselves.

SUMMARY

Counseling-based outpatient programs based upon Cognitive Behavioral Therapy or 12-step facilitation methods are currently the most common form of medical treatment for substance use disorders, and both are highly supported by research studies for their consistent and long-term outcomes. Brief interventions have been shown to be an effective intervention for problem drinking and it is recommended that they be incorporated into primary care medicine on a regular basis. Opioid Substitution treatment has been shown to be an extremely effective treatment for opioid dependence, especially when combined with additional outpatient counseling. Additional psychosocial and pharmacotherapies have been demonstrated to improve outcomes in certain populations as well. Contingency management techniques have been shown to be particularly useful in

conjunction with opioid substitution treatments and cognitive behavioral therapies, and more generally may be a helpful adjunct to improve treatment outcomes. Family and couples therapy improves outcomes when this treatment option is available. Inpatient SUD treatments are successful and should be considered for patients who are unable to consistently attend outpatient programs. Naltrexone treatment may be helpful for reducing craving in alcohol dependent patients. Other similar treatments (e.g. acamprosate) may be available soon. Disulfiram for alcoholism and naltrexone for opioid addiction may be helpful in certain subpopulations of substance users, however, there is not strong evidence for their general use.

UNANSWERED QUESTIONS

1) How can we encourage non-treatment seeking addicts into treatment? How can subjects who leave treatment be re-engaged? Nearly 75% of patients with identified SUDs do not enter SUD treatment. Finding methods to encourage these patients to receive treatment is essential for reducing the impact of SUDs in our population.

2) Are there populations that predictably do well in one form of therapy versus another? Do different treatments work better for different age groups or sexes? For whom is inpatient treatment needed?

3) When is it safe to end treatment? When and for how long is relapse prevention needed? How often do people need "booster" interventions? When, if ever, should one discontinue medication-based treatments?

4) Are brief interventions equally effective for treatment of non-alcohol substance use disorders?

5) Why and how do people "spontaneously" recover? What can be done to encourage this process?

6) Who is likely to be able to moderate substance use and who need be encouraged to abstain?

7) What components of formal treatment are important for effectiveness? What combinations of treatment modalities lead to optimal outcomes? Are some treatment methods incompatible with others?

8) How much counseling is necessary in conjunction with pharmacotherapies? Once stable abstinence is attained in these treatments, is psychosocial counseling still necessary/worthwhile?

9) What is the long-term efficacy of therapies targeting drugs of abuse such as amphetamines, sedatives, marijuana and hallucinogens, for which few long-term randomized studies have been conducted?

PRACTICE RECOMMENDATIONS

For Problematic Alcohol Use/Substance Abuse
    Brief interventions
For Substance Dependence/Addiction
    CBT or 12 step-facilitation
    Self-help
For Alcohol dependent patients
    Naltrexone
For Opioid-dependent patients
    Opioid Substitution treatment
For patients in stable relationships
    Behavioral Couples Therapy
For non-treatment seeking populations
    Motivational Interviewing

REFERENCES

Allsop S, Saunders B, Phillips M, Carr A. (1997). A trial of relapse prevention with severely dependent male problem drinkers. Addiction 92: 61-74.

Anderson P, Scott E. (1992) The effect of general practitioners' advice to heavy drinking men. Br J Addict 87: 891-900.

Baer JS, Kivlahan DR, Blume AW, McKnight P, Marlatt GA. (2001) Brief intervention for heavy-drinking college students: 4-year follow-up and natural history. Am J Public Health 91: 1310-6.

Bale RN, Zarcone VP, Van Stone WW, Kuldau JM, Engelsing TM, Elashoff RM. (1984) Three therapeutic communities. A prospective controlled study of narcotic addiction treatment: process and two-year follow-up. Arch Gen Psychiatry 41:185-91.

Bale RN, Van Stone WW, Kuldau JM, Engelsing TM, Elashoff RM, Zarcone VP Jr. (1980) Therapeutic communities vs methadone maintenance. A prospective controlled study of narcotic addiction treatment: design and one-year follow-up. Arch Gen Psychiatry 37:179-93

Burge SK, Amodei N, Elkin B, Catala S, Andrew SR, Lane PA, Seale JP. (1997) An evaluation of two primary care interventions for alcohol abuse among Mexican-American patients. Addiction 92: 1705-16.

Caddy GR, Addington HJ Jr, Perkins D. (1978) Individualized behavior therapy for alcoholics: a third year independent double-blind follow-up. Behav Res Ther 16: 345-362.

Calsyn DA, Wells EA, Saxon AJ, Jackson TR, Wrede AF, Stanton V, Fleming C. (1994) Contingency management of urinalysis results and intensity of counseling services have an interactive impact on methadone maintenance treatment outcome. J Addict Dis 13: 47-63.

Carroll KM, Nich C, Ball SA, McCance E, Frankforter TL, Rounsaville BJ. (2000) One-year follow-up of disulfiram and psychotherapy for cocaine-alcohol users: sustained effects of treatment. Addiction 95:1335-49.

Carroll KM, Sinha R, Nich C, Babuscio T, Rounsaville BJ. (2002) Contingency management to enhance naltrexone treatment of opioid dependence: a randomized clinical trial of reinforcement magnitude. Exp Clin Psychopharmacol. 10(1):54-63.

Catalano RF, Gainey RR, Fleming CB, Haggerty KP, Johnson NO. (1999) An experimental intervention with families of substance abusers: one-year follow-up of the focus on families project. Addiction 94(2):241-54.

Chapman PLH, Huygen I. (1988) An evaluation of three treatment programmes for alcoholism : an experimental study with 6- and 18-month follow-up. Brit J Addict 83: 67-81.

Chick J, Lloyd G, Crombie E. (1985) Counselling problem drinkers in medical wards: a controlled study. Br Med J 290: 965-7.

Chick J, Ritson B, Connaughton J, Stewart A, Chick J. (1988) Advice versus extended treatment for alcoholism: a controlled study. Brit J Addict 83: 159-170.

Crits-Christoph P, Siqueland L, Blaine J, Frank A, Luborsky L, Onken LS, Muenz LR, Thase ME, Weiss RD, Gastfriend DR, Woody GE, Barber JP, Butler SF, Daley D, Salloum I, Bishop S, Najavits LM, Lis J, Mercer D, Griffin ML, Moras K, Beck AT. (1999) Psychosocial treatments for cocaine dependence: National Institute on Drug Abuse collaborative cocaine treatment study. Arch Gen Psychiatry 56: 493-502.

Department of Health and Human Services Publication No. (SMA) 94-2075. (1994) "Chapter 4 of TAP 11: Treatment for Alcohol and Other Drug Abuse: Opportunities for Coordination". Accessed online at: http://www.treatment.org/Taps/Tap11/tap 11chap4.html on 7/30/03.

Edwards G, Orford J, Egert S, Guthrie S, Hawker A, Hensman C, Mitcheson M, Oppenheimer E, Taylor C. (1977) Alcoholism: a controlled trial of "treatment" and "advice". J Stud Alcohol 38: 1004-31.

Edwards G, Guthrie S. (1967) A controlled trial of inpatient and outpatient treatment of alcohol dependency. Lancet 11:555-9

Elvy GA, Wells JE, Baird KA. (1988) Attempted referral as intervention for problem drinking in the general hospital. Brit J Addict 83: 83-89.

Epstein DH, Hawkins WE, Covi L, Umbricht A, Preston KL. (2003) Cognitive-behavioral therapy plus contingency management for cocaine use: Findings during treatment and across 12-month follow-up. Psychol Addict Behav 17: 73-82.

Epstein EE, McCrady BS. (1998) Behavioral couples treatment of alcohol and drug use disorders: current status and innovations. Clin Psychol Rev 18(6):689-711.

Fals-Stewart W, Birchler GR, O'Farrell TJ. (1996) Behavioral couples therapy for male substance-abusing patients: effects on relationship adjustment and drug-using behavior. J Consult Clin Psychol 64(5): 959-72.

Fals-Stewart W, Kashdan TB, O'Farrell TJ, Birchler GR. (2002) Behavioral couples therapy for drug-abusing patients: effects on partner violence. J Subst Abuse Treat 22(2):87-96.

Fals-Stewart W, O'Farrell TJ, Birchler GR. (1997) Behavioral couples therapy for male substance-abusing patients: a cost outcomes analysis. J Consult Clin Psychol 65(5):789-802.

Farabee D, Rawson R, McCann M. (2002) Adoption of drug avoidance activities among patients in contingency management and cognitive-behavioral treatments. J Substance Abuse Treat 23: 343-350.

Finney JW, Hahn AC, Moos RH. (1996) The effectiveness of inpatient and outpatient treatment for alcohol abuse: the need to focus on mediators and moderators of setting effects. Addiction 91: 1773-96.

Fleming MF, Barry KL, Manwell LB,

Johnson K, London, R. (1997) Brief physician advice for problem alcohol drinkers. A randomized controlled trial in community-based primary care practices. JAMA 277: 1039-45.

Fleming MF, Mundt MP, French MT, Manwell LB, Stauffacher EA, Barry KL. (2002) Brief physician advice for problem drinkers: long-term efficacy and benefit-cost analysis. Alcohol Clin Exp Res 26: 36-43.

Fuller RK, Branchey L, Brightwell DR, Derman RM, Emrick CD, Iber FL, James KE, Lacoursiere RB, Lee KK, Lowenstam I. (1986) Disulfiram treatment of alcoholism. A Veterans Administration cooperative study. JAMA 256:1449-55

Foy DW, Nunn LB, Rychtarik RG. (1984) Broad-spectrum behavioral treatment for chronic alcoholics: effects of training controlled drinking skills. J Consult Clin Psychol 52: 218-230.

Gallant D. (1999) Alcohol. In Textbook of Substance abuse Treatment. Eds. Marc Galanter and Herbert D. Kleber. American Psychiatric Press, Washington, DC, pgs. 413-422.

Garbutt JC, West SL, Carey TS, Lohr KN, Crews FT. (1999) Pharmcological treatment of alcohol dependence: a review of the evidence. JAMA 281: 1318-25.

Gonzales RA, Weiss F. (1998) Suppression of ethanol-reinforced behavior by naltrexone is associated with attenuation of the ethanol-induced increase in dialysate dopamine levels in the nucleus accumbens. J Neurosci 18: 10663-71.

Graham K, Annis HM, Brett PJ, Venesoen P. (1996) A controlled field trial of group versus individual cognitive-behavioural training for relapse prevention. Addiction 91: 1127-39.

Greenwood GL, Woods WJ, Guydish J, Bein E. (2001) Relapse outcomes in a randomized trial of residential and day drug abuse treatment. Subst Abuse Treat 20:15-23.

Griffith JD, Rowan-Szal GA, Roark RR, Simpson DD. (2000) Contingency management in outpatient methadone treatment: a meta-analysis. Drug Alcohol Depend 58(1-2):55-66.

Gunne LM, Gronbladh L. (1981) The Swedish methadone maintenance program: a controlled study. Drug Alcohol Depend 7:249-56

Guydish J, Sorensen JL, Chan M, Werdegar D, Bostrom A, Acampora A. (1999) A randomized trial comparing day and residential drug abuse treatment: 18-month outcomes. j Consult Clin Psychol 67: 428-34.

Heinala P, Alho H, Kiianmaa K, Lonnqvist J, Kuoppasalmi K, Sinclair JD. (2001) Targeted use of naltrexone without prior detoxification in the treatment of alcohol dependence: a factorial double-blind, placebo-controlled trial. J Clin Psychopharmacol 21:287-92.

Higgins ST, Budney AJ, Bickel WK, Hughes JR, Foerg F, Badger G. (1993) Achieving cocaine abstinence with a behavioral approach. Am J Psychiatry 150(5):763-9.

Higgins ST, Budney AJ, Bickel WK, Foerg FE, Donham R, Badger GJ. (1994) Incentives improve outcome in outpatient behavioral treatment of cocaine dependence. Arch Gen Psychiatry. 51(7):568-76.

Higgins ST, Budney AJ, Bickel WK, Badger GJ, Foerg FE, Ogden D. (1995) Outpatient behavioral treatment for cocaine-dependence: One-year outcome. Exp Clin Psychopharmacol 3: 205-212.

Higgins ST, Petry NM (1999). Contingency management. Incentives for sobriety. Alcohol Res Health. 23(2):122-7.

Higgins ST, Wong CJ, Badger GJ, Haug Ogden DE, Dantona RL. (2000) Contingent Reinforcement Increases Cocaine Abstinence During Outpatient Treatment and 1 year of follow-up. J

Consult Clin Psychol 68: 64-72.

Judson BA, Carney TM, Goldstein A. (1981) Naltrexone treatment of heroin addiction: efficacy and safety in a double-blind dosage comparison. Drug Alcohol Depend 7:325-46.

Kakko J, Svanborg KD, Kreek MJ, Heilig M. (2003) 1-year retention and social function after buprenorphine-assisted relapse prevention treatment for heroin dependence in Sweden: a randomised, placebo-controlled trial. Lancet 361:662-8.

Kelley ML, Fals-Stewart W. (2002) Couples-versus individual-based therapy for alcohol and drug abuse: effects on children's psychosocial functioning. J Consult Clin Psychol 70(2):417-27.

Keso L, Salaspuro M. (1990) Inpatient treatment of employed alcoholics: a randomized clinical trial on Hazelden-type and traditional treatment. Alcohol Clin Exp Res 14:584-9.

Kirchmayer U, Davoli M, Verster A. (2002) Naltrexone maintenance treatment for opioid dependence. Cochrane Database Syst. Rev. CD001333.

Kleber H. (1999) Opioids: Detoxification. In Textbook of Substance abuse Treatment. Eds. Marc Galanter and Herbert D. Kleber. American Psychiatric Press, Washington, DC, pgs. 413-422.

Kosten TR, Schottenfeld R, Ziedonis D, Falcioni J. (1993) Buprenorphine versus methadone maintenance for opioid dependence. J Nerv Ment Dis 181:358-64

Kristenson H, Ohlin H, Hulten-Nosslin MB, Trell E, Hood B. (1983) Identification and intervention of heavy drinking in middle-aged men: results and follow-up of 24-60 months of long-term study with randomized controls. Alcohol Clin Exp Res 7: 203-9.

Krystal JH, Cramer JA, Krol WF, Kirk GF, Rosenheck RA. (2001) Naltrexone in the treatment of alcohol dependence. N Engl J Med 345:1734-9

Lam JA, Jekel JF, Thompson KS, Leaf PJ, Hartwell SW, Florio L. (1995) Assessing the value of a short-term residential drug treatment program for homeless men. J Addict Dis 14:21-39.

Landabaso MA, Iraurgi I, Jimenez-Lerma JM, Sanz J, Fernadez de Corres B, Araluce K, Calle R, Gutierrez-Fraile M. (1998) A randomized trial of adding fluoxetine to a naltrexone treatment programme for heroin addicts. Addiction 93:739-44

Landabaso MA, Iraurgi I, Sanz J, Calle R, Ruiz de Apodaka J, Jimenex-Lerma JM, Gutierrez-Fraile M. (1999) Naltrexone in the treatment of alcoholism: two-year follow up results. Eur J Psychiatry 13: 97-105.

Lerner A, Sigal M, Bacalu A, Shiff R, Burganski I, Gelkopf M. (1992) A naltrexone double blind placebo controlled study in Israel. Isr J Psychiatry Relat Sci 29: 36-43.

Li TK. (2000) Pharmacogenetics of responses to alcohol and genes that influence alcohol drinking. J Stud Alcohol 61: 5-12.

Ling W, Wesson DR, Charuvastra C, Klett CJ. (1996) A controlled trial comparing buprenorphine and methadone maintenance in opioid dependence. Arch Gen Psychiatry 53:401-7

Longabaugh R, Wirtz PW, Beattie MC, Noel N, Stout R. (1995) Matching treatment focus to patient social investment and support: 18-month follow-up results. J Consult Clin Psychol 63: 296-307.

Manwell LB, Fleming MF, Mundt MP, Stauffacher EA, Barry KL. (2000) Treatment of problem alcohol use in women of childbearing age: results of a brief intervention trial. Alcohol Clin Exp Res 24: 1517-24.

Marlatt GA, Baer JS, Kivlahan DR, Dimeff LA, Larimer ME, Quigley LA, Somers JM, Williams E. (1998) Screening and brief intervention for high-risk college student drinkers: results from a 2-year follow-up assessment. J Consult Clin Psychol 66: 604-15.

Marques AC, Formigoni ML. (2001) Comparison of individual and group cognitive-behavioral therapy for alcohol and/or drug-dependent patients. Addiction 96: 835-46.

Mattick RP, Hall W. (1996) Are detox-ification programmes effective? Lancet 347: 97-100.

Maxwell S, Shinderman M. (1999) Optimizing response to methadone maintenance treatment: use of higher-dose methadone. J Psychoactive Drugs 31:95-102

McCrady B, Longabaugh R, Fink E, Stout R, Beattie M, Ruggieri-Authelet A. (1986) Cost-effectiveness of alcoholism treatment in partial hospital versus inpatient settings after brief inpatient treatment: 12 month outcomes. J Consult Clin Psychol 54: 708-13.

McCrady BS, Stout R, Noel N, Abrams D, Nelson HF. (1991) Effectiveness of three types of spouse-involved behavioral alcoholism treatment. Br J Addict 86(11):1415-24.

McKay JR, Alterman AI, Cacciola JS, O'Brien CP, Koppenhaver JM, Shepard DS. (1999) Continuing care for cocaine dependence: comprehensive 2-year outcomes. J Consult Clin Psychol 67: 420-7

McKay JR, Alterman AI, McLellan AT, Snider EC, O'Brien CP. (1995) Effect of random versus nonrandom assignment in a comparison of inpatient and day hospital rehabilitation for male alcoholics. J Consult Clin Psychol 63:70-8.

McLachlan JFC, Stein RL. (1982) Evaluation of a day clinic for alcoholics. J Stud Alcohol 43:261-72.

Miller WR, Benefield RG, Tonigan JS. (1993) Enhancing motivation for change in problem drinking: a controlled comparison of two therapist styles. J Consult Clin Psychol 61: 455-61.

Miller WR. (1978) Behavioral treatment of problem drinkers: a comparative outcome study of three controlled drinking therapies. J Consult Clin Psychol 46: 74-86.

Miller WR, Rollnick S. (1991) Motivational Interviewing: Preparing people to change addictive behavior. Guilford Press: New York.

Miller WR, Taylor CA, West JC. (1980a) Focused versus broad-spectrum behavior therapy for problem drinkers. J Consult Clin Psychol 48: 590-601.

Miller WR, Taylor CA. (1980b) Relative effectiveness of bibliotherapy, individual and group self-control training in the treatment of problem drinkers. Addict Behav 5: 13-24.

Miller WR, Meyers RJ, Tonigan JS. (1999) Engaging the unmotivated in treatment for alcohol problems: a comparison of three strategies for intervention through family members. J Consult Clin Psychol 67: 688-697.

Monti PM, Rohsenow DJ, Swift RM, Gulliver SB, Colby SM, Mueller TI, Brown RA, Gordon A, Abrams DB, Niaura RS, Asher MK. (2001) Naltrexone and cue exposure with coping and communication skills training for alcoholics: treatment process and 1-year outcomes. Alcohol

Moyer A, Finney JW, Swearingen CE, Vergun P. (2002) Brief interventions for alcohol problems: a meta-analytic review of controlled investigations in treatment-seeking and non-treatment seeking populations. Addiction 97: 279-292.

Newman RG, Whitehill WB. (1979) Double-blind comparison of methadone and placebo maintenance treatments of narcotic addicts in Hong Kong. Lancet 2:485-8

Nilssen O. (1991) The Tromso study:

identification of and a controlled intervention on a population of early-stage risk drinkers. Prev Med 20: 518-28.

Oei TP, Jackson P. (1980) Long-term effects of group and individual social skills training with alcoholics. Addict Behav 5: 129-36.

O'Farrell, TJ. (1993) A behavioral marital therapy couples group program for alcoholics and their spouses. In TJ O'Farrell (Ed.), Treating Alcohol Problems: Marital and Family Interventions (pp. 170-209). New York: Guilford Press.

O'Farrell TJ. (1999) Behavioral Couples Therapy for Alcoholism and Drug Abuse. Int J Psychosocial Reh 14(4).

O'Farrell TJ, Murphy CM. (1995) Marital violence before and after alcoholism treatment J Consult Clin Psychol. 63(2):256-62.

Office of National Drug Control Policy (2001) The Economic Costs of Drug Abuse in the United States, 1992-1998. http://www.whitehousedrugpolicy.gov/publications/pdf/economic_costs98.pdf, accessed on 5/30/03.

Peng GS, Wang MF, Chen CY, Chou HC, Li TK, Yin SJ. (1999) Involvement of actaldehyde for full protectin against alcoholism by homozygosity of the variant allele of mitochondrial aldehyde dehydrogenase gene in Asians. Pharmacogenetics 9: 463-76.

Persson J, Magnusson PH. (1989) Early intervention in patients with excessive consumption of alcohol: a controlled study. Alcohol 6: 403-408.

Petry NM, Tedford J, Martin B. (2001) Reinforcing compliance with non-drug-related activities. J Subst Abuse Treat 20(1):33-44.

Petry NM, Martin B, Cooney JL, Kranzler HR. (2000) Give them prizes, and they will come: contingency management for treatment of alcohol dependence. J Consult Clin Psychol 68(2):250-7.

Petry NM, Martin B. (2002) Low-cost contingency management for treating cocaine- and opioid-abusing methadone patients. J Consult Clin Psychol 70(2): 398-405.

Petry NM. (2000) A comprehensive guide to the application of contingency management procedures in clinical settings. Drug Alcohol Depend 58(1-2):9-25.

Powell BJ, Penick EC, Read MR, Ludwig AM. (1985) Comparison of three outpatient treatment interventions: a twelve-month follow-up of men alcoholics. J Stud Alcohol 46:309-12

Preston KL, Umbricht A, Epstein DH. (2002) Abstinence reinforcement maintenance contingency and one-year follow-up. Drug Alcohol Dependence 67: 125-137.

Preston KL, Umbricht A, Wong CJ, Epstein DH. (2001) Shaping cocaine abstinence by successive approximation. J Consult Clin Psychol 69(4):643-54.

Preston KL, Umbricht A, Epstein DH. (2000) Methadone dose increase and abstinence reinforcement for treatment of continued heroin use during methadone maintenance. Arch Gen Psychiatr 57(4): 395-404.

Project MATCH Research Group. (1997) Matching alcoholism treatments to client heterogeneity: Project MATCH posttreatment drinking outcomes. J Stud Alcohol 58: 7-29.

Rawson RA,Tennant FS. (1984) Five-year follow-up of opiate addicts with naltrexone and behavior therapy. NIDA Res Monogr 49: 289-95.

Rawson RA, Huber A, McCann M, Shoptaw S, Farabee D, Reiber C, Ling W. (2002) A comparison of contingency management and cognitive-behavioral approaches during methadone maintenance treatment for cocaine dependence. Arch Gen Psychiatry 59: 817-824.

Richmond R, Heather N, Wodak A, Kehoe L, Webster I. (1995) Controlled evaluation of a general practice-based brief intervention for excessive drinking. Addiction 90: 119-32.

Robertson I, Heather N, Dzialdowski A, Crawford J, Winton M. (1986) A comparison of minimal versus intensive controlled drinking treatment interventions for problem drinkers. Brit J Clin Psych 22: 185-194.

Romelsjo A, Andersson L, Barner H, Borg S, Granstrand C, Hultman O, Hassler A, Kallqvist A, Magnusson P, Morgell R. (1989) A randomized study of secondary prevention of early stage problem drinkers in primary health care. Br J Addict 84: 1319-27.

Rubio G, Jimenez-Arriero MA, Ponce G, Palomo T. (2001) Naltrexone versus acamprosate: one year follow-up of alcohol dependence treatment. Alcohol Alcohol 36:419-25

Substance Abuse and Mental Health Services Administration (SAMHSA) (2001) National Household Survey on Drug Abuse (NHSDA). http://www.samhsa.gov/oas/nhsda.htm#N HSDAinfo accessed on 5/30/03.

San L, Pomarol G, Peri JM, Olle JM, Cami J. (1991) Follow-up after a six-month maintenance period on naltrexone versus placebo in heroin addicts. Br J Addict 86:983-90

Sannibale C. (1988) The differential effect of a set of brief interventions on the functioning of a group of 'early-stage' problem drinkers. Australian Drug and Alcohol Review 7: 147-155.

Sanchez-Craig M, Leigh G, Spivak K, Lei H. (1989) Superior outcome of females over males after brief treatment for the reduction of heavy drinking. Br J Addict 84: 395-404.

Sanchez-Craig M, Davila R, Cooper G. (1996) A self-help approach for high-risk drinking: effect of an initial assessment. J Consult Clin Psychol 64: 694-700.

Saunders B, Wilkinson C, Phillips M. (1995) The impact of a brief motivational intervention with opiate users attending a methadone programme. Addiction 90:415-24.

Saxon AJ, Wells EA, Fleming C, Jackson TR, Calsyn DA. (1996) Pre-treatment characteristics, program philosophy and level of ancillary services as predictors of methadone maintenance treatment outcome. Addiction 91:1197-209.

Schumacher JE, Mennemeyer ST, Milby JB, Wallace D, Nolan K. (2002) Costs and effectiveness of substance abuse treatments for homeless persons. J Ment Health Policy Econ. 5(1):33-42.

Scott E, Anderson P. (1990) Randomized controlled trial of general practitioner intervention in women with excessive alcohol consumption. Drug Alcohol Review 10: 313-321.

Sees KL, Delucchi KL, Masson C, Rosen A, Clark HW, Robillard H, Banys P, Hall SM. (2000) Methadone maintenance vs 180-day psychosocially enriched detoxification for treatment of opioid dependence: a randomized controlled trial. JAMA 283:1303-10.

Silverman K, Wong CJ, Umbricht-Schneiter A, Montoya ID, Schuster CR, Preston KL. (1998) Broad beneficial effects of cocaine abstinence reinforcement among methadone patients. J Consult Clin Psychol 66(5):811-24.

Silverman K, Wong CJ, Higgins ST, Brooner RK, Montoya ID, Contoreggi C, Umbricht-Schneiter A, Schuster CR, Preston KL. (1996) Increasing opiate abstinence through voucher-based reinforcement therapy. Drug Alcohol Depend. Jun;41(2):157-65.

Sinclair JD. Evidence about the use of naltrexone and for different ways of using it in the treatment of alcoholism. Alcohol Alcohol 36: 2-10.

Spivak K, Sanchez-Craig M, Davila R. (1994)

Assisting problem drinkers to change on their own: effect of specific and non-specific advice. Addiction 89: 1135-1142.

Sobell MB, Sobell LC. (1973) Alcoholics treated by individualized behavior therapy: one year treatment outcome. Behav Res Ther 11: 599-618

Sobell MB, Sobell LC. (1976) Second year treatment outcome of alcoholics treated by individualized behavior therapy: results. Behav Res Ther 14: 195-215.

Sobell LC, Sobell MB, Leo GI, Agrawal S, Johnson-Young L, Cunningham JA. (2002) Promoting self-change with alcohol abusers: a community-level mail intervention based on natural recovery studies. Alcohol Clin Exp Res 26: 936-948.

Srisurapanont M, Jarusuraisin N. (2002) Opioid antagonists for alcohol dependence. Cochrane Database Syst Rev: CD001867.

Stein LI, Newton JR, Bowman RS. (1975) Duration of hospitalization for alcoholism. Arch Gen Psychiatry 32:247-52.

Stephens RS, Roffman RA, Curtin L. (2000) Comparison of extended versus brief tretaments for marijuana use. J Consult Clin Psychol 68:898-908.

Stephens RS, Roffman RA, Simpson EE. (1994). Treating adult marijuana dependence: a test of the relapse prevention model. J Consult Clin Psychol 62: 92-99.

Strain EC, Stitzer ML, Liebson IA, Bigelow GE. (1993) Methadone dose and treatment outcome. Drug Alcohol Depend 33:105-17.

Streeton C, Whelan G. (2001) Naltrexone, A relapse prevention maintenance treatment of alcohol dependence: A meta-analysis of randomized controlled trials. Alcohol Alcohol 36:544-552.

Stitzer ML, Iguchi MY, Felch LJ. (1992) Contingent take-home incentive: effects on drug use of methadone maintenance patients. J Consult Clin Psychol. 60(6):

927-34.

Stitzer ML, Bickel WK, Bigelow GE, Liebson IA. (1986) Effect of methadone dose contingencies on urinalysis test results of polydrug-abusing methadone-maintenance patients. Drug Alcohol Depend. 18(4): 341-8.

Vogler RE, Compton JV, Weissbach TA. (1975) Integrated behavior change techniques for alcoholics. J Consult Clin Psychol 43: 233-43.

Vogler RE, Weissbach TA, Compton JV, Martin GT. (1977) Integrated behavior change techniques for problem drinkers in the community. J Consult Clin Psychol 45: 267-79.

Wallace P, Cutler S, Haines A. (1988) Randomized controlled trial of general practitioner intervention in patients with excessive alcohol consumption. Brit Med J 297: 663-668.

Walsh DC, Hingson RW, Merrigan DM, Levenson SM, Cupples LA, Heeren T, Coffman GA, Becker CA, Barker TA, Hamilton SK, McGuire TG, Kelly CA. (1991) A randomized trail of treatment options for alcohol-abusing workers. N Engl J Med 325:775-82.

Weiss RD. (1999) Inpatient treatment. In Textbook of Substance abuse Treatment. Eds. Marc Galanter and Herbert D. Kleber. American Psychiatric Press, Washington, DC, pgs. 413-422.

White JM, Danz C, Kneebone J, La Vincente SF, Newcombe DA, Ali RL. (2002) Relationship between LAAM-methadone preference and treatment outcomes. Drug Alcohol Depend 66:295-301.

Wilson A, Davidson WJ, Blanchard R, White J. (1978) Disulfiram implantation. A placebo-controlled trial with two-year follow-up. J Stud Alcohol 39:809-19.

Winters J, Fals-Stewart W, O'Farrell TJ, Birchler GR, Kelley ML. (2002) Behavioral couples therapy for female substance-abusing patients: effects on substance use and relationship adjustment. J Consult Clin Psychol 70(2):344-55.

Wutzke SE, Conigrave KM, Saunders JB, Hall WD. (2002) The long-term effectiveness of brief interventions for unsafe alcohol consumption: a 10-year follow-up. Addiction 97: 665-75.

Yandoli DE, Eisler I, Robbins C, Mulleady G, Dare C. (2002) A comparative study of family therapy in the treatment of opiate users in a London drug clinic. J Fam Ther Vol 24(4), Nov, pp. 402-422

Zweben A, Pearlman S, Li S. (1988) A comparison of brief advice and conjoint therapy in the treatment of alcohol abuse: the results of the marital systems study. Brit J Addict 83: 899-916.

PREVENTION OF YOUTH SMOKING

Alessandra N. Kazura and Raymond Niaura

INTRODUCTION

Recent survey data demonstrate a promising decline in youth smoking rates, and prevention efforts need to be optimized to continue this trend. According to the Monitoring the Future Survey, daily smoking by high school seniors in 2002 has decreased to 16.9% from an all time high of 28.8% in 1976 (Johnston et al, 2002b). Additionally, the annual incidence of new smokers among 12-17 year olds has decreased from 1.1 million in 1997 to 747,000 in 2000 (USDHHS, 2002). Later age of onset of smoking experimentation has also been reported, with initial use by grade 6 declining from 20% for the class of 1986 to 15% for the class of 2001 (Johnston et al., 2002a). In this chapter, we summarize youth tobacco use trends and then highlight successful, evidence-based prevention programs. We comment on risk profiles that may signal resilience or vulnerability to smoking uptake and we discuss gaps in our knowledge of prevention efficacy and effectiveness in youth subpopulations. Finally, we identify promising examples of new strategies for preventing youth tobacco use.

Tobacco Use Trends

A comprehensive understanding of youth tobacco use requires attention to patterns of use by age and cohort, gender, ethnicity, location, and other sociodemographic factors. While smoking rates have declined across the majority of subgroups measured by the Monitoring the Future Survey (Johnston et al., 2002b), variation in prevalence rates can be observed among these subgroups. For example, last 30-day prevalence rates of 12.0% and 12.7% were observed for White and Hispanic eighth grade students, but only 7.7% for Black students. Thirty-day smoking rates in

eighth grade students were lowest in the West, at 7.5%, and highest in the South of the United States, at 13.0%. Even more striking differences were noted between students with parents in the highest and lowest educational levels, with 30-day prevalence rates of 5.8% and 20.5%, respectively. Declines in smoking have been attributed to increases in youth perception of risk and disapproval of smoking, anti-smoking media campaigns, and increases in cigarette prices (Johnston et al., 2002b).

Cigarettes remain the most common tobacco product used by youth, but other tobacco products are important to address and may contribute to unique morbidity and mortality concerns. For ninth through twelfth grade students, the last 30-day prevalence of smokeless tobacco use was 8.2% in 2001, while the cigar smoking rate was 15.2% (Grunbaum et al., 2002). Bidis, which are hand rolled cigarettes imported from India, may find favor with some youth; nicotine concentrations are typically higher in bidis than standard cigarettes (NIDA, 2000). Embalming fluid dipped cigarettes (street names include "illy", "wets", and "fry" and may also refer to marijuana based products), have made appearances in some communities and are particularly of concern because of acute toxicity associated with the chemical additives (Modesto-Lowe, 2002; Weiner, 2000: Moriarity, 1996).

Although the delivery of nicotine, and therefore risk of nicotine dependence, is common to all forms of tobacco products, prevention and cessation efforts may need to be tailored to the specific types of tobacco used by youth. For example, only 45% of high school seniors perceive great health risk from regular use of smokeless tobacco compared to 73% endorsing great risk from smoking a pack or more of cigarettes per day

(Johnston et al, 2002c). In addition, different forms of tobacco are likely to be associated with different youth subcultures, such as the association of chewing tobacco with sports such as baseball.

Development of Smoking and Nicotine Dependence

The progression from initial use of cigarettes to nicotine dependence can be conceptualized as a series of stages (USDHHS, 1994). *Preparation* is the stage prior to actual use of cigarettes during which attitudes about smoking are shaped positively toward smoking. The "Trying Stage" is defined as the smoking of the first few cigarettes and is the point of smoking initiation. Experimentation incorporates a range of repeated, but still irregular smoking, while the rate of smoking picks up and becomes established over a range of situations at the "Regular Use" stage. In this model, the final stage is "Addicted or Dependent" and follows a period of regular use of cigarettes. As defined by DSM-IV criteria, nicotine dependent smokers are characterized by at least three of the following symptoms occurring in the same 12-month period: 1) tolerance, 2) withdrawal, 3) use of larger amounts or over a longer time period than intended, 4) persistent desire or unsuccessful attempts to control use, 5) spending considerable time in activities needed to obtain, use or recover from the effects of use (e.g. chain-smoking), 6) reduced time in important activities because of use; and 7) use despite knowledge of having a physical or psychological problem related to use (American Psychiatric Association 1994). The duration and quantity of use necessary for dependence symptoms to develop remains incompletely characterized, but may occur very early---within weeks--- for at least some adolescent smokers (DiFranza et al., 2000). Craving, or a strong desire to smoke during conditions of deprivation, is also considered a typical feature of nicotine dependence (American Psychiatric Association 1994). While adolescent nicotine dependence is generally recognized by researchers and clinicians, the evidence base is considerably lagging behind that for adult dependent smokers (for a comprehensive review of this topic, see Shadel et al., 2000).

The first few experiences inhaling cigarette smoke are thought to be typically unpleasant, but with repeated use, tolerance to aversive effects and increasing experience of pleasurable effects may manifest rapidly (Pomerleau, 1995). As nicotine intake rates increase, symptoms of nicotine dependence are reported by some youth before daily smoking patterns begin. While specific developmental processes of dependence are not well described, the occurrence of nicotine dependence in adolescents is supported by a preponderance of evidence. This evidence includes youth reports of feeling addicted, feeling subjective effects and reasons for sustained smoking, consumption of substantial levels of nicotine, experience of withdrawal symptoms, and difficulty in quitting tobacco use (Lynch et al., 1994). Withdrawal symptoms in adolescents include strong urges to smoke, nervousness, tension, irritability, hunger, concentration difficulties, dysphoria, and insomnia (Rojas et al., 1998; Killen et al., 2001; Prokhorov et al., 2001). Of course, progression is not inevitable, and the majority of youth who try and experiment with cigarettes do not become addicted to them (Pomerleau, 1995).

Risk Profiles

A variety of intrinsic and extrinsic factors are associated with risk of smoking uptake. Factors such as sociodemographic characteristics and environmental characteristics are primarily associated with smoking initiation, while peer smoking influences, and personal characteristics such as tobacco use attitudes and mental health

Table 1: Risk Factors for Youth Smoking Uptake

Risk Factors	Initiation	Regular use/dependence
Sociodemographic factors		
Low socioeconomic status	X	X
Developmental stage	X	
Male gender	X	
Environmental factors		
High accessibility	X	X
High advertising	X	X
Parental tobacco use	X	X
Sibling tobacco use	X	
Peer tobacco use	X	X
High normative expectations	X	
Low social support	X	X
Parenting factors	X	X
Behavioral factors		
Low academic achievement	X	X
Presence of other problem behaviors	X	X
Low tobacco refusal skills	X	X
High intentions to smoke	X	
Experimentation	X	X
Personal factors		
High knowledge of consequences	X	
Functional meanings of tobacco use	X	X
Low subjective expected utility	X	X
Low self-esteem/self-image	X	X
Low self-efficacy	X	X
Personality factors	X	X
Psychological well-being	X	X
Presence of mood disorders	X	X
Presence of externalizing disorders	X	X
Biological factors		
Genetic	X	X
In utero exposure		X

Adapted from: Centers for Disease Control and Prevention. *Preventing Tobacco Use Among Young People. A Report of the Surgeon General.* Washington, DC: U.S. Government Printing Office, 1994. 123.

problems, also predict progression of smoking. A number of family factors have been associated with youth risk for smoking uptake. In a prospective study of 808 ethnically diverse children followed from age 10-11 to age 21, Guo et al. found that baseline parental smoking status, family monitoring and rules, and family bonding were all significant predictors of smoking initiation (Guo, 2000). Higher levels of family bonding and monitoring were protective against daily smoking, even in the presence of parental smoking.

Genetic risk factors have been identified over the last decade, although the biological mechanisms for these are still unknown (Sullivan and Kendler, 1999). Based on reviews of twin, family, and adoption studies, Sullivan and Kendler estimate the genetic liability to smoking initiation to be about 60% and to nicotine dependence to be about 70% Common genes are thought to be the causal mechanism behind the strong associations found between lifetime smoking and lifetime depression; this has been modeled in a population-based register of adult female twins (Kendler et al., 1993). At this time, genetic profiling does not have a role in evidence-based prevention strategies.

Evidence-based Prevention Strategies
School-Based Prevention

A summary of selected school-based prevention interventions can be found in Table 2. For reviews of youth tobacco prevention strategies through the early 1990's, readers are referred to the 1994 report of the Institute of Medicine, Growing Up Tobacco Free, and the 1995 Report of the Surgeon General, Preventing Tobacco Use in Young People (Lynch, 1994; USDHHS, 1994). Reviews of school-based prevention strategies based on information-deficit and affective education models found them to be ineffective in decreasing tobacco uptake; furthermore, concerns were raised about possible inadvertent promotion of interest in tobacco use (Lynch, 1994). On the other hand, efficacy has been demonstrated for many social-influences based general drug prevention programs, with small to moderate effect sizes reported (Sussman et al., 2001).

In 1994, the Centers for Disease Control and Prevention published recommendations for school-based prevention programs, drawing upon current research of protective and risk factors, as well as on results of school intervention studies conducted in previous years (CDC, 1994).

Table 2: Longitudinal Randomized Controlled Interventions for Prevention of Youth Tobacco Use

Social Influences Smoking Prevention Program Cameron et al., 1999.	N = 4466 6th- 8th grade students in 100 schools (Ontario, Canada).	This study compared the effects of nurse versus teacher delivered prevention interventions and workshop versus self-preparation of the intervention providers. The program was based on a social influences model. The intervention was delivered across the study years.	Smoking rates were lower in high-risk intervention schools (16.0%) versus control (26.9%) among students followed from Grade 6 to Grade 8 (about 2.5 years). No significant differences were found for low risk schools, and no significant differences found for teacher versus nurse delivered interventions, or by interventionist training method.

Good Behavior Game and Mastery Learning Curriculum Kellam et al., 1998.	N = 2311 1st grade students in 19 urban public schools.	Three group design with 2 cohorts: 1) Good Behavior Game – teacher delivered classroom management intervention designed to reduce aggressive and disruptive behaviors; 2) Mastery Learning Curriculum – an enriched curriculum to raise reading achievement; 3) control.	At the 7 year follow-up, smoking initiation was lower for the "best behaving" tertile of boys in the Good Behavior Game group compared to control (RR = 0.13; 95% CI – 0.03, 0.62). There was a non-statistically significant trend for all boys (RR = 0.58 (95% CI = 0.33, 1.00) in cohort 1, RR= 0.62 (95% CI = 0.29, 1.29). Girls' smoking was not reduced.
Hutchinson Smoking Prevention Project Peterson et al.2000.	N = 8388 3rd grade students in 40 school districts (state of Washington).	Social learning theory/social influences based intervention vs. observation control. "Best practices" included observational learning, self-efficacy enhancement, refusal skills, family support building over 65 sessions.	There was no significant intervention effect for daily smoking rates at either the 12th grade, or 2-years post high school follow-up periods. No significant intervention effects were found for other measured smoking outcomes or for subgroups determined a priori.
Family-Based			
Family Matters Study Bauman et al, 2001.	N = 1326 12-14 year olds plus parent recruited by random digit dialing, representative of US population with phone (48 states)	This was based on value expectancy theory, Health Belief Model, social learning theory, social inoculation theory. Two group study: 1) 4 mailings plus follow-up phone counseling with parent provided by a health educator; 2) untreated control.	Follow-up rate was 86.2% at 12 months. Smoking onset decreased in the treatment group with OR = 1.30, p = .037; after control for design effect OR = 1.27, p = .059. Program effect positive for non-Hispanic Whites but not other racial/ethnic groups with effect size of 0.25.
Iowa Brief Family Intervention Study Spoth et al., 2001.	N = 667 6th grade students plus parents, 30 rural Iowa schools	Three group design: 1) Preparing for the Drug Free Years (PDFY) based on pro-social bonding model; 2) Iowa Strengthening Family Program (ISFP) based on resiliency and social-ecological theories of adolescent development; 3) control.	At the 10th grade follow-up (about 4 years), a significant reduction in smoking initiation was found for ISFP compared to control with a relative reduction of 34.8% (p < .01).

Family-School Partnership and Classroom-Centered intervention Storr et al., 2002.	N = 678 1st grade students Predominately African American.	Three group design: 1) Classroom-Centered (CC) targeted teacher management of child behavioral risks for substance use - aggression, shyness and inattention; 2) Family-School Partnership added parent-teacher communication and parent management of child behaviors to CC; 3) control.	At the 6 year follow-up, smoking was reduced in both intervention conditions compared to control: OR for CC = 0.55 (95% CI = 0.34-0.96); OR for FSP = 0.69 (95% CI = 0.50-0.97).
Project Toward No Drug Abuse Sussman et al., 2002.	N = 2468 High school students in 42 schools.	Three field trials, 2 with alternative high schools. The intervention consisted of twelve 40-minute classroom delivered sessions based on motivation-skills-decision-making model. Delivery was by project health educators and by students was compared in one of the trials.	No reduction was found for last 30-day cigarette smoking in 2 of 3 trials, but a 27% relative reduction of smoking was found in the health educator led condition compared to control in 3rd trial (p< .05). A baseline smoking rate of 57% was observed in this study. Follow-up was at 1 year for all 3 trials.
Community-Based			
Mass media and school intervention Flynn et al., 1994.	N = 5458 4th-6th grade students in 4 communities	A four-year mass media campaign plus school-based intervention was compared to a school-based intervention alone.	At two years post-intervention, daily smoking rates were lower in the media plus school group, OR = 0.62, 95% CI = 0.49, 0.78 (absolute smoking rates not provided). Only 38% of the original sample received "full exposure" to interventions and were included in this outcome analysis.

School-Based			
Computer-based out-of-school intervention Ausems et al., 2002.	N = 3, 349 11 – 12 year old students in 156 schools (The Netherlands)	This was based on a social influence model. Four conditions were compared: 1) a seven lesson in-school program; 2) three computer-tailored letters sent to the students' homes; 3) in-school plus computer-tailored letters; 4) control.	The tailored letters resulted in the lowest level of smoking initiation compared to control (10.4% versus 18.1%) and continuation (13.1% versus 23.5%), at the 6 month follow-up. No significant effects were found for the in-school program alone, or for the combined interventions versus the letters alone.
Life Skills Training Botvin et al., 1995.	N = 5954 7th grade students in 56 schools	This was a three group design based on a social influences model: 1) active intervention with teachers trained with workshops and consultations; 2) active intervention with teachers trained with videotapes; 3) "treatment as usual" control. Active intervention was delivered over 15 classes in 7th grade and 10 booster sessions in 9th grade and involved teaching skills for resisting drugs.	The 12th grade follow-up rate (5 years) was 60.4%. Weekly and monthly smoking rates were lower in the two experimental groups compared to control. For monthly smoking, rates were 27% and 26% for the intervention conditions versus 33% for control; for weekly, 23% and 21% versus 27% (p < .05). Stronger effects were found for the high fidelity to program groups.

These recommendations are as follows:

1. Develop and enforce a school policy on tobacco use.

2. Provide instruction about the short- and long-term negative physiologic and social consequences of tobacco use, social influences on tobacco use, peer norms regarding tobacco use, and refusal skills.

3. Provide tobacco-use prevention education in kindergarten through 12th grade; this instruction should be especially intensive in junior high or middle school and should be reinforced in high school.

4. Provide program-specific training for teachers.

5. Involve parents or families in support of school-based programs to prevent tobacco use.

6. Support cessation efforts among students and all school staff who use tobacco.

7. Assess the tobacco-use prevention program at regular intervals.

The details for each of these elements are provided at http://www.cdc.gov/nccdphp/dash/healthtopics/tobacco/guidelines/index.htm.

The Hutchinson Smoking Prevention Project rigorously tested a state-of-the-art social influences approach for schools that was recommended by panels of experts at the

Centers for Disease Control and Prevention and the National Cancer Institute (Peterson et al., 2000). Over 8300 students were enrolled in the study in grade 3, and then followed through grade 12. Schools were randomly assigned to intervention and control conditions (20 schools each), with matching for school district size, location, and smoking prevalence. The intervention was grounded in social learning theory, and built upon previously tested social influences interventions. Intervention elements included observational learning, correction of erroneous perceptions of social norms of smoking, self-efficacy enhancement, reinforcement of nonsmoking behavior, skills for identification of advertising and other social influences, refusal skills building, and enlisting family support for nonsmoking (Peterson et al., 2000). The intervention was initiated with third grade students, with follow-up sessions over 7 years. Intervention content and process was matched to age-specific interests and developmental capabilities of the students. Trained classroom teachers implemented the intervention and maintained a high rate of delivery of key intervention components. A 94% retention rate was achieved at the final assessment point. Despite sufficient statistical power to detect even small differences, no differences in smoking behaviors were detected between intervention and control schools. Daily smoking rates at grade 12 were 24.7% and 24.4% for girls at control and experimental schools; rates for boys were 26.7% and 26.3%. While these results were disappointing, a number of prevention scientists have cautioned against concluding that the social influences model is ineffective. Specific criticisms have been directed at the absence of important elements of social-influences strategies, such as communication and decision-making skills development, as well as questions about the setting issues, such as school-level risk for

smoking (Cameron et al., 2001; Sussman et al., 2001).

A school-based multi-drug prevention program, Life Skills Training (LST), was tested in over 56 public schools in the state of New York (Botvin et al., 1995). The intervention was based on specific drug refusal skill development in a context of a general competence enhancement approach that emphasized development of self-management and social skills. LST involved classroom instruction and rehearsals of decision-making, problem-solving, personal control, assertiveness and social skills, peer interaction skills, and drug refusal skills. General skills such as assertiveness were applied to specific drug related situations, such as peer pressure to use drugs. Self-esteem enhancement was also part of the curriculum. These lessons were provided in 15 sessions in the 7th grade, 10 sessions in 8th grade, and 5 sessions in 9th grade. Six thousand 7th grade students were randomized at the level of the school to one of three study conditions. Two experimental groups were compared to a control group. The two experimental groups delivered LST; however, teachers received formal one-day training and implementation feedback in the first group, while teachers in the second group received two hours of videotape training and no implementation feedback. At the follow-up in the 12th grade, smoking, alcohol, and marijuana use were all found to be significantly lower in the intervention group. Sixty percent of the original sample completed the 12th grade follow-up assessment (62%). Monthly smoking rates were 27% in the experimental group in which teachers received formal training and feedback compared to 33% in the control group (p < 0.05). Weekly smoking rates were also lower in the first experimental group (23% vs. 27%; p < 0.05). Smoking rates were also lower in the videotape trained teachers group compared to control, with monthly smoking rates of 26% vs. 33% (p < 0.01) and weekly smoking rates of 21% vs. 27% (p < 0.05). Outcomes varied considerably across schools, with better outcomes observed in schools delivering the intervention with higher fidelity to intervention component delivery, based on secondary analyses of the sub sample that received 60% or more of the intervention during grades 7 through 9.

Kellam et al. (1998) report on two early elementary school prevention interventions, the Good Behavior Game and the Mastery Learning curriculum. These interventions were designed to decrease aggressive and disruptive behaviors, which are associated with increased rates of tobacco use. Teachers in classrooms assigned to the Good Behavior Game intervention were instructed in behavior management strategies to reduce aggressive and disruptive behaviors such as fighting, shouting out of turn, and teasing. Children were placed in teams, and teams were rewarded with points when no member exhibited the proscribed behaviors during the game sessions. The Mastery Learning intervention consisted of an enriched academic curriculum designed to raise reading achievement scores. It included setting of high expectations, small instructional units, use of formative testing, and individualized correction methods. Schools were randomly assigned to either of the two intervention or control conditions and 2311 1st grade students were enrolled. At the seven-year post-intervention follow-up, a significant delay in smoking uptake was found for boys in the Good Behavior game condition compared to control (RR = 0.62, 95% confidence interval = 0.40; p = .04). Furthermore, results were better for well-behaved boys. A trend towards delays in smoking was also observed for the Mastery Learning group, but the difference was not significant compared to control.

School smoking risk level may be a determinant of intervention efficacy. Cameron et al. (1999) found that students at Canadian public elementary schools defined as "high risk" on the basis of 6th grade student smoking rates were responsive to a social influences program compared to control schools (end of 8th grade smoking rate of 16.0% versus 26.9%), while smoking rates in low risk schools did not significantly differ from control. A model-based estimated odds ratio for smoking by study condition suggested that a smoking rate of 20% or more predicted response to the intervention. Of note, in this study, results did not significantly differ based on the interventionist role (teachers versus nurses) or training method (self-preparation versus workshop training).

Although smoking uptake continues to occur throughout adolescence, the majority of randomized clinical prevention trials have targeted pre-adolescents. Project Towards No Drug Abuse is a motivation-skills-decision-making intervention model that was developed and tested in three separate field trials, involving 2468 students (Sussman et al., 2002). Multiple risk behaviors were addressed in this study, including tobacco use, use of alcohol, marijuana and other drugs, weapon carrying and victimization. The active intervention consisted of twelve 40-minute sessions delivered in the classroom. These lessons were systematically organized to address content derived from the theoretical model, including correction of myths about drug use, introduction to smoking cessation materials, and decision-making skills development. Sessions were designed to be interactive. Project Toward No Drug Abuse has been tested in the field in a variety of settings, with different combinations of content delivery channels. Sessions delivered by a study health educator were compared to those delivered by a combination school staff and a study health educator and to a student self-instruction condition, as well as to non-intervention controls. Two of the field trials involved "continuation" schools that provided service to high-risk students; 30-day cigarette use was more than twice the rate of that in the traditional high schools. While several other targeted risk behaviors were reduced in all three field trials, cigarette use was not affected in two of the field trials. In the third trial that involved continuation schools, students receiving health educator delivered sessions experienced lower rates of smoking compared with self-instruction and control classrooms (relative reduction of 27%). The follow-up period for each trial was 1 year.

Storr et al. (2002) tested a combined family and school-based approach in a prevention program with first grade students in a predominately African American public school system. This program was universal in its design, that is, it was delivered to all children, not just subsets of children at high risk for tobacco use initiation. Children were randomly assigned to one of three interventions: the Family –School Partnership classroom (FSP), classroom-centered intervention only (CC), and a control classroom. Early child behavioral risk factors for later substance use--problems with aggression, shyness, and attention--were targeted through enhancing teacher management skills in the CC intervention. The FSP intervention added teacher-parent communications and enhancement of parent management skills to the CC intervention components. Both the CC and FSP program resulted in lower rates of smoking at the 6 year follow-up: the CC intervention had an adjusted relative risk of 0.57 (95% CI = 0.34 – 0.96), and the FSP intervention had an adjusted relative risk of 0.69 (95% CI = 0.50 – 0.97).

Individualized, computer-tailored letters mailed to students at home resulted in lower six month smoking initiation and continuation rates in a study conducted in The Netherlands (Ausems et al., 2002). In this study, 3349 11-12 year old students were randomized to one of four conditions: 1) an in-school, 7 lesson prevention program implemented by teachers; 2) an out-of-school intervention consisting of 3 weekly tailored letters to students that were mailed to students' homes; 3) the in-school plus the out-of-school intervention; 4) control condition. Intervention content was based on a social influences program. The letters were computer-tailored based on student responses to a baseline questionnaire on smoking intention, behavior, attitudes, refusal self-efficacy, and social norms. At the 6 month outcome, self-reported smoking initiation and continuation rates were significantly lower in the out-of-school letter condition compared to control: 10.4% versus 18.1% and 13.1% versus 23.5%, respectively. The in-school program did not outperform the control condition, and it did not significantly reduce smoking in the combined condition when compared to the letters condition alone.

Few cost-effectiveness analyses of successful interventions have been published. Wang et al. (2001) report a saving of $13, 316 per life-year saved and $8,482 per quality-adjusted life year saved for the Project Toward No Tobacco Use (TNT) intervention cost of $16, 403 ($13.29 per student). TNT consisted of a 2-year efficacy trial of a 10-lesson school-based tobacco prevention curriculum for junior high students (Dent et al., 1995). Standard economic evaluation techniques included measurement of program implementation costs, estimation of the numbers of life years and quality adjusted life years saved, estimation of the lifetime medical costs for smokers versus nonsmokers, selection of costs in 1990 dollars to correspond with the intervention period, and discounting costs at a 3% annual rate in keeping with recommendations from the Panel on Cost-effectiveness in Health and Medicine (Gold et al., 1996). An intermediate outcome of number of established smokers that were prevented was used, and then this was translated into the number of life years and quality adjusted life years saved by the intervention. Life years saved was based upon Rogers and Powell-Griner's estimates that never smokers have a life expectancy of 2.1 years more than former smokers, 3.5 years more than light smokers, and 14.2 years longer than heavy smokers (Rogers and Powell-Griner 1991) In this analysis, Wang et al. (2001) started with 14 year olds, and modeled their smoking status at 26 years, with and without the TNT intervention at 26 years. Intervention costs included health educator training costs, health educator salaries, and manuals for the health educators and the students. The savings modeled in these analyses compare quite favorably to cost-effectiveness analyses of breast cancer screening and smoking cessation programs for adults.

Family-Based Interventions

Results are very promising for several recently published outcomes of family-based interventions. The Iowa Brief Family Intervention Study demonstrated significantly reduced rates of cigarette use in family-based interventions compared to control (Spoth et al., 2001). Both of the interventions, the Preparing for Drug Free Years and the Iowa Strengthening Families Program, addressed prevention of alcohol and marijuana use, in addition to tobacco use. Families were recruited from 33 randomly assigned school sites: 667 6th grade students were followed through grade 10.

The Preparing for Drug Free Years (PDFY) intervention condition was based on social control theory, and emphasized prosocial bonding as a key intervention component. Parent groups attended five weekly 2-hour sessions, with children joining parents for one of these sessions. Content focused on educating parents about risk factors for substance abuse, and building skills for establishing behavior guidelines, monitoring compliance and consequences,

managing conflict, enhancing parent-child bonds, and enhancing child participation in family tasks. Children were taught to resist peer influences for drug use, supported by parents.

The Iowa Strengthening Families Program (ISFP) was based on resiliency and social ecological models of adolescent development. Parents and children attended seven 2-hour sessions, the first hour of which parents and children met separately in groups, followed by joint parent-child groups. Parents were instructed in clarification of expectations, use of appropriate discipline, management of emotions and communications, and peer resistance. Skills were practiced in the parent-child sessions. Both intervention groups used videotapes to standardize content.

Overall attendance rates were high for both intervention conditions: 94% attended three or more sessions and 61% attended all five sessions for the PDFY intervention, and 94% attended five or more sessions and 62% attended all seven sessions for the ISFP intervention. Substance use was lower in both intervention conditions compared to control. The relative reduction in "ever" use of cigarettes compared to the control condition was 12.5% for the PDFY intervention and 34.8% for the ISFP intervention (the later was statistically significant at the $p < .01$). Increased emphasis on family interactions, with skills rehearsals within sessions, is hypothesized as the likely source for the better outcome of ISFP compared to PDFY.

The Family Matters Study, conducted by Bauman and colleagues (Bauman et al., 2001), is a population-based experimental study designed to prevent both alcohol and tobacco use. The intervention was based on the Health Belief Model, social learning theory, and value expectancy theory. Adolescents, ages 12 to 14 years, and their families (N = 1316) were recruited by a random digit dial procedure and randomized to intervention versus control condition. The intervention consisted of 4 successive mailed booklets followed by telephone contact by a health educator. Booklets focused on 1) motivation and engagement; 2) education about general family characteristics associated with risk and protection from substance use; 3) focus on tobacco and alcohol specific factors; and 4) resistance to pro-tobacco and alcohol peer and media influences. At the 12-month follow-up, smoking initiation rates were 16.4% lower in adolescents in the intervention condition compared to controls. This effect was moderated by race/ethnicity, with an effect size of 0.25 for non-Hispanic White youth and 0.15 for the whole sample. The program did not have a statistically significant effect on alcohol use. Of note, this intervention is relatively inexpensive, with a delivery cost of about $140 per parent-adolescent dyad, and could be widely disseminated with important public health value in reducing smoking uptake.

Wakefield et al. (2000) examined the impact of smoking restrictions on adolescent smoking in a cross-sectional survey study of 17, 287 high school students. Bans on smoking in the home were protective against smoking, even after controlling for the smoking status of the parents; students endorsing home smoking bans had a lower 30 day smoking prevalence rate (OR = 0.79; 95% CI = 0.67-0.91, p <0.001). Although the effect size was lower than with home smoking bans, community restrictions in public places were also protective (OR = 0.91; 95% CI = 0.83 – 0.99, p = 0.03). School smoking bans were only protective if the ban was perceived as being enforced (OR = 0.86; 95% CI = 0.77 – 0.94, p < 0.001).

Community-Based Prevention

Media campaigns and tobacco control policy interventions are the two major community-based strategies for reducing adolescent smoking. Youth appear to be particularly sensitive to increases in cigarette costs, with reductions of 7% per price increase of 10% modeled in econometric analyses, although studies of changes in trajectory of uptake are much needed (Chaloupka et al., 1998).

Flay et al. reviewed media research and added behavioral science constructs to generate recommendations for successful prevention campaigns (Flay et al., 1980). Elements judged to be critical to successful communication and behavior change included generation of motivation and interest, targeting of specific issues, repetition of messages across time and media sources, provision of specific information to support behavioral change, and provision of contacts for further information and help.

Although often conceptualized as universal interventions, media campaigns can also be targeted to high risk populations. Flynn et al. (1997) tested a media campaign addition to a school smoking campaign. The media component was specifically developed to reach youth at high risk. The sample consisted of 2718 4th – 6th grade students in 4 communities: the two communities receiving the media intervention plus the school-based intervention were matched to two communities receiving the school-based intervention only. Students were assessed prior to the interventions, with post-intervention follow-up five years later. High-risk students were characterized as having either personal smoking experience and/or the presence of regular smokers among family or peers (Worden et al., 1988). In addition, high-risk students were subdivided into "rebels" and "conformists," based on their attitudes about smoking. The media intervention provided television and radio messages that were developed with the input from focus groups conducted with students and from consultation with experts in mass media communications, psychologists, and health educators. Additional input from survey data and from showings of the prepared spots to students and a panel of experts were used to guide the final selection. The spots were aired with purchased time during high appeal programs, and they deliberately did not contain any unifying logos to prevent association with an authority source. The spots gave educational messages that were coordinated with the school intervention, and they were tailored for the range of developmental levels of the sample. The communities received an average of 540 television spots and 350 radio spots each of the four intervention years. Among high risk students, the combined media and school intervention resulted in lower smoking rates at follow-up (Odds Ratio = 0.71; Confidence Interval = 0.56, 0.90). As predicted, the higher risk youth also reported more television and radio use than the lower risk youth. Although smoking rates were lower in both high and low risk youth in the media intervention communities, the effect of the intervention was larger for the high-risk youth. Study limitations include problems with matching communities across regions of the country and missing data that resulted in loss of 52% of the sample in the final outcome analyses. Nonetheless, this study introduced a novel method for combining intervention channels with universal reach but with messages targeted to a high-risk population.

Health Care-Based Prevention

Preventive care guidelines have promoted smoking prevention in pediatric health care for over a decade (Glynn, 1989). Smoking cessation interventions by internists and other adult health care providers effectively increase adult smoking cessation rates, but prevention of smoking in pediatric settings has not been demonstrated (Fiore et al., 1996). Our knowledge of guideline implementation is largely based on cross-sectional surveys of physicians and patients.

Tobacco control counseling does not appear to be routine. Only 25% of adolescents and young adults in a large, nationally representative sample recalled any health care provider comments about smoking (Baker, 1995). Less than half of the adolescents surveyed in a large longitudinal study of smoking risk factors in Memphis reported recall of physician advice not to smoke, and only 43.2% recalled physician screening for smoking status (Alfano et al., 2002). Physician self-report surveys tend to result in higher counseling rates. Thorndike et al. (1999) analyzed data from the 1991-1996 National Ambulatory Medical care Surveys (5087 MDs; 16,648 visits), and found screening rates of 72.4% and counseling rates of only 1.6% for all adolescents aged 11-21. Screening and counseling rates did not increase across the survey years. The counseling rate for adolescents who were known to be smokers was also quite low, at 16.9% of visits. In a 1999 survey of pediatricians and family practitioners in western New York state, physicians reported asking most adolescents about smoking status (91%) and reinforcing abstinence with most nonsmokers (84%), but inquiries about parental and peer smoking status were lower (56% and 41%, respectively) (Klein et al., 2001). Zapka et al. (1999) found that the majority of pediatricians in her Massachusetts sample endorsed prevention counseling with children and adolescents, although counseling rates were not independently validated. However, other studies of pediatric health care provider screening and counseling practices report much lower rates, e.g. tobacco counseling was provided during only 1.5% of all visits and 4.1% of well child visits included in the National Ambulatory Medical Care Survey and the National Hospital Ambulatory Medical Care Survey (Tanski et al., 2003).

Tailoring

Most of the prevention studies that have been discussed are intended as universal reach and intervention strategies. Siddiqui et al. (1996) examined characteristics of study participants in a number of longitudinal prevention programs and reported that study dropouts were more likely to be smokers. Dropouts were more likely to have lower academic achievement, to have lower levels of resistance skills, and to have lower levels of tobacco and health knowledge. Among ethnic groups, Black youth were more likely to be missing at follow-up.

Can tailoring of prevention programs improve prevention outcomes? In addition to concerns raised by differential attrition rates in studies, the need for tailoring is suggested by the variation in tobacco use rates and trends across sociodemographic groups as well as our knowledge of other risk and protective factors.

Through the early 1990s, our knowledge of smoking uptake processes has been largely based on studies of White, suburban populations. Similarly, effective interventions were typically tested with White majority samples. Focus groups conducted by Parker and colleagues with African American and Latino adolescents did not find differences in reasons for smoking or for youth identified ideas for prevention programming compared to those described by White youth in prior studies (Parker et al., 1996). In contrast, other investigators have described different smoking uptake patterns when modeling ethnicity and family influences as predictors, and family influences may play a stronger role relative to peer influences in some minority populations (Kegler et al., 2002; Robinson and Klesges, 1997; Sussman et al., 1987).

Botvin et al. demonstrated effectiveness for a social resistance/competence enhancement intervention in a predominately Hispanic, urban sample of 7th grade students (Botvin et al., 1992). The intervention, previously tested with White, suburban students, was revised with modifications in reading level, illustrative examples, and situations used for skills training (Botvin et al., 1989b). There was no direct comparison of the efficacy of the intervention between ethnic groups, but a mediating model suggested that the same processes were active in this predominately Hispanic sample as were active in the earlier White samples. Botvin et al. (1989) also demonstrated feasibility and acceptability of a similar intervention in a predominately Black, urban sample.

Sussman et al. (1995) tested smoking prevention videotapes developed to target African American adolescents. Two videotapes were compared to each other in one study, and both videotapes were compared to discussion groups led by an African American graduate student in the second study. One videotape was designed to be for generic appeal, and the other was designed for target audience appeal. The storyline was similar in both of the tapes, but clothing, music, setting, and language differed. Based on pre- and post-test assessments, both videotapes were well received, but neither appeared to have a differential effect on short-term smoking outcomes than the discussion groups. As in the previously described study, comparisons were not made across ethnic groups.

Direct comparisons of targeted versus universal school-based programs for high-risk youth are needed, but universal programs have been demonstrated to be effective in reducing smoking. Griffin et al. (2003) reported on an analysis of a subset of high risk youth (N = 802) included in a randomized clinical trial of the Life Skills Training Program for prevention of multiple drugs of abuse (program previously described). Risk was defined in two ways: "social risk" on the basis of number of friends who use, and "academic risk" on the basis of school performance. At baseline in 7th grade, the rate of smoking was 10%, with no significant difference between experimental and control groups. Attrition from the study was predicted from pre-intervention lifetime smoking history. The outcome analysis was based on a composite smoking behavior score; a significant effect was observed for the intervention condition compared to control.

Although gender-based differences in smoking patterns have been observed, literature searches did not identify interventions that were specifically tailored to these differences. Similarly, our literature searches did not identify tobacco-specific interventions targeted and tailored to families at high-risk for child tobacco uptake, although risk factors such as parent smoking behaviors and parenting styles have been incorporated into the universal family-based interventions that have been described.

SUMMARY AND CONCLUSION

The field of youth smoking prevention has benefited from important advances over the last decade. Experimental testing of theory driven interventions have provided promising strategies for reduction of youth smoking. Progress has been made in the development of promising strategies for reaching minority youth. Several studies have begun the process of testing interventions targeted to youth at high risk for smoking due to behavioral concerns, as well as analyzing the efficacy of universal programs in a subset of high risk youth. While the preponderance of evidence-based studies continues to use the school as the intervention delivery channel, interventions have moved beyond the classroom, to family and community, with encouraging results. In addition, interventions that combine delivery channels have been added to the list of prevention strategies.

Despite the successes of the last two decades, considerable room remains for innovation in this field. The exploration of targeted interventions is incomplete and may become particularly salient for catching the youth who continue to smoke despite implementation of the best universal strategies. Even universal strategies have not exhausted theoretical approaches, such as identification and intervention with "hot" (affective) and "cold" (rational decision-making) processes involved in risk behaviors, as suggested by Clayton and others (Clayton et al., 2000). Psychiatric symptoms such as depressed mood, stress, attention problems, and conduct problems are known to be associated with smoking in studies of adolescents as well as adults, yet few prevention or early intervention strategies have measured these factors and compared them in smoking versus nonsmoking youth (Upadhyaya et al., 2002). Advances in our understanding of genetic processes of youth smoking uptake are anticipated in the near future, and these will likely require innovations in intervention approaches, including careful attention to the ethics of clinical communication and policy associated with behavioral genetics.

Improved strategies are needed to disseminate and sustain successful interventions. Some of the solutions for this may require a shift in thinking from short term to long term planning, even as interventions are initially conceptualized and developed. Swisher (2000) has proposed guidelines for sustainability of prevention programs that include systematic planning for institutionalization of successful interventions, professional development for practitioners and researchers, long term and early planning for sustainability, less crisis orientation, and community specific adaptations of interventions. Given the number and range of evidence-based interventions for smoking prevention, this shift is well justified.

REFERENCES

Alfano CM, Zbikowski SM, Robinson LA, Klesges RC, Scarinci IC (2002) Adolescent reports of physician counseling for smoking. Pediatrics 109:E47.

American Psychiatric Association (1994). Diagnostic and Statistical Manual of Mental Disorders, Fourth Edition [DSM-IV]. Washington, DC: American Psychiatric Press.

Ausems M, Mesters I, van Breukelen G, De Vries H (2002) Short-term effects of a randomized computer-based out-of-school smoking prevention trial aimed at elementary schoolchildren. Prev Med 34:581-9.

Baker L (1995) Health-care provider advice on tobacco use to persons aged 10-22 Years- United States, 1993. MMWR 44:826-30.

Bauman KE, Foshee VA, Ennett ST, Pemberton M, Hicks KA, King TS, Koch GG (2001) The influence of a family program on adolescent tobacco and alcohol use. Am J Public Health 91:604-10.

Botvin GJ, Baker E, Dusenbury L, Botvin EM, Diaz T (1995) Long-term follow-up results of a randomized drug abuse prevention trial in a white middle-class population. JAMA 273:1106-12.

Botvin GJ, Batson HW, Witts-Vitale S, Bess V, Baker E, Dusenbury L (1989a) A psychosocial approach to smoking prevention for urban black youth. Public Health Rep 104:573-82.

Botvin GJ, Dusenbury L, Baker E, James-Ortiz S, Botvin EM, Kerner J (1992) Smoking prevention among urban minority youth: assessing effects on outcome and mediating variables. Health Psychol 11:290-9.

Botvin GJ, Dusenbury L, Baker E, James-Ortiz S, Kerner J (1989b) A skills training approach to smoking prevention among Hispanic youth. J Behav Med 12:279-96.

Cameron R, Best JA, Brown KS (2001) Re: Hutchinson Smoking Prevention Project: long-term randomized trial in school-based tobacco use prevention--results on smoking. J Natl Cancer Inst 93:1267-8; discussion 1269-71.

Cameron R, Brown KS, Best JA, Pelkman CL, Madill CL, Manske SR, Payne ME (1999) Effectiveness of a social influences smoking prevention program as a function of provider type, training method, and school risk. Am J Public Health 89:1827-31.

Centers for Disease Control and Prevention (1994) Guidelines for school health programs to prevent tobacco use and addiction. J Sch Health 64:353-60.

Chaloupka FJ (1998) Economics. Addicted to Nicotine: A National Research Forum, pp 39-41.

Clayton RR, Scutchfield FD, Wyatt SW (2000) Hutchinson Smoking Prevention Project: a new gold standard in prevention science requires new transdisciplinary thinking. J Natl Cancer Inst 92:1964-5.

Dent CW, Sussman S, Stacy AW, Craig S, Burton D, Flay BR (1995) Two-year behavior outcomes of project towards no tobacco use. J Consult Clin Psychol 63:676-7.

DiFranza JR, Rigotti NA, McNeill AD, Ockene JK, Savageau JA, St Cyr D, Coleman M (2000) Initial symptoms of nicotine dependence in adolescents. Tob Control 9:313-9.

Fiore M, Bailey W, Cohen S, Dorfman S, Goldstein M, Gritz E, Heyman R, Hollbrook J, Jaen C, Kottke T, Lando H, Mecklenbrg R, Mullen P, Nett L, Robinson L, Stitzer M, Tommasello A, Villejo L, Wewers M (1996) Smoking Cessation: Clinical Practice Guideline No.

18. Rockville, MD: Agency for Health Care Policy and Research, Public Health Service, U.S. Department of Health And Human Services.

Flay BR, DiTecco D, Schlegel RP (1980) Mass media in health promotion: an analysis using an extended information-processing model. Health Educ Q 7:127-47.

Flynn BS, Worden JK, Secker-Walker RH, Pirie PL, Badger GJ, Carpenter JH (1997) Long-term responses of higher and lower risk youths to smoking prevention interventions. Prev Med 26:389-94.

Glynn TJ, Manley MW (1989) How to Help Your Patients Stop Smoking. A National Cancer Institute Manual for Physicians. Bethesda, Maryland: Smoking, Tobacco and Cancer Program, Division of Cancer Prevention and Control, National Cancer Institute.

Gold MR, Gold SR, Weinstein MC, eds. (1996) Cost-effectiveness in health and medicine. New York, NY: Oxford University Press.

Griffin KW, Botvin GJ, Nichols TR, Doyle MM (2003) Effectiveness of a universal drug abuse prevention approach for youth at high risk for substance use initiation. Prev Med 36:1-7.

Grunbaum JA, Kann L, Kinchen SA, Williams B, Ross JG, Lowry R, Kolbe L (2002) Youth risk behavior surveillance--United States, 2001. J Sch Health 72:313-28.

Guo (2000) Family Influences on the Risk of Daily Smoking Initiation from Adolescence to Young Adulthood. Boston, MA: NIDA.

Johnston L, O'Malley P, Bachman J (2002a) Monitoring the Future National Survey Results on Drug Use, 1975-2001. Bethesda, MD: National Institute on Drug Abuse.

Johnston L, O'Malley P, Bachman J (2002b) Teen smoking declines sharply in 2002, more than offsetting large increases in the early 1990s. Ann Arbor, MI: University of Michigan News and Information Services.

Johnston LD, O'Malley PM, Bachman JG (2002c) Monitoring the Future National Results on Adolescent Drug Use: Overview of Key Findings, 2001. Bethesda, MD: National Institute on Drug Abuse.

Kegler MC, McCormick L, Crawford M, Allen P, Spigner C, Ureda J (2002) An exploration of family influences on smoking among ethnically diverse adolescents. Health Educ Behav 29:473-90.

Kellam SG, Anthony JC (1998) Targeting early antecedents to prevent tobacco smoking: findings from an epidemiologically based randomized field trial. Am J Public Health 88:1490-5.

Kendler KS, Neale MC, MacLean CJ, Heath AC, Eaves LJ, Kessler RC (1993) Smoking and major depression. A causal analysis. Arch Gen Psychiatry 50:36-43.

Killen, JD, Ammerman S, Rojas N, Varady J, Haydel F, Robinson TN (2001). Do adolescent smokers experience withdrawal effects when deprived of nicotine? Exp Clin Psychopharmacol 9(2): 172-82.

Klein JD, Levine LJ, Allan MJ (2001) Delivery of smoking prevention and cessation services to adolescents. Arch Pediatr Adolesc Med 155:597-602.

Lynch B, Bonnie R, Committee on Preventing Nicotine Addiction in Children and Youths, Institute of Medicine (1994) Growing Up Tobacco Free: Preventing Nicotine Addiction in Children and Youth. Washington, D.C.: National Academy Press.

Modesto-Lowe V (2002) Illy users in Connecticut: two case reports. Subst Abus 23:255-7.

Moriarty AL (1996) What's "new" in street drugs: "illy". J Pediatr Health Care 10:41-3.

National Institute on Drug Abuse (2000) Bulletin Board, NIDA Notes, 15(1).

Parker VC, Sussman S, Crippens DL, Scholl D, Elder P (1996) Qualitative development of smoking prevention programming for minority youth. Addict Behav 21:521-5.

Peterson AV, Jr., Kealey KA, Mann SL, Marek PM, Sarason IG (2000) Hutchinson Smoking Prevention Project: long-term randomized trial in school-based tobacco use prevention--results on smoking. J Natl Cancer Inst 92:1979-91.

Pomerleau OF (1995) Individual differences in sensitivity to nicotine: implications for genetic research on nicotine dependence. Behav Genet 25:161-77.

Prokhorov AV, Hudmon KS, de Moor, CA, Kelder SH, COnroy JL, Ordway N (2001). Nicotine dependence, withdrawal symptoms, and adolescents' readiness to quit smoking. Nicotine Tob Res 3(2): 151-5.

Robinson LA, Klesges RC (1997) Ethnic and gender differences in risk factors for smoking onset. Health Psychol 16: 499-505.

Rogers RG, Powell-Griner E (1991) Life expectancies of cigarette smokers and nonsmokers in the United States. Soc Sci Med 32(10): 1151-9.

Rojas NL, Killen JD, Haydel KF, Robinson TN (1998) Nicotine dependence among adolescent smokers. Arch Pediatr Adolesc Med 152(2): 151-6.

Shadel, WG, Shiffman S, Niaura R, Nichter M, Abrams DA (2000) Current models of nicotine dependence: what is known and what is needed to advance understanding of tobacco etiology among youth. Drug Alcohol Depend 59 Suppl 1: S9-22.

Siddiqui O, Flay BR, Hu FB (1996) Factors affecting attrition in a longitudinal smoking prevention study. Prev Med 25:554-60.

Spoth RL, Redmond C, Shin C (2001) Randomized trial of brief family interventions for general populations: adolescent substance use outcomes 4 years following baseline. J Consult Clin Psychol 69:627-42.

Storr CL, Ialongo NS, Kellam SG, Anthony JC (2002) A randomized controlled trial of two primary school intervention strategies to prevent early onset tobacco smoking. Drug Alcohol Depend 66:51-60.

Sullivan PF, Kendler KS (1999) The genetic epidemiology of smoking. Nicotine Tob Res 1:S51-7; discussion S69-70.

Sussman S, Dent CW, Flay BR, Hansen WB, Johnson CA (1987) Psychosocial predictors of cigarette smoking onset by white, black, Hispanic, and Asian adolescents in Southern California. MMWR Morb Mortal Wkly Rep 36 (Suppl 4):11S-16S.

Sussman S, Dent CW, Stacy AW (2002) Project towards no drug abuse: a review of the findings and future directions. Am J Health Behav 26:354-65.

Sussman S, Hansen WB, Flay BR, Botvin GJ (2001) Re: Hutchinson Smoking Prevention Project: long-term randomized trial in school-based tobacco use prevention--results on smoking. J Natl Cancer Inst 93:1267; discussion 1269-71.

Sussman S, Parker VC, Lopes C, Crippens DL, Elder P, Scholl D (1995) Empirical development of brief smoking prevention videotapes which target African-American adolescents. Int J Addict 30:1141-64.

Swisher JD (2000) Sustainability of prevention. Addictive Behaviors 25:965-73.

Tanski SE, Klein JD, Winickoff JP, Auinger P, Weitzman M (2003) Tobacco counseling at well-child and tobacco-influenced illness visits: opportunities for improvement. Pediatrics 111:E162-7.

Thorndike AN, Ferris TG, Stafford RS, Rigotti NA (1999) Rates of U.S.

physicians counseling adolescents about smoking. J Natl Cancer Inst 91:1857-62.

Upadhyaya HP, Deas D, Brady KT, Kruesi M (2002). Cigarette smoking and psychiatric comorbidity in children and adolescents. J Am Acad Child Adolesc Psychaitry 41(11): 1294-305.

U.S. Department of Health and Human Services (1994) Preventing Tobacco Use Among Young People: A Report of the Surgeon General. Atlanta, GA: U.S.Department of Health and Human Services, Public Health Service, Centers for Disease Control and Prevention, National Center for Chronic Disease Prevention and Health Promotion, Office on Smoking and Health.

U.S. Department of Health and Human Services, Substance Abuse and Mental Health Services Administration (2002) Results from the 2001 National Household Survey on Drug Abuse: Volume I. Summary of National Findings: NHSDA Series H-17. Rockville, MD: Office of Applied Studies.

Wakefield M, Banham D, Martin J, Ruffin R, McCaul K, Badcock N (2000) Restrictions on smoking at home and urinary cotinine levels among children with asthma. Am J Prev Med 19:188-92.

Wang LY, Crossett LS, Lowry R, Sussman S, Dent CW (2001) Cost-effectiveness of a school-based tobacco-use prevention program. Arch Pediatr Adolesc Med 155:1043-50.

Weiner AL (2000) Emerging drugs of abuse in Connecticut. Conn Med 64:19-23.

Worden JK, Flynn BS, Geller BM, Chen M, Shelton LG, Secker-Walker RH, Solomon DS, Solomon LJ, Couchey S, Costanza MC (1988) Development of a smoking prevention mass media program using diagnostic and formative research. Prev Med 17:531-58.

Zapka JG, Fletcher K, Pbert L, Druker SK, Ockene JK, Chen L (1999) The perceptions and practices of pediatricians: tobacco intervention. Pediatrics 103:e65.

EVIDENCE-BASED RECOMMENDATIONS FOR THE TREATMENT OF TOBACCO DEPENDENCE

Ludmila Cofta-Gunn, Kelli L. Wright, David W. Wetter

INTRODUCTION

Smoking related diseases claim an estimated 440,000 American lives each year (CDC, 1994a) and smoking is the leading cause of preventable morbidity and mortality in the United States (CDC, 1994b). Adult male and female smokers lose an average of 13.2 and 14.5 years of life, respectively, because they smoke (CDC, 2002a). The health benefits of quitting smoking are substantial and include a decreased risk of lung cancer, other cancers, heart disease, stroke, and chronic obstructive pulmonary disease and emphysema (Godtfredsen et al., 2002) (See Volume II chapters 1, 4, 5, 6). Smoking cessation has also been shown to decrease risk for a variety of other conditions and disorders including slowed healing of wounds, infertility, and peptic ulcer disease (http://www.lungusa.org/tobacco/secondhand _factsheet99.html, 2003). Moreover, environmental tobacco smoke (ETS) is listed as a known human carcinogen, indicating that there is a cause and effect relationship between exposure to tobacco smoke and human cancer incidence (NCI, 1999). ETS causes about 3,000 lung cancer deaths annually among adult nonsmokers in the United States and as many as 35,000 deaths from ischemic heart disease (CDC, 2002a). ETS has also been linked to serious respiratory problems in children, as well as increased risk for sudden infant death syndrome (CDC, 2002a).

Smoking imposes significant economic costs on society. Each pack of cigarettes sold in the United States has been estimated to cost the nation $7.18 in medical care costs and lost productivity (CDC, 2002a). Estimates suggest that smoking causes over $150 billion in annual health-related economic losses including $81.9 billion in mortality-related productivity losses and $75.5 billion in excess medical expenditures (CDC, 2002a). Per year, the economic cost for each smoker in the United States is estimated to be $3,391 (CDC, 2002a).

Unfortunately, although the prevalence of smoking declined 40 percent between 1965 and 1990, it has been virtually unchanged thereafter (CDC, 1999). Despite concerted public health efforts, the proportion of smokers in 2000 (23.2%) is only slightly lower than that reported in 1990 (25.5%) and 1995 (24.7%; http://www.lungusa.org/data/ 2002, 2003). The reason why smoking prevalence remains unchanged may be that both cessation and initiation rates have stabilized in the last several years (CDC, 2002b) and may have reached an equilibrium reflected by stable prevalence rates. Smoking prevalence is significantly higher among men (27.6%) than among women (22.1%) and in certain sociodemographic groups—34% among Alaskan American natives; 35.4% among individuals who attended but did not complete high school; and 29% among individuals 44 years of age or younger (CDC, 1999). Higher smoking prevalence is strongly associated with lower socioeconomic status (SES) and with comorbid psychiatric disorders such as depression, substance abuse, and schizophrenia (Lasser et al., 2000).

Despite the health and societal consequences of smoking, many health care providers fail to treat tobacco use consistently and effectively. Smoking status was identified in only 67% of primary healthcare visits and help in quitting smoking was offered on only 21% percent of smokers' clinic visits (Thorndike et al., 1998). Furthermore, when treatment is provided, it is typically to those smokers already diagnosed with tobacco-related diseases (Thorndike et al., 1998). These findings are surprising in light of substantial evidence that all smoking cessation treatments are known to be extremely cost-effective relative to other disease prevention interventions and disease treatments. For this reason, they are referred to as the "gold standard" of chronic disease prevention interventions (Fiore et al., 2000). Intensive interventions may have a lower cost per life-year saved than brief interventions (Cromwell et al., 1997), but brief treatments are cost-effective as well (Fiore et al., 1995; Glynn et al., 1990; Jaen et al., 1997).

The Agency for Health Care Policy and Research addressed the smoking problem by conducting a research project that was published as the *Smoking Cessation Clinical Practice Guideline* (Fiore et al., 1996). That document was later updated as the *Treating Tobacco Use and Dependence Clinical Practice Guideline* (the *Guideline;* Fiore et al., 2000) by the U.S. Department of Health and Human Services. This chapter reviews results from the *Guideline* and highlights its primary recommendations. Developments in smoking cessation clinical research that have been published after the *Guideline* are then discussed, focusing on a systematic review of randomized controlled trials of pharmacologic and behavioral approaches to treatment. This review results in evidence-based recommendations for smoking cessation interventions. Effective treatments are then summarized and organized as to how they might be used within three different intervention programs. Key areas for future research are discussed and resources for health care professionals are listed. The chapter focuses on cessation rather than prevention - a topic that necessitates its own review (see Volume 1, Chapter 8).

CLINICAL PRACTICE GUIDELINE
Guideline origins

The original *Guideline* (Fiore et al., 1996)

became an influential blueprint for treating nicotine dependence and brought about significant changes in numerous areas such as the education of clinicians, the monitoring of tobacco use status, and provision of treatment in health care settings. Important new research on tobacco use and treatment that was published subsequent to the original *Guideline* necessitated an update of that document. The revised *Guideline* was published in 2000 (Fiore et al., 2000) and covered research published from 1975 to 1999. The *Guideline* is the most comprehensive compilation and synthesis of research on the treatment of nicotine dependence to date.

Guideline Development Procedures and Methods

The 2000 *Guideline* was developed by a panel of experts in tobacco use and dependence and was influenced by two goals: (1) identify effective treatment strategies, and (2) formulate easy to disseminate recommendations appropriate for diverse clinical settings and patient populations. Peer-reviewed randomized placebo controlled clinical trials were judged to provide the highest level of evidence for the evaluation of treatment efficacy, although recommendations were based on the available evidence and expert opinion if randomized clinical trials were unavailable. The *Guideline* evaluated treatments for tobacco users as well as interventions targeting clinician and health care delivery system behavior. Primary tobacco use prevention and community-level interventions were not addressed by the *Guideline*.

The analytic technique used in the *Guideline* was meta-analysis. This statistical approach evaluates the effect of a selected variable (i.e., treatment) on outcome (i.e., smoking status) across a range of similar studies. The selection of studies included in the meta-analyses was accomplished in several steps. Only peer-reviewed, random-ized controlled studies of a tobacco-use treatment published in English between January 1, 1975 and January 1, 1999 where randomization took place at the patient level and follow-up results were reported for at least 5 months after quitting were considered. Over 180 eligible articles were identified and over 500 additional articles were utilized as well.

Outcome data included abstinence at follow-ups of between 5 months and 3 years. Both biochemically verified abstinence and self-reported abstinence without biochemical verification were included. Follow-up data included "intent-to-treat" where the number of participants abstinent at follow-up was divided by number of participants randomized to treatment (with participants lost to follow-up being considered smokers), as well as "completer" data where the denominator was the number of participants who had completed treatment. Other types of follow-up data (i.e., non-abstinence related data) were not included.

The meta-analyses were conducted using logistic regression with random effects modeling. The initial step was the selection of eligible studies relevant to the topic being evaluated. For instance, in evaluating self-help treatments, the first step was the selection of studies that included a self-help intervention. Next, the treatment and control groups in each study were evaluated for confounders, and the confounded groups were eliminated from analyses. At least two studies with suitable control conditions had to be available for a topic to be included in the meta-analyses, and the analyzed treatment or variable had to be similar enough in the selected studies to justify combining the studies.

The results of meta-analyses were evaluated using odds ratios and 95% confidence intervals. Comparisons of odds ratios were only made within the same meta-analysis. Additionally, abstinence percentages and 95% confidence intervals were computed to facilitate interpretation.

Recommendations resulting from meta-analyses included strength-of-evidence ratings based on the following criteria:

A – Multiple well-designed randomized clinical trials; direct relevance of the trials to the recommendation; consistent pattern of findings.

B – Some evidence from randomized clinical trials in support of the recommendation; scientific support not optimal (e.g., too few trials, trials inconsistent, trials not directly relevant).

C – Consensus of the *Guideline* panel in the absence of relevant randomized controlled trials.

The same scales rating strength of evidence were used throughout the chapter. Treatment effectiveness was evaluated based on significant differences in abstinence rates.

Clinical Treatment Model

The *Guideline* is based on a treatment model designed to be implemented in health care settings (Figure 1). The model emphasizes that each patient seen by a health care professional in a clinical setting should be assessed for, and have documented, his or her tobacco use status (current, former, or never user). Persons who have never smoked or who previously smoked but have been abstinent for an extended period of time do not need intervention. Former smokers who quit recently should receive a relapse prevention intervention. Current smokers should be advised to quit and their motivation to quit should be assessed. Those willing to quit should either receive a brief clinical intervention or a referral to an intensive clinical treatment. A typical brief clinical intervention includes help with a quit plan including setting a quit date, practical counseling that teaches problem solving and coping skills, help with intra- and extra-

Figure 1. Treatment Model for Tobacco Use and Dependence

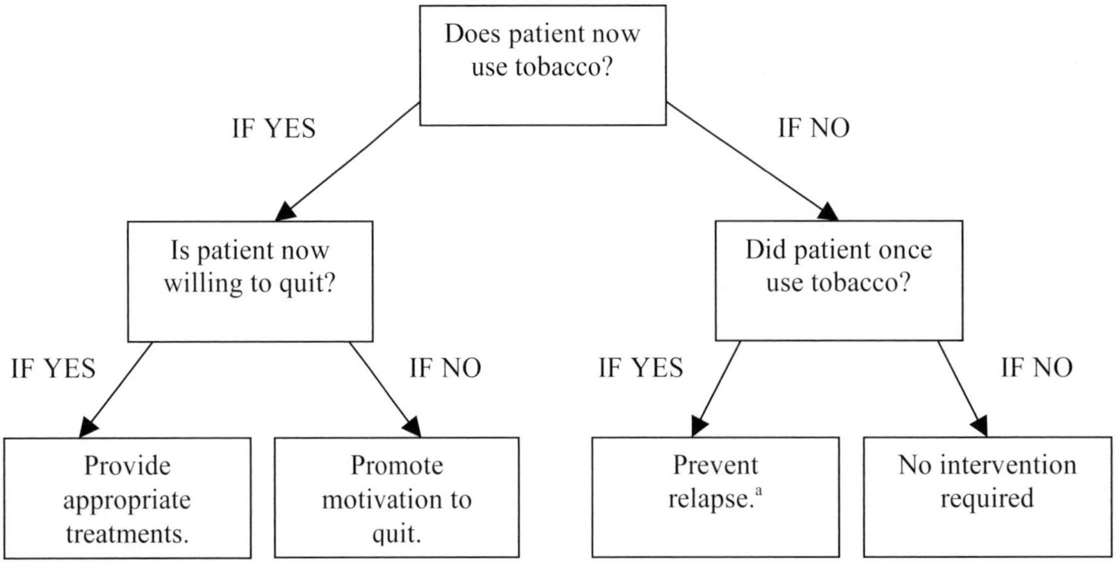

ᵃ Relapse prevention interventions are not necessary in the case of the adult who has not used tobacco for many years

Source: Fiore, M. C., et al. (2000). Treating tobacco use and dependence . Rockville, MD: U.S. Department of Health and Human Services, Public Health Service, Agency for Health Care Policy and Research.

treatment social support, recommendations for pharmacotherapy except in special circumstances, and supplementary materials. Follow-up contact should be scheduled by phone or in person. Intensive nicotine dependence treatments are provided by clinicians specially trained in such approaches.

Smokers unwilling to quit should be offered a brief intervention designed to enhance their motivation to quit. The intervention should point out why quitting is personally relevant, address acute, long-term, and environmental risks of smoking, emphasize the benefits of quitting, help identify impediments to quitting, and address how to overcome those impediments. This intervention should be repeated every time a

smoker, who is unwilling to quit, appears at a clinic.

Chronic Disease Model

The *Guideline* views nicotine dependence as a chronic disease. Like other chronic diseases, nicotine dependence may consist of cycles of relapse and remission over an extended period of time. The *Guideline* emphasizes that a failure to acknowledge the chronic character of nicotine dependence may result in a failure to effectively treat this condition. On the other hand, an understanding of the relapsing nature of the disorder leads to the provision of ongoing rather than one-time care. A chronic disease model helps clinicians perceive relapse as a disease stage rather than a failure of either the clinician or patient. It also helps clinicians appreciate the importance of counseling smokers about their condition and offering them pharmacological treatments in the same way as is done for other chronic diseases.

Key Findings and Recommendations
Pharmacotherapy

The *Guideline* identified five first-line and two second-line smoking cessation medications, and encouraged the use of these medications except in special circumstances, such as medical counterindications, smoking less than 10 cigarettes a day, or pregnancy/breast feeding. Tobacco users attempting to quit should be encouraged to use one or a combination of efficacious pharmacological treatments. In the pharmacotherapy studies reviewed by the *Guideline*, participants typically received counseling. Thus, the *Guideline* encouraged the use of a multi-component approach with pharmacotherapy as a vital element of such an approach.

First-Line Medications

First-line medications have been proven safe and effective and have been approved by the U.S. Food and Drug Administration for the treatment of smoking cessation. These pharmacotherapies have demonstrated empirical efficacy and should be considered first for treatment of nicotine dependence except in cases of contraindications.

Bupropion SR (Sustained Release Bupropion)

Two large multicenter studies met criteria for inclusion in the analysis comparing bupropion SR to placebo. It was shown that use of bupropion SR doubles long-term rates of abstinence relative to placebo medication. Recommendation: Bupropion SR is an efficacious pharmacotherapy for smoking cessation that smokers should be encouraged to use (Strength of Evidence = A).

Nicotine Replacement Therapy (NRT)

Four separate analyses were conducted to compare the nicotine gum, inhaler, spray, and patch to placebo, respectively. Results demonstrated that gum improves long-term abstinence by approximately 30-80% as compared to placebo gum, whereas the inhaler, spray, and patch more than double long-term rates of abstinence over that of placebo. Recommendation: NRT is available in the form of gum, inhaler, nasal spray, and transdermal patch. All four types have been proven efficacious for smoking cessation and their use should be encouraged (Strength of Evidence = A).

There were three studies that met criteria for inclusion in the analysis of nicotine patch use in over-the-counter settings, which revealed that patch use nearly doubled abstinence rates when compared with placebo. Recommendation: Over-the-counter nicotine patch treatment is more efficacious than placebo and its use should be encouraged (Strength of Evidence = B).

Results of two nicotine gum studies suggest that the 4 mg gum is more effective than the 2 mg gum in highly dependent smokers. Recommendation: Nicotine gum should be offered in the 4 mg rather than 2 mg dosage to highly dependent smokers (Strength of Evidence = B).

Second-Line Medications

Although second-line pharmacotherapies have evidence of efficacy for the treatment of tobacco dependence, they play a more limited role than first-line medications. This is because the FDA has not approved their indication for tobacco dependence treatment and there are more concerns regarding potential side effects.

Clonidine

The meta-analysis of five studies comparing clonidine to placebo demonstrated that the use of clonidine approximately doubles abstinence.

Recommendation: Clonidine is an effective smoking cessation intervention and may be used under a physician's care as a second-line treatment for tobacco dependence (Strength of Evidence = A).

Nortriptyline

The analysis of nortriptyline included two studies. Results suggested that nortriptyline increases abstinence rates relative to placebo.

Recommendation: Nortriptyline is an efficacious smoking cessation intervention and may be used under a physician's care as a second-line treatment for tobacco dependence (Strength of Evidence = B).

Combination Nicotine Replacement Therapy

Three studies met selection criteria and were included in the analysis of combination nicotine replacement therapy. The results showed that combination therapy increased long-term rates of abstinence relative to nicotine replacement monotherapy. Because there is limited data regarding the safety of such treatment, its use is recommended only with patients unable to quit with a single type of pharmacotherapy.

Recommendation: Combining the nicotine patch with either the nicotine gum or nicotine nasal spray is a more effective treatment than a single form of nicotine replacement. Patients should be encouraged to use combined treatment if they are unable to quit using a single type of first-line pharmacotherapy (Strength of Evidence = B).

Behavioral Treatments
Brief Clinical Interventions

Of the seven studies included in the meta-analysis of physician advice to quit smoking, the modal length of intervention was 3 minutes or less. Results showed that such brief physician advice significantly increased long-term smoking abstinence. A meta-analysis of session length (see below) revealed that both minimal (3 minutes or less) and low-intensity (3-10 minutes) interventions significantly increased abstinence rates. A separate analysis of total contact time (see below) confirmed that interventions lasting 1-3 and 4-30 minutes were effective.

Recommendation: Physician advice to quit is effective. All physicians should strongly advise every patient who smokes to quit (Strength of Evidence = A).

Recommendation: Minimal and low-intensity interventions are effective. All tobacco users should be offered at least minimal intervention (Strength of Evidence = A).

Intensity of Clinical Interventions

Intensity of clinical interventions involving person-to-person contact was examined in three separate meta-analyses addressing session length (forty three studies), total contact time (thirty five studies), and the number of sessions (forty five studies). The analyses revealed a strong dose-response relation between treatment intensity and outcome. Sessions longer than 10 minutes, total contact time of 30 minutes or more, and at least four sessions per treatment appeared particularly effective.

Recommendation: More intensive inter-ventions (both in terms of session length and total contact time) demonstrate a greater effect than less intensive interventions and should be used when feasible (Strength of Evidence = A).

Recommendation: Four or more sessions of in-person treatment appear particularly effective in increasing rates of smoking abstinence. Whenever possible, clinicians should meet with individuals quitting tobacco four times or more (Strength of Evidence = A).

Clinician Type

Twenty-nine studies were included in the meta-analysis of the effectiveness of different types of clinicians. Results are consistent across a variety of clinicians, with no increase in abstinence rates associated with any one type of clinician.

Recommendation: Interventions delivered by various types of clinicians are effective. All clinicians should provide interventions for smoking cessation (Strength of Evidence = A).

Thirty-seven studies met selection criteria and were included in the examination of the effectiveness of incorporating multiple clinicians in smoking cessation interventions. The term, multiple clinicians, refers to number of different "types" of clinicians, not the total number of clinicians regardless of type. Specifically, research shows that treatment delivered by multiple types of clinicians significantly increases abstinence relative to treatment where there is no clinician. Data also demonstrates a nonsignificant trend for increased effectiveness of multiple types of clinicians as compared to a single type.

Recommendation: Interventions delivered by multiple clinician types are more effective than those delivered by one type of clinician. Therefore, the delivery of interventions by more than a single type of clinician is encouraged (Strength of Evidence = C).

Treatment Format

The analysis of fifty-eight studies examining different types of formats demonstrated that proactive telephone, group, and individual counseling all increase smoking abstinence rates as compared to no intervention.

Recommendation: Proactive telephone, group, and individual counseling are effective and should be used in smoking cessation interventions (Strength of Evidence = A).

Fifty-four studies showed that treatments using more than two formats increased abstinence rates compared to those incorporating only a single type of format.

Recommendation: Delivering smoking cessation treatment in multiple types of formats is more effective than a single format and is encouraged (Strength of Evidence = A).

Types of Counseling and Behavioral Treatments

The analyses of sixty-two studies examining the effectiveness of various types of counseling and behavioral treatment revealed four specific categories of therapy that significantly increase abstinence rates as compared to no treatment controls: (1) provision of practical counseling (e.g., skills training, stress management); (2) provision of intra-treatment social support; (3) helping smokers obtain social support outside of treatment; and (4) aversive smoking. Aversive smoking techniques (e.g., rapid smoking, rapid puffing) usually involve considerable discomfort on the part of the smoker and may even involve a health risk. Thus, they should include medical screening and supervision, and should be offered to smokers who desire such an approach.

Recommendation: Practical counseling, provision of intra-treatment social support, and helping smokers obtain social support outside of treatment are effective and should be included in smoking cessation interventions (Strength of Evidence = B).

Recommendation: Aversive smoking techniques are effective and may be used with smokers requesting such treatment or who have been unsuccessful with other types of treatment (Strength of Evidence = B).

The above analyses included six studies on the effectiveness of diet and physical activity but these behavioral interventions did not significantly increase abstinence rates. A separate analysis was conducted on acupuncture and did not reveal its efficacy as a smoking cessation intervention. The data regarding hypnosis and physiological feedback were insufficient to address the efficacy of these approaches for smoking cessation.

Special Populations
Gender

Although smoking cessation clinical trials demonstrated that the same treatments benefit both men and women, research suggested that some treatments may be more effective for men relative to women (e.g., nicotine replacement therapy). This may be due to differences in barriers and stressors faced by the two genders. For instance, women are more likely to experience depression and have greater weight control concerns. Therefore, interventions addressing these topics may increase abstinence rates in women.

Recommendation: The same treatments for smoking cessation are effective for men and women and are recommended for both genders, except in the case of the pregnant smoker (Strength of Evidence = B).

Pregnant Women

Studies with less than 5 months follow-up were included in this meta-analysis because of the need for preparturition data. Seven studies met inclusion criteria and revealed that extended or augmented treatments (i.e., interventions offering more intensive counseling than minimal advice, self-help materials, and referral to a smoking cessation program) produced significantly higher rates of smoking cessation in pregnant women than usual care. The use of pharmacotherapies was suggested as a treatment option for those unable to quit with the help of other methods. However, the clinician and the patient who choose this option must be aware of potential risks of different pharmacotherapies for the fetus. In addition, none of these medications were tested for smoking cessation in pregnant women. Thus, clinicians and their patients must balance the risks and unknown efficacy of pharmacotherapy among pregnant women with the known risks of continued smoking.

Recommendation: Due to the serious risks of smoking during pregnancy, pregnant smokers should be offered extended or augmented psychosocial intervention that exceeds minimal quit advice (Strength of Evidence = A).

Recommendation: Because quitting smoking at any point during pregnancy can result in benefits to both the fetus and the mother, treatment should be offered throughout the course of pregnancy (Strength of Evidence = B).

Recommendation: Pharmacological therapy should be considered when a pregnant woman is unable to quit, and potential benefits of quitting outweigh the risks of pharmacotherapy and continued smoking (Strength of Evidence = C).

Ethnic Minorities

Whereas studies have demonstrated the effectiveness of various treatments for smoking cessation across minority groups, there is no consistent evidence that interventions designed for specific ethnic groups increase quit rates. However, clinicians should ensure that cessation counseling and self-help materials are delivered in language understood by the smoker and incorporate culturally appropriate examples.

Recommendation: Smoking cessation interventions have proven effective across ethnic minority groups. Members of these different groups should be offered treatments recommended for the general population (Strength of Evidence = A).

Recommendation: When possible, tobacco cessation treatment should be modified for appropriate use in the different ethnic populations with which they are used (Strength of Evidence = C).

Hospitalized Smokers

Four studies met criteria and were relevant for the analysis comparing smoking cessation treatment to usual care for hospitalized patients. Results suggested that augmented smoking cessation interventions can increase abstinence rates in these patients.

Recommendation: Smoking cessation treatments have been shown to be effective for hospitalized patients and should be provided to smokers in the hospital setting (Strength of Evidence = B).

Smokers with Psychiatric Comorbidity and/or Chemical Dependency

There was insufficient evidence to determine whether smokers with psychiatric comorbidity and/or chemical dependency would benefit from treatments tailored to their condition. For this reason, the *Guideline* recommended the use of treatments proven to be effective in the general population.

Recommendation: Smokers with comorbid psychiatric conditions should be provided with smoking cessation interventions proven to be effective in the general population (Strength of Evidence = C).

Recommendation: Because bupropion SR and nortriptyline are efficacious in the general population and also effectively treat depression, they should be considered for the treatment of tobacco dependence in smokers with current or past depression (Strength of Evidence = C).

Recommendation: Because evidence indicates that smoking cessation treatment does not interfere with chemical dependency recovery, smokers receiving treatment for substance use should be provided with treatments proven to be effective in the general population (Strength of Evidence = C).

Special Topics
Post-Cessation Weight Gain

Although no separate analysis was conducted regarding this topic, the *Guideline* panel reviewed available studies that addressed weight gain and agreed as to the following recommendations.

Recommendation: The clinician should acknowledge that quitting smoking is often followed by weight gain. In addition, the clinician should recommend physical activity and diet as means to control weight after quitting, as well as suggest that quitters focus on smoking cessation rather than weight control in the initial stages of abstinence (Strength of Evidence = C).

Recommendation: For those smokers extremely concerned about weight gain, it may be appropriate to recommend bupropion SR or nicotine replacement therapy, as they have been shown to delay weight gain after quitting smoking (Strength of Evidence = B).

Treatment Matching

The *Guideline* panel examined evidence regarding a stepped-care model of tobacco dependence treatment, as well as individually tailored interventions. The concept of stepped care refers to an approach where more intensive and more expensive treatments are provided to smokers who have failed with less intensive low-cost treatments, until the treatment is intensive enough to be successful. Although both stepped care and individual tailoring demonstrated some empirical support, the data was not sufficient to conclude that either approach significantly increases abstinence rates over nontailored counseling approaches of similar intensity. Thus, the *Guideline* panel recommended that additional research in these areas be conducted.

Key Recommendations

The main recommendations of the *Guideline* are listed below.

1) As a chronic condition, nicotine dependence may require repeated interventions.

2) Effective smoking cessation treatments

exist and may lead to long-term or permanent abstinence.

3) Every smoker should be offered treatments identified as effective if she/he is willing to quit or should be provided with a brief intervention to enhance his/her motivation to quit.

4) Clinicians and health care delivery systems should consistently identify, document, and treat every tobacco user seen in a health care setting.

5) Brief smoking cessation treatments are effective and every smoker should be offered at least such a treatment.

6) There is a strong dose-response relation between the intensity of smoking cessation counseling and its effectiveness.

7) Among different types of counseling and behavioral therapies, three proved most effective and should be used with all smokers willing to quit: practical counseling (problem solving/coping skills training), intra-treatment social support, and help with finding extra-treatment social support.

8) Pharmacotherapies for smoking cessation are effective and should be offered to all smokers willing to quit except when contraindicated. The first-line pharmacotherapies include bupropion SR and nicotine replacement therapy (nicotine gum, nicotine inhaler, nicotine nasal spray, and nicotine patch). The second-line pharmacotherapies include clonidine and nortryptyline. Over-the-counter nicotine patches have been found effective and should be recommended to smokers by clinicians.

9) Because smoking cessation treatments are cost-effective compared to other medical treatments, the treatments identified as effective in the *Guideline* should be covered by health insurance plans.

Comparison to the 1996 Guideline

In comparison to the previous 1996 *Guideline*, the updated version of the *Guideline* revealed significant advances in nicotine and tobacco research and treatment. For instance, even stronger evidence emerged for dose-response relation between counseling intensity and effectiveness. New counseling modes, such as telephone counseling and treatments that focus on building external social support, also demonstrated efficacy. Lastly, since the 1996 *Guideline* was published, many new effective pharmacological treatments have been developed and propagated among clinicians.

NEW DEVELOPMENTS IN THE FIELD

A thorough overview of research addressing efficacious smoking cessation interventions is the primary aim of this chapter. This effort was guided by two underlying goals: (1) to update recommendations made by the *Guideline* and (2) to examine content areas, new treatment approaches, and target populations for which minimal or no data existed at the time the *Guideline* was published. As in the *Guideline*, only peer-reviewed, randomized controlled studies, with follow-up results at a timepoint at least 5-months post-quit date, were selected for review.

The following summary of evidence is divided into sections that represent three broad groupings of smoking cessation interventions: pharmacological treatments, behavioral treatments, and special topics and populations. Recommendations, based on strength-of-evidence ratings, conclude each category.

Pharmacological Treatments

Since the publication of the 2000 *Guideline*, advances in the pharmacological treatment of smoking cessation have been made in the following areas: (1) application of bupropion in novel populations and in combination with other pharmacotherapies; (2) new modes of delivery and varying doses of NRT; and (3) use of other pharmacological agents.

Bupropion

Several studies examined the efficacy of bupropion in special populations including African Americans, chronically ill patients, smokers formerly treated with bupropion for smoking cessation, and recent quitters. Results from these studies are summarized below and shown in Table 1.

One study compared the use of bupropion sustained release (SR) to placebo in a large sample of African American smokers, showing a significant increase in 6-months post-quit abstinence rates with bupropion use (Ahluwalia et al., 2002). Similarly, Tashkin et al. (2001) examined patients diagnosed with chronic obstructive pulmonary disease and found a significantly higher rate of smoking cessation at 6 months post-quit in those treated with bupropion as compared to patients receiving a placebo medication. Gonzales and colleagues (Gonzales et al., 2001) tested the use of bupropion in a sample of smokers formerly treated by bupropion and found significantly higher 6-month post-quit abstinence rates in the treatment group as compared to the placebo group. In a sample of recent quitters, bupropion use was associated with a significant improvement in abstinence rates maintained for 18 months post-quit (Hays et al., 2001).

Two studies examined the efficacy of bupropion in small samples of smokers with schizophrenia (Evins et al., 2001; George et al., 2002). Bupropion had a significant effect on short-term end-of-treatment smoking abstinence rates (George et al., 2002) and was associated with smoking reduction at 6 months post-quit (Evins et al., 2001). Table 1 also lists comparisons of bupropion to other pharmacotherapies for smoking cessation treatment in the general population.

Specifically, an investigation of bupropion and nortriptyline, conducted by Hall and colleagues (Hall et al., 2002), found both medications to improve long-term abstinence when compared to a placebo. The difference in abstinence rates between bupropion and nortriptyline was not significant. Another study by Jorenby et al. (Jorenby et al., 1999) found bupropion to significantly increase the rates of long-term smoking cessation as compared to the nicotine patch. However, the patch in this study was not more effective than placebo.

Summary of Evidence:

1. The *Guideline* found bupropion to be an efficacious treatment for smoking cessation in the general population and also recommended its use in special populations. The recent research supports this recommendation and provides additional evidence indicating that bupropion is an efficacious treatment for smoking cessation in African Americans, patients with chronic obstructive pulmonary disease, smokers formerly treated with bupropion for smoking cessation, and recent quitters. Therefore, its use in these subgroups should be encouraged (Strength of Evidence = A).

2. Bupropion shows some promise in facilitating smoking reduction and cessation in persons with schizophrenia and may be considered in the treatment planning for this recalcitrant population of smokers. This conclusion is based on two small studies, and only one of them showed a short-term cessation effect (Strength of Evidence = C).

3. Bupropion was found to be no less effective than nortriptyline and more effective than the patch in the initiation and maintenance of long-term abstinence, thus providing further support for its

Table 1. Pharmacological Treatments: Bupropion

Study	Participants per Group	Intervention	Outcome
Bupropion SR vs. placebo Ahluwalia et al., JAMA 2002: 468-74.	N=600 African American smokers (n=300 per group)	Bupropion SR 300mg per day vs. placebo for 7 weeks All participants received motivational counseling.	<u>6 weeks PQ: 7-day PP (BC)</u> Bupropion SR = 36% Placebo = 19% $p<.001$ <u>26 weeks PQ: (BC)</u> Bupropion SR = 21% Placebo = 13.7% $p<.02$ Intent-to-treat procedures were used.
Bupropion SR vs. placebo Tashkin et al., The Lancet 2001: 1571-75.	N=404 smokers with mild or moderate chronic obstructive pulmonary disease (bupropion n=204; placebo n=200)	Bupropion SR 300mg per day vs. placebo for 12 weeks. All participants received smoking cessation counseling.	<u>6 weeks PQ: 28-day PP (BC)</u> Bupropion SR = 28% Placebo = 16% $p<.003$) <u>11 weeks PQ: continuous from wk 3 (BC)</u> Bupropion = 18% Placebo = 10% $p<.05$ <u>25 weeks PQ: continuous from wk 3 (BC)</u> Bupropion = 16% Placebo = 9% $p<.05$ Intent-to-treat procedures were used.
Bupropion SR vs. placebo Gonzales et al., Clinical Pharmacology & Therapeutics 2001: 438-444.	N=450 smokers who had previously used bupropion in a smoking cessation attempt (bupropion n=226; placebo n=224)	Bupropion SR 300mg per day vs. placebo for 12 weeks All participants received brief individual counseling as standard-of-care.	<u>6 weeks PQ: 28 day PP (BC)</u> Bupropion = 27% Placebo = 5% $p<.001$) <u>23 weeks PQ: continuous from week 4 (BC)</u> Bupropion = 12% Placebo = 2% $p<.001$ Intent-to-treat procedures were used.
Bupropion SR vs. placebo for relapse prevention Hays et al., Annals of Internal Medicine 2001; 423-33.	N=784 smokers who were motivated to quit smoking (bupropion n=214; placebo n=215)	Bupropion SR 300mg per day vs. placebo for 45 weeks All participants received bupropion SR 300mg per day for the initial 7 weeks of the trial.	<u>51 weeks PQ: 7-day PP (BC)</u> Bupropion = 55.1% Placebo = 42.3% $p=.008$ <u>77 weeks PQ: 7-day PP (BC)</u> Bupropion = 47.7% Placebo= 37.7% $p=.034$ <u>103 weeks PQ: 7-day PP (BC)</u> Bupropion = 41.6% Placebo = 40% ns <u>Median time to relapse</u> Bupropion = 156 days Placebo = 65 days $p=.021$ Intent-to-treat procedures were used.

Bupropion SR vs. placebo Evins et al., Nicotine & Tobacco Research 2001: 397-403.	N=18 stable outpatients with schizophrenia (n=9 per group)	Bupropion SR 150mg per day vs. placebo All participants received concurrent cognitive-behavioral therapy program	<u>20 weeks PQ: smoking reduction (BC)</u> Expired-air CO was reduced more in bupropion-treated patients, compared with placebo. $p<.03$ No participant dropout.
Bupropion SR vs. placebo George et al., Biological Psychiatry 2002: 53-61.	N=32 outpatients with schizophrenia (n=16 per group)	Bupropion SR 300mg per day vs. placebo for 10 weeks All participants received smoking cessation behavioral group therapy.	<u>8 weeks PQ: 7-day PP (BC)</u> Bupropion SR = 50% Placebo = 12.5% $p<.05$ <u>6 months PT: 7-day PP</u> Bupropion SR = 18.8% Placebo = 6.3% ns Intent-to-treat procedures were used.
Two (medical management vs. psychological intervention) X three (bupropion SR vs. nortriptyline vs. placebo) design Hall et al., Archives of General Psychiatry 2002: 930-6.	N=220 smokers (n per cell ranged from 35 to 38)	Bupropion SR 300mg per day Nortriptyline drug dose titrated until a serum level of 50-150ng/mL was obtained Medical management: physician advice Psychological intervention: 5 group smoking cessation sessions	<u>19 weeks PQ: 7-day PP (BC)</u> Bupropion = 24.5% Nortriptyline = 22% Placebo = 16.5% $p<.05$ Bupropion was equally as effective as nortriptyline. Intent-to-treat procedures were used.
Bupropion SR vs. nicotine patch vs. bupropion SR plus nicotine patch vs. placebo Jorenby et al., The New England Journal of Medicine 1999: 685-91.	N=893 smokers (n=244, 244, 245, 160 for bupropion, nicotine patch, bupropion plus patch, and placebo groups, respectively)	Bupropion SR 300mg/day vs. nicotine patch vs. bupropion SR 300mg/day plus patch vs. placebo Treatment duration was 9 weeks. All patients received individual counseling during treatment and follow-up periods.	<u>51 weeks PQ: 7-day PP (BC)</u> Bupropion = 30.3% Bupropion plus patch = 35.5% Nicotine patch = 16.4% Placebo = 15.6% Bupropion vs. placebo ($p<.001$) Bupropion plus patch vs. placebo ($p<.001$) Bupropion vs. patch ($p<.001$) Bupropion plus patch vs. patch alone ($p<.001$) Bupropion plus patch vs. bupropion alone (ns) Patch vs. placebo (ns) Intent-to-treat procedures were used.

BC = biochemically confirmed; PP = point-prevalence; PQ = post-quit date; PT = post-treatment, ns= not significant
*abstinence type not reported
**rates not reported

application in the treatment of smoking cessation. However, the latter finding needs to be interpreted with caution because the patch was not found effective in this study (Strength of Evidence = B).

Nicotine Replacement Therapy
The latest studies testing the efficacy of

NRT focused on new modes of delivery and higher doses (Table 2). Shiffman and colleagues (Shiffman et al., 2002) evaluated the nicotine lozenge and found significant treatment effects compared to placebo that were maintained at one year post-quit. Wallstrom, Nilsson, & Hirsch (2000) examined the nicotine sublingual tablet. The tablet was found to increase continuous abstinence at 6 weeks, 3 months, and 6 months post-quit when compared to placebo. Abstinence rates were not significantly different at 1 year post-quit. A combination treatment of nicotine inhaler and nicotine patch proved more efficacious than the inhaler and placebo patch at 12 weeks post-quit, but not at 6 months post-quit (Bohadanaet al., 2000).

Several studies compared varying doses of the nicotine patch. In two studies, higher doses were compared to both lower doses and to the placebo patch. Hughes and colleagues (Hughes et al., 1999) compared 21 mg, 35 mg, and 42 mg dosages to placebo in heavy smokers. They found a significant overall effect of dose on abstinence up to 52 weeks post-cessation. However, the dose-response curve was shallow and higher doses were not significantly different from lower doses at any time point. In another study, 25 mg and 15 mg

dosages differed from one another, as well as from placebo, in terms of continuous abstinence at 12 months post-quit (Tonnesen et al., 1999). Using data from the Transdermal Nicotine Study Group (1991), Daughton and colleagues (Daughton et al., 1999) found that continuous abstinence rates were higher for the 21 mg patch dose than for 7 mg, 14 mg or placebo at 48 to 62 months post-quit.

Summary of Evidence.
1. Studies show that novel NRT modes of delivery (nicotine lozenge and nicotine sublingual tablet) as well as new combinations (nicotine inhaler and nicotine patch) are efficacious and provide new treatment alternatives. However, these recommendations are based on only one randomized clinical trial for each of these new modes or combinations. The studies regarding the lozenge, the subligual tablet, and the inhaler-and-patch combination are viewed as stand-alone evidence because the evidence reviewed in the *Guideline* concerned other NRT modes of delivery and combinations than the ones reviewed here (Strength of Evidence = B).
2. Studies comparing the efficacy of different doses of the nicotine patch

Table 2. Pharmacological Treatments: Nicotine Replacement Therapy

Study	Participants per Group	Intervention	Outcome
Nicotine polacrilex lozenges vs. placebo Shiffman et al., Archives of Internal Medicine 2000: 1267-76.	N=1818 smokers Parallel arms testing 2mg and 4mg lozenges Low dependence smokers: 2mg (n=459) vs. placebo (n=458) High dependence smokers: 4mg (n=450) vs. placebo (n=451)	4mg nicotine lozenges vs. placebo lozenges for 24 weeks 2mg nicotine lozenges vs. placebo lozenges for 24 weeks Participants were provided with sufficient lozenges for the labeled maximum use of 20 per day. Lozenge use was to stop after 6 months. All participants received brief behavioral counseling.	6 weeks PQ: 28-day PP (BC) 4mg lozenges = 48.7% Placebo = 20.8% *p*<.001 2mg lozenges = 46.0% Placebo = 29.7% *p*<.001 Significant treatment effects were maintained for a full year PQ. Intent-to-treat procedures were used.

Nicotine sublingual tablets vs. placebo Wallstrom et al., Addiction 2000: 1161-71.	N=247 smokers (nicotine tablet n=123; placebo n=124)	2mg sublingual tablets vs. placebo tablets for 3 months Highly dependent smokers were instructed to use two tablets per hour, up to a maximum of 40 tablets per day; low dependent smokers were instructed to use one tablet per hour, up to a daily maximum of 20. All participants received brief advice to quit smoking and a guide to smoking cessation.	<u>6 weeks PQ: continuous abstinence (BC)</u> Nicotine tablets = 50% Placebo = 29% *p<.001* <u>3 months PQ: continuous abstinence (BC)</u> Nicotine tablets = 42% Placebo = 23% *p<.001* <u>6 months PQ: continuous abstinence (BC)</u> Nicotine tablets = 33% Placebo = 18% *p<.005* <u>12 months PQ: continuous abstinence (BC)</u> Nicotine tablets = 23% Placebo = 15% *ns* Intent-to-treat procedures were used.
Nicotine patch plus nicotine inhaler vs. placebo patch plus nicotine inhaler Bohadana et al., Archives of Internal Medicine 2000: 3128-34.	N=400 (n=200 per group)	15 mg nicotine patch plus 10mg nicotine inhaler vs. placebo patch plus 10mg nicotine inhaler As indicated, all participants received the 10mg nicotine inhaler.	<u>6 weeks PQ: continuous abstinence (BC)</u> Patch + inhaler = 60.5% Placebo + inhaler = 47.5% *p<.009* <u>12 weeks PQ: continuous abstinence (BC)</u> Patch + inhaler = 42% Placebo + inhaler = 31% *p<.02* <u>6 months PQ: continuous abstinence (BC)</u> Patch + inhaler = 25.0% Placebo + inhaler = 22.5% not significant (*p=.56*) <u>12 months PQ: continuous abstinence (BC)</u> Patch + inhaler = 19.5% Placebo plus inhaler = 14.0% ns Intent-to-treat procedures used.
Higher dose nicotine patches vs. standard dose nicotine patches vs. placebo Tonnesen et al., European Respiratory Journal 1999: 238-46.	N=3575 smokers randomized to 5 treatment arms.	Participants were allocated to one of five daily treatments: 25mg nicotine patches for 22 weeks, 25mg patches for 8 weeks, 15mg patches for 22 weeks, 15mg patches for 8 weeks, or placebo patches. No additional treatment components were reported.	<u>12 months PQ: continuous abstinence (BC)</u> 25mg patch for 22 weeks = 15.4% 25mg patch for 8 weeks = 15.9% 15mg patch for 22 weeks = 13.7% 15mg patch for 8 weeks = 11.7% Placebo = 9.9%. 15mg vs. placebo (*p<.05*) 25mg vs. 15mg (*p<.03*) 25mg vs. placebo (*p<.001*) There was no significant difference in success rate between the two active treatment durations. Intent-to-treat procedures were used.

Higher dose nicotine patch vs. lower dose nicotine patch vs. placebo Hughes et al., Nicotine Tobacco Research 1999: 169-74.	N=1039 smokers who smoked – 30 cigarettes per day Participants were randomly assigned in a double-blind manner to one of the four treatment arms. (n per group not specified in the article)	Compared 0, 21, 35, and 42mg/day 24-hour patches for 6 weeks usage followed by 10 weeks of tapering. All subjects received a stop-smoking booklet, 7 sessions of group behavioral counseling for smoking cessation, and brief individual counseling.	<u>12 weeks PQ: continuous abstinence (BC)</u> 42mg patch = 39% 35mg patch = 30% 21mg patch = 24% Placebo patch = 16% 42, 35, 21mg vs. placebo ($p<.01$) <u>6 months PQ: continuous abstinence (BC)</u> 42mg patch = 26% 35mg patch = 20% 21mg patch = 20% Placebo patch = 13% 42, 35, 21mg vs. placebo ($p<.01$) <u>12 months PQ: continuous abstinence (BC)</u> 42mg patch = 19% 35mg patch = 9% 21mg patch = 13% Placebo patch = 7% 42, 35, 21mg vs. placebo ($p<.01$) Active doses were not significantly different from one another at any time point. Intent-to-treat procedures were used.
21mg vs. 14mg vs. 7mg vs. placebo nicotine patches Daughton et al., Preventive Medicine 1999: 113-118.	N=724 (21mg n=193; 14mg n=202; 7mg n=127; placebo n=202) Patient population is from the Transdermal Nicotine Study Group (JAMA 1991: 3133-3138).	Participants were randomized to 21, 14, 7, or 0mg nicotine patch groups. All participants received group smoking cessation counseling.	<u>4 to 5 years PQ: continuous abstinence (BC)</u> 21mg patch = 20.2% 14mg patch = 10.4% 7mg patch = 11.8% Placebo patch = 7.4% 21mg vs. 14mg ($p=.007$) 21mg vs. 7mg ($p=.05$) 21mg vs. placebo ($p<.001$) Intent-to-treat procedures were used.

BC = biochemically confirmed; PP = point-prevalence; PQ = post-quit date; PT = post-treatment; ns= not significant
*abstinence type not reported   **rates not reported

produced mixed results. Higher than standard doses did not prove more efficacious than standard doses. However, among standard doses, the highest ones were more efficacious than the lower ones. This conclusion is based on two well-controlled randomized trials. This evidence indicates that higher standard doses are preferred over the lower ones unless medically contraindicated (Strength of Evidence = B).

Other Pharmacological Agents

In addition to testing bupropion and NRT in new populations or new combinations, studies in the area of pharmacological treatments examined other agents (Table 3). Three antidepressants not used as quit

Table 3. Other Pharmacological Treatments

Study	Participants per Group	Intervention	Outcome
Fluoxetine vs. placebo Blondal et al., Addiction 1999: 1007-15.	N=100 (fluoxetine n=48; placebo n=52)	Fluoxetine 20mg/day vs. placebo All participants received nicotine inhaler and supportive group treatment	6 weeks PQ: continuous abstinence (BC) Fluoxetine = 54% Placebo = 48% *ns* 3 months PQ: continuous abstinence (BC) Fluoxetine = 40% Placebo = 40% *ns* 6 months PQ: continuous abstinence (BC) Fluoxetine = 29% Placebo = 33% *ns* 12 months PQ: continuous abstinence (BC) Fluoxetine = 21% Placebo = 23% *ns* No participant dropout.
Fluoxetine vs. placebo Niaura et al., Journal of Consulting and Clinical Psychology 2002: 887-96.	N=989 smokers (60mg n=328; 30mg n=328; placebo n=333)	10 weeks of fluoxetine 60mg/day vs. fluoxetine 30mg/day vs. placebo. All participants received 9 sessions of individual cognitive-behavioral therapy for smoking cessation.	32 weeks PQ: 7-day PP (BC) Fluoxetine 60mg = 15% Fluoxetine 30mg = 16% Placebo = 18% *ns* Intent-to-treat procedures were used.
Sertraline vs. placebo Covey et al., American Journal of Psychiatry 2002: 1731-37.	N=134 smokers with a history of major depression (sertraline n=68; placebo n=66)	Sertraline for 12 weeks (titrated up to 200mg/day for weeks 4 through 10) vs. placebo All participants received cognitive behavioral counseling.	6 weeks PQ: 7-day PP (BC) Sertraline = 33.8% Placebo = 28.8% *ns* 32 weeks PQ: 7-day PP (BC) Sertraline = 16.7% Placebo = 11.8% *ns* No moderating effects of single or recurrent major depression, depressed mood at baseline, nicotine dependence level, or gender were observed. Intent-to-treat procedures were used.
Paroxetine vs. placebo Killen et al., Journal of Consulting and Clinical Psychology 2000: 883-9.	N=224 smokers (paroxetine 40mg n=75; paroxetine 20mg n=75; placebo n=74)	Paroxetine 40mg/day vs. paroxetine 20mg/day vs. placebo All participants received transdermal nicotine system and behavioral treatment.	4 weeks PQ: 7-day PP (BC) Paroxetine 40mg = 57% Paroxetine 20mg = 48% Placebo = 45% *ns* 10 weeks PQ: 7-day PP (BC) Paroxetine 40mg = 39% Paroxetine 20mg = 33% Placebo = 36% *ns* 26 weeks PQ: 7-day PP (BC) Paroxetine 40mg = 27% Paroxetine 20mg = 21% Placebo = 25% *ns* Intent-to-treat procedures used.

Two (medical management vs. psychological intervention) X three (bupropion SR vs. nortriptyline vs. placebo) design Hall et al., Archives of General Psychiatry 2002: 930-6.	N=220 smokers (n per cell ranged from 35 to 38)	Bupropion SR 300mg per day Nortriptyline drug dose titrated until a serum level of 50-150ng/mL was obtained Medical management: physician advice Psychological intervention: 5 group smoking cessation sessions	<u>19 weeks PQ: 7-day PP (BC)</u> Bupropion = 24.5% Nortriptyline = 22% Placebo = 16.5% p<.05 Bupropion was equally as effective as nortriptyline Intent-to-treat procedures were used.
Naltrexone vs. placebo Covey et al., Journal of Addictive Diseases 1999: 31-40.	N=68 smokers who smoked at least 20 cigarettes daily (n=30 for naltrexone; n=38 for placebo)	Naltrexone 75mg vs. placebo daily for 4 weeks. All participants were seen weekly for individual smoking cessation therapy.	<u>4 weeks PQ: 7-day PP (BC)</u> Naltrexone = 46.7% Placebo = 26.3% *ns* <u>6 months PQ: self-reported abstinence*</u> Naltrexone = 27% Placebo = 15% *ns* Intent-to-treat procedures were used.
Naltrexone vs. nicotine patch vs. placebo Wong et al., Addiction 1999: 1227-37.	N=100 smokers (naltrexone/nicotine patch n=26; naltrexone/placebo patch n=23; placebo naltrexone/nicotine patch n=25; placebo naltrexone/placebo patch n=26)	Twelve weeks of either placebo-only, naltrexone only, placebo with nicotine patch, or naltrexone with nicotine patches. Naltrexone dose was 50mg/day. Nicotine patch was 21mg for 8 weeks and 14mg for 4 weeks. All participants received smoking cessations counseling.	<u>12 weeks PQ: 7-day PP (BC)</u> Naltrexone = 22% Placebo = 19% Naltrexone plus patch = 46% Placebo plus patch = 48% Only the main effect of patch was significant (*p*=.006). <u>24 weeks PQ: 7-day PP (BC)</u> Naltrexone = 17% Placebo = 15% Naltrexone plus patch = 35% Placebo plus patch = 32% *ns* Intent-to-treat procedures were used.

BC = biochemically confirmed; PP = point-prevalence; PQ = post-quit date; PT = post-treatment; ns= not significant
*abstinence type not reported
**rates not reported

smoking medications before were tested for their effectiveness in smoking cessation - fluoxetine (Blondal et al., 1999; Niaura et al., 2002), sertraline (Covey et al., 2002), and paroxetine (Killen et al., 2000). These antidepressants were used in combination with the NRT and/or behavioral treatments. None produced significantly higher abstinence rates compared to placebo. Nortriptyline, an antidepressant that was not FDA-approved for smoking cessation but that was recommended in the *Guideline* as a second line medication, was compared to bupropion and placebo in a study by Hall and colleagues (Hall et al., 2002). Both nortriptyline and bupropion were found efficacious compared to placebo but there was no difference in their respective efficacies (Hall et al., 2002). Naltrexone, an opioid antagonist, has been used as a treatment for alcohol dependence. However, neither of two placebo-controlled studies testing its effectiveness for smoking cessation found a significant effect of naltrexone used either alone (Covey et al., 1999) or in combination with the patch (Wong et al., 1999).

Summary of Evidence.
1. The latest studies on pharmacological treatments have not identified new agents that are effective for smoking cessation. The efficacy of fluoxetine, sertraline, paroxetine, and naltrexone was not confirmed. However, with the exception of one fluoxetine trial, sample sizes were small in those studies, especially those on naltrexone. The efficacy of new pharmacological agents discussed here may be worth further examination. Based on current evidence, they are not recommended for smoking cessation.

2. Nortriptyline along with bupropion remain the only antidepressants that have empirically demonstrated efficacy. Two nortriptyline studies reviewed by the *Guideline* confirmed its efficacy. A recent placebo-controlled randomized trial reviewed in this section showed that nortriptyline may be as effective as bupropion. Thus, nortriptyline is recommended as a smoking cessation medication. Because of its side-effects, it should be offered to those who cannot quit using the first-line pharmacotherapies (Strength of Evidence = A).

Behavioral Treatments

Since the publication of the *Guideline*, behavioral treatments known to be effective were tested (1) in special populations and (2) in different real-world settings. In addition, (3) other behavioral approaches such as exercise and acupuncture were evaluated.

Behavioral Treatments in Special Populations

Targeted special populations included women with weight-related issues, low-income smokers, and smokers with various chronic conditions such as HIV, diabetes, and recurrent depression (Table 4). Two studies addressed weight-related issues among women smokers because the majority of weight-concerned smokers are female (Meyers et al., 1997). Perkins and colleagues (Perkins et al., 2001) tested a cognitive-behavioral therapy aimed at reducing weight concerns in female smokers by helping them accept modest weight gain and by improving their body image. The three-arm randomized trial included cognitive-behavioral therapy geared toward reducing weight concerns with no dieting instruction, weight control counseling with dieting, and standard smoking cessation counseling with no weight-related topics. Cognitive behavioral therapy with no dieting instruction produced significantly higher abstinence rates at 12 months post-quit than did standard cessation counseling. The traditional behavioral weight control program that included dieting was not more effective than standard counseling (Perkins et al., 2001). Another trial tested a very low energy diet in women who had relapsed previously because of postcessation weight gain (Danielsson et al., 1999). All participants received nicotine gum and a combination smoking cessation and weight control counseling, with or without the low energy diet. The diet proved efficacious compared to no diet as it resulted in a significantly higher abstinence rate at 1 year post-quit. Smoking cessation in low-income populations poses a particular challenge because of the limited resources of these smokers as well as the fact that they are a part of a culture with higher than average smoking rates (Solomon & Flynn, 1993). Proactive telephone peer support combined with free nicotine patch compared to the patch only promoted short-term (3-month post-quit) but not long-term (6-month post-quit) abstinence in low-income women (Solomon et al., 2000). A similar result was obtained in a study testing the effectiveness of brief behavioral counseling and clinician advice among

Table 4. Behavioral Treatments for Special Populations.

Study	Participants per Group	Intervention	Outcome
Cognitive-behavioral therapy (CBT) for weight concerns vs. weight control counseling (WCC) vs. standard counseling (SC) alone Perkins et al., Journal of Consulting and Clinical Psychology 2001: 604-613.	N=219 women smokers concerned about weight gain (WCC n=72; CBT n=72; SC n=75)	CBT to promote the acceptance of modest weight gain, discourage dieting, and reduce concerns about cessation-related weight gain vs. WCC to attenuate weight gain after quitting smoking, largely by reducing between-meal snacking vs. SC - standard cognitive-behavioral smoking cessation counseling with no weight-related topics. All participants received standard counseling.	<u>6 months PQ: continuous (BC)</u> CBT = 28% WCC = 18% SC = 12% CBT vs. SC (*p*<.05) WCC vs. SC (ns) <u>12 months PQ: continuous (BC)</u> CBT = 21% WCC = 13% SC = 9% CBT vs. SC (*p*<.05) WCC vs. SC (ns) Intent-to-treat procedures were used.
Low energy diet vs. control Danielsson et al., British Medical Journal 1999: 490-4.	N=287 women smokers who had gained weight in previous attempts to quit (diet group n=137; no diet group n=150)	Very low energy diet (Nutrilett 1.76 MJ per day) vs. no diet. All participants received nicotine gum and a combination of standard smoking cessation counseling and weight control counseling.	<u>1 year PQ: continuous (BC)</u> Diet = 28% Control = 16% *p*<.05 Intent-to-treat procedures were used.
Peer support for smoking cessation vs. control Solomon et al., Preventive Medicine 2000: 68-74.	N=214 Medicaid-eligible women smokers of childbearing age (peer support n=106; control n=108)	Proactive telephone peer support vs. no peer support. All participants received free nicotine patches.	<u>3 months PQ: 7-day PP (BC)</u> Peer support = 42% Control = 28% *p*=.03 <u>6 months PQ: 7-day PP (BC)</u> Peer support = 23% Control = 19% *ns* Intent-to-treat procedures were used.
Brief smoking cessation intervention vs. control Glasgow et al., American Journal of Public Health 2000: 786-9.	N=1154 female smokers in low-income Planned Parenthood clinics (intervention n=578; control n=576)	Brief smoking cessation intervention (BI) that involved a 9-minute video, 12-15 minutes of behavioral counseling, and follow-up telephone calls vs. control (no BI, standard care only - SC). All participants received standard care (clinician advice to quit).	<u>6 weeks PT: 7-day PP</u> BI = 10.2% SC = 6.9% *p*<.05 <u>6 months PT: 30-day PP (BC)</u> BI = 6.4% SC = 3.8% *ns* Intent-to-treat procedures were used.
Multicomponent intervention including feedback about genetic susceptibility to lung cancer vs. control McBride et al., Cancer, Epidemiology, Biomarkers & Prevention 2002: 521-8.	N=557 low-income African-American smokers (intervention n=372; control n=185).	Feedback on genetic susceptibility to lung cancer combined with motivational telephone counseling (GSF) vs. enhanced usual care (EUC; provider advice to quit) All participants received the nicotine patch and self-help materials.	<u>3 months PT: 7-day PP (BC)</u> GSF = 19% EUC = 10% *p*<.006 <u>9 months PT: 7-day PP (BC)</u> GSF = 15% EUC = 10% *ns* Intent-to-treat procedures were used.

Smoking cessation intervention vs. control Canga et al., Diabetes Care 2000: 1455-60.	N=280 diabetic smokers (intervention n=147; control n=133)	Smoking cessation intervention (SCI) consisting of nurse-delivered counseling, a negotiated cessation date, and optional patch for heavy smokers vs. usual care (UC) All participants received usual diabetic care including advice to quit.	6 months PQ: 5-month PP (BC) SCI = 21.1% UC = 5.3% $p<.001$ Intent-to-treat procedures were used.
Nurse-managed, peer-led smoking cessation intervention vs. control Wewers et al., Journal of the Association of Nurses in AIDS Care 2000: 37-44.	N=15 HIV-positive smokers (intervention n=8; control n=7)	Nurse-managed, peer-led intervention consisting of 8 weeks of weekly face-to-face or telephone counseling, skills training, and 6 weeks of 21mg nicotine patch (SCI) vs. advice to quit (UC). All participants received standard written smoking cessation self-help materials.	6 weeks PQ: 7-day PP (BC) SCI = 62.5 UC = 0% $p=.002$ 8 months PT: 7-day PP(BC) SCI = 62.5% UC = 0% $p=.002$ 6 weeks PQ: continuous (BC) SCI = 62.5% UC = 0% $p=.002$ 8 months PT: continuous(BC) SCI = 50% UC = 0% $p=.006$ Intent-to-treat procedures were used.
Cognitive-behavioral treatment for depression vs. control Brown et al., Journal of Consulting and Clinical Psychology 2001: 471-480.	N=179 smokers with past major depressive disorder (intervention n=86; control n=93)	Cognitive-behavioral treatment for depression plus standard care (CBT-D) vs. standard care only (ST). All participants received standard care (cognitive-behavioral smoking cessation treatment).	1 month PT: 7-day PP (BC) CBT-D = 39.5% ST = 30.1% ns 6 months PT: 7-day PP (BC) CBT-D = 24.4% ST = 24.7% ns 12 months PT: 7-day PP (BC) CBT-D = 32.5% ST = 24.7% ns In smokers with recurrent depression: 1, 6, 12 months PT: 7-day PP (BC) CBT-D = higher abstinence rates** than ST across all timepoints $p=.02$ Intent-to-treat procedures were used.

BC = biochemically confirmed; PP = point-prevalence; PQ = post-quit date; PT = post-treatment; ns= not significant
*abstinence type not reported
**rates not reported

women in low-income Planned Parenthood clinics. Compared to advice only, the counseling and advice was associated with a higher abstinence rate at 6 weeks but not at 6 months post-treatment (Glasgow et al., 2000). A trial that focused on low-income African American smokers (McBride et al., 2002) examined the efficacy of a treatment including feedback on genetic susceptibility to lung cancer, telephone-based motivational counseling, the patch, and self-help materials. Compared to enhanced usual care (provider advice to quit, the nicotine patch and self-help materials), the experimental treatment produced higher abstinence rates at 3 but not 9 months post-treatment.

Behavioral treatments were also examined in smokers with chronic diseases. A behavioral intervention for diabetic smokers consisting of counseling, quit date negotiation, and optional nicotine patch produced significantly higher abstinence rates at 6 months post-quit when compared to usual care for diabetic smokers (advice to quit; Canga et al., 2000). In a small pilot study on HIV-positive smokers, the intervention consisted of telephone and face-to-face counseling, coping skills training, and the patch. Counseling was delivered by HIV-positive ex-smokers trained by a nurse in smoking cessation counseling. The intervention yielded significantly higher end-of-treatment and 8-month post-treatment abstinence rates when compared to standard smoking cessation self-help materials (Wewers et al., 2000). Finally, a cognitive-behavioral treatment for depression added to a standard smoking cessation treatment was compared to the standard treatment alone. The depression plus smoking cessation treatment was associated with higher abstinence rates up to 12 months post-treatment among smokers with recurrent but not nonrecurrent major depressive disorder (Brown et al., 2001).

Summary of Evidence.
1. Two approaches to weight issues among women proved efficacious as smoking cessation treatments: a very low energy diet and a cognitive-behavioral treatment aimed at the reduction of weight concerns rather than weight gain per se. Both approaches were more effective than a traditional weight control program and produced long-term abstinence effects. However, these treatments were only tested in one study each. The results

indicate that either a strict diet or counseling aimed at reducing weight concerns can be offered to female smokers with weight-related issues (Strength of Evidence = B).
2. Behavioral treatments are effective in low-income populations but only short term. This conclusion is based on three trials. However, the study populations did not overlap in all three trials as two included low-income female smokers and one low-income African American smokers. As pointed out by the Guideline, in the absence of more effective treatments targeted specifically at special populations, these smokers should be offered the same behavioral treatments that are used with success in the general population (Strength of Evidence = B).
3. Behavioral treatments were effective in populations with chronic conditions such as diabetes, HIV, and recurrent depression. However, each population was examined in only one study. In addition, the study of HIV patients had a very low number of participants, and cognitive behavioral therapy for depression was an effective cessation treatment in patients with recurrent but not non-recurrent depression. Given the fact that behavioral treatments are already known to be effective across a wide range of smoker populations, they can be offered in the special populations listed here (Strength of Evidence = B).

Behavioral Treatments in Real-World Settings

A considerable number of studies tested the efficacy of behavioral treatments in real-world settings such as hospitals, out-patient clinics, pharmacies, and quitlines (Table 5). The Guideline concluded that behavioral treatments provided to hospital in-patients are effective. Several recent studies tested hospital-based smoking cessation interventions delivered during admission or

Table 5. Behavioral Treatments in Real-World Settings.

Study	Participants per Group	Intervention	Outcome
Hospital-based intervention vs. usual care Hajek et al., British Medical Journal 2002: 1-5.	N=540 smokers admitted to hospital after myocardial infarction or for cardiac bypass surgery who expressed interest in stopping smoking (intervention n=274; control n=266).	Intervention delivered at admission (HBI) lasting 20-30 minutes including carbon monoxide reading, special booklet, quiz, contact with other people giving up, declaration of commitment to give up, and sticker in patient's notes vs. brief verbal advice and standard booklet (UC). All participants received usual care as described above.	6 weeks PT: continuous (BC) HBI = 60% UC = 59% ns 12 months PT: continuous (BC) HBI = 37% UC = 41% ns Intent-to-treat procedures were used.
Hospital-based smoking cessation intervention vs. usual care Feeney et al., Internal Medicine Journal 2001: 470-5.	N=198 current smokers admitted to coronary care with acute myocardial infarction (intervention n=96; usual care n=102)	Intervention (HBI) consisting of pre-discharge physician consultation, quit smoking manual, and individualized coping skills training, and post-discharge weekly telephone counseling for 4 weeks vs. pre-discharge educational video (UC). All participants were advised to quit by a cardiologist and given supportive telephone counseling at 3, 6, and 12 months post-discharge.	12 months post-discharge: continuous abstinence (BC) HBI = 39% UC = 2% $p<.001$ Intent-to-treat procedures were used.
Hospital-based directly mailed smoking cessation intervention vs. usual care Schofield et al., Preventive Medicine 1999: 527-34	N=4158 smokers recently discharged from the hospital (intervention n=2099; usual care n=2059)	Hospital-based intervention (HBI): personalized letter with physician advice to quit smoking plus self-help materials mailed 1 to 2 weeks after discharge vs. unspecified usual care (UC). No additional treatment components were reported.	6 months post-discharge: 7-day PP (self-reported) Intervention = 17% Usual care = 15% ns 12 months post-discharge: 7-day PP (BC) Intervention = 12% Usual care = 13% ns Discharged patients with smoking-related health risks in the intervention group were significantly more likely to be abstinent at 12 month post-discharge than patients in the control condition for whom smoking was not highly relevant to medical diagnosis ($p<.05$).** Intent-to-treat procedures were not used.

Ultrasound photographs of atherosclerotic plaques vs. usual care Bovet et al., Preventive Medicine 2002: 215-220.	N=153 (intervention n=74; usual care n=79)	Ultrasonography of carotid and femoral arteries (USG) plus usual care vs. usual care (UC; quit-smoking physician advice). All participants received quit-smoking physician advice.	<u>6 months PT: 7-day PP (self-reported</u> USG = 17.6% UC = 6.3% *p*=.031 Intent-to-treat procedures were <u>not</u> used (2 of 155 participants were lost to followup).
Self-help intervention vs. usual care McBride et al., Preventive Medicine 1999: 133-138.	N=580 female smokers who had been screened for cervical cancer during the prior month (intervention n=288; usual care n=292)	Self-help intervention (SHI): booklet, smoking and reproductive health information, and 3 telephone counseling calls vs. usual care (UC; standard clinical follow-up, no formal smoking cessation intervention). All participants received UC, as described above.	<u>3 months PT: 7-day PP (BC)</u> SHI = 10.9% UC = 10.5% *ns* <u>12 months PT: 7-day PP (BC)</u> SHI = 10.6% UC = 15.5% *ns* Intent-to-treat procedures were used.
Pharmacy-based smoking cessation program vs. usual care Maguire et al., Addiction 2001: 325-331.	N=484 smokers (intervention n=265; usual care n=219)	Structured pharmacy-based smoking cessation program (counseling, information leaflet, 4 weekly then 3 monthly follow-ups for advice as needed) vs. usual care (UC; ad-hoc pharmacist advice). No additional treatment components were reported.	<u>12 months PT: continuous abstinence (BC)</u> Intervention = 14.3% UC = 2.7% *p*<.001 Intent-to-treat procedures were used.
Proactive telephone counseling vs. optional telephone counseling Zhu et al., New England Journal of Medicine 2002: 1087-1093.	N=3283 smokers calling a real-life quitline (proactive phone counseling n=1973; optional phone counseling n=1309)	Seven proactive counseling calls vs. option to call and receive counseling All participants received self-help materials.	<u>12 months PQ: self reported 1-month PP</u> Proactive counseling = 9.1% Optional counseling = 6.9% *p*<.001). Intent-to-treat procedures were used.
Callback telephone counseling vs. usual care Borland et al., Addiction 2001: 881-889.	N=998 smokers calling a statewide "Quitline" service (intervention n=497; usual care n=501)	Callback telephone counseling and self-help materials vs. usual care (UC; self-help materials alone). All participants received self-help materials.	<u>12 months post-baseline: self-reported 9-month PP</u> Telephone counseling = 11.2% Usual care = 5.7% *p*<.01. Intent-to-treat procedures were used.

BC = biochemically confirmed; PP = point-prevalence; PQ = post-quit date; PT = post-treatment; ns= not significant
*abstinence type not reported
**rates not reported

after discharge. A brief multicomponent intervention delivered during hospital admission to patients with myocardial infarction or admitted for bypass surgery did not produce significantly different abstinence rates compared to usual care consisting of advice and a booklet (Hajek et al., 2002). Two studies focused on post-discharge interventions. An intervention for myocardial infarction patients started with pre-discharge advice to quit and individualized coping skills training. It continued post-discharge with telephone counseling weekly for 4 weeks and then at 2, 3, 6, and 12 months (Feeney et al., 2001). Compared to usual care (pre-discharge advice to quit, educational video, and in-person supportive counseling at follow-up), the intervention was associated with higher abstinence rates at 12 months post-treatment. In another study testing a hospital-delivered post-discharge intervention, the intervention did not significantly differ from usual care (Schofield et al., 1999). However, there was an interaction between treatment and medical diagnosis. Original diagnoses were aggregated by experts into two categories: conditions highly related to smoking and conditions not highly related to smoking. Patients in the treatment group diagnosed with conditions highly related to smoking were significantly more likely to be abstinent at 12 months post-treatment than patients in the control group diagnosed with conditions not highly related to smoking (Schofield et al., 1999).

Two studies tested smoking cessation interventions integrated into disease risk screening procedures. In an intervention following cardiovascular risk screening, smokers were shown ultrasound photographs of their own atherosclerotic plaques. The intervention was associated with significantly higher abstinence rates at 6 months post-treatment than physician advice alone (Bovet et al., 2002). A self-help intervention following cervical cancer screening did not improve abstinence rates at 3 and 12 months post-treatment when compared to standard clinical follow-up (McBride et al., 1999b).

A pharmacy-based intervention was tested in one study and proved efficacious (Maguire et al., 2001). The intervention consisted of smoking cessation counseling, self-help materials, 4 weekly follow-ups, and monthly follow-ups as needed. The intervention was associated with significantly higher abstinence rates at 12 months post-treatment compared to ad-hoc pharmacist advice.

Two studies looked at smoking cessation interventions delivered by a real-world quitline to smokers who called the quitline. In one study, all callers assigned to the intervention condition received telephone counseling while callers in the control condition received telephone counseling only if they requested it. The intervention was associated with a significantly higher abstinence rate at 12 months post-quit (Zhu et al., 2002). Among smokers calling another quitline, the intervention consisted of a series of brief counseling calls scheduled around the quit date. This intervention added to self-help materials was associated with a significantly higher abstinence rate at 12 months post-baseline than self-help materials alone (Borland et al., 2001).

Summary of evidence

1. Studies reviewed by the *Guideline* demonstrated that treatments effective in the general population are effective in hospital patients. However, among three recent studies, two failed to show treatment effect. One of those studies had a very large sample but did not find an overall intervention effect. The study that found an effect compared augmented intervention to a very minimal intervention, suggesting that the treatment effect was due to increased treatment intensity. Hospital-based interventions require further research. In the meantime, hospitalized and discharged patients should be offered treatments found effective in the general population (Strength of Evidence = B)

2. It appears that interventions accompanying a risk screening procedure hold

some promise but require further research. This conclusion is based on two studies only. One of them showed that such an intervention was effective and the other did not. The sample used in the former study was small. Both compared a multicomponent treatment to very little or no treatment rather than to a treatment of similar intensity. Thus, smoking cessation interventions integrated into disease risk screening procedures hold some promise but it would be premature to unequivocally recommend them at this time (Strength of Evidence = C).

3. One study compared a pharmacy-based behavioral intervention to less intensive usual care and found it effective. This confirms that more intensive behavioral treatments are more effective than the less intensive ones. Pharmacy-based behavioral interventions are recommended (Strength of Evidence = B).

4. Two studies tested behavioral interventions delivered via telephone quitlines. In both studies, more intensive interventions were more effective than less intensive interventions. Thus, the conclusion reached by the *Guideline* that intensive behavioral treatments are more effective than the less intensive ones was confirmed in real-life quitline settings (Strength of Evidence = A).

Non-traditional Behavioral Treatments

Several studies tested non-traditional interventions for smoking cessation such as physical exercise and acupuncture (Table 6). A study by Marcus and colleagues (Marcus et al., 1999) among women smokers compared a vigorous exercise program combined with a cognitive-behavioral cessation program to the cessation program alone. The two treatments were matched on contact time. The exercise condition significantly increased continuous abstinence rates at end-of-treatment, 3, and 12 months post-treatment. Two studies examined

the use of acupuncture for smoking cessation. One study tested three different interventions: acupuncture combined with cessation education, sham acupuncture combined with cessation education, and acupuncture alone (Bier et al., 2002). The three treatments significantly differed from each other with respect to end-of-treatment but not 18-months post-treatment abstinence rates. The combination of acupuncture and education was significantly more effective than either sham acupuncture with education or acupuncture alone. Sham acupuncture with education was significantly more effective than acupuncture alone. In the second study, presumed anti-smoking acupoints stimulation was compared to a control condition using stimulation of acupoints presumably not related to smoking. Differences in cessation rates were not reported. The intervention was associated with significantly lower blood cotinine levels at both end of treatment and 8 months post-treatment (He et al., 2001).

Summary of Evidence.

1. Vigorous physical exercise was shown to be effective for smoking cessation among women in one well-controlled study. However, studies including physical exercise reviewed by the *Guideline* did not yield significant results. Thus, a vigorous exercise approach holds some promise and can be offered to smokers motivated to quit (Strength of Evidence = C).

2. Studies on acupuncture produced mixed results. One study showed a short-term but not a long-term effect of acupuncture in combination with an educational program. However, acupuncture alone was less effective than both acupuncture combined with education and sham acupuncture combined with education. This suggests an acupuncture by education effect but not an acupuncture effect. The other study demonstrated a

Table 6. Nontraditional Behavioral Treatments

Study	Participants per Group	Intervention	Outcome
Exercise vs. control Marcus et al., Archives of Internal Medicine 1999: 1229-34.	N=281 healthy, sedentary female smokers (intervention n=134; control n=147)	Vigorous exercise plus cognitive-behavioral smoking cessation program (CBT) vs. CBT only with matched contact time. All participants received 12 sessions of group CBT smoking cessation counseling.	End-of-treatment: continuous abstinence (BC) Exercise = 19.4% Control = 10.2% p=.03 6 months PT: continuous abstinence (BC) Exercise = 16.4% Control = 8.2% p=.03 12 months PT: continuous abstinence (BC) Exercise = 11.9% Control = 5.4% p=.05 Intent-to-treat procedures were used.
Acupuncture vs. acupuncture plus educational cessation program vs. sham acupuncture plus educational cessation program Bier et al., American Journal of Public Health 2002: 1642-47.	N=141 smokers (acupuncture n=38; acupuncture/education n=45; sham acupuncture/education n=58)	True acupuncture alone vs. true acupuncture plus a smoking cessation educational program vs. sham acupuncture plus a smoking cessation educational program No additional treatment components were reported.	End-of-treatment: self-reported 7-day PP Acupuncture = 10% Acupuncture + education = 40% Sham acupuncture + education = 22% p=.023 18 months PT: self-reported 7-day PP Acupuncture = 20% Acupuncture plus education = 40% Sham acupuncture plus education = 22% p=ns Intent-to-treat procedures were not used.
Acupuncture vs. control He et al., Preventive Medicine 2001: 364-72.	N=46 smokers (acupuncture n=26; control n=20).	Presumed anti-smoking acupoints stimulation vs. stimulation of acupoints presumably not related to smoking No additional treatment components were reported.	End-of-treatment: smoking reduction (BC) Intervention, as compared to control, was associated with significantly lower blood cotinine levels (p<.05) 8 months PT: smoking reduction (BC) Intervention, as compared to control, was associated with significantly lower blood cotinine levels (p<.05). Intent-to-treat procedures were not used.

BC = biochemically confirmed; PP = point-prevalence; PQ = post-quit date; PT = post-treatment; ns= not significant
*abstinence type not reported
**rates not reported

long-term effect of acupuncture but used smoking reduction rather than cessation as outcome. Both studies used small samples and did not use intent-to-treat procedures where those lost to follow-up are considered smokers. The studies reviewed by the *Guideline* did not confirm the efficacy of acupuncture. Thus, the data to date are not supportive of acupuncture and this area requires further well-controlled research (Strength of Evidence C).

Special Topics and Special Populations

In addition to research testing various pharmacological and behavioral treatments for smoking cessation, a significant number of recent studies were devoted to topics and populations of special interest. Those studies can be grouped into two categories: (1) studies testing the efficacy of tailored/individualized treatments; the majority used new computer-based technologies; and (2) studies testing the efficacy of new approaches to smoking cessation and relapse prevention in pregnant and postpartum women.

Tailored/Individualized Treatments

Studies testing the efficacy of tailored/individualized treatments (See Volume 1, Chapter 1) for smoking cessation are listed in Table 7. Six studies in this category tested the effectiveness of interventions tailored to participants' stage of change. The transtheoretical model of behavior change (Prochaska & DiClemente, 1983) posits that behavior change progresses through several stages: precontemplation (no intention to change behavior in the next 6 months), contemplation (intention to change within 6 months), preparation (intention to take action within the next month), action (active involvement in behavior change for less than 6 months), and maintenance (sustained behavior change for at least 6 months).

Of the six tailored interventions, two proved efficacious. A stage-based self-help booklet and a counseling letter tailored to stage of change and other relevant characteristics was effective in increasing abstinence rates when compared to a no intervention control group (Etter & Perneger, 2001). Another stage-matched intervention consisted of mailed reports and self-help manuals (Prochaska et al., 2001). The reports included feedback on the participants' current stage of change, provided stage-matched coping strategies, and referred individuals to the relevant section of the self-help manual. This intervention was associated with significantly higher abstinence rates than the control assessment-only condition at 24 months post-baseline.

On the other hand, two trials testing similar stage-based interventions did not yield significant treatment effects. In a study with three arms, a stage-matched letter was compared to a non-tailored letter and to a no intervention condition. No differences were found among the three conditions (Lennox et al., 2001). In a desktop computer-administered treatment, stage-matched information and motivational modules did not yield differences when compared to the control condition (computer-administered sessions on health topics unrelated to smoking (O'Neill et al., 2000).

Two studies tested stage-based interventions in special populations. One randomized trial targeted smokers with low readiness to quit and administered three interventions: three stage-matched letters, a single stage-matched letter, or a standarized self-help guide. The letters were also tailored based on self-reported outcome expectations, self-efficacy, and smoking behavior. There were no significant outcome differences among groups (Dijkstra et al., 1999). Another study using a stage of change approach focused on African Americans. All participants received a health care provider

Table 7. Tailored Treatments.

Study	Participants per Group	Intervention	Outcome
Computer-tailored mail-in intervention vs. control Etter & Perneger, Archives of Internal Medicine 2001: 2596-2601.	N=2934 daily smokers (n=1467 per group)	Personalized counseling letters and stage-based booklets vs. no intervention No additional treatment components were reported.	7 months post-baseline: self-reported 7-day PP Intervention = 8.0% Control = 3.3% p<.001 Intent-to-treat procedures were used.
Staged-based intervention vs. control Prochaska et al., Addictive Behaviors 2001: 583-602.	N=4144 smokers (intervention n=1358; control n=2786)	Stage-matched self-help booklet and counseling letter vs. control assessment-only condition No additional treatment components were reported.	12 months post-baseline: self-reported 7-day PP Intervention = 17% Control = 13.8% p<.05 24 months post-baseline: self-reported 7-day PP Intervention = 24.9% Control = 19.0% p<.05 Intent-to-treat procedures were not used.
Computer tailored vs. non-tailored letter intervention vs. control Lennox et al., British Medical Journal 2001: 1-7.	N=2553 smokers (tailored letter group n=857; non-tailored group=846; no letter group n=850)	Computer tailored letter based on smoking cessation stage of change vs. non-tailored, standard letter on smoking cessation vs. no letter control group (letter of thanks for participation in the study). No additional treatment components were reported.	6 months PT: 7-day PP (BC) Tailored letter = 3.5% Non-tailored letter = 4.4% Control = 2.6% ns Intent-to-treat procedures were used.
Computer administered intervention targeting cigarette smoking based on stages of change (CAS) vs. computer administered control intervention (CAC) O'Neill et al., American Journal of Health Promotion 2000: 93-96.	N=65 undergraduates (n=31 in the intervention group; n=34 in control)	CAS (6 computer modules matched to participants stage of readiness to quit smoking) vs. CAC (3 computer modules dealing with health-related topics other than smoking) Control modules were equivalent to intervention modules in length and general format. No additional treatment components were reported.	1 month PT: self-reported continuous abstinence Intervention = 19.4% Control = 15.2% ns 3 months PT: self-reported continuous abstinence Intervention = 30.0% Control = 21.2% ns 7 months PT: self-reported continuous abstinence Intervention = 29.6% Control = 31.0% ns Intent-to-treat procedures were not specified.

Two types of tailored smoking cessation self-help interventions vs. standardized smoking cessation self-help guide vs. control Dijkstra et al., Preventive Medicine 1999: 203-211.	N=843 smokers low in self-reported readiness to quit (tailored groups n=214 and 206; standardized group n=215; control group n=208)	Three consecutive tailored letters (MT) vs. single tailored letter (ST) vs. standardized self-help guide (SHG) vs. no self-help materials (CO) Tailoring was based on stage of change, outcome expectations, self-efficacy, and smoking behavior. No additional treatment components were reported.	<u>6 months PT: self-reported 7-day PP</u> MT = 3.2% ST = 4.4% SHG = 3.5% CO = 5.5% *ns* Intent-to-treat procedures were used.
Two types of tailored intervention approaches vs. control Lipkus et al., Nicotine & Tobacco Research 1999: 77-85.	N=160 African-American smokers (tailored interventions n=55 and 52; control n=53)	Health care provider prompting intervention with tailored print communications (HCP) vs. prompting intervention with tailored print communications and tailored telephone (HCPT) counseling vs. health care provider prompting intervention (HC) alone All participants received the health care provider prompting intervention.	<u>16 months PT: self-reported 30-day PP</u> HCP = 32.7% HCPT = 19.2% HC = 13.2% HCP vs. HC (*p*<.05) HCP vs. HCPT (not significant) HCPT vs. HC (not significant) Intent-to-treat procedures were used.
Personalized mail intervention vs. standard mail intervention vs. control Becona & Vazquez, Journal of Consulting and Clinical Psychology 2001: 33-40.	N=300 (n=100 for each group)	Personalized written feedback combined with a standard mail intervention vs. standard mail intervention alone vs. no treatment control (control participants were promised treatment after a 6-month period) No additional treatment components were reported.	<u>End-of-treatment: 7-day PP (BC)</u> Personalized intervention = 51% Standard intervention = 37% Control = 0% Personalized , Standard vs. Control (*p*<.001) <u>3 months: 7-day PP (BC)</u> Personalized intervention = 37% Standard intervention = 22% Control = 1% Personalized , Standard vs. Control (*p*<.001) <u>6 months: 7-day PP (BC)</u> Personalized intervention = 32% Standard intervention = 19% Control = 1% Personalized , Standard vs. Control (*p*<.001) Intent-to-treat procedures were used.

BC = biochemically confirmed; PP = point-prevalence; PQ = post-quit date; PT = post-treatment; ns= not significant   *abstinence type not reported   **rates not reported prompting intervention and were randomized into one of the three conditions: tailored print communications, tailored print communications and tailored telephone counseling, or no tailored intervention. Tailored print communications combined with health care provider prompting was associated with higher abstinence rates at 16 months post-treatment than health care provider prompting alone. Tailored print communications combined with tailored telephone counseling and health care provider prompting did not significantly differ from the other conditions (Lipkus et al., 1999).

Finally, compared to a standard mailed self-help intervention, personalized written feedback based on self-reported smoking behavior, motivation, and use of coping strategies was associated with higher abstinence rates up to 6 months post-treatment (Becona & Vazquez, 2001).

Summary of Evidence.
1. Studies on tailored interventions produced mixed results. Two of the three studies that produced positive results used large samples but had other weaknesses. One study compared the tailored intervention to no intervention and thus did not isolate the effect of tailoring (Etter & Perneger, 2001). The other study had loss to follow-up that differed by treatment group

(Prochaska et al., 2001). The third study was well designed and used intent-to-treat procedures, but had a small sample (100 per study arm; Becona & Vazquez, 2001). In addition, the *Guideline* did not recommend tailored treatments because of insufficient data. In sum, although tailored interventions hold some promise, further well-designed research is needed. (Strength of Evidence = C)

Pregnant/Postpartum Women
Another topic that stimulated a substantial number of new studies was smoking during and after pregnancy (Table 8). Only two of eight new studies in this area reported a significant treatment effect. Enhancement of external social support, financial incentives, and a brief educational intervention produced higher quit rates at 8 months gestation and 2 months postpartum than did a brief educational intervention alone (Donatelle et al., 2000). In another study of women who quit during pregnancy, a relapse prevention intervention was delivered pre-and postpartum or prepartum only (McBride et al., 1999a). The control condition consisted of a self-help booklet. The intervention delivered pre-and postpartum compared to both the prepartum intervention and the control condition was associated with significantly higher abstinence rates at 8 weeks and 6

Table 8. Treatments for Pregnant/Postpartum Women

Study	Participants per Group	Intervention	Outcome
Educational intervention, social support, and financial incentives vs. control Donatelle et al., Tobacco Control 2000: iii67-iii69.	N=220 pregnant smokers at 28 or less weeks gestation (intervention n=112; control n=108)	Peer support and $50/month vouchers vs. educational intervention alone All participants were given brief educational counseling: verbal and written information on the importance of smoking cessation.	8-month gestation: 7-day PP (BC) Intervention = 32% Control = 9% *p*<.0001 2 months postpartum: 7-day PP (BC) Intervention = 21% Control = 6% *p*<.0009 Intent-to-treat procedures were used.

Pre/postpartum intervention vs. prepartum intervention vs. control McBride et al., American Journal of Public Health 1999: 706-711.	N=897 smokers who quit during pregnancy (pre/post n=306; prepartum n=294; control n=297)	Pre- and postpartum telephone counseling plus relapse prevention kit vs. prepartum phone counseling and relapse prevention kit vs. self-help booklet only All participants received the self-help booklet.	<u>8 weeks postpartum: 7-day PP (BC)</u> Pre/postpartum = 39% Prepartum = 35% Control = 30% Pre/postpartum, prepartum vs. control ($p<.05$) <u>6 months postpartum: 7-day PP (BC)</u> Pre/postpartum = 33% Prepartum = 24% Control = 26% Pre/postpartum vs. prepartum, control ($p<.05$) <u>12 months postpartum: 7-day PP (BC)</u> Pre/postpartum = 25% Prepartum = 23% Control = 24% not significant Intent-to-treat procedures were used.
Nicotine patch vs. control Wisborg et al., Obstetrics & Gynecology 2000: 967-971.	N=250 pregnant women who smoked ten or more cigarettes after the first trimester (experimental n=124; control n=126)	15mg patch for 8 weeks, then 10mg for 3 weeks vs. placebo patch All women received smoking cessation counseling and reading materials.	<u>1 year after start of intervention: continuous abstinence (BC)</u> Nicotine patch = 21% Placebo patch = 19% *ns* Intent-to-treat procedures were used.
Computerized telephone counseling vs. motivational counseling vs. control Ershoff et al., American Journal of Preventive Medicine 1999: 161-168.	N=332 smokers who self-reported to be active smokers at their initial prenatal appointment (telephone counseling n=120; motivational counseling n=101; usual care n=111).	Computerized telephone cessation program based on interactive voice response technology vs. telephone counseling from nurse educators using motivation interviewing techniques vs. usual care All participants received usual care self-help booklets tailored to smoking patterns, stage of change, and lifestyle of pregnant smokers.	<u>End-of-pregnancy: 7-day PP (BC)</u> Telephone counseling = 18.2% Motivational counseling = 23.3% Control = 16.4% *ns* No participants lost to follow-up.
Smoking cessation intervention vs. control Panjari et al., Australian and New Zealand Journal of Obstetrics and Gynaecology 1999: 312-317.	N=732 pregnant smokers (study group n=339; control n=393).	Four individual behavioral counseling sessions delivered by a midwife trained in smoking cessation vs. standard care. All women received standard antenatal care, which included the distribution of a smoking and pregnancy pamphlet during a group information session.	<u>34-36 weeks gestation: 7-day PP (BC)</u> Intervention = 11.9% Control = 9.8% *ns* Intent-to-treat procedures were <u>not</u> used.

| Smoking cessation intervention vs. control

Hajek et al., Addiction 2001: 485-494.	N=1120 pregnant smokers or recent quitters in third month of pregnancy (treatment group n=545; control n=575)	Brief counseling and written materials tailored to women's cessation goals, arrangement for continuing self-help support, and feedback on carbon monoxide levels vs. usual anti-smoking advice No additional treatment components were reported.	At birth: 7-day PP (BC) Intervention = 22% Control = 20% *ns* 6 months postpartum: continuous abstinence (BC) Intervention = 7% Control = 8% *ns* Intent-to-treat procedures were used.
Relapse prevention intervention vs. control

Van't Hof et al., Tobacco Control 2000; ii64-ii66. | N=277 smokers who quit during pregnancy (intervention n=133; control n=144) | Post-delivery, in-hospital nurse-delivered relapse prevention counseling vs. no intervention

All participants received standard pediatrician-delivered care | 6 months postpartum: self-reported relapse rate Intervention = 41% Control = 37% *ns*

Intent-to-treat procedures were not used. |
| Relapse prevention intervention vs. control

Johnson et al., Nursing Research 2000: 44-52. | N=251 smokers who quit during pregnancy (intervention n=125; control n=126). | Nurse-delivered postpartum relapse prevention counseling vs. no treatment

No additional treatment components were reported. | 6 months postpartum: continuous abstinence (BC) Intervention = 37.6% Control = 27% *ns* Intent-to-treat procedures were used. |

BC = biochemically confirmed; PP = point-prevalence; PQ = post-quit date; PT = post-treatment; ns= not significant
*abstinence type not reported
**rates not reported

months postpartum but not at 12 months postpartum. The studies with no significant treatment effect compared the nicotine patch to placebo (Wisborg et al., 2000), a computerized telephone cessation program and motivational counseling intervention to usual care (self-help booklet plus brief physician advice; Ershoff et al., 1999), midwife-delivered individual cessation counseling to usual care (prenatal care and quit smoking pamphlet; Panjari et al., 1999), midwife-delivered counseling, written materials, and carbon monoxide feedback to usual antismoking advice (Hajek et al., 2001), and nurse-delivered postpartum relapse prevention counseling to standard pediatric care with no relapse prevention treatment (Johnson et al., 2000; Van't Hof et al., 2000).

Summary of Evidence.
1. These findings demonstrate that the issue of smoking during pregnancy and postpartum remains a major challenge.

Research reviewed by the *Guideline* confirmed that augmented behavioral interventions are more effective in this population than minimal advice. Of the two studies that yielded significant results, one focused on smoking cessation and one on relapse prevention. These results suggest that multifaceted cessation programs that include the enhancement of external social and financial support might be effective. Study results also suggest that relapse prevention programs delivered during both prepartum and postpartum periods may be more efficacious than programs delivered prepartum only, at least with respect to short-term abstinence (Strength of Evidence B).

DISCUSSION
Effective Treatment
Our review shows that a wide array of effective smoking cessation treatments are

available for smokers who want to quit and clinicians who want to help them. These options include several pharmacological and behavioral treatments that can be combined to create various kinds of smoking cessation programs. The clinician can choose a program that is best suited both to the needs of the quitter and to available resources. Below we present three such programs most typically found in the real world: a brief intervention program, an intensive intervention program, and a quitline program. Our recommendations are based on the *Guideline* and more recent evidence presented earlier in this chapter. Table 9 lists effective smoking cessation treatments and their relevance to brief, intensive, and quitline programs. Treatments in Table 9 are grouped based on their type. They are all effective and their order is not related to their efficacy levels.

Table 9. Effective Smoking Cessation Treatments[a] and Their Relevance to the Type of Intervention Program (Brief, Intensive or Quitline)

Treatment	Relevance	Source
Pharmacological Treatments		
1. Bupropion SR (Sustained Release)		
• In the general population	B, I, Q	The *Guideline,* New Developments
• In African Americans, patients with chronic obstructive pulmonary disease, smokers who previously used bupropion, and recent quitters	B, I, Q	New Developments
2. Nicotine Replacement Therapy (NRT)		
• Patch (including over-the-counter patch), gum, inhaler, and nasal spray	B, I Q	The *Guideline*
• Gum: 4 mg compared to 2 mg in highly dependent smokers	B, I Q	The *Guideline*
• Combination NRT: patch/gum, patch/spray, patch/inhaler	B, I, Q	The *Guideline* New Developments
• Highest standard dose compared to lower doses (21 mg compared to 14 mg and 7 mg; 25 mg compared to 15 mg)	B, I, Q	New Developments
• Nicotine lozenge and nicotine sublingual tablet	B, I, Q	New Developments
3. Clonidine	B, I	The *Guideline*
4. Nortriptyline	B, I	The *Guideline,* New Developments
Behavioral Treatments		
1. Brief Clinical Interventions		
• Physician advice to quit	B	The *Guideline*
• Minimal interventions (3 minutes or less)	B	The *Guideline*
2. Low-intensity interventions (3-30 minutes of total person-to-person contact time)	Q	The *Guideline*
3. Intensive Clinical Interventions		
• Session length of at least 10 minutes	I, Q	The *Guideline*
• Total person-to-person contact time at least 30 minutes	I, Q	The *Guideline*
• Four or more sessions of person-to-person contact	I, Q	The *Guideline*
4. Clinician Type		
• Clinician-delivered interventions across various clinician types	B, I	The *Guideline*
• Multiple clinician types compared to one type	I	The *Guideline*
5. Treatment Format		
• Proactive telephone counseling	B, I, Q	The *Guideline*
• Group counseling,	I	The *Guideline*
• Individual counseling	B, I, Q	The *Guideline*
• Multiple formats compared to single format	B, I	The *Guideline*

6. Types of Counseling/Behavioral Treatments		
• Practical counseling (e.g., skills training, stress management)	B, I, Q	The *Guideline*
• Social support as a part of treatment	B, I, Q	The *Guideline*
• Help with obtaining external social support	B, I, Q	The *Guideline*
• Aversive smoking	I	The *Guideline*
7. Behavioral Interventions in Real-Life Settings		
• Hospital-based interventions	B, I	The *Guideline*, New Developments
• Pharmacies	B, I	New Developments
• Telephone quitlines	Q	New Developments
8. Behavioral Treatments in Special Populations		
• low-income populations	B, I, Q	New Developments
• patients with diabetes and HIV	B, I, Q	New Developments
• cognitive-behavioral therapy for depression among patients with recurrent depression.	I	New Developments
Special Topics/Special Populations		
1. Treatments effective in the general population are effective in special populations	B, I, Q	The *Guideline*, New Developments
2. Post-cessation weight gain		
• Bupropion SR to delay weight gain in smokers with weight concerns	B, I, Q	The *Guideline*
• NRT to delay weight gain in smokers with weight concerns	B, I, Q	The *Guideline*
• Very low energy diet	I	New Developments
• Cognitive behavioral therapy reducing weight concerns among women with weight issues	I	New Developments
4. Pregnant Women		
• Extended/augmented psychosocial interventions, throughout pregnancy	I	The *Guideline*
• Multifaceted interventions that include enhancement of external social support and financial incentives	I	New Developments
• Relapse prevention programs delivered both pre- and postpartum	I	New Developments

B – brief clinical interventions, I – intensive clinical interventions, Q – quitline programs
[a] effective treatments with Strength of Evidence ratings A or B are included

Pharmacotherapy

Pharmacotherapy is a vital component of smoking cessation interventions and should be offered to all smokers who want to quit. A variety of smoking cessation medications are now available with some offered over the counter and others by prescription only. First-line medications are considered safe and effective, and have been approved by the FDA for treatment of tobacco dependence. Unless contraindicated, those medications should be considered first as a part of a smoking cessation intervention. Second-line medications are ones for which there is efficacy evidence but which have more concerns over possible side effects and have not been FDA-approved for treatment of tobacco dependence. These medications should be considered on a case-by-case basis after the use of first-line medications has been excluded. Second-line pharmacotherapies require medical supervision and are thus not well suited to conditions where such supervision is not available.

Pharmacotherapy can be incorporated into any type of smoking cessation program. Therefore, the recommendations for the use of smoking cessation medications are presented first and apply to all three programs described below. Specific guidelines for the use of pharmacotherapies are listed in Table 10.

Table 10. Recommendations for Pharmacotherapy.

Pharmacotherapy	Recommendation

1. General Guidelines	• All smokers willing to quit should be offered pharmacotherapy, except in special circumstances (e.g., pregnancy)
	• Choice of a specific pharmacotherapy should be guided by the following factors:
	  – Clinician familiarity with the medication
	  – Availability of prescription
	  – Contraindications for selected patients
	  – Patient preference
	  – Previous patient experience with a specific medication
	  – Patient characteristics (e.g., depression history, weight issues)

2. First-line Medications: Bupropion SR	• If prescription is available and there are no medical contraindications, offer bupropion • Special considerations: If there is a history of depression and/or weight issues, offer bupropion
3. First-line Medications: NRT	• If prescription is not available and/or there are medical contraindications against bupropion, recommend over-the-counter nicotine patch • 21 mg patch is recommended for those who smoke 10 or more cigarettes per day; lower patch dosages are recommended for those who smoke less • If the patch is not well tolerated and/or did not work in the past, and/or *ad libitum* dosing is preferred, offer nicotine gum (over-the-counter only) • 4mg gum is recommended for highly dependent smokers • If the gum is not well tolerated or not acceptable, and prescription is available, offer nicotine spray or inhaler • If prescription is available, the gum, spray or inhaler are not well tolerated and/or oral NRT administration is preferred, offer nicotine lozenge or sublingual tablet • Special considerations: If a patient has a history of difficulty quitting and/or is unable to quit with a single NRT, offer a combination of the patch with gum, spray, or inhaler. • Special considerations: If there are weight issues and bupropion cannot be used, offer NRT
4. Second-line Medications: Clonidine and Nortriptyline	• If prescription is available and either of the considerations below apply, offer clonidine or nortriptyline • If first-line medications are contraindicated, use one of the second line medications • If first-line medications are not helpful, use one of the second line medications • Patient's medical history and tolerance of side-effects should guide the choice of either clonidine or nortriptyline • Special considerations: patients with a history of depression who cannot or choose not to use bupropion should be offered nortriptyline
5. Special Populations	• Pharmacotherapies effective in the general population can be used in special populations unless medically contraindicated • Bupropion has been tested and proven effective in African Americans, patients with chronic obstructive pulmonary disease, smokers who previously used bupropion, and recent quitters

298

Brief Interventions

The benefits of providing treatment to smokers are overwhelmingly evident but time limitations have hindered efforts to offer such help. Perhaps the most important evidence-based message for clinicians is that brief smoking cessation interventions, including those lasting only 3 minutes or less, are effective. This means that smoking cessation interventions can and should be delivered to all smokers by any type of clinician, in all clinical settings.

To be able to offer at least a brief inter-vention to all smokers, clinicians should routinely ask all patients about their smoking status. Although any clinician can offer such treatment, brief strategies are especially relevant to those healthcare professionals who see large numbers of patients, even if only for very short periods of time (i.e., physicians, nurses, dentists, pharmacists, etc.). A brief intervention may consist of as little as advice to quit, but a short intervention should go beyond that and include the provision of very basic smoking cessation strategies (see Table 11).

Table 11. Recommendations for Brief Interventions.[a]

Brief Intervention Component	Recommendation
1. Smoking Status Assessment	• All patients seen in a clinical setting should be asked about their smoking status • Smoking status of each patient should be documented
2. Advice to Quit	• All smokers should be advised to quit in a clear, strong, and personalized manner

3. Motivation to Quit Assessment and Enhancement	• All smokers who are advised to quit should be asked whether they are willing to do so
	• For smokers not ready to make a quit attempt, clinicians should use a brief motivation promotion intervention
	• The intervention should address
	   – Relevance of quitting to the patient's health, social, and family situation
	   – Negative consequences of smoking
	   – Benefits of quitting smoking
	   – Barriers to quitting
	• The motivation enhancement intervention should be repeated every time an unmotivated patient is seen by a clinician

4. Treatment Options	• If a patient is willing to use an intensive treatment and such a treatment is available, refer the patient to it • If an intensive person-to-person treatment is not available, offer a brief intervention and refer to a quitline • A brief intervention should include both pharmacological and behavioral components

5. Pharmacotherapy[b]	• All smokers willing to quit should be offered pharmacotherapy, except in special circumstances (e.g., pregnancy)
	• Choice of a specific pharmacotherapy should be guided by the following factors:
	   – Clinician familiarity with the medication
	   – Availability of prescription
	   – Contraindications for selected patients
	   – Patient preference
	   – Previous patient experience with a specific medication
	   – Patient characteristics (e.g., depression history, weight issues)

6. Behavioral Intervention	• Clinician should negotiate the quit date with all smokers willing to quit, preferably within the next two weeks
	• Choice of a specific behavioral strategies should be guided by the following factors:
	  – Availability of resources
	  – Time limitations
	  – Patient characteristics

a. Brief Behavioral Strategies	• Advise the patient to tell family, patients, and coworkers about quitting and request their understanding (enhancement of external social support)
	• Provide a supportive clinical environment (intratreatment social support)
	• Provide practical counseling
	  – Briefly educate the patient about symptoms of nicotine withdrawal and how to cope with them
	  – Advise to remove tobacco products form his/her environment and avoid smoking places
	  – Advise to avoid alcohol
	  – Advise to anticipate triggers and challenges
	  – Emphasize the importance of total abstinence
	  – Advise to encourage housemates to quit with the patient
	• Provide supplementary educational materials

b. Clinician Type and Clinical Setting	• Any type of clinician can deliver a brief intervention • A brief intervention can be delivered in any clinical setting, for example during a routine physical exam, during a hospital stay or at a pharmacy
c. Follow-Up	• If possible/applicable, a clinicians should schedule a follow-up, preferably within the first week of the quit date
7. Special Populations	• Brief interventions effective in the general population can be offered in special populations • Some special populations such patients with recurrent depression, HIV, women with weight issues, and pregnant women may particularly benefit from a referral to an intensive program

[a] Adapted from: Fiore, M. C., et al. (2000). Treating tobacco use and dependence . Rockville, MD: U.S. Department of Health and Human Services, Public Health Service, Agency for Health Care Policy and Research.
[b] Specific types of pharmacotherapy and recommendations are listed in Table 10.

Brief interventions like all other types of smoking cessation interventions can and should offer pharmacotherapy. Specific strategies for a brief intervention program are listed in Table 11.

Intensive Interventions

Another very important evidence-based message for clinicians is that there is a strong dose-response relationship between smoking cessation treatment intensity and its efficacy. More intensive treatments produce higher abstinence rates than do less intensive or brief interventions.

These interventions are often delivered by clinicians specializing in the treatment of nicotine dependence. However, all appropriately trained clinicians with the necessary resources can provide valuable opportunities for patients to quit smoking. All smokers willing to quit should be informed about intensive treatment options and referred to an intensive program if they express strong willingness to participate. It is important to note that the feasibility of this approach is determined by logistical factors such as time constraints and resource availability.

The efficacy of intensive treatments is by no means limited to selected segments of the population of smokers but some subpopulations may particularly benefit from such programs. Examples include pregnant women or smokers unable to quit with less intensive interventions. Intensive treatments should incorporate pharmacotherapy. Detailed strategies for intensive interventions are highlighted in Table 12.

Table 12. Recommendations for Intensive Interventions.[a]

Intensive Intervention Component	Recommendation
1. Assessment of Willingness to Participate in an Intensive Intervention	• Due to the strong relation between dose and response to treatment, the willingness to participate in an intensive intervention should be assessed for every smoker who is motivated to quit and seen in any type of a healthcare setting • Smokers willing to receive an intensive intervention should be referred to such a program

2. Quit Plan	• Once in the program, the smoker's quit date should be negotiated and scheduled preferably no later than 2 weeks ahead
	• The smoker should be advised to
	  – Tell family, friends, and coworkers about quitting and request their support
	  – Prior to quitting, avoid smoking in usual places
	  – Remove tobacco product from his/her environment

3. Pharmacotherapy[b]	• All smokers willing to quit should be offered pharmacotherapy in conjunction with counseling interventions, except in special circumstances (e.g., pregnancy)
	• Pharmacotherapy type should be selected by the following factors:
	  – Clinician familiarity with the medication
	  – Availability of prescription
	  – Contraindications for selected patients
	  – Patient preference
	  – Previous patient experience with a specific medication
	  – Patient characteristics (e.g., depression history, weight issues)

4. Clinician Type	• Various types of clinicians are effective and should provide intervention.

5. Behavioral Treatment Intensity	• The recommended intensity is
	  – Session duration longer than 10 minutes
	  – At least 4 separate sessions
	  – No less than 30 minutes of total contact time

6. Behavioral Treatment Format	• Both individual and group face-to-face counseling have been shown to be effective • The use of proactive telephone counseling has demonstrated efficacy and is recommended • If possible, treatment should be delivered in multiple formats

7. Types of Counseling	• Counseling should involve three components: (1) problem solving/skills training; (2) intra-treatment social support; and (3) securing support outside of the treatment setting.

a. Problem Solving/Skills Training	Problem solving/skills training should teach the smoker to
	• Identify triggers for smoking and high risk situations which increase the likelihood of smoking. Typical lapse triggers include:
	  – Negative affect
	  – Presence of other smokers
	  – Drinking alcohol
	  – Experiencing urges
	  – Time pressure
	• Develop problem-solving skills to cope with high-risk situations:
	  – Anticipate and avoid temptations
	  – Use cognitive strategies to reduce negative mood
	  – Change lifestyle to reduce stress, enhance quality of life, and promote pleasure
	• Employ basic educational information about smoking and successful quitting provided face-to-face and via self-help materials whenever available. Basic facts are:
	  – Smoking is an addiction
	  – Even a puff increases relapse risk
	  – Withdrawal typically peaks 1-3 weeks after quitting
	  – Withdrawal symptoms include negative mood, urges, and difficulty concentrating

b. Intra-treatment Support	The clinician should
	• Provide encouragement including belief in patient's ability to quit and information that
	  – Effective treatments are available
	  – Half of ever-smokers have quit
	• Demonstrate caring and concern for the patient
	  – Ask how the patient feels about quitting
	  – Express concern and willingness to help
	  – Empathize with the patient's fears, difficulties, and ambivalent feelings related to quitting
	• Facilitate discussion about the quitting process. Ask about the patient's:
	  – Reasons to quit
	  – Concerns about quitting
	  – Success achieved
	  – Difficulties encountered

c. Extra-treatment Support	The clinician should
	• Teach patient how to obtain social support
	  – If possible, show videotapes that model support requesting skills
	  – Practice requesting support from family, friends, and coworkers
	  – Help patient in creating a smoke-free home
	• Encourage patient to seek such support
	  – Help patient identify supportive others
	  – Call the patient to remind him/her to seek support
	  – Inform about helplines and quitlines
	• Arrange outside support for patient
	  – Call and mail letters to supportive others
	  – If possible, invite others to cessation sessions
	  – If possible, assign patients to be "buddies" for one another

8. Aversive Smoking	• If the smoker has been unsuccessful with other treatments, requests aversive techniques, and medical supervision is available, offer an aversive smoking intervension (e.g., rapid smoking or rapid puffing)
9. Special Populations	• Intensive interventions effective in the general population can be offered in special populations • Pregnant women should receive as intensive of a treatment as possible with special emphasis on enhancement of external social support, financial incentives, and relapse prevention delivered both pre- and postpartum • Smokers with recurrent depression may particularly benefit from cognitive-behavioral therapy for depression • Female smokers with weight issues can be offered very low energy diet or cognitive-behavioral therapy aimed at reducing weight concerns
10. Follow-up	• If possible, a clinicians should schedule a follow-up, preferably within a month of the last counseling session • Those who relapse should be offered an intensive treatment program

[a] Adapted from: Fiore, M. C., et al. (2000). Treating tobacco use and dependence . Rockville, MD: U.S. Department of Health and Human Services, Public Health Service, Agency for Health Care Policy and Research.
[b] Specific types of pharmacotherapy and recommendations are listed in Table 10.

Quitline Interventions

A quitline is a region, state or nation-wide telephone-based smoking cessation service that is often free and available to all smokers who call it. Quitlines are now available in most states and their number is rapidly growing. Quitline interventions have been proven to be effective and will likely emerge as a frontrunner in the fight against tobacco use because they offer an unprecedented opportunity for reducing smoking rates in the general public, as well as among hard-to-reach subgroups of the smoking population (e.g., pregnant, low income, and ethnic minority smokers).

The attractiveness of quitline interventions consists of their wide availability and ability to overcome usual barriers to treatment such as time limitations, transportation, or day care. Quitlines can be used from the smoker's home and usually offer flexible schedules including evening and weekend calls.

Quitline interventions can and should be combined with pharmacotherapy. Depending on the availability of prescriptions, quitlines may offer a broader range of pharmacological options or encourage a smoker to use over-the-counter NRT. Specific strategies for a quitline intervention program are listed in Table 13.

KEY AREAS FOR FUTURE RESEARCH

Although smoking cessation interventions have been extensively researched, there are several areas of research that require more attention for the whole field to progress more rapidly. These areas include (1) individually tailored treatments, (2) treatments targeted at special populations, (3) pregnancy smoking cessation and postpartum relapse, (4) pharmacotherapy comparisons and mechanisms of action, and (5) methodological issues related to behavioral interventions.

Tailored Treatments

Continued research is needed on tailored approaches including the use of new technologies as the efficacy of these approaches has not been established. An important methodological issue regarding tailored treatments is that studies need to be

Table 13. Recommendations for Quitline Interventions.[a]

Quitline Intervention Component	Recommendation

1. Quit Plan	• For each smoker who calls the quitline, his/her quit date should be negotiated and scheduled preferably no later than 2 weeks ahead
	• The smoker should be advised to
	  – Tell family, friends, and coworkers about quitting and request their support
	  – Prior to quitting, avoid smoking in usual places
	  – Remove tobacco product from his/her environment

2. Pharmacotherapy[b]	• If prescription is available within or in conjunction with the quitline and there are no contraindications, the smoker should be offered bupropion • If prescription is not available and there are no contraindications, callers should be encouraged to use over-the-counter patch • Other NRT modes can be considered depending on prescription availability, smokers's preference, and past experience
3. Behavioral Treatment Format	• All callers should be offered telephone counseling • All callers should receive supplemental educational self-help materials

4. Counseling Intensity	• The recommended intensity is
	  – Call duration longer than 10 minutes
	  – At least 4 separate calls
	  – No less than 30 minutes of total contact time
	• If there are time constraints, counseling time of less than 30 minutes may be considered

5. Types of Counseling	• Counseling should involve three components: (1) problem solving/skills training; (2) intra-treatment social support; and (3) securing support outside of the treatment setting.

a. Problem Solving/Skills Training	Problem solving/skills training should teach the smoker to
	• Identify triggers for smoking and high risk situations which increase the likelihood of smoking. Typical lapse triggers include:
	  – Negative affect
	  – Presence of other smokers
	  – Drinking alcohol
	  – Experiencing urges
	  – Time pressure
	• Develop problem-solving skills to cope with these high-risk situations:
	  – Anticipate and avoid temptations
	  – Use cognitive strategies to reduce negative mood
	  – Change lifestyle to reduce stress, enhance quality of life, and promote pleasure
	• Employ basic educational information about smoking and successful quitting provided face-to-face and via self-help materials whenever available. Basic facts are:
	  – Smoking is an addiction
	  – Even a puff increases relapse risk
	  – Withdrawal typically peaks 1-3 weeks after quitting
	  – Withdrawal symptoms include negative mood, urges, and difficulty concentrating

b. Intra-treatment Support	The counselor should
	• Provide encouragement including belief in patient's ability to quit and information that
	  – Effective treatments are available
	  – Half of ever-smokers have quit
	• Demonstrate caring and concern for the patient
	  – Ask how the patient feels about quitting
	  – Express concern and willingness to help
	  – Empathize with the patient's fears, difficulties, and ambivalent feelings related to quitting
	• Facilitate discussion about the quitting process. Ask about the patient's:
	  – Reasons to quit
	  – Concerns about quitting
	  – Success achieved
	  – Difficulties encountered

c. Extra-treatment Support	The counselor should
	• Teach patient how to obtain social support
	  – Practice requesting support from family, friends, and coworkers
	  – Help patient in creating a smoke-free home
	• Encourage patient to seek such support
	  – Help patient identify supportive others
	  – Call the patient to remind him/her to seek support
	  – Inform about helplines and quitlines
	• Arrange outside support for patient, for instance call and mail letters to supportive others

6. Follow-Up	• If possible/applicable, a clinicians should schedule a follow-up, preferably within a month of the last counseling session • Those who relapsed should be offered another quitline intervention or referred to a more intensive treatment program

[a] Adapted from: Fiore, M. C., et al. (2000). Treating tobacco use and dependence . Rockville, MD: U.S. Department of Health and Human Services, Public Health Service, Agency for Health Care Policy and Research.
[b] Specific types of pharmacotherapy and recommendations are listed in Table 10

well designed so the effect of tailoring is isolated. A tailored treatment should be compared to a similar nontailored treatment of the same duration and intensity rather than to no treatment or basic standard care. Regarding treatment contents, studies on tailored treatments should include other dimensions in addition to stages of change, for instance smoking behavior, self-efficacy, outcome expectations, and the use of coping strategies. More basic research on individual differences among smokers is needed as the findings of such research will provide a better foundation for treatment tailoring.

Targeted Treatments for Special Populations

Effective treatments targeted specifically at special populations are scarce. For example, there are insufficient data on treatments targeted at racial/ethnic minorities. Only three recent studies met our review criteria and these studies were devoted exclusively to African Americans. One tested a pharmacotherapy effective in the general population (bupropion), one tested a novel multicomponent behavioral treatment not targeted specifically at this racial minority, and the third tested an individually tailored behavioral treatment rather than a racially targeted intervention. Data on treatments targeted at other non-white ethnicities were not available. More research is also needed on how to best help smokers with comorbidities such as depression, schizophrenia, and alcohol/chemical dependency.

Another special population that requires more research are highly dependent smokers who have difficulty quitting using standard approaches. One way to target such smokers is stepped care. This concept refers to the approach where more intensive and more expensive treatments are provided to those smokers who fail with less intensive low-cost treatments, until the treatment is intensive enough to be effective. This concept has not been sufficiently tested and its efficacy remains unknown.

Cessation in Pregnancy and Postpartum Relapse

Among special populations, pregnant smokers and former smokers at risk for postpartum relapse pose a particular challenge. Although smoking prevalence during pregnancy declined in all age and racial/ethnic groups between 1989-1998, 12.9% of all pregnant women in 1998 reported prenatal smoking (USDHHS, 2001). In addition, among the 30-50% of female smokers who quit during pregnancy, 60-80% relapse within 1 year postpartum (McBride et al., 1999a; Stotts et al., 2000). Research in this area has been abundant but few effective treatments have been developed. Some targeted approaches such as extended psychosocial interventions, multifaceted interventions that include enhancement of external social support and financial incentives, and relapse prevention programs delivered both pre- and postpartum have been shown to be effective among pregnant female smokers. However, a high proportion of recent studies produced nonsignificant results. For example, the nicotine patch did not prove effective among pregnant women who smoked after the first trimester. Among behavioral cessation treatments that did not prove effective were telephone counseling combined with in-person motivational counseling, midwife-delivered counseling, and a multicomponent program consisting of brief counseling, tailored written materials, and feedback on carbon monoxide levels. Among relapse prevention programs that did not prove effective were two postpartum nurse-delivered relapse prevention counseling programs. Thus, there is a need for continued research that would help refine smoking cessation and relapse prevention treatments for this population.

Pharmacotherapies

Despite a growing number of pharmacological agents proven effective for smoking cessation, relatively little is known about these agents' mechanisms of action. For example, why NRT is effective remains unclear. NRT reduces withdrawal symptoms, but withdrawal reduction has not been demonstrated to account for the effectiveness of NRT (Hughes, 1993). One possible mechanism may be that NRT breaks the connection between smoking cues and nicotine intake. During ad lib smoking, nicotine reinforcement due to smoking is paired with a myriad of environmental and interoceptive cues. However, during NRT use, those cues are no longer paired with nicotine intake. Consequently, the stimuli that were associated with smoking are no longer linked to nicotine reinforcement and this should reduce cue-induced craving and withdrawal. Another possibility is that NRT, by maintaining steady state blood nicotine levels, makes smoking less pleasurable. Therefore, a slip may be less likely lead to a full-blown relapse. Likewise, it has not been established whether bupropion is effective due to its antidepressant action or through some other effects on brain neurochemistry (Piasecki & Baker, 2001). This knowledge is important as it provides the basis for the development of better pharmacotherapies in the future.

More research is also needed on efficacy comparisons between different pharmaco-therapies. There have been very few such studies, and some that did make such comparisons, arouse generalizability concerns. For example, in a study comparing bupropion with the patch, bupropion was more effective than the patch but the patch did not differ from placebo (Jorenby et al., 1999).

Methodological Issues in Behavioral Treatments Research

The area of behavioral treatments is in need of more rigorous research on treatment structural elements. Structural characteristics such as treatment intensity and treatment format have been shown to be important predictors of treatment efficacy, but different elements of treatment tend to be correlated and careful research is needed to tease apart their respective effects. For example, counseling session length and counseling format may be correlated in such a way that longer sessions tend to involve face-to-face contact while shorter sessions tend to be telephone-based. Thus, to examine the effect of session length one should compare interventions using different session lengths but the same format. Unfortunately, there are few methodologically rigorous studies that purposely manipulate a single element of treatment (Piasecki & Baker, 2001).

A similar methodological issue refers to research on new types of behavioral treat-ments. This evidence presents interpretation problems because newer studies tend to test multicomponent treatment packages and do not rigorously assign different treatment contents to different study arms. For example, a study concerned with the efficacy of motivational interviewing for smoking cessation should include a study arm where the intervention consists of a similar treatment package without motivational contents. Instead, a multicomponent intervention that includes but is not limited to the new treatment is often compared to basic standard care (Piasecki & Baker, 2001).

SUMMARY

Smoking cessation treatment is an important part of chronic disease prevention. In the United States, tobacco use is the single most preventable cause of morbidity and mortality (CDC, 1994b). Indeed, tobacco dependence itself should be perceived as a chronic disease and clinicians should seize every opportunity to treat it. By assessing each patient's smoking status, advising smokers to quit, and offering appropriate treatment options, clinicians can play a critical role in offsetting the disastrous health effects of tobacco use. Fortunately, effective treatments are available and can be incorporated into any clinical context or practice model. By encouraging cessation and treating nicotine dependence, clinicians will contribute to their patients' health and well-being, thus fulfilling the chief mission of their profession.

RESOURCES FOR HEALTH PROFESSIONALS

Out of numerous smoking cessation resources available for clinicians, important and quality resources are listed below.

1. "Treating Tobacco Use and Dependence - Clinical Practice Guideline", The Office of the Surgeon General
   http://www.surgeongeneral.gov/tobacco/default.htm
   The official website of the Surgeon General Office offers valuable information for clinicians and as well as consumer materials. *The Guideline* used as a reference throughout this text is available there in several versions:
   - "Treating Tobacco Use and Dependence - Clinical Practice Guideline" - Full Text

- "Treating Tobacco Use and Dependence - Clinical Practice Guideline. Summary"
- "Treating Tobacco Use and Dependence - Clinical Practice Guideline. Quick Reference Guide for Clinicians"

A consumer guide called "You Can Quit Smoking. Consumer Guide" is also available.

Hard copies of "Treating Tobacco Use and Dependence: A Clinical Practice Guideline" and "You Can Quit Smoking. Consumer Guide" are also available by calling 1-800-358-9295 or writing to Publications Clearinghouse, P.O. Box 8547, Silver Spring, MD 20907-8547.

2. Tobacco Information and Prevention Source (TIPS), Center for Disease Control and Prevention (CDC)
http://www.cdc.gov/tobacco/index.htm

TIPS is an official website of the Office on Smoking and Health (OSH), a division within the National Center for Chronic Disease Prevention and Health Promotion which is one of the CDC centers. OSH is responsible for leading and coordinating strategic efforts aimed at preventing tobacco use, promoting smoking cessation, protecting nonsmokers from environmental tobacco smoke, and eliminating tobacco-related health disparities. The website includes but is not limited to educational materials, quit advice, information on tobacco-related research, and information on tobacco control.

3. Database and Educational Resource for Treatment of Tobacco Dependence
http://treatobacco.net

Treatobacco.net is a source of evidence-based data and practical support for the treatment of tobacco dependence. It is aimed at physicians, nurses, pharmacists, dentists, psychologists, researchers, policy makers, regulators and anyone interested in the issues connected with tobacco use. All the information in Treatobacco.net is collected and reviewed by a panel of international experts,

and is updated to include the latest research. Treatobacco.net is produced and maintained by the Society for Research on Nicotine and Tobacco, in collaboration with the World Bank, Centers for Disease Control and Prevention, the World Health Organization, the Cochrane Group and a panel of international experts.

REFERENCES

Ahluwalia JS, Harris KJ, Catley D, Okuyemi KS, Mayo MS. (2002) Sustained-release bupropion for smoking cessation in African Americans. JAMA 288: 1-17.

Becona E, Vazquez F. (2001) Effectiveness of personalized written feedback through a mail intervention for smoking cessation: A randomized-controlled trial in Spanish smokers. J Consul Clin Psychol 69: 33-40

Bier ID, Wilson J, Studt P, Shakleton M. (2002) Auricular acupuncture, education, and smoking cessation: A randomized, sham-controlled trial. Am J Public Health 92: 1642-47.

Blondal T, Gudmundsson L J, Tomasson K, Jonsdottir D, Hilmarsdottir H, Kristjansson F, Nilsson F, Bjornsdottir U. (1999) The effects of fluoxetine combined with nicotine inhalers in smoking cessation--A randomized trial. Addiction 94: 1007-1015.

Bohadana A, Nilsson F, Rasmussen T, Martinet Y. (2000) Nicotine inhaler and nicotine patch as a combination therapy for smoking cessation: A randomized, double-blind, placebo-controlled trial. Arch Int Med160: 3128-34.

Borland R, Segan C.J, Livingston PM, Owen N. (2001) The effectiveness of a callback counselling for smoking cessation: A randomized trial. Addiction 96: 881-89.

Bovet P, Perret F, Cornuz J, Quilindo J, Paccaud F. (2002) Improved smoking cessation in smokers given ultrasound photographs of their own atherosclerotic plaques. Prev Med 34: 215-20.

Brown RA, Kahler CW, Niaura R, Abrams, DB, Sales SD, Ramsey SE, Goldstein MG, Burgess ES, Miller IW. (2001) Cognitive-behavioral treatment for depression in smoking cessation. J Consult Clin Psychol 69: 471-80.

Canga N, De Irala J, Vara E, Duaso MJ, Ferrer A, Martinez-Gonzalez MA. (2000) Intervention study for smoking cessation in diabetic patients: A randomized controlled trial in both clinical and primary care settings. Diabetes Care 23: 1455-60.

CDC. (1994a) Medical - care expenditures attributable to cigarette smoking--United States, 1993. Morb Mortal Wkly Rep 43:469-472.

CDC. (1994b) Surveillance for smoking-attributable mortality and years of potential life lost, by state -- United States, 1990. MorbMortal Wkly Rep 43: 1-8.

CDC. (1999) Cigarette smoking among adults -- U. S. 1997. MMWR 48: 993-6.

CDC. (2002a) Annual smoking - attributable mortality, years of potential life lost, and economic costs -- U.S., 1995-1999. Morb Mortal Wkly Rep 51: 300-303.

CDC. (2002b)Cigarette smoking among adults -- United States, 2000. Morb Mortal Wkly Rep 51: 642-645.

Covey LS, Glassman AH, Stetner F. (1999) Naltrexone effects on short-term and long-term smoking cessation. J Addict Dis 18: 31-40.

Covey LS, Glassman AH, Stetner F, Rivelli S, Stage K. (2002) A randomized trial of sertraline as a cessation aid for smokers with a history of major depression. Am J Psychiatry 159: 1731-37.

Cromwell J, Bartosch WJ, Fiore MC, Hasselblad V, Baker T. (1997) Cost-effectiveness of the Clinical Practice Recommendations in the AHCPR Guideline for Smoking Cessation. JAMA 278: 1759-1766.

Danielsson T, Rossner S, Westin A. (1999) Open randomised trial of intermittent very low energy diet together with nicotine gum for stopping smoking in women who gained weight in previous attempts to quit. Br Med J l 319: 490-4.

Daughton DM, Fortman SP, Glover ED, Hatsukami, DK, Heatley SA, Lichtenstein E, LTM R, Killen JD, Nowak RT, Ullrich F, Patil KD, Renard SI. (1999) The smoking cessation efficacy of varying doses of nicotine patch delivery systems 4 to 5 years post-quit day. Prev Med 28: 113-118.

Dijkstra A, De Vries HD, Roijackers J. (1999) Targeting smokers with low readiness to change with tailored and nontailored self-help materials. Prev Med 28: 203-11.

Donatelle RJ, Prows SL, Champeau D, Hudson D. (2000) Randomised controlled trial using social support and financial incentives for high risk pregnant smokers: Significant Other Supporter (SOS) program. Tob Control 9: iii67-iii69.

Ershoff DH, Quinn VP, Boyd NR, Stern J, Gregory M, Wirtschafter D. (1999) The Kaiser Permanente prenatal smoking-cessation trial: When more isn't better, what is enough? Am J Prev Med 17: 161-8.

Etter J, Perneger TV. (2001) Effectiveness of a computer-tailored smoking cessation program: A randomized trial. Arch Int Med 161: 2596-2601.

Evins AE, Mays VK, Rigotti NA, Tisdale T, Cathre C, Goff DC. (2001) A pilot trial of dupropion added to cognitive behavioral therapy for smoking cessation in schizophrenia. Nicotine Tob Res 3: 397-403.

Feeney GF, McPherson A, Connor JP, McAlister A, Young RM, Garrahy P. (2001) Randomized controlled trial of two cigarette quit programmes in coronary care patients after myocardial infarction. Int MedJ 31: 470-75.

Fiore MC, Bailey WC., Cohen SJ, Dorfman SF, Goldstein MG, Gritz ER, Heyman RB, Jaen CR, Kottke TE, Lando HA, Meclenburg RE, Dollan Mullen P, Nett LM, Robinson L, Stitzer ML, Tommasello AC, Villejo L, Wewers ME. (2000) Treating tobacco use and dependence . Rockville, MD: U.S. Department of Health and Human Services, Public Health Service, Agency for Health Care Policy and Research.

Fiore MC, Baily WC, Cohen SJ, Goldstein MG, Gritz ER, Heyman RB, Holbrook J, Jaen CR, Kottke TE, Lando H, Mecklenburg R, Mullen PD, Nett LM, Robinson L, Stizer ML, Tommasello A, Villejo L, Wewers ME. (1996) Smoking Cessation. Clinical Practice Guideline No. 18 : U.S. Department of Health and Human Services, Public Health Service, Agency for Health Care Policy and Research.

Fiore MC, Jorenby DE, Schensky AE, Smith SS, Bauer RR, Baker TB. (1995) Smoking status as the new vital sign: effect on assessment and intervention in patients who smoke [see comments]. Mayo Clin Proc 70: 209-13.

George TP, Vessicchio JC, Termine A, Bregartner TA., Feingold A, Rounsaville BJ, Kosten TR. (2002) A placebo controlled trial of bupropion for smoking cessation in schizophrenia. Biol Psychiatry 52: 53-61.

Glasgow RE, Whitlock EP, Eakin EG, Lichtenstein E. (2000) A brief smoking cessation intervention for women in low-income planned parenthood clinics. Am J Public Health 90: 786-89.

Glynn TJ, Manley MW, Pechacek TF. (1990) Physician-initiated smoking cessation program: the National Cancer Institute trials. Prog Clin Biol Res 339: 11-25.

Godtfredsen NS, Holst C, Prescott E, Vestbo J, Osler M. (2002) Smoking reduction, smoking cessation, and mortality: A 16-year follow-up of 19,732 men and women from the Copenhagen centre for prospective population studies. Am J Epidemiol 156: 994-1001.

Gonzales DH, Nides MA, Ferry LH, Kustra RP, Jamerson BD, Segall N, Herrero LA, Krishen A, Sweeney A, Buaron K, Metz A. (2001) Bupropion SR as an aid to smoking cessation in smokers treated previously with bupropion: a randomized placebo-controlled study. Clin Pharmacol Ther 69: 438-44.

Hajek P, Taylor TZ, Mills P. (2002) Brief intervention during hospital admission to help patients to give up smoking after myocardial infarction and bypass surgery: Randomised controlled trial. Br Med J 324: 1-6.

Hajek P, West R, Lee A, Foulds J, Owen L, Eiser JR, Main N. (2001) Randomized controlled trial of a midwife-delivered brief smoking cessation intervention in pregnancy. Addiction 96: 485-94.

Hall SM, Humfleet GL, Reus VI, Munoz RF, Hartz DT, Maude-Griffin R. (2002) Psychological intervention and antidepressant treatment in smoking cessation. Arch Gen Psychiatry 59: 930-36.

Hays JT, Hurt RD, Rigotti NA, Niaura R, Gonzales D, Durcan MJ, Sachs DP, Wolter TD, Buist SB, Johnston A, White JD. (2001) Sustained-release bupropion for pharmacologic relapse prevention after smoking cessation. Ann Intern Med, 135: 423-33.

He D, Medbo JI, Hostmark, AT. (2001) Effect of acupuncture on smoking cessation or reduction: An 8-month and 5-year follow-up study. Prev Med, 33: 364-72.

http://www.lungusa.org/data/2002. (2003). American Lung Association.

http://www.lungusa.org/tobacco/secondhand_factsheet99.html. (2003). American Lung Association.

Hughes JR. (1993) Pharmacotherapy for smoking cessation. Unvalidated assumptions, anomalies, and suggestions for future research. J Consult Clin Psych 61: 751-760.

Hughes JR. (1996) The future of smoking cessation therapy in the United States. Addiction 91: 1797-1802.

Hughes JR, Lesmes GR, Hatsukami DK, Richmond RL, Lichtenstein E, Jorenby DE, Broughton JO, Fortmann SP, Leischow SJ, McKenna JP, Rennard SI, Wadland WC., Heatley SA. (1999). Are higher doses of nicotine replacement more effective for smoking cessation? Nicotine TobRes 1: 169-174.

Jaen CR, Stange KC., Tumiel LM, Nutting P. (1997) Missed opportunities for prevention: smoking cessation counseling and the competing demands of practice. J Fam Pract 45: 348-54.

Johnson JL, Ratner PA, Bottorff JL, Hall W, Dahinten S. (2000) Preventing smoking relapse in postpartum women. Nurs Res 49: 44-52.

Jorenby DE, Leischow SJ, Nides MA, Rennard SI, Johnston JA, Hughes AR, Smith SS, Muramoto ML, Daughton DM, Doan K, Fiore MC., Baker TB. (1999) A controlled trial of sustained-release bupropion, a nicotine patch, or both for smoking cessation. N Engl J Med 340: 685-91.

Killen JD, Fortmann SP, Schatzberg AF, Hayward C, Sussman L, Rothman M, Strausberg L, Varady A. (2000) Nicotine patch and paroxetine for smoking cessation. J Consult Clin Psychol 68: 883-9.

Lasser K, Boyd JW, Woolhandler S, Himmelstein D, McCormick D, Bor DH. (2000) Smoking and mental illness: A population-based prevalence study. JAMA 284: 2606-2610.

Lennox AS, Osman LM, Reiter E, Robertson R, Friend J, McCann I, Skatun D, Donnan PT. (2001) Cost effectiveness of computer tailored and non-tailored smoking cessation letters in general practice: Randomised controlled trial. Br MedJ 322,: 1-7.

Lipkus IM, Lyna PR, Rimer BK. (1999) Using tailored interventions to enhance smoking cessation among African-Americans at a community health center. Nicotine Tob Res 1: 77-85.

Maguire TA, McElnay JC, Drummond A. (2001) A randomized controlled trial of a smoking cessation intervention based in community pharmacies. Addiction 96: 325-31.

Marcus BH, Albrecht AE, King TK, Parisi AF, Pinto BM, Roberts M, Niaura RS, Abrams DB. (1999) The efficacy of exercise as an aid for smoking cessation in women: A randomized controlled trial. Arch Intern Med 159: 1229-34.

McBride CM, Bepler G, Lipkus IM, Lyna P, Samsa G, Albright J, Datta S, Rimer B K. (2002) Incorporating genetic susceptibility feedback into a smoking cessation program for African-American smokers with low income. Cancer Epidemiol Biomarkers Prev 11: 521-8.

McBride CM, Curry SJ, Lando HA, Pirie PL, Grothaus LC, Nelson JC. (1999a) Prevention of relapse in women who quit smoking during pregnancy. Am J Public Health 89: 706-11.

McBride CM, Scholes D, Grothaus LC, Curry SJ, Ludman E, Albright J. (1999b) Evaluation of a minimal self-help smoking cessation intervention following cervical cancer screening. Prev Med 29: 133-38.

Meyers AW, Klesges RC, Winders SE, Ward KD, Peterson BA, Eck LH. (1997) Are weight concerns predictive of smoking cessation? A prospective analysis. J Consult Clin Psychol 66: 448-452.

NCI. (1999). Health effects of exposure to environmental tobacco smoke: The report of the California Environmental Protection Agency (99-4645). Bethesda: U.S. Department of Health and Human Services, National Institutes of Health, National Cancer Institute.

Niaura R, Spring B, Borrelli B, Hedeker D, Goldstein MG, Keuthen N, DePue J, Kristeller J, Ockene J, Prochazka A, Chiles JA, Abrams DB. (2002) Multicenter trial of fluoxetine as an adjunct to behavioral smoking cessation treatment. J Consult Clin Psychol 70: 887-96.

O'Neill HK, Gillispie MA, Slobin K. (2000) Stages of change and smoking cessation: A computer-administered intervention program for young adults. Am J Health Promotion 15: 93-96.

Panjari M, Bell R, Bishop S, Astbury J, Doery J. (1999) A randomized controlled trial of a smoking cessation intervention during pregnancy. Australian and New Zealand Journal of Obstetrics and Gynaecology 39: 312-17.

Perkins KA, Marcus MD, Levine MD, D'Amico D, Miller A, Broge M, Ashcom J, Shiffman S. (2001) Cognitive-behavioral therapy to reduce weight concerns improves smoking cessation outcome in weight-concerned women. J Consult Clin Psychol 69: 604-13.

Piasecki TM, Baker TB. (2001) Any further progress in smoking cessation treatment? Nicotine & Tobacco Research 3: 311-323.

Prochaska JO, DiClemente CC. (1983) Stages and processes of self-change of smoking: Toward an integrative model of change. J Consul Clin Psychol 51: 390-5.

Prochaska JO, Velicer WF , Fava JL, Rossi JS, Tsoh JY. (2001) Evaluating a population-based recruitment approach and a stage-based expert system intervention for smoking cessation. Addictive Behaviors 26: 583-602.

Schofield PE, Hill DJ, Johnston CI, Streeton JA. (1999) The effectiveness of a directly mailed smoking cessation intervention to Australian discharged hospital patients. Prev Med 29: 527-34.

Shiffman S, Dresler CM, Hajek P, Gilburt S, Targett DA, Strahs KR. (2002) Efficacy of a nicotine lozenge for smoking cessation. Archives of Internal Medicine 162: 1267-76.

Solomon LJ, Flynn BS. (1993) Women who smoke. In: Nicotine addiction principles and management (C. T. Orleans & J. Slade, eds.), pp. 339-349. New York: Oxford University Press.

Solomon LJ, Scharoun GM, Flynn BS, Secker-Walker RH, Sepinwall D. (2000) Free nicotine patches plus proactive telephone peer support to help low-income women stop smoking. Prev Med 31: 68-74.

Stotts AL, DiClemente CC, Carbonari JP, Mullen PD. (2000) Postpartum return to smoking: Staging a "suspended" behavior. Health Psychol 19(4): 324-32.

Tashkin D. (2001) Smoking cessation in patients with chronic obstructive pulmonary disease: A double-blind, placebo-controlled, randomised trial. Lancet 357: 1571-75.

Thorndike AN, Rigotti NA, Stafford RS, Singer DE. (1998) National patterns in the treatment of smokers by physicians. JAMA 279: 604-8.

Tonnesen P, Paoletti P, Gustavsson G, Russell MA, Saracci R, Gulsvik A, Rijcken B, Sawe U. (1999) Higher dose nicotine patches increase one-year smoking cessation rates: Results from the European CEASE trial. European Respiratory Journal 13: 238-46.

USDHHS. (2001). Women and smoking.

Van't Hof SM, Wall MA, Dowler DW, Stark MJ. (2000). Randomised controlled trial of a postpartum relapse prevention intervention. Tobacco Control 9: iii64-iii66.

Wallstrom M, Nilsson F, Hirsch J. (2000) A randomized, double-blind, placebo-controlled clinical evaluation of a nicotine sublingual tablet in smoking cessation. Addiction 95: 1161-71.

Wewers M, Neidig JL, Kihm KE. (2000) The feasibility of a nurse-managed, peer-led tobacco cesstion intervention among HIV-positive smokers. Journal of the Association of Nurses in AIDS Care 11: 37-44.

Wisborg K., Henriksen TB, Jespersen LB, Secher NJ. (2000) Nicotine patches for pregnant smokers: A randomized controlled study. Obstetrics & Gynecology 96: 967-71.

Wong GY, Wolter TD, Croghan GA, Croghan IT, Offord KP, Hurt RD. (1999) A randomized trial of naltrexone for smoking cessation. Addiction 94: 1227-37.

Zhu S, Anderson CM, Tedeschi GJ, Rosbrook B, Johnson CE, Byrd M, Gutierrez-Terrell E. (2002) Evidence of real-world effectiveness of a telephone quitline for smokers. N Eng J Med 347: 1087-93.

DUAL DIAGNOSIS DISEASE MANAGEMENT

Robert E. Drake

INTRODUCTION

This chapter addresses the problem of co-occurring severe mental illness and substance use disorder, also called dual diagnosis. Co-occurrence of chronic illnesses is of course widespread and refers to many co-occurring conditions. The term "dual diagnosis" has been used to refer to the specific population of people with co-occurring severe mental illness (defined as major mental illness such as schizophrenia or bipolar disorder with prolonged disability) and substance use disorder (defined as abuse of or dependence on alcohol or other psychoactive drugs). This population is heterogeneous diagnostically and in many other ways, but constitutes a definable clinical entity because state mental health programs are responsible for their care. Dual diagnosis is less than optimal as a term because there are many dually diagnosed populations and because most of the individuals in this group have multiple rather than dual impairments. Several other terms, e.g., mentally ill substance abuser, have been proposed for patients with severe mental illness and co-occurring substance use disorder. Nevertheless, dual diagnosis and co-occurring disorders remain the most commonly used terms and will be used synonymously in this chapter.

The problem of co-occurring substance use disorders among young patients with severe mental illnesses such as schizophrenia and bipolar disorder living in the community became apparent to clinicians and researchers by the early 1980s (e.g., Caton, 1981; Pepper et al., 1981). Since then two important findings have been clearly established. First, substance abuse is a common comorbidity among adults with severe mental illness. Along with many clinical studies, community surveys such as the Epidemiologic Catchment Area Study (Regier et al., 1990) and the National Comorbidity Study (Kessler et al., 1996) have established that approximately 50% of persons with severe mental illnesses self-report difficulties that are consistent with a diagnosis of substance use disorder. Assuming that patients tend to underreport substance abuse and that having co-occurring disorders rather than a single disorder increases the likelihood of treatment (Regier et al., 1990) yields the conclusion that substantially over half of all treated patients with severe mental illnesses have a co-occurring substance use disorder. Thus, clinicians should assume that the typical patient has a dual diagnosis rather than a single diagnosis.

The second robust finding regarding co-occurrence is that patients with dual diagnosis have a much greater rate of negative outcomes than similar patients who have mental illness alone. The negative outcomes are presumed to be causally related to the presence of substance use disorder, particularly since they tend to improve rapidly when abstinence occurs (Drake and Brunette, 1998). Negative outcomes related to co-occurrence include higher rates of relapse (Swofford et al., 1996), hospitalization (Haywood et al., 1995), victimization (Goodman et al., 1997), violence (Steadman et al., 1998), incarceration (Abram and Teplin, 1991), homelessness (Caton et al., 1994), and serious infections such as HIV and hepatitis (Rosenberg et al., 2001).

Evolution of Clinical Interventions

Since the problem of dual diagnosis became apparent in the early 1980s, clinical interventions have rapidly developed and evolved. Initial studies documented that parallel treatment, consisting of separate and traditional interventions in mental health settings and substance abuse settings, was ineffective (Ridgely et al., 1987). Thus the need to integrate mental health and substance abuse interventions within the same programs became apparent. Following initial efforts, it also became clear that community mental health centers were more equipped than were substance abuse programs to provide integrated treatment for patients with dual diagnosis, simply because community mental health centers already offered a comprehensive array of interventions that included medication management, case management, family psychoeducation, housing services, vocational rehabilitation, crisis services, and other supports that were essential for people with severe mental illnesses. These comprehensive services would have been prohibitively expensive for substance abuse treatment programs to duplicate, while it was relatively easy to add substance abuse interventions to the existing comprehensive community mental health programs. One exception, an area where the substance abuse treatment system had greater capacity, was in residential treatment, and many existing residential treatment programs for substance abusers were modified to provide integrated treatment.

The next step involved studies of integrated treatments during the 1980s. These studies demonstrated that adding substance abuse counseling within community mental health centers for people with dual disorders was often ineffective, because the patients were not easily engaged in treatment and were not motivated to pursue abstinence (Hellerstein et al., 1995; Lehman et al., 1993; Mercer-McFadden et al., 1997). Clinicians became aware that outreach and motivational interventions needed to be part of a dual diagnosis program in order to engage the patients (Mercer-McFadden et al., 1997). Studies also showed that dual diagnosis patients did not easily fit into residential

substance abuse programs (Drake, Mercer-McFadden et al., 1998).

Current outpatient dual diagnosis programs therefore involve comprehensive community mental health services plus substance abuse interventions that are specifically tailored for persons with severe mental illness. Many books and manuals for clinicians are available, and some of these are described at the end of this chapter. Current residential treatment programs have also been modified extensively to offer integrated treatment in a less intensive approach for dual diagnosis patients.

A series of open clinical trials demonstrated that these comprehensive integrated interventions were effective in engaging patients in treatment, helping them to reduce and eliminate their substance abuse, and helping them to stabilize their mental illness (e.g., Detrick and Stepock, 1992; Drake et al., 1993; Durrell et al., 1993; Meisler et al., 1997). Similarly, modifications of traditional residential treatment programs, such as therapeutic communities, seemed to be more effective (Sacks, 1997) than traditional residential treatment programs.

FINDINGS FROM RECENT CONTROLLED TRIALS

Beginning in the mid-1990s, controlled research studies of comprehensive dual diagnosis programs began to appear. Although these studies demonstrate a variety of positive outcomes, which we review next, they also are limited by serious methodological problems, including inconsistency of interventions, heterogeneity of patients, difficulties with measures, variable lengths of follow-up, small samples, failures to engage patients, high attrition, and treatment drift (Drake, Mercer-McFadden et al., 1998).

Table 1 shows a summary of the recent controlled studies, including design, participants, interventions and outcomes.

Recent Controlled Studies of Dual Diagnosis Interventions

Study	Design	Participants	Interventions	Outcomes
Godley et al., 1994	Experiment, treatment for 2 years	n = 38 dual diagnosis patients	Integrated intensive case management plus substance abuse counseling vs. non-integrated services	Intensive case management group had fewer days of drug use
Jerrell and Ridgely, 1995	Quasi-experiment, treatment for 18 months	n = 132 dual diagnosis patients	behavioral skills training vs. 12-step counseling; case management vs. 12-step counseling	Behavioral skills training group had fewer substance abuse symptoms than 12-step group. 12-step + case management was more effective than 12-step alone.
Drake et al., 1997	Quasi-experiment, treatment for 18 months	n = 217 homeless, dual diagnosis patients	Integrated intensive case management, substance abuse counseling, and housing supports vs. non-integrated services	Integrated treatment group had greater treatment progress and greater reductions in alcohol severity
Carmichael et al., 1998	Experiment in 2 sites; Quasi-experiment in 1 site	n = 208 dual diagnosis patients	Integrated mental health and substance abuse treatment vs. non-integrated treatment	Integrated treatment group had greater improvement in alcohol abuse and drug abuse
Ho et al., 1998	Quasi-experiment, 6-month treatment intervals	n = 179 dual diagnosis patients	Integrated day treatment plus assertive community treatment and skills training vs. integrated day treatment	The group with enhanced assertive community treatment and skills training had greater rates of abstinence
Drake et al., 1998	Experiment, treatment for 3 years	n = 203 dual diagnosis patients	Integrated assertive community treatment plus substance abuse counseling vs. non-integrated services	Integrated treatment group had greater treatment progress and decreased alcohol severity
Kasprow et al., 1999	Quasi-experiment, outcome at discharge following several years of residential treatment	n = 385 dually diagnosed veterans	Residential treatment facilities that specialized in integrated mental health and substance abuse treatment vs. similar residential facilities that specialized in substance abuse treatment	Patients in integrated treatment had faster return to independent community living but no differences in substance abuse outcomes.
McHugo et al., 1999	Quasi-experiment, treatment for 3 years	n = 87 dual diagnosis patients	Assertive community treatment teams with high fidelity for dual diagnosis treatment vs. similar teams with low fidelity	Patients in high-fidelity programs had greater reductions in alcohol and drug use and higher rates of substance abuse remission
Brunette et al., 2001	Quasi-experiment	n = 86 dual diagnosis patients, f/u one year after residential tx	Long-term integrated mental health and substance abuse residential treatment (average 400 days) vs. short-term integrated residential treatment (average 66 days)	Patients discharged from long-term programs were more likely to maintain abstinence

316

Study	Design	Participants	Interventions	Outcomes
Barraclough et al., 2001	Experiment, treatment for 9 months	n = 36 patients with schizophrenia and substance abuse	Motivational counseling, family psychoeducation, and cognitive behavioral therapy vs. usual services	Experimental group had more days of abstinence
Aguilera et al., 2001	Quasi-experiment	n = 225 dual diagnosis patients	Residential treatment with integrated mental health and substance abuse interventions vs. residential treatment with substance abuse focus	Integrated treatment group had more successful program completers and less recidivism, but substance abuse outcomes not reported.

This table includes true experiments (randomized studies) and quasi-experiments (controlled studies with non-equivalent comparison groups). Because most of these studies take place in the context of comprehensive mental health services, this review focuses on the substance abuse treatment components and on substance abuse as an outcome.

Several features of these 11 studies warrant attention. First, there are few true experiments, and the true experiments have limitations, such as small study group size (Barraclough et al., 2001; Godley et al., 1994), treatment drift (i.e. that the treatments became more alike over time) (Drake et al., 1998), and highly selected participants with supportive families (Barraclough et al., 2001). Second, eight studies address comprehensive outpatient programs, and three address residential programs. Even among the outpatient and among the residential studies, there is little consistency of specific experimental interventions or of control group interventions. Thus, no two studies are strictly comparable.

Third, the participants in most of these studies are heterogeneous diagnostically with respect to mental illness diagnoses, substance abuse diagnoses, treatment history, and other important characteristics such as motivational level. Heterogeneity can of course easily obscure outcomes. For example, outpatient treatment is generally used for initial treatment, and residential treatment is usually reserved for outpatient non-responders, but the differences between patients in the residential and outpatient studies is unclear. Fourth, because dual diagnosis patients are difficult to engage and retain in treatment, attrition was high in many studies (e.g., 31% in Jerrell and Ridgely, 1995). Studies that included assertive outreach tended to have much better retention in treatment and research (Drake et al., 1998).

Fifth, studies examined various aspects of substance abuse using a variety of measures. Compared with non-mentally ill substance abusers, patients with co-occurring disorders tend to use smaller amounts of substances, have different consequences of their use, and have less of the physiological syndrome of dependence (Wolford et al., 1999). These distinctions render traditional instruments less useful, but few new instruments have been validated, and a consensus has not yet developed on how best to assess substance use in dually diagnosed patients. The relatively consistent finding is nevertheless that the experimental groups do better on at least one substance abuse outcome (and usually on other outcomes such as hospitalization not shown in the table), while the control or comparison groups never do better and often do worse on a variety of outcomes. Finally, in addition to other factors that threaten generalizability, two of the recent studies (Barraclough et al., 2001; Aguilera et al., 2001) come from other countries (the United Kingdom and Honduras) that have mental health care systems that are quite different from public mental health programs in the U.S.

Given the remarkable complexity and non-comparability of studies, the limited consistency of outcomes is remarkable. As we review next, the most consistent finding is that programs with greater integration of mental health and substance abuse interventions tend to have better outcomes.

Principles of Dual Diagnosis Interventions

There are different ways to interpret the findings of the studies shown in Table 1. Because the specific interventions and combinations differ so widely across studies and because well done randomized controlled trials with representative patients are so difficult to conduct with this population, it is impossible at this point to say that any specific intervention is effective for dual diagnosis patients. This was the conclusion of an earlier Cochrane review that considered only the most rigorous studies (Ley et al., 1999). Such a conclusion ignores the principle of evidence-based medicine that clinicians should use the best available evidence within a hierarchy of evidence (Guyatt and Rennie, 2002). It also ignores the observation that several principles of care are consistent across many successful dual diagnosis programs (Drake et al., 2001). My colleagues and I have therefore argued that while specific interventions are refined and until research on specific interventions and combinations is available, the existing evidence should be used to abstract principles of dual diagnosis programs that appear to be effective (Drake, Mercer-McFadden et al., 1998). Taking this approach, several principles of dual diagnosis treatment can be identified.

Integration of interventions. All of the recent studies support the basic notion of combining, or integrating, mental health and substance abuse interventions. Integration means that one clinician or team takes responsibility for helping the patient learn to manage and recover from both illnesses (Minkoff, 1989; Osher and Kofoed, 1989). Mental health and substance abuse interventions are combined and specifically tailored to fit persons with co-occurring disorders. The patient does not have to travel to different programs, does not have to make sense of conflicting messages, and does not have to relate to independent clinicians. The advantages of integration are immediately obvious in outpatient and residential programs in terms of engagement and retention. Note that integration does not mean that programs or systems of care exchange memoranda of agreement. To be successful, integration must occur at the level of clinical interaction. Most programs accomplish integration by establishing multidisciplinary teams, which include substance abuse treatment experts along with mental health experts.

Stages-wise interventions. Effective programs incorporate the concept of stages of treatment (Carey, 1996; McHugo et al., 1995; Osher and Kofoed, 1989). In the simplest conceptualization, stages of treatment include (a) forming a trusting relationship with the patient (i.e., engagement), (b) helping the engaged patient to develop the motivation to pursue recovery (i.e., persuasion), (c) helping the motivated patient to acquire skills and supports for controlling illnesses and pursuing personal goals (i.e., active treatment), and (d) helping the patient in stable remission to develop and use strategies for maintaining recovery (i.e., relapse prevention).

Rather than move linearly through stages, patients sometimes enter services at advanced levels, sometimes skip over or pass rapidly through stages, and often relapse to earlier stages. Moreover, they may be in different stages with respect to recovery from mental illness and from substance abuse. Nevertheless, the concept of stages has proven useful to program planners and clinicians because patients at different stages respond to different stage-specific interventions. For example, patients at the engagement stage typically need attention to basic needs and to establishing a relationship with a clinician. They do not benefit from abstinence-oriented group interventions, which are appropriate and central for patients in the active treatment stage.

Assertive outreach. Many dually diagnosed patients have difficulty in accessing services and participating consistently in treatment (Owen et al., 1997). Effective programs therefore engage patients and members of their support systems by providing assertive outreach, usually through some combination of intensive case management and meetings in the patient's residence (Mercer-McFadden et al., 1997).

For example, homeless persons with dual diagnosis often benefit from outreach, help with housing, and time to develop a trusting relationship prior to any formal treatment. These approaches enable patients to engage in and maintain needed relationships with a consistent program over months and years. Without such efforts, noncompliance and dropouts are high (Hellerstein et al., 1995).

Motivational interventions. The majority of dual diagnosis patients have little readiness for abstinence-oriented treatment (Test et al., 1989; Ziedonis and Trudeau, 1997). Many also lack motivation to manage their psychiatric illnesses and to pursue education, employment, or other adult roles. Effective programs therefore incorporate motivational interventions that are designed to help patients become ready for more definitive interventions that are aimed at illness self-management (Barraclough et al., 2001; Carey, 1996). For example, patients who are so demoralized, symptomatic, or confused that they mistakenly believe that alcohol and cocaine are helping them to cope better than medications require education, support, and counseling to develop hope and a realistic understanding of illnesses, drugs, treatments, and goals. Motivational interventions involve helping the individual to identify his or her own goals and then to recognize, through a systematic examination of the individual's ambivalence, that not managing one's illnesses interferes with attaining those goals (Miller and Rollnick, 1991). Recent research demonstrates that patients who lack motivation can be helped with motivational interventions (Carey et al., 2002).

Counseling. Once patients are motivated to manage their own illnesses, they need to develop skills and supports to control symptoms and to pursue an abstinent lifestyle. Effective programs provide some form of counseling that promotes cognitive and behavioral skills at this stage. The counseling takes different forms and formats, e.g., group, individual, family, or a combination (Mueser et al., 1998). Few studies have compared specific approaches to counseling. Several research groups are actively working to refine cognitive-behavioral approaches to mental health and substance abuse counseling for dual diagnosis patients. These approaches often incorporate motivational sessions at the beginning of counseling and as needed in subsequent sessions rather than as separate interventions.

Social support interventions. In addition to helping the patient to build skills for illness self-management and pursuing goals, effective programs also focus on strengthening the immediate social environment to help the patient to modify behavior. These activities, which recognize the role of social networks in recovery from dual diagnosis (Alverson et al., 2000), comprise peer group, social network, or family interventions. A range of different interventions seem to be effective, provided the patient attends consistently, suggesting that social support rather than specific model of treatment may be the critical component.

Long-term perspective. Effective programs recognize that recovery tends to occur over months or years. People with severe mental illness and substance abuse do not usually develop stability and functional improvements quickly, even in intensive treatment programs, unless they enter treatment at an advanced stage (Drake, Mercer-McFadden et al., 1998). Instead, they tend to improve over months and years in conjunction with a consistent dual diagnosis program. Effective programs therefore take a long-term, community-based perspective that includes rehabilitation activities to prevent relapses and to enhance gains.

<u>Comprehensiveness</u>. Learning to lead a symptom-free, abstinent lifestyle that is satisfying and sustainable often requires transforming many aspects of one's life, e.g., habits, stress management, friends, activities, and housing. Therefore, in effective programs attention to substance abuse as well as mental illness is insinuated into all aspects of the existing mental health program and service system rather than isolated as a discrete substance abuse treatment intervention. Inpatient hospitalization, assessment, crisis intervention, medication management, money management, laboratory screening, housing, and vocational rehabilitation incorporate special features that are tailored specifically for dual diagnosis. For example, hospitalization is considered a component of the system that supports movement toward recovery by providing diagnosis, stabilization, and linkage with outpatient dual diagnosis interventions (Greenfield et al., 1995). Similarly, housing and vocational programs can be used to support the dually diagnosed individual in acquiring skills and supports needed for recovery (Drake and Mueser, 2000).

RESEARCH QUESTIONS

Several research questions are pressing. Some of these are at the level of clinical interventions, while others are at the level of systems issues. Refining and testing specific interventions is clearly a priority and should be done with routine patients rather than with highly compliant or otherwise non-representative patients. Individual, group, and family interventions will undoubtedly be more effective as they are standardized, tested, and improved. They will also be more easily disseminated as training materials and fidelity measures become available. Several important investigations are underway in this area. For example, Carey and her colleagues (Carey et al., 2002) are testing motivational interviewing approaches with unmotivated

patients; Bellack and his colleagues (Bellack and DiClemente, 1999) are currently testing group interventions; and Mueser and his colleagues (Mueser and Fox, 2002) are testing family interventions.

An open question is how to sequence and combine interventions. Researchers need to test different interventions and different combinations of interventions for patients who are at different stages of recovery. Thus, for example, it may be important to study one set of interventions, such as patient and family psychoeducation combined with outreach and motivational counseling, for patients who are not yet engaged in treatment and motivated to pursue abstinence, and an entirely different set of interventions, such as individual and group behavioral counseling for those who are engaged and actively trying to achieve sustained abstinence.

All of the recent studies examine current abusers as a heterogeneous group. Another priority might be to develop and test interventions for four specific groups based on treatment needs: (1) patients with no history of substance abuse, (2) patients who have a history of abuse but are currently in remission, (3) current abusers who have not yet failed outpatient dual diagnosis treatment, and (4) patients who are non-responders to basic outpatient approaches. The approximately 40-50% of patients who have never had a problem with substance abuse probably deserve accurate psychoeducation regarding prevention, if only because they will undoubtedly be exposed to social pressures to use substances while participating in mental health programs. Similarly, the 20-30% of patients who have a history of substance use disorder but are currently in remission are undoubtedly prone to relapse and deserve some type of relapse prevention intervention. Finally, taking an algorithmic approach to dual diagnosis treatment suggests that the patients who do not respond to basic outpatient substance abuse counseling (individual, group, or family) should be offered secondary interventions. In fact, some data are already available for a number of secondary interventions, such as disulfiram, clonazepam, intensive family treatments, trauma interventions, and long-term residential interventions (see, e.g., Brunette et al., 2001; Mueser et al., 2003; Zimmet et al., 2000).

Beyond developing and testing interventions for routine patients in routine treatment systems, transforming systems of care is a challenge for administrators and services researchers. Thus, for example, the field needs studies of training procedures for all clinicians, of financing and contracting mechanisms, and of computerized decision support systems. Systematic interventions at the system level, rather than small programs utilizing highly trained specialized clinicians, will be required to impact on a problem that affects the majority of patients. The National Evidence-based Practices Project, which is studying the process of practice implementation in routine mental health settings, is one example of a system-level study (Drake et al., 2001).

RESOURCES

Many recent books describe integrated mental health and substance abuse treatment for clinicians (e.g., Brunette et al., 2003; Daley et al., 1993; Mueser et al, 2003; Watkins et al., 2001). These are all excellent resources. The Daley book involves modification of traditional 12-step procedures. The Watkins book is geared toward students. The Mueser text is for mental health practitioners and goes into detail regarding many different aspects of treatment. The Brunette book is actually a multi-media toolkit that offers training videos and extensive educational materials for different stakeholder groups.

REFERENCES

Abrams K, Teplin L. (1991) Co-occurring disorders among mentally ill jail detainees: Implications for public policy. Am Psychol 46:1036-1044.

Aguilera R, Anderson A, Gabire E, Merlo M, Paredes T, Pastrana R. (1999) A clinical impact evaluation of integrated and disease specific substance abuse program models in Honduras. Int J Psychophysoc Rehab 3:97-167.

Alverson H, Alverson M, Drake RE. (2000) An ethnographic study of the longitudinal course of substance abuse among people with severe mental illness. Community Ment Health J 36:557-569.

Barrowclough C, Haddock G, Tarrier N, Lewis S, Moring J, O'Brien R, Schofield N, McGovern J. (2001) Randomized controlled trial of motivational interviewing and cognitive behavioral intervention for schizophrenia patients with associated drug or alcohol misuse. Am J Psychiatry 158:1706-1713.

Bellack AS, DiClemente CC. (1999) Treating substance abuse among patients with schizophrenia. Psychiatr Serv 50:75-80.

Brunette MF, Drake RE, Woods M, Hartnett T. (2001) A comparison of long-term and short-term residential treatment programs for dual diagnosis patients. Psychiatr Serv 52:526-528.

Brunette MR, Drake R, Lynde D, and the Integrated Dual Disorders Treatment Group. (2003) Toolkit for Integrated Dual Disorders Treatment. Rockville, MD: Substance Abuse and Mental Health Services Administration.

Carey KB. (1996) Substance use reduction in the context of outpatient psychiatric treatment: A collaborative, motivational, harm reduction approach. Community Ment Health J 32:291-306.

Carey KB, Carey MP, Maisto SA, Purnine DM. (2002) The feasibility of enhancing psychiatric outpatients' readiness to change their substance abuse. Psychiatr Serv 53:602-608.

Carmichael D, Tackett-Gibson M, Dell O. (1998) Texas Dual Diagnosis Project Evaluation Report 1997-1998. College Station, TX: Texas A&M University, Public Policy Research Institute.

Caton C. (1981) The new chronic patient and the system of community care. Hosp Community Psychiatry 32:475-478.

Caton C, Shrout P, Eagle P, Opler L, Felix A, Dominguez B. (1994) Risk factors for homelessness among schizophrenic men: A case-control study. Am J Public Health 84:265-270.

Daley DC, Moss HB, Campbell F. (1993) Dual disorders: Counseling Clients with Chemical Dependency & Mental Illness. Center City, MN: Hazelden.

Detrick A, Stiepock V. (1992) Treating persons with mental illness, substance abuse, and legal problems: The Rhode Island experience. In Innovative Community Mental Services. (Stein, LI ed), pp 65-77. San Francisco, CA: Jossey-Bass.

Drake RE, Brunette MF. (1998) Complications of severe mental illness related to alcohol and other drug use disorders. In Recent Developments in Alcoholism. pp 285-299. New York: Plenum Publishing Company.

Drake RE, Essock SM, Shaner A, Carey KB, Minkoff K, Kola L, Lynde D, Osher FC, Clark RE, Richards L. (2001) Implementing dual diagnosis services for clients with severe mental illness. Psychiatr Serv 52:469-476.

Drake RE, Goldman HH, Leff HS, Lehman F, Dixon L, Mueser KT, Torrey WC. (2001) Implementing evidence-based practices in routine mental health service settings. Psychiatr Serv 52:179-182.

Drake RE, McHugo GJ, Clark RE, Teague GB, Xie H, Miles K, Ackerson TH. (1998) Assertive community treatment for patients with co-occurring severe mental illness and substance use disorder: A clinical trial. Am J Orthopsychiatry 68:201-215.

Drake RE, McHugo G, Noordsy DL. (1993) Treatment of alcoholism among schizophrenic outpatients: Four-year outcomes. Am J Psychiatry 150:328-329.

Drake RE, Mercer-McFadden C, Mueser KT, McHugo GJ, Bond GR. (1998) Review of integrated mental health and substance abuse treatment for patients with dual disorders. Schizophr Bull 24:589-608.

Drake RE, Mueser KT. (2000) Psychosocial approaches to dual diagnosis. Schizophr Bull 26:105-118.

Drake RE, Yovetich NA, Bebout RR, Harris M, McHugo GJ. (1997) Integrated treatment for dually diagnosed homeless adults. J Nerv Ment Dis 185:298-305.

Durell J, Lechtenberg B, Corse S, Frances R. (1993) Intensive case management of persons with chronic mental illness who abuse substances. Hosp Community Psychiatry 44:415-416.

Godley SH, Hoewing-Roberson R, Godley MD. 1994 Final MISA Report, Bloomington, IL: Lighthouse Institute.

Goodman LA, Rosenberg SD, Mueser KT, Drake RE. (1997) Physical and sexual assault history in women with serious mental illness: Prevalence, correlates, treatment, and future research directions. Schizophr Bull 23:685-696.

Greenfield SF, Weiss RD, Tohen M. (1995) Substance abuse and the chronically mentally ill: A description of dual diagnosis treatment services in a psychiatric hospital. Community Ment Health J 31:265-278.

Guyatt G, Rennie D, 2002 Users' Guides to the Medical Literature, Chicago, IL: American Medical Association.

Haywood TW, Kravitz HM, Grossman LS. (1995) Predicting the "revolving door" phenomenon among patients with schizophrenic, schizoaffective, and affective disorders. Am J Psychiatry 152:865-861.

Hellerstein DJ, Rosenthal RN, Miner CR. (1995) A prospective study of integrated outpatient treatment for substance-abusing schizophrenic patients. Am J Addictions 42:33-42.

Ho AP, Tsuang JW, Liberman RP, Wang R, Wilkins JN, Eckman TA, Shaner AL. (1999) Achieving effective treatment of patients with chronic psychotic illness and comorbid substance dependence. Am J Psychiatry 156:1765-1770.

Jerrell JM, Ridgely MS. (1995) Comparative effectiveness of three approaches to serving people with severe mental illness and substance abuse disorders. J Nerv Ment Dis 183:566-576.

Kasprow WJ, Rosenheck R, Frisman L, DiLella D. (1999) Residential treatment for dually diagnosed homeless veterans: A comparison of program types. The Am J Addictions 8:34-43.

Kessler RC, Nelson CB, McGonagle KA, Edlund MJ, Frank RG, Leaf PJ. (1996) The epidemiology of co-occurring addictive and mental disorders: Implications for prevention and service utilization. Am J Orthopsychiatry 66:17-31.

Lehman A, Myers C, Thompson J, Corty E. (1993) Implications of mental and substance use disorders. J Nerv Ment Dis 181:365-370.

Ley A, Jeffery DP, McLaren S, et al. (February 1999) Treatment programmes for people with both severe mental illness and substance misuse. The Cochrane Library.

McHugo GJ, Drake RE, Burton HL, Ackerson TH. (1995) A scale for assessing the stage of substance abuse treatment in persons with severe mental illness. J Nerv Ment Dis 183:762-767.

McHugo GJ, Drake RE, Teague GB, Xie H. (1999) Fidelity to assertive community treatment and client outcomes in the New Hampshire dual disorders study. Psychiatr Serv 50:818-824.

Meisler N, Blankertz L, Santos AB, McKay C. (1997) Impact of assertive community treatment on homeless persons with co-occurring severe psychiatric and substance use disorders. Comm Ment Health J 33:113--122.

Mercer-McFadden C, Drake RE, Brown NB, Fox RS. (1997) The community support program demonstrations of services for young adults with severe mental illness and substance use disorders 1987-1991. Psychiatr Rehab J 20:13-24.

Minkoff KT. (1989) An integrated treatment model for dual diagnosis of psychosis and addiction. Hosp Community Psychiatry 40:1031-1036.

Mueser KT, Drake RE, Noordsy DL. (1998) Integrated mental health and substance abuse treatment for severe psychiatric disorders. J Prac Psychiatr Behav Health 4:129-139.

Mueser KT, Fox L. (2002) A family intervention program for dual disorders. Community Ment Health J 38:253-270.

Mueser KT, Noordsy DL, Drake RE, Fox L. (2003) Integrated Treatment for Dual Disorders: Effective Intervention for Severe Mental Illness and Substance Abuse. Guilford Press.

Mueser KT, Noordsy DL, Fox L, Wolfe R. (2003) Disulfiram treatment for alcoholism in severe mental illness. Am J Addictions 12:242-252.

Osher FC, Kofoed LL. (1989) Treatment of patients with psychiatric and psychoactive substance use disorders. Hosp Community Psychiatry 40:1025-1030.

Pepper B, Krishner MC, Ryglewicz H. (1981) The young adult chronic patient: Overview of a population. Hosp Community Psychiatry 32:463-469.

Regier DA, Farmer ME, Rae DS, Locke BZ, Keith SJ, Judd LL, Goodwin FK. (1990) Comorbidity of mental disorders with alcohol and other drug abuse. JAMA 264:2511-2518.

Ridgely MS, Osher FC, Goldman HH, Talbott JA. 1987 Executive Summary: <u>Chronic Mentally Ill Young Adults with Substance Abuse Problems: A Review of Research, Treatment, and Training Issues.</u> Baltimore: The University of Maryland Task Force on Chronic Mentally Ill Young Adults with Substance Problems.

Rosenberg SD, Goodman LA, Osher FC, Swartz M, Essock SM, Butterfield MI, Constantine N, Wolford GL, Salyers M. (2001) Prevalence of HIV, Hepatitis B and Hepatitis C in people with severe mental illness. Am J Public Health 91:31-37.

Sacks, S. (1997) Final Report: <u>Therapeutic Community-Oriented Supported Housing for MICAs.</u> New York: Center for Therapeutic Community Research.

Steadman HJ, Mulvey EP, Monahan J, Robbins PC, Appelbaum PS, Grisso T, Roth LH, Silver E. (1998) Violence by people discharged from acute psychiatric inpatient facilities and by others in the same neighborhoods. Arch Gen Psychiatry 55:393-401.

Swofford C, Kasckow J, Scheller-Gilkey G, Indrbitzin LB. (1996) Substance use: A powerful predictor of relapse in schizophrenia. Schizophr Research 20:145-151.

Watkins TR, Lewellen A, Barrett M. (2001) <u>Dual Diagnosis: An Integrated Approach to Treatment.</u> Thousand Oaks, CA: Sage Publications.

Wolford GL, Rosenberg SD, Drake RE, Mueser KT, Oxman TE, Hoffman D, Vidaver RM, Luckoor R, Carrieri KL. (1999) Evaluation of methods for detecting substance use disorder in persons with severe mental illness. Psychology of Addict Behav 13:313-326.

Zimmet SV, Strous RD, Burgess ES, Kohnstamm S, Green IA. (2000) Effects of clozapine on substance use in patients with schizophrenia and schizoaffective disorders: A retrospective survey. J Clin Pharmacol 20:94-98.

META-ANALYSIS OF LONG-TERM EFFECT OF PSYCHOSOCIAL INTERVENTIONS ON PAIN IN ADULTS WITH CANCER

Elizabeth C. Devine

INTRODUCTION

Pain is a common symptom among individuals with cancer. It has been estimated that approximately 75% of individuals with cancer will at some point during the course of their illness have pain from their cancer (Bonica, 1990). Others have noted that the majority of adults receiving treatment for their cancer at some point have cancer pain that impairs their quality of life and functionality with the severity of pain increasing as the stage of cancer increases (Carr et al., 2002). Likewise, the need to improve pain management in individuals with cancer has been widely noted (Cleeland et al., 1994; Coyle et al., 1990; Wells, 2000). In response to this need, in recent years there have been efforts to improve pain management for individuals with cancer (Jacox et al., 1994; Jadad & Browman, 1995; Zech et al., 1995).

Analgesics are the mainstay of pain management, yet analgesics may cause undesired effects such as sedation, nausea, constipation, and/or renal or liver toxicity. In order to determine the effect of adjunctive pain therapies in adults with cancer, researchers have tested the effect of various non-pharmaceutical interventions such as education, psychosocial, and/or cognitive/behavioral interventions (hereafter referred to as psychoeducational interventions). While several relevant systematic reviews of this topic have been done (Devine, 2003; Carroll & Seers, 1998; Devine & Westlake, 1995; Pan et al., 2000; Smith et al., 1994; Thomas & Weiss, 2000; Trijsburg et al., 1992; van Fleet, 2000; Wallace, 1997) most of these reviews do not include the recent studies, many include both randomized and nonrandomized studies, some lack critical information about the review methodology

used (e.g., search strategies and inclusion criteria for studies), some include studies with both adults and children without separate analysis, some include studies with a wide range of painful chronic conditions, most provide narrative summaries of the statistical analyses of treatment effect in individual studies rather than quantitative analysis of effect size values (e.g., the quantitative estimate of a treatment's effect on pain), and none are focused on the longer-term effect of psychoeducational interventions on pain.

PURPOSE

The primary purpose of this meta-analysis was to determine the long-term effect of selected psychoeducational interventions on pain in adults with cancer. Secondary purposes were to determine whether there is a stronger research base for the long-term effect on pain of some types of psychoeducational interventions than others, and also, if possible, to determine whether publication bias, a Hawthorne effect, measurement reactivity, or a floor effect on pain offered plausible alternative explanations for the findings.

METHODS

Meta-analytic methods described by Hedges and Olkin (1985) were used to summarize and analyze the effect of psychoeducational interventions on pain in adult oncology patients.

Sample

Literature identification strategies included searches of the following computerized data bases: Cumulative Index to Nursing and Allied Health Literature, *PubMed®*, *Dissertation Abstracts International*, *PsycLIT®*, and the *Cochrane Database of Systematic Reviews.*

Key words for the computerized searches included cancer/neoplasms, patient/client education, counseling, behavioral therapy, guided imagery, hypnosis, relaxation therapy, music, and pain. Reference lists of relevant studies and reviews also were examined.

Three selection and four exclusion criteria for studies were used. Studies were selected if they (a) involved provision of a psycho-educational intervention to adults with cancer; (b) used a randomized experimental design; and (c) included an outcome measure of pain for which an effect size value was discernable. Studies were excluded if they (a) examined related but different research questions (e.g., is a psychoeducational intervention as effective as pharmacotherapy for pain?), (b) had fewer than 5 subjects in each treatment condition (i.e., the treatment and control groups), (c) included treatment and control groups that were not selected from the same setting(s), or (d) included only post-treatment data that were collected less than three weeks after the treatment was initiated. It had been the original intent of the reviewer to exclude outcomes that were not measured 12 or more months after the treatment was initiated. Unfortunately, since so few of the identified studies met this criterion, it was expanded to three weeks.

There also were three exclusion criteria for outcomes. Effect size values were excluded from analysis if they were (a) derived from treatment and control groups that were apparently nonequivalent, (b) from measures that were inappropriate, or (c) measured less than three weeks after the initiation of the treatment. The criteria indicative of treatment and control group nonequivalence were as follows. Effect size values were not used if the difference between treatment and control groups on pretest scores was an effect size value of 1.0 or more, or if the ratio of treatment to control group standard deviations was less than .25 or greater than 4. Since pain is a highly personal, subjective experience, measures of provider-rated pain were judged to

be inappropriate, and as such were not used. If a study measured a specific outcome on multiple occasions, only effect size values calculated from measures obtained three weeks or more after the treatment was initiated were used in the meta-analysis.

Measures

Characteristics of the study, the sample, the treatment, the setting, and the outcomes were coded to facilitate description and analysis. Study characteristics included publication form and date, professional preparation of the first author, manner of assignment of subjects to treatment condition, and type of control group. Sample characteristics of age, gender, ethnicity, and type of cancer were coded. Treatment characteristics included the content, timing, duration, frequency, and mode of delivery of the experimental intervention. Setting characteristics included the country and the site where the intervention occurred (hospital, clinic, or community). Outcomes were coded according to the actual measure, the timing and manner of data collection, sample size, and direction and magnitude of treatment effect. The outcome selected for analysis was self-reported pain. Use of analgesics was not included in analysis because the direction of "beneficial" effect is unclear (e.g., while in some instances decreased pain might be indicated by lower analgesic usage, in other instances encouraging subjects to use pre-scribed medications appropriately could result in them increasing their use of analgesics). Reliability of coding these characteristics from research reports was calculated for a more extensive meta-analysis (e.g., one that was not limited to long-term, randomized studies). Based on percentage agreement, intercoder agreement was acceptable (87%) (Devine, 2003).

Procedures

The scale-free, size-of-effect statistic used in this meta-analysis was based on Cohen's (1969) population statistic δ, which represents the standardized mean difference between treatment and control groups measured in standard deviation units. The effect size statistic provides information about both the direction and magnitude of treatment effect. The basic formula for the effect size statistic is: $\delta = [(M_c - M_e)S]$. When control group (M_c) and experimental group means (M_e) and the pooled within-group standard deviation (S) were not available in the research report, δ was calculated from selected statistics (e.g., t values or exact p values) if these as well as the direction of effect was reported or from proportions using formulas and tables provided by Glass, McGraw, and Smith (1981) and Rosenthal (1994). Hedges and Olkin (1985) demonstrated that small studies overestimate the population effect size value (δ). Using procedures described by Hedges and Olkin, the effect of small-sample bias was removed by multiplying the effect size statistic δ by a coefficient that included information on the sample sizes of the experimental and control groups, resulting in the statistically unbiased effect size statistic d.

Studies with large sample size provide more stable estimates of δ than studies with small sample size. To give greater weight to studies with larger sample sizes, each effect size value (d) was weighted by the inverse of its variance before averaging the effect size values across studies (Hedges & Becker, 1986; Hedges & Olkin, 1985). Because d values calculated from proportions have a different sampling distribution than d values calculated from means or t values, their variances were calculated using a procedure derived by L. V. Hedges (personal communication, June 14, 1991). In this paper, d_+ was used to represent the average, weighted, unbiased, estimate of effect. According to Cohen (1969), δ values of .20, .50, and .80 correspond with small, medium, and large effects. The effect size statistic δ conveys

information about both the direction and magnitude of the difference in mean scores between two populations. It is calculated by dividing the difference between population means by the standard deviation in the populations, which are assumed to be equal. It is a metric-less estimator since, no matter the original scale (e.g., a 0-10 pain scale or the McGill Pain questionnaire), it communicates the magnitude of the difference between means in standard deviation units. The direction of the difference is communicated by knowing the order of subtraction of the two means and whether a positive or negative value was obtained. Since population values are not known, as described earlier, it is estimated from sample data. For example, if the average pain scores were as follows (experimental treatment group mean = 7, N = 40, SD = 2 and control treatment group = 8, N = 40, SD = 2) and the experimental group mean was subtracted from the control group mean and this difference (i.e., 1.0) was divided by the pooled within-group standard deviation (i.e., 2.0) then the effect size value would equal +0.5, a medium positive effect).

For all effect size values, the convention was adopted to ascribe them a positive sign when the experimental group reported less pain than the control group and a negative sign when the control group reported less pain. In almost all instances when pretreatment and post-treatment scores were reported on the same outcome, a pretreatment d value was calculated and the observed post-treatment effect size value was adjusted for any pretreatment difference between groups by subtracting the d value estimated from pretest data from the d value estimated from posttest data. An exception to this procedure was made for two studies involving bone marrow transplant patients. In these studies it was anticipated that prescribed medical therapies related to their bone marrow transplantation were likely to cause patients to develop oral mucositis and experience mouth pain that was likely to last for several weeks. In those two studies pretreatment pain was both irrelevant to the outcome of interest (pain from oral mucositis) and negligible in all groups. Only posttest pain scores from those studies were used in the meta-analysis.

<u>Unit of statistical analysis.</u> While effect size values for individual measures of self-reported pain are included in Tables 1 and 2, studies were allowed to contribute only one effect size value (d) to any estimate of effect obtained by averaging effect size values across multiple studies (i.e., d_+). Because some studies had multiple measures of self-reported pain, and/or multiple experimental treatment groups each of which were contrasted with the control group, several procedures were needed to obtain the single effect size value for self-reported pain for each study (the sample of studies). The decision rules, for determining the single effect size value for each study, are described in detail elsewhere (Devine, 1992; Devine & Reifschneider, 1995). They include the following: when there were two or more measures of self-reported pain in the study, all effect size values for these measures of pain calculated for the comparison between the experimental treatment group and the control group were averaged to provide a single estimate of effect for that experimental treatment from the study. When there were multiple experimental treatment groups in a single study, the following decision rules were used. If the primary researcher made a prediction about which experimental treatment group would have the largest effect on pain, the effect size value calculated for that experimental treatment group was selected to represent the study. If no prediction was made, in most instances the effect size values for pain were averaged across all experimental treatment groups. However, if the design was factorial, the effect size value for the experimental treatment group that received the largest number of treatment components (factors) was selected to represent the study. When results and hence effect size

values were only available for subgroups that were not relevant for the current meta-analysis (e.g., separate analysis for those also receiving nursing home care services as part of usual care and for those not receiving these services), sample-size weighted average effect size values were calculated using the effect-size values calculated for each of the sub-groups.

A modified sample of studies was used for the analysis of the effect of each type of treatment on pain. Using the modified sample of studies, a study could be represented by more than one effect size value as long as only one effect size value (d) from the study was used in the calculation of any average, weighted, unbiased estimate of effect (d_+). For example, in a study with two experimental treatment groups (e.g., education only and relaxation only), the effect size value for each of those treatments was included in the appropriate type-of-treatment subgroup. But, if a study had two experimental treatment groups that received the same treatment content (e.g., only the mode of treatment delivery varied) the effect size values for the two experimental groups in that study would be averaged in order to obtain a single effect size value for the appropriate type-of-treatment subgroup.

RESULTS

Twenty-five studies of the effect of psycho-educational interventions on self-reported pain in adults with cancer were identified for which an effect size value could be calculated (Devine, 2003). Only 19 of these included random assignment to treatment condition. Of these 19 studies, one study did not clearly specify the study duration, three studies measured the outcome immediately after the treatment, five studies followed patients from 7 to 14 days, seven studies followed patients between three weeks and two months, and three studies followed patients between 12 and 15 months. Since the focus of this review is on longer-term effects, it includes 15 studies that followed patients for three weeks or longer. Ten of these were included in the earlier edition of this chapter and 5 were added in 2004. (Tables 1 and 2).

When multiple reports of the same research were available, these were reviewed for relevant information and included in the reference list. However, for analysis all research reports based on a single sample of subjects were considered a single study.

Study characteristics

The fifteen studies were published between 1983 and 2004. Fourteen of studies were published in a journal and one was found only in doctoral dissertation format. Of the twelve studies for which professional preparation of the first author was discernable, a nurse was the first author in four studies (58%) and a physician was the first author in three studies (33%). Most of the studies ($n = 12$) included usual care for the setting as the control treatment, while the other 3 included a control treatment that involved both usual care for the setting and a placebo or an alternate treatment that was administered by the researchers. Sample sizes in the studies ranged from 29 to 313 with the median sample size being 116.

Subject characteristics

The 15 studies included data from 1,738 adults with cancer. As reported in 14 studies, average age of subjects ranged between 33 and 64 years. Five of the studies included only women and none included only men. Only 5 studies reported the race and/or ethnicity of subjects and in many of these studies, 98-100% of subjects were Caucasian. In the study by Miaskowski et al. (2004) 84% of subjects were Caucasian and in the study by Dalton et al. (2004) 63% were Caucasian. In no instances were separate analyses of treatment effect reported by age, gender or race/ethnicity.

In fourteen studies the type of malignancy was reported. In five of these studies, 70 percent or more of subjects were women with breast cancer. In six other studies, subjects included adults with a variety of types of cancer and no single type of cancer was the majority. Two studies included only adults with a hematological malignancy, and one study included only women with gynecologic cancer.

Documented pain was an identified selection criterion in only 8 of the 15 studies. In two other studies pain was expected to occur in the weeks following bone marrow transplantation. In the other five studies the presence or expected development of pain was presumably assumed. In some studies it may be possible to obtain a crude estimate of expected pain level in the absence of treatment (baseline pain), by examining pretreatment pain level. Variability in baseline pain is a very important issue because when the expected level of pain, in the absence of an experimental intervention, is relatively mild, it is less likely that an intervention will be found to reduce pain because there is little room for reducing pain. Typically, this phenomenon is called a floor effect. Using the pretest level of pain as the indicator of baseline pain may only be reasonable for studies of somewhat shorter duration. For studies lasting 12 months or longer, pretreatment pain level is less likely to be a good predictor of the expected pain level in the absence of treatment at the posttest time period.

Pain prior to the psychoeducational intervention typically was reported for present pain intensity or usual/average pain intensity. To provide a single estimate of baseline pain for each study, in most instances, reported pain level prior to the treatment was averaged across treatment and control groups. In a few instances, pretest scores on pain were not relevant since they were measured prior to ablative chemotherapy given in anticipation of bone marrow transplantation. In those instances, the posttest pain intensity in the control group was used to estimate anticipated pain level in the absence of treatment (baseline pain). In the studies reviewed, various measures of present or usual pain were used, but a 0-10 numeric scale was the most common. In order to analyze the baseline pain level across studies, results from other scales (e.g., 0-5 or 0-100) were converted using linear interpolation to the corresponding value on a 0-10 scale. Once all scores were on a 0-10 scale, it was found that baseline pain varied from 1.8 to 8.0. Based on the criterion: when pain interferes with a cancer patient's functions such as activity, mood or sleep, Serlin and associates (1995) have found that on a 0 to 10 pain scale, scores of 1 to 4 correspond with mild pain, scores of 4 to 6 correspond with moderate pain, and scores of 7 to 10 correspond with severe pain. To provide a somewhat more conservative assessment, in this review when average baseline present/usual pain was 3 or less or when the baseline average worst pain was 4 or less it was assessed that the baseline pain was relatively mild and that the study was likely to have floor effect on the outcome pain.

Based on these criteria it was likely that four studies had a floor effect on pain. With scores on, or converted to, a 0 to 10 pain scale, baseline present or usual pain was 3 or less in three of the studies (Goodwin, et al., 2001; Speigel & Bloom, 1983; Given, et al., 2004). Since the first two of these studies followed subjects for 12 months or more, it may be possible that pretest baseline pain scores are somewhat less relevant than if the study had been of shorter duration, but Goodwin and associates did note an interaction effect with baseline pain. They found that even though, when analyzed across all subjects, there was a statistically significant beneficial effect on pain, there was no significant effect on pain among those that had low pain upon entry into the study. In the study by Given and associates this low level of baseline pain may have contributed to the relatively small effect found on the outcome pain. The researchers did note an interaction between severity of symptoms at baseline and the effect of the treatment with a larger effect being found in those with more

severe symptoms at baseline. In the study by Ward and associates (2000) usual or current pain was not reported, but average worst pain at the pretest was less than 4 on a 0-10 scale.

In two other studies it was difficult to assess baseline pain since pretest pain level was not reported. In those studies baseline pain could only be judged by examining the posttest incidence of pain in the control group. In the study by Rimer and associates (1987), at the posttest 76% of subjects in the control group had more than mild pain. In the study by Maguire and associates (1983), 61% of subjects in the control group reported at least some arm pain at the posttest. In neither of these instances was a floor effect on pain clearly evident.

Setting characteristics

Sixty-seven percent of the studies ($n = 10$) were conducted in the United States of America. The other 5 studies were divided between the United Kingdom ($n = 2$), Canada ($n = 1$), and Australia ($n = 2$). Three of the studies (20%) were conducted exclusively in an inpatient hospital setting, 4 (27%) were conducted exclusively in some type of outpatient treatment facility and 2 (13%) were conducted exclusively in the home. The other six studies involved a combination of settings, such as those involving initial instruction in an intervention (e.g., relaxation training) in the outpatient oncology clinic with subsequent self-administration of the intervention that was done in the subject's home.

Treatment characteristics

At least one effect size value could be coded for 20 experimental treatment groups identified in the 15 studies in the sample (see Tables 1 and 2). Analysis of the narrative descriptions of treatments revealed that experimental interventions included one, or more than one, of the following general categories of content: education (e.g., didactic content about pain and pain treatment), cognitive/behavioral counseling.

Table 1. Study characteristics and direction and magnitude of effect of treatment on pain of studies lasting one year or longer.

Study Author, Journal: Date	Subjects, sample size used in analysis, attrition, and baseline pain (e.g., at pretest)[1]	Interventions	Outcome measure of pain, effect size, timing of posttest measure/method of measurement
Group support vs usual care Goodwin, Leszcz, Ennis, Koopmans, Vincent, Guther, et al. New England Journal of Medicine 2001: 1719-26.	Adults with metastatic breast cancer Treatment: $n = 99$; Control: $n = 44$ Attrition: 90 lost to study (note: mortality at one year approximately 65%) Average pain intensity at pretest: 1.83 on 0 – 10 scale	Treatment: weekly group meetings lasting 90 minutes for 1 year or longer if beneficial. Therapy goal to foster support and encourage expression of emotions about cancer and its effects on their lives. Coping strategies discussed. Monthly session provided for family and friends. Control: usual care plus every 4-6 months all in study were sent educational materials about breast cancer and its treatment as well as relaxation and nutrition	VAS (pain experience) $d = .36$ VAS (suffering/hurt) $d = .22$ Authors noted an interaction with baseline pain: minimal effect in those with low pain. Subjects completed a questionnaire at baseline and one year later.
Education and counseling vs usual care Maguire, Brooke, Tait, Thomas, & Sellwood. Clinical Oncology 1983: 319-24.	Adults having modified radical mastectomy for breast cancer Treatment: $n = 75$; Control: $n = 77$ Attrition: 20 lost to study Pain at pretest was not reported. At posttest 61% in control group had pain.	Treatment: education and counseling by a specialist nurse in hospital, at discharge, and every 2 months to monitor progress until well adapted Topics: instruction in arm exercises, advise on prostheses, feelings related to loss of breast and social adjustment were discussed Control: usual care	% with arm pain $d = .26$ Subjects reported pain to the researcher 12-18 months after surgery
Group therapy vs usual care Spiegel & Bloom, Psychosomatic Medicine 1983: 333-9	Metastatic breast cancer Treatment: $n = 30$; Control: $n = 24$ Attrition: 23 lost to study. Analyses done on 54 who completed data collection at 2 points in time. Individual regression used to interpolate missing data. Average pain sensation at baseline: 2.5 on 0 – 10 scale	Treatment: weekly 90-minute group therapy sessions for one year. One of the two treatment groups participated in self hypnosis exercises (Results for the two treatment groups were not reported separately in detail. Both had less pain than control subjects, and hypnosis was reported to have an additive analgesic effect Control: usual care	VAS (sensation) $d = .68$ VAS (suffering/pain) $d = .59$ Pain frequency $d = .01$ Pain duration $d = .35$ At baseline and again 12 months later subjects rated their pain and responded to inquiries about the cause of their pain

Note: [1] Pain intensity rating at the pretest (across all groups). This information is not available for all studies. values $d=$ the standardized mean difference measured in standard deviation units VAS = Visual Analogue Scale

Table 2. Study characteristics, direction and magnitude of effect of treatment on pain for studies lasting at least 3 weeks, but less than 1 year.

Study Author, Journal: Date	Subjects, sample size used in analysis, attrition, and baseline pain (e.g., at pretest)[1]	Interventions	Outcome measure of pain, effect size values), and timing of posttest measure
Tailored cognitive behavioral therapy vs standard cognitive behavioral therapy vs usual care Dalton, Keefe, Carlson, Youngblood, Pain management Nursing 2004 3-18	Adult receiving care for cancer pain. Major types of cancer: Breast, lung, lymphoma, colorectal Treatment 1: $n = 43$; Treatment 2: $n = 45$; Control: $n = 33$ Attrition: at 6 months 93 lost to study [54 of whom died or had disease progression or complications] Average pain severity at pretest: 4.3 on a 0 – 10 scale	Treatments 1 and 2 included 5 50-minute sessions, three of which could be delivered by phone. Homework and a pain diary were completed. Treatment 1 was predicted to have the larger effect. **Treatment 1:** Profile-Tailored Cognitive Behavioral Therapy included cognitive behavioral content that was selected in order to match the individual's score on the six scales of the Biobehavioral Pain Profile questionnaire. The scales included: Environmental, loss of control, health care avoidance, past/current experiences, physiological responsivity, and thoughts of disease progression. **Treatment 2:** Standard Cognitive Behavioral Therapy included teaching patients the relationship between pain and emotions as well as how to use coping, problem solving, relaxation, and self control strategies and how to modify cognitive distortions and distressing thoughts to promote personal control. Imagery or distraction, social reinforcement, and positive self-statements were used **Control:** Usual care which included a range of educational and supportive techniques	**Treatment 1** 1 month VAS (pain severity) $d = .73$[a] VAS (pain intensity) $d = .64$[a] 6 months VAS (pain severity) $d = .46$[a] VAS (pain intensity) $d = .18$[a] **Treatment 2** 1 month VAS (pain severity) $d = .18$[a] VAS (pain intensity) $d = -.35$[a] 6 months VAS (pain severity) $d = .75$[a] VAS (pain intensity) $d = .37$[a] Patients kept a pain diary for one week prior to the 1 month and six month data collection time period. Data from patient diaries collected one week after the intervention were not used in this meta-analysis. Means and standard deviations were obtained from the researcher.

Table 2 continued

Study	Subjects	Interventions	Outcome measure
Pain education program vs usual care de Wit, van Dam, Zandbelt, van Buuren, van der Heijden, Leenhouts, & Loonstra, Pain 1997: 55-69	Adults with cancer experiencing pain. Major types of cancer: Breast, genitourinary Without home care: Treatment: $n = 106$; Control: $n = 103$ With home care: Treatment: $n = 53$; Control: $n = 51$ Attrition: 78 lost from study Average present pain intensity at pretest 3.3 on a 0 – 10 scale	**Treatment:** 30 -60 minutes education (plus audiotape and booklet) with two 5-15 minute follow-up phone calls. Topics: pain, medication, side effects, myths, nonpharmacologic interventions for pain, & what to do if pain control inadequate. Topics tailored for prior knowledge and relevance to specific patient. **Control:** usual care	Subgroups with and without home care (HC) were reported separately. Pain subscale from EOERC[2] $d = .35^a$ (without HC) $d = -.19^a$ (with HC) VAS (present pain intensity)[2] $d = .65^a$ (without HC) $d = -.30^a$ (with HC) VAS (average pain intensity)[2] $d = .61^a$ (without HC) $d = -.16^a$ (with HC) VAS (worst pain intensity)[2] $d = .43^a$ (without HC) $d = -.14^a$ (with HC) No effect size value could be calculated for: MPQ Questionnaires completed at baseline and after 2, 4, & 8 weeks. Outcomes measured at 2 weeks after pretest were excluded.
Individualized multidimensional patient therapy programs vs usual care Farzanegan Dissertation: 1989	Adult referred to pain clinic for cancer-related pain and started on scheduled analgesics Treatment: $n = 15$; Control: $n = 14$ Attrition: 1 lost from control group Average pain intensity at pretest: 80 on 0 – 100 scale	**Treatment:** Four sessions of individualized patient therapy spaced 1-2 weeks apart. Topics: information about pain treatment; relaxation techniques (progressive relaxation, controlled breathing, guided imagery); disease related counseling; home practice of relaxation. **Control:** usual care in pain clinic	MPQ: Sensory $d = -.44^a$ Affective $d = 1.31^a$ Evaluative $d = .37^a$ VAS (pain intensity) $d = -.28^a$ At baseline and 4-5 weeks later subjects completed a questionnaire on pain.

Table 2 continued

Study	Subjects	Interventions	Outcome measure
Cognitive behavioral vs usual care Given, Given, Rahbar, Jeon, McCorkle, Cimprich, Galecki, Kozachik, Brady, Fisher-Malloy, Courtney, Bowie, Journal of Clinical Oncology 2004: 507-16	Adults with solid tumors undergoing first course of chemotherapy Major types of cancer: breast, lung Treatment: $n = 118$; Control: $n = 119$ Attrition: 70 lost to study Pain severity at pretest: 2.4 on a 10-point scale. Sixty-four percent of subjects were prescribed analgesics at week 20. This was comparable between groups ($p = .52$)	**Treatment:** Based on Bandura's approach to developing self-efficacy, the nurse and patient identified problems, the nurse proposed interventions, and together they assessed patient's ability to perform the proposed cognitive and behavioral strategies. Four types of behavioral strategies were used: providing self-care management information, problem solving, communications with providers, and counseling/support. For pain these included medication management, distraction with music, managing environment or side effects, increasing communications with physician, verbalizing emotions and pain management preferences. Other strategies were used for other symptoms **Control:** standard care.	Pain severity at 10 weeks $d = .15^a$ Pain severity at 20 weeks $d = .05^a$ Subjects were interviewed at baseline, at 10 weeks and at 20 weeks. Multiple symptoms were assessed. Effect size values were calculated only for pain. A significant interaction between severity of all symptoms at baseline and effect on all symptoms was noted; those with more symptoms had a larger effect from the treatment. Means and standard deviations were obtained from the researcher.
Support, coping skills, & problem solving vs usual care Sandgren, McCaul, King, O'Donnell, & Foreman, Oncology Nursing Forum 2000: 683-88	Recently diagnosed women with stage I or II breast cancer with 91% of subjects receiving adjuvant therapy during study. Treatment: $n = 24$; Control: $n = 29$ Attrition: 9 lost from study Pain at pretest 57.1 on a 100 point scale where a higher score indicates less pain	**Treatment:** Ten therapy sessions by phone were conducted across 4 months. The intervention included emotional support, instructions in coping skills, strategies for managing anxiety and stress, and interventions to solve patient-generated problems. Strategies used/taught included cognitive restructuring, encouraging emotional expression, nonspecific support, and diaphragmatic breathing for relaxation **Control:** usual care	Pain subscale[2] $d = .30$ Subjects reported pain by telephone at baseline, 4 months, and 10 months. [Baseline value used as covariate, covariate adjusted posttest means analyzed].

Table 2 continued

Study	Subjects	Interventions	Outcome measure
Education *vs* usual care Miaskowski, Dodd, West, Schumacher, Paul, Tripathy, Koo, Journal of Clinical Oncology 2004: 1713-20	Adults with cancer experiencing pain from bone metastasis Major types of cancer: breast, prostate, and lung Treatment: $n = 93$; Control: $n = 81$ Attrition: 38 lost to study Average pain intensity at pretest: 3.9 on a 10-point scale.	**Treatment:** The treatment was called PRO-SELF. Academic detailing related to pain management was done with the patient and family care giver by clinical nurse specialists. The session was tailored to meet identified learning needs. Patients were taught how to use a weekly pill box and scripts were provided to promote communications with physicians about unrelieved pain. Written education about pain and side effects management was provided. The PRO-SELF nurse called patients during weeks 2, 4, and 5 and visited the patient at home during weeks 3 and 6; they assessed pain scores and medication intake. Content was reinforced and patients coached as needed. Coaching included adjusting analgesic intake within the scope of the prescription, pain assessment, strategies to prevent or relieve side effects, and discussing any needed changes in pain management plan with their provider. The intervention took about 3.65 hours to deliver (West et al, 2003). **Control:** standard care: subjects were provided with the patient version of the Cancer Pain Guideline published by the Agency for Health Care Policy and Research. Advised to record every evening their pain level and analgesics taken that day. Adherence with pain management diary was asses-sed by research nurses 3 times at home and 3 times by phone.	Average pain[2] $d = .77$[a] Least pain[2] $d = .57$[a] Worst pain[2] $d = .46$[a] Subjects recorded their pain level every evening in a pain management diary. Means and standard deviations were obtained from the researcher.
Education *vs* usual care Rimer, Levy, Keintz, Fox, Engstrom, & MacElwee, Patient Education and Counseling 1987: 267-77	Adults with cancer being treated with narcotics for nonsurgical pain. Major types of cancer: lung, colo-rectal and breast Treatment: $n = 127$; Control: $n = 103$ Attrition: 35 lost to study At the posttest 76% of controls had > mild pain.	**Treatment:** 15 minutes of education about pain management included printed materials. Topics: analgesic regime for pain, rationale for compliance, debunking myths about tolerance and addiction, aids to promote implementation of analgesic regimen **Control:** usual care	% with no/mild pain $d = .49$ Subjects reported pain intensity to a nurse in person at the pretest and over the phone four weeks later.

336

Study	Subjects	Interventions	Outcome measure
Relaxation and guided imagery vs usual care Sloman, Nursing Clinics of North America 1995: 697-709. Sloman, Brown, Aldana, & Chee, Contemporary Nurse 1994[3]: 6-12	Hospitalized adults with cancer pain Many types of cancer Treatment 1: $n = 20$; Treatment 2: $n = 20$ Control: $n = 20$ Attrition: 7 lost from study. Additional subjects randomly assigned to balance groups. Pain intensity at pretest: 2.5 on 0 – 5 scale	**Treatment 1:** Twice weekly session with nurse-administered relaxation and guided imagery; encouraged to practice on their own 2 times a day and to use whenever in pain **Treatment 2:** Twice weekly session with audio-tape-guided relaxation and guided imagery encouraged to practice 2 times a day using the audio-tape, and to use whenever in pain **Control:** usual care	<u>Treatment 1</u> MPQ: Sensory $d = .66$[a] Affective $d = .07$[a] Present pain intensity $d = .86$[a] VAS (worst pain) $d = 1.08$[a] <u>Treatment 2</u> MPQ: Sensory $d = .51$[a] Affective $d = .28$[a] Present pain intensity $d = .99$[a] VAS (worst pain) $d = .71$[a] Subjects completed questionnaires about pain at the pretest and 3 weeks later (10% completed it at home and mailed it to the researcher).
Cognitive behavioral interventions vs placebo Syrjala, Cummings, & Donaldson, Pain 1992: 137-46	Adults having a bone marrow transplant for a hematological malignancy Treatment 1: $n = 12$; Treatment 2: $n = 11$ Attention Control: $n = 12$ Attrition: 22 lost to the study Usual care control group not used in meta-analysis because gender distribution significantly different. Pain in control group at week 3: 38 on 0 – 100 scale.	**Treatment 1:** Hypnosis explained and concern elicited. Hypnosis induction with relaxation and imagery. Additional phrases related to health, well-being, self-control, and enhanced coping. Inductions taped and provided for daily self-administration. **Treatment 2:** Progressive muscle relaxation & brief autogenic relaxation (also tape provided for daily self-administration); cognitive restructuring of uncomfortable experiences; procedural and sensation information; short-term goal setting for self-care with monitoring progress; and meaning of illness and treatment explored. **Control:** Equal time spent with therapist, conversation dictated by patient, no coping skills introduced. All treatments administered 90 minutes twice before admission and then 30 minutes twice a week for 4 weeks	**Treatment 1** VAS (intensity of mouth or throat pain) $d = .52$ **Treatment 2** VAS (intensity of mouth or throat pain) $d = .44$ Subjects recorded pain daily for past 24 hours and results were averaged for the week. Only data for the 3rd week after transplant was used.

Table 2 continued

Study	Subjects	Interventions	Outcome measure
3 treatments vs usual care Syrjala, Donaldson, Davis, Kippes, & Carr, Pain 1995: 189–98	Adults having a bone marrow transplant for a hematological malignancy Treatment 1: $n = 24$; Treatment 2: $n = 23$ Treatment 3: $n = 24$; Control: $n = 22$ Attrition: 67 were lost to the study Pain in control group at week 3 = 34.4 on 0 – 100 scale.	**Treatment 1:** Relaxation and imagery (as in Treatment 2); cognitive restructuring self-defeating cognitions; distracting attention from noxious physical sensations; short-term goal setting for self-care with monitoring progress; incorporating visions of favorite places and people into imagery; discouraging goal setting that could not be controlled; and problem solving. Written and one-on-one instructions plus audiotapes provided for daily self-administration. **Treatment 2:** Information on pain and nausea. Deep breathing, progressive muscle relaxation and imagery with brief autogenic relaxation and additional phrases/images about well-being, strength, competence and comfort. Written and one-on-one instructions plus audiotapes provided for daily self-administration. **Treatment 3:** Psychotherapeutic support related to affective status and current situation. Positive reframing and information about the normal course of pain and about medical treatment. **Control:** Usual care All three experimental treatments were administered 90 minutes twice before admission and then 30 minutes twice a week for 5 weeks	**Treatment 1**[2] VAS (intensity of mouth or throat pain) $d = .64$ **Treatment 2**[2] VAS (intensity of mouth or throat pain) $d = .27$ **Treatment 3**[2] VAS (intensity of mouth or throat pain) $d = .47$ Subjects recorded pain daily for past 24 hours and results were averaged for the week. Only data for the 3rd week after transplant was used
Individually tailored information vs usual care Ward, Donovan, Owens, Grosen, & Serlin, Research in Nursing and Health 2000: 393-405.	Adults with progressive or metastatic gynecologic cancer experiencing pain in last 2 weeks Treatment: $n = 13$; Control: $n = 14$ Attrition: 17 lost to the study Worst pain intensity at baseline: 3.96 on 0 – 10 scale	**Treatment:** Individually tailored information about barriers to and side effects from pain management with analgesics. Content prompted by data from questionnaires on barriers to pain management and side effects from analgesics. Booklet was provided, questions were answered, and a follow up phone call was made for clarification. **Control:** Usual care	Brief Pain Inventory[2]: Worst pain $d = -.59$[a] Interferes with life $d = -.28$[a] No effect size values could be calculated for: two subscales: "least pain in last week" and "pain now". Subjects recorded pain at baseline and again at 1 month and 2 month follow up periods. Questionnaire distributed by non-treatment provider or mailed.

Table 2 continued

Study	Subjects	Interventions	Outcome measure
Individually tailored education vs general education/discussion about living with cancer Yates, Edwards, Nash, Aranda, Purdie, Najman, Skerman, Walsh, Patient Education and Counseling 2004:227-37.	Adults with cancer pain in last two weeks or on opioids for cancer pain. Major types of cancer: breast, colorectal, lung, or head and neck Treatment: $n = 94$; Control: $n = 90$ Attrition: 44 lost to the study Average pain intensity at baseline: 4.1 on 0 – 10 scale	**Treatment:** Individually tailored education about cancer pain management, communicating with health care providers about pain and reducing reluctance to take analgesics. The initial treatment was provided in the outpatient department and lasted about 30 minutes. Content provided was prompted by an assessment of patient's barriers to effective pain management. The intervention included targeted information giving, collaborative problem solving, and practicing cognitive and behavioral strategies for overcoming identified barriers to effective pain management. A booklet was provided. The second intervention was by telephone one week later and lasted about 15 minutes. Pain control was assessed, use and barriers using recommended strategies was discussed. Pain management plan reinforced and revised as needed **Control:** General education about living with cancer provided in the outpatient department and by follow-up phone call. Control intervention of equivalent time as experimental intervention.	Brief Pain Inventory: Average pain $d = .06^a$ Distress from pain $d = .28^a$ Impact from pain $d = .27^a$ Questionnaires were completed at baseline and after 1 & 8 weeks and returned by mail. If follow-up phone calls were needed about the questionnaires, these were made by non-treatment providers. Pain measured at 1 week after the treatment was excluded. Groups differed somewhat at baseline with the control group containing a higher percentage of individuals with breast cancer and a higher percentage of married persons. The groups did not differ by gender.

Note: [1] Pain intensity rating at the pretest (across all groups). This information is not available for all studies. $d =$ the standardized mean difference measured in standard deviation units [2] Multiple effect size values for the same outcome measure over time are averaged. [3] Duplicate report of the same research EOERC = pain scale from the European Organization for Research and Treatment of Cancer Core Quality of Life Questionnaire MPQ = McGill Pain Questionnaire VAS = Visual Analogue Scale , [a] adjusted for pretest differences between groups ($d_{post-test} - d_{pretest}$)

Classifying interventions was very challenging since most interventions included multiple types of treatment content. Cognitive-behavioral strategies were the most frequently occurring type of treatment. Traditional relaxation-based cognitive behavioral strategies such as relaxation, guided imagery, hypnosis and/or deep breathing were included in 12 of the 20 experimental interventions. Non-relaxation-based cognitive-behavioral strategies such as cognitive restructuring, distraction, problem solving, positive self-statements, practicing communicating with physicians, using a pill box, strategies to alleviate side-effects, self-monitoring of pain or progress were common types of treatment content in interventions labeled as cognitive-behavioral. These same types of treatment content also were commonly included in interventions that were not labled as cognitive-behavioral in nature. Some interventions that were labeled by the researchers as educational or counseling in nature included activities such as problem solving, practicing communicating with physicians about pain, etc.. In other instances researchers described that coping strategies were suggested or discussed, and while these may have been cognitive-behavioral strategies, the actual the nature of these interventions was not specified.

Nine of the experimental interventions studied included education (e.g., didactic content about pain and pain treatment). It was also common for these interventions to include information about the myths associated with analgesic medications and instructions in the appropriate use of analgesics. While some of these interventions also included a general description of nonpharmacological interventions for pain (e.g., relaxation or distraction), if detailed instructions with return demonstration or practice were included, the content was considered cognitive/behavioral rather than simply educational. In only five instances did the experimental treatments involve primarily education. In four of these,

the education provided was tailored to the needs of the subject. In one, standardized education was provided. In the other three experimental interventions education was combined with other types of content (e.g., cognitive /behavioral or psychosocial counseling).

Seven of the experimental interventions studied included psychosocial counseling. In four instances coping strategies were suggested to the individuals receiving psychosocial counseling, but the counseling appeared to be the predominant content. (i.e., Goodwin et al., 2001; Spiegel & Bloom, 1983; Syrjala et al., 1995, Treatment 3, Sandgren et al, 2000). In the other experimental interventions the psychosocial counseling was combined with either multiple other types of content without apparent emphasis on the counseling content..

Threats to Validity

Restricting the sample to studies with random assignment to treatment condition eliminated a major potential threat to the internal validity of the review. However, other threats to valid inference are possible. Of concern are the possible threats to validity based on publication bias, a floor effect on pain, measurement reactivity, and a Hawthorn effect (Cook & Campbell, 1979; Rosenthal, 1979). Studies potentially threatened by a publication bias, are those published in a journal. Studies threatened by a floor effect on pain are those in which baseline pain (the expected level of pain in the absence of the experimental treatment) was low (e.g., on a 0 to 10 pain scale, less than 3 for current/usual pain or less than 4 for worst pain). Studies potentially threatened by a Hawthorn effect are those without a control group that received a placebo or alternate treatment delivered by the researcher, and studies potentially threatened by high measurement reactivity are those in which posttest pain level was reported verbally to the researcher who provided the treatment. In Table 3, the effect size values based on the sample of studies is reported for each study that is not threatened by each of the identified threats to validity. Unfortunately, due to the small sample size of relevant studies and the distribution of the threats to validity, only limited analyses were possible. When analyses were restricted to the 8 studies with no documented floor effect on pain and data collection by a method other than verbal report of pain to the researcher who provided the experimental intervention, the effect size value was statistically significant, and homogeneous (d_+ = .44, 95% confidence interval = .27; .61; Q = 4.6, df = 7). This provides some empirical evidence that when the threats to validity based on a floor effect on the outcome and high measurement subjectivity are not present, moderate sized effects still are evident.

Effect on Pain

Pain was measured using self-report. The McGill Pain Questionnaire and various visual analogue-type scales were the tools most frequently used to assess pain. In order to avoid over weighting studies with multiple outcome measures of self-reported pain or studies with multiple experimental treatment conditions, the sample of studies was used in which each study provided only 1 d value to each analysis.

Effect size values based on the sample of studies ranged from -.44 to +.65 with 87% of the studies demonstrating a positive treatment effect on pain that was d = .20 or larger. When results were aggregated across all studies, a small to moderate-sized, statistically significant, homogeneous beneficial effect on pain was found (d_+ = .34; 95% confidence interval = .23; .45; Q = 13.9, df =14). Given the relatively small number of studies in the review and the extent to which treatment components varied between studies, only limited quantitative analysis of effect of specific types of treatments on pain was possible.

Cognitive/behavioral interventions. Three studies tested the effect of cognitive/behavioral

interventions alone. In all three instances the interventions tested were relaxation-based interventions (e.g., relaxation with guided imagery or self-hypnosis). Effect size values based on the modified sample of studies ranged from .27 to .65 (Table 4). When these were aggregated there was a statistically significant, homogeneous, moderately-sized beneficial effect on pain (d_+ = .48, 95% confidence interval = .12; .84; Q = .9, df = 2). In three other studies, both relaxtion-based and non relaxation-based cognitive behavioral interventions were used. Effect size values based on the modified sample of studies ranged from .20 to .64 with two of the three being .50 or larger (Table 4). When these were aggregated the effect was of small to moderate size, but not statistically significant, (d_+ = .32, 95% confidence interval = -.05; .69; Q = 3.3, df = 2). It should be noted that the study with the lowest effect size value did have a likely floor effect on the outcome pain.

Education. Five studies tested the effect of education alone. Effect size values based on the modified sample of studies ranged from -.44 to .49 (Table 4). When aggregated there was not a statistically significant effect on pain (d_+ = .29, 95% confidence interval = -.08; .67; Q = 7.9, df = 4). It should be noted that there was wide variability within the effect size values.

Psychosocial counseling. Six studies included interventions with psychosocial counseling. In three of these studies, while coping strategies also were included in the intervention, it appeared from the descriptions of the intervention that psychosocial counseling was the predominant content in the interventions. Effect size values based on the modified sample of studies for these four studies ranged from .29 to .47 (Table 4). When aggregated there was a statistically significant, homogeneous, small-to-moderately-sized beneficial effect on pain (d_+ = .35, 95% confidence interval = .11; .58; Q = .34, df = 3).

Multiple types of content. Three studies included interventions that included content from two or more categories (e.g., education, cognitive/behavioral treatment, and psycho-social counseling). Effect size values based on the modified sample of studies ranged from .24 to .44 (Table 4). Even though all three effect size values were positive and of small or moderate size, when aggregated there was not a statistically significant, beneficial effect on pain (d_+ = .29, 95% confidence interval = -.06; .64; Q = .17, df = 2)

DISCUSSION

Only three randomized studies of the effect of psychoeducational interventions on pain were located in which there was follow-up for 12 or more months. In contrast with most of the other twelve studies in this review, in those three studies it was not a selection criteria that the potential subjects reported being in pain or were scheduled to have a procedure that was expected to cause them to be in pain for several weeks (e.g., bone marrow transplantation) and when pretest level of pain was reported it was relatively low (e.g., 1.8 on a 10-point scale in Goodwin et al., 2001 and 2.5 on a 10-point scale in Spiegel & Bloom, 1983) or it was not measured (Maguire et al., 1983). As such, these studies, all of which included only breast cancer patients, provided a better test of whether the experimental intervention would moderate the development of pain over time rather than whether it would reduce pain that existed upon enrollment in the study. In all three of these studies at least a small effect on pain was found at the 12-15 month follow-up period. In two of these studies only individuals with metastatic breast cancer were included and the intervention included weekly group support meetings, although in one of the studies (Spiegel & Bloom) some participants also were taught self-hypnosis. The third study included individuals who had had a modified radical mastectomy and the intervention included disease-specific individual counseling and education about arm exercises and the use of a prosthesis. Generalizability of these three studies is limited by three major factors. First, for the two studies that did not include only disease-specific content (e.g., arm exercises after surgery), all subjects had breast cancer and so our ability to generalize these results on the effect of psychosocial counseling to individuals with other types of cancer is untested. Second, two of the three studies were about 20 years old and were conducted at a time when usual care for the prevention and treatment of cancer pain was quite different from current practice. Third, both the vari-ability and lack of specificity of the inter-ventions tested were of concern. The nature and content of the psychosocial counseling was described only generally. Of these three studies, the one by Goodwin and associates is particu-larly important because it was recent, its intervention was relatively clearly specified (i.e., weekly group meetings providing psycho-social counseling and discussion of coping strategies, in addition to monthly support sessions for family and friends), it had an alternate-treatment control group, and it yielded a statistically significant effect on pain. The differences in treatment effectiveness between interventions with different types of treatment content were not remarkable except for the subset of studies that tested the effect of education alone, which included the one study with a negative effect size value (Ward et al., 2000). Of greater note was the variability in experimental treatment content within each type-of- treatment subgroup and the substantial variability in effect size values obtained for the outcome pain within each of those subgroups. It is very encouraging that all but two of the effect size values based on the modified sample of studies was both positive and .20 or larger. This suggests that there is a high probability that several types of psychoeducational intervention may be helpful in the long-term prevention or reduction of pain. However, our enthusiasm must be tempered by the fact that strong evidence based

Table 3 Studies not threatened by a publication bias, a Hawthorne Effect, high measurement reactivity, or a floor effect on pain and the effect size value for the study, based on the sample of studies

No Publication Bias	No Hawthorne Effect	Lower Measurement Reactivity	No Floor Effect on Pain
Farzanegan, 1989: d = .24	Goodwin, et al. 2001: d = .29 Syrjala, et al., 1992: d = .64 Yates, et al., 2004: d = .20	Dalton, et al., 2004: d = .50 de Wit, et al., 1997: d = .27 Farzanegan, 1989: d = .24 Goodwin, et al. 2001: d = .29 Miaskowski, et al., 2004: d = .60 Sloman, 1995: d = .65 Syrjala, et al., 1992: d = .52 Syrjala, et al., 1995: d = .64 Ward, et al., 2000: d = -.44 Yates, et al., 2004: d = .20	Dalton, et al., 2004: d = .50 de Wit, et al., 1997: d = .27 Farzanegan, 1989: d = .24 Maguire, et al., 1983: d = .26 Miaskowski, et al., 2004: d = .60 Rimer, et al. 1987: d = .49 Sandgren, et al., 2000: d = .30 Sloman, 1995: d = .65 Syrjala, et al., 1992: d = .52 Syrjala, et al., 1995: d = .64 Yates, et al., 2004: d = .20

Table 4 Effect size values based on the modified sample of studies by predominate type of treatment provided

Cognitive Behavioral (CB)	Education	Psychosocial support plus coping strategies	No predominate type of treatment
Relaxation-Based 1. Sloman, 1995, Relaxation and guided imagery: d = .65 2. Syrjala et al., 1992, Treatment 1, hypnosis, relaxation, and guided imagery: d = .52 3. Syrjala et al., 1995, Treatment 2, deep breathing, progressive muscle and brief autogenic, relaxation and imagery: d = .27 CB with Relaxation and Non-Relaxation-based Treatments 4. Syrjala et al., 1995, Treatment 1, relaxation and guided imagery, cognitive restructuring, distraction, goal setting: d = .64 Tailored CB with Relaxation and Non-Relaxation-based Treatments 5. Dalton et al., 2004, CB therapies used were tailored to Biobehavioral Pain Profile d = .50 6. Given et al., 2004, CB therapies used were tailored to identified problems d = .2	Standardized Education 1. Rimer, et al., 1987, Education on pain management: d = .49 Tailored Education 2. de Wit, et al., 1997, Education on pain management tailored to knowledge: d = .27 3. Miaskowski et al., 2004 Education on pain management, side effects management, and communicating with health care providers about pain tai-lored to meet learning needs : d = .60 4. Ward et al., 2000, Education on the bar-riers to and side effects from taking analge-sics tailored to identified barriers: d = -.44 5. Yates et al., 2004, Education about pain management, communicating with health care providers about pain, and reducing reluctance to take analgesics tailored to identified barriers: d = .20	Goodwin et al., 2001, Group support and coping strategies: d = .29 Sandgren et al., 2000, Emotional support provided by phone and instruction in coping skills: d = .30 Spiegel et al., 1983, Group therapy plus some subjects taught self-hypnosis: d = .41 Syrjala et al., 1995, Treatment 3, psychotherapeutic support and positive reframing: d = .47	Farzanegan, 1989, Education, relaxation, guided imagery, and counseling: d = .24 Maguire et al., 1983, Arm exercises after radical mastectomy, edu-cation about prosthesis, and counseling: d = .26 Syrjala et al., 1992, Treatment 2, relaxation, cognitive restructuring, goal setting, and information about procedures and sensations: d = .44

on multiple replications of specific experimental treatments is lacking. The subsets of experimental interventions with similar types of treatment content were very small and in several instances, the aggregated effect size values were not statistically significant even though all of the effect size values in that subset were positive. The ability to examine both the relative effectiveness of different types of treatments and the plausibility of alternative explanations for the findings based on threats to validity were severely limited by the small number of relevant studies identified. Even when the types of experimental treatment content provided were grouped according to a very broad conceptualization of construct replication and the modified sample of studies was used, only from three to five studies contributed an effect size value to analyses of effect on pain by each type of treatment. With so few studies in each subset, it must be noted that if only a few additional studies with quite different outcomes were found and added to the review, the conclusions of the review could be reversed. Even the most fundamental research questions on the long-term effect of psychoeducational interventions on pain in adults with cancer remain less than fully answered. These include: 1) what types of psychoeducational intervention have a long-term effect on pain in adults with cancer, 2) how long does the effect last, 3) how frequently should the treatment be re-administered to achieve optimal effect on pain, 4) can the effect be generalized to and across different types of individuals (e.g., gender, socioeconomic status, ethnicity) and 5) can the effect be generalized to and across the different types of pain that are found in adults with cancer.

This lack of certainty arises from the fact that there are still relatively few randomized controlled studies on this topic as well as from the prevalence of methodological and reporting weaknesses in the research conducted to date.

These weaknesses can be organized according to the interventions tested, the populations sampled, and the methods used. All too frequently the intervention tested in a study included multiple types of treatment content, was poorly described, and was contrasted with a usual care control treatment that was even more poorly described. Without confidence in the exact nature of the experimental and control treatments and the fact that these treatments differ in substantial and systematic ways, it is unclear to what construct one might attribute observed differences in outcome or whether a lack of difference in outcome might be attributable to a lack of substantial difference between experimental and control treatments.

Usual care for the setting cannot be withheld and when patients are in pain it is likely that usual care will include some psychoeducational interventions (e.g., education about analgesics, coping strategies, booklets on distraction or relaxation) in addition to an analgesic regime. If the patient remained in pain it would be expected that over time the usual care provided would be modified in ways to attempt to reduce the patient's pain. For this reason, in the future it may be profitable to expand the meta-analysis to look at the effect of the interventions during the first three weeks after the treatment The types of psychoeducational interventions examined in this review are the same as those that are recommended in widely disseminated clinical practice guidelines for the management of cancer pain (Jacox et al., 1994).

Research also suggests that many patients will treat their own pain with psychoeducational interventions without having been taught these interventions by researchers. Dalton (1987) reported that 50% of their subjects used nonpharmacologic interventions (including massage and distraction) to control their pain. Gaston-Johansson, Fall-Dickson, Nada, and associates (2000) reported that prior to receiving an experimental intervention for pain that included relaxation, 35% of subjects reported using relaxation for pain. Based on a survey of 80 women with cancer pain, Arathuzik (1991) reported that 20 coping strategies for pain were used by 20% or more of their sample. These strategies included remaining calm (68.8%), relaxing muscles (50%), visualization (47.5%), and putting pain out of their thoughts (41.2%). While this widespread use nonpharmacological interventions for pain suggests that these types of treatments for pain are acceptable to many individuals, when various uncontrolled and undocumented non-pharmacological interventions for pain happen concurrently with or as part of usual care, it can severely interfere with an adequate assessment of the effectiveness of an experimental intervention for pain. Variability in the usual care provided between subjects and between studies can be a major factor leading to variability in treatment outcome and hence the calculated effect size values. This can arise when the same treatment overlaps extensively with the content provided in usual care in some studies and only overlaps only minimally in other studies. Even if the treatment is effective, when there is exten-sive overlap between the treatment provided to both treatment and control groups, this will tend to minimize the observed between-group differences in outcome because both groups have actually received similar treatments. When usual care varies between subjects in a study this will tend to inflate the standard deviation on the outcome and hence decrease the effect size value. The problem of uncon-trolled usual care interventions will continue to grow as nonpharmacologic interventions for pain become more widely used. Care must be taken to describe the content of the control treatment (both usual care and relevant self-administered treatments) lest it appear that experimental interventions are ineffective when the root cause for a lack of between-group difference in outcome is a lack of substantial difference between the experimental and con-trol

treatments received. The study by de Witt and associates (1997) provides an interesting case in point as to what may happen when the control treatments differ. They had two subsets of subjects: those who, based on need, received home-care nursing services after discharge from the hospital as part of usual care, and those who did not need or receive these services. While there may have been many differences between these two subsets of subjects, such as their ability to perform daily activities or chance differences due to ineffective random assignment, one obvious difference between the subgroups is the control treatment received. Those receiving home care services from nurses would have ready access to pain-relevant education and interventions, particularly if their pain were not well controlled. Dramatic differences in the outcome of this education-based experimental intervention also were noted, with a moderately sized beneficial effect being found in the "no home care" subgroup ($d = .51$), and a small negative effect in the home care group ($d = -.20$).

In terms of populations studied, the practical difficulties involved in doing pain research in adults with cancer are well acknowledged (Kerr, 1995). Cancer is not a single disease and pain associated with cancer often is complex in nature. Pain in cancer patients may be due to the tumor itself, treatment for the cancer, or a comorbid condition. It is frequently the case that cancer patients have pain from two or more sources. For example, among 200 patients in a cancer pain clinic, Banning, Sjogren, & Henriksen (1991) found that 75% of patients had pain from two or more causes and Twycross & Fairfield (1983) reported that 80 of 100 cancer patients in hospice had pain in two or more anatomically distinct sites. This level of complexity in the phenomenon being studied (i.e., pain) is difficult to control or account for in research. The optimal intervention could vary with the type of pain (e.g., nociceptive versus neuropathic). When the type of pain being studied is unspecified, this potential

345

relationship between the type of intervention and type of pain remains unexplored. While some studies in this review specified the pain they wanted reported upon (e.g., by referring the subject to their arm or mouth pain) most did not. Also, the effect of assessing only one level of pain intensity when multiple pains are present is unknown. It also is problematic when either relevant subgroups (e.g., ethnic minorities) are not adequately represented in the research or when analyses of treatment effectiveness by relevant subgroups (e.g., gender) are not conducted and reported.

Doing long-term research with patients who are seriously ill with cancer is a major challenge. In the 15 studies in this review, attrition ranged from 7% to 71% with 60% of studies having attrition greater than 20%. Factors occurring over time that are well beyond the control of the researchers, such as mortality from the cancer, medical conditions requiring an alteration of the cancer treatment protocol, and the development of the need for hospice care can increase attrition from studies on pain management.' High attrition is a problem that can affect both the internal and external validity of research.

In terms of research methods, the gold standard for judging treatment effectiveness typically involves having results from many large, randomized, double-blind placebo trials of the same treatment conducted in the population of interest. Concern about the methodological and reporting quality of clinical research is not new. This concern is evidenced in the Consolidated Standards of Reporting Trials (CONSORT) statement (http://www.consort-statement.org). Initially issued in 1996 and revised in 1999, the CONSORT statement includes a checklist of 22 items that were selected because they have been associated with biased estimates of treatment effect. Tools of this nature can help researchers design better studies and report them in a more interpretable manner and they

can provide consumers of research with a framework within which to assess reported research. Some common reporting weaknesses in the research in this meta-analysis included deficiencies in reporting of the intervention tested, the methods used to generate and implement random allocation to treatment condition, and any blinding of treatment providers or data collectors that was used.

Despite the challenges inherent in research on pain, if researchers are to maximize the usefulness of their research on the effect of psychoeducational interventions on pain in adults with cancer, it is essential that they address the complex nature of the phenomenon pain as well as other concurrent therapies being used for pain and describe both in their research reports. We must continue to look to new research in order to strengthen or challenge the conclusions that have been based on the research available to date.

REFERENCES

Arathuzik D. (1991) Pain experience for metastatic breast cancer patients. Unraveling the mystery. Cancer Nurs 14: 41-48.

Banning A, Sjogren P, Henriksen H. (1991) Pain causes in 200 patients referred to a multidisciplinary cancer pain clinic. Pain 45: 45-48.

Bonica JJ. (1990) The management of pain. In: Cancer pain (Bonica JJ, ed), pp. 400-460. Philadelphia: Lea & Febiger.

Carr D, Goudas L, Lawrence D, Pirl W, Lau J, DeVine D, Kupelnick B, Miller K. (July 2002) Management of Cancer Symptoms: Pain, Depression, and Fatigue. Evidence Report/Technology Assessment No. 61 (Prepared by the New England Medical Center Evidence-based Practice Center under Contract No 290-97-0019) AHRQ Publication No. 02-E032. Rockville, MD: Agency for Healthcare Research and Quality.

Carroll D, Seers K. (1998) Relaxation for the

relief of chronic pain: a systematic review. J Adv Nurs 27: 476-487.

Cleeland CS, Gonin R, Hatfield AK, Edmonson JH, Blum RH, Stewart JA, Pandya KJ. (1994) Pain and its treatment in outpatients with metastatic cancer. N Engl J Med 330: 592-596.

Clotfelter CE. (1999) The effect of an educational intervention on decreasing pain intensity in elderly people with cancer. Oncol Nurs Forum 26: 27-33.

Cohen J. (1969) Statistical power analysis for the behavioral sciences. New York: Academic Press.

Cook TD, Campbell DT. (1979) Quasi-experimentation design and analysis issues for field settings. Boston: Houghton Mifflin.

Coyle N, Adelhardt J, Foley KM, Portenoy RK (1990) Character of terminal illness in the advanced cancer patient: pain and other symptoms during the last four weeks of life. J Pain Symptom Manage 5: 83-93.

Dalton JA, Keefe FJ, Carlson J, Youngblood R. (2004) Tailoring cognitive-behavioral treatment for cancer pain. Pain Management Nursing 5: 3-18.

de Wit R, van Dam F, Zandbelt L, van Buuren A, van der Heijden K, Leenhouts G, Loonstra S. (1997) A pain education program for chronic cancer pain patients: follow-up results from a randomized controlled trial. Pain 73: 55-69.

Devine, EC. (2003). Meta-analysis of the effect of psychoeducational interventions on pain in adults with cancer. Oncol Nurs Forum 30: 75-89.

Devine EC. (1992) Effects of psychoeducational care for adult surgical patients: a meta-analysis of 191 studies. Patient Education and Counseling 19, 129-142.

Devine EC, Reifschneider E. (1995) A meta-analysis of the effects of psychoeducational care in adults with hypertension. Nurs Res 44:237-245.

Devine EC, Westlake SK. (1995) The effects of psychoeducational care provided to adults with cancer: meta-analysis of 116 studies. Oncol Nurs Forum 22:1369-1381.

Farzanegan ZM. (1989) Effects of individualized patient therapy programs on pain, psychological distress, and quality of life of cancer patients. Unpublished doctoral dissertation, University of Southern California, Los Angeles, CA.

Gaston-Johansson F, Fall-Dickson JM, Nanda J, Ohly KV, Stillman S, Krumm S, Kennedy MJ. (2000) The effectiveness of the comprehensive coping strategy program on clinical outcomes in breast cancer autologous bone marrow transplantation. Cancer Nurs 23: 277-285.

Given C, Given B, Rahbar M, Jeon S, McCorkle R, Cimprich B, Galecki A, Kozachik S, Brady A, Fisher-Malloy MJ, Courtney K, Bowie E. (2004) Effect of a cognitive behavioral intervention on reducing symptom severity during chemotherapy. J Clin Oncology 22: 507-516.

Glass GV, McGraw ML, Smith ML. (1981) Meta-analysis in social research. Beverly Hills: Sage.

Goodwin PJ, Leszcz M, Ennis M, Koopmans J, Vincent L, Guther H, Drysdale E, Hundleby M, Chochinov HM, Navarro M, Speca M, Hunter J. (2001) The effect of group psychosocial support on survival in metastatic breast cancer. N Engl J Med 345: 1719-1726.

Hedges LV, Becker BJ. (1986) Statistical methods in the meta-analysis of research on gender differences. (S Hyde & MC Linn, eds), pp. 14-50. The psychology of gender. Baltimore: Johns Hopkins University Press.

Hedges LV, Olkin I. (1985) Statistical methods for meta-analysis. San Diego: Academic Press.

Jacox A, Carr DB, Payne R. (1994) New clinical-practice guidelines for the management of pain in patients with cancer. N Engl J Med 330: 651-655.

Jadad AR, Browman GP. (1995) The WHO

analgesic ladder for cancer pain management. Stepping up the quality of its evaluation. JA MA 274: 1870-1873.

Kerr IG. (1995) Clinical trials to study pain in patients with advanced cancer: practical difficulties. Anticancer Drugs 6 S: 18-28S.

Maguire P, Brooke M, Tait A, Thomas C, Sellwood R. (1983) The effect of counselling on physical disability and social recovery after mastectomy. Clin Oncol 9: 319-324.

Miaskowski C, Dodd M, West C, Schumacher K, Paul SM, Tripathy D, Koo P. (2004) Randomized clinical trial of the effectiveness of a self-care intervention to improve cancer pain management. J Clinical Oncology 22: 1713-1720.

Pan CX, Morrison RS, Ness J, Fugh-Berman A, Leipzig RM. (2000) Complementary and alternative medicine in the management of pain, dyspnea, and nausea and vomiting near the end of life. A systematic review. J Pain Symptom Management 20: 374-387.

Rimer B, Levy MH, Keintz MK, Fox L, Engstrom PF, MacElwee N. (1987) Enhancing cancer pain control regimens through patient education. Patient Education and Counseling 10: 267-277.

Rosenthal R. (1979) The "file drawer problem" and tolerance for null results. Psychological Bulletin 86: 638-641.

Sandgren AK, McCaul KD, King B, O'Donnell S, Foreman G. (2000). Telephone therapy for patients with breast cancer. Oncology Nursing Forum 27: 683-688.

Serlin RC, Mendoza TR, Nakamura Y, Edwards KR, Cleeland CS. (1995). When is cancer pain mild, moderate or severe? Grading pain severity by its interference with function. Pain 61: 277-284.

Sloman R. (1995) Relaxation and the relief of cancer pain. Nursing Clinics of North America 30: 697-709.

Sloman R, Brown P, Aldana E, Chee E. (1994) The use of relaxation for the promotion of comfort and pain relief in persons with advanced cancer. Contemporary Nurse 3: 6-12.

Smith MC, Holcombe JK, Stullenbarger E. (1994) A meta-analysis of intervention effectiveness for symptom management in oncology nursing research. Oncol Nur Forum 21: 1201-1209.

Spiegel D, Bloom JR. (1983) Group therapy and hypnosis reduce metastatic breast carcinoma pain. Psychosomatic Medicine 45: 333-339.

Syrjala KL, Cummings C, Donaldson GW. (1992) Hypnosis or cognitive behavioral training for the reduction of pain and nausea during cancer treatment: a controlled clinical trial. Pain 48: 137-146.

Syrjala KL, Donaldson GW, Davis MW, Kippes ME, Carr JE. (1995) Relaxation and imagery and cognitive-behavioral training reduce pain during cancer treatment: a controlled clinical trial. Pain 63: 189-198.

Thomas EM, Weiss SM. (2000) Nonpharmacological interventions with chronic cancer pain in adults. Cancer Control 7: 157-164.

Trijsburg RW, van Knippenberg FC, Rijpma SE. (1992) Effects of psychological treatment on cancer patients: a critical review. Psychosomatic Medicine 54: 489-517.

Tycross RG, Fairfield SS. (1983) <u>Symptom control in far advanced cancer: Pain relief</u>. London: Pitman Books.

van Fleet S. (2000) Relaxation and imagery for symptom management: improving patient assessment and individualizing treatment. Oncol Nurs Forum 27: 501-510.

Wallace KG. (1997) Analysis of recent literature concerning relaxation and imagery interventions for cancer pain. Cancer Nurs, 20: 79-87.

Ward S, Donovan HS, Owen B, Grosen E, Serlin R. (2000) An individualized intervention to overcome patient-related barriers to pain management in women with gynecologic cancers. Res Nurs Health 23: 393-405.

Wells N. (2000) Pain intensity and pain interference in hospitalized patients with cancer. Oncol Nurs Forum 27: 985-991.

West CM, Dodd MJ, Paul SM, Schumacher K, Tripathy D, Koo P, Miaskowski C. (2003) The PRO-SELF©: Pain control program-An effective approach for cancer pain management. Oncol Nurs Forum 30: 65-73.

Yates P, Edwards H, Nash R, Aranda S, Purdie D, Najman J, Skerman H, Walsh A (2004) A randomized controlled trial of a nurse-administered educational intervention for improving cancer pain management in ambulatory settings. Patient Education and Counseling 53: 227-237.

Zech DF, Grond S, Lynch J, Hertel D, Lehmann KA. (1995) Validation of World Health Organization Guidelines for cancer pain relief: a 10-year prospective study. Pain 63: 65-76.

BIOPSYCHOSOCIAL MANAGEMENT OF CHRONIC PAIN

Robert J. Gatchel and Yuan Bo Peng

As summarized by the American Pain Society, pain is a prevalent and costly problem; 50 million Americans report serious chronic pain, and it is estimated that pain costs Americans an estimated $100 billion per year. Pain is defined by the International Association for the Study of Pain as "An unpleasant sensory and emotional experience associated with actual or potential tissue damage, or described in terms of such damage". Pain is always associated with a subjective feeling. With the same stimuli, individuals may experience or report a different severity of pain. In general, there are three interacting components of pain: discriminative, affective-motivational, and cognitive (Casey, 1999).

Pain is usually broadly classified as acute, chronic, or recurrent, depending on its time course (Gatchel & Oordt, 2003). **Acute pain** is usually indicative of tissue damage, and it is characterized by momentary intense noxious sensations (i.e., nociception). It serves an important biological signal of potential tissue/physical harm. Some anxiety may initially be precipitated, but prolonged physical and emotional distress usually is not. Indeed, anxiety, if mild, can be quite adaptive in that it stimulates behaviors needed for recovery, such as the seeking of medical attention, rest and removal from the potentially harmful situation. As the nociception decreases, acute pain usually subsides.

Chronic pain is defined as pain that lasts six months or longer, well past the normal healing period one would expect for its protective biological function. Arthritis, back injuries, and cancer can produce chronic pain syndromes and, as the pain persists, it is often accompanied by emotional distress such as depression, anger and frustration. Such pain can also often significantly interfere with activities of daily living.

Recurrent pain refers to intense, episodic pain, reoccurring for more than three months. Recurrent pain episodes are usually brief (as are acute pain episodes); however the reoccurring nature of this type of pain makes it similar to chronic pain in that it is very distressing to patients. Such episodes may develop without a well-defined cause, and then may begin to generate an array of emotional reactions, such as anxiety, stress, depression and helplessness. Often, pain medication is used to control the intensity of the recurrent pain, but it is not usually helpful in reducing the frequency of the episodes that a person experiences. It should also be noted that, many times, patients find it difficult to distinguish between chronic and recurrent pain. Patients will often present with chronic-like symptoms from prolonged episodes of, say, headache or back pain. These do not always fit the description of chronic pain, but are usually persistent and can be as disabling.

Of course, the above types of pain require different treatment approaches (Gatchel, 1996). In discussing back pain rehabilitation, for example, **primary care** is applied usually to acute cases of pain of limited severity. Basic symptom control methods are utilized in relieving pain during the normal early healing period. Frequently, some basic psychological reassurance that the acute pain episode is temporary, and will soon be resolved, is quite effective. **Secondary care** represents "reactivation" treatment administered to those patients who do not improve simply through the normal healing process. It is administered during the transition from acute (primary) care to the eventual return to work. Such treatment has been designed in order to promote return to productivity before advanced physical deconditioning and significant psychosocial barriers to returning to work occur. At this phase, more active psychosocial intervention may need to be administered to those patients who do not appear to be progressing. Finally, **tertiary care** requires an interdisciplinary and intensive treatment approach. It is intended for those patients suffering the effects of physical deconditioning and chronic disability. In general, it differs from secondary treatment in regard to the intensity of rehabilitation services required, including psychosocial and disability management. Such an approach will be more comprehensively reviewed later in this chapter.

Behavioral therapies have been developed and are beginning to be evaluated for the treatment of chronic pain. However, they are not yet commonly used or available in mainstream healthcare settings. As identified by the NIH Technology Assessment Panel, there are five barriers to integration of behavioral therapies into chronic pain treatment: 1) overemphasis on the biomedical model; 2) lack of standardization among the techniques included under "behavioral and relaxation therapies"; 3) patient noncompliance and physician reluctance to prescribe such therapies; 4) lack of consistent reimbursement by insurers for such services; 5) ill-defined credentialing criteria for providers of such services (Caudill, 1997). These barriers start to dissolve with the development of the bio-psychosocial model of pain.

Before reviewing the various behavioral approaches to the management of chronic pain, it is important to first discuss the underlying theoretical model of pain upon which these approaches are based--**the biopsychosocial model of pain**. Today, this biopsychosocial model is accepted as the most heuristic perspective to the understanding and treatment of chronic pain disorders (Gatchel, 2005; Turk & Monarch, 2002). This model views physical disorders such as pain as the result of a complex and dynamic interaction among physiological, psychological and social factors that perpetuate and may even worsen the clinical presentation. Each individual experiences pain uniquely, as the result of the range of psychological, social and economic factors that can interact with physical pathology to modulate that individual's report of symptoms and subsequent disability. The development of this biopsychosocial approach has grown rapidly during the past decade, and a great deal of scientific knowledge has been produced in this short period of time concerning the best care of individuals with complex pain problems, as well as pain prevention and coping techniques.

As Turk and Monarch (2002) and Gatchel (2005) have discussed in their comprehensive reviews of the biopsycho-social perspective on chronic pain, people differ significantly in how frequently they report physical symptoms, in their tendency to visit physicians when experiencing identical symptoms, and in their responses to the same treatments. Often, the nature of a patient's response to treatment has little to do with his or her objective physical condition. For example, White and colleagues (1961) have noted that less than one-third of all individuals with clinically significant symptoms consult a physician. On the other hand, from 30%-50% of patients who seek treatment in primary care do not have specific diagnosable disorders (Dworkin & Massoth, 1994)! Turk and

Monarch (2002) also make the distinction between disease and illness in better understanding chronic pain. The term disease is basically used to define "an objective biological event" that involves the disruption of specific body structures or organ systems caused by either anatomical, pathological or physiological changes. Illness, in contrast, is generally defined as a "subjective experience or self-attribution" that a disease is present. An illness will produce physical discomfort, behavioral limitations, and psychosocial distress. Thus, illness refers to how a sick individual and members of his or her family live with, and respond to, symptoms and disability. This distinction between disease and illness is analogous to the distinction made between pain and nociception. Nociception involves the stimulation of nerves, especially nociceptors, that convey information about tissue damage to the brain. Nociception does not always lead to the experience of pain. For example, pain is not perceived immediately by wounded soldiers and athletes. Patients with cingulectomy can experience both noxious and innocuous sensory inputs without eliciting aversiveness (Wilson & Chang, 1974). Pain, on the other hand, is a more subjective perception that is the result of the transduction, transmission and modulation of sensory input. This input may be filtered through a person's genetic composition, prior learning history, current physiological status, and sociocultural influences. Pain, therefore, cannot be comprehensively assessed without a full understanding of the individual who is exposed to the nociception. The biopsychosocial model focuses on illness, which is the result of the complex interaction of biological, psychological and social factors. With this perspective, a diversity in pain or illness expression (including its severity, duration and psychosocial consequences) can be

expected. The inter-relationships among biological changes, psychological status, and the sociocultural context all need to be taken into account in fully understanding the pain patient's perception and response to illness. A model or treatment approach that focuses on only one of these core sets of factors will be incomplete. Indeed, the treatment efficacy of a biopsychosocial approach to pain has consistently demonstrated the heuristic value of this model (Gatchel, 2005; Turk & Monarch, 2002).

THE BIOPSYCHOSOCIAL APPROACH TO CHRONIC PAIN MANAGEMENT

Thus, the biopsychosocial approach to chronic pain management appropriately conceptualizes pain as a complex and dynamic interaction among physiological, psychological and social factors that often results in, or at least maintains, pain. It cannot be broken down into distinct, independent psychosocial or physical components. Each person also experiences pain uniquely. The complexity of pain is especially evident when it persists over time, as a range of psychological, social and economic factors can interact with pathophysiology to modulate a patient's report of pain and subsequent disability. The model utilizes physiological, biological, cognitive, affective, behavioral and social factors, as well as their inter-play, when explaining a patient's report of pain.

There is now a revolution in developing a more comprehensive, biopsychosocial understanding of pain. Besides the greater appreciation of psychosocial factors that contribute to the pain process, there is a growing understanding of how endocrine modulation of pain mechanisms occur. Also, research on pain mechanisms and pathways has greatly expanded in scope during the past decade, including the use of a wide array of techniques such as anatomical, electrophysiological, genetic, molecular biological and pharmacological approaches. Technical advances have also improved methods for identifying brain regions involved during various neurological and psychiatric conditions. This synergy across disciplines will hopefully lead to the most effective methods to manage pain, because it will help us in understanding how the nervous system senses, interprets and responds to pain (Gatchel, 1999).

As noted earlier, Gatchel (2005) and Turk (2002) have provided a more comprehensive review of the biopsychosocial perspective on chronic pain. Earlier, Turk (1999) had also indicated that, within a biopsychosocial context, pain problems need to be "... viewed longitudinally as ongoing, multifactorial processes in which there is a dynamic and reciprocal interplay among biological, psychological, and social cultural factors that shapes the experience in responses of patients." (p. 20). Thus, in order to comprehensively assess pain, one must be certain to account for such potential interactions before prescribing the best treatment regimen, individualized for a particular patient with pain.

The Initial Assessment Phase

When embracing a biopsychosocial model, a "step-wise approach" to assessment is recommended (Gatchel, 2000; Gatchel, 2005), which proceeds from global indices of biopsychosocial concomitants of pain to more detailed evaluations of specific diagnoses. Likewise, a "stepped-care framework" for managing pain is also advocated (Gatchel, 2005). Table 1 presents some commonly used psychosocial instruments for the assessment of patients experiencing pain. A comprehensive description of these instruments can be found in Gatchel (2001a) and Turk and Melzack (2001). Again, it should be kept in mind that no one type of assessment measure can usually "capture" all the important characteristics when considering a patient's report of pain. Rather, integrating a number of assessment tools is needed.

It should also be kept in mind that pain is a cardinal symptom of disease. Pain, though, sometimes does not fit neatly into an "evaluative-curative model" of medical care. Regardless, however, the evaluation of pain should include a medical history, physical examination, and appropriate medical tests. Indeed, recently, several important organizations in the United States have developed new standards for the evaluation of pain. The Joint Commission on Accreditation of Healthcare Organizations (JCAHO) requires that pain severity be documented using a pain scale. Additionally, patients' own words to describe their pain, pain location, duration, aggravating and alleviating factors, present pain management regimen and effectiveness, the effects of pain, the patient's pain goal, and a physical examination are all to be documented upon initial assessment (2000). Indeed, physicians are now required to consider pain as a **"fifth vital sign"** (added to pulse, blood pressure, core temperature, and respiration).

The Commission for the Accreditation of Rehabilitation Facilities (CARF) has also developed new guidelines for the assessment of patients with pain who are candidates for rehabilitation programs. This requires not only a medical evaluation, but also evaluation of patient functioning, physical assessment, psychosocial assessment, social and vocational assessments, and spirituality referral when indicated. It requires that the participants in the assessment are the patient, physician, and a psychologist. Additional assessments may be made by a physical therapist, occupational therapist, vocational specialist

1. LISTING OF COMMONLY USED PSYCHOSOCIAL INSTRUMENTS FOR THE ASSESSMENT OF PATIENTS EXPERIENCING PAIN.

Beck Anxiety Inventory (BAI)
Beck Depression Inventory-2 (BDI-2)
Chronic Pain Coping Inventory
Clinical Observational Techniques of Pain Behavior
Fear Avoidance Beliefs Questionnaire (FABQ)
Medical Outcomes Study Short Form (SF-36)
McGill Pain Questionnaire
Million Behavioral Health Inventory
Million Visual Analog Scale
Millon Behavioral Medicine Diagnostic (MBMD)
Minnesota Multiphasic Personality Inventory-2 (MMPI-2)
Multidimensional Pain Inventory (MPI)
Oswestry Pain Disability Questionnaire
Quantified Pain Drawing
Pain Disability Questionnaire
Roland and Morris Disability Questionnaire
Sickness Impact Profile (SIP)
Structured Clinical Interview for the DSM-IV
Symptom Checklist-90 Revised (SCL-90R)
The Coping Strategies Questionnaire
The Ways of Coping Questionnaire-Revised

and a biofeed-back therapist. Assessment criteria for entry into a pain management rehabilitation program must be matched to predicted outcomes, frequency of service, intensity of service, and duration of service. Pediatric patients must also have their family included as a part of the assessment team.

The Pain Management Phase

Pain, especially when it becomes chronic in nature, often cannot be "cured" but only managed. This is also true for other chronic medical conditions such as hypertension, diabetes, asthma, etc. There is *no* known cure for these chronic medical disorders, and they can only be managed. Moreover, currently, a major trend in the pain management literature is a movement away from the "homogeneity of pain patients

myth," and towards an attempt *to* match treatment *to* specific assessment outcomes of patients (e.g., Turk & Gatchel, 1999b; Turk & Okifuji, 2001). Because groups of patients may differ in psychosocial and behavioral characteristics, even when the medical diagnosis is identical, such patient differences and treatment matching is important to consider. Traditionally, patients with the same medical diagnosis or set of symptoms were "lumped" together (e.g., chronic back pain, fibromyalgia, neuropathic pain, cancer pain), and then treated in the same way, as though "one size fits all." However, it has been demonstrated that there are differential responses of pain patients with the same diagnosis to the same treatment. As a result, it is now important that treatment should be individually tailored for each patient based upon the careful biopsychosocial assessment of that particular patient. It is often the case that two chronic low back patients, for example, will require slightly different treatment programs because of differences in their physical, psychosocial or socioeconomic presentations. Turk and Okifuji (2001) have provided a comprehensive review of the importance of this treatment-matching process, and literature to support the greater clinical efficacy of such a matching approach strategy. Indeed, taking the approach of delineating homogeneous subgroups among patients with pain will provide an extremely important basis for the future development of even more specific, optimal treatment regimens for these different subgroups of patients.

An example of one such approach to treatment-matching that shows great promise is the use of the Multidimensional Pain Inventory (MPI), also known as the West Haven-Hale Multidimensional Pain Inventory (1985). The MPI was initially developed to measure three psychological dimensions of pain: 1) patient self-reported pain and the effect of that pain; 2) response of significant others to the communication of pain patients; and 3) level of activities of daily living. The instrument was shown to have good psychometric properties. Subsequently, Turk and Rudy (1988) developed a classification system based on the MPI, which categorized patients according to three subgroups that predicted response to treatment: dysfunctional, interpersonally distressed and adaptive copers. According to this classification system, dysfunctional subgroup patients are hypothesized not to respond as well to intervention as would patients in the other two subgroups. Indeed, a study by Asmundson, Norton and Alterdings (1997) demonstrated that patients with chronic low back pain who were classified as dysfunctional on the MPI reported more pain-specific fear and

avoidance than did patients in the other two subgroups. Such characteristics were, in turn, related to poorer coping ability in these dysfunctional chronic pain patients.

Turk and Okifuji (1998) have reviewed other research demonstrating the utility of the MPI with other chronic pain conditions, including headache, TMJ pain and fibromyalgia. Assessment of such MPI profiles will help to "tailor" the needs for treatment strategies to account for the different personality characteristics of patients, For example, patients with an interpersonally distressed profile may need additional clinical attention addressing interpersonal skills to perform effectively in a group-oriented treatment program. Pain patients with dysfunctional and interpersonally distressed profiles display more indications of acute and chronic personality differences relative to adaptive coper profile patients, and they would therefore require more clinical management (Etscheidt et al., 1995). Such additional attention, however, would not necessarily be essential for adaptive coper profile patients.

Interdisciplinary Pain Management
As earlier noted in this Chapter, when pain becomes chronic, a more intensive tertiary care or interdisciplinary treatment approach is required because of the significant effects of physical deconditioning and chronic disability. This approach requires the most coordinated type of care, and is used with the most costly pain problems. The critical elements of this interdisciplinary approach include the following:
- Formal, repeated quantification of physical deficits to guide, individualize and monitor physical training/reconditioning progress.
- Psychosocial and socioeconomic assessment to guide, individualize, and monitor disability behavior-

oriented interventions and outcomes.

- Multimodal disability management program using cognitive-behavioral approaches.
- Psychopharmacological interventions for detoxification and psychological management.
- Interdisciplinary, medically directed team approach with formal staffing, frequent team conferences, and low staff-to-patient ratios.
- Ongoing outcome assessment utilizing standardized objective criteria.

There have been a number of reviews that have documented the clinical and cost effectiveness of such interdisciplinary bio-psychosocial treatment programs for chronic pain patients relative to less intensive, single-modality treatment programs (Deschner & Polatin, 2000; Gatchel, 1999; Turk, 2002; Wright & Gatchel, 2002). Such interdisciplinary programs are required for chronic pain patients who have complex needs and requirements. Although they represent a small minority of pain patients, there nevertheless is a significant number of patients who have failed to benefit from the combination of spontaneous healing and short-term, symptom-focused primary or secondary care treatment. They have also become financial burdens on their insurance carriers, as well as the health care system in general. Such patients have often failed to experience significant pain relief after repeated and extended contacts with several different physicians and other health care providers. Psychosocial distress, physical deconditioning, secondary gains and losses, and medication issues often complicate their presentation. Therefore, this stage of treatment is much more complex and demanding of pain-management specialists. As such, the strengths of multiple

disciplines working together to address complex issues confronting chronic pain patients is definitely needed. The overall therapeutic focus should be toward patient independence and autonomy, while acknowledging when certain physical limitations cannot be overcome. The Commission on Accreditation of Rehabilitation Facilities (CARF) requires that a certified pain-management team include at least a physician, specialized nurse, a physical therapist and a clinical psychologist or psychiatrist. However, often, an occupational therapist is required when return-to-work and vocational retraining issues become important in managing chronic pain patients.

Finally, one variant of chronic pain management program - functional restoration - has been extensively reviewed by Mayer and Polatin (2000). The clinical effectiveness of functional restoration has been well documented. The interdisciplinary treatment team consists of the following:

- The physician serves as a medical director of the treatment plan, and he/she must have a firm background in providing medical rehabilitation for these types of pain disorders frequently encountered. Formal training may vary from anesthesiology, orthopedic sur-gery, neurology, psychiatry, occupational medicine to internal medicine. The physician has to assume a direct role in the medical management of the patients' pain by providing the medical history to the treatment team, and by taking direct responsibility for medication management for any other medical interventions. At times, other team members and outside consultants may be involved in the medical treatment of the patient, but it is the physician's primary responsibility to coordinate these medical contributions to the patient's care.

- Although not all programs use nursing services, any pain management program which provides anesthesiology services involving injections, nerve blocks, and other medical procedures will require a nurse. The nurse assists the physician, follows up the procedures, and may interact with patients in the role of case manager, as well as providing patient education. The nurse may be viewed as a physician-extender and educator who has a strong impact on the patient.

- Although the physician and nurse play a major role in managing the physical status of patients, the psychologist or psychiatrist plays the leading role in the day-to-day maintenance of the psycho-social aspects and status of the patient's care. Significant psychosocial barriers to positive outcomes of the treatment (such as emotional distress and depression, as well as functional, legal, and work-related issues) may develop as a patient progresses from acute through subacute to the chronic stage of a pain syndrome. The psychologist is responsible for performing a full psychosocial evaluation, which includes identification of psycho-social barriers, and the assessment of the patient's psychological strengths and weaknesses. A cognitive-behavioral treatment approach can then be utilized to address important psychosocial issues such as pain-related depression, anxiety, fear, as well as psychopathology. A cognitive-behavioral treatment approach has

been found to be the most appropriate modality for chronic pain patients in a program such as this.

- The physical therapist interacts daily with the patient regarding any physical progression issues towards recovery. Effective communication with other team members is crucial in order that the patients' fear of exercise will not interfere with their reconditioning effort. The physical therapist also helps to educate the patient by addressing the physiological bases of pain, and teaching ways of reducing the severity of pain episodes through the use of appropriate body mechanics and pacing.

- The occupational therapist is involved in both physical and vocational aspects of the patient's treatment. A great majority of patients participating in an inter-disciplinary program are likely not to be working because of their pain and, often, they have become pessimistic about the prospect of returning to work. The occupational therapist needs to address these vocational issues and the physical determinants on underlying disability. This therapist also plays an important educational role in teaching patients techniques for managing pain on the job in ways that do not jeopardize their employment status. Finally, the occupational therapist can play an important role as case manager in contacting employers to obtain job descriptions, possible job accommodations, and other information, as well as vocational retraining if necessary.

- Constant, effective communication among all treatment personnel is required, during which patient progress can be discussed and evaluated. This is important so patients hear the same treatment philosophy and message from each of the treatment team members. Indeed, many times, patients are in conflict about their own future treatment and may seek out any conflict between team members and use it to compromise treatment goals.

- A formal interdisciplinary treatment team meeting should occur at least once a week to review patient progress and to make any modifications in the treatment plan for each patient. Individually tailoring treatment for patients is essential.

- Evaluating and monitoring treatment outcomes in a systematic fashion is essential for not only treatment outcome evaluations, but also for quality assurance purposes for the treatment team.

EFFECTS OF COMPLEMENTARY AND ALTERNATIVE MEDICINE ON CHRONIC PAIN

Complementary and alternative medicine (CAM), as defined by National Center for Complementary and Alternative Medicine (NCCAM), part of the NIH, is *"a group of diverse medical and health care systems, practices, and products that are not presently considered to be part of conventional medicine"* (2002). Complementary medicine is used together with conventional medicine. An example of a complementary therapy is using aromatherapy to help lessen a patient's discomfort following surgery. Alternative medicine is used in place of conventional medicine. An example of an alternative therapy is using a special diet to treat cancer instead of under-going surgery, radiation, or chemotherapy that has been recommended by a conventional doctor. NCCAM classifies CAM therapies into five categories, or domains:

- Alternative Medical Systems. Alternative medical systems are built upon complete systems of theory and practice. Often, these systems have evolved apart from and earlier than the conventional medical approach used in the United States. Examples of alternative medical systems that have developed in Western cultures include homeopathic medicine and naturopathic medicine. Examples of systems that have developed in non-Western cultures include traditional Chinese medicine and Ayurveda.

- Mind-Body Interventions. NCCAM defines mind-body medicine as "behavioral, psychologic, social and spiritual approaches to medicine not commonly used." Mind-body medicine uses a variety of techniques designed to enhance the mind's capacity to affect bodily function and symptoms. Some techniques that were considered CAM in the past have become mainstream (for example, patient support groups and cognitive-behavioral therapy). Other mind-body techniques are still considered CAM, including relaxation, meditation, imagery, hypnosis, prayer, mental healing, biofeedback, and therapies that use creative outlets such as art, music, or dance.

- Biologically Based Therapies. Biologically based therapies in CAM use substances found in nature, such as herbs, foods, and vitamins. Some examples include dietary supplements, herbal products, and the use of other so-called natural but as yet scientifically unproven therapies (for example, using shark cartilage to treat cancer).

- Manipulative and Body-Based Methods. Manipulative and body-based methods in CAM are based on manipulation and/or movement of one or more parts of the body. Some examples include chiropractic or osteopathic manipulation, and massage.

- Energy Therapies. Energy therapies involve the use of energy fields. They are of two types: Biofield therapies are intended to affect energy fields that purportedly surround and penetrate the human body. The existence of such fields has not yet been scientifically proven. Some forms of energy therapy manipulate biofields by applying pressure and/or manipulating the body by placing the hands in, or through, these fields. Examples include qi gong, Reiki, and Therapeutic Touch.

- Bioelectromagnetic-based therapies involve the unconventional use of electromagnetic fields, such as pulsed fields, magnetic fields, or alternating-current or direct-current fields.

In the United States, an estimated 60 million Americans used alternative medicine in 1990, at an estimated cost of $13.7 billion (Eisenberg et al., 1993). In addition, the estimated number of annual visits to providers of alternative medicine amounted to 425 million visits, which far exceeded the number of visits to all primary-care physicians in the United States (388 million visits). Another important finding is that 70% of patients who acknowledged using alternative therapy never mentioned it to their physicians. This may impose a potential drug overdose danger to the patients because some of the herbal remedies do have similar or synergistic action as prescribed drugs. Physicians, therefore, need to evaluate patients fully for their possible use of alternative medical therapies. Eisenberg (1997) provided a comprehensive strategy for physicians: 1) review safety and efficacy issues related to alternative medical therapies; and 2) arrange for follow-up visits to monitor for potentially harmful side effects. Because of these concerns, The National Cancer Institute's Office of Cancer CAM identified the challenges for scientifically rigorous research of CAM (e.g., diagnosis, prevention, and treatment) in cancer pain research.

- The development of appropriate controls, shams, and placebo interventions
- Development of CAM interventions for research: individualized vs. standardized approaches
- Development of "new drugs": FDA regulations
- Development of Phase III trials vs. Phase I/II developmental trials in CAM research
- Ethical issues related to CAM symptom research
- CAM symptom research: implication for statistics
- Tools and measurement issues in CAM cancer symptom research

CAM can be implemented as part of the strategies in the treatment of chronic pain, including approaches like acupuncture, massage, and chiropractic and various herbal remedies. The efficacy of alternative medicine therapies such as acupuncture and chiropractic and various mind-body techniques for treating various chronic pain syndromes has been extensively evaluated (Berman et al., 1998; Berman et al., 2004; Davis, 1997). However, these approaches cannot be used as the sole treatment modality. Rather, they should be used as complementary approaches with other conventional approaches. Other alternative or complementary approaches that are beginning to be used in the area of pain management include hypnosis, massage therapy, and herbalism. Also, recent studies have demonstrated the effectiveness of acupuncture for low back pain. In one such study, Ghoname and colleagues (1999) compared the effectiveness of percutaneous electrical nerve stimulation (PENS), which is a form of acupuncture, to transcutaneous electrical nerve stimulation and low back exercise therapies in patients with chronic low back pain. A sham PENS procedure was also included, in the design to control for possible placebo effects. A pre- to post-treatment assessment randomized design was used. The results clearly demonstrated that the acupuncture (PENS) treatment was significantly more effective in decreasing self-reported pain and medication use as well as in improving physical activity, quality of sleep, and a sense of well-being, relative to the other three conditions. Moreover, 81% of the patients stated that they would be willing to pay money out of pocket to receive PENS therapy, compared to only 4% to 9% who stated this regarding other treatment modalities. The close relationship of acupuncture and electroacupuncture with endorphins (enkephalin, beta-endorphin, endomorphin, and dynorphin) has been summarized (Han, 2004), in the treatment of various kinds of chronic pain including low back pain and diabetic neuropathic pain.

About one-third of all rheumatology patients in the USA had used CAM in the preceding year (Rao et al., 2003). In a recent comprehensive review of the effectiveness of CAM on musculoskeletal conditions, Ernst (2004) summarizes the trial data for or against CAM as a symptomatic treatment for back pain, fibromyalgia, neck pain, osteoarthritis and rheumatoid arthritis. Those common therapeutic and diagnostic techniques used in CAM turned out to be positive (Autogenic training, Hypnotherapy, Massage, and Yoga), negative (Applied kinesiology, Chelation therapy, Chiropractic, Colonic irrigation, Iridology, Macrobiotic diet, and Spiritual healing), and uncertain (Alexander technique, Aromatherapy, Osteopathy, and Reflexology). Treatments that have shown a significant promise in the treatment of musculoskeletal conditions are acupuncture (for back pain, fibromyalgia, and osteoarthritis), herbal medicine (for back pain, osteoarthritis, and rheumatoid arthritis), massage (for back pain), spinal manipulation (for fibromyalgia), supplements (for osteoarthritis and rheumatoid arthritis), and homoeopathy/ diets (for rheumatoid arthritis). There is no recommended CAM treatment for neck pain.

As CAM has received more attention over the past 10 years, close to 6500 CAM randomized controlled trials have been identified (University of Maryland Complementary Medicine Program, 2005).

EFFECTS OF COPING ON CHRONIC PAIN

Any discussion of chronic pain would be incomplete without reviewing how coping processes and variables can affect such an illness. Coping is a dynamic process that is conceptualized as "the person's cognitive and behavioral efforts to manage (reduce, minimize, master or tolerate) the internal and external demands of the person-environment transaction that is appraised as taxing or exceeding the person's resources" (Folkman et al., 1986). With the implementation of cognitive methods in chronic pain management, patients are taught to replace helplessness and hopelessness with resourcefulness and hope. There is a strong relationship between beliefs and coping and adjustment to chronic pain (Jensen et al., 1991). Patients can avoid catastrophizing (a negative self-statement and overly negative thoughts and ideas) if they believe they can control their pain. Boothby and colleagues (1999) have provided an excellent review of the research literature on the effects of coping on pain. This review includes pain related to chronic illnesses and procedures, such as rheumatoid arthritis, sickle cell disease, fibromyalgia, knee-replacement surgery, breast cancer surgery, temporomandibular disorders, headache, and low back pain. On the basis of their comprehensive review of the empirical literature, Boothby and colleagues came to a number of general conclusions that have practical and clinical implications:

- There appears to be a negative association between passive coping strategies (such as wishful thinking and praying/hoping) and positive adaptation. Such passive strategies have the potential to interfere with improvement. Therefore, chronic pain management should encourage patients to take a very active role in their recovery.

- Again, other passive coping strategies such as the use of pain-contingent rest, guarding or bracing behaviors to avoid injury, and the use of sedative-hypnotic medication for dealing with chronic pain, should be discouraged. Although these strategies may produce short-term reductions in discomfort and pain, they have strong potential for reducing physical functioning, thus weakening muscles and tendons and leading to greater future discomfort/pain.

- Discouraging specific passive strategies (such as rest and catastrophizing)

may be more appropriate than telling patients to avoid all passive strategies. A compromise might need to be made between combinations of both passive as well as more active coping strategies.

- It is probably more practical to teach and encourage specific active coping strategies, such as relaxation, stress management and cognitive restructuring. This can be done on both an individual, as well as a group, basis.

In another review of the effect of mind-body therapies for the management of pain, Astin (2004) suggests a beneficial effect of combining stress management, coping skills training, cognitive restructuring and relaxation therapy for chronic low back pain; cognitive-behavioral therapy when combined with an educational/ informational component can be effective for rheumatoid and osteoarthritis; relaxation and thermal biofeedback can be effective for migraine; imagery, hypnosis, and relaxation can reduce pain from invasive medical procedures.

CLINICAL- AND COST-EFFECTIVENESS OF TREATMENTS FOR CHRONIC PAIN

Recent data indicate that the number of Americans using pain management programs has increased 64% from 1998 to 2000 (Marketdata Enterprises, 2001). Moreover, an estimated 7.9 million Americans sought some treatment for their chronic pain in 2000, an increase from the 4.8 million who sought treatment in 1998. Back and neck pain were the most chronic pain conditions. With such an increase, an important question is whether such pain management programs are clinically effective, as well as cost-effective. We briefly summary the strenght of evidence supporting various treatments for chronic pain in Table 2.

361

Table 2.   Effectiveness of Treatments for Chronic Pain

Treatment Modality	Pain Syndromes Tested	Strengths/Weaknesses of Treatment	Evidence Rating*
EFFECTIVE TREATMENTS			
Multidisciplinary pain centers	All chronic pain disorders	Cost-effective, reduces disability	A
Cognitive behavioral therapy	All chronic pain disorders	Cost-effective, reduces pain	B
Spinal cord stimulators	Patients with unremitting pain for whom all other interventions have failed	Long-term effectiveness (> 1 year) not known	C
Implantable drug delivery devices	Patients with unremitting pain for whom all other interventions have failed	Long-term effectiveness (> 1 year) not known	C
Hypnotherapy	Chronic pain	Rarely used/tested	C
Acupuncture	Back pain, fibromyalgia, osteoarthritis	Rarely used/tested	C
Spinal manipulation	Fibromyalgia	Often overused	C
UNDER INVESTIGATED TREATMENTS			
Alexander technique	Cannot be determined	Not known	D
Aromatherapy	Cannot be determined	Not known	D
Osteopathy	Cannot be determined	Not known	D
Reflexology	Cannot be determined	Not known	D
INEFFECTIVE TREATMENTS			
Autogenic training	Chronic pain	Rarely used/tested	D
Massage and Yoga	Back pain	Rarely used/tested	D
Herbal medicine	Back pain, osteoarthritis, rheumatoid arthritis	Purity of herbs often not known	D
Homeopathy/diets	Rheumatoid arthritis	Rarely used/tested	D
Applied kinesiology	Cannot be determined	Not known	F
Chelation therapy	Cannot be determined	Not known	F
Colonic irrigation	Cannot be determined	Not known	F
Iridology	Cannot be determined	Not known	F
Macrobiotic diet	Cannot be determined	Not known	F

*   A= Strong evidence of effectiveness; consistently shown to be effective in well designed RCTs

B= Substantial evidence of effectiveness; shown to be effective in some well designed RCTs

C= Weak evidence of effectiveness; evidence from small or non-randomized trials

D= Little to no evidence of effectiveness; no evidence of effectiveness in small or non-randomized trials

F= Substantial evidence against effectiveness; no evidence of effectiveness in well-designed RCTs

Turk (2002) recently provided a comprehensive review of effectiveness data for the most common treatments for patients with chronic pain. In this review, Turk examined and compared representative published studies that evaluated conservative (standard) care, pharmacological treatments, surgery, spinal cord stimulators, implantable drug delivery systems, and pain rehabilitation programs. He considered treatment effectiveness outcome criteria such as pain reduction, medication use, functional activities, health care utilization, and the closure of any disability compensation cases. It should be noted that Turk cautioned the reader when interpreting his results, especially when comparisons have been made between treatments and across studies, because there were major differences in the pain syndromes evaluated, the inclusion and outcome criteria utilized, the variable drug dosages prescribed, the comparability of the treatments evaluated, as well as the definition of "chronic" used across the various studies.

On the basis of this review, Turk (2002) concluded that there are currently little data available that can systematically identify the specific characteristics of patients who most likely would benefit from any of the pain treatment methods. He indicates that: "Studies are needed that answer the question: What treatments delivered in what ways are most effective for patients with what set of characteristics with the least iatrogenic complications and adverse events? Successful answers to this question will permit more clinically effective and cost-effective ways to treat the difficult population of patients with chronic pain." (p. 363). At this time, however, a number of general conclusions can be made. These are listed below.

- Comprehensive pain rehabilitation programs provide significantly better treatment outcomes for variables such as functional activities, return-to-work, medication use, health care utilization and closure of disability claims relative to other treatments. They improve overall functioning of chronic pain sufferers. Moreover, they are associated with substantially fewer iatrogenic consequences and adverse events.

- Overall, these pain rehabilitation programs are also significantly more cost effective than the more expensive spinal cord stimulators, implantable drug delivery systems, surgery and conservative care, even for carefully selected patients. In addition, they are associated with potentially significant cost savings in both health care expenditures and disability payments.

- Treatment with spinal cord stimulators also appears to result in improvements of pain and functioning in patients; however, this is only the case when carefully selecting certain patients. This is also true for surgery and implantable drug delivery systems.

- Unfortunately, outcome studies of pharmacological treatments are quite limited because extant studies have rarely considered outcomes other than improvements in pain severity, as well as adverse side effects and complications associated with the medications.

These above conclusions were based on several seminal studies. For example, the reduction of pain after treatment in comprehensive pain rehabilitation programs has been reported to be statistically significant in a number of meta-analyses (Flor et al., 1992 Guzman et al., 2001; Morley et al., 1999). Its cost effectiveness has also been demonstrated (Turk, 2002). It should also be pointed out that one important component in most comprehensive pain rehabilitation programs- cognitive-behavioral treatment- has been shown in a literature review to significantly help chronic pain patients reduce self-reported pain, distress and pain behavior, as well as improve their daily functioning (McCracken & Turk, 2002).

In terms of other treatment modalities, several studies have reported significant pain reduction with spinal cord stimulators in carefully selected chronic pain patients (North et al., 1991). In a review of 39 such studies for low back pain, Turner and colleagues (1995) reported that an overall average of 59% of patients had at least a 50% reduction in pain. Finally, a number of investigations have reported a significant reduction in chronic pain with the use of implantable drug delivery systems (Hassenbusch et al., 1991; Paice et al., 1996). Again, though, the key to the potential success of these modalities is the careful selection of patients appropriate for such treatment. In a special section of the *Clinical Journal of Pain* edited by Gatchel (2001b), many of these issues have been addressed.

SUMMARY AND CONCLUSIONS

As Gatchel and Turk (1999) and Gatchel (2005) have concluded on the basis of a review of the literature on the treatment of chronic pain patients, the overall therapeutic results produced by interdisciplinary pain treatment programs are quite promising, with clinically significant changes displayed not only in self-reported pain and mood, but also in important socioeconomic variables such as return-to-work and the use of the health care system. Moreover, Turk and Gatchel (1999a) calculated a savings of over $1 million over a period of 19 years for each patient treated at an interdisciplinary pain-management center. Turk (2002) has also more recently summarized the cost savings of such programs. In this Chapter, it was also emphasized that more research is greatly needed to evaluate what combinations of variables are most important to prescribe the most efficient and effective therapeutic "package" in an interdisciplinary treatment program. As Turk and Gatchel (1999b) had concluded, "There are no data available to determine what set of patients with what characteristics are most likely to benefit from what set of treatment modalities, provided in what type of format." Future investigation is needed to address this important issue so as to increase the efficiency in time, cost and outcome of this promising interdisciplinary treatment approach to chronic pain management. Finally, an emphasis on the biopsychosocial model of pain was presented, as well as making the distinction between disease and illness to better understand chronic pain. The biopsychosocial model focuses on illness, which is the result of a complex interaction of biological, psychological and social factors. With this perspective in mind, it becomes obvious that pain, especially when it becomes chronic in nature, often cannot be "cured" but only managed. Such pain-management approaches were reviewed, including more recent CAM approaches, with a final emphasis on how coping processes and variables can affect an illness such as chronic pain. Finally, for a more comprehensive review of behavioral procedures used in the management of different types of pain, the reader is referred to the second edition of *Psychological Approaches to Pain Management: A Practitioner's Handbook* by Turk and Gatchel (2002), as well as *Clinical Essentials of Pain Management* by Gatchel (2005).

REFERENCES

Asmundso GJG, Norton GR, Alterdings MD. (1997) Fear and avoidance in dysfunctional chronic back pain patients. *Pain 69*: 231-236.

Astin JA. (2004) Mind-body therapies for the management of pain. *Clin J Pain 20*: 27-32.

Berman BM, Jonas W, Swyers JP. (1998) Issues in the use of complementary/ alternative medical therapies for low back pain. *Physical Med Rehab Clin North America 9*(2): 497-513.

Berman BM, Smith WB, Ernst E, Soeken L, Tall JM, Raja SN, et al. (2004) Special topics series. Complementary and Alternative Medicine. *Clin J Pain 20*: 1-32.

Boothby JL, Thorn BE, Stroud MW, Jensen MP. (1999) Coping with pain. In RJ Gatchel & DC Turk (Eds.), *Psychosocial Factors in Pain: Critical Perspectives*. New York: Guilford.

Casey KL. (1999) Forebrain mechanisms of nociception and pain: Analysis through imaging. *PNAS 96*: 7668-7674.

Caudill MA. (1997) Clinical implications of the NIH technology and assessment conference addressing behavioral treatment of chronic pain. *Mind Body Medicine 2*: 207-213.

Davis CM (Ed.). (1997) *Complementary Therapies and Rehabilitation*. Thorofare, NJ: Slack.

Deschner M, Polatin PB. (2000) Interdisciplin-ary programs: Chronic pain management. In TG Mayer, RJ Gatchel & PB Polatin (Eds.), *Occupational Musculoskeletal Disorders: Function, Outcomes & Evidence* (pp. 629-637). Philadelphia: Lippincott, Williams & Wilkins.

Dworkin SF, Massoth DL. (1994) Temporo-mandibular disorders and chronic pain: Disease or illness? *J Prosthetic Dentistry, 72*(1): 29-38.

Eisenberg DM. (1997) Advising patients who seek alternative medical therapies. *Ann Int Med 127*(1): 61-69.

Eisenberg DM, Kessler RC, Foster C, Norlock FE, Calkins DR, Delbanco TL. (1993) Unconventional medicine in the United States. *New Engl J Med 328*: 246-252.

Ernst E. (2004) Musculoskeletal conditions and complementary/alternative medicine. *Best Practice Res Clin Rheumatol 18*: 539-556.

Etscheidt MA, Steiger HG, Braverman B. (1995) Multidimensional pain inventory profile classifications and psychopathology. *J Consult Clin Psychol 51*: 29-36.

Flor H, Fydrich T, Turk DC. (1992) Efficacy of multidisciplinary pain treatment centers: A meta-analytic flow. *Pain 49*: 221-230.

Folkman S, Lazarus RS, Gruen RJ, DeLongis A. (1986) Appraisal, coping, health status and psychological symptoms. *J Personality Social Psychol 50*: 571-579.

Gatchel RJ. (1996) Psychological disorders and chronic pain: Cause and effect relation-ships. In RJ Gatchel & DC Turk (Eds.), *Psychological Approaches to Pain Management: A Practitioner's Handbook* (pp. 33-52). New York: Guilford.

Gatchel RJ. (1999) Perspectives on Pain: A Historical Overview. In R. J. Gatchel & D. C. Turk (Eds.), *Psychosocial Factors in Pain: Critical Perspectives* (pp. 3-17). New York: Guilford Publications.

Gatchel RJ. (2000) How practitioners should evaluate personality to help manage chronic pain patients. In RJ Gatchel JN Weisberg (Eds.), *Personality Characteristics of Patients with Pain*. Washington, DC: American Psychological Association.

Gatchel RJ. (2001a) *A Compendium of Outcome Instruments for Assessment and Research of Spinal Disorders*.

LaGrange, IL: North American Spine Society.

Gatchel RJ. (2001b) Special section editor: Pretreatment screening of patients with pain--Introduction. Clin J Pain 17: 191.

Gatchel RJ. (2005) Clinical Essentials of Pain Management. Washington, DC: American Psychological Association.

Gatchel RJ, Oordt MS. (2003) Clinical Health Psychology and Primary Care: Practical Advice and Clinical Guidance for Successful Collaboration. Washington, DC: American Psychological Association.

Gatchel RJ, Turk DC. (1999) Inter-disciplinary treatment of chronic pain patients. In RJ Gatchel & DC Turk (Eds.), Psychosocial Factors in Pain: Critical Perspectives (pp. 435-444). New York: Guilford.

Ghoname EA, Craig WF, White PF, Ahmed HE, Hamza MA, Henderson BN, et al. (1999) Percutaneous electrical nerve stimulation for low back pain: A randomized crossover study [published erratum appears in JAMA 1999 May 19; 281(19):1795). JAMA 281(9): 818-823.

Guzman J, Esmail R, Karjalinen K, Malmivaara A, Irvin E, Bombadier C. (2001) Multidisciplinary rehabilitation for chronic low back pain: Systematic review. BMJ 322: 1511-1516.

Han JS. (2004) Acupuncture and endorphins. Neurosci Let 361: 258-261.

Hassenbusch SJ, Stanton-Hicks MD, Soukup J, et al. (1991) Sufentanil citrate and morphine/bupivacaine as alternative agents in chronic epidural infusions for intract-able noncancer pain. Neurosurgery 29: 76-82.

Jensen MP, Turner JA, Romano JM, Karoly P. (1991) Coping with chronic pain: A critical review of the literature. Pain 47: 249-283.

Joint Commission on Accreditation of Healthcare Organizations. (2000) Pain Assessment and Management: An Organizational Approach. Oakbrook, IL: Author.

Kerns RD, Turk DC, Rudy TE. (1985) The West Haven-Yale Multidimensional Pain Inventory. Pain 23: 345-356.

Marketdata Enterprises. (2001) Chronic Pain Management Clinics. A Market Analysis. Tampa, FL: Author.

Mayer TG, Polatin PB. (2000) Tertiary nonoperative interdisciplinary programs: The functional restoration variant of the outpatient chronic pain management program. In TG Mayer, RJ Gatchel PB Polatin (Eds.), Occupational Musculo-skeletal Disorders: Function, Outcomes & Evidence (pp. 639-649). Philadelphia: Lippincott, Williams & Wilkins.

McCracken LM, Turk DC. (2002) Behavioral and cognitive-behavioral treatment for chronic pain. Spine 27: 2564-2573.

Morley S, Eccleston C, Williams A. (1999) Systematic review and meta-analysis of randomized controlled trials of cognitive behavior therapy and behavior therapy for chronic pain in adults, excluding headache. Pain 80:1-13.

National Center for Complementary and Alternative Medicine. (2002) What is CAM? Retrieved January 12, 2004, from http://nccam.nih.gov/health/whatiscam/

North RG, Ewend MG, Lawton MT. (1991) Failed back surgery syndrome: 5-year follow-up after spinal cord stimulator implantation. Neurosurgery 28: 692-699.

Paice JA, Penn RD, Shott S. (1996) Intraspinal morphine for chronic pain: A retrospective, multicenter study. J Pain Symp Manage 11: 71-80.

Rao JK, Kroenke K, Mihaliak KA, Grambow C, Weinberg M. (2003) Rheumatology patients' use of complementary therapies: Results from a one-year longitudinal study. Arthritis and Rheumatism 49: 619-625.

Turk D, Okifuji A. (1998) Directions in prescriptive chronic pain management based on diagnostic characteristics of the patient. APS Bulletin 8: 5-11.

Turk D, Rudy T. (1988) Toward an empirically derived taxonomy of chronic pain patients: Integration of psychological assessment data. J Consult Clin Psychol 56: 233-238.

Turk DC. (2002) Clinical effectiveness and cost effectiveness of treatment for patients with chronic pain. Clin J Pain 18: 355-365.

Turk DC, Flor H. (1999) Chronic pain: A biobehavioral perspective. In RJ Gatchel & DC Turk (Eds.), Psychosocial Factors in Pain: Critical Perspectives (pp. 18-34). New York: Guilford.

Turk DC, Gatchel RJ. (1999a) Multi-disciplinary programs for rehabilitation of chronic low back pain patients. In WH Kirkaldy-Willis TN Bernard, Jr. (Eds.), Managing Low Back Pain (4th ed., pp. 299-311). New York: Churchill Livingstone.

Turk DC, Gatchel RJ. (1999b) Psychosocial factors and pain: Revolution and evolution. In RJ Gatchel & DC Turk (Eds.), Psychosocial Factors in Pain: Critical Perspectives. New York: Guilford.

Turk DC, Gatchel RJ. (Eds.) (2002) Psychological Approaches to Pain Management: A Practitioner's Handbook (2nd ed.). New York: Guilford.

Turk DC, Melzack R. (2001) Handbook of Pain Assessment (2nd ed.). New York: Guilford.

Turk DC, Monarch ES. (2002). Biopsycho-social perspective on chronic pain. In DC Turk & RJ Gatchel (Eds.) Psychological Approaches to Pain Management: A Practitioner's Handbook (2nd ed.) New York: Guilford.

Turk DC, Okifuji A. (2001) Matching treatment to assessment of patients with chronic pain. In DC Turk & R Melzack (Eds.), Handbook of Pain Assessment (2nd ed.). New York: Guilford.

Turner JA, Loeser JD, Bell KG. (1995) Spinal cord stimulation for chronic low back pain: A systematic literature synthesis. Neurosurgery 37: 1088-1096.

University of Maryland Complementary Medicine Program. (2005) CM Field Registry. Retrieved January 12, 2005 from http://www.compmed.umm.edu/cochrane/registry.html

White KL, Williams F, Greenberg BG. (1961) The etiology of medical care. New Engl J Med 265: 885-886.

Wilson DH, Chang AE. (1974) Bilateral anterior cingulectomy for the relief of intractable pain. Confinia Neurologica 36: 61-68.

Wright AR, Gatchel RJ. (2002) Occupational musculoskeletal pain and disability. In DC Turk & RJ Gatchel (Eds.), Psychological Approaches to Pain Management: A Practitioner's Handbook, 2nd Edition (pp. 349-364). New York: Guilford.

MANAGEMENT OF MIGRAINE AND TENSION-TYPE HEADACHES

Kenneth A. Holroyd

EPIDEMIOLOGY

Recurrent headaches are prevalent and are associated with substantial individual and societal burden. Approximately 18% of women and 6% of men (e.g., 28 million individuals in the U.S.;Lipton et al., 2001) experience migraine. Approximately 36% of women and 42% of men experienced a tension-type headache in the last year, with 2.8% of women and 1.4% of men experiencing tension-type headaches more than 15 days per month (Rasmussen et al., 1991; Schwartz et al., 1998).

Missed workdays and impaired work function resulting from migraine costs employers about $13 billion a year and direct medical costs run about $1 billion per year (Hu et al., 1999). Because tension-type headaches are more prevalent than migraine, they associated with greater societal costs even though they are associated with less disability (Rasmussen and Lipton, 2000). As the frequency or severity of either migraine or tension-type headaches increases, the impact of headaches on functioning increases (Holroyd et al., 2000; Lipton et al.,, 2000). Consequently, a relatively a small portion (< 50%) of individuals with frequent or severe headaches account for over 80% of the disability and costs associated with these disorders (Lipton et al., 1997; Schwartz et al., 1998). These individuals are an important target group for disease management programs.

DIAGNOSIS

The International Headache Society (IHS; Olesen, 1988) classification system for headache disorders employs operational diagnostic criteria modeled after those in the *Diagnostic and Statistical Manual of Mental Disorders* (DSM-IV;American Psychiatric Association, 1994). Primary headache disorders are distinguished from secondary headaches that result from an underlying disease and account for 95% of headache problems. The two most prevalent primary headache disorders -migraine and tension-type headache- are the main drivers of disability and health care costs. Specific diagnostic criteria for these two disorders are currently under revision but the revised diagnostic should be available on the IHS website (www.i-h-s.org) by the publication of this volume. The possibility of a secondary cause for headaches, of course, must be ruled out by physical and neurological exam and indicated tests before a diagnosis of a primary headache disorder can be made.

HEADACHE PRECIPITANTS

Headache triggers are ordered according to the strength of supporting evidence in Table 2. General population studies indicate stress, sleep difficulties, and hormonal factors (relevant particularly for migraine) are the triggers most frequently identified by headache sufferers (Rasmussen, 1993). *Stress* is the most frequently identified headache precipitant for both migraine and tension-type headache (Rasmussen, 1993). Headaches may be triggered by stress or by relaxation following a period of stress ("let down headaches"). *Sleep* difficulties are commonly identified as a headache trigger, with insufficient sleep, oversleeping, or an irregular sleep schedule identified as most common sleep precipitants (Sahota and Dexter, 1990; Rasmussen, 1993). Fluctuations in *reproductive hormones* (menarche, menstruation, pregnancy, menopause, hormone replacement therapy) are associated with headache disorders, particularly migraine (for a review see Silberstein and Merriman,

Table 1. Commonly Reported Headache Triggers and Empirical Support for Reported Trigger*

Trigger Factor	Migraine?	Other Headache?
Strong Evidence**		
Stress	Yes	Yes
Menstruation	Yes	Yes
Caffeine Withdrawal	Unknown	Yes
Visual Stimuli (e.g., lights)	Yes	Yes
Weather Changes	Yes	Yes
Moderate Evidence		
Nitrates	Yes	Yes
Fasting	Probable	Yes
Sleep Disturbances	Possible	Yes
Wine	Yes	Yes
MSG	Unknown	Yes
Aspartame	Yes	Yes
Limited Evidence		
Smoking	Not proven	Unknown
Odors	Not proven	Not proven
Chocolate	Not proven	Not proven
Tyramine (e.g., aged cheeses)	Not proven	Not proven

*Adapted from Martin and Behbehani (2002)
**Strength of evidence is defined as follows: 1) strong-at least two prospective randomized-controlled or diary studies confirming an association with no dissenting studies, 2) moderate-at least one randomized controlled trial or a prospective diary study confirming an association with no dissenting studies or a prospective diary study confirming an association with no dissenting studies, or two supporting studies with one dissenting study.

1997). Close to 30% of people with headaches, primarily those with migraine, report that *dietary factors*, such as skipping or delaying meals, or ingesting specific foods, beverages, or ingredients sometimes trigger their headaches (Robbins, 1994). *Environmental stimuli* (e.g., glare, chemical odors) also are commonly identified as headache triggers.

PSYCHOSOCIAL COMPLICATIONS
Medication Overuse Headaches

Medication overuse or "rebound" headaches resemble chronic tension-type or chronic migraine headaches; however, it is the frequent use of prescription or nonprescription analgesic medications or abortive medications (combination analgesics, opiates, nonopioid analgesics, barbiturates, ergots, and other abortive agents including triptans) that is inducing headaches or aggravating the original tension-type or migraine headaches (Diener, 2000; Limmroth et al., 2002; Silberstein and Dongmei, 2002). Medication overuse headache has been estimated to occur in at least 30% of people treated in headache centers (Diener, 2000). Overuse of combination analgesics, that contain a simple analgesic plus an opiate or barbiturate, appears to alter headache features (e.g., reduce associated migraine symptoms such as photophobia and phonophobia) and increase the number of days headaches occur on the other hand, overuse of triptans may increase the frequency of migraines without dramatically altering the features of the migraine attack. Medication overuse headaches can only be managed effectively if the use of the offending medications is reduced or eliminated (Diener, 2000;

Silberstein and Dongmei, 2002). The use of all acute medications must be limited (most recommendations limit use to three or fewer days per week). Opioid and combination analgesics (see below) may be particularly problematic in this regard. NSAIDS and COX-2 inhibitors may be less likely than other simple or combination analgesics to induce rebound headaches, but are not free from this problem (Silberstein et al., 2002).

Co-Morbid Psychiatric Disorders

Epidemiological studies (Merikangas et al.,, 1990; Breslau and Davis, 1993; Merikangas et al.,, 1993; Breslau, Davis et al.,, 1994; Breslau, Merikangas et al., 1994) confirm that the prevalence of mood and anxiety disorders is elevated in migraine sufferers (relative risk typically between 2 and 3). Longitudinal data further argue that the association between mood disorders and migraine is bi-directional: for example, Breslau and colleagues (Breslau, Davis et al., 1994; Breslau, Merikangas et al. ,1994) found that migraine increased the risk of a *subsequent* episode of major depression (adjusted relative risk = 4.8), but the presence of major depression also increased the risk of *subsequently* developing migraine (adjusted relative risk = 3.3).

The prevalence of both anxiety and mood disorders also appears to be elevated in chronic tension-type headache, at least in clinical samples. Over 40% of chronic tension-type headache sufferers in primary care settings, and even higher percentages of chronic tension-type headache sufferers seen in specialty settings, receive either an anxiety or mood disorder diagnosis (Goncalves and Monteiro, 1993; Guidetti et al., 1998; Puca et al., 1999; Holroyd et al., 2000).

The presence of a co-morbid anxiety or mood disorder appears to increase the disability associated with either tension or migraine headaches so effective management of psychiatric disorders is likely to be important for improvements in functioning (Holroyd et al., 2000; Lipton et al., 2000).

MEDICAL MANAGEMENT
Goals and Treatments

There are four goals of medication treatment.

Acute - Symptomatic. The goal of symptomatic therapy is reduce pain. Symptomatic medications include analgesics prescribed primarily to reduce pain, such as nonsteroidal anti-inflammatory drugs (NSAIDS, COX-2 inhibitors), combination analgesics, typically containing a simple analgesic plus a barbiturate (e.g., butalbital) or opioid (i.e., codeine), and opioids alone (e.g., oxycodone). The use of all acute medications must be limited to avoid rebound headaches (Silberstein et al., 2002).

Acute - Abortive. If taken early in the migraine episode the goal of abortive therapy is to interrupt the migraine process, preventing a full blown migraine from developing; if taken later in the migraine episode a more realistic goal is to reduce migraine symptoms. Abortive medications include NSAIDS, Cox-2 inhibitors, ergotamine derivatives and, especially, serotonin-receptor agonists (triptans such as sumatriptan, rizatriptan, naratriptan, zolmitriptan, almotriptan and eletriptan). These agents must be used no more than two to three days per week to avoid rebound headaches (Goadsby et al., 2002; Silberstein et al., 2002).

Acute - Antiemetic. The goal of antiemetic therapy is to reduce nausea and control vomiting. Antiemetics also improve the absorption of some oral medications, including analgesics and may have anti-migraine effects themselves. Antiemetics (e.g., prochlorperazine, metoclopramide) are used to treat the nausea and vomiting associated with migraines. Patients who experience nausea and vomiting are instructed to take an antiemetic before or along with their analgesic (Silberstein et al., 2002).

Preventive. The goal of preventive therapy is to reduce the frequency of headaches. Preventive or prophylactic medications for migraine include beta-blockers (e.g., propranolol), calcium channel blockers (verapimil), antidepressants (tricyclic, serotonin-reuptake inhibitors, and MAO inhibitors), anticonvulsants (e.g., divalprox sodium) and NSAIDS (Goadsby et al., 2002). Antidepressants (mostly tricyclics) are the primary preventive medications for tension-type headache.

Efficacy

The Agency for Health Care Quality and Research[1] sponsored a comprehensive evaluation of evidence for medical, behavioral and physical treatments for migraine, and for behavioral treatments for tension-type headache. The resulting evidence reports prepared by the Duke University Center for Clinical Health Policy Research provide a synthesis of evidence for the efficacy of current therapies for migraine and tension-type headache (Goslin et al., 1999; Gray, Goslin et al., 1999; Gray, McCrory et al., 1999a).

The evidence reports for migraine evaluated every pertinent trial of acute or preventive medication and, where appropriate, employed meta-analytic techniques to integrate finding across trials. For example, 21 separate trials of propranolol HCl, the most extensively evaluated preventive medication, were examined, with 12 of the propranolol trials providing information necessary for the calculation of a treatment effect size (Gray, Goslin et al., 1999). The resulting meta-analysis revealed that propranolol has yielded a highly reliable, but moderate size treatment effect (effect size = .55, 95% confidence interval .42 to .69). No other preventive medications proved reliably more effective, though timolol (a beta blocker) divalproex sodium (an anticonvulsant) and amitriptyline (a tricyclic antidepressant) had

similarly strong empirical support and over 30 medications had some degree of empirical support.

The AHCQ meta-analyses (Gray, McCrory et al., 1999b) and subsequent published meta-analyses (e.g.,Ferrari et al. 2001), for example, revealed that 30% to 40% of people are pain-free two hours after taking an oral triptan as acute therapy for migraine. The three original evidence reports-two on acute therapies (self-administered and perenterally administered) and one on preventive therapies -plus updates of newer acute (triptan) therapies can be found at the Duke University's Center for Clinical Health Policy Research website at www.clinpol.mc.duke.-edu .

The AHCQR evidence reports provided the stimulus for the formation of the US Headache Consortium, an affiliation of influential medical organizations[2] created to develop clinical guidelines for the management of migraine. The US Headache Consortium clinical guidelines, which provide the skeleton of a disease management plan for migraine, have been published in brief in *Neurology* (Silberstein and Rosenberg, 2000), and in detail on the American Academy of Neurology WEB site at www.aan.com. This guideline emphasizes drug therapies, but also address behavioral therapies, as will be discussed below.

BEHAVIORAL MANAGEMENT
Behavioral Interventions

Behavioral interventions emphasize the *prevention* of headaches, although the same headache management skills can be used to influence the severity of headaches as well. The long-term goals of behavior therapy include reduced frequency and severity of headaches, reduced headache-related disability and affective distress, reduced reliance on poorly tolerated or unwanted pharmacotherapy, and enhanced personal control of headaches.

Relaxation Training

Relaxation skills (Bernstein and Carlson, 1993) presumably enable headache sufferers to exert control over headache-related physiological responses and, more generally, to lower sympathetic arousal. Relaxation may provide an activity break, as well as help individuals achieve a sense of mastery or self-control over their symptoms. Patients are instructed to practice a graduated series of relaxation techniques 20-30 minutes per day, and, as they master brief relaxation techniques, to integrate relaxation into daily life.

Biofeedback Training

Thermal (hand warming) feedback-feedback of skin temperature from a finger-and electromyographic (EMG) feedback-feedback of electrical activity from muscles of the scalp, neck, and sometimes the upper body-are the most commonly used biofeedback modalities, although electroencephalographic ("neurofeedback") and cephalic vasomotor biofeedback are also used experimentally (Schwartz, 1995). Thermal and cephalic vasomotor biofeedback emphasize the self-regulation of blood flow, EMG emphasizes the self-regulation of muscle activity, and neurofeedback is hypothesized to teach the self-regulation of cortical excitability. However, each of these biofeedback procedures also teach individuals to reduce arousal, to monitor physiological cues that signal the onset of headaches and to take actions to prevent headaches and abort the onset of an immanent headache. As with relaxation training, patients practice the self-regulation skills they learn during biofeedback training for about 20-30 minutes per day, and, as they master headache management skills, they are encouraged to integrate use of these skills into their day.

Cognitive-Behavior (Stress Management) Therapy

Cognitive-behavior therapy focuses upon the cognitive and affective precipitants and components of headache (Blanchard and Andrasik, 1985; Holroyd, Lipchik et al., 2001; Lipchik et al., 2002). Cognitive-behavioral interventions direct patients' attention to the role their thoughts and behavior play in generating stress (and stress-related headaches), and in increasing headache-related disability. Patients monitor the circumstances in which their headaches occur, including their thoughts and feelings prior to the onset of headaches. Once a headache-related stressful situation is identified the patient and counselor collaboratively identify of a cognitive target. The target cognitions may be stress-generating *thoughts* or an underlying *belief* or assumption that distills the common meaning or theme from many stress-generating thoughts. For example, a patient who reported experiencing frequent headaches in response to new sales goals that she feared she was unable to meet recorded the thought "I have let the company down (by not meeting this month's sales goal)". This thought appeared (on the basis of other evidence) to be related to the belief that "If I fail to meet this goal or make a mistake, I am a failure." Stress-generating beliefs most commonly reflect perfectionism, excessive need for approval, and excessive need for control.

Challenging Stress-Generating Thoughts. When the identified cognitive target involves stress-generating thoughts, adaptive coping statements can be generated to interrupt the flow of these thoughts. Methods of challenging stress-generating thoughts might include the evaluation of evidence for the stress-generating thought: "Lets see what evidence we can find for (the statement implicit or explicit in the stress-generating thought)". The counselor then assists the patient in finding both confirming and disconfirming evidence for this thought and in weighing the evidence. Alternative adaptive coping statements are used to challenge stress-generating thoughts. For example, to combat the thought "I'll never meet my sales goal by the end of the month," adaptive coping statements might include statements such as "At this time, there is no way to tell how far I'll get this month. Instead I'll focus on the task at hand and I'll see how far I get" and "I'll focus on what I can do; if I need to, I'll find a way to work toward meeting my goal next month." A useful coping statement is typically stated in the patient's own words and framed within the patient's belief system so that it undermines problematic beliefs "from within." Adaptive coping statements can be particularly helpful in short circuiting stress-generating thoughts that occur in reaction to specific, circumscribed, and time limited stressors.

Challenging Stress-generating Beliefs. When the identified cognitive target involves a stress-generating belief, the patient may be pushed to examine this belief. Stress-generating beliefs can be challenged in much the same way as stress-generating thoughts. Other techniques for working with stress-generating beliefs include "decatastrophizing" or the "what if" technique, and cost and benefit analysis (see Beck and Emery, 1985). For example, perfectionistic beliefs such as "I must never make a mistake, or I am a failure" are often defended on the grounds that they are necessary for high achievement. However, when the costs as well as the benefits of this belief are listed it can highlight costs such as time devoted to unimportant tasks (they need to be done perfectly), anxiety ("I might fail") and frustration (" I have to do better") in achievement situations, and avoidance of opportunities (exploring new opportunities requires a tolerance for initial failure).

Alternative views techniques that encourage the patient to generate alternative explanations for events that confirm a stress-generating belief can be particularly helpful. The patient might be asked "What might Ann (a respected friend, relative or co-worker) think if you refused this new responsibility?" or "What would you say to Ann if she was asked to do this and declined with the explanation that her workload was full?" It can be helpful in working with alternative views to reverse roles with the patient, where the therapist plays the patient, adopting and defending the patient's belief system, while the patient plays the therapist, attempting to challenge the targeted dysfunctional belief. For example, the woman described above who failed to meet the sales goal for one month might be asked, "What would you say to a colleague who failed to meet the sales goal?" or "What would think about a colleague if he or she didn't meet this goal?"

All sessions culminate in a homework assignment that is designed to continue or extend the work done in the session. Homework assignments that are developed collaboratively and incorporate input from the patient are most likely to be carried out. Typical homework tasks include engaging in a specific behavior that is avoided because of a stress-generating belief; asking a significant other what he or she would think of this behavior; or collection of additional diary data on thoughts, feelings and behaviors in stressful situations. For example, a patient who believes "I must be perfect, never make a mistake, or I am a failure" might be asked to intentionally make a small mistake and carefully record the consequences. Alternatively, the patient might inquire of coworkers (or family members, if more appropriate) how they would feel and think about the patient if the patient made a specific feared mistake.

Integrating Treatment Techniques

Typically, the above treatment techniques are not used in isolation, but used in the context of therapy that teaches multiple headache management skills and tailors headache management skills to the clinical characteristics of the client's headaches, as well as to their life situation. In addition to providing information about the clinical characteristics and pathophysiology of headaches, and orienting the patient to what is involved in behavioral headache management, this might include exercises to identify headache triggers and early warning signs, exercises to teach patients how to evaluate the effectiveness of their medications and to effectively use headache medications, strategies for coping with headaches that continue occur despite self-management efforts, the development of a migraine management plan, including a plan for coping with any reoccurrence of headaches that might occur following treatment (see Table 2 for a sample treatment protocol). Further details can be found in Lipchik and colleagues (2002).

Treatment Formats

Treatment can be administered either individually or in a group, and can be administered in a clinic-based treatment format or in a home-based treatment format.

Clinic-Based Treatment Format

Clinic-based treatment typically involve 6 to 12 weekly sessions, 45 to 60 minutes in length if treatment is administered individually, and 60 to 120 minutes in length if treatment is administered in a group. This treatment format provides more health care provider time and attention, and allows the provider greater opportunity to directly observe the patient than does a home-based treatment format, but requires the patient to travel more frequently to the clinic, and thus is more costly. Descriptions of clinic-based treatment are available in Blanchard and Andrasik (1985) for individual treatment, and Scharff (1994) and Nash and colleagues (in press) for group treatment.

Home-Based Treatment Format

Home-based or minimal-contact treatment involves 3 to 4 monthly treatment sessions 45 to 60 minutes in length for individual sessions, or 60 to 120 minutes in length for group sessions. Clinic visits introduce headache management skills and address problems encountered in acquiring or implementing these skills. Patient manuals and audiotapes guide the actual learning and refinement of headache management skills that occurs at home with phone contacts. For example, in Table 3 the material covered in all weeks that are not in bold (weeks 2, 3, 4, 6, 7,8, 10, 11, 12 for migraine) is covered in workbooks and audiotapes that are used at home, with learning supervised and questions addressed in phone calls. Lipchik, Holroyd and Nash (2002) and Blanchard and Andrasik (1985) provide more detailed descriptions of home-based treatment.

Table 2: Typical Structure for Behavioral Treatment*

Week	Migraine	Tension-type Headache
1	Orientation to self-management of headaches	Same
	Explanation of headaches & treatment	Same
	Introduction of progressive muscle relaxation, deep breathing, muscle stretches, imagery.	Same
2	Brief forms of relaxation	Same
	Begin monitoring of migraine triggers/ warning signs	Begin monitoring headache warning signs & headache-related stressors.
3	Address difficulties with home practice	Same
	Introduce cue-controlled relaxation, relaxation by recall, autogenic phrases.	Same

4	Application of quick relaxation skills to daily activities.	Same
5	Address problems in using relaxation skills Identify headache triggers & warning signs Effective use of migraine medications Review pain coping skills. Develop a plan for responding to warning signs & to migraines	Same Identify headache-related warning signs & stresses Continue refinement of basic relaxation skills <u>or</u> introduce either advanced (1) stress-management skills, or (2) EMG biofeedback training Review pain coping skills
6	Apply & refine plan for responding to warning signs & to migraines	Apply & refine relaxation, stress-management skills or biofeedback skills
7	Address problems & refine plan for responding to warning signs & migraines.	Address problems in the application of relaxation, stress-management, or biofeedback skills.
8	Continue evaluation and refinement of plan for responding to warning signs & migraines.	Continue to evaluate & refine relaxation, stress-management or biofeedback skills
9	Continue with basic headache management skills <u>or</u> introduce either advanced (1) stress-management, or (2) thermal (hand-warming) biofeedback training skills	Identify most useful headache management skills for this patient Develop a long-term headache management plan, including coping with anticipated problems following treatment and relapse prevention.
10	Practice & evaluate relaxation, stress-management or biofeedback skills.	
11	Address difficulties in application of chosen headache management skill.	
12	Apply & refine relaxation, stress-management or biofeedback skills. Identify most useful headache management activities for this patient	
13	Develop long-term headache management plan, including coping with anticipated problems following treatment and relapse prevention.	

See Lipchik, Holroyd & Nash (2002), and Blanchard & Andrasik (1985) for more detailed descriptions of treatment techniques

Session Structure

With either treatment format, clinic sessions typically involve: (1) a review of self-monitoring forms and homework, (2) a discussion of any difficulties encountered in learning and applying headache management skills, (3) the presentation of the rationale for the new headache management skill that will be focus of the present session, (4) instruction and practice in this new skill, (4) formulation of a homework assignment, and (5) summary.

375

Efficacy

Migraine.

The Agency for Health Care Quality and Research sponsored evidence reports included an evaluation of the evidence for behavioral treatments for migraine (Goslin et al. 1999). Table 3 presents a synopsis of results from trials where outcome data could be obtained and where at least 6 patients were included per treatment group. Figure 1 presents summary data, both the effect size (top) and the percentage reduction in migraine (bottom) data from their meta-analysis. Unfortunately, only about half (N = 39) of the available (N = 70) controlled trials could be included in the AHCRQ meta-analysis, because early behavioral treatment studies often failed to report data necessary for effect size calculations. (The small number of trials included in the AHCPR meta-analysis may explain the relatively large confidence intervals evident in Figure 1.) However, additional analyses suggested that, even if all trials could have been included, the conclusions would not have changed significantly. Furthermore, results from this meta-analysis are consistent with results from other more inclusive meta-analyses (e.g., Blanchard et al., 1980; Holroyd and Penzien, 1990; Blanchard, 1992). On the basis of this evidence report The US Headache Consortium Clinical Guidelines for the Management of Migraine (Campbell et al., 2000) conclude "Relaxation training, thermal biofeedback combined with relaxation training, EMG biofeedback, and cognitive-behavioral therapy may be considered as treatment options for the prevention of migraine".

Tension-type headache

Table 4 similarly summarizes results from trials evaluating behavioral treatments for tension-type headache. Effect size and percent improvement data from the evidence report on the management of tension-type headache prepared for the AHCQR is presented in Figure 2 (McCrory et al., 2001). It can be seen that the four behavioral treatments have each yielded a 40% to 50% reduction in tension-type headache activity when results are averaged across trials. This evidence report concludes "Behavioral treatments for tension-type headache have a consistent body of research indicating efficacy" (p.7). As in the evidence report on the treatment of migraine, only a portion (N =35) of the identified trials (N = 107) could be included in the formal meta-analysis. Nonetheless, additional analyses again suggested that overall findings would not change dramatically in this larger pool of trials. Meta-analyses conducted for the evidence report are also consistent with results from earlier, more inclusive meta-analyses (Blanchard et al., 1980; Holroyd and Penzien, 1986; Bogaards and ter Kuile, 1994) that used different statistical techniques. are also consistent with results from earlier, more inclusive meta-analyses (Blanchard et al., 1980; Holroyd and Penzien, 1986; Bogaards and ter Kuile, 1994) that used different statistical techniques.

Integrating Drug and Psychological Therapies

Migraine

Holroyd and Penzien (1991) compared the results reported in 25 trials of the preventive drug propranolol HCl and in35 trials of combined thermal biofeedback plus relaxation that included over 2400 patients. Nearly identical outcomes were reported with propranolol HCl and thermal biofeedback plus relaxation: each treatment yielded, on average, a 55% reduction in migraine activity, while (pill) placebo yielded only a 12% reduction in migraine activity.

Two trials also have examined the benefits of combining propranolol HCl with thermal biofeedback training. Holroyd et al. (N = 33 ;1995) compared the effectiveness of (home-based) TBF alone and when combined with (60 to 180 mg/day) propranolol HCl.

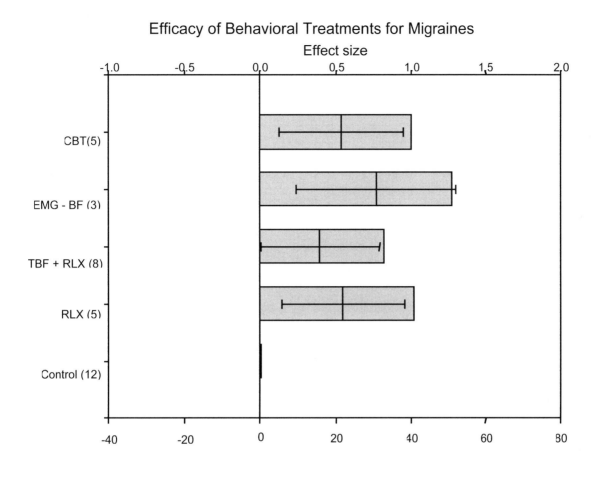

Figure 1: Effect size with 95% confidence interval (top axis) and percent reduction in migraine (bottom axis). CBT = Cognitive-behavior therapy; EMG-BF = Electromyographic biofeedback training; TBF + RLX = Thermal biofeedback training plus relaxation training; RLX = Relaxation training; Control = Headache monitoring control. Adapted from Goslin et al (1999)

Table 3: Results of Studies Evaluating Behavioral Treatments for Migraine

Study	Treatment type	# Imprv'd /N * (%)	Before Tx	After Tx	%** Improvement	Measure ***	Results
Andreychuk and Skriver, 1975	Self –hypnosis (n = 10)	-	87.5	55.1	37%	HI	No significant differences in improvement. Both groups showed significant improvement from pre-to "posttreat." (thermal BF, p = 0.01; self-hypnosis, p = 0.025.
	Thermal BF + relax. (AT phrases) (n = 9)	-	132.1	24.1	82%	HI	
Barrios, 1980±	Relax (PRM) (n = 8)	-	4.00	3.75	06%	HF	No differences among groups (p-values not given). All treatments combined improved from pre to "posttreat." (p < 0.01).
	Thermal BF + AT phrases (n = 7)	-	6.57	4.00	39%	HF	
	Social Skills (beh. mgmt) (n = 9)	-	6.89	3.56	48%	HF	
Bild and Adams, 1980±	Control (WL) (n = 6)	-	2.40	2.00	17%	HF	EMG BF was not significantly better than the WL group (p-value not given). BVP BF group excluded.
	EMG BF (n = 6)	-	2.20	1.40	36%	HF	
Blanchard, Appelbaum, Radnitz et al., 1990±	Control (WL) (n = 30)	6/30 (20%)	2.51	2.53	-01%	HI	The BF groups improved from pre- to posttreat, relative to WL group (p = 0.004). The pseudomeditation group also improved compared to WL (p-value not given). There were no significant differences in efficacy among the three active groups.
	Placebo (pseudomeditation) (n = 24)	9/24 (38%)	3.07	1.94	37%	HI	
	Thermal BF + relax. (PMR) (n = 32)	17/32 (53%)	3.53	2.05	42%	HI	
	Thermal BF + relax. (PMR) + cog. ther. (n = 30)	15/30 (50%)	3.37	1.90	44%	HI	

Study	Treatment type	# Imprv'd /N * (%)	Before Tx	After Tx	%** Improvement	Measure ***	Results
Blanchard, Nicholson, Radnitz et al., 1991[±]	Control (WL) (n = 13)	1/13 (8%)	2.98	3.44	-15%	HI	Each thermal BF group improved relative to the WL group (p < 0.05, each comparison). Neither BF group was significantly more effective than the other (p-value not given).
	Thermal BF (+ AT phrases) with no home practice (n = 23)	11/23 (48%)	3.76	2.92	22%	HI	
	Thermal BF (+AT phrases) with home practice (n = 23)	12/23 (52%)	3.91	2.65	32%	HI	
Blanchard, Theobold, Williamson et al., 1978[±]	Control (WL) (n = 10)	-	0.85	0.66	22%	HI	Authors reported that the active groups were each significantly more effective than the WL group (p < 0.05, both cases). There was no statistically significant differences between thermal BF and relax. (no p-value given). At one year follow-up (Silver, Blanchard, Williamson, et al., 1979) there were no significant differences between the two treatment groups.
	Relax. (PMR) + home practice (n = 10)	6/11 (55%)	0.98	0.17	83%	HI	
	Thermal BF + relax. (AT phrases) + home practice (n = 10)	9/13 (69%)	0.70	0.21	70%	HI	
Brown, 1984[±]	Placebo (subconscious recording) (n = 13)	-	1.00	1.07	-07%	HI	The two active groups did not differ significantly from each other. However, the two active groups combined showed greater improvement than placebo (p < .01) pretreat. to treat; p < .05 pretreat. to f/up).
	Response group (relax.) (n = 13)	-	1.00	0.50	50%	HI	

Study	Treatment type	# Imprv'd /N* (%)	Before Tx	After Tx	%** Improvement	Measure ***	Results
Daly, Donn, Galliher, et al., 1983±	Relax. ([PMR] + AT phrases) (n = 11)	6/11 (55%)	0.68	0.63	08%	HI	There were no significant differences among the three groups (p = 0.245). Each group improved from pre- to posttreat. (p < 0.05, ea. case). At 1 year follow up (Daly, Zimmerman, Donn et al., 1985) patients maintained improvements with all three treatments.
	EMG BF + relax. (AT phrases) (n = 10)	7/10 (70%)	0.59	0.25	58%	HI	
	Thermal BF + relax. (AT phrases) (n = 10)	8/10 (80%)	0.76	0.37	51%	HI	
Friedman and Taub, 1984	Control (WL) (n = 10)	-	-	-	-	HF	The WL group did not improve from pretreat. to 3 mo (no p-value given). However, from 6 to 12 mo., the active groups combined improved significantly (p < 0.001). (The WL group provided no data beyond 3 mo.).
	Relax. (n = 8)	-	26.7	25.3	03%	HF	
	Thermal BF + no home practice (n = 7)	-	11.3	8.9	21%	HF	
Gauthier, Côte, and French, 1994	Thermal BF + no home practice (n = 9)	2/9 (22%)	2.67	2.73	-02%	HI	The "home practice" thermal BF group was significantly more improved than the "no home practice" group (p < 0.05).
	Thermal BF + home practice (n = 8)	5/8 (68%)	3.18	1.85	42%	HI	
Gauthier, Lacroix, Côte, et al., 1985±	Control (WL) (n = 7)	N/S	11.8	10.2	14%	HF	There were no significant differences in efficacy between the two BF groups (p - values not given).
	Thermal BF (n = 8)	5/8 (63%)	13.6	5.5	60%	HF	
	BVP BF (n = 7)	4/7 (57%)	10.0	5.2	48%	HF	

Study	Treatment type	# Imprv'd /N* (%)	Before Tx	After Tx	%** Improvement	Measure ***	Results
Holroyd, France, Cordingley, et al., 1995	Relax. + thermal BF (n = 14)	8/14 (57%)	5.21	2.63	50%	HI	Relax. + thermal BF + propanolol decreased significantly more than relax.+ thermal BF alone (p < 0.05).
	Relax. + thermal BF + propanolol HCl (n = 13)	12/13 (92%)	6.11	1.83	70%	HI	
Holroyd, Holm, Hursey, et al., 1988	Ergotamine tartrate + compliance training (home-based) (n = 18)	11/18 (61%)	7.55	4.81	36%	HI	Both treatment groups improved significantly from pre- to posttreat., but neither group was better than the other (no p-values given). At three year follow-up (Holroyd, Holm, Penzien et al., 1989) both groups were improved relative to pretreat. (p < 0.01).
	Thermal BF + relax. (home-based) (n = 19)	10/19 (53%)	7.79	4.59	41%	HI	
Janssen and Neutgens, 1986	(migraine only) Relax. (AT phrases) (n = N/S)	-	0.72	0.59	18%	HI	From treatment (wks. 12 & 13) to f/up (wks. 25 & 26) there were no significant differences between the two treatment groups in M-Only pts (p = 0.634) or in pts with mixed M + TTH (p = 0.052). Both treatment groups improved from pretreatt. to f/up (no p-values given).
	(migraine only) Relax. (PMR) (n = N/S)	-	0.83	0.56	33%	HI	
	(mixed M + TTH) Relax. (AT phrases) (n = N/S)	-	0.64	0.58	09%	HI	
	(mixed M + TTH) Relax. (PRM) (n = N/S)	-	0.87	0.51	41%	HI	

Study	Treatment type	# Imprv'd /N* (%)	Before Tx	After Tx	%** Improvement	Measure***	Results
Jurish, Blanchard, Andrasik, et al., 1983	Thermal BF + relax. (n = 21)	11/21 (52%)	3.45	2.13	38%	HI	ANOVA showed a non significant difference between the two treatment groups (p = .09). However, clinically significant improvements were more frequent in minimal contact (15/19 pts) than clinic-based treatment (11/21) (p < .01).
	Thermal BF + relax. (minimal therapist contact) (n = 19)	15/19 (79%)	3.59	1.47	59%	HI	
Kewman and Roberts, 1980±	Control (WL) (n = 11)	-	1.23	1.0	19%	HF	No significant difference between the thermal BF (increased temp.) and WL group.
	Thermal BF (increase temp.) (n = 11)	-	0.98	0.85	13&	HF	
Lacroix, Clarke, Bock, et al., 1983	Relax. (PMR) (n = 7)	-	4.00	1.50	63%	HF	No Significant differences among the groups. All groups combined improved from pre- to posttreat. (p < 0.01).
	EMG BF (n = 9)	-	2.50	2.00	20%	HF	
	Thermal BF (n = 9)	-	4.00	0.55	86%	HF	
Lake, Rainey, and Papsdorf, 1979±	Control (WL) (n = 6)	-	1.00	1.17	-17%	HI	Only EMG BF superior to WL at posttreat. (p = 0.0076). Three BF groups combined superior to WL at f/up (p = 0.048).
	EMG BF (n = 6)	-	1.00	0.48	52%	HI	
	Thermal BF + Relax. (n = 6)	-	1.00	0.70	30%	HI	
	Thermal BF + cog. ther. (RET) (n = 6)	-	1.00	0.79	21%	HI	

Study	Treatment type	# Imprv'd /N* (%)	Before Tx	After Tx	%*** Improvement	Measure ***	Results
Machado, and Gomez de Machado, 1985	Control (WL) (n = 7)	-	8.80	10.6	-20%	HI	The two active groups better than WL (p < 0.001). Both active groups improved significantly from pre- to posttreat., but the WL did not.
	Relax. (modified PRM) (n = 5)	-	2.60	1.20	54%	HI	
	Relax. (modified PRM) + thermal BF (n = 7)	-	6.00	0.80	87%	HI	
Mathew, 1981	*MIGRAINE ONLY*						For the migraine-only pts, each active group improved significantly more than did the controls (no p-values given). Comparisons of BF + relax. with preventive drug therapies were not reported. The propanolol-alone group improved by 62%, and the amitriptyline-alone group improved by 42%, with the former treatment being significantly better than the latter (p < 0.01).
	Control (abortive ergotamine) (n = 33)	-	3.40	2.72	20%	HI	
	Propanolol (n = 38)	-	4.12	1.57	62%	HI	
	Amitriptyline (n = 32)	-	3.93	2.28	42%	HI	
	Biofeedback (EMG + thermal) + relax. (n = 31)	-	3.50	2.28	35%	HI	
	Propanolol + amitriptyline (n = 38)	-	4.08	1.47	64%	HI	
	Propanolol +biofeedback (n = 33)	-	4.22	1.1	74%	HI	
	Amitriptyline + biofeedback (n = 38)	-	3.78	1.89	48%	HI	
	Propanolol + amitriptyline + biofeedback (n = 30)	-	4.31	1.17	73%	HI	

Study	Treatment type	# Imprv'd /N* (%)	Before Tx	After Tx	%** Improvement	Measure ***	Results
	Mixed M + TTH Control (abortive ergotamine) (n = 35)	-	8.12	6.6	18%	HI	For mixed M + TTH authors report BF + relax. by itself did not appear to be the treatment of choice, but significantly contributed to better results as an adjunct. Statistical comparisons involving BF + relax. were not reported.
	Mixed M + TTH Propanolol (n = 38)	-	6.7	3.24	52%	HI	
	Mixed M + TTH Amitriptyline (n = 31)	-	7.78	3.12	60%	HI	
	Mixed M + TTH Biofeedback (EMG + thermal) + relax. (n = 31)	-	8.06	4.20	48%	HI	
Mathew, 1981 (cont.)	Mixed M + TTH Propanolol + amitriptyline (n = 36)	-	7.36	2.51	69%	HI	
	Mixed M + TTH Propanolol + biofeedback (n = 34)	-	6.32	2.41	62%	HI	
	Mixed M + TTH Amitriptyline + biofeedback (n = 39)	-	7.10	2.42	66%	HI	
	Propanolol + amitriptyline + biofeedback (n = 37)	-	7.84	1.89	76%	HI	

Study	Treatment type	# Imprv'd /N* (%)	Before Tx	After Tx	%** Improvement	Measure***	Results
McCrady, Wauquier, McNeil, et al., 1994±	Placebo (self-relax.) (n = 12)	3/12 (25%)	1.19	1.24	-04%	HI	BF group improved more than the placebo group (no p-value given).
	EMG BF + thermal BF + relax. (AT phrases) (n = 11)	6/11 (55%)	1.28	1.00	22%	HI	
Mitchell and Mitchell, 1971 (Study 1)	Relax. (PRM) application (n = 7)	-	1.00	0.76	24%	HF	Relax + cog. ther. better than relax (p < .01) and WL (p < .01).
	Relax. + cog. ther. (combined desensitization) (n = 7)	-	1.00	0.24	76%	HF	
Mitchell and Mitchell, 1971 (Study 2)	Control (WL) (n = 5)	-	1.00	0.93	07%	HF	Relax. + cog. ther. better than WL (p < .05).
	Relax. + cog. ther. (systematic desensitization) (n = 5)	-	1.00	0.59	41%	HF	
Mullinex, Norton, Hack, et al., 1978±	Placebo (false thermal BF) (n = 5)	1/5 20%	1.00	0.92	08%	HI	Authors reported that the two groups showed similar improvements. Study lacks power due to small sample size
	Thermal BF (n = 6)	2/6 33%	1.00	0.78	21%	HI	

Study	Treatment type	# Imprv'd /N* (%)	Before Tx	After Tx	%** Improvement	Measure ***	Results
Nicholson and Blanchard, 1993±	Control (WL) (n = 5)	1/5 20%	1.00	0.90	10%	HI	Statistical significance not reported.
	Relax. (PMR) + cog. ther. (stress-coping or problem solving) + thermal BF (n = 5)	3/5 60%	1.00	0.54	46%	HI	
Penzien, Johnson, Carpenter, et al., 1990	Propranolol (n = 11)	6/11 (55%)	-	-	44%	HI	No significant differences between treatments.
	Relax. + thermal BF + cog. ther. (coping skills, home-based) (n = 11)	5/11 (46%)	-	-	42%	HI	
Richardson and McGrath, 1989±	Control (WL) (n = 17)	3/17 (18%)	15.53	15.20	02%	HF	Significant differences between each of the active groups and the WL group (no p-values given), but no difference between the two active groups (no p-value given).
	Cog. ther. + relax. (PMR) – Minimal therapist contact (n = 15)	5/15 (33%)	14.5	10.5	28%	HF	
	Cog. ther. + relax. (PMR) – clinic-based (n = 15)	7/15 (47%)	15.47	8.32	46%	HF	

Study	Treatment type	# Imprv'd /N* (%)	Before Tx	After Tx	%** Improvement	Measure ***	Results
Sargent, Solbach, Coyne, et al., 1986	Control (WL) (n = 34)	-	6.33	5.79	09%	HF	No significant difference between active treatments. All four groups improved from pretreat. to f/up, with the three active groups combined being significantly better than WL (p = 0.016).
	Relax. (AT phrases) (n = 34)	-	6.84	5.86	14%	HF	
	EMG BF (n = 34)	-	6.95	5.27	24%	HF	
	Thermal BF (n = 34)	-	6.99	5.51	21%	HF	
Sorbi and Tellegen, 1984[±]	Relax. (AT phrases) + cog. ther. (stress-coping) (n = 10)	-	0.20	0.094	53%	HF	Both treatment groups significantly improved from pre- to posttreat. ("with thermal BF," p < 0.05; "without thermal BF," p < 0.01). No significant differences between treatments.
	Relax. (AT phrases) + cog. ther. (stress-coping) + thermal BF (n = 11)	-	0.27	0.15	44%	HF	
Sorbi and Tellegen, 1986[±]	Relax. (AT phrases) (n = 13)	-	0.19	0.11	40%	HF	Authors stated that "[t]he effects did not differ between the two types of training." Both treatment groups showed significant reductions from pre-to posttreat. (p < .01 for relax.; p < .05 for cog. ther.) At 3 yrs both groups had maintained the improvements previously achieved (relax., 38%; cog. ther., 36%).
	Cog. ther. (stress mgmt) (n = 16)	-	0.12	0.08	31%	HF	

Study	Treatment type	# Imprv'd /N* (%)	Before Tx	After Tx	%** Improvement	Measure ***	Results
Sovak, Kunzel, Sternbach, et al., 1981	Drug therapy (propranolol + analgesics) (n = 20)	9/20 (45%)	-	-	-	-	No significant difference between treatments.
	Thermal BF + relax. (AT phrases) (n = 28)	15/28 (54%)	-	-	-	-	
Wittchen, 1983±	Control (WL) (n = 10)	-	3.5	3.0	14%	HF	Each active group improved significantly from pre- to posttreat. (p < 0.05, ea. treatment group), but the WL group did not improve (p-value not given).
	Psychological ther. (n = 10)	-	2.4	1.7	29%	HF	
	Acupuncture ther. (n = 10)	-	3.4	1.6	53%	HF	

Adapted from: Duke University Center for Clinical Health Policy Research. (1999). *Behavioral and Physical Treatments for Migraine Headache (Technical Review 2.2)* (No. PB127946). Durham, NC: Agency for Health Care Policy and Research.

Key: AT = autogenic training; BF = biofeedback; BVP = Blood Volume Pulse; cog. = cognitive; EMG = electromyograph; f/up = follow-up; freq. = frequency; HA = headache; HCl = hydrogen chloride; HI = headache index (measure that takes severity and duration into account); M = migraine; mo. = month; n = number of patients; N/S = non-specified; PMR = progressive muscle relaxation; posttreat. = posttreatment; pretreat. = pretreatment; pt = patient; ther. = therapy; relax. = relaxation; TTH = tension-type headache; w/ = with; w/o = without; WL = wait-listed; yr = year

* Number clinically improved (typically >50% improvement)/number of treated patients (percent clinically improved)

** Average percentage reduction in headache measure

*** Outcome measure reported here

± Studies covered in metanalysis shown in figure 1

Table 4: Results from Studies Evaluating Behavioral Treatments for Tension-Type Headache

Study	Treatment type	# Imprv'd /N* (%)	Before Tx	After Tx	%** Improvement	Measure ***	Results
Andrasik and Holroyd, 1980	EMG BF (n = 10)	-	-	-	-	HI	EMG biofeedback yielded significantly greater improvement than HA monitoring at posttreat., 6-week and 3-year f/up(p < 0.05); latter Andrasik and Holroyd (1983).
	No treatment (HA monitoring) (n = 10)	-	-	-	-	HI	
	Two other treatments excluded (n = 19)	-	-	-	-	-	
Appelbaum, Blanchard, Nicholson et al., 1990±	PMR minimal-contact format (n = 16)	8/16 (50%)	5.10	2.4	-	HI	The two active treatment groups were significantly more improved than WL control (p = 0.05). There was no significant difference between the two active treatment groups.
	PMR + CBT minimal-contact (n = 17)	9/17 (53%)	5.53	3.1	-	HI	
	WL control (n = 8)	1/8 (13%)	5.80	5.0	-	HI	
Arena, Bruno, Hannah et al., 1995±	Frontal EMG BF (n = 8)	4/8 (50%)	-	-	43.8%	HI	Trapezius EMG was significantly better than PMR (p < 0.05) with no significant difference between the two EMG groups.
	Trapezius EMG BF (n = 10)	10/10 (100%)	-	-	74%	HI	
	PMR (n = 8)	3/8 (37.5%)	-	-	33.9%	HI	

Study	Treatment type	# Imprv'd /N* (%)	Before Tx	After Tx	%** Improvement	Measure***	Results
Attanasio, Andrasik, and Blanchard, 1987[±]	PMR + CBT (office-based) (n = 7)	5/7 (71%)	5.6	2.6	-	HI	No significant differences between the three treatment groups.
	PMR + CBT (home-based) (n = 8)	5/8 (62.5%)	6.1	3.7	-	HI	
	PMR (home-based) (n = 6)	3/6 (50%)	5.2	3.2	-	HI	
Bernal, 1982	Hypnosis (suggestions for deep relax) (n = 6?)		18	16	-	HI	All three active treatments showed significant improvements from pretreat to treat ($p < .05$ or better) while sham EMG BF did not improve.
	EMG BF (n = 6?)		24	23	-	HI	
	Alternating hypnosis/EMG BF (n = 6?)		-	-	-	HI	
	Sham (non-contingent) EMG BF (n = 6?)		21	18	-	HI	
Blanchard, Appelbaum, Radnitz et al., 1990[±]	PMR (n = 19)	6/19 (32%)	5.63	3.82	32%	HI	PMR + CBT was significantly ($p < 0.02$) better than both pseudo-meditation and WL control. There was no significant difference between the two active treatment groups.
	PMR + CBT (stress coping) (n = 16)	10/16 (62.5%)	5.82	3.20	45%	HI	
	Pseudomeditation control (n = 16)	7/16 (44%)	5.23	4.63	11%	HI	
	WL control (n = 15)	3/15 (20%)	5.05	4.45	12%	HI	

Study	Treatment type	# Imprv'd /N* (%)	Before Tx	After Tx	%** Improvement	Measure ***	Results
Chesney and Shelton, 1976±	EMG BF	-	4.83	2.83	41%	HF	Relax. alone and BF + relax. were both significantly better than WL control (p < 0.05).
	Relax. (deep muscle and rapid)	-	5.33	1.33	75%	HF	
	EMG BF plus relax.	-	5.83	1.33	78%	HF	
	WL control	-	4.17	4.67	-12%	HF	
Cox, Freundlich, and Meyer, 1975±	EMG BF + relax. (cue-controlled breathing) (n = 9)	8/9 (89%)	1.69	0.63	63%	HI	EMG BF + relax. more improved than placebo (p < 0.05) and equivalent to relax. alone.
	Relax. (PMR + cue-controlled breathing) (n = 9)	4/9 (44%)	1.35	0.63	53%	HI	
	Medication placebo (n = 9)	2/9 (22%)	1.55	1.25	19%	HI	
	WL control	-	4.17	4.67	-12%	HF	
Cram, 1980	EMG BF (reduction) (n = 8?)	-	-	-	42%	HI	Both EMG BF groups better than WL in last 2 weeks treat. Both EMG BF groups improved from pretreat.
	EMG BF (stability training) (n = 8?)	-	-	-	1%	HI	
	Bogus medication (control) (n = 8?)	-	-	-	-	HI	
	Headache monitoring (control) (n = 8?)	-	-	-	8%	HI	

Study	Treatment type	# Imprv'd /N* (%)	Before Tx	After Tx	%** Improvement	Measure ***	Results
Daly, Donn, Galiher, et al., 1983[±]	EMG BF + relax (n = 9)	7/9 (78%)	.89	.47	-	HI	No statistical analysis reported.
	Thermal BF + relax (autogenic phrases) (n = 8)	6/8 (75%)	.91	.22	-	HI	
12 mfu described in Daly, Zimmerman, Donn et al., 1985	Relax (PMR) (n = 8)	3/8 (38%)	1.13	.84	-	HI	
Figueroa, 1982	PMR+ cog. beh. ther. (n = 5)	-	4.9	3.2	-	HF	PMR + CBT was significantly better than both psychotherapy and WL control at posttreat. and f/up (p < 0.05).
	Psychotherapy (n = 5)	-	2.9	4.0	-	HF	
	WL control (n = 5)	-	4.5	5.1	-	HF	
Gada, 1984[±]	EMG BF + PMR (n = 30)	20/30 (67%)	5.5	2.4	-	HI	No difference between treatment groups. Both treatment groups improved significantly from pre-to post-treat. (p < 0.01).
	PMR (n = 28)	19/28 (68%)	5.2	2.5	-	HI	
Hart, 1982	EMG BF from frontal region (n = 12)	0/12 (0%)	1.8	1.4	-	HA (N/S)	Greater improvement in the relax. group than in the BF groups (p < 0.05). 27/32 patients followed at 6 and 12-mo. assessments. Results unchanged except that 4/10 pts in EMG frontal group reported > 70% improvement.
	EMG BF from neck (n = 10)	0/10 (0%)	2.9	-	-	HA (N/S)	
	Relax.; taped procedure (n = 10)	4/10 (40%)	1.6	0.8	-	HA (N/S)	

Study	Treatment type	# Imprv'd /N* (%)	Before Tx	After Tx	%** Improvement	Measure***	Results
Haynes, Griffin, Mooney et al., 1975±	EMG BF (n = 8)	-	82.1	20.9	-	HI	Both EMG BF and relax. significantly better than control (p < 0.01).
	Relax.; taped relaxation during treatment sessions (n = 8)	-	102.3	18.6	-	HI	
	Control group (relax. without instructions) (n = 5)	-	68.7	87.8	-	HI	
Holroyd and Andrasik, 1978±	CBT (n = 10)	-	127.5	35.7	-	HI	Two active treatment groups and the HA discussion group differed significantly from the WL control group (p < 0.05), but did not differ from one another.
	CBT + relax. (n = 7)	-	183.4	57.2	-	HI	
	Headache discussion group (control) (n = 7)	-	132.4	61.8	-	HI	
	WL (n = 9)	-	152.1	147.9	-	HI	
Holroyd, Andrasik, and Noble, 1980±	EMG BF (n = 8)	7/8 (88%)	164.8	55.5	66%	HI	The EMG BF group, but not the bogus meditation group, was significantly better than WL control at posttreat. and f/up (p < 0.05). Patients more likely to be significantly improved in EMG BF group than two control groups (p < 0.01).
	Bogus meditation (control) (n = 9)	2/9 (22%)	151.9	133.0	12%	HI	
	WL control (HA monitoring) (n = 11)	3/11 (27%)	155.8	137.1	19%	HI	

Study	Treatment type	# Imprv'd /N* (%)	Before Tx	After Tx	%** Improvement	Measure ***	Results
Holroyd, Andrasik, and Westbrook, 1977[±]	CBT (n = 9)	-	92.5	25.4	73%	HI	CBT significantly better than EMG BF and WL control at posttreat. and at 15- week f/up (p < 0.05). Follow-up described in Holroyd & Andrasik (1982).
	EMG BF (n = 10)	-	102.3	76.0	26%	HI	
	WL control (n = 9)	-	95.1	100.8	-6%	HI	
Holroyd, Nash, Pingel et al., 1991[±]	Relax. + CBT (n = 19)	7/19 (37%)	2.17	0.96	-	HI	Significant improvement from pre to posttreat. in both the behavioral treatment group (p < 0.001) and the amitriptyline group (p < 0.01). Relax. + cog. beh.ther. significantly better than amitriptyline (p < 0.001).
	Amitriptyline (n = 17)	3/17 (18%)	2.04	1.49	-	HI	
Holroyd, O'Donnell, Stensland et al., 2000[±]	TCA (n = 53)	20/53 (38%)	2.8	1.7	-	HI	At trial endpoint (8 mo. after beginning treatment) CBT + relax. + TCA were more improved than placebo (p < 0.01 or better); individual treatments and combined treatment did not differ significantly. Combined treatment was found to be better than individual treatments in percentage of patients improved (p < 0.0063 or better).
	CBT + relax. + placebo medication (n = 49)	17/49 (35%)	2.8	1.8	-	HI	
	CBT + relax.+ TCA (n = 53)	34/53 (64%)	2.8	1.6	-	HI	
	Placebo medication (n = 48)	Not reported	2.7	2.5	-	HI	

Study	Treatment type	# Imprv'd /N* (%)	Before Tx	After Tx	%** Improvement	Measure ***	Results
Hutchings and Reinking, 1976	EMG BF (n = 6?)	-	-	-	66%	HI	The two EMG BF groups showed significantly better results than did the relax. group (p < 0.05).
	EMG BF + relax. (n = 6?)	-	-	-	20%	HI	
	PMR, passive volition, and AT (n = 6?)						
Janssen, 1983	EMG BF + PMR (n = 6?)	-	100	58	42%	HI	H-test showed trend H = 5.10 2 df; p <0.08.
	EMG BF (no instructions to relax) (n = 6?)	-	100	68	32%	HI	
	WL control (n = 6?)	-	100	112	-12%	HI	
Kondo and Canter, 1977±	EMG BF (n = 10)	-	5.4	1.0	81%	HF	Patients in the true EMG group reported significantly fewer HAs than did patients in the placebo EMG group at post-treat. (p < 0.005).
	Placebo (non-contingent) EMG BF (n = 10)	-	5.4	3.5	35%	HF	
Martin and Mathews, 1978	EMG BF (n = 12)	-	39.4	29.25	-	HI	No difference between two treatments at posttreat or f/up. Significant improvement with treatment (p <.01).
	PMR (audiotape) (n = 12)	-	34.7	31.9	-	HI	
Mosley, Grothues, and Meeks, 1995±	Relax. (n = 10)	4/10 (40%)	7.18	5.29	26%	HI	Both relax. (p < 0.05) and relax.+ CBT(p < 0.001) were significantly better than WL control. Relax. + CBT was also significantly better than relax. alone (p < 0.05).
	Relax.+ CBT (n = 11)	7/11 (64%)	7.80	3.73	52%	HI	
	WL control (n = 9)	0/9 (0%)	7.26	7.13	1.8%	HI	

Study	Treatment type	# Imprv'd /N* (%)	Before Tx	After Tx	%** Improvement	Measure***	Results
Murphy, Lehrer, and Jurish, 1990[±]	Group CBT (n = 12)	9/12 (75%)	3.5	2.3	-	HF	CBT yielded greater improvement than relax. (p < 0.02). More patients clinically improved in CBT than relax. (p < 0.05).
	Group relax. (n = 11)	2/11 (18%)	3.7	2.9	-	HF	
Paiva, Nunes, Moreira et al., 1982[±]	EMG BF (n = 8)	-	1.21	0.42	-	HF	At posttreat only EMG BF significantly improved (p <.05).
	Sham EMG BF (n = 8)	-	2.00	1.19	-	HF	
	Diazepam (n = 8)	-	1.72	1.26	-	HF	
	Placebo (n = 8)	-	2.17	1.98	-	HF	
Rokicki, Holroyd, France et al., 1997[±]	EMG BF + relax. (PMR) (n = 29)	-	2.1	1.4	33%	HI	EMG BF + relax. group showed significantly greater improvement than did controls (p < 0.05).
	HA monitoring control (n = 13)	-	2.4	2.5	-4%	HI	
Schlutter, Golden, and Blume, 1980	EMG BF + PMR (n = ?)	-	-	-	-	HD	No difference between treatments. Treated patients improved (e.g., 14 HA hours/week, p <.01).
	EMG (n = ?)	-	-	-	-	HD	
	Hypnosis (hypnotic analgesia) (n = ?)	-	-	-	-	HD	

Study	Treatment type	# Imprv'd /N* (%)	Before Tx	After Tx	%** Improvement	Measure***	Results
Spinhoven, Linssen, van Dyck et al., 1992	Self-hypnosis (n = 23)	-	3.3	3.0	-	HI	No difference between treatments. Treated patients improved (p <.05).
	Relax (autogenic training) (n = 23)	-	2.9	2.5	-	HI	
ter Kuile, Spinhoven, Linssen et al., 1994±	Relax. (AT) (n = 41)	-	24.2	16.2	33%	HI	Only relax. differed significantly from controls at posttreat. (p < 0.05).
	CBT + relax. (n = 40)	-	27.2	22.5	17.3%	HI	
	WL control (n = 53)	-	25.9	25.4	1.9%	HI	
Tobin, Holroyd, Baker et al., 1988±	Relax. (home-based) (n = 12)	-	3.10	1.99	-	HI	Posttreat. scores were significantly lower in the relax. + CBT group than in the relax. alone group (p < 0.05). Improvements maintained at 3 mo. f/up.
	Relax. (home-based) + CBT (n = 12)	-	3.08	0.74	-	HI	
Vaccaro and Feindler, 1980	CBT (n = 7)	-	2.6	1.7	-	HF	HA frequency improved significantly from pre- to posttreat. in both cog. beh. and relax. groups (p < 0.01).
	Relax. (n = 6)	-	1.1	0.5	-	HF	

Adapted from: McCrory, D., Penzien, D., Hasselblad, V., & Gray, R. (2001). *Behavioral and Physical Treatments for Tension-Type and Cervicogenic Headache* (No. 2085). DesMoines, Iowa: Foundation for Chiropractic Education and Research.

Key: AT = autogenic training; BF = biofeedback; BVP = Blood Volume Pulse; cog. = cognitive; EMG = electromyograph; f/up = follow-up; freq. = frequency; HA = headache; HD = headache duration (hours); HCl = hydrogen chloride; HF = headache frequency; HI = headache index (measure that takes severity and duration into account); M = migraine; mo. = month; n = number of patients; N/S = non-specified; PMR = progressive muscle relaxation; posttreat. = posttreatment; pretreat. = pretreatment; pt = patient; ther. = therapy; relax. = relaxation; TCA = tricyclic antidepressants; TTH = tension-type headache; w/ = with; w/o = without; WL = wait-listed; yr = year

* Number clinically improved (typically >50% improvement)/number of treated patients (percent clinically improved)

** Average percentage reduction in headache measure

*** Outcome measure reported here

± Studies included in metanalysis shown in figure

Efficacy of Treatments for Tension-type Headache

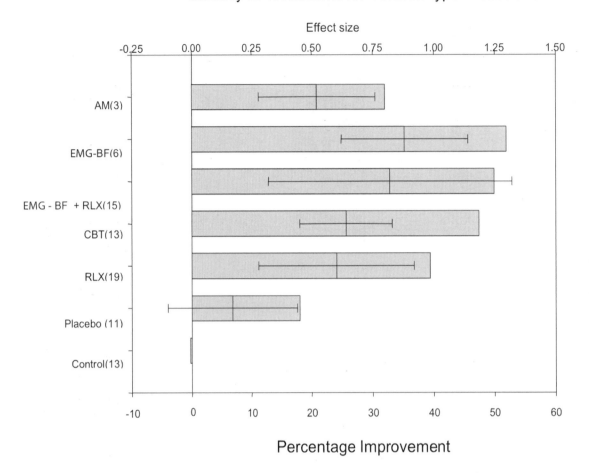

Figure 2: Effect size with 95% confidence interval (top axis) and percent reduction in tension-type headache activity (bottom axis). AM = AmitriptylineHCl; EMG-BF = Electromyographic biofeedback training; EMG-BF + RLX = electromyographic biofeedback training plus relaxation training; CBT = Cognitive-behavior therapy; RLX = Relaxation training; Placebo = Pseudotherapy or false biofeedback training; Control = Headache monitoring control. Adapted from McCrory et al (2001)

Propranolol significantly enhanced the effectiveness of TBF on measures of migraine activity, analgesic medication use and quality of life. Earlier Mathew (1981) also found that (60 to 120 mg/day) propranolol HCl increased the effectiveness of a 10 session multi-modal (EMG and thrermal) biofeedback training package; however, propranolol HCl tended to produce larger reduction in migraine activity than biofeedback training, and about the same reductions as the combined treatment (see Table 4). However, the high dropout rate (38% of patients) from biofeedback training alone raises the possibility that outcomes with this treatment were compromised by poor patient compliance.

Holroyd and colleagues (1998) have proposed tentative algorithms for decisions about whether to offer drug or behavioral treatment or their combination.

Tension-type headache

It can be seen in Figure 2 that that results reported in trials of behavioral treatments have been comparable to results reported in trials of the primary preventive drug amitriptyline HCL. Two studies also provide information about the benefits of combined psychological and drug therapy for tension-type headache. Reich (N = 50 ;1993) examined the benefits of adding amitriptyline (to 75 mg./day) to an intensive (30 session) multiple site EMG biofeedback training protocol. The combination of amitriptyline HCl and EMG biofeedback training yielded more rapid improvement in tension-type headache activity than EMG biofeedback training alone; however, beginning at month 8 and continuing through the 24-month evaluation period the combined treatment showed no advantage over EMG biofeedback training alone. In fact at the 20- and 24-month observation periods - after withdrawal from amitriptyline HCl - patients who received EMG biofeedback training alone recorded significantly fewer hours of headache activity than patients who received the combined treatment. Holroyd and colleagues (N = 203 ; Holroyd, O'Donnell et al., 2001) examined the separate and combined effects of cognitive-behavior (stress-management) therapy and tricyclic antidepressant medication for chronic tension-type headaches see Table 4). Patients received one of four treatments: tricyclic antidepressant (amitriptyline HCl to 100 mg./day or nortriptyline HCl to 75 mg./day) medication, medication placebo, limited-contact CBT (three clinic sessions) plus antidepressant medication, or CBT plus placebo. Antidepressant medication and cognitive-behavior therapy yielded similar reductions in chronic tension-type headaches, analgesic medication use, and headache-related disability at a 6-month follow-up evaluation (8 months after beginning treatment), but improvements tended to be more rapid in the two-antidepressant medication conditions than with CBT alone (See Figure 3). However, the combined treatment was more likely (64 % of patients) to produce clinically significant (≥ 50%) reductions in tension-type headaches, than either antidepressant medication alone (38 % of patients) or CBT (35 % of patients) alone.

FUTURE DIRECTIONS

Identification of effective interventions - even the formulation of empirically based clinical practice guidelines - fails to produce effective disease management. Clinical practice guidelines typically are adopted only sporadically in a minority of settings. Formidable barriers impede the implementation of disease management programs in the primary care setting where the majority of patients are treated (Cabana et al., 1999). Thus, a disease management program that relies primarily on disseminating information about empirically supported disease treatments is thus doomed to failure in most settings.

The cost-effective management of chronic disorders in general, and headache disorders in particular, requires not only empirically based clinical guidelines, but also a health care delivery system structured to implement these guidelines consistently and appropriately. Deficiencies in the delivery of health care services to individuals with chronic disorders, whether the disorder is headaches, depression or diabetes are now widely recognized. These deficiencies result, in large part, because the health also a health care delivery system structured to implement these guidelines consistently and appropriately.

Figure 3: Mean Headache Index Scores following various therapies

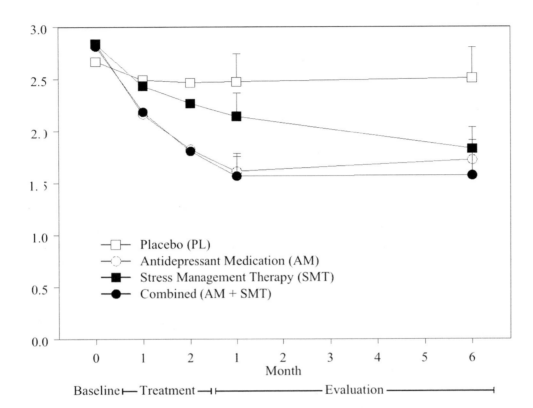

Figure 3: Mean Headache Index scores at baseline, during treatment (dose adjustment), and (with standard error) at one-month and six month evaluations. Headache Index is calculated as a mean of daily headache ratings (range 0-10) over one-month periods. Adapted form Holroyd et al.(2001)

Deficiencies in the delivery of health care services to individuals with chronic disorders, whether the disorder is headaches, depression or diabetes are now widely recognized. These deficiencies result, in large part, because the health care system is set up to diagnose and treat acute illness (Holroyd and Creer, 1986; Von Korff et al., 1997). As a result, key services are not delivered effectively to individuals with chronic disease.

Individuals with chronic disease are likely to benefit when education and psychosocial and medical interventions are integrated, when regular monitoring of signs and symptoms is integrated into proactive follow-up care, and when health care teaches and supports the performance of behavioral disease management activities (Wagner et al., 1996). Effective chronic disease management often requires changes in the health care system. The majority of individuals with headache disorders, or for that matter other chronic disorders, are seen in primary care, not in specialty medical, behavioral medicine, or mental health settings. The 12-minute primary care visit will therefore need to be restructured or supplemented to effectively incorporate educational and psychosocial interventions and proactive monitoring of patients in primary practice. Experiments in this area include the increased use of proactive phone contacts, the use of mini-clinics where patients with the same or related disorders are periodically scheduled for the same time period, so that educational and psychosocial services delivered by nurses, health educators, or psychologists can be more readily integrated into the primary care visit. Promising results with the management of recurrent headache disorders have been reported with the use of such supplementary services (Blumenfeld and Tischio, 2003; Mulligan et al., 2003; Smith et al., 2003). Clinic information systems, which often serving primarily medical-record keeping and scheduling functions, also will need to be restructured to better support effective care for chronic conditions. Information systems then might then also identify patients in need of special attention, who, for example, are using analgesics excessively or who are currently depressed; at the same time, this system could present from empirically from relevant empirically based clinical guidelines directly to the primary care physician to encourage the use of empirically based treatments. New ways of incorporating expertise in psychosocial interventions into primary practice will also be needed. Experiments in the last decade include the creation of expert teams of nurses, health educators and psychologists who are available for immediate phone consultation during the patient visit, or who are periodically available in the primary care setting to see patients *with* the primary care physician. These consultation procedures, unlike more traditional consultation services that often produce little more than a written report with recommendation, will, over time, increase primary care physicians' knowledge of psychosocial assessment and treatment procedures.

It is important that behavioral scientist-clinicians be actively in current efforts to restructure health care health care delivery for disease management. Effective use will need to be made of existing behavioral science knowledge if we are to develop interventions that help patients successfully carry out sometimes difficult disorder management activities over extended periods of time (Bodenheimer et al., 2002). Behavioral clinician-scientists will need to rethink the way psychosocial treatment is administered; psychosocial interventions in primary care are taking a different form than psychosocial interventions administered in a specialty behavioral medicine or mental health setting. Behavioral science knowledge also will need to be incorporated into the design of medical information systems if these information systems are to support health care providers and patients in their disease management activities.

RECOMMENDED READINGS

Borkum, J. (in press). Chronic headaches: biology, psychology and behavioral treatment. Hillsdale: New Jersey, Laurence Erlbaum.

Holroyd, K. A. (2002). "Assessment and psychological treatment of recurrent headache disorders." J Consult Clin Psychol 70: 656-677.

Goslin, R., R. Gray, et al. (1999). Behavioral and physical treatments for migraine headache. Technical review 2.2. February 1999. Prepared for the Aency for Health Care Policy and Research under contract No. 290-94-2025. Available at: http://www.clinpol.mc.duke.edu.

Silberstein, S. D., Lipton, R. B. et al., Eds. (2001). Wolff's Headache and

Other Headache Pain. New York, NY, Oxford University Press.

FOOTNOTES

[1] Previously the Agency for Health Care Policy and Research

[2] American Academy of Family Physicians, American Academy of Neurology, American Headache Society, American College of Emergency Physicians, American College of Physicians, American Osteopathic Association & National Headache Foundation

REFERENCES

American Psychiatric Association (1994) Diagnostic and Statistical Manual of Mental Disorders. Washington, DC, American Psychiatric Press.

Ashina, Messoud (2002) "Nitric oxide synthase inhibitors for the treatment of chronic tension-type headache." Expert Opin Pharmacother 3: 395-399.

Beck AT, Emery G. (1985) Anxiety Disorders and Phobias: A cognitive Perspective. New York, Basic Books.

Bernstein DA,Carlson CR. (1993) Progressive relaxation: Abbreviated methods. Principles and practice of stress management, 53-85 (P. Lehrer and R. L. Woolfolk). New York, The Guilford Press.

Blanchard EB. (1992) "Psychological treatment of benign headache disorders." J Consult Clin Psychol 60: 537-551.

Blanchard EB, Andrasik F. (1985) Management of chronic headaches: A psychological approach. Elmsford, NY, Pergamon Press.

Blanchard EB, Andrasik F. (1980) Migraine and tension headache: A meta-analytic review. Behav Ther 11: 613-631.

Blumenfeld A, Tischio M. (2003) Center of excellence for headache care: Group model at Kaiser Permanente. Headache 403: 431-440.

Bodenheimer T, Lorig K, Holman H, Grumbach K. (2002) Patient self management of chronic disease in primary care. JAMA 288(19): 2469-2475.

Bogaards MC, ter Kuile MM. (1994) Treatment of recurrent tension headache: A meta-analytic review. Clin J Pain 10: 174-190.

Breslau N, Davis GC. (1993) Migraine, physical health and psychiatric disorder: A prospective epidemiologic study in young adults. J Psychiatr Res 27: 211-221.

Breslau N, Davis GC, Schultz LR, Peterson EL. (1994) Migraine and major depression: A longitudinal study. Headache 34: 387-393.

Breslau N, Merikangas K, Bowden CL. (1994) Comorbidity of migraine and major affective diorders. Neurology 44(suppl 7): S17-S22.

Cabana MD,Rand CS, Powe NR, Wu AW, Wilson MD, Abboud PA, Rubin HR. (1999) Why don't physicians follow clinical practice guidelines? JAMA 282: 1458-1465.

Campbell JK,Penzien DB. (2000) Evidence-based guidelines for migraine headache: Behavioral and physical treatments, US Headache Consortium. 2001. http://www.aan.com/public/practiceguidelines/headache_gl.htm

Diener HC.. (2000) Headache associated with chronic use of substances. The Headaches, 871-877 (H.-C. Diener and C. Dahlof). Philadelphia, Lippincott, Williams, & Wilkins.

Ferrari MD,Roon KI, Lipton RB, Goadsby PJ. (2001) Oral triptans (serotonin 5-HT1B/1D agonists) in acute migraine treatment: a meta-analysis of 53 trials. Lancet 358: 1668-1675.

Goadsby PJ, Lipton RB, Ferrari MD. (2002) Migraine-current understanding and treatment. N Engl J Med 346: 257-270.

Goncalves JA, Monteiro P. (1993) Psychiatric analysis of patients with tension-type headache. Tension-Type Headache: Classification, Mechanisms, and Treatment, 167-172 (J. Olesen and J. Schoenen). New York, Raven Press.

Goslin R, Gray R. (1999) Behavioral and physical treatments for migraine headache. Technical Review 2.2, Duke Center for Health Policy Research (prepared for Agency for Health Care Policy and Research). 2003. http://www.clinpol.mc.duke.edu

Gray R, Goslin R, et al. (1998) New 5-HT1 agonists (triptans), Duke Center for Health Policy Research (prepared for the US Headache Consortium). 2003. http://www.clinpol.mc.duke.edu

Gray R, Goslin R. (1999) Drug treatments for the prevention of migraine headache, Duke Center for Health Policy Research (prepared for Agency for Health Care Policy and Research). 2003. http://www.clinpol.mc.duke.edu

Gray R, McCrory D, et al. (1999a) Parental drug treatments for acute migraine headache, Duke Center for Health Policy Research (prepared for Agency for Health Care Policy and Research). 2003. http://www.clinpol.mc.duke.edu

Gray R, McCrory D, et al. (1999b) Self-administered drug treatments for acute migraine headache, Duke Center for Health Policy Research (prepared for Agency for Health Care Policy and Research). 2003. http://www.clinpol.mc.duke.edu

Guidetti V, Galli F, Fabrizi P, Giannantoni AS, Napoli L, Bruni O, Trillo S. (1998). Headache and psychiatric comorbidity: Clinical aspects and outcome in an 8 year follow-up study. Cephalalgia 18: 455-62.

Holroyd K, Stensland M, Lipchik GL, Hill KR, O'Donnell FS, Cordingley G. (2000). Psychosocial correlates and impact of chronic tension-type headaches. Headache 40: 3-16.

Holroyd KA, Creer T. (1986) Self-management of chronic disease: Handbook of Clinical Interventions and Research. New York, Academic Press.

Holroyd KA, France JL, Cordingley GE, Rokicki LA, Kvaal SA, Lipchik GL, McCool HR. (1995) Enhancing the effectiveness of relaxation/thermal biofeedback training with propranolol HCI. J Consult Clin Psychol 63: 327-330.

Holroyd KA, Lipchik GL. (1998) Psychological management of recurrent headache disorders: Empirical basis for clinical practice. Best practice: Developing and promoting empirically supported interventions, 193-212 (K. S. Dobson and K. D. Craig). Newbury Park, CA, Sage.

Holroyd KA, Lipchik GL. (2001) Behavioral management of recurrent headache disorders. Wolff's Headache and Other Headache Pain, 562-598 (S. D. Silberstein, R. B. Lipton and D. J. Dalessio). New York, NY, Oxford University Press.

Holroyd KA, O'Donnell FJ, Stensland M, Lipchik GL, Cordingley GE, Carlson BW. (2001) Management of chronic tension-type headache with tricyclic antidepressant medication, stress-management therapy, and their combination: a randomized controlled trial. JAMA 285: 2208-2215.

Holroyd KA,Penzien DB. (1986). Client variables in the behavioral treatment of recurrent tension headache: A meta-analytic review. J Beh Med 9: 515-536.

Holroyd KA, Penzien DB.(1990). Pharmacological vs. nonpharmacological prophylaxis of recurrent migraine headache: A meta-analytic review of clinical trails. Pain 42: 1-13.

Holroyd KA,Penzien DD, Cordingley GE. (1991) Propranolol in the management of recurrent migraine: A meta-analytic review. Headache 31: 333-340.

Hu XH, Markson LE, Lipton RB, Stewart WF, Berger ML. (1999) Burden of Migraine in the United States: Disability and economic costs. Arch Intern Med 159: 813-818.

Limmroth V, Katsarava Z, et al. (2002) Features of medication overuse headache following overuse of different acute headache drugs. Neurology 59: 1011-1014.

Lipchik GL, Holroyd K, et al. (2002) Cognitive-behavioral management of recurrent headache disorders: a minimal-therapist contact approach. Psychological approaches to pain management, 356-389 (D. C. Turk and R. S. Gatchel). New York, Guilford Pubs.

Lipton RB, Hamelsky SW, et al. (2000) Migraine, quality of life, and depression: a population based study. Neurology 55: 629-635.

Lipton RB, Hamelsky SW, et al. (2001) Epidemiology and impact of headache. Wolff's Headache and Other Headache Pain, 85-107 (S. D. Silberstein, R. B. Lipton and D. J. Dalessio). New York, NY, Oxford University Press.

Lipton RB,Stewart WF, et al. (1997). Burden of migraine: Societal costs and therapeutic opportunities. Neurology 48 (Suppl. 3): S4-S9.

Martin VT, Behbehani MM. (2002) Towards a rationale understanding of migraine trigger factors. Med Clin North Am.

Mathew NT. (1981) Prophylaxis of migraine and mixed headache: A randomized controlled study. Headache 21: 105-109.

McCrory D, Penzien D. (2001) Behavioral and Physical Treatments for Tension-Type and Cervicogenic Headache. DesMoines, Iowa, Foundation for Chiropractic Education and Research.

Merikangas KR, Angst J, Isler H. (1990) Migraine and psychopathology: Results of the Zurich cohort study of young adults. Arch Gen Psychiat 47: 894-852.

Merikangas KR, Merikangas JR, Angst J. (1993) Headache syndromes and psychiatric disorders: Association and family transmission. J Psychiatr Res 27: 197-210.

Mulligan M, Bernstein A. (2003) Headache clinic small group appointments in a health maintenance organization (HMO): Impact on disability, resource utilization, quality of life, and patient satisfaction. Headache 43(5 s94): 557.

Nash JM, Park ER. (in press) Cognitive-behavioral group treatment for disabling headache. J Clin Pain.

Olesen JC. (1988) Classification and diagnostic criteria for headache disorders, cranial neuralgias, and facial pain: Headache Classification Committee of the International Headache Society. Cephalalgia 8 (Suppl. 7).

Puca F, Genco S, Prudenzano MP, Savarese M, Bussone F, D'Amico D, Cerbo R, Gala C, Coppola MT, Gallai

V, Firenze C, Sarchielli P, Guazzelli M, Guidetti V, Manzoni G, Grannella F, Muratorio A, Bonuccelli U, Nuti A, Nappi G, Sandrini G, Verri AP, Sicuteri F, Marabini S. (1999) Psychiatric Comorbidity and psychosocial stress in patients with tension-type headache from headache centers in Italy. Cephalalgia 19: 159-164.

Rasmussen BK. (1993) Migraine and tension-type headache in a general population: Precipitating factors, female hormones, sleep pattern and relation to lifestyle. Pain 53: 65-72.

Rasmussen BK, Jensen R, Schroll M, Olesen J. (1991) Epidemiology of headache in a general population - a prevalence study. J Clin Epidemiol 44(11): 1147-1157.

Rasmussen BK, Lipton RB. (2000) Epidemiology of tension-type headache. The Headaches, 545-550 (J. Olesen, P. Tfelt-Hansen and K. M. A. Welch). Philadelphia, Lippincott Williams & Wilkins.

Reich BA, Gottesman M. (1993) Biofeedback and psychotherapy in the treatment of muscle contraction/tension-type headache. Headache Diagnosis and Interdisciplinary Treatment, 167-180 (C. D. Tollison and R. S. Kunkel). New York, Urban & Schwartzenberg.

Robbins L. (1994) Precipitating factors in migraine: A retrospective review of 494 patients. Headache 34: 214-216.

Sahota PK, Dexter JD. (1990) Sleep and headache syndromes: A clinical review. Headache 35: 80-84.

Scharff L, Marcus DA. (1994) Interdisciplinary outpatient group treatment of intractable headache. Headache 34: 73-78.

Schwartz BS, Stewart WF, et al. (1998) A population-based study of the epidemiology of tension-type headache. JAMA 279: 381-383.

Schwartz MS. (1995) Biofeedback: A practitioner's guide. New York, Guilford Press.

Silberstein SD, Dongmei L. (2002) Drug overuse and rebound headache. Curr Pain Headache Rep 6: 240-247.

Silberstein SD, Lipton RB, et al. (2002) Headache in clinical practice. London, England, Martin Dunitz.

Silberstein SD, Merriman G. (1997) Sex hormones and headache. Blue books of practical neurology: Headache, 143-176 (P. Goadsby and S. D. Silberstein). Boston, Butterworth Heinemann.

Silberstein SD, Rosenberg J. (2000) Multispecialty consensus on diagnosis and treatment of headache. Neurology 54: 1553-1554.

Smith T, Hilgeman J, et al. (2003) Focused migraine interventions improve the coordination of care in a provider group setting. Headache 43(5 s96): 554.

Von Korff M, Gruman J, et al. (1997) Collaborative management of chronic illness. Ann Intern Med 127(12): 1097-1102.

Wagner EH, Austin BT, et al. (1996) Improving outcomes in chronic illness. Managed Care Quarterly 4: 12-25.

APPENDIX A:
Clinical Trials in Tables 3 & 4

Andrasik F, Holroyd KA. (1980) A test of specific and nonspecific effects in the biofeedback treatment of tension headache. J Consult Clin Psychol 48: 575-586.

Andrasik F, Holroyd KA. (1983) Specific and nonspecific effects in the biofeedback treatment of tension headache: 3-year follow-up. J Consult Clin Psychol 51: 634-636.

Andreychuk T, Skriver C. (1975) Hypnosis and biofeedback in the treatment of migraine headache. Int J Clin Exp Hypn 23(3): 172-183.

Appelbaum KA, Blanchard EB, Nicholson NL, Radnitz C, Kirsch C, Michultka D. (1990) Controlled evaluation of the addition of cognitive strategies to a home-based relaxation protocol for tension headache. Beh Ther 21: 293-303.

Arena JG, Bruno GM, Hannah SL, Meador KJ. (1995) A comparison of frontal electromyographic biofeedback training, trapezius electromyographic biofeedback training, and progressive muscle relaxation therapy in the treatment of tension headache. Headache 35(7): 411-419.

Attanasio V, Andrasik F, Blanchard EB. (1987) Cognitive therapy and relaxation training in muscle contraction headache: efficacy and cost-effectiveness. Headache 27(5): 254-260.

Barrios F. (1980). Social skills training and psychosomatic disorders. In D. Rathjen & J. Foreyt (Eds.), Social Competence: interventions for children and adults (pp. 271-301). New York: Pergamon.

Bernal G. (1982) A study of the differential effectiveness of biofeedback and hypnosis for the treatment of tension headaches. In Proceedings of the Biofeedback Society of America, Chicago, IL.

Bild R, Adams HE. (1980) Modification of migraine headaches by cephalic blood volume pulse and EMG biofeedback. J Consult Clin Psychol 48((1)): 51-57.

Blanchard EB, Appelbaum KA, Nicholson NL, Radnitz CL, Morrill B, Michultka D, Kirsch C, Hillhouse J, Dentinger MP. (1990) A controlled evaluation of the addition of cognitive therapy to a home-based biofeedback and relaxation treatment of vascular headache. Headache 30: 371-376.

Blanchard EB, Appelbaum KA, Radnitz C, Morrill B, Michultka D, Kirsch C, Guarnieri P, Hillhouse J, Eveans DD, Jaccard J. (1990) A controlled evaluation of thermal biofeedback adn thermal biofeedback combined with cognitive therapy in the treatment of vascular headache. J Consult Clin Psychol 58: 216-224.

Blanchard EB, Nicholson NL, Radnitz CL, Steffek BD, Appelbaum KA, Dentinger MP. (1991) The role of home-practice in thermal biofeedback. J Consult Clin Psychol 59: 507-512.

Blanchard EB, Nicholson NL, Taylor AE, Steffek BD, Radnitz CL, Appelbaum KA. (1991) The role of regular home-practice in the relaxation treatment of tension headache. J Consult Clin Psychol 59: 467-470.

Blanchard EB, Theobold DE, Williamson DA, Silver BV, Brown DA. (1978) Temperature biofeedback in the treatment of migraine headaches. Archives of General Psychiatry 35: 581-588.

Brown J. (1984). Imagery coping strategies in the treatment of migraine. Pain 18(2): 157-167.

Chesney MA, Shelton JL. (1976) A comparison of muscle relaxation and electromyogram biofeedback treatments for muscle contraction headache. J Beh Ther Exp Psychiatr 7: 221-225.

Cox DJ, Freundlich A, Meyer RG. (1975) Differential effectiveness of electromyograph feedback, verbal relaxation instructions, and medication placebo with tension headaches. J Consult Clin Psychol 43(6): 892-898.

Cram J. (1980). EMG Biofeedback and the treatment of tension headaches: a systematic analysis of treatment components. Behav Ther 11: 699-710.

Daly EJ, Donn PA, Galliher MJ, Zimmerman JS. (1983) Biofeedback applications to migraine and tension headaches: A double-bind outcome study. BiofeedSelf-Regul 8: 135-152.

Daly EJ, Zimmerman JS, Donn PA, Galliher MJ. (1985) Psychophysiological treatment of migraine and tension headaches: a 12-month follow-up. Rehab Psychol 30(1): 3-10.

Figueroa JL. (1982) Group treatment of chronic tension headaches: A comparative treatment study. Beh Mod 6: 229-239.

Friedman H, Taub HA. (1984) Brief psychological training procedures in migraine treatment. Am J Clin Hypn 26(3): 187-200.

Gada GT. (1984) A comparative study of efficacy on EMG bio-feedback and progressive muscle relaxation in tension headache. Indian J of Psychiat 26: 121-127.

Gauthier J, Cote G, French D. (1994) The role of home practice in the thermal biofeedback treatment of migraine headache. J Consult Clin Psychol 62: 180-184.

Gauthier JG, Lacroix R, Cote A, Doyon J, Drolet M. (1985) Biofeedback control of migraine headaches: A comparison of two approaches. Biofeed Self-Regul 10: 139-159.

Hart JD. (1982, March 1982) EMG biofeedback and relaxation training in the treatment of tension headache: a psychophysiological evaluation. Paper presented at the Biofeedback Society of American, Chicago, IL.

Haynes SN, Griffen P, Mooney D. (1975) Electromyographic biofeedback and relaxation instructions in the treatment of muscle contraction headaches. Beh Ther 6: 672-678.

Holroyd KA, Andrasik F. (1978) Coping and the self-control of chronic tension headache. J Consult Clin Psychol 46: 1036-1045.

Holroyd KA, Andrasik F, Noble J. (1980) A comparison of EMG biofeedback and a credible pseudotherapy in treating tension headache. J Beh Med 3: 29-39.

Holroyd KA, Andrasik F, Westbrook T. (1977) Cognitive control of tension headache. Cog Ther Res 1:121-133.

Holroyd KA, France JL, Cordingley GE, Rokicki LA, Kvaal SA, Lipchik GL, McCool HR. (1995) Enhancing the effectiveness of relaxation/thermal biofeedback training with propranolol HCI. J Consult Clin Psychol 63: 327-330.

Holroyd KA, Holm JE, Hursey K.G, Penzien DB, Cordingley GE, Theofanous AG, Richardson SC, Tobin DL. (1988) Recurrent vascular headache: home-based behavioral treatment vs. abortive pharmacological treatment. J Consult Clin Psychol 56: 218-223.

Holroyd KA, Holm JF, Penzien DB, Cordingley GE, Hursey KG, Martin NJ, Theofanous A. (1989). Long-term maintenance of improvements achieved with (abortive) pharmacological and nonpharmacological treatments for migraine: Preliminary findings. Biofeed Self Regul 14(4): 301-308.

Holroyd KA, Nash JM, Pingel JD, Cordingley GE, Jerome A. (1991) A comparison of pharmacological (amitriptyline HCl) and nonpharmacological (cognitive-behavioral) therapies for chronic tension headaches. J Consult Clin Psychol 59: 387-393.

Holroyd KA, O'Donnell F, Stensland M. (2000) Management of chronic tension-type headache with (tricyclic) antidepressant medication, stress-management therapy and their combination: a randomized controlled trial. Unpublished Manuscript.

Hutchings DF, Reinking RH. (1976) Tension headaches: what form of therapy is most effective? Biofeed Self Regul 1(2): 183-190.

Janssen K. (1983) Differential effective-ness of EMG-feedback versus combined EMG-feedback and relaxation instructions in the treatment of tension headache. 27(3): 243-53.

Janssen, K., & Neutgens, J. (1986) Autogenic training and progressive relaxation in the treatment of three kinds of headache. Behaviour Research and Therapy, 24, 199-208.

Jurish SE, Blanchard EB, Andrasik F, Teders SJ, Neff DF, Arena JG. (1983) Home- versus clinic-based treatment of vascular headache. J Consult Clin Psychol, 51: 743-751.

Kewman D, Roberts AH. (1980) Skin temperature biofeedback and migraine headache: A double-blind study. Biofeed Self-Regul 5: 327-345.

Kondo C, Canter A. (1977) True and false electromyographic feedback: effect on tension headache. J Abnorm Psychol 86(1): 93-95.

Lacroix J, Clarke M, Bock JC, Doxey N, Wood A, Lavis S. (1983) Biofeed-back and relaxation in the treatment of migraine headaches: comparative effectiveness and physiological correlates. J Neurol Neurosurg Psychiatry 46(6): 525-532.

Lake A, Rainey J, Papsdorf JD. (1979) Biofeedback and rational emotive therapy in the management of migraine headache. J Appl Behav Anal 12: 127-140.

Machado H, Gomez de Machado A. (1985) The effectiveness of psycho-physiological techniques in the treatment of migraine headaches: a cross-cultural study in a Honduran population.

Martin PR, Mathews AM (1978) Tension headaches: Psychophysiological investigation and treatment. J Psychosom Res 22: 389-399.

Mathew NT. (1981) Prophylaxis of migraine and mixed headache: A randomized controlled study. Head-ache 21: 105-109.

McCrady A, Wauquier A, McNeil A, Gerard G. (1994) Effect of biofeedback-assisted relaxation on migraine headache and changes in cerebral blood flow velocity in the middle cerebral artery. Headache 34: 424-428.

Mitchell K, Mitchell D. (1971) Migraine: an exploratory treatment application of programmed behaviour therapy techniques. J Psychosom Res 15(2): 137-157.

Mosley TH, Grotheus CA, Meeks WM. (1995) Treatment of tension headache in the elderly: A controlled eval-uation of relaxation training and relaxation combined with cognitive-behavior therapy. J Clin Geropsychol 1: 175-188.

Mullinix J, Norton BJ, Hack S, Fishman MA. (1978) Skin temperature biofeedback and migraine. Headache 17: 242-244.

Murphy AI, Lehrer PM, Jurish S. (1990) Cognitive coping skills training and relaxation training as treatments for tension headaches. Beh Ther 21: 89-98.

Nicholson NL, Blanchard EB. (1993) A controlled evaluation of behavioral treatment of chronic headache in the elderly. Behav Ther 24(3): 67-76.

Paiva T, Nunes JS, Moreria A, Santos J, Teixeira J, Barbosa A. (1982) Effects of frontalis EMG biofeedback and diazepam in the treatment of tension headache. Headache 22: 216-220.

Penzien D, Johnson C, Carpenter D, Holroyd K. (1990) Drug vs. behavioral treatment of migraine: Long-acting propranolol vs. home-based self-management training. Headache 21: 300.

Richardson GM, McGrath PJ. (1989) Cognitive-behavioral therapy for migraine headaches: A minimal-therapist-contact approach versus a clinic-based approach. Headache 29: 352-357.

Rokicki LA, Holroyd KA, France CR, Lipchik GL, France JL, Kvaal SA. (1997) Change mechanisms associated with combined relaxation/EMG biofeedback training for chronic tension headache. Appl Psychophysiol Biofeed 22: 21-41.

Sargent J, Solbach P, Coyne L, Spohn H, Fegerson J. (1986) Results of a controlled, experimental, outcome study of non-drug treatments with a control of migraine headaches. J Beh Med 9: 291-323.

Schlutter LC, Golden C, Blume HG. (1980). A comparison of treatments for prefrontal muscle contraction headache. Br J Med Psychol 53: 47-52.

Silver B, Blanchard EB, Williamson DA, Theobald DE, Brown DA. (1979) Temperature biofeedback and relaxation training in the treatment of migraine headaches: One-year follow-up. Biofeed Self Regul 4: 359-366.

Sorbi M, Tellegen B. (1984) Ways of appraisal and coping in migraine provoking situations. Gedrag: Tijdschrift voor Psychologie 12(5): 5-15.

Sorbi M, Tellegen B. (1986) Differential effects of training in relaxation and stress-coping in patients with migraine. Headache 26(9): 473-481.

Sovak M, Kunzel M, Sternbach RA, Dalessio DJ. (1981) Mechanism of the biofeedback therapy of migraine: Volitional manipulation of the psychophysiological background. Headache 21: 89-92.

Spinhoven P, Linssen A, et al. (1992) Autogenic training and self-hypnosis in the control of tension headache. Gen Hosp Psychiatry 14(6): 408-415.

ter Kuile M, Spinhoven P, Linssen ACG, Zitman FG, Van Dyck R, Rooijmans HGM. (1994) Autogenic training and cognitive self-hypnosis for the treatment of recurrent headaches in three different subject groups. Pain 58: 331-340.

Tobin DL, Holroyd KA, Baker A, Reynolds RVC, Holm JE. (1988) Development and clinical trial of a minimal contact, cognitive-behavioral treatment for tension headache. Cog Ther Res 12: 325-339.

Vaccaro D, Feindler E. (1980) A comparison of cognitive and behavioral control of tension headaches. Paper presented at the AABT 14th annual convention, New York, NY.

Wittchen HA. (1983) A biobehavioral treatment program (SEP) for chronic headache patients. In: Perspectives in Research on Headache (K. A. Holroyd, B. Schlote & H. Zenz, Eds.), (pp. 183-192) Hogrefe, Toronto.

BEHAVIORAL TREATMENT OF PERSISTENT INSOMNIA

Charles M. Morin

INTRODUCTION

Insomnia is among the most frequent health complaints in medical practice and the most common of all sleep disorders in the adult population. Persistent insomnia is associated with significant morbidity and with increased health care costs (Breslau et al., 1996; Ford and Kamerow, 1989; Walsh, 2004). In the United States, about 10% of people suffer from chronic insomnia and the direct costs of insomnia have been estimated to be $13.9 billion per year (Walsh, 2004). Despite its high prevalence and burden for the individual and society, insomnia often goes unrecognized and remains untreated. Most patients who initiate treatment do so without professional consultation and often resort to a host of alternative remedies (herbal/dietary supplements) of unknown risks and benefits. When insomnia is brought to the attention of a health-care provider, typically a primary care physician, treatment is often limited to medication. Hypnotic medications may be clinically indicated and useful in some selected situations, but psychological and behavioral factors are almost always involved in perpetuating sleep disturbances over time and such factors must be addressed when treating persistent insomnia. This chapter reviews the evidence regarding the efficacy, effectiveness, and feasibility of psychological and behavioral interventions for insomnia.

Diagnostic Features and Definition

Insomnia entails a spectrum of complaints reflecting dissatisfaction with the quality, duration, or efficiency of sleep. These complaints may involve problems with falling asleep at bedtime, waking up in the middle of the night and having difficulty going back to sleep, waking up too early in the morning with an inability to return to sleep and, a complaint of nonrestorative or poor sleep quality. In addition, complaints of daytime fatigue, problems with memory and concentration, and mood disturbances (e.g., irritability, dysphoria) are typically associated with insomnia and are often the primary concerns prompting patients to seek treatment (Morin and Espie, 2003).

Several indicators are useful to evaluate the clinical significance of insomnia and the need for treatment. These markers include the severity, frequency, and duration of sleep difficulties and their associated daytime consequences. Although there is no standard definition, sleep-onset insomnia and sleep-maintenance insomnia are respectively defined by a latency to sleep onset and/or time awake after sleep onset greater than 30 minutes, with a corresponding sleep efficiency, the percentage of time devoted to sleep that was spent asleep, lower than 85 percent. Likewise, early morning awakening can be operationalized by a complaint of waking up earlier (more than 30 minutes) than desired, with an inability to go back to sleep, and before total sleep time reaches 6.5 hrs. Total sleep time alone is not a good index to define insomnia because there are individual differences in sleep needs. Some people may function well with as little as 5-6 hours of sleep and would not necessarily complain of insomnia, while others needing 9-10 hours may still complain of inadequate sleep. Thus, it is necessary to consider the impact of insomnia on a person's life to judge its clinical significance. As such, there must be evidence of impairments in social or occupational functioning or significant distress to make a diagnosis of insomnia.

A distinction is also made between situational/acute insomnia, a condition lasting a few days and often associated with life events or jet-lag, short-term/subacute insomnia (lasting between one and four weeks), and persistent insomnia, lasting more than one month. In sum, the diagnosis of insomnia is based on a subjective complaint of difficulties initiating and/or maintaining sleep, present three of more nights per week and lasting more than one month, that cause clinically significant distress or impairments of daytime functioning. Insomnia may be a secondary symptom of several conditions including medical, psychiatric, substance abuse and other sleep disorders; or, it can be a disorder in itself as in primary insomnia (American Psychiatric Association, 1997; American Academy of Sleep Medicine, 1997)

Prevalence and Significance of Insomnia

One-third of the adult population reports some insomnia symptoms, 9%-12% experience additional daytime consequences, and 6% meet criteria for an insomnia syndrome (Ohayon, 2002). In primary care medicine, about 20% of patients report signficant sleep disturbances (Hohagen et al., 1993). Insomnia is secondary to a medical, psychiatric, or other sleep disorder in more than 60% of the cases and is a primary syndrome in the remaining 40%. Insomnia is more prevalent among women, middle-aged and older adults, shift workers, and patients with medical or psychiatric disorders. Difficulties initiating sleep are more common among young adults, and problems maintaining sleep are more frequent among middle-aged and elderly adults. Persistent insomnia can produce a significant burden for the

individual and for society, as evidenced by reduced quality of life, increased absenteeism and reduced productivity at work, and higher health-care costs (Ford and Kamerow, 1989; Simon and VonKorff, 1997; Walsh, 2004). It is also associated with increased risk of depression and chronic use of hypnotics and, among older adults with cognitive impairments, sleep disturbances may hasten placement in nursing home facilities.

Psychological and Behavioral Treatments

Treatment options for insomnia include basic sleep hygiene education, psychological and behavioral interventions, pharmacotherapy, and a variety of complementary and alternative therapies. The focus of this chapter is on the non-pharmacological therapies and, more specifically, on behavioral interventions that have been validated for persistent insomnia. These methods include sleep restriction (Spielman et al., 1987), stimulus control therapy (Bootzin et al., 1991), relaxation-based interventions, cognitive strategies, sleep hygiene education, and combined cognitive-behavioral therapy. A summary of those interventions is provided in Table 1; more extensive descriptions are available in other sources (Morin, 1993; Morin and Espie, 2003).

Table 1: Psychological and Behavioral Treatments for Primary Insomnias	
Therapy	**Description**
Stimulus control therapy	A set of instructions designed to reassociate the bed/bedroom with sleep and to re-establish a consistent sleep-wake schedule: (1) Go to bed only when sleepy; (2) get out of bed when unable to sleep; (3) use the bed/bedroom for sleep only (no reading, watching TV, etc); (4) arise at the same time every morning; (5) no napping.
Sleep restriction therapy	A method to curtail time in bed to the actual sleep time, thereby creating mild sleep deprivation, which results in more consolidated and more efficient sleep.
Relaxation training	Clinical procedures aimed at reducing somatic tension (e.g., progressive muscle relaxation, autogenic training) or intrusive thoughts (e.g., imagery training, meditation) interfering with sleep.

Table 1 cont.	
Cognitive therapy	Psychotherapeutic method aimed at changing faulty beliefs and attitudes about sleep, insomnia, and the next day consequences. Other cognitive strategies are used to control intrusive thoughts at bedtime and prevent excessive monitoring of the daytime consequences of insomnia.
Sleep hygiene education	General guidelines about health practices (e.g., diet, exercise, substance use) and environmental factors (e.g., light, noise, temperature) that may promote or interfere with sleep. This may also include some basic information about normal sleep and changes in sleep patterns with aging.
Cognitive-behavior therapy	A combination of any of the above behavioral (e.g., stimulus control, sleep restriction, relaxation) and cognitive procedures.

The main objectives of psychological and behavioral approaches are to target those factors that perpetuate or exacerbate sleep disturbances. Such features may include hyperarousal, poor sleep habits, irregular sleep-wake schedules, and misconceptions about sleep and the consequences of insomnia. Although numerous factors can precipitate insomnia, when it becomes a persistent problem, psychological and behavioral factors are almost always involved in perpetuating it over time; hence, the need to target those factors directly in treatment (Spielman and Glovinsky, 1991). Another goal of treatment is to teach patients self-management skills to cope more adaptively with residual sleep disturbances that may persist even after therapy.

Evidence for Efficacy, Durability, and Generalizability

Two sources of evidence can be used to summarize treatment efficacy, including mean effect sizes obtained from meta-analyses and outcomes from individual studies using a randomized clinical trial design. Table 2 provides a summary of effect sizes obtained from four meta-analyses (Morin et al., 1994; Murtagh and Greenwood, 1995; Smith et al., 2002), inlcuding one that focused exclusively on the treatment of insomnia in older adults (Pallesen, 1998). Table 3 provides a summary of treatment studies evaluating the

efficacy of psychological and behavioral treatments for both primary and secondary insomnia. Only randomized clinical trials published since 1990 and providing follow-ups of a minimum duration of three months are listed in the table; other studies not meeting these criteria (e.g., case series) may also be discussed in the text but are not listed in that table. For each listed study, patients' demographics, types of treatment, duration of treatment and follow-ups, and a summary of outcomes are presented.

Evidence for efficacy. Clinical findings from more than 50 clinical trials (> 2000 patients) conducted in the 80's and early 90's and evaluating non-pharmacological interventions for insomnia have been summarized in two meta-analyses (Morin et al., 1994; Murtagh and Greenwood, 1995). Two additonal meta-analyses have been conducted including one that focused on older adults (Pallesen, 1998) and another one on comparative outcomes between psychological and pharmacological approaches (Smith et al., 2002). One additional review/practice parameters paper commissioned by the American Academy of Sleep Medicine (Morin et al., 1999) also summarized the findings of non-pharmacological interventions for insomnia. Evidence from these different sources show that behavioral interventions produce reliable changes in several sleep parameters (see Table 2), including sleep-onset latency (effect sizes (d, the mean difference in standard deviation units) ranging from 0.41 to 1.05), number of awakenings (0.25-0.83), duration of awakenings (0.61-1.03), total sleep time (0.15-0.49), and sleep quality ratings (0.94-1.14). Based on Cohen's criteria, the magnitude of those therapeutic effects is large (i.e., $d > 0.8$) for sleep latency and sleep quality and moderate (i.e., $d > 0.5$) for other sleep parameters. Effect sizes are apparently smaller for studies conducted with older adults (all studies conducted prior to 1998), although more recent studies have shown that older adults respond to treatment as well as young and middle-adults (this issue is discussed further below). Effect sizes for behavioral interventions are similar to those obtained for benzodiazepine-receptor agonists (Smith et al., 2002; Nowell et al., 1997), with a slight advantage for psychological treatment on measures of sleep onset latency and sleep quality and for pharmacotherapy on total sleep time. When transformed into a percentile rank, these data indicate that approximately 70% to 80% of patients with insomnia benefit from psychological and behavioral treatments.

Table 2. Summary of treatment outcomes (mean effect sizes (d)) based on meta-analyses.

Authors	SOL	FNA	WASO	TST	SQ
Morin et al. (1994)	0.88	0.53	0.65	0.42	n/a
Murtagh & Greenwood (1995) [a]	0.87 (0.58 - 1.16)	0.63 (0.63 - 0.63)	n/a	0.49 (0.49– 0.49)	0.94 (0.28– 1.60)
Pallesen et al. (1998) [a]	0.41 (0.24 - 0.58)	0.25 (0.01 - 0.49)	0.61 (0.42 - 0.80)	0.15 (-0.02- 0.31)	n/a
Perlis et al. (2002) [b] Pharmacotherapy Behavioral Therapy	0.45 (0.28) 1.05 (0.76)	0.97 (1.00) 0.83 (1.30)	0.89 (0.29) 1.03 (0.19)	0.84 (0.76) 0.46 (0.62)	1.20 (1.30) 1.44 (1.20)

[a] The 95% CI is reported with each effect size.
[b] The standard deviation is reported with each effect size.
Note: SOL=sleep onset latency; FNA = frequency of nighttime awakenings; WASO= wake after sleep onset; TST=total sleep time; SQ = sleep quality; n/a = not available.

In terms of absolute changes across sleep parameters, data from quantitative reviews show that treatment reduces subjective sleep-onset latency from an average of 60-65 minutes at baseline to about 35 minutes post-treatment. The duration of awakenings is decreased from an average of 70 minutes at baseline to about 38 minutes following treatment. Total sleep time is increased by 30 minutes, from 6 hours to 6.5 hours after treatment, and ratings of sleep quality are enhanced with treatment. Thus, for the average insomnia patient, treatment effects may be expected to reduce sleep onset latency and wake after sleep onset by an average of about 50% and to bring the absolute values of those sleep parameters below or near the 30-min cut-off criterion initially used to define sleep-onset or maintenance insomnia. Treatment effects are similar for sleep-onset and sleep-maintenance problems, although fewer studies have targeted the later type and particularly early morning awakening problems. Overall, findings from meta-analyses represent fairly conservative estimates of treatment effects as they are based on averages computed across all psychological and behavioral interventions and insomnia diagnoses (i.e., primary and secondary). On the other hand, although the majority of patients benefit from treatment, it appears that only a small proportion (20%-30%) of them achieves full remission and that a significant proportion of patients continues to experience residual sleep disturbances (Espie et al., 2001; Morin et al., 1999a).

Treatment outcome has been documented primarily with prospective daily sleep diaries. Several studies have complemented those findings with data from polysomnography (Edinger et al., 2001; Morin et al., 1999b; Jacobs et al., 1993) and with wrist-actigraphy (Hauri, 1997; Espie et al., 2001; Guilleminault et al., 1995). Although the magnitude of improvements is usually smaller on those objective measures, they parallel clinical changes reported on daily sleep diaries. For example, in a study of older adults with sleep maintenance insomnia (Morin et al., 1999b), average baseline values for wake time after sleep onset were 62 min for diaries and 73 min for polysomnographic measures. Post-treatment means were 29 min for the diary and 35 min for polysomnography, yielding improvement rates of 54% and 51%, respectively for the two assessment methods. In a study of sleep-onset insomnia (Jacobs et al., 1993), baseline sleep latencies were 77 min (diary) and 84 min (polysomnography); at post-treatment, these values had decreased to 19 min and 21 min. respectively, on both measurement methods. In another study (Edinger et al., 2001), sleep efficiency increases of 8% and 12% were obtained for PSG and diary measures respectively following CBT. Collectively, these findings indicate that treatment does not only alter sleep perception on daily diaries, but also produce objective changes on PSG sleep continuity measures. Except for a modest increase in stages 3-4 following sleep restriction, there is little evidence of changes in sleep stage with psychological and behavioral treatment.

Comparative effectiveness of therapies.

Comparative studies of behavioral interventions have shown that stimulus control and sleep restriction therapies are more effective than relaxation and sleep hygiene education (Engle-Friedman et al., 1992; Edinger et al., 2001; Friedman et al., 1991; Lichstein et al., 2001; Morin et al., 1994; Murtagh and Greenwood, 1995). Sleep restriction tends to produce better outcomes than stimulus control in terms of improving sleep efficiency and sleep continuity, but it also decreases total sleep time during the initial intervention. There is a trend for relaxation methods focusing on cognitive arousal (i.e., reducing intrusive thoughts at bedtime) to yield slightly greater improvements than those targeting somatic arousal. Although some basic education about sleep is incorporated to almost all behavioral interventions of insomnia, sleep hygiene education produces little impact on sleep when used as the only intervention (Edinger & Sampson, 2003; Engle-Friedman et al., 1992). Formal cognitive therapy has not been evaluated as a single treatment modality, although it is increasingly incorporated as one key therapeutic component in multifaceted interventions (Edinger et al., 2001; Espie et al., 2001; Morin et al., 1999).

Psychological, behavioral, and cognitive interventions are not incompatible with each other and can easily be combined. As indicated in Table 3, multi-component therapy is becoming the standard approach to treating insomnia. This approach typically includes a behavioral (stimulus control, sleep restriction and, sometimes, relaxation), a cognitive (cognitive restructuring therapy), and an educational (sleep hygiene) component, hence the name cognitive-behavior therapy (CBT). There is no strong evidence that this multi-component approach is more effective than any of its single components. However, the appeal of this approach may come from the fact that it is consistent with a multi-

Table 3. Randomized Clinical Trials of Psychological and Behavioral Interventions for Insomnia with Follow-Ups of at Least 3 Months (1990-2004)

Author(s) (year)	Patients N, % of female, mean age	Diagnosis	Treatment conditions	Treatment (Weeks/hrs) Follow-Up (months)	Outcomes
Baillargeon et al. (2003)	65 58.0 67.4	Primary insomnia and hypnotic-dependent insomnia	Medication taper; Combined taper + CBT (sleep restriction, stimulus control, cognitive therapy, sleep hygiene)	8/12 12	A greater proportion of participants in the combined treatment group reported complete hypnotic withdrawal at posttreatment (77% vs. 38%) and at 12-month FU (70% vs. 24%). No sleep data reported.
Bastien et al. (2004)	45 64.4 41.8	Primary insomnia	CBT (individual); CBT (group); CBT (telephone consultations)	8/ 8 (ind.) 8/12 (group) 8/3 (tel.) 6	All treatment modalities produced significant improvements in WASO, TWT and SE that were maintained for 6 months after treatment completion. At post-treatment, 64% of participants had SE > 80%. TST increased from post to 3-month FU.
Currie et al. (2000)	60 55.0 45.0	Insomnia secondary to chronic pain	CBT (stimulus control, sleep restriction, education, cognitive therapy, relaxation); Wait-list control	7/14 3	Treated patients improved more than controls on SOL (55 min to 28 min), SE (72% to 85%), WASO, and sleep quality. They also showed less motor activity on nocturnal actigraphy recordings. Benefits well maintained at FU. No group difference in pain ratings, depressive symptoms, and medication use.

Note: SOL=sleep onset latency; WASO=wake after sleep onset; SE=sleep efficiency; TST=total sleep time; TWT=total wake time; PSG=polysomnography; CBT=cognitive behavior therapy; FU=longest available follow-up; NA = information not available.

Table 3 continued

Author(s) (year)	Patients N, % of female, mean age	Diagnosis	Treatment conditions	Treatment (Weeks/hrs) Follow-Up (months)	Outcomes
Edinger et al. (2001)	75 46.7 55.8	Primary insomnia	CBT (sleep restriction, stimulus control, cognitive therapy/education); Progressive muscle relaxation; Placebo (psychological)	6/6 6	CBT produced larger subjective reductions of WASO (54%) than relaxation (16%) or placebo (12%). PSG changes were smaller but CBT was also more effective. Clinically significant improvements achieved by 64% of CBT, 12% of relaxation, and 8% of placebo patients. Sleep changes maintained at 6 months FU.
Edinger & Sampson (2003)	20 10 51.0	Primary insomnia	CBT (abbreviated version); Sleep hygiene information	2/1 3	Six of ten patients treated with CBT obtained at least a 50% reduction in WASO compared to none among the 10 patients in the control sleep hygiene education group.
Engle-Friedman et al. (1992)	53 66.0 59.6	N/A	Sleep hygiene; Sleep hygiene/relaxation; Sleep hygiene/stimulus control; Wait-list control	4/4 24	Improvements on measures of SOL and number of awakenings in all treatments but not in the control condition. Stimulus control more effective at post and 2-year FU. No changes on PSG measures.
Espie, Inglis, Tessier et al. (2001)	139 68.3 51.4	Primary insomnia	CBT (stimulus control, sleep restriction, relaxation, cognitive therapy); Wait-list control	6/5 12	Significant reductions of SOL (61 to 28 min) and WASO in CBT but not in control. Significant increase of TST at FU; 84% of patients initially using hypnotics remained drug-free at follow-up.
Friedman et al. (1991)	22 63.6 69.2	Primary insomnia	Sleep restriction; Relaxation	4/4 3	Improvement rates for sleep restriction were twice that of relaxation (33% vs 16% for WASO). SE was increased from 67% to 83% with sleep restriction; total sleep time was increased by 51 minutes at FU from baseline.

416

Table 3 continued

Author(s) (year)	Patients N, % of female, mean age	Diagnosis	Treatment conditions	Treatment (Weeks/hrs) Follow-Up (months)	Outcomes
Friedman et al. (2000)	39 66.7 64.2	Primary insomnia	Sleep hygiene/sleep restriction; Sleep hygiene/sleep restriction + optional daytime nap; Sleep hygiene	4/NA 3	Few between- and within- group differences in treatment efficacy. Sleep diary data showed that SE increased more rapidly in the conditions including sleep restriction. TST (derived from actigraphy data) was lower at the end of treatment and returned near baseline levels at FU for the three conditions.
Guillemi-nault et al. (1995)	30 56.3 44.0	Primary insomnia	Stimulus control/sleep hygiene; Stimulus control/sleep hygiene/ exercise; Stimulus control/sleep hygiene/ bright light	4/NA 9-12	All three conditions improved on measures of SOL and TST but only the bright light condition showed statistically significant changes over time. Outcome corroborated with actigraphy.
Hauri (1997)	26 73.1 47.7	Primary insomnia	Sleep hygiene/relaxation; Sleep hygiene/relaxation /medication; Wait-list control	6/6 10	The two treatments were more effective than control at posttreatment. At FU, subjects treated with the behavioral approach alone had a higher SE (83%) than the combined intervention (79%). Actigraphy used to document outcome.
Jacobs et al. (2004)	63 69.8 47.1	Primary insomnia	CBT (sleep hygiene, stimulus control, relaxation, cognitive therapy); Pharmacotherapy (zolpidem 10 mg); Combined CBT + Pharmacotherapy; Placebo (medication)	6/2.5 12	CBT produced the greatest changes in SOL and SE, yielded the largest number of good sleepers after treatment and produced best long-term outcomes. Combined treatment provided no advantage over CBT alone. For example, SOL was reduced by 50% in CBT (68 min to 34 min), 47% in combined therapy, 18% in pharmacotherapy, and 11% for placebo.

Table 3 continued

Author(s) (year)	Patients N, % of female, mean age	Diagnosis	Treatment conditions	Treatment (Weeks/hrs) Follow-Up (months)	Outcomes
Lichstein et al. (2000)	44 50 68.6	Insomnia associated with medical or psycholo-gical conditions	Multi-component behavioral treatment (sleep hygiene, stimulus control, relaxation); Wait-list control	4/4 3	Treated participants showed greater improvement on WASO, SE, and sleep quality than control participants. WASO reduced by 31 min at follow up relative to 8 min in controls; SE increased by 11% (vs. 3%). 57% of treated patients showed clinical improvement in SE compared with 19% of untreated group. No difference in outcomes between patients with insomnia secondary to psychological or medical conditions.
Lichstein et al. (2001)	74 72.6 68.03	Primary insomnia	Relaxation; Sleep restriction; Placebo (psychological)	6/5 12	All three conditions improved subjective but not PSG-defined sleep parameters. Effect sizes was small at post treatment (0.2) and moderate (around 0.5) at follow-up. Sleep restriction was the most effective treatment.
Mimeault & Morin (1999)	54 59.2 50.8	Primary insomnia	Self-help CBT manual; Self-help CBT manual plus weekly phone consultation; Wait-list control	NA/6 3	The two treatments showed significant changes on SE and TWT, whereas the control did not. The addition of a phone consultation provided a slight advantage during treatment but not at follow-up.
Morgan et al. (2003)	209 67.5 65.4	Primary insomnia and hypnotic-dependent insomnia	CBT (stimulus control, relaxation, cognitive therapy, sleep hygiene, medication withdrawal); Treatment as usual	6/6 6	CBT showed greater improvement on subjective measures of sleep quality and continuity and greater decrease of hypnotic medications. Evidence of significant cost offsets at follow up, accounted for by reductions of usage of sleep medications and health care services.

Table 3 continued

Author(s) (year)	Patients N, % of female, mean age	Diagnosis	Treatment conditions	Treatment (Weeks/hrs) Follow-Up (months)	Outcomes
Morin et al. (1993)	24 70.8 67.1	Primary insomnia	CBT (stimulus control, sleep restriction, cognitive therapy, education); Wait-list control	8/12 12	CBT was effective in reducing WASO and in increasing SE (69% à 83%). Results were corroborated by PSG data. Therapeutic gains were maintained at 3 and 12-month FU.
Morin, Colecchi, et al. (1999)	78 64.0 65.0	Primary insomnia	CBT (stimulus control, sleep restriction, sleep hygiene, cognitive therapy); Pharmacotherapy; CBT + Pharmacotherapy; Placebo (medication)	8/12 24	The three active treatments were more effective than placebo at posttreatment. The combined approach improved sleep more than either single component. CBT participants sustained their clinical gains at FU, whereas those treated with medication alone did not.
Morin et al. (2004)	76 50.0 62.5	Primary insomnia and hypnotic-dependent insomnia	CBT (stimulus control, sleep restriction, cognitive therapy, sleep hygiene); Medication taper; Combined CBT + taper	10/15 12	90% reduction in the quantity and 80% in the frequency of benzodiazepine use; 63% were drug-free at posttreatment. No group differences on these measures. Modest but significant improvement of sleep during treatment in all three conditions: SE (71 to 74%), TWT (142 to 112 min.), TST (359 to 326 min.) in all three conditions. Patients receiving CBT showed additional sleep improve-ments (e.g., TWT decreased from 137 to 93 min).
Pallesen et al. (2003)	55 83.6 69.8	Primary insomnia	Sleep hygiene/ relaxation Sleep hygiene/ stimulus control; Wait-list control	4/2 6	No significant differences in treatment effect between the intervention types. SE and life satisfaction both in favour of sleep hygiene plus stimulus control. ES associated with pre-post treatment change on sleep measures are of medium size. Treatment effects were maintained in both groups.

Table 3 continued

Author(s) (year)	Patients N, % of female, mean age	Diagnosis	Treatment conditions	Treatment (Weeks/hrs) Follow-Up (months)	Outcomes
Rybarcsyk et al. (2002)	38 57.8 67.8	Insomnia associated with medical illness	CBT (stimulus control, sleep restriction, cognitive therapy, relaxation, sleep hygiene); Relaxation; Wait-list control	8/12 4	Compared to control, CBT group had significant improvement on five of seven self-reported sleep measures. Clinically significant changes at follow up were obtained for 54 % of CBT patients, 35 % of relaxation patients and 6% of controls.
Sanavio et al. (1990)	40 65.0 39.6	Primary insomnia	EMG biofeedback; Cognitive therapy; Stimulus control/relaxation; Wait-list control	2/6 36	All three treatments more effective than reducing SOL (37% vs 1%) and WASO 1%). Benefits were maintained at 1 and 3

Note: SOL=sleep onset latency; WASO=wake after sleep onset; SE=sleep efficiency; TST=total sleep time; TWT=total wake time; PSG=polysomnography; CBT=cognitive behavior therapy; FU=longest available follow-up; NA = information not available.

dimensional etiological model of persistent insomnia and that it addresses different facets presumed to perpetuate sleep disturbances (Espie, 2002; Morin and Espie, 2003; Spielman and Glovinsky, 1991).

A few studies have examined what specific components of multi-faceted interventions contribute most to treatment outcomes. In a follow-up study of patients who had completed CBT for insomnia, Harvey and colleagues (Harvey et al., 2002) found that the most critical ingredients associated with long-term sleep improvements were stimulus control and sleep restriction, followed by cognitive restructuring. Relaxation was the most frequently endorsed component (79% of respondents), but it did not predict improvement on any of the sleep outcome variables. Other studies have examined the association between changes in sleep beliefs and attitudes and sleep improvements. Reductions of dysfunctional sleep cognitions during treatment were correlated with sleep improvements at post-treatment, and fewer dysfunctional cognitions at post-treatment were associated with better maintenance of sleep changes over time (Edinger et al., 2001; Morin et al., 2002). With increasing evidence that CNS hyperarousal is implicated in primary insomnia, there is a need for greater attention to identify the biological, as well as the psychological, mechanisms responsible for sleep changes.

Long-term outcomes.

A fairly robust finding across behavioral treatment studies is that treatment produces stable changes in sleep patterns over time. All studies listed in Table 3 have follow-ups of a minimum duration of three months (average of 9 months). The data indicate that changes in sleep latency and wake after sleep onset observed at post-treatment are well maintained after treatment completion, and sometimes up to 24 and even 36 months later (Engle-Friedman et al., 1992; Morin et al., 1999b; Sanavio et al., 1990). Although interventions that restrict the amount of time spent in bed may yield only modest

increases (and even a reduction) of sleep time during the initial treatment period, this parameter is usually improved at follow-ups, with total sleep time often exceeding 6.5 hours. Long-term outcome must be interpreted cautiously, however, as few studies report long-term follow-ups and, among those that do, attrition rates increase over time. In addition, it is important to keep in mind that a substantial proportion of those patients with chronic insomnia who benefit from short-term therapy may remain vulnerable to recurrent episodes of insomnia in the long-term. As such, there is a need to develop and evaluate the effects of long-term, maintenance therapies to prevent or minimize the frequency and severity of those episodes (Jindal et al., 2004).

Generalizability of treatment outcomes.

Until recently, most treatment studies had focused on primary insomnia in otherwise healthy, young, and medication-free patients. An important question that naturally arose was whether the findings obtained in those studies generalized to patients with comorbid medical or psychiatric disorders. Findings from clinical case series (Morin et al., 1994; Dashevsky and Kramer, 1998; Perlis et al., 2000) suggest that patients with medical and psychiatric conditions can also benefit from insomnia-specific treatment, even though these patients continue to have more symptoms following therapy than with those who suffer from primary insomnia. Recent controlled studies have also shown that cognitive-behavior therapy is effective for treating insomnia associated with chronic pain (Currie et al., 2000), cancer (Quesnel et al., 2003), and with various medical conditions in older adults (Lichstein et al., 2000; Rybarczyk et al., 2002). In general, the findings from secondary insomnia studies indicate that baseline and post-treatment scores on insomnia symptom measures are usually more severe among patients with comorbid psychiatric and medical disorders, but the absolute changes on those outcomes during treatment are comparable to patients with primary insomnia.

Insomnia is age-related and there is a significant increase in the use of sleep medications as people grow older. The natural quesiton is how effective are behavioral interventions for insomnia in older adults? Although findings from earlier studies (see Pallesen, 1998 for a review) suggest that older adults did not respond to behavioral treatment as well as younger adults, more recent studies have clearly shown that this segment of the population responds just as well to insomnia treatment, particularly when they are well screened for other sleep disorders that may increase in incidence in older age (e.g., restless legs syndrome, sleep apnea). Indeed, nine of the twenty studies listed in Table 3 were conducted with older adults presenting with either primary insomnia or insomnia associated with comorbid medical or psychological conditions (e.g., Friedman et al., 2000; Lichstein et al., 2000; 2001; Morin et al., 1993; 1999; 2004; Morgan et al., 2003; Pallesen et al., 2003; Rybarcsyk et al., 2002). Behavioral treatment is also beneficial with medicated as well as with unmedicated patients with insomnia. Three clinical trials have recently shown that a supervised, structured, and time-limited withdrawal program, with or without cognitive-behavior therapy, can facilitate discontinuation of hypnotic medications among older adults with insomnia who are prolonged users (Baillargeon et al., 2003; Morin et al., 2004; Morgan et al., 2003).

Unresolved research questions

Despite significant progress made in the treatment of insomnia over the last decade, there are still several unresolved issues for the future. These issues are concerned with the specificity of treatment effects, as well as with their magnitude and clinical significance; the transfer of knowledge, more specifically dissemination of evidence-based treatments and improving access to behavioral interventions in most healthcare systems, remains a challenge.

First, although there is evidence supporting the *efficacy* of psychological and behavioral treatment for insomnia, there is still little information about the *specificity* of this treatment modality and its active therapeutic mechanisms responsible for sleep improvements. With a few notable exceptions which have used attention-placebo conditions (Edinger et al., 2001; Lichstein et al., 2001), most clinical trials of behavioral therapies have used wait-list control groups, precluding the unequivocal attribution of treatment effects to any specific ingredient of psychological and behavioral treatment. The lack of a pill-placebo control equivalent in psychological outcome research makes it difficult to determine what percentage of the variance in outcomes is due to specific therapeutic ingredients (i.e., restriction of time in bed, cognitive restructuring), the measurement process (i.e., self-monitoring), or to non-specific factors (e.g., therapist attention, patients' expectations).

Another challenge for the future is to optimize outcome. Although the majority of individuals treated with behavioral interventions are considered treatment responders, only a minority (15-20%) achieve full remission, and a subtantial proportion continue experiencing residual, though occasional, sleep difficulties. Some ongoing clinical trials are currently examining the optimal dosage of therapy (Edinger et al., 2000) and whether the addition of long-term, maintenance and individualized therapy, would enhance outcome. Additional clinical trials are also examining whether the addition of sleep medication to behavioral intervention improves or worsens short- and long-term outcome. As current evidence suggest that behavioral interventions are indicated primarily for persistent insomnia, and medication for acute insomnia, there is also a need to examine more closely the role of behavioral therapy for situational insomnia. This is an important question because inidividuals who initiate hypnotic medication for acute insomnia may be at risk of staying on this treatment regimen longer than is initially intended.

Despite increasing evidence documenting the costs and morbidity of insomnia on quality of life, abseenteeism and reduced productivity at work, there is still little evidence that sleep improvements, either with behavioral or medication therapies, lead to significant reduction of this morbidity (see Morgan et al., 2003; Morin, 2003). This remains an important challenge because there is a significant discrepancy between the estimated prevalence of insomnia and the actual number of individuals who receive treatment. A related isssue is that it is often assumed that medication is less expensive and produces faster results than the more costly and time-consuming behavioral interventions. However, with the evidence suggesting that treatment gains are much better sustained over time with behavioral interventions, one might hypothesize that behavioral interventions would also be more cost-effective than pharmacological therapy. Randomized and prospective clinical trials evaluating cost-effectiveness of alternative therapies would be very informative to document this critical issue.

On the practical side, an important challenge for the future will be to more efficiently disseminate the evidence that is currently available. Despite the accumulation of data-based evidence suggesting that behavioral therapy is as effective as medication in the short-term, and more effective in the long-term, insomnia remains, for the most part, untreated; and, when treatment is initiated, it is typically limited to pharmacotherapy. There is a need to increase both physicians' and mental-health practitioners' knowledge of empirically-validated behavioral interventions for insomnia and, of course, increase access to such interventions through primary care services. Some studies have recently documented the usefullness of different treatment implementation models using nurse practitioners (Espie et al., 2001), internet (Ström et al., 2004), telephone consultations (Bastien et al., 2004), and self-

help materials (Mimeault and Morin, 1999) that would facilitate access to those interventions.

Useful Ressources for Health Professionals

Treatment manuals and reference materials

Morin CM, Espie CA. Insomnia: a clinical guide to assessment and treatment. New York: Kluwer Academic/Plenum Publishers; 2003.

Morin CM, Insomnia: psychological assessment and management. New York, NY: Guilford Press; 1993.

Perlis M, Lichstein (2003). (Eds.). *Treatment of sleep disorders : Principles and practice of behavioral sleep medicine.* New York, NY: John Wiley & Sons.

www.therapyadvisor.org (NIMH site promoting scientifically-based psychotherapy)

Professional and Research Organizations

American Academy of Sleep Medicine
www.aasmnet.org

National Center for Sleep Disorders Research
www.nhlbi.nih.gov/about/ncsdr

Patient Support and Advocacy Groups

American Insomnia Association
www.americaninsomniaassociation.org

National Sleep Foundation
www.sleepfoundation.org

REFERENCES

American Psychiatric Association (1994). Diagnostic and Statistical Manual of Mental Disorders (DSM-IV). Washington, DC: American Psychiatric Association.

American Sleep Disorders Association (1997). International Classification of Sleep Disorders: Diagnostic and Coding Manual. Revised ed. Rochester, MN: American Sleep Disorders Association.

Baillargeon L, Landreville P, Verreault R, Beauchemin J-P, Morin CM. (2003). Discontinuation of benzodiazepines among older insomniacs adults treated through cognitive-behavioral therapy combined with gradual tapering: a randomized trial. CMAJ 169:1015-1020.

Bastien C, Morin, CM, Ouellet MC, Blais FC, Bouchard S. (2004). Cognitive-behavior therapy for insomnia: comparison of individual therapy, group therapy, and telephone consultations. J Consul Clin Psychol 4:653-659.

Bootzin RR, Epstein D, Wood JM. (1991). Stimulus control instructions..In: Hauri P, editor. Case Studies in Insomnia (19–28). New York (NY): Plenum Press.

Breslau N, Roth T, Rosenthal L, Andreski P. (1996). Sleep disturbance and psychiatric disorders: a longitudinal epidemiological study of young adults. Biol Psychiatry 39:411-418.

Currie SR, Wilson KG, Pontefract AJ, deLaplante L. (2000). Cognitive-behavioral treatment of insomnia secondary to chronic pain. J Consul Clin Psychol 68:407-416.

Dashevsky B, Kramer M. (1998). Behavioral treatment of chronic insomnia in psychiatrically ill patients. J Clin Psy 59:693-399.

Edinger JD, Sampson WS. (2003). A primary care "friendly" cognitive behavioral insomnia therapy. Sleep 26:177-82.

Edinger JD, Wohlgemuth WK, Radtke RA, Marsh GR, Quillian E. (2001). Cognitive behavioral therapy for treatment of chronic primary insomnia: a randomized controlled trial. JAMA 285:1856-1864.

Edinger JD, Wohlgemuth WK, Radtke RA, Marsh GR, Quillian E. (2001). Does cognitive-behavioral insomnia therapy alter dysfunctional beliefs about sleep? Sleep 24:591-599.

Edinger JD, Wohlgemuth WK, Radtke RA, Marsh GR. (2000). Dose response effects of behavioral insomnia therapy. Sleep 23:310.

Espie CA, Inglis SJ, Harvey L. (2001). Predicting clinically significant response to cognitive behavior therapy for chronic insomnia in general medical practice: analyses of outcome data at 12 months posttreatment. J Consul Clin Psychol 69:58-66.

Espie CA, Inglis SJ, Tessier S, Harvey L. (2001). The clinical effectiveness of cognitive behaviour therapy for chronic insomnia: implementation and evaluation of a sleep clinic in general medical practice. Behav Res Ther 39:45-60.

Espie CA. (2002). Insomnia: conceptual issues in the development, persistence, and treatment of sleep disorders in adults. Annual Review of Psychology 53:215-243.

Ford DE, Kamerow DB. (1989). Epidemiologic study of sleep disturbances and psychiatric disorders: an opportunity for prevention? JAMA 262:1479-1484.

Friedman L, Bliwise D, Yesavage JA, Salom SR. (1991). A preliminary study comparing sleep restriction and relaxation treatments for insomnia in older adults. J Gerontology 46:1-8.

Friedman L, Benson K, Noda A, Zarcone V, Wicks DA, O'Connell K, Brooks JO, Bliwise D, Yesavage J. (2000). An actigraphic comparison of sleep restriction and sleep hygiene treatments for insomnia in older adults. J Geriatr Psychiatry Neurol 13:17-27.

Guilleminault C, Clerk A, Black J, Labanowski M, Pelayo R, Claman D. (1995). Nondrug treatment trials in psychophysiological insomnia. Arch Intern Med 155:838-844.

Harvey L, Inglis SJ, Espie CA. (2002), Insomniacs' reported use of CBT components and relationship to long-term clinical outcome. Behav Res Ther 40:75-83.

Hauri PJ. (1997). Insomnia: can we mix behavioral therapy with hypnotics when treating insomniacs? Sleep 20:1111-1118.

Hohagen F, Rink K, Kappler C, et al. (1993). Prevalence and treatment of insomnia in general practice: a longitudinal study. Eur Arch Psychiatry Clin Neurosci 242:329-336.

Jacobs GD, Benson H, Friedman R. (1993). Home-based central nervous system assessment of a multifactorial behavioral treatment of chronic sleep-onset insomnia. Behav Ther 24:159-174.

Jacobs GD, Pace-Schott EF, Stickgold R, Otto MW. (2004). Cognitive behavior therapy and pharmacotherapy for insomnia: A randomized controlled trial and direct comparison. Arch Intern Med 164:1888-1896.

Jindal RD, Buysse DJ, Thase ME. (2004). Maintenance treatment of insomnia: what can we learn from the depression literature? Am J Psychiatry 161:19-24.

Lichstein KL, Peterson BA, Riedel BW, Means MK, Epperson, MT, Aguillard RN. (1999). Relaxation to assist sleep medication withdrawal. Behavior Modification 23:379-402.

Lichstein KL, Riedel BW, Wilson NM, Lester KW, Aguillard RN. (2001). Relaxation and sleep compression for late-life insomnia: a placebo-controlled trial. J Consult Clin Psychol 69:227-239.

Lichstein KL, Wilson NM, Johnson CT. (2000). Psychological treatment of secondary insomnia. Psychol Aging 15:232-240.

Mimeault V, Morin CM. (1999). Self-help treatment for insomnia: bibliotherapy with and without professional guidance. J Consult Clin Psychol 67:511-519.

Morgan K, Dixon S, Mathers N, Thompson J, Tomeny M. (2003). Psychological treatment for insomnia in the management of long-term hypnotic drug use: A pragmatic randomized controlled trial. British J Gen Prac 53:923-928.

Morin CM, Bastien C, Guay B, Radouco-Thomas M, Leblanc J, Vallières, A, Blais FC. (2004). Insomnia and chronic use of benzodiazepines: a randomized clinical trial of supervised tapering, cognitive- behavioral therapy, and a combined approach to facilitate benzodiazepine discontinuation. Am J Psy 161:332-342.

Morin CM, Blais FC, Savard J. (2002). Are changes in beliefs and attitudes about sleep related to sleep improvements in the treatment of insomnia? Behav Res Ther 40:741-752.

Morin CM, Colecchi C, Stone J, Sood R, Brink D. (1999b). Behavioral and pharmacological therapies for late-life insomnia: a randomized clinical trial. JAMA 281:991-999.

Morin CM, Culbert JP, Schwartz SM. (1994;). Nonpharmacological interventions for insomnia: a meta-analysis of treatment efficacy. Am J Psychiatry 151:1172-1180.

Morin CM, Espie CA. (2003). Insomnia: a clinical guide to assessment and treatment. New York: Kluwer Academic/Plenum Publishers.

Morin CM, Hauri PJ, Espie CA, Spielman AJ, Buysse DJ, Bootzin RR. (1999a). Nonpharmacologic treatment of chronic insomnia. Sleep 22:1134-1156.

Morin CM, (1993). Insomnia: psychological assessment and management. New York, NY: Guilford Press.

Morin CM, Stone J, McDonald K, Jones S. (1994). Psychological management of insomnia: a clinical replication series with 100 patients. Behav Ther 25:291-309.

Morin CM. (2003). Measuring outcome in randomized clinical trials of insomnia therapies. Sleep Med Rev 7:263-279.

Murtagh DRR, Greenwood KM. (1995). Identifying effective psychological treatments for insomnia: a meta-analysis. J Consult Clin Psychol 60:79-89.

Nowell PD, Mazumdar S, Buysse DJ, Dew MA, Reynolds CF 3rd, Kupfer DJ. (1997) Benzodiazepines and zolpidem for chronic insomnia: a meta-analysis of treatment efficacy. JAMA 278:2170-2177.

Ohayon M. (2002). Epidemiology of insomnia: what we know and what we still need to learn. Sleep Med Rev 6:97-111.

Pallesen S, Nordhus IH, Kvale G, Nielsen GH, Havik OE, Johnsen BH, Skjotskift S. (2003). Behavioral treatment of insomnia in older adults: an open clinical trial comparing two interventions. Behav Res Ther 41:31-48.

Perlis M, Aloia M, Millikan A, Boehmler J, Smith M, Greenblatt D, et al. (2000). Behavioral treatment of insomnia: a clinical case series study. J Behav Med 23:149-161.

Quesnel C, Savard J, Simard S, et al. (2003). Efficacy of cognitive-behavioral therapy for insomnia in women treated for non-metastatic breast cancer. J Consul Clin Psychol 71:189-200.

Rybarczyk B, Lopez M, Benson R, Alsten C, Stepanski E. (2002). Efficacy of two behavioral treatment programs for comorbid geriatric insomnia. Psychol Aging 17:288-298.

Simon G, VonKorff M. (1997). Prevalence, burden, and treatment of insomnia in primary care. Am J Psychiatry 154: 1417-1423.

Smith MT, Perlis ML, Park A, Smith MS, Pennington J, Giles, DE, Buysse, DJ. (2002). Comparative meta-analysis of pharmacotherapy and behavior therapy for persistent insomnia. Am J Psy 159:5-11.

Spielman AJ, Glovinsky PB. (1991). The varied nature of insomnia. In: Hauri P, editor. Case Studies in Insomnia. New York (NY): Plenum Press 1-15.

Spielman AJ, Saskin P, Thorpy MJ. (1987). Treatment of chronic insomnia by restriction of time in bed. Sleep 10:45-56.

Ström S, Pettersson R, Andersson G. (2004). Internet-Based Treatment for Insomnia: a Controlled Evaluation. J Cons Clin Psychol 72:113-120.

Walsh JK. (2004) Clinical and socio-economic correlates of insomnia. J Clin Psychiatry 65(8): 13-19.

PRIMARY PREVENTION OF OBESITY

Nancy E. Sherwood and Robert W. Jeffery

INTRODUCTION

Obesity is a major public health problem in the United States. Increases in the prevalence of obesity over the last few decades have been dramatic in all age and social groups, heightening concern about health risks for children, adolescents, and adults (Center for Disease Control and Prevention, 2002a, 2002b; Kuczmarski et al., 1994; Mokdad et al., 1999; Must et al., 1999). Currently, over half of US adults and 15% of US children and adolescents are overweight and upward trends in prevalence show no sign of slowing (Center for Disease Control and Prevention, 2002a, 2002b). A continuation of current trends seems quite likely to lead to substantial increases in the number of people affected by obesity-related health conditions and in premature mortality (National Heart, Lung and Blood Institute, 1999; World Health Organization, 1997). Increased obesity is also likely to promote increases in psychosocial comorbidities, including binge eating disorder, depression, social bias, and discrimination (Falkner et al., 1999; Gortmaker et al., 1993; Marcus, 1993; Wadden and Stunkard, 1985). The economic burden of obesity is also sizeable. It adversely affects the costs of individual health care including obesity treatment and premature disability and death contribute to lost productivity (Oster et al., 1999; Thompson et al., 1998; Wolf and Colditz, 1996). Estimates of the total economic burden of obesity are as high as $100 billion per year (Wolf, 1998).

Given the alarming increase in obesity and the difficulty and cost of treating it, more and more attention is being paid to how it can be prevented. Although the field of obesity treatment has been making advances for over 30 years, research on obesity prevention is just emerging. The primary prevention of obesity is rapidly becoming a public health priority. It has been argued that prevention of weight gain may be easier, less costly and more effective than treating obesity after it has fully developed (World Health Organization, 1997). The goal of the chapter is to review the literature on primary prevention strategies for obesity and to discuss implications for future research in this area.

Although individuals are at risk for unhealthy weight gain at any point in their lives, several risk periods for excessive weight gain have specifically been identified and discussed: early adolescence, young adulthood (25 to 34 years of age), and for women, pregnancy and menopause (Obarzanek and Pratt, 2003; Wing, 1998). Additionally, certain population sub-groups have been identified as at particularly high risk for obesity and thus in need of preventive services (e.g., American Indians, African American females) (Cabellaro et al., 1998; Obarzanek and Pratt, 2003). This review focuses on intervention studies that have sought to prevent obesity by improving eating behavior and/or activity patterns. It includes prevention programs that have been conducted across different age and cultural groups. To identify obesity prevention studies, we conducted a computerized search of English-language peer-reviewed literature (in MEDLINE), searched our own files, consulted with colleagues, and searched the references of identified papers. Four studies with adults and ten studies with children or adolescents were identified. The review is restricted to studies in which prevention of obesity or weight gain was the specific goal and that utilized randomization to treatment and comparison groups. An overview of the studies is shown in Table 1.

427

Children and Adolescents

Primary prevention of obesity in childhood and adolescence is a critical need. Childhood-onset obesity is related to an increased likelihood of obesity later in life. The likelihood of persistence of obesity from childhood to adulthood is related to the degree and duration of obesity, family adiposity and age of the child. A recent study that tracked 854 infants over 21-29 years found that among obese 6 year olds about 50% remained obese. However, by the age of 10-14 years, 80% of obese children with at least one obese parent remained obese (Whitaker et al., 1997). Although obesity-associated morbidities occur most frequently in adults, consequences of excess weight, such as type 2 diabetes, are now occurring with greater frequency among obese adolescents (Fagot-Campagna et al., 2000). Obesity prevention programs for youth that have been conducted in both school and community-based settings are reviewed.

School-based Obesity Prevention Programs

Schools have the potential to make valuable contributions to the prevention of childhood obesity. More than 95% of youth, ages 5-17 are enrolled in school, and no other institution has as much continuous and intensive contact with children during their first two decades of life. The availability of classroom health education, physical education programs, food service, health services, and family contact make schools an attractive target for providing obesity interventions in a comprehensive manner. Although a number of school-based health promotion interventions have been conducted that focus on reduction of risk for cardiovascular disease (Nader et al., 1999), or on promoting healthy eating (Baranowski et al., 2000) and physical activity (Sallis et al., 1997), the small number of school-based studies that have focused specifically on obesity prevention are reviewed here.

Pathways

Across both genders and the age span, American Indians have a high prevalence of obesity and obesity-related health problems (Story et al., 2001). Pathways was a multisite school-based study designed to reduce the prevalence of obesity in American Indian school children (Cabellaro et al., 1998). Pathways was based on a partnership between five universities and seven American Indian communities: Gila River Indian Community, Tohono O'odham (University of Arizona); White Mountain Apache, San Carlos Apache (Johns Hopkins University); Oglala Lakota, Sicangu Lakota (University of Minnesota); and Navajo (University of New Mexico). Forty-one schools were randomized to either intervention (n = 21) or control (n = 20) conditions. Four integrated intervention components delivered in grades 3 through 5 included a classroom curriculum, school food service, physical activity, and family component. The classroom curriculum consisted of culturally appropriate lessons that focused on promoting healthful, low-fat eating behaviors, and increasing physical activity. The lessons were presented to each intervention school via two 45-minute sessions per week for a 12-week period during each school year. The school food service component involved working with food service staff to lower the amount of fat in breakfast and lunch meals to no more than 30% of total. The physical activity component included modifications in the frequency and quality of physical education classes (e.g., a minimum of three 30-minute sessions per week), the introduction of classroom activity breaks, and encouragement of active play during recess periods. The family intervention component included take-home materials for families and family gatherings at a school. After 3 years, no significant differences in the primary outcome variable (percent body fat) were observed (Lohman et al., 2001).

Table 1. Description of obesity prevention studies and major outcomes

Study Name	Study Type and Population	Intervention Description	Major Outcomes
Pathways Lohman et al., 2001; Himes et al., 2001; Going et al., 2001	Multi-site, group randomized trial 1: 21 schools 2: 20 schools from seven American Indian Communities	1: 3-year, multi-component intervention (e.g., classroom curriculum, school food service, physical activity, and family components) delivered in grades 3-5. 2: Control	No significant effect for BMI or PBF at 3 years. There were reductions in school service fat calories and child-reported fat intake.
Planet Health Gortmaker et al., 1999	Group randomized trial 1: 5 schools 2: 5 schools	1: 2-year, multidisciplinary (e.g., language arts, math, science and social studies), multi-component (e.g., classroom curriculum, physical activity, fitness funds) intervention 2: Control	**Obesity prevalence among girls at 2 years:** 1: 20.3%, 2: 23.7%, p< .03 **Greater remission of obesity among girls at 2 years:** 1: 31.5%, 2: 19.1%, p < .04
Robinson et al., 1999	Randomized trial 1: 1 school 2: 1 school	1: 6-month, 18-lesson classroom curriculum to reduce TV, videotape, and videogame use. 2: Control	**At 6 months,** **Decreased BMI:** 1. 18.7 (3.8), 2: 18.8 (3.8), p <.002 **Decreased Triceps skinfold thickness:** 1. 15.5 (6.0), 2: 16.5 (5.3), p < .002 **Decreased Waist circumference:** 1: 63.6 (9.0), 2: 64.7 (8.9) , p < .001 **Decreased Waist to hip ratio:** 1:0.83 (0.06), 2:0.84 (0.05), p <.001 There were also significant decreases in TV watching.
Dance for Health Flores et al., 1995	Randomized trial 1: 43 students 2: 38 students	1: 12-week "Dance for Health" physical activity curriculum (3 times per week) and health education curriculum (2 times per week) 2: Control	Decrease in BMI among girls at 12 weeks: 1: 22.1 (6.0), 2: 22.5 (4.4) , p < .05
Stolley and Fitzgibbon 1997	Randomized trial of African American girls and their mothers 1: 32 2: 33	1: 11-week culturally-tailored intervention based on the "Know Your Body" Program 2: Control	No significant differences in BMI were found. Intervention girls reported lower percent of calories from fat compared to control girls
GO GIRLS! Resnicow et al. 2000	Uncontrolled trial 1: 57 overweight, adolescent African American girls	1: 6-month culturally tailored program with three components: 1) interactive educational/behavioral sessions; 2) physical activity (e.g., dance); 3) Food preparation	No significant BMI, PBF, physical activity, or dietary intake differences between "high" and "low" attenders.

Study Name	Study Type and Population	Intervention Description	Major Outcomes
GEMS: Baylor Baranowski et al. (2003)	Randomized trial of 8 year old African American girls 1: 19 2: 16	1: 12-week program including a 4-week summer day camp followed by an 8-week Internet component for girls and their parents 2: 4-week Control summer day camp and 8-week general health Internet component for girls and their parents	No significant BMI, dietary intake or physical activity differences
GEMS: Stanford Robinson et al. (2003)	Randomized trial of 8-10 year old African American girls 1: 28 2: 33	1: 12-week program including dance classes offered five days per week and a home-based media use reduction program 2: Health Education program to promote healthful diet and physical activity including monthly community health lectures and newsletters	No significant BMI, dietary intake or physical activity differences
GEMS: Minnesota Story et al. (2003)	Randomized trial of 8-10 year old African American girls 1: 26 2: 28	1: 12-week program including a two day per week after school program with physical activity and nutrition components and a family-based component 2: Monthly Saturday morning program focused on self-esteem and cultural enrichment	No significant BMI, dietary intake or physical activity differences
GEMS: Memphis Beech et al. (2003)	Randomized trial of 8-10 year old African American girls 1: 21 child-targeted 2: 21 parent-targeted 3: 18	1: 12-week program targeting children, weekly 90 minute sessions focused on physical activity and nutrition. 2: 12-week program targeting parents, weekly 90 minute sessions focused on physical activity and nutrition. 3: : Monthly program meetings designed to enhance and prevent declines in self-esteem	No significant BMI. or physical activity differences. Girls in the parent-targeted intervention reported consuming fewer sweetened beverages compared to control girls.

Study Name	Study Type and Population	Intervention Description	Major Outcomes
Pound of Prevention-Pilot Forster et al. (1988)	Randomized trial 1: 110 2: 109	1: 12-month intervention including monthly newsletters, financial incentives and an optional 4-session education course 2: Control	**Decrease in weight at 1 year:** 1: -2.1 lbs (0.6), 2: -0.3 lbs (0.6), p < .03
Pound of Prevention Jeffery and French (200)	Randomized trial 1: 197 Education Only 2: 198 Education Plus Lottery 3: 414	1: 3-year intervention including monthly newsletters, optional in-person and home-based activities 2: 3-year intervention including monthly newsletters, optional in-person and home-based activities, and financial incentives 3: Control	No significant weight, dietary intake or physical activity differences.
Klem et al. (2000)	Randomized trial 1: 33 Group 2: 32 Correspondence 3: 37	1: 10-week intervention with weekly group meetings 2: 10-week intervention with weekly mailed lessons 3: Control	**Decrease in weight at 10-weeks between Group and Control:** 1: -1.9^a kg. (1.8), 2: -1.1 ^{a,b} (2.1), 3: -0.2^a (1.3). p < .03. No significant weight differences were observed at 6-month follow-up.
Women's Healthy Lifestyle Project Kuller et al. (2001)	Randomized trial 1: 260 2: 275	1: 5-year cognitive-behavioral program including 10 weekly sessions, 5 biweekly sessions, 3 bimonthly group meetings and group, mail or phone contact every 2-3 months 2: Control	**Decrease in weight at 6, 18, 30, 42, and 54 month follow-up:** 6 months, 1: -10.7 lbs, 2: -0.5 lbs, p < .05 18 months, 1: -6.7 lbs, 2: -0.6 lbs, p < .05 30 months, 1: -4.7 lbs, 2: +2.1 lbs, p < .05 42 months, 1: -2.2 lbs, 2: +3.6 lbs, p < .05 54 months, 1: -0.2 lbs, 2: +5.2 lbs, p < .05

Abbreviations: BMI=body mass index, PBF=percent body fat,

However, the Pathways intervention was effective at reducing fat calories in the school food service, and the reported fat intake among participants (Himes et al., 2001). Promising trends for physical activity increases in the intervention schools were observed (Going et al., 2001).

Planet Health

Planet Health was a school-based health behavior intervention program designed to reduce the prevalence of obesity among youth in grades 6-8 (Gortmaker et al., 1999). Ten schools were randomized to either intervention (n = 5) or control (n = 5) conditions. The interdisciplinary intervention took place over a 2-year period. Planet Health sessions focused on four behavioral changes: reducing television viewing to less than 2 hours a day, increasing moderate and vigorous physical activity, decreasing consumption of high fat foods, and increasing consumption of fruits and vegetables to five a day or more. A unique aspect of Planet Health was its interdisciplinary curriculum approach. The intervention material was integrated into instruction for traditional subject areas (i.e., language arts, math, science and social studies) and physical education classes. Each intervention school received the Planet Health program of teacher training workshops, classroom lessons, physical education materials, wellness sessions and fitness funds. Each year, the four behavioral goals were addressed in one lesson per major subject area, so that a total of 16 core lessons were taught per year. An additional lesson developed a 2-week school-wide "Power Down" campaign to reduce television viewing at home. The physical education component of the curriculum included thirty 5-minute microunits during each school year. Physical education materials included student self-assessment and goal setting related to both inactivity and activity. Students were encouraged to replace inactive time with moderate and vigorous activity. Monetary incentives of $400 to $600 were made available to teachers in intervention schools who submitted proposals for student activities consistent with Planet Health themes. Two-year outcome evaluation of the Planet Health program was promising. A gender difference in the effectiveness of the intervention was noted, with girls responding more positively than boys. Obesity prevalence among girls in the control schools increased from 21.5% to 23.7% over the 2-year intervention period, while obesity prevalence among girls in the intervention schools decreased from 23.6% to 20.3%. Controlling for baseline levels of obesity, the prevalence of obesity among girls

in the intervention schools was reduced compared to girls in the control schools (OR = 0.47, 95% CI = 0.24-0.93, p < .03). Additionally, greater remission of obesity among girls in the intervention schools compared to the control schools was observed (OR = 2.16, 95% CI = 1.07-4.35, p < .04). Examination of changes in the behavioral targets revealed that reductions in television viewing were associated with decreases in obesity among the girls; a similar effect was not reported for boys.

School-based Media Use Reduction

Robinson (1999) conducted a randomized controlled trial to examine the effects of a school-based intervention focused on reducing television, videotape and video game use on changes in adiposity, physical activity and dietary intake in third and fourth grade children. One school received the intervention and one school served as the control group. The intervention consisted of an 18 lesson, 6-month classroom curriculum to reduce media use.

Key intervention components included: self-monitoring of media use, a 10-day "TV Turn-Off" period, encouragement of limiting media use to 1 hour per day, parent newsletters, and "TV allowance" gadgets in each home that allowed parents to control the total amount of television access time per week. Children were also encouraged to become selective viewers of the media and advocates for reduced media use. Six-month outcome data showed that children in the intervention school showed significant relative decreases in body mass index (BMI; Adjusted change=-0.45, CI=-0.73 to -0.17, p < .002), tricep skin-fold thickness (Adjusted change=-1.47, CI=-2.41 to -0.54, p < .002), waist circumference (Adjusted change=-2.30, CI=-3.27 to -1.33, p < .001), and waist-to-hip ratios (Adjusted change=-0.02 (-0.03 to -0.01) compared to children in the control school. Statistically significant decreases in children's reported TV watching and meals eaten in front of the TV were observed in the intervention group relative to the controls. No significant differences between the two schools, however, were observed for changes in high fat food intake, moderate-to-vigorous physical activity, or fitness.

Dance for Health

Dance for Health (Flores, 1995) was a 12-week school-based intervention program designed to maintain or decrease weight and increase physical activity among low-income African American and Hispanic students. Forty-three students were randomized to Dance for Health and 38 to usual physical activity. Those in the intervention class received a health education curriculum twice a week and a mandatory dance oriented physical education class three times a week. The dance curriculum included 40 minutes for moderate-to-high intensity dance to culturally appealing, student chosen music, and 10 minutes for warm-up and cool down. The 25-session health education component addressed nutrition, exercise, obesity, unhealthy weight practices smoking prevention, substance abuse, stress management, and peer pressure. The 30-minute sessions included 10 minutes of didactics and 20 minutes of more interactive activities. Outcome evaluations were more promising for girls compared to boys. Girls in the intervention group had a significantly greater change in BMI compared to girls in the control group (intervention girls, -0.8 % change; control girls, +0.3% change).

Community-based Obesity Prevention Studies

Although the majority of health promotion programs for children have been provided in school settings, community-based programs represent untapped potential for obesity prevention interventions (Yung and Hammond, 1997). Although the school

environment confers many advantages including the reduction of barriers of cost and transportation and the provision of access to a large, already assembled population, schools may be limited in their ability to focus on culturally unique needs and characteristics because they typically serve children of different ethnic and cultural backgrounds. In contrast, many community-based health and social service organizations primarily serve one ethnic minority group and have positive reputation and connections in the community (Isaacs and Benjamin, 1991). Given the advantage community-based programs have in tailoring interventions for specific cultural groups, to date, community-based obesity prevention programs described in the literature have been targeted towards African American girls who are at particularly high risk for obesity and associated health consequences.

Obesity Prevention for African American Girls

Stolley and Fitzgibbon (1997) conducted the first published community-based obesity prevention study for African American girls. Participants were 65 African American girls and their mothers who lived in the inner city of Chicago and attended a local tutoring program. Interested mothers and daughters were randomized to either the treatment or attention placebo control group. Upon completion of baseline assessments, the groups attended separate one-hour program sessions for an 11-week period. The culturally tailored intervention program, based on the Know Your Body Program, focused on adopting a low-fat, low-calorie diet and increased physical activity. Key culturally-tailored components of the intervention included: 1) incorporating parental participation; 2) holding the program at the tutoring site for easy access and safety; 3) incorporating participants' food preferences and ease of access to specific foods into the dietary change component of the program; 4) using culturally relevant music and dance for intervention activities; and 5) using appropriate materials from magazines geared towards African Americans. Although no treatment effects on BMI were reported, results showed significant differences between the treatment and control mothers for daily saturated fat intake and percentage of calories from fat. Daughters in the treatment group also reported lower percent calories from fat relative to girls in the control group.

GO GIRLS!

GO GIRLS! was a pilot, community-based, nutrition and physical activity program designed for inner city, overweight African American girls (Resnicow et al., 2000). Participants were overweight (BMI $\geq$ 85th percentile for age and sex), 11 to 17 year-old African American girls who were recruited through public housing developments. Given the developmental nature of the program, no control group was included. The 6-month program included biweekly group sessions for the first 4 months and weekly sessions for the last 2 months. Each session included three components: 1) an interactive educational or behavioral session focused on program goals; 2) 30 to 60 minutes of physical activity (e.g., Hip Hop, Funk and "Afrobics" aerobic dance); and 3) preparation and tasting of low-fat, portion-controlled recipes (e.g., low-fat macaroni and cheese, oven "fried" chicken). Results showed that girls who were classified as "high attenders" (e.g., girls who attended at least half of the sessions) reported lower total energy and percentage of energy intake from fat at follow-up compared to "low attenders" although these differences were not statistically significant. No statistically significant differences between "high" and "low" attenders were observed for measures of physical activity, BMI, and percent body fat.

Girls health Enrichment Multi-site Studies (GEMS)

Phase I of GEMS was a National Heart, Lung, and Blood Institute-sponsored multicenter research program to develop and test 12-week pilot interventions to prevent excessive weight gain in 8 to 10 year old African-American girls (Obarzanek and Pratt, 2003). The GEMS initiative was funded given the lack of available information regarding what types of interventions, delivery channels and settings, and intervention messages would be most effective for preventing obesity in African American girls. Four field centers participating in GEMS (University of Memphis, University of Minnesota, Baylor College of Medicine, and Stanford University) independently developed and tested their own interventions but shared common eligibility criteria and key measurements. Since the pilot studies had a relatively short intervention period of 12 weeks and include small numbers of girls, they were not powered to detect statistically significant differences in weight, diet and activity outcomes. However, the descriptions of the programs and results provide valuable information in this developing area of research.

The Baylor GEMS Pilot Study: The Fun, Food and Fitness Project (Baranowski et al., 2003).

Thirty-five 8-year-old African American girls and their parents or caregivers were randomly assigned to the treatment (n = 19) or control (n = 16) condition. Intervention goals were as follows: 1) increase girls' fruit and vegetable consumption; 2) increase girls' intake of water; and 3) increase girls' participation in moderate to vigorous physical activity to 60 minutes per day. The intervention condition included a four-week summer day camp followed by an 8-week Internet intervention component for girls and their parents. The intervention day camp included training in dance, educational games to increase physical activity and fruit and vegetable intake, snack recipe preparation, goal setting, buddy groups, and the use of camp cheers as mnemonics for decision making, problem-solving and asking behaviors. The intervention websites for girls and parents featured a different message each week (e.g., fun physical activity at home, choosing fruits and vegetables for snacks). The girls intervention website featured a comic book with characters who attended the GEMS summer camp and were trying to obtain the diet and activity goals, problem solving activities, review of goal attainment for the previous week's goal, opportunities to set new goals, a photo album of girls from camp, an "ask the expert" feature, and linkages to websites that might be of interest to girls. The intervention parent web-site mirrored the girl website and included a comic book featuring parent/child interactions that modeled desired parenting behaviors, a parent poll of how best to encourage lifestyle changes, goal-setting activities, recipes, an "ask the expert" feature, and links to other websites, including the girls' website. The control condition included a "usual" 4-week summer day camp followed by an 8-week Internet program that asked girls to log-on once a month and provided links to general health and homework websites. The control parent website offered links to the girls' website as well as other websites with information on general health issues. Results showed no significant differences in BMI either at the end of the summer camp or at the end of the 12-week intervention period. However, at the end of the summer camp, there was a trend for lower BMI among the heavier girls in the intervention group compared to the heavier girls in the control group. Although trends were in the hypothesized direction, no significant treatment group differences were observed for physical activity or dietary intake behaviors.

The Stanford GEMS Pilot Study (Robinson et al., 2003)

Sixty-one 8 to 10 year old African American girls and their parents or caregivers were randomly assigned to the treatment (n = 28) or control (n = 33) condition. Intervention goals were to increase time spent in moderate-to-vigorous physical activity and to decrease time spent engaging in sedentary activity. GEMS Jewels dance classes were offered 5 days per week at three neighborhood community centers. Girls were encouraged to attend the dance classes as often as possible during the 12-week intervention period. Each daily session lasted for up to 2.5 hours (3:30 to 6:00 p.m.), beginning with a one-hour homework period and a healthful snack followed by 45 to 60 minutes of moderate-to-vigorous dance. Classes included traditional African dance, Hip-Hop, and Step. Each session ended with a 30-minute GEMS talk that focused on the meaning and importance of dance in the girls' lives and the African-American community and culture. Additional activities included costume creation, videotaping, and performances for families and friends. Female African American college students and recent college graduates with dance expertise led the sessions. The START (Sisters Taking Action to Reduce Television) intervention included five lessons delivered during home visits over the 12-week intervention period. A female African-American intervention specialist scheduled lesson times with each family and delivered the intervention to the participating girl and other family members who were available. The strategies promoted for reducing television viewing included nonselective reductions in total hours and/or access to television; selective reductions by day, time, context, or content; and displacement of viewing time with other activities (e.g., dance). Specific behaviors included self-monitoring, a 2-week TV-turnoff, and budgeting viewing hours. The lessons incorporated African and African-American history and cultural themes. Families were also given electronic TV time managers to help with budgeting TV time (TV Allowance, Miami, FL). Additionally, five newsletters were mailed to parents/guardians to reinforce the lessons and communicate updates on dance class activities. Girls and families randomized to the control group received a state-of-the-art information-based health education program that focused on promoting healthful diet and activity patterns. The control intervention included monthly community health lectures delivered by volunteers from the African-American task forces of the local chapters of the American Heart Association and the American Diabetes Association and 11 "Felicia's Healthy News Flash" newsletters mailed to girls and 5 "Stanford GEMS Health Report" newsletters mailed to parents. Newsletter content focused on reducing risks for obesity, heart disease, stroke, hypertension, and diabetes and included age-appropriate and culturally targeted educational materials from federal health agencies. Results showed that, although not statistically significant, there was a trend for girls in the intervention group to have a lower BMI at follow-up compared to girls in the control group. Nonsignificant trends for lower waist circumference; increased after-school physical activity; and reduced television, videotape, and video game were also observed. The treatment group significantly reduced reported household television viewing and dinners eaten while watching television.

The Minnesota GEMS Pilot Study: An After-School Obesity Prevention Program
(Story et al., 2003)

Fifty-four 8 to 10 year old African American girls and their parents or caregivers were randomly assigned to the treatment (n = 26) or control (n = 28) condition. Girls in the intervention group participated in a 12-week

after-school program called "Girlfriends for KEEPS," where KEEPS stood for Keys to Eating, Exercising, Playing, and Sharing. Intervention goals included: 1) increasing frequency of participation in sustained, moderate-to-vigorous intensity activities; 2) decreasing time spent in sedentary activities; 3) promoting enjoyment, physical competence, and self confidence in a range of physical activities; 4) decreasing consumption of high-fat foods; 5) increasing consumption of fruits and vegetables; 6) decreasing consumption of sweetened beverages; and 7) adopting healthy weight-related eating practices (e.g., portion size awareness, eating when hungry). Intervention meetings, designed in a "club meeting" format, were held twice a week for one hour after school at each of the three elementary schools. The intervention was taught by trained African-American GEMS staff. Club activities were comprised of fun, culturally appropriate, interactive, hands-on activities that emphasized skill building and practice of the particular health behavior message for that week. Weekly messages included drinking water more often than soda pop, increasing the consumption of fruits and vegetables, drinking low-fat milk, selecting low-fat foods for snacks, eating smaller portions of snacks, choosing smaller-sized and lower-fat entrees in fast food restaurants, increasing physical activity, watching less television, and enhancing self-esteem. A healthful snack, sometimes prepared by the girls, was offered at each club meeting. Girls participated in physical activity for a minimum of 20 minutes during each session. A variety and choice of activities were included such as dancing (ethnic, hip hop, aerobic), double-dutch jump rope, relay races, tag, and step aerobics. To keep girls' interest and participation, incentives were built into the program for attendance, setting short-term goals, and completing activities. These included attendance beads that together made a bracelet by the end of the intervention, water bottles, pedometers, jump ropes, and t-shirts. The intervention also included a family component designed to reinforce and support the healthy eating and physical activity messages delivered in the after-school program. The family component included weekly family packets sent home to the parents, family night events, encouragement telephone calls to parents to reinforce and support diet and activity goals they set for their family, and organized neighborhood walks. Girls randomized to the control condition participated in the "GEMS Club", a non-nutrition/physical activity low-intensity program that focused on promoting positive self-esteem and cultural enrichment. Participants attended monthly Saturday morning meetings (three meetings during the 12-week period), which included arts and crafts, self-esteem activities, creating memory books, and a workshop on African percussion instruments. Result showed no significant treatment group differences in BMI upon completion of the 12-week intervention period. However, promising trends were noted with girls in the intervention group showing higher levels of physical activity relative to girls in the control group at the follow-up measurement.

The Memphis GEMS Pilot Study: Child- and Parent-Targeted Interventions (Beech et al., 2003)

Sixty 8 to 10 year old African American girls were randomized to one of three groups: 1) a child-targeted intervention program; 2) a parent/caregiver-targeted program; or 3) a control condition. The child- and parent-targeted interventions were similar, allowing for evaluation of two different approaches to obtain the same objectives. Intervention goals included: 1) choosing a nutritionally balanced eating plan, including the reduction of high-fat food intake (particularly fast foods); 2) increasing water consumption and reducing

sweetened beverage intake; 3) increasing fruit and vegetable intake; and 4) promoting nutrition-related healthy behaviors and the recognition of health-compromising behaviors such as eating while watching television, meal skipping, and snacking when not hungry; 5) increasing the frequency of moderate to vigorous physical activity; 6) decreasing the frequency of sedentary behaviors; and 7) promoting enjoyment and self-efficacy in physical activity. The child-targeted intervention entitled "GEMS Jamboree" included weekly 90-minute intervention sessions for 12 weeks. Program structure included the following: 1) an introduction consisting of a welcome and a discussion of the basic concepts for the day (15 minutes); 2) a "Movin' It" physical activity component (30 minutes); 3) a "Munchin' It" nutrition component (30 minutes); and 4) a "Taking it Home" segment (15 minutes) in which the concepts of the day were reviewed, incentives (small gifts) were given, and motivation for healthy eating and the maintenance of physical activity were provided. The primary activity for the physical activity component was hip-hop aerobics. The nutrition component included interactive strategies designed to promote the dietary intake goals (e.g., taste testing, food preparation, food art). The parent-targeted intervention entitled "Eating and Activity Skills for Youth" (EASY) also included weekly 90-minute intervention sessions during the 12-week period. Program structure included: 1) "EASY Moves", a dance-based physical activity component; 2) "EASY Tips", a didactic nutrition segment; and 3) "EASY Fun", a segment alternating food preparation and nutrition-related games. The weekly intervention concluded with a session used to reinforce key points and to provide take-home materials (i.e., healthy recipes and small thematic incentives related to the weekly concepts). Childcare was provided, with non-nutrition or physical activity-related activities designed for the 8 to 10 year old daughters. Girls randomized to the control group attended three monthly 90-minute sessions over the 12-week pilot study that focused on improving self-esteem. Control group activities included arts and crafts, "friendship-building"/social support-type activities (e.g., "trust" games), and enjoyable games. Personalized greeting cards and general health information were mailed to participants bimonthly to maintain contact and build rapport. Results showed that compared to girls in the comparison condition, girls in the active conditions combined showed a nonsignificant trend for reduced BMI and waist circumference. Statistically significant intervention effects were observed for sweetened beverages, with girls in the parent-targeted intervention consuming fewer sweetened beverages compared to girls in the control group. No significant treatment group effects were observed for the physical activity or other dietary intake variables.

Two field centers from GEMS Phase I, the University of Memphis and Stanford University, are currently evaluating 2-year obesity prevention interventions for pre-adolescent African American girls in full-scale randomized trials

Adulthood

Both normal weight and overweight individuals are at risk for weight gain during adulthood. Between the ages of 30 and 55 years, average weight gain per year among adults in the US is .5 to 1 kg (Williamson et al., 1991). Slowing this rate of weight gain may help reduce the population impact of obesity. Behavior changes required to achieve and maintain large weight losses are difficult for most people. However, the premise behind weight-gain prevention programs is that behavior changes needed to prevent or reverse small weight gains with age may be easier to sustain.

Pound of Prevention (POP)

The POP studies (Forster et al., 1988; Jeffery and French, 1997, 1999) were the first completed obesity prevention studies in adults. The POP program was based on the hypothesis that gradual weight gain in adults is due in large part to the fact that people are not very attentive or motivated to correct the small changes in weight that lead to obesity or the small changes in eating and exercise habits that could prevent these weight gains. The goal of the POP interventions were to encourage participants to make small changes in their eating and activity habits to prevent weight gain with age. In the initial POP study, 219 participants were randomized to either weight-gain prevention treatment or no treatment for a 1-year period. Participants in the treatment group received monthly newsletters relating to weight management, participated in a financial incentive system, and were offered an optional four-session education course in the sixth month of the program. Significant treatment effects for weight change were found. At 1-year follow-up, participants in the intervention group showed a new weight loss of 1.8 lb compared to participants in the control group. Moreover, 82% of the intervention participants maintained or lost weight compared to 56% of control group participants.

In the full-scale POP study, participants were randomized to one of three conditions: Control (n = 414), Education (n = 197) , or Education Plus Lottery (n = 198) (Jeffery and French, 1999). Participants in the two education groups received monthly newsletters for 3 years that focused on five program messages. Education messages included: 1) paying attention to weight by self-weighing ≥ 1 time per week; 2) eating two servings of fruit per day; 3) eating three servings of vegetables each day; 4) reducing intake of high-fat foods; and 5) walking three times a week for ≥ 20 minutes. Participants returned a prestamped postcard each month on which they recorded adherence to program messages and their current weight. Participants in the Education Plus Lottery condition were offered a $100 lottery drawing each month for members who returned their postcards. Once every 6 months, participants were invited to participate in additional intervention in-person and home-based activities. Activities included four-session weight control classes, aerobics classes, a correspondence weight-loss course, and a home-based walking "marathon" competition. Participants in the POP study were on average 38 years old and were primarily female. About half of the participants were married. The average BMI was about 26 in the control and education + incentive groups, but was 27.5 in the education only group. Of note, study population included 400 low-income participants recruited from low-income neighborhoods and WIC clinics.

Participants returned an average of 68% of the newsletter postcards across the 3-year intervention period. Upon completion of the study, 80% reported having read most or all of the newsletters. Twenty-five percent of the participants participated in ≥ 1 supplementary activity (e.g., POP marathon, weight-loss correspondence course). Of note, the supplementary correspondence options were considerably more popular than the in-person opportunities (Sherwood et al., 1998). The overall mean weight change observed in the study population over 3 years was a gain of 1.7 kg, approximately .5 kg per year. Sixty-three percent of participants gained weight whereas only 37% maintained or lost weight. Point estimates for weight gain were slightly lower in both intervention groups than in the control group at each year. However, these differences fell far short of statistical significance. No significant intervention group differences were observed for energy intake, fat intake, or exercise. Significant group differences were observed for self-weighing frequency and a healthy weight-loss

practice index that included behaviors such as increasing fruit and vegetable intake and increasing exercise that were promoted by the POP program. Although POP was not successful in achieving its primary objective, several aspects of the results were informative. Newsletter mailings were shown to be a cost-effective way of communicating with large numbers of people over an extended period of time. Favorable behavioral, knowledge, and weight trends in the intervention groups were encouraging.

Obesity Prevention for Women

Klem et al. (2000) evaluated the acceptability of three different formats for prevention of weight gain among 25 to 34 year old women. One hundred two recruited participants were randomly assigned to one of three treatment formats: a weekly group meeting focused on modest dietary and physical activity changes, a weekly correspondence course with similar content, and a no-treatment control group who received a lifestyle brochure. After participants were assigned to a treatment group, they were asked whether they were willing to participate in that treatment format. Participants who refused were omitted from the study. Although similar numbers of randomized women verbally agreed to participate in their assigned treatment, a greater percentage of women actively participated in the correspondence option. Program efficacy was assessed by examining weight change at posttreatment (10 weeks) and 6-month follow-up. Of the 55 women who participated in the measurement session at the end of the 10-week intervention, participants in the group format showed the largest short-term changes in weight (group format: mean = -1.9 kg, sd = 1.8; correspondence format: mean = -1.1 kg, sd = 2.1; and control group: mean = -0.2 kg, sd = 1.3; $p < .03$). At 6-month follow-up, however, no significant treatment group differences in weight loss were observed.

Women's Healthy Lifestyle Project

The Women's Healthy Lifestyle Project tested the hypothesis that reducing consumption of saturated fat and cholesterol by decreasing total and fat calories and moderately increasing physical activity among "healthy" women would prevent the rise in LDL cholesterol and weight gain during menopause (Kuller et al., 2001; Simkin-Silverman et al., 1998 ; Simkin-Silverman et al., 1995). The intensive phase of the intervention consisted of 10 weekly sessions and then biweekly sessions for an additional 10 weeks. The maintenance phase included 3 monthly group meetings; 3 bimonthly group meetings; and group, mail, or telephone contact every 2 to 3 months thereafter. Additionally, participants were invited to attend a 6-week refresher program and received quarterly newsletters. Social and educational gatherings were held two to three times per year. Intervention goals were as follows: 1) lower fat intake to 25% of daily calories; 2) lower saturated fat intake to 7%; 3) lower cholesterol to 100 mg/day; 4) increase level of moderate intensity physical activity; and 5) prevent future weight gain by achieving a modest weight loss in all participants. Normal weight participants with a BMI < 24.4 were given a 5-lb weight-loss goal, mildly overweight participants with a BMI 24.5 to 26.4 were given a 10-lb weight-loss goal, and moderately overweight participants with a BMI ≥ 26.5 were given a 15-lb weight-loss goal. Both groups attended follow-up visits at 6, 18, 30, 42, and 54 months. Attendance at the follow-up visits averaged 93%, with 95% returning for the 54-month assessment. Across all the time periods, there was a significant weight change difference between the intervention and comparison group. Among women in the comparison group who participated in the assessments only and received no intervention, weight remained stable initially and then the typical increases in weight over time were observed so that at the end of the study participants were on average 5 lb heavier. Women in the intervention group initially lost weight and then gradually gained weight over time. Due to the initial weight loss, however, at the end of the 54-month period, women in the intervention group were at about their baseline weight as opposed to 5 lb heavier.

SUMMARY AND RECOMMENDATIONS

The field of obesity prevention has emerged in response to the worsening obesity epidemic and the lack of long-term success of obesity treatment programs. It has been suggested that obesity prevention may be more effective than obesity treatment, however, work in this area is in the early stages and empirical data supporting this view are lacking. This chapter has reviewed several weight-gain prevention programs targeted towards youth, adults, and specific ethnic groups. Programs have been conducted in both school and community settings, have been generally well received by participants, and have shown positive behavior change trends. To date, outcome evaluations have not yielded consistent effects on BMI and obesity prevalence. Considerably more work needs to be done in the area of obesity prevention before conclusions can be made about its efficacy and definitive recommendations can be made about best practices. Given the current state of obesity prevention, we suggest preliminary recommendations, areas for further investigation, and challenges for the primary prevention of obesity.

Recruitment and Retention

Recruitment and retention of participants in obesity prevention trials is a critical first step toward reducing the prevalence of obesity. Obesity prevention programs must be tailored to the audience of interest and packaged in such a way as to be attractive and accessible to participants. The majority of obesity prevention programs published in the literature have been successful in recruiting and retaining participants. The most impressive long-term follow-up rate was observed in the Women's Healthy Lifestyle trial with 95% of participants completing a 54-month follow-up assessment (Kuller et al., 2001). Community-based programs targeting youth have also shown high retention rates, however, such programs have been short-term, ranging from 10 weeks to 6 months. Maintaining high levels of interest and participation among youth and families over longer periods of time may be challenging.

Recruitment messages for obesity prevention programs have ranged from emphasizing preventing weight gain specifically (Jeffery and French, 1999) to focusing on more general messages of promoting healthy eating and physical activity (Baranowski et al., 2003; Beech et al., 2003; Robinson et al., 2003; Story et al., 2003). Recruitment messages need to capture the attention of the audience of interest. Obesity prevention programs targeting youth must focus not only on the health benefits of participation, but also on the social benefits of taking part. Another key issue for obesity prevention programs is attracting a target audience of normal weight adult participants. Participants in weight-gain prevention programs to date have tended to be heavier, with normal weight individuals less likely to participate. Since even normal weight adults are at risk for weight gain with age, strategies for attracting such participants to obesity programs are needed.

The optimal treatment modality for different audiences also needs further attention. Research with adults suggests a stronger preference for correspondence versus in-person programs (Klem et al., 2000;

Sherwood et al., 1998). Participants in the POP program were significantly more likely to take part in correspondence options compared to face-to-face program options. Klem et al. also reported that participants were more likely to take part in a correspondence program versus an in-person group program. However, short-term results suggested that participants in the in-person program lost more weight compared to those in the correspondence program. The efficacy of face-to-face programs may be enhanced by the greater accountability, structure, and support that is provided by this modality. Strategies for enhancing the intensity and effectiveness of correspondence programs are needed given their popularity and potential to reach a larger audience. A combination of initial face-to-face sessions and subsequent correspondence options as used in the Women's Healthy Lifestyle trial may be a viable option. Future weight-gain prevention efforts should focus on ways of increasing impact of correspondence contacts (e.g., tailoring of messages, increased frequency) and modalities for correspondence options (e.g., mail- or phone-based strategies, internet programs).

Intervention Goals

Refining intervention goals for obesity prevention is another key area for future investigation. Weight-gain prevention programs have tended to use strategies "inherited" from obesity treatment research. Diet-related intervention recommendations have included reductions in energy intake, fat intake and sweetened beverages, and increases in fruit and vegetable intake. Activity-related messages have included a focus on increasing time spent in moderate-to-vigorous physical activity and decreasing time spent in sedentary pursuits, primarily television viewing. An open question is whether weight-gain prevention strategies should be different from obesity treatment strategies, and, if so, in what ways should they be different?

The optimal specificity and intensity of obesity prevention messages deserves further investigation. The Pound of Prevention program included five messages: 1) paying attention to weight by self-weighing ≥ 1 time per week; 2) eating two servings of fruit per day; 3) eating three servings of vegetables each day; 4) reducing intake of high-fat foods; and 5) walking three times a week for ≥ 20 minutes (Jeffery and French, 1999). Although four of the five messages were quite specific, the message regarding reducing intake of high-fat foods was fairly general. Increasing the specificity of this message may have helped participants to better understand and adhere to program goals. For example, the Women's Healthy Lifestyle trial included specific recommendations about percent of calories from fat and saturated fat (Kuller et al., 2001).

In addition to greater specificity, obesity prevention messages may need to be more intense. An example of a more intense program goal could be the recommendation to lose weight as a weight-gain prevention strategy. Participants in the Women's Healthy Lifestyle trial were given a weight-loss goal depending upon their starting weight (Kuller et al., 2001). Evaluation data showed that women in the intervention group initially lost weight although they gradually gained weight over time. Due to the initial weight loss, however, at the end of the 54-month follow-up period, women in the intervention group were at about their baseline weight compared to women in the control group, who were approximately 5 lb heavier on average. These data suggest that modest weight-loss goals may be effective in preventing weight gain for as long as 5 years and are consistent with the results of two recent observational studies that have shown that weight losses of unknown cause over periods of 1 or 2 years are typically followed by weight regain, but that

there are net benefits relative to no weight loss lasting as long as 4 years (Field et al., 2001; Jeffery et al., 2002).

In addition to determining the optimal intensity and specificity of obesity prevention messages, more information is needed about what goals to include for which subgroups of individuals. Dietary intake goals in prevention programs have included recommendations about specific food groups (e.g., increases in fruit and vegetable intake, reductions in sweetened beverages, increases in water consumption) and macronutrient intake (e.g., reductions in fat intake). Obesity prevention programs may also need to include messages about total energy intake. Activity-related goals have included both increases in physical activity and decreases in sedentary behavior. Media use reduction appears to be a promising obesity prevention strategy among youth and should be explored as a strategy for adult populations. Weight-gain prevention programs also focus on behavioral strategies such as self-monitoring weight and teaching individuals to respond to small weight gains by making moderate behavioral changes such as increasing physical activity and/or decreasing caloric intake. Little information in known, however, about which of the above noted factors is most strongly associated with success in preventing excessive weight gain.

To summarize, challenges for obesity prevention programs include: 1) optimal recruitment and retention strategies and treatment modalities for different audiences; 2) increasing the intensity and specificity of program messages; 3) increasing the intensity and duration of programs; and 3) strategies for sustaining motivation for behavioral changes.

REFERENCES

Baranowski T, Baranowski J, Cullen KW, Thompson DI, Nicklas T, Zakeri IF, Rochon J. (2003) The Fun, Food and Fitness Project (FFFP): The Baylor

GEMS pilot study. Ethn Dis 13 (Suppl 1): S1-30-S1-39.

Baranowski T, Davis M, Resnicow K, Baranowski J, Doyle C, Lin LS, Smith M, Wang DT. (2000) Gimme 5 fruit and vegetables for fun and health: Outcome evaluation. Health Educ Behav 27:96-111.

Beech BM, Klesges RC, Kumanyika SK, Murray DM, Klesges L, McClanahan B, Slawson D, Nunnally C, Rochon J, McLain-Allen B, Pree-Cary J. (2003) Child- and parent-targeted interventions: The Memphis GEMS pilot study. Ethn Dis 13(Suppl 1): S1-40-S1-53..

Cabellaro B, Davis S, Davis CE, Ethelbah B, Evans M, Lohman T, Stephenson L, Story M, White J. (1998) Pathways: A school-based program for the primary prevention of obesity in American Indian children. J Nutr Biochem 9: 535-543.

Centers for Disease Control and Prevention (2002a). Prevalence of overweight among children and adolescents: United States, 1999-2000. Accessed on 1/15/03: http://www.cdc.gov/nchs/products/pubs/pubd/hestats/overwght99.htm

Centers for Disease Control and Prevention (2002b) Prevalence of overweight and obesity among adults: United States, 1999-2000. Accessed on 1/15/03: http://www.cdc.gov/nchs/products/pubs/pubd/hestats/obese/obse99.htm

Fagot-Campagna A, Pettitt DJ, Engelgau MM, Burrows NR, Geiss LS, Valdez R, Beckles GL, Saaddine J, Gregg EW, Williamson DF, Venkat Narayan KM. (2000) Type 2 diabetes among North American children and adolescents: An epidemiologic review and a public health perspective. J Pediatr 136:664-672.

Falkner NH, French SA, Jeffery RW, Neumark-Sztainer D, Sherwood NE, Morton N. (1999) Mistreatment due to weight: Prevalence and sources of perceived mistreatment in women and men. Obes Res 7:572-576.

Field AE, Wing RR, Manson JE, Spiegelman DL, Willett WC. (2001) Relationship of a large weight loss to long-term weight change among young and middle-aged US women. Int J Obes Relat Metab Disord 25:1113-1121.

Flores R. (1995) Dance for health: Improving fitness in African American and Hispanic adolescents. Public Health Rep 110:189-193.

Forster JL, Jeffery RW, Schmid TL, Kramer FM. (1988) Preventing weight gain in adults: A Pound of Prevention. Health Psychol 7:515-525.

Going SB, Stone E, Harnack L, Thompson J, Norman J, Stewart D, Corbin C, Hastings C, Eklund J; The Pathways Collaborative Research Group. (2001) The effects of the Pathways Obesity Prevention Program on physical activity in American Indian school children. Fed Am Soc Experi Biol 15:abstract 836.4.

Gortmaker SL, Must A, Perrin JM, Sobol AM, Dietz WH. (1993) Social and economic consequences of overweight in adolescence and young adulthood [see comments]. N Engl J Med 329:1008-1012.

Gortmaker SL, Peterson K, Wiecha J, Sobol AM, Dixit S, Fox MK, Laird N. (1999) Reducing obesity via a school-based interdisciplinary intervention among youth: Planet Health. Arch Pediatr Adolesc Med 153:409-418.

Himes JH, Cunningham-Sabo L, Gittelsohn J, Harnack L, Ring K, Suchindran C, Thompson J, Weber J; The Pathways Collaborative Research Group. (2001) Impact of the Pathways intervention on dietary intake of American Indian school children. Fed Am Soc Experi Biol 15:abstract 836.3.

Isaacs M, Benjamin M. (1991) Toward a Culturally Competent System of Care: Programs which Utilize Culturally Competent Principles, II. Washington,

DC: CASSP Technical Assistance Center, Center for Child Health and Mental Health Policy, Georgetown University Child Development Center.

Jeffery RW, French SA. (1997) Preventing weight gain in adults: Design, methods and one year results from the Pound of Prevention study. Int J Obes Relat Metab Disord 21:457-464.

Jeffery RW, French SA. (1999) Preventing weight gain in adults: The Pound of Prevention study. Am J Public Health 89:747-751.

Jeffery RW, McGuire MT, French SA. (2002) Prevalence and correlates of large weight gains and losses. Int J Obes Relat Metab Disord 26:969-972.

Klem ML, Viteri JE, Wing RR. (2000) Primary prevention of weight gain for women aged 25-34: The acceptability of treatment formats. Int J Obes Relat Metab Disord 24:219-225.

Kuczmarski RJ, Flegal KM, Campbell SM, Johnson CL. (1994) Increasing prevalence of overweight among US adults: The National Health and Nutrition Examination Surveys, 1960-1991. JAMA 272:205-211.

Kuller LH, Simkin-Silverman LR, Wing RR, Meilahn EN, Ives DG. (2001) Women's Healthy Lifestyle Project: A randomized clinical trial: Results at 54 months. Circulation 103:32-37.

Lohman TG, Going S, Stewart D, Cabellaro B, Stevens J, Himes J, Weber J, Thompson J, Davis E, Norman J; The Pathways Collaborative Research Group. (2001) The effect of Pathways Obesity Prevention Study on body composition in American Indian children. Fed Am Soc Experi Biol 15:abstract 836.9.

Marcus M. (1993) Binge eating in obesity. In: Binge Eating, Nature, Assessment, and Treatment (Fairburn CG, Wilson GT, eds), pp 77-96. New York, NY: Guilford Press.

Mokdad AH, Serdula MK, Dietz WH, Bowman BA, Marks JS, Koplan JP. (1999) The spread of the obesity epidemic in the United States, 1991-1998. JAMA 282:1519-1522.

Must A, Spadano J, Coakley EH, Field AE, Colditz G, Dietz WH. (1999) The disease burden associated with overweight and obesity. JAMA 282: 1523-1529.

Nader PR, Stone EJ, Lytle LA, Perry CL, Osganian SK, Kelder S, Webber LS, Elder JP, Montgomery D, Feldman HA, Wu M, Johnson C, Parcel GS, Luepker RV. (1999) Three-year maintenance of improved diet and physical activity: The CATCH cohort. Arch Pediatr Adolesc Med 153:695-704.

National Heart, Lung and Blood Institute. (1999) Clinical guidelines on the identification, evaluation, and treatment of overweight and obesity in adults. Bethesda, MD: NIH, NHLBI.

Obarzanek E, Pratt CA. (2003) Girls health Enrichment Multi-site Studies (GEMS): New approaches to obesity prevention among young African-American girls. Ethn Dis 13(Suppl 1): S1-1-S1-5.

Oster G, Thompson D, Edelsberg J, Bird AP, Colditz GA. (1999) Lifetime health and economic benefits of weight loss among obese persons. Am J Public Health 89:1536-1542.

Resnicow K, Yaroch AL, Davis A, Wang DT, Carter S, Slaughter L, Coleman D, Baranowski T. (2000) GO GIRLS!: Results from a nutrition and physical activity program for low-income, overweight African American adolescent females. Health Educ Behav 27:616-631.

Robinson TN. (1999) Reducing children's television viewing to prevent obesity: A randomized controlled trial. JAMA. 282:1561-1567.

Robinson TN, Killen JD, Kraemer HC, Wilson DM, Matheson DM, Haskell WL, Pruitt LA, Powell TM, Owens AS,

Thompson NS, Flint-Moore NM, Davis GJ, Emig KA, Brown RT, Rochon J, Green S, Varady A. (2003) Dance and reducing television viewing to prevent weight gain in African-American girls: The Stanford GEMS pilot study. Ethn Dis 13(Suppl 1):S1-65-S1-77.

Sallis JF, McKenzie TL, Alcaraz JE, Kolody B, Faucette N, Hovell MF. (1997) The effects of a 2-year physical education program (SPARK) on physical activity and fitness in elementary school students. Sports, Play and Active Recreation for Kids. Am J Public Health 87:1328-1334

Sherwood NE, Morton N, Jeffery RW, French SA, Neumark-Sztainer D, Falkner NH. (1998) Consumer preferences in format and type of community-based weight control programs. Am J Health Promo 13:12-18.

Simkin-Silverman LR, Wing RR, Boraz MA, Meilahn EN, Kuller LH. (1998) Maintenance of cardiovascular risk factor changes among middle-aged women in a lifestyle intervention trial. Womens Health 4:255-271.

Simkin-Silverman L, Wing RR, Hansen DH, Klem ML, Pasagian-Macaulay AP. Meilahn EN, Kuller LH. (1995) Prevention of cardiovascular risk factor elevations in healthy premenopausal women. Prev Med 24:509-517.

Stolley MR, Fitzgibbon ML. (1997) Effects of an obesity prevention program on the eating behavior of African American mothers and daughters. Health Educ Behav 24:152-164.

Story M, Davis S, Ethelbah B, Himes J, Holy Rock B, Stephenson L, Stevens J, Stone E; The Pathways Collaborative Research Group. (2001) Childhood obesity: A priority for prevention in American Indian school children. Fed Am Soc Experi Biol 15:abstract 836.10.

Story M, Sherwood NE, Himes JH, Davis M, Jacobs DR, Cartwright Y, Smyth M,

Rochon J. (2003) An after-school obesity prevention program for African-American girls: The Minnesota GEMS pilot study. Ethn Dis 13(Suppl 1):S1-54-S1-64.

Thompson D, Edelsberg J, Kinsey KL, Oster G. (1998) Estimated economic costs of obesity to US business. Am J Health Promot 13:120-127.

Wadden TA, Stunkard AJ. (1985) Social and psychological consequences of obesity. Ann Intern Med 103:1062-1067.

Whitaker RC, Wright JA, Pepe MS, Seidel KD, Dietz WH. (1997) Predicting obesity in young adulthood from childhood and parental obesity. N Engl J Med 337:869-73.

Williamson DF, Kahn HS, Byers T. (1991) The 10-year incidence of obesity and major weight gain in black and white US women aged 30-55 years. Am J Clin Nutr 53:1515S-1518S.

Wing RR. (1998) Obesity. In: Behavioral Medicine and Women: A Comprehensive Handbook (Blechman EA, KD Brownell KD, eds), pp 397-401. New York, NY: Guilford Press.

Wolf AM. (1998) What is the economic case for treating obesity. Obes Res 6(suppl):2S-7S.

Wolf AM, Colditz GA. (1996) Social and economic effects of body weight in the United States. Am J Clin Nutr 63:466S-469S.

World Health Organization. (1997, June) Obesity: Preventing and managing the global epidemic. Report of a WHO Consultation on Obesity, Geneva, Switzerland.

Yung B, Hammond W. (1997) Community-based interventions. In: Health-Promoting and Health-Compromising Behaviors Among Minority Adolescents (Wilson D, Rodriguez J, Taylor W, eds), pp. 269-297. Washington, DC: American Psychological Association.

BEHAVIORAL MANAGEMENT OF OBESITY

G. Ken Goodrick and Suzanne Kneuper

INTRODUCTION

The World Health Organization has defined obesity as a Body Mass Index above 30 kg/m^2 (weight/height^2) (WHO, 1998). In 1999, 34% of Americans were overweight (BMI between 25 and 29.9), and 27% were obese (National Center for Health Statistics, 1999). Although the rapid increase in prevalence of obesity over the last 20 years is unlikely to continue, current trends indicate that all Americans will be overweight by the year 2230 (Foreyt and Goodrick, 1995). Obesity is associated with an enormous burden of physical, economic and emotional suffering (Wadden et al., 2002).

The cause of obesity is a gradual accretion of stored energy as adipose tissue due to a surplus of calories taken in over calories expended in metabolism and activity. Obesity can be prevented and controlled if eating and exercise behaviors can be modified and the improvements maintained indefinitely. In ancient times, without modern technology, most people had to labor daily, and there were few foods processed to have high caloric density. Today however, under conditions of individual freedom to eat and (not) exercise ad libitum, an abundant food supply that is processed to increase appetite, and a reduced need to engage in physical activity, humans seem to become obese, even in cultures that value thinness.

Increases in obesity can be attributed to an individual's failure to eat and exercise prudently due to:

a) a lack of skill or knowledge about how to perform the prescribed behaviors
b) internal psychological factors that limit motivation to change behavior (low self-esteem, previous failure experiences)
c) susceptibility to external influences that operate through psychological paths to encourage overeating and underexercising (food marketing, restaurant practices, behavioral contagion, promulgation of the value of inactive leisure such as viewing TV while in a stuffed recliner chair, lack of time due to modern life)
d) external influences that operate through physiological paths to induce overeating (exposure to food stimuli that induce increases in appetite)
e) internal influences that operate through physiological paths to induce overeating (history of restrictive dieting that potentiates appetite and reduces eating control)
f) learning that overeating feels good and can alleviate negative emotions
g) experiencing exercise as aversive due to a low fitness level
h) some combination of the above factors

This chapter will discuss how best to alter eating and exercise patterns to manage obesity. It will be limited to efforts that target free-living adult individuals. These efforts hope to produce changes in the person that will result in sustained improvements in eating and exercise. These behavioral approaches generally try to address the causes listed above by training the person to develop skills to counteract the psychophysiological and social/cultural influences that are associated with imprudent behavior. The general model is shown in Figure 1.

After an assessment of eating and exercise patterns, a new behavior plan is designed. A person could then adopt the new patterns. However, there are many factors that may adversely influence behavior

Figure 1: Behavioral Treatment of Obesity

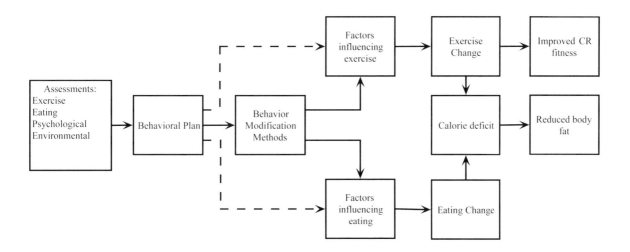

change attempts. Behavior modification methods may be helpful in overcoming these influences.

This chapter examines the effectiveness of behavior modification in the treatment of obesity. This will be achieved by:

a) studying the etiology of obesity as it informs treatment design
b) defining the "best" treatment goals for "best" practices
c) describing behavior modification methods
d) discussing influences on eating and the best practices for eating control
e) discussing influences on exercise and the best practices for exercise control
f) summarizing the approaches with the best outcomes in research settings
g) pointing out methodological problems that make evaluation difficult
h) focusing on possible reasons for the poor long-term success rate of behavioral treatments
i) presenting areas for future research to improve treatment success

ETIOLOGY

The human body is genetically programmed to store excess calories as fat (Bouchard, 1994). The excess intake of calories over calories expended in exercise is clearly the result of environmental changes attendant upon the modernization of society. Several studies show that when people move from more primitive to more modern environments, obesity increases (reviewed by Wadden et al., 2002), and that obesity decreases when they move back to primitive areas (McDermott et al., 1998).

It is commonly thought that overeating is the major contributing factor to obesity in our society. However, there is evidence that decreases in physical activity may be the key factor (Bennett, 1995). An investigation of obesity trends in Britain showed that, from 1950 to 1990, obesity increased dramatically but total energy intake, and percent intake from fat, remained about the same. However, the correlation between prevalence of obesity and car ownership was high, and across all social classes, there was a high correlation between obesity and hours of television viewing, and with inactive lifestyle (Prentice and Jebb, 1995). Surveys in the U.S. indicate a reduction in energy and fat intake over a period of increasing obesity, supporting the argument that reductions in physical activity may be key (Weinsier et al., 1998). The modern environment encourages overeating through an abundant food supply that is modified to enhance sales through processing that adds fat and sugar, and through competitive portion sizing (larger sells more). There is no biological drive to increase activity in response to over consumption of food, so maintaining a positive energy balance requires no willpower (Peters et al., 2002). A low level of daily energy expenditure has been found to be strongly correlated with rate of weight gain (Ravussin et al., 1988).

Implication for behavioral treatments

Overall, a treatment needs to go beyond prescription of lifestyle behaviors, but to teach skills that will help the patient resist the influences of the modern food and exercise environments. Clearly a major emphasis needs to be increasing physical activity. Controlling calorie density and portion sizes in the diet are equally important. Avoiding inadequate sleep may also prove to be important.

DEFINITION OF "BEST" IN THE CONTEXT OF "BEST PRACTICES"

Health professionals should provide treatments that have been shown to optimize health. Often patients are motivated to lose weight for cosmetic reasons. This can be a problem. Some methods of weight loss, such as restrictive dieting, can decrease health, exacerbate eating disorders, or instigate metabolic changes that ultimately lead to greater obesity (Foreyt and Goodrick, 1991; Goodrick, 1999). Realistic treatment results may fall short of the patient's desire to look thin (Wadden et al., 2002), causing conflict with the therapist and feelings of frustration

that may increase the likelihood of loss of eating control and relapse. Counseling to negotiate treatment goals based on health rather than appearance may be vital to long-term psychophysiological success. Some patients will achieve significant and lasting weight loss, but at the cost of chronic obsessional dieting and worrying about weight. For psychological health, patients need to accept weight-loss limitations, improve body image, stop obsessing about weight, and focus on relationships and occupation. Much of the health benefit of weight loss is seen in the first 10% of loss (NHLBI, 1998), and average long-term success is about 10-15% of pretreatment weight. A dynamic model has been derived to predict the benefits of sustained weight loss (Oster et al., 1999). Depending on age, gender, and initial BMI, a sustained 10% weight loss may (1) reduce the expected number of years of life with hypertension, hypercholesterolemia, and type 2 diabetes by 1.2 to 2.9, 0.3 to 0.8, and 0.5 to 1.7, respectively; (2) reduce the expected lifetime incidence of CHD and stroke by 12 to 38 cases per 1000 and 1 to 13 cases per 1000, respectively; (3) increase life expectancy by 2 to 7 months; and (4) reduce expected lifetime medical care costs of these 5 diseases by $2200 to $5300. Thus, the patient should be counseled to accept these parameters of success.

The "best" practices should result in improvements in physical fitness through chronic exercise, as this has been shown to be related to decreases in all-cause mortality across degrees of obesity (Blair and Brodney, 1999; Farrell et al., 2002). Decrease in waist circumference is another possible indicator of improved risk for hypertension, diabetes, and dyslipidemia. Goals of less than 102 cm for men, and 88 cm for women have been suggested (Janssen et al., 2002). However, waist reductions down to these goals may be unrealistic, as a

10% reduction in weight is the current recommended goal. Another worthy goal is control of blood lipids to reduce risk of cardiovascular disease. Total cholesterol should be below 200, and HDL above 40 mg/dL. LDL should be less than 130 mg/dL (NHLBI, 1998). These may be achieved through changes in diet and increased exercise.

The concept of "healthy weight" describes a weight or body mass index associated with minimal risk for morbidity or mortality. Careful epidemiological analyses have shown that the relative risk of death is generally lowest at a BMI in the range 19.0 to 21.9 kg-m^{-2}. However, for women younger than 75 y this range extends to 24.9, and for women over 75 there may be a protective effect up to a BMI of 31.9. For men over 75, a protective effect may exist up to a BMI of 24.9. Other than for these age effects, mortality risk increases with increasing BMI (Dietz et al., 1999). In treating the individual patient, it should be recognized that weight-associated problems result from a cascade of events related to abnormal blood concentrations of insulin, glucose, or lipids that occur when fat cells become full and insulin-insensitive, and lose their protective functions; attention to these indices should be paramount in evaluating the benefits of weight management (Abernathy et al., 1996).

Implications for behavioral treatments

Unfortunately most studies and clinics evaluate success using weight-loss as the outcome. Ideally, determination of best practices would compare reductions in risk factors as well as improvements in physical fitness.

OVERVIEW OF BEHAVIOR MODIFICATION METHODS

Behavioral principles were first applied to the treatment of obesity in the late 1960s and early 1970s. This approach assumes that the behaviors related to regulation of body weight (eating and exercise behaviors) have a learned component, and thus can be relearned or modified. Behaviorists believe that in order to change eating and exercise behaviors, it is important to alter the environmental cues and the reinforcers that control these behaviors (Wing, 2002). The emphasis of treatment has shifted to focus mostly on energy balance. Behavioral treatment of obesity is grounded in the basic premise of changing daily habits or behaviors in order to achieve the desired goal. The focus is on eating behaviors, attitudes, social support, exercise, nutrition, and other factors related to eating (Brownell and Kramer, 1994). The nucleus of this model is the evaluation of the antecedents and consequences that influence behavior. Treatment is geared toward modifying the situations that promote eating, eating behavior itself, and the consequences or events that follow eating. Comprehensive programs have broadened to employ general behavioral principles in areas such as nutrition, physical activity, social support, and cognitive psychology as they relate to weight control (Brownell and Stunkard, 2002).

Behavioral techniques are used in conjunction with other approaches, including medication or surgery (Aronne, 2002). The major commercial weight loss centers such as Weight Watchers, Diet Center, and NutriSystem have integrated behavior modification into their programs.

The principal methods of behavior modification for weight management are shown in Table 1. The wide variety of methods, and the non-standard application of such methods across studies make it difficult to evaluate the effectiveness of any one method.

Without attention control groups, it cannot be determined if results are due to treatment or to the nonspecific factors related to therapeutic contact (Foreyt et al., 1981). Also, when dealing with free-living adults, some apply the methods of self-management and some do not. The use of a method, such as self-monitoring, and success in a program may both be due to a third, motivational factor inherent in the subject and independent of any external application from therapists.

Table 1. Behavior Modification Treatment Components for Weight Control

COMPONENT	DESCRIPTION	EXAMPLES
Self-monitoring	Recording of target behaviors and factors associated with behaviors	Food and exercise diaries, recording of moods and situations associated with overeating or under-exercising
Stimulus Control	Restricting environmental factors associated with inappropriate behaviors	Staying away from tempting, high-fat foods, eating and exercising in structured situations
Contingency management	Rewarding good behavior-withholding reward for bad behavior	Prizes for achievement of behavioral goals
Changing behavior parameters	Alter target behavior	Slow down eating, self-regulate exercise intensity
Cognitive-behavior modifications	Change thinking patterns related to target behaviors	Counter social pressure to be thin to reduce temptation to diet. Focus on health rather than appearance
Relapse Prevention	Identify situational variables associated with relapse	Use problem solving to develop coping strategies. Overcome feelings of failure and try again
Social Support	Getting help from other people going through same struggle	Regular meetings to share experiences and solutions, encouragement, help through crises
Social Influence	Specific activities to counter social environment	Rewards for group achievement to build team spirit; patients give mini-lectures; patients receive training in how to give telephone support to others; group study of advertising and social pressures to overeat and under-exercise

Notwithstanding the methodological difficulties that prevent a clear proof of the efficacy of these methods, it is generally accepted that self-monitoring is crucial to successful self-management, that stimulus control in terms of environment change or avoidance can positively affect eating and exercise behaviors, and social support can improve results (Poston et al., 2000; Foreyt et al., 1993; Baker et al., 1993; Boutelle et al., 1998; Kayman et al., 1990).

CONTROL OF EATING
Environmental Influences

There have been many environmental changes in the last few decades that may influence eating habits. The major changes have been described (French et al., 2001):

a) Increase in the absolute amount of fat in the food supply per capita.

b) Availability and increased serving size of soft drinks, and reduction in milk consumption have resulted in a 131% increase in soda consumption from 1978-1996. One-third of total sugar consumption, which averages twice the recommended level, is attributable to soft drinks (Tippett and Cleveland, 1999).

c) Restaurant eating has increased dramatically, portion sizes have also become giant, and percent calories from fat is higher than in meals eaten at home (Young and Nestle, 2002).

d) Marketing of food on television has increased dramatically, and the most advertised are the least recommended by health authorities.

e) Food costs have been dropping relative to family income, making it easier to buy more calories.

Implications for treatment

Teach nutrition so that the patient can select a low-calorie density diet. Teach skills for food selection control at restaurants and social gatherings.

Teaching reduction in dietary fat content rather than caloric restriction has been shown to be effective in weight management as part of an overall eating and physical activity program (Riebe et al., 2003).

Diet Influences

For optimal weight management, the diet should help produce a calorie deficit (if assessment indicates too many calories being eaten even with a good exercise program), and it should help reduce cardiovascular risks. The Institute of Medicine now recommends that 20 to 35% of calories should come from fat, 45 to 65%

from carbohydrates, and 10 to 35% from protein. Daily fiber intake should be 38 grams. The flexibility in terms of macronutrient content reflects the lack of consensus from research using a wide variety of diets, most of which can produce weight loss (Couzin, 2002). There is good evidence from a meta-analysis of ad libitum dietary intervention studies that a reduction in dietary fat without intentional restriction of energy intake is associated with weight loss, and losses are greater for heavier subjects (Astrup et al., 2000). However, some advocate a higher-fat diet, up to 40% of calories, to help individuals achieve a sense of satiation associated with increased eating control, as long as the fat is monounsaturated (e.g. olive oil) (Willett, 2001). In long-term trials varying dietary fat content between 18% and 40%, no consistent effect on body fat has been found (Willett, 2002). The increase in obesity in the U.S. has occurred during a period when fat content of the diet has decreased, further suggesting that an emphasis on fat reduction may not prove fruitful in efforts to stem the tide of obesity.

The food industry is in the business of selling as much food as it can. Processing of foods to increase calorie density beyond their natural state is one way to increase consumption. Flavor enhancements and manipulation of the fat-carbohydrate ratio can increase calorie intake beyond physiological needs (Sclafani, 2001).

A current area of dispute is the role of dietary glycemic index in weight control. Some propose that the current increase in obesity in the industrialized world is due to the popularity of high-carbohydrate, low-fat diet suggestions. These diets include foods with high glycemic indices, causing postprandial hypoglycemia leading to subsequent hunger and overeating, and to hyperinsulinemia. This is associated with the promotion of postprandial carbohydrate oxidation at the expense of fat oxidation, thus altering fuel partitioning in a way that may lead to body fat gain. In contrast, diets based on low-fat foods with low glycemic indices may enhance weight control because they promote satiety, minimize postprandial insulin secretion, and maintain insulin sensitivity (Brand-Miller et al., 2002).

Implications for Treatment

Behavior change may need to go beyond eating fewer calories because some diets may be more conducive to eating control. Proper nutrition to reduce cardiovascular risks is also indicated.

Psychological Processes in Eating Control

One of the chief reasons given by patients who come for behavioral treatment is that they feel unable to control their eating (Goodrick, 1999). For the health professional dealing with obesity or eating disorders, the problem is how to help the patient who reports lack of control over eating. The feeling of being out of control is distressing, because the patient feels that he or she should be able to control calorie intake; failure to do so is viewed as a lack of willpower or character. Our cultural traditions in the Western world stem from thousands of years of teachings defining a good person as one in whom the mind has control over the base instincts. As Cicero said, "Reason should direct and appetite obey." Obesity is often taken as a sign of personal failing. In pre-industrial society, obesity was a sign of sloth and/or gluttony compared to all others who had to toil for a living, and who were too poor to overindulge in food. Even though about one half of the population is overweight, and the causes of obesity are clearly not associated with personal character, the stigma against the obese remains.

One answer to this problem for some is to view obesity as the result of a disease characterized by lack of control over eating, or as an *addiction*. Although "addiction" is not clearly defined in medicine or psychiatry, the concept allows patients to view themselves as victims of physiological processes that are not their fault. The problems with this model of overeating as a disease have been thoroughly reviewed by Wilson (1991). The "symptoms" of the disease include perceived loss of eating control, cravings, preoccupation with food, and sometimes denial and secrecy. Overeating is alternated with restrictive dieting, and eating is used to regulate emotions and to cope with stress in a manner similar to the use of psychotropic drugs. However, these symptoms can be better explained as the result of normal physiological processes in the control of eating in response to the very abnormal situation of the modern human. This abnormal situation includes:

- Sedentary behavior patterns and an abundance of high-calorie density food
- A natural facility for weight gain as an adaptive physiological response
- A strong desire to control weight
- A dependence upon restrictive dieting to control weight
- Psychophysiological responses to dieting that enhance appetite
- Periodic loss of control of eating with weight gain
- Feelings of inadequacy due to the perception that one should be able to control eating.

This describes the well-known "dieters dilemma" (Bennett and Gurin, 1982).

If eating dyscontrol is not an addiction, then what is it? Much of the overweight public perceives it as a problem that is not amenable to self-control. The demand for appetite suppressant medication is very high. Sales of nutritional supplements for appetite control, and for devices that claim to help in weight control continue to rise. Many of the overweight have struggled for years, only to see their weight slowly increase; it is no wonder that they perceive themselves as out of control, and needing a "magic pill." At the same time, therapists are struggling to get patients to alter their eating and exercise habits towards a new, permanent lifestyle, that most seem to abandon within a few years, as evidenced by the regain likely for the vast majority of those so treated.

Overweight individuals' attempts to control weight through restrictive dieting apparently involve the assumption that they can control their eating. However, eventually they come to the realization that much of their eating is out of their cognitive control. "Cognitive" control and "physiological control" of eating are not separate processes -- they are interactive. For example, cognitive activities concerning food (thoughts, viewing of food pictures) can change physiological processes associated with increased appetite, such as pancreatic reflex discharge of insulin and glucagon (Bellisle, 1995). Physiological events, such as drop in blood sugar associated with insulin increase, precipitate cognitions of food that lead to eating (Campfield et al., 1996). The affective response to a food stimulus changes as a function of the internal energy status; a pleasant food becomes less pleasant after much of it is eaten (Bellisle, 1995). The classic mind-body problem thus blurs our ability to describe the nexus of causality in eating control. The situation becomes more complex with the realization that mental activities, and control of eating behavior, operate to a large extent under the influence of the physical and social environment.

Virtually all patients presenting for weight management treatment have a history of restrictive dieting attempts. Dieting may give rise to a preoccupation with food, and attempts to suppress such thoughts in order to gain eating control may actually lead to

an increase in such thoughts, and failure of eating control (Ward et al., 1996). Severe dieting, such as very low calorie diets, may cause some patients to become binge eaters (Telch and Agras, 1993).

Clinical experience and research (Sjoberg and Persson, 1979) show that when those with weight concerns attempt to control eating using restrictive diets, they often arrive at a psychophysiological state characterized by an apparent conflict between desires to lose weight and compulsion to eat. This state includes muddled thinking about original weight-loss goals, and eating discordant with intention (Ruderman, 1986). Overeating may result from a motivated shift to lower levels of self-awareness, as an escape from painful feelings of personal inadequacy (Heatherton and Baumeister, 1991). Relapse from diet regimens seem to occur upon exposure to food at mealtime, either when socializing or when alone, when happy, tense, angry, or depressed, or when bored (Grilo et al., 1989). Over-eating often seems to be an activity done in response to emotional distress, or to the perception that one has "blown" a diet by eating some forbidden food (Heatherton et al., 1990).

The lifetime prevalence rates for depression and potential binge eating disorder are high among overweight adults (Linde et al., 2004). While initial weight loss and regular exercise may help with mood, negative emotional states are often associated with poor eating control, and may need to be addressed before standard behavior modification methods are applied.

In summary, patients who report problems in eating control most likely have a history of restrictive dieting that may potentiate psychological aspects of appetite. They report eating as a form of self-medication for negative affective states, and also in response to social influences with positive affective states. All this occurs in an environment of abundant food, much of which has been processed to maximize appetite. When rats are placed into such an environment, they eat more and become obese, but they are not motivated to try to control themselves to avoid stigmatization. Many humans placed into such an environment (the industrialized world) present with the complaint of obesity and report the perception that they can't control their eating; indeed, some feel they are "addicted" to food.

Implications for treatment

Behavioral treatment programs may need to recognize that many patients feel they cannot self-manage their eating behaviors. For some, this is based on bitter experience. It should be established that patients are comfortable with a self-management approach. Otherwise provision of external support through close contact and peer groups may be helpful.

Physiological Processes in Eating Control

Parallels have been drawn between overeating and drug addiction, since both behavioral syndromes involve intense cravings and loss of self-control (Goodrick, 1999). There may be similar physiological mechanisms that mediate both food and drug reward. For example, sweet cravings are associated with opiate addiction (Willenbring et al., 1989), and opiate withdrawal is often eased by eating of sweets (Morabia et al., 1989). The opiate antagonist naloxone has been shown to reduce taste preferences, and reduced calorie intake from snacks in binge eaters; preferences for sweet, high-fat foods were especially affected (Drewnowski et al., 1992). Since binge eaters report a pattern of compulsive overeating that can be triggered by such palatable foods, and since the eating seems to alleviate some negative mood states, the parallel to drug dependence is compelling.

As discussed above, most patients presenting with the complaint of uncontrolled eating have a history of restrictive dieting. Food deprivation increases the reward value of food (Berridge, 1991), possibly by sensitizing the opioid reward system (Carr and Simon, 1984). Multiple episodes of food restriction, typical of dieting in humans, make rats supersensitive to the effects of the appetite-stimulating effect of brain opioids, through mechanisms that may overlap with those associated with opioid involvement in drug addiction (DeVry et al., 1989; Carr and Papadouka, 1994). Obese humans characterized by large weight fluctuations (presumably from bouts of restrictive dieting) show elevated preferences for sugar and fat mixtures compared to obese persons with stable weight (Drewnowski et al., 1991). From an adaptive viewpoint, it makes sense that an animal would want to eat more after a period of starvation, to make up for lost weight. However, the potentiation of eating seems to persist even after normal weight is regained (Hagan and Moss, 1991), setting the stage for obesity as a long-term outcome of restrictive dieting. Overeating after restrictive dieting may also be due to feedback signals from lean and fat tissues. Unfortunately, dieters typically regain lost fat faster than they regain lost fat-free mass (FFM), so that when fat mass is restored, there is still a hunger signal due to reduced FFM; the resultant eating also adds to the fat mass, making the post-diet individual fatter than before a diet (Dulloo et al., 1997).

The dopamine (DA) reward theory posits that DA release in the nucleus accumbens (NAc) reinforces any behavior, and acetylcholine (ACh) inhibits behavior. Opioid links have been identified in this eating reward circuit that projects from the hypothalamus to the NAc. Food deprivation lowers DA levels in the Nac, and raises ACh (Pothos et al., 1995). This led Hoebel (1997) to speculate that during food restriction (dieting) alternative behaviors such as binge eating or drug abuse may occur to restore DA levels. The sights, sounds, and smells of food may also trigger DA release through conditioning (Schultz et al., 1997), thus potentiating eating in an environment filled with food stimuli (i.e., modern society). Reductions in striatal DA D2 receptors have been found in pathologically obese patients, similar to the reductions found in drug-addicted subjects. The DA D2 receptor levels were found to have an inverse relationship to the body mass index of the obese subjects, suggesting that overeating may be an attempt to compensate for a reduced sensitivity of DA D2 reward circuits. (Wang et al., 2004). In pathologically obese patients, treatment with DA agonists may be helpful in the treatment of obesity, by reducing the amount of food consumption needed to obtain a satisfying level of DA in the brain (Cincotta et al., 1997; Cincotta and Meier, 1996). A trial using Buproprion SR showed some promise for this therapeutic mechanism (Anderson et al., 2002).

Implications for Treatment

Based on the above discussion, what can be done to help those with eating dyscontrol? In terms of treatment for the obese, the following seem to be indicated (Foreyt and Goodrick, 1994):

- Avoidance of restrictive dieting regimes. Reduction in calorie density may provide satiety, good nutrition, and minimal physiological reactivity. Regularity of eating to avoid excessive hunger may enhance perceptions of self-control.
- Emphasis on social support and interpersonal skills. While it is not clear whether eating disorders can be construed as "addictions," it may be that some patients will need greater support to resist the temptations to overeat, to which they might succumb if left alone.

The only weight management programs that seem to have had a long-term effect are those based on the continuous care model that assumes a lifetime of clinical contact and scrutiny (Perri et al., 1992). This again raises the question whether behavioral treatment methods work apart from the social scrutiny associated with the implementation of any treatment (Foreyt et al., 1981).

- The patient's attribution of self-blame for overeating needs to be replaced with an explanation of the biopsychosocial model, showing that symptoms are the result of a mismatch between organism and environment.
- Adjunctive pharmaceutical approaches that may alter physiological reward paths to promote prudent eating in those who manifest particular difficulty in self-control. In addition to the Bupropion dopamine-antagonist approach, Sibutramine, which produces its therapeutic effects by norepinephrine, serotonin and dopamine reuptake inhibition, has been shown to produce small but significant weight losses (Nisoli and Carruba, 2000; Wirth and Krause, 2001), but adverse side effects and cost need to be taken into account when decisions are made to resort to pharmacological approaches.

CONTROL OF EXERCISE

Leisure-time physical activity has been steadily decreasing in the U.S. (US Dept Health Human Services, 1996), and most occupations have become more sedentary over the last few decades. These trends have no doubt contributed to the increasing prevalence of obesity. Observations of animals have shown that most adult mammals exercise only when necessary, and rest otherwise. This natural tendency to conserve energy may explain why humans fail to get healthful exercise when placed in an environment that is very different from the environment to which humans had become adapted through evolution.

Environmental Influences

Television and the Internet now allow humans to sit still and receive stimulation that satisfies the brain's need for information and perceptual excitement. Television is the main leisure-time activity of Americans, who average 28 hours per week, which is about 10 times as much time as they spend on exercise (Nielsen Media Research, 2000). The rise in obesity has been associated with an increasing use of automobiles and reduction in walking (US Dept Health Human Services, 2000). Although there is free access to public exercise facilities (parks), the public generally is utilizing them less and less, probably because we have become accustomed to the comfort of climate-controlled residences, and partly because there is a fear of attack by criminal elements. There has been a substantial growth in health clubs over the last 20 years, but obese adults may be reluctant to patronize them due to fear to perceived stigmatization.

Implications for Treatment

Treatment providers have little power to change American lifestyle insofar as television and perceived crime are concerned. However, integrating behavioral recommendations into current lifestyle may be one answer. An example of this is the provision of a treadmill that a person can use to get a healthful walk while watching TV in the comfort and safety of his/her home (Jakicic, 1999, see table). Also, reducing television viewing time has been shown to reduce obesity in children (Robinson, 1999).

Exercise Parameters

Findings from research in exercise adherence counseling indicate that an

intervention involving behavior modification, and using a continuous care model involving periodic contact, may be most effective. King and associates (King et al., 1988; King et al., 1995) have found that home-based exercise can result in good adherence when combined with brief baseline instruction and continuing telephone contact. Adherence rates for home-based programs can be greater than for group-based exercise (King et al., 1995). Home-based exercise has also been found to be superior to group-based exercise in terms of long-term exercise participation and treatment adherence in a weight management program (Perri et al., 1997). A review of exercise adherence studies (Hillsdon and Thorogood, 1996) found: a) interventions that encourage walking, and do not require attendance at a facility are most likely to lead to sustainable increases in overall physical activity; b) brisk walking has the greatest potential of increasing overall activity levels of a sedentary population while meeting public health recommendations; and c) all the home-based exercise studies in which researchers provided a means of telephone contact with subjects had positive results. Further research is needed to determine if systems using telephonic reporting of regimen adherence can provide the additional motivation for patients to overcome barriers to self-management of chronic diseases (Piette, 2000).

Chronic exercise can improve mood and sense of well-being, feelings of energy, and may also reduce negative body image, improve self-efficacy and self-esteem, and enhance positive coping style (Baker and Brownell, 2000). This can lead to increased motivation and commitment to exercise, as exercise becomes a self-reinforcing behavior, as contrasted with inactivity that leads to low perceived energy and reduced motivation to exercise (Foreyt and Goodrick, 2001; Goodrick, 1999; Foreyt et al., 1995). However, unless exercise intensity is matched with current fitness level, the hedonic response to exercise can be negative. Women with low fitness levels are more likely to report psychological distress after high-intensity exercise bouts, while high-fit women do not experience negative affect (Blanchard, et al., 2001). Consistent with these considerations, sedentary adults have been found to be more likely to adhere to exercise prescriptions if they exercise at a high frequency (5-7 x/w) versus a low frequency (3-4 x/w), and if the exercise is of a lower intensity (45-55% of maximum heart rate reserve) rather than higher (65-75%) (Perri et al., 2002).

Obese women have lower exercise capacity than lean women, reporting more musculoskeletal pain during strenuous exercise (Hulens et al., 2001). Adults who do not exercise often perceive of exercise as an activity that will decrease their feelings of energy- they think of exercise as a burden, while those who exercise moderately and regularly think of exercise as an energy-boosting behavior (Riddle, 1980; Goodrick et al., 1994). This points out the importance of using a self-regulated intensity approach (Goodrick et al., 1994) to ensure optimal hedonic response at each level of fitness development during adoption of physical activity habits.

According to Social Cognitive Theory (Bandura, 1986), a behavior is more likely to become a habit if it has intrinsic reward value (enjoyable) and the individual has a high level of behavioral capability (skill level). Thus, individuals continue to participate in an activity that they enjoy and that they can do well. Conversely, individuals discontinue an activity that they dislike and/or an activity that they feel incompetent to perform. The theory also predicts that an activity will be discontinued if external/social pressure is applied to motivate an individual to perform an activity-- and

usually this is necessary if the activity is not perceived as self-rewarding. Pressure to exercise has been shown to predict *less* exercise later in life (Taylor et al., 1999).

Implications for treatment
An exercise treatment should:
- Teach an exercise program that is experienced as enjoyable by focusing on the positive psychological effects
- Be sensitive to individual differences in fitness level by using a self-regulated-intensity approach.

EVIDENCE OF EFFECTIVENESS OF BEHAVIORAL TREATMENTS
Uncontrolled Studies

There are two studies that demonstrate how much weight loss a person can expect to achieve and maintain indefinitely, following behaviors that are healthful and that do not involve obsessive, perfectionistic thinking. The National Weight Control Registry is a web-based registry for adults who have maintained a loss of at least 30 lbs for at least 1 year. Data from this registry (which now lists over 3500 people with an average weight loss of 30 kg maintained for 5.5 years) have implications for successful weight loss and maintenance (Wing and Hill, 2001). Among the characteristics of registrants that seem to be associated with successful weight control are:
1. They generally eat a low-fat (24% of calories from fat), high-carbohydrate diet with moderate calorie amounts.
2. They avoid fried foods, and substitute low-fat for high-fat foods, reduce portion size, and have fewer snack episodes than those who have not been able to control weight.
3. They use behavior change strategies taught in weight-control classes, particularly self-monitoring of weight and behaviors.

4. They get a lot of exercise (2545 kcal per week for women, 3293 for men), averaging about 1 hour a day of brisk walking or an equivalent exercise.

Importantly, registrants report no adverse psychological effects of weight control (Klem et al., 1998).

Another study (Cormillot and Fuchs, 1990) observed the weight loss maintenance success of 2500 women in Argentina who used sensible behavioral approaches. A formula was derived to help people predict a realistic "possible weight" based on the success of many others.

A realistic possible weight is equal to:
Ideal weight (100 lbs plus 5 lbs for each inch over 5 feet in height)
> Plus

(Age + Number of years overweight) times 0.22
> Plus

(Maximum weight ever) divided by 10
> Minus

4.4

This formula generally results in a goal weight that is higher than most patients desire, so an important part of counseling is to convince the patient that this is the best he/she can do.

Implications for Treatment

The above studies show that reasonable behavior changes, when maintained indefinitely, can result in maintained weight losses that are significant from a health standpoint if not from a cosmetic standpoint. They also show that a healthful lifestyle can be well tolerated and even enjoyed.

Controlled Studies

Some recent behavioral treatment studies that randomized subjects to treatment conditions, and that recorded at least 12-month follow-up data are described in Table

2. The target behaviors vary, with some addressing diet, others addressing exercise, and some both. They also vary to the extent they incorporated behavior modification methods. Because of this variance, it is difficult to make direct comparisons across studies in order to conclude what treatment is optimal. The studies tend to take place in university research settings providing free treatments, and many subjects were in the higher socioeconomic levels. Under these settings, the likelihood of long-term participation in a study is more likely. Thus, generalizability to the reality of a fee-for-service obesity clinic, or to inner-city, racial minority settings is problematic. Additionally, as mentioned above, the lack of attention or health education control groups makes it impossible to determine whether the results are due to the effects of specific treatments, or due to the non-specific effects of being in a study combined with specific diet and exercise instructions. The intensity of many of the interventions over an extended period may be contraindicated for replication in settings where financial resources are limited. The studies suffice to show that significant weight loss can be achieved. It remains now to determine how best to perform similarly effective interventions in a more cost-beneficial manner.

The Perri et al. (1988) study represents an effort to maximize the influence of social support, exercise and continued contact. This is the best and most successful representation of behavior modification, as it covers exercise, diet, and social support. The social influence approach (see Table 1) may be critical to help offset the strong influence of our current culture and advertising that promote gluttony and sloth.

The study by Goodrick et al. (1994) compared diet-only, exercise-only and combination approaches. After one year, the combination group led with a loss of 5.7 kg, followed by the diet-only group losing 4.7

458

Table 2: Selected Controlled Studies

Study	Sample	Design	Intervention	Primary Findings
Perri et al., 1988	120 obese adults	20-week treatment, then maintenance programs Outcomes: Weight change at 12 and 18 months	. Diet + Exercise . Behavior modification . Random assignment to four maintenance conditions: 1. Contact maintained with therapists (CM) 2. CM plus social influence (SI) support groups 3. CM plus exercise 4. CM plus SI plus exercise	All maintenance conditions maintained 83% of their 12.5 kg loss. Subjects in CMP plus SI plus exercise had a mean loss from baseline of 13.6 kg at 18 months.
Goodrick et al., 1994	102 obese adults, 50% male	Treatment for 12 weeks, with 11 follow-up meetings over the next 40 weeks Outcomes: Adherence to exercise at least 3x/week for >20 min each bout	Behavior modification Random assignment to: 1. Diet only 2. Exercise only (self-regulated intensity-SRI) 3. Exercise (SRI) and Diet	Each group had 35% adhering to criterion at baseline. Percent of subjects meeting exercise criterion (exercise at least 3x/week for >20 min each bout) at 12 months (intention to treat) was: 1. Diet only-29 % 2. Exercise only- 55% 3. Exercise and Diet- 49%
Skender et al., 1996		Same study as above, long-term weight outcomes		Weight loss at 1 and 2 years (intention to treat): 1. Diet Only: -4.7 kg, +1.1 kg 2. Exercise Only: -2.0 kg, -1.6 kg 3. Exercise and Diet: -5.7 kg, -1.1 kg
Stevens et al., 2001	1191 adults, 110-165% of ideal body weight	3 to 4 years of lifestyle intervention, versus usual care. Blood pressure was target.	14 weekly, 6 biweekly, then monthly groups. At 18 months, other options made available to maintain participation. Nutrition and physical activity self-management; self-monitoring, goal setting, action plans, and avoiding eating triggers	Weight loss at 18 and 36 months: Intervention: -2.0 kg, -0.2 kg Usual Care: +0.7 kg, +1.8 kg Blood pressure lower in intervention group at all time points. Risk ration for hypertension in intervention group was 0.81 (CI, 0.70 to 0.95) at 36 months

Study	Sample	Design	Intervention	Primary Findings
Ditschu-neit et al., 1999	100 obese adults who were referred to an obesity center at an university hospital; criteria: BMI 25-40 and 18+ age	Phase 1 (weight loss): 3-mo, prospective, randomized, parallel intervention of 2 diets. Phase 2 (weight loss/maintenance): case-control, diet and meal replacements for all subjects. Outcomes: Mean weight loss	. Meal replacements . Behavior modification: diaries only . Phase 1: energy restricted diets of conventional foods (n=50) vs. meal replacements (n=50); Phase 2: energy-restricted diet of meal replacement for all subjects	14% of the energy-restricted diet and 42% of the meal replacement groups had reduced their body weight by >10% of their initial weight (9.7 kg).
Andersen et al., 1999	40 obese women (mean BMI 32.9); age 21-60; seen in a university weight management program	16 wks randomized controlled trial with 1-year follow-up Outcomes: changes in body weight, body composition, cardiovascular risk profiles, and physical fitness at 16 weeks and a 1 year	. Physical Activity . Behavior modification: activity monitors only . All got low-fat diet (1,200 kcal/day) Random assignment to: 1. structured aerobic exercise 2. lifestyle activity	Weight loss: 1: 8.3 kg for aerobic 2: 7.9 kg for lifestyle aerobic group lost significantly less fat-free mass than lifestyle (0.5 vs. 1.4 kg); During 1 year follow up, aerobic group regained more than lifestyle group (1.6 vs. 0.08 kg); Serum triglyceride levels and total cholesterol levels did not differ from groups or baseline

Study	Sample	Design	Intervention	Primary Findings
Jakicic et al. 1999	148 sedentary women (mean BMI 32.8, age 36.7) in a university-based weight control program	18 month randomized trial Outcomes: body weight, body composition, cardiorespiratory fitness, and exercise adherence	. Behavior modification . 18-month weight control program with 3 groups: 1. long-bout exercise 2. multiple short-bout exercise, or 3. multiple short-bout exercise with home exercise equipment using a treadmill	Weight loss was significantly greater in home exercise equipment with multiple short-bout exercise (10 kg), but long-bout exercise was not significant when compared to the other two groups; home exercise group maintained a higher level of exercise than both other groups at 13 to 18 months of treatment; all groups increased cardiorespiratory fitness; weight loss at 18 months was significantly greater in 200 min/wk (14 kg) compared to 150-200 min/wk (10 kg) or less than 150min/wk (6 kg).
Knowler et al., 2002	3284 overweight adults with impaired glucose tolerance	RCT with: . Placebo . Metformin . Lifestyle	. 16 lessons one-to-one with case manager, with additional monthly sessions and group meetings. . Behavior modification to achieve: 1. low-calorie, low-fat diet 2. 150 minutes of physical activity/week	Weight loss at 1,2,3, and 4 years (kg): Lifestyle: -6.5, -5.5, -4.1, -3.9 Placebo: no weight loss (no change in physical activity) Lifestyle risk reduction for diabetes 58% (CI: 48 to 66%)

Study	Sample	Design	Intervention	Primary Findings
Jeffery et al., 2003	202 overweight adults	RCT Behavior therapy with 1000 cal/week of exercise versus 2500 cal/week	. Group 1: Behavior therapy, nutrition and exercise, small groups weekly for 6 months, biweekly for next 6 months, monthly for 6 months. 1000 cal exercise/week . Group 2: As above, but 2500 cal exercise/week, with more social support, and with exercise coaches after each group session. Also $3 reward for achieving weekly goal	Weight losses (kg) at 6, 12 and 18 months: Group 1: 8.1, 6.1, 4.1 Group 2: 9.0, 8.5, 6.7
Klem et al., 1997	784 adults	Self-selected subjects who report weight management success	. 50% lost weight in formal programs using behavioral methods . They tend to self-monitor, use social support, and problem solving approaches . Their diet is 24% calories from fat . They expend 11830 kJ/week (2800 calories) through physical activity	Average initial loss = 30 kg Minimum maintained weight loss 13.6 kg, maintained for at least 5 years

kg, and the exercise-only group losing 2.0 kg. In this study, there was an attempt to teach sedentary obese adults who claimed they did not enjoy exercise to develop an exercise habit based on self-regulated intensity. Subjects were taught to exercise at an intensity that always felt invigorating but never strenuous. They were taught to focus on the pleasant aspects of exercise and its short- and long-term effects. In large part, most subjects ended up reporting that they enjoyed exercise. The reasons given among those who stopped exercising were not related to exercise, but seemed to involve life interferences, such as divorce or changing jobs. This study also used self-monitoring and stimulus control as behavior modification methods.

A two-year follow-up of this study (Skender et al., 1996) found that the diet-only group had regained to 1.1 kg heavier than baseline, the combination group regaining 4.6 kg, and the exercise-only group regaining only 0.4 kg, resulting in the best long-term result. Subjects gave the impression that the diet component was not enjoyable, and may have led to less success in those groups that had that component. Exercise was perceived by most subjects as enjoyable, and perhaps this helped in exercise maintenance.

Since many patients report a lack of control of eating, a convenient way to avoid food decisions is to have a meal replacement. The Ditschuneit et al. (1999) study showed that using a meal replacement (Slimfast can) once daily for dinner could have a sustained and significant effect. In this study, only diary-keeping was employed as a behavior modification measure.

The Andersen et al. (1999) study shows that structured aerobics classes and lifestyle activity interventions can produce about the same results, and when combined with a 1200 kcalorie/day diet can result in fair weight loss Perhaps the most interesting

study involved the provision of motorized treadmills in the homes of obese female subjects (Jakicic, 1999). Given the convenience of home-based exercise compared to the cost of health clubs and the dangers of public parks, and considering that treadmills can be used during normal television viewing periods, this approach needs further investigation as a way to get Americans physically fit.

In a study focusing on the prevention of hypertension, a large sample of adults received behavioral self-management training over 3 to 4 years (Stevens et al., 2001). At 18- and 36- month assessments, the intervention group showed slightly better weight results, and the risk for hypertension at 36 months was reduced to 81% compared to the usual care condition. This shows the value of looking at endpoints other than weight to determine the value of behavioral interventions.

In the Diabetes Prevention Program, 3284 adults were randomly assigned to placebo, Metformin or to a behavioral lifestyle intervention (low calorie, low-fat diet, 150 minutes of physical activity/wk) (Knowler et al., 2002). The lifestyle intervention involved 16 one-to-one counseling sessions, followed by monthly groups. This was much more intensive than typical behavioral programs. Weight loss at one year was 6.5 kg, tapering off to a loss of 3.9 kg at 4 years. The most important finding was not weight loss but a risk reduction for diabetes of 58%. Less intensive methods for motivating similar behavioral changes could have dramatic effects on the reduction of diabetes.

Because those listed in the National Weight Control Registry performed more exercise than was typically prescribed in behavioral programs, Jeffery et al. (2003) compared typical (1000 cal/wk) with a high exercise regimen (2500 cal/wk). The high exercise group received more social support, and were seen by exercise coaches regularly. They also received $3 after meeting weekly goals. From the 12th to 18th months of the study, the high exercise group averaged about 2.5 kg greater weight loss than the low exercise group. It remains to be seen how many people will put forth a significantly higher level of effort and time for exercise to achieve a relatively small advantage in weight, even though other health benefits no doubt are obtained.

The results of the National Weight Control Registry are shown in Table 2 as well. By comparison, the results of the registrants are far better than those of any controlled study. The challenge is to discover what motivational and environmental factors may account for the success of the registrants, and to find out how to translate these to others.

Views from Reviews
Several meta-analyses of behavioral treatments of obesity have concluded that the results of group treatments have not changed substantially over the last 20 years (Foreyt and Goodrick, 1993; Wing 2002). Patients initially lose 10-15% of body weight and then regain one third of lost weight in the year following treatment, with increasing regain over time. The one-year percent of weight lost has increased slightly from 6.1% to 7.8% over the last 30 years (Wadden et al., 2004), with gradual return to baseline within 5 years (Wadden et al., 1989). Reviewing 17 studies, and using success criteria of either maintenance of all weight lost (or further loss), or maintenance of at least 9 kg of initial weight loss, Ayyad and Andersen (2000) found an overall success rate of 15% at 3 or more years follow-up. The rate of successful weight loss and maintenance among population-based samples may indicate an even more dismal picture. Among 911 obese adults surveyed in Finland, only 6% had lost 5% or more of

their body weight and maintained this loss for up to 9 years (Sarlio-Lahteenkorva et al., 2000). The NIH Evidence Report on weight control (1998) concluded that behavior therapy produced a weight loss of 4 kg over 4 years when applied to diet and exercise methods.

As mentioned above, methodological inadequacies in treatment studies make it difficult to determine if behavior modification approaches are more effective than specific behavior information and attention from therapists. It is difficult to separate out studies that are diet only or exercise only versus behavior modification with diet and exercise, and comparison groups chosen do not allow a determination of the unique effect of behavioral methods (Orzano et al., 2004). A study that casts doubt on the value of behavior modification training involved overweight women who were helped to lose weight using prepared meals (Hensrud et al., 1994). Without participation in any weight-loss educational program, and without receiving any behavior modification training, they lost an average 10 kg. During several years of follow-up, there was a regain of lost weight in most cases. Their long-term results were as good as those following relatively intensive behavior modification programs. This raises questions about the efficacy of such intensive programs, and provides further support to the contention that eating and exercise behaviors are largely under the control of psychophysiological factors that are not strongly influenced by training patients to self-manage.

FUTURE DIRECTIONS
The general lack of long-term success of weight management treatments indicates that most humans, when placed in an environment that allows sedentary lifestyle and ad libitum eating of calorie-dense foods, will adjust behaviors in a way that results in

gradual deposition of excess body fat. The mechanisms controlling these behaviors appear to occur at a sub-cognitive level, as social norms favor thinness and overweight people express negative affect concerning their inability to control weight.

Six areas for future research need to be explored:

1. Examining the parameters of behaviors to discover what facilitates self-management: Given that adherence to weight management behaviors needs to continue indefinitely, behavioral interventions need to be tested that provide a balance between effectiveness in producing a calorie change, and tolerability. Theoretically, sensible eating can be enjoyable. The registrants of the National Weight Control Registry provide an example of a low-calorie density eating style that is healthful and not perceived as self-punitive. Currently, there is no evidence to recommend the use of one dietary approach over another for long-term weight control (Wadden et al., 2004; Dansinger et al., 2005). Likewise, more research is needed to develop exercise programs that are perceived as enjoyable and energizing (e.g., Good-rick et al., 1994). In general more exercise is better, with 2800 cal/wk perhaps being an upper limit applicable to most people.

2. Exploring cost-effective ways to apply a continuing care model: Obesity is a chronic condition requiring continuing contact to enhance motivation for adherence. Future research is needed to test less intensive and less expensive approaches. Bibliotherapy, computer-assisted therapy, interactive web sites, and free or low-cost self-help groups based in worship or other non-profit centers have shown promise (Latner, 2001).

3. Obesity and Perceived Energy: Approaching obesity treatment as an energy-enhancing intervention integrates exercise, nutrition and sleep, and may be more

appealing to patients as it has the potential to improve mood (Foreyt and Goodrick, 2001). Obesity is associated with daytime sleepiness even in the absence of sleep apnea (Vgontzas et al., 1998). This may be related to the insufficient exercise and excessive caloric intake characteristic of the lifestyle of most obese persons. Lack of exercise is associated with reduced feelings of energy (Thayer, 1996). The high-calorie density diet of many obese persons is associated with increased tiredness and sleep in rats (Danguir, 1987), and a high-fat diet has been found to be associated with reduced energy expenditure and less physical activity compared to an isocaloric, high-carbohydrate diet in humans, possibly mediated by changes in thyroid hormone profile consistent with a reduction in metabolic energy expenditure (Baldini et al., 1994).

Many obese patients complain of low energy, and the popularity of weight-loss supplements containing guarana extract and ephedra may be explained by the positive psychological effects of these energy-boosters, especially when compensating for the potential reduction in energy related to calorie restriction (Foreyt and Goodrick, 2001).

Feelings of low energy generally are associated with negative mood states. For obese adults with a history of restrained eating, negative moods are associated with increased likelihood for emotional overeating or binge eating episodes that seem to be used to regulate negative affect (Lynch et al., 2000; Goodrick, 2000).

In our recent studies with obese subjects, the average sleep duration was 7 hours. This duration is consistent with national polls. Sleep deprivation ultimately produces sleepiness, fatigue, impaired coping abilities and negative mood. Dysphoric mood secondary to sleep insufficiency may also precipitate overeating episodes (Thayer, 1996; Foreyt and Goodrick, 2001).

The increase in obesity in the U.S. during the 20th century was accompanied by a decrease in sleep duration from 9 hours to the current 7 hours. Sleep loss can produce marked alterations in glucose metabolism and endocrine function (Spiegel et al., 1999), suggesting that sleep loss, even in the absence of disordered breathing, may promote insulin resistance. Sleep loss also increases the severity of obesity-associated sleep-disordered breathing, resulting in a feedforward cascade of negative effects that not only worsens the sleep problem, but contributes to the development of adverse metabolic consequences such as insulin resistance, further weight gain, and diabetes (Tasali and Van Cauter, 2002). Conversely, weight loss improves sleep-related breathing and in some individuals cures sleep-disordered breathing. Thus, both from the standpoint of avoiding negative-affect overeating from low energy, and from the standpoint of avoiding metabolic consequences, sleep adequacy should be an integral part of any obesity treatment.

4. Examining how the environmental influences can be altered by changing the environment: Ideally this would involve the removal of high-calorie density foods from the marketplace (unlikely to occur), and the provision of convenient, safe, and inexpensive exercise facilities (parks, corporate fitness centers, home treadmills).

5. Applying stronger contingencies for behaviors: Despite an attempt to make behaviors convenient and enjoyable, there may still be a need to apply external motivation to counteract the temptation of our modern environment. Methods might include taxing artificially calorie-dense foods, providing financial incentives through employers or insurance programs for physical fitness improvement and maintenance, or requiring regular exercise as a condition of employment or for receiving welfare benefits. Despite American myths about individualism and self-reliance, the U.S. government has a long tradition of regulating ostensibly private behavior (Kersh and Morone, 2002). For problems related to alcohol, illegal drugs, tobacco, and sexuality, the government has stepped in with regulatory laws to protect the public health from the effects of citizens' private habits. Considering the increasing costs of obesity in terms of diabetes and cardio-vascular diseases, the time may be approaching that the government will need to control the freedom to eat and be sedentary. Many obese adults who perceive themselves to be unable to self-control may embrace external control as helpful to them, while others will fight against any attempt to curtail individual liberties.

6. Proving the beneficial health effects of weight-loss maintained over long periods. Although all the indications point to the health benefits of long-term weight loss, definitive studies have yet to be done. This is due to the high relapse rate in studies, and the length of time and sample size needed for a study to detect group differences for calculations of relative risk for various disease endpoints. Planning for such research is now ongoing at the NIH.

7. Assess potential eating disorders and address integrated treatment with weight management. Binge eating disorder (BED) and night eating syndrome (NES) are frequently seen in obese patients. The psychological characteristics of BED are similar to those for bulimia, leading some to classify BED as a mental disorder. NES has not been studied long enough for a clear classification as a mental disorder. In many obese patients, unusual eating patterns reflective of dyscontrol may be found, and may interfere with behavioral approaches to weight management. More research is needed to determine how best to assess abnormal eating behaviors, and how best to address them in the behavioral treatment of obesity (Tanofsky-Kraff and Yanovski, 2004). Although some patients with BED have psychological profiles similar to bulimia, binge eaters can achieve as much success as non-bingers in standard behavioral treatments (Gladis et al., 1998).

8. Recognizing that obesity is the result of an organism-environment mismatch that affects the entire population. To illustrate this perspective, one must imagine a dog breeder with 50 fine, pedigreed German shepherds. Suppose his assistant failed to let the dogs exercise, and fed them pizza, resulting in fat dogs. One would not blame the dogs, nor try to cajole them into avoiding pizza, or to get more exercise within the confines of their cages. Clearly the solution is to alter the environment by letting the dogs loose to an exercise area, and by limiting them to quality dog food. The obesity problem would eventually disappear. An "animal husbandry" approach should now be considered for humans. Obesity can no longer be construed as a problem for individuals, but as a problem for the population, requiring action by food suppliers, exercise facilitators, or, if these do not change voluntarily, by the government. While behavioral treatment of individuals may help some, it is now appropriate to use behavior modification methods both on corporations and government entities to effect changes at the population/environmental level, and also on the public generally to help them accept the need for such large-scale control measures (Tillotson, 2004).

CONCLUSIONS

1. Behavioral treatment of obesity has been demonstrated. Eating and exercise patterns have been shown to result in moderate improvements in weight and health risks. Attainment of an optimal weight in terms of health risk rarely occurs.

2. Motivating individuals to adhere to these behavioral patterns appears to be difficult in the face of psychophysiological processes involved in the interaction between humans and the current modern environment. As a result, most persons regain lost weight. Adjunctive pharmacotherapies with acceptable cost/benefit outcomes need further research.

3. Behavior modification may help some to change their behaviors, but the evaluation research has methodological problems that make it difficult to determine if the methods are more effective than general educational and exhortatory approaches.

4. Future research should examine the potential of energy-enhancement approaches, lower-cost, long-term interventions, and the feasibility of policies that promote healthful behaviors without excessive government intervention.

5. Future research needs to use standardized treatment methods, including standardization of treatment manuals, contact time, therapist training, and behavioral recommendations and assessments.

REFERENCES

Abernathy RP, Black DR (1996) Healthy body weights: an alternative perspective. Am J Clin Nutr 63(3 Suppl): 448S-451S.

Andersen RE, Wadden TA, Bartlett SJ, Zemel B, Verde TJ, Franckowiak SC (1999) Effects of lifestyle activity vs structured aerobic exercise in obese women: a randomized trial. JAMA 281:335-340.

Arrone L J (2002) Treatment of Obesity in the Primary Care Setting. Handbook of Obesity Treatment (Wadden TA and Stunkard AJ, ed), pp 388. The Guilford Press: New York London.

Astrup A, Grunwald GK, Melanson El, Saris WH, Hill JO (2000) The role of low-fat diets in body weight control: a meta-analysis of ad libitum dietary intervention studies. Int J Obes 24:1545-1552.

Ayyad C, Andersen T (2000) Long-term efficacy of dietary treatment of obesity: a systematic review of studies published between 1931 and 1999. Obes Rev 1:113-119.

Baker CW, Brownell KD. (2000) Physical activity and maintenance of weight loss: physiological and psychological mechanisms. In: Physical Activity and Obesity (Bouchard C, ed), pp 311-328. Champaign, IL: Human Kinetics.

Baker RC, Kirschenbaum DS (1993) Self-monitoring may be necessary for successful weight control. Behav Ther 24:377-94.

Baldini LG, Schoeller DA, Dietz WH (1994) Metabolic differences in response to a high-fat vs. a high-carbohydrate diet. Obes Res 2:348-354.

Bandura A (1986) Social foundations of thought and action. Englewood Cliffs, NJ: Prentice-Hall,.

Bellisle, F (1995). Sensory afferents and the control of eating behavior (meeting report). Appetite, 24, 55-56.

Bennett, WI (1995). Beyond overeating. N Engl J Med 332: 673-674.

Bennett WI and Gurin J (1982). The Dieter's Dilemma. New York: Basic Books.

Berridge KC (1991) Modulation of taste affect by hunger, caloric satiety and sensory-specific satiety in the rat. Appetite 16:103-120.

Blair SN, Brodney S (1999) Effects of physical inactivity and obesity on morbidity and mortality: current evidence and research issues. Med Sci Sports Exerc 31(Suppl 11): S646-S662.

Blanchard CM, Rodgers WM, Spence JC, Coureya KS (2001) Feeling state responses to acute exercise of high and low intensity. J Sci Med Sport 4:30-38.

Bouchard CB (1994) Genetics of obesity: overview and research direction. In: The Genetics of Obesity (Bouchard CB, ed), pp223-233. Boca Raton, FL: CRC press.

Boutelle KN, Kirschenbaum DS (1998) Further support for consistent self-monitoring as a vital component of successful weight control. Obes Res 6:219-24

Brand-Miller JC, Holt SH, Pawlak DB, McMillan J (2002) Glycemic index and obesity. Am J Clin Nutr 76: 281S-285S.

Brownell KD and Kramer FM (1994) Behavioral Management of Obesity. In: Obesity Pathophysiology Psychology and Treatment (Blackburn GL and Kanders BS, eds), pp 231-240. Chapman and Hall: New York.

Brownell KD, Stunkard AJ (2002) Goals of obesity treatment. In: Eating Disorders and Obesity: A Comprehensive Handbook (2nd ed) (Fairburn CG, Brownell KD eds), New York, NY: Guilford.

Campfield, L.A., Smith, F.J., Rosenbaum, M., and Hirsch , J. (1996). Human eating: evidence for a physiological basis using a modified paradigm. Neurosci Biobehav Rev 20:133-137.

Carr KD and Papadouka V (1994) The role of multiple opioid receptors in the potentiation of reward by food restriction. Brain Res 639:253-260.

Carr KD and Simon EJ (1984) Potentiation of reward by hunger is opioid mediated. Brain Res 297: 369-373.

Cincotta AH and Meier AH (1997) Bromocriptine (Ergoset) reduces body weight and improves glucose tolerance in obese diabetics. Diabetes Care 19: 667-670.

Cincotta AH, Tozzo E, Scislowski PWD (1997) Bromocriptine/SKF38393 treatment ameliorates obesity and associated metabolic dysfunctions in obese (ob/ob) mice. Life Sci 61:951-956.

Cormillot A, Fuchs A (1990) The possible weight. Int J Obes 14(Suppl 2): 10.

Couzin J (2002) IOM Panel weights in on diet and health. Science 297:1788-1789

Danguir J (1987) Cafeteria diet promotes sleep in rats. Appetite 8:49-53.

De Vry J, Donselaar I, and Van Ree JM (1989) Food deprivation and acquisition of intravenous cocaine self-administration in rats: effect of naltrexone and haloperidol. J Pharmacol Experiment Ther 251:735-740.

Ditschuneit HH, Flechtner-Mors M, Johnson TD, Adler G (1999) Metabolic and weight-loss effects of a long-term dietary intervention on obese patients. Am J Clin Nutr 69: 198-204.

Drewnowski A, Krahn DD, Demitrack MA, Nairn K, Gosnell BA (1992) Taste responses and preferences for sweet high-fat foods: evidence for opioid involvement. Physiol Behav 51:371-379.

Drewnowski A, Kurth CL, and Rahaim JE (1991) Taste preferences in human obesity: environmental and familial factors. Amer J Clin Nutr 54:635-641.

Dulloo AG, Jacquet J, and Girardier L (1997) Poststarvation hyperphagia and body fat overshooting in humans; a role for feedback signals from lean and fat tissues. Amer J Clin Nutr 65:717-723.

Farrell SW, Braun L, Barlow CE, Cheng YJ, Blair SN (2002) The relation of body mass index, cardiorespiratory fitness, and all-cause mortality in women. Obes Res 10:417-423.

Foreyt JP, Brunner RL, Goodrick GK, Cutter G, Brownell KD, St Jeor ST (1995) Psychological correlates of weight fluctuation. Int J Eat Disord 17:263-273.

Foreyt, JP, Goodrick, GK (1991). Factors common to successful therapy for the obese patient. Med Sci Sports Exerc 23: 292-297.

Foreyt JP, Goodrick GK (1993) Evidence for success of behavior modification in weight loss and control. Ann Intern Med 119:698-701.

Foreyt JP, Goodrick GK (1994) The ultimate triumph of obesity. Lancet 346:134.

Foreyt JP, Goodrick GK (1994) Attributes of successful approaches to weight loss and control. Appl Prev Psychol 3:209.

Foreyt JP, Goodrick GK (2001) Dieting and weight loss: the energy perspective. Nutr Rev 59:S25-S26.

Foreyt JP, Goodrick GK, Gotto AM (1981) Limitations of behavioral treatment of obesity: Review and analysis. J Behav Med 4:159- 174.

French SA, Story M, Jeffery RW (2001) Environmental influences on eating and physical activity. Annu Rev Public Health 22:309-335.

Gladis MM, Wadden TA, Vogt R, Foster G, Kuehnel RH, Bartlett SJ. (1998) Behavioral treatment of obese binge eaters: do they need different care? J Psychosom res 44:375-384.

Goodrick GK (1999) Energy, Peace, Purpose. New York, NY: Berkley.

Goodrick GK (2000) Inability to control eating: addiction to food or normal response to abnormal environment? Drugs Soc 15:123-140.

Goodrick GK, Foreyt JP (1991) Why treatments for obesity don't last. J Am Diet Assoc 91:1243-1247.

Goodrick GK, Malek JN, Foreyt JP (1994) Exercise adherence in the obese: self-regulated intensity. Med Exer Nutr Health 3:335-338.

Grilo CM, Shiffman S, and Wing RR (1989) Relapse crises and coping among dieters. J Consult Clin Psychol 57: 488-495.

HaganMM, and Moss DE (1991) An animal model of bulimia nervosa: opioid sensitivity to fasting episodes. Pharmacol Biochem Behav 39:421-422.

Heatherton TF, and Baumeister RF (1991) Binge eating as escape from self-awareness. Psychol Bull 110:86-108.

Heatherton TF, Polivy J, and Herman CP (1990) Restrained eating: Some current findings and speculations. Psychol Addict Behav 4:100-106.

Hensrud DD, Weinsier RL, Darnell BE, Hunter GR (1994) A prospective study of weight maintenance in obese subjects reduced to normal body weight without weight-loss training. Am J Clin Nuttr 60:688-9.

Hoebel BE (1997) Neuroscience and appetitive behavior research: 25 years. Appetite 29: 119-133.

Hillsdon M, Thorgood M (1996) A systematic review of physical activity promotion strategies. Br J Sports Med 30:84-89.

Hoebel BE (1997) Neural systems for reinforcement and inhibition of behavior: Relevance to eating, addiction and depression. In: Understanding quality of life: Scientific perspectives on enjoyment and suffering (Kahnerman D, Diener E and Schwarz N eds), Russell Sage Foundation.

Hulens M, Vansant G, Lysens R, et al. (2001) Exercise capacity in lean versus obese women. Scand J Med Sci Sports 11:305-309.

Jakicic JM, Winters C, Lang W, Wing RR (1999) effects of intermittent exercise and use of home exercise equipment on adherence, weight loss, and fitness in overweight women: a randomized trial. JAMA 282: 1554-1560.

Janssen I, Katzmarzyk PR, Ross R (2002) Body mass index, waist circumference, and health risk: evidence in support of current National Institute of health guidelines. Arch Intern Med 162:2074-2079.

Jeffery RW, Wing RR, Sherwood NE, Tate DF (2003) Physical activity and weight loss: does prescribing higher physical activity goals improve outcome? Am J Clin Nutr 78:684-689.

Kayman S, Bruvold W, Stern JS (1990) Maintenance and relapse after weight loss in women: behavioral aspects. Am J Clin Nutr 52:800-807.

Kersh R, Morone J (2002) The politics of obesity: seven steps to government action. Health Aff 21:142-153.

King AC, Kaskell WL, Young DR et al. (1995) Long-term effects of varying intensities and formats of physical activity on participation rates, fitness, and lipoproteins in men and women aged 50-65 years. Circulation 91:2596-2604.

King AC, Taylor CB, Haskell WL, Debusk RF (1988) Strategies for increasing early adherence to and long-term maintenance of home-based exercise training in healthy middle-aged men and women. Am J Cardiol 61:628-32.

Klem ML, Wing RR, McGuire MT, Seagle HM, Hill JO (1997) A descriptive study of individuals successful at long-term maintenance of substantial weight loss. Am J Clin Nutr. 6:239-46.

Klem ML, Wing RR, McGuire MT, Seagle HM, Hill JO (1998) Psychological symptoms in individuals successful at long-term maintenance of weight loss. Health Psychol 17:336-345.

Knowler WC, Barrett-Connor E, Fowler SE, Hamman RF, Lachin JM, Walker EA, Nathan DM (2002). Reduction in the incidence of type 2 diabetes with lifestyle intervention or Metformin. New Engl J Med 346:393-403.

Latner JD (2001) Self-help in the long-term treatment of obesity. Obes Rev 2:87-97.

Linde JA, Jeffrey RW, Levy RL, Sherwood NE, Utter J, Pronk NP, Boyle RG (2004) Binge eating disorder, weight control self-efficacy, and depression in overweight man and women. Int J Obes 28:418-425.

Lynch WC, Everingham A, Dubitzky J et al. (2000) Does binge eating play a role in the self-regulation of moods? Integr Physiol Behav Sci 35:298-313.

McDermott R, O'Dea R, Rowley K, Knight S, Burgess P (1998) beneficial impact of the homelands movement on health outcomes in central Australian aborigines. Aust NZ J Pub Health 22:653-658.

Morabia, A., Fabre, J., Chee, E., Zeger, S., Orsat, E., and Robert, A. (1989). Diet and opiate addiction: A quantitative assessment of the diet of non-institutionalized opiate addicts. Brit J Addict 84:173-180.

National Center for Health Statistics (1999) Prevalence of overweight and obesity among adults: United States, 1999. Washington, DC.

NIH (1998). Clinical guidelines for the identification, evaluation and treatment of overweight and obesity in adults- the evidence report. Obes Res 6:51S-209S.

Nielsen Media Research (2000) 2000 Report on television: The First 50 years. New York, NY: AC Nielsen Co.

Nisoli E, Carruba MO.(2000) An assessment of the safety and efficacy of sibutramine, an anti-obesity drug with a novel mechanism of action. Obes Rev 1:127-39.

Orzano AJ, Scott JG (2004) Diagnosis and treatment of obesity in adults: an applied evidence-based review. J Am Board Fam Pract 17:359-369.

Oster S, Thompson D, Edelsberg J, Bird AP, Colditz GA (1999) Lifetime health and economic benefits of weight loss among obese persons. Am J Public Health 89:1536-42.

Perri MG, Anton SD, Durning PE et al. (2002) Adherence to exercise prescriptions: effects of prescribing moderate versus higher levels of intensity and frequency. Health Psychol 21:452-458.

Perri MG, Martin AD, Leermakers EA, Sears SF, Notelovitz M (1997) Effects of group- versus home-based exercise in the treatment of obesity. J Consult Clin Psychol 65:278-85.

Perri MG, McAllister DA, Gange JJ, Jordan RC, McAdoo G, Nezu AM. Effects of four maintenance programs on the long-term management of obesity. J Consult Clin Psychol 56:529-534.

Perri MG, Nezu AM, Viegener BJ (1992) Improving the long-term management of obesity: Theory, research, and clinical guidelines. New York, NY: Wiley.

Peters JC, Wyatt HR, Donahoo WT, Hill JO (2002) From instinct to intellect: the challenge of maintaining healthy weight in the modern world. Obes Rev 3:69-74.

Piette JD (2000) Interactive voice response systems in the diagnosis and management of chronic disease. Am J Managed Care 6:817-827.

Poston WSC, Foreyt JP (2000) Successful management of the obese patient. Am Fam Physician 61:3615-22.

Pothos EN, Creese I, Hoebel BG (1995) Restricted eating with weight loss selectively decreases extracellular dopamine in the nucleus accumbens and alters dopamine response to amphetamine, morphine, and food intake. J Neurosci 15:6640-50.

Prentice AM, Jebb SA (1995) Obesity in Britain: gluttony or sloth? BMJ 311:437-439.

Ravussin E, Lillioja S, Knowler WC et al. (1988) Reduced rate of energy expenditure as a risk factor for body-weight gain. N Engl J Med 318:467-472.

Riddle PK (1980) Attitudes, beliefs, behavioral intention, and behavior of women and men toward regular jogging. Res Quart ExercSport, 51, 663-674.

Riebe D, Greene GW, Ruggiero L, Stillwell KM, Blissmer B, Nigg CR, Caldwell M (2003). Evaluation of a healthy-lifestyle approach to weight management. Prev Med 36:45-54.

Robinson TN (1999). Reducing children's television viewing to prevent obesity: a randomized controlled trial. JAMA 282:1561-7.

Ruderman A J (1986) Dietary restraint: A theoretical and empirical review. Psycholog Bull 99:247-262.

Sarlio-Lahteenkorva S, Rissanen A, Kaprio J (2000) A descriptive study of weight-loss maintenance: 6 and 15 year follow up of initially overweight adults. Int J Obes 24:116-125.

Schultz W, Dayan P, and Montague PR (1997) A neural substrate of prediction and reward. Science, 275, 1593-1599.

Sclafani A (2001) Psychobiology of food preferences. Int J Obes 25 (Suppl5):S13-S16.

Sjoberg L, Persson L-O (1979) A study of attempts by obese patients to regulate eating. Addict Behav 4:349-359.

Skender ML, Goodrick GK, Del Junco DJ, Reeves RS, Darnell L, Gotto AM, Foreyt JP (1996) Comparison of 2-year weight loss trends in behavioral treatments of obesity: diet, exercise, and combination interventions. J Am Diet Assoc 96:342-346.

Spiegel K, Leproult R, Van Cauter E (1999) Impact of sleep debt on metabolic and endocrine function. Lancet 354:1435-1439.

Stevens VJ, Obarzanek E, Cook NR, Lee IM, Appel LJ, Smith West D, Milas NC, Mattfeldt-Beman M, Belden L, Bragg C, Millstone M, Raczynski J, Brewer A, Singh B, Cohen J for Trials for the Hypertension Prevention Research Group (2001). Long-term weight loss and changes in blood pressure: results of the Trials of Hypertension Prevention, phase II.Ann Intern Med134:1-11.

Tanofsky-Kraff M, Yanovski SZ (2004) Eating disorder or disordered eating? Non-normative eating patterns in obese individuals. Obes Res 12:1361-1366.

Tasali E, Van Cauter E (2002) Sleep-disordered breathing and the current epidemic of obesity: Consequence or contributing factor? Am J Resp Crit Care Med 165:562-563.

Taylor WC, Blair SN, Cummings SS, Wun CC, Malina RM (1999). Childhood and adolescent physical activity patterns and adult physical activity. Med Sci Sports Exerc 31:118-123.

Telch CF, Agras WS (1993) The effects of a very low calorie diet on binge eating. Behav ther 24:177-193.

Thayer RE (1996). The origin of everyday moods: managing energy, tension and stress. New York, NY: Oxford Univ Press.

Tillotson JE (2004) America's obesity: conflicting public policies, industrial economic development, and unintended human consequences. Annu Rev Nutr 24:617-643.

Tippett KS, Cleveland LE (1999) How current diets stack up: comparison with dietary guidelines. In: America's Eating Habits: Changes and Consequences (Frazao E, ed) Washington, DC: USDA/Econ Res Serv.

USDHHS Centers for Disease Control and Prevention, National Center for Chronic Disease prevention and Health Promotion (1996) Physical activity and health: a report of the Surgeon General. Atlanta, GA: 1996.

USDHHS (2000) Health People 2010. Washington, DC: USDHHS

Vgontzas AN, Bixler EO, Tan TL et al.(1998) Obesity without sleep apnea is associated with daytime sleepiness. Arch Intern Med 158:1333-1337.

Wadden TA, Brownell KD, Foster GD (2002) Obesity: responding to the global epidemic. J Consult Clin Psychol 70:510-525.

Wadden TA, Butryn ML, Byrne KJ (2004). Efficacy of lifestyle modification for long-term weight control. Obes Res 12:151S-162S.

Wang GJ, Volkow ND, Thanos PK, Fowler JS (2004) Similarity between obesity and drug addiction as assessed by neurofunctional imaging: a concept review. J Addict Dis 23: 39-53.

Weinsier RL, Hunter GR, Heini AF, Goran MI, Sell SM (1998) The etiology of obesity: relative contribution of metabolic factors, diet, and physical activity. Am J Med 105:145-150.

Willenbring ML, Morley JE, Krahn DD, Carlson GA, Levine AS, Shafer RB (1989) Psychoneuroendocrine effects of methadone maintenance. Psychoneuro-endocrinology 14: 371-391.

Willet WC (2001) Eat, drink and be healthy. The Harvard Medical School guide to healthy eating. New York, NY: Simon and Schuster Source,.

Willett WC (2002) Dietary fat plays a role in obesity: no. Obes Rev 3:59-68.

Willett WC, Dietz WH, Colditz GA (1999) Primary care: guidelines for healthy weight. N Engl J Med 341: 427-434.

Wilson GT (1991) The addiction model of eating disorders: a critical analysis. Adv Behav Res Ther 13:27-72.

Wing RR, Hill JO (2001) Successful weight loss maintenance. Annu Rev Nutr 21:323-341.

Wing RR (2002) Behavioral Weight Control. In: Handbook of Obesity Treatment (Wadden TA and Stunkard AJ, eds), pp 340-351. New York, NY: Guilford.

Wirth A, Kraus J (2001). Long-term weight loss with sibutramine: a randomized controlled trial. JAMA 286:1331-9.

World Health Organization (1998) Obesity: Preventing and Managing the Global Epidemic. Geneva, Switzerland: Author.

Young LR, Nestle M (2002) The contribution of expanding portion sizes to the US obesity epidemic. Am J Public Health 92:246-249.

The letters *f* or *t* following a page number refer to a figure or table on that page.

The letters *f* or *t* following a page number refer to a figure or table on that page.

D

The letters *f* or *t* following a page number refer to a figure or table on that page.

The letters *f* or *t* following a page number refer to a figure or table on that page.

The letters *f* or *t* following a page number refer to a figure or table on that page.

J

K

L

M

The letters *f* or *t* following a page number refer to a figure or table on that page.

The letters *f* or *t* following a page number refer to a figure or table on that page.

The letters *f* or *t* following a page number refer to a figure or table on that page.

The letters *f* or *t* following a page number refer to a figure or table on that page.

The letters *f* or *t* following a page number refer to a figure or table on that page.

The letters *f* or *t* following a page number refer to a figure or table on that page.

The letters *f* or *t* following a page number refer to a figure or table on that page.

The letters *f* or *t* following a page number refer to a figure or table on that page.

The letters *f* or *t* following a page number refer to a figure or table on that page.

The letters *f* or *t* following a page number refer to a figure or table on that page.

The letters *f* or *t* following a page number refer to a figure or table on that page.